Industrial Policy, Innovation and Economic Growth: The Experience of Japan and the Asian NIEs

Industrial Policy, Innovation and Economic Growth: The Experience of Japan and the Asian NIEs

Edited by

Poh-Kam Wong

*Centre for Management of Innovation and
Technopreneurship (CMIT)
Faculty of Business Administration
National University of Singapore*

and

Chee-Yuen Ng

*International Development Research Institute
Foundation for Advanced Studies on International Development
Japanese Ministry of Foreign Affairs*

SINGAPORE UNIVERSITY PRESS
NATIONAL UNIVERSITY OF SINGAPORE

© 2001 Singapore University Press
Yusof Ishak House
31 Lower Kent Ridge Road
Singapore 119078

Fax: (65) 774-0652
E-mail: supbooks@nus.edu.sg
Website: http://www.nus.edu.sg/SUP

ISBN 9971-69-255-4 (paper)

Typeset by: Scientifik Graphics (Singapore) Pte Ltd
Printed by: Seng Lee Press Pte Ltd

CONTENTS

v

PREFACE

The role of industrial and technology policy in economic development has been a controversial issue in the literature on economic development of developing countries. In particular, the positive role of the state in the rapid economic growth of East Asia has been questioned in the light of the recent Asian financial crisis which has ravaged growth in much of East Asia. The East Asian Miracle has been alleged to be the East Asian Mirage instead, while the continued weakness of the Japanese economy has been used to discredit the role of industrial policy of any kind.

In response to such sweeping negation of the role state intervention, this volume provides a careful historical analysis of the development experience of the five most advanced countries in East Asia — Japan and the four Asian NIEs (Taiwan, Korea, Singapore and Hong Kong) — to provide a more balanced interpretation of the role and contribution of industrial and technology policy in these five countries. Written by indigenous scholars from the respective countries, the chapters provided in-depth review of the role of the state in industrial development of each of the countries in general as well as in specific selected industries (e.g. electronics, textiles). These detailed country chapters, together with a synthetic chapter written by the editors, show clearly that the five East Asian countries have pursued quite diverse development strategies, and hence the role of the state has been quite varied. While state intervention has generally played a positive role in promoting economic growth in the early stages of industrialization, some of the countries have suffered from policy inertia and institutional dysfunction in later years. Synthesizing from the experience of these five more advanced East Asian economies, a "transitional developmental state" approach is suggested for other developing countries seeking to draw lessons from the experience of East Asia.

The editors would like to acknowledge the generous financial support provided by the Sasakawa Peace Foundation (SPF) of Japan to the Centre for Management of Innovation and Technopreneurship at the National University of Singapore, for a research project from which the chapters for this book are drawn. We are also grateful to the various constructive comments provided by various scholars on East Asian development on earlier drafts of the papers. In particular, we would like to thank the following three institutions for co-organizing with us forums to discuss the findings from our study with scholars from Japan, US and Europe: The Institute for Asia-Pacific Studies, Waseda University, which hosted a forum in Tokyo in Sept. 1999; Berkeley Roundtable on International Economy (BRIE), University of California, Berkeley, which hosted a forum in Berkeley in Jan. 2000; and the Asian Research Centre, Copenhagen Business School, which hosted a forum in Copenhagen in March 2000.

CONTRIBUTORS

Ha-Joon Chang is Assistant Director of Development Studies, Faculty of Economics and Politics, University of Cambridge. He has served as consultant to UNCTAD, World Bank, ADB, UNDP, UNIDO, and WIDER on issues including the role of the government in industrial development, role of institutions in economic development, globalization and transnational corporations, the East Asian development experience, and intellectual property rights and economic development. He is a member of the Editorial Board of Cambridge Journal of Economics, and a member of the Advisory Panel for the Human Development Report, 1999, of UNDP, 1998–99. He obtained his B.A. in Economics from the Seoul National University, and his M. Phil. and Ph.D. in Economics and Politics from the University of Cambridge.

Been-Lon Chen is currently Professor of Economics at the National Central University in Taiwan. He is also a research fellow of Economics at the Academia Sinica, Taiwan. His research interests are Macroeconomics, Economic Development, and Information and Uncertainty. Professor Chen has published papers in Contemporary Economic Policy, International Economic Review, Journal of Economics, Journal of Economics and Dynamics Control, Journal of International Trade and Economic Development, and Journal of Economic Integration. He has also been a referee for Asian Economic Review, Journal of International Trade and Economic Development, Review of Development Economics, and Review of International Economics. Professor Chen received his Ph.D. in Economics from University of California, L.A., USA.

Tain-Jy Chen is currently Professor of Economics at National Taiwan University. He is also Consultant for Chung-Hua Institution for Economic Research, Taiwan. His research interests are in international economics and economic development. Professor Chen has co-authored a book, *Political Economy of US-Taiwan Trade (1995)* and edited a book, *Taiwanese Firms in Southeast Asia: Networking Across Borders (1998)*, in addition to professional writings in numerous academic journals.

Stephen W.K. Chiu is Associate Professor in Sociology at The Chinese University of Hong Kong. His research interests are in development, social movement, and industrial sociology. His publications include *East Asia and the World Economy (1995)*, *City-States in the Global Economy: Industrial Restructuring in Hong Kong and Singapore (1997)*, *Dynamics of Social Movement in Hong Kong (forthcoming)* and a number of book chapters and journal articles on economic restructuring and industrial relations. Professor Chiu received his Ph.D. from Princeton University, USA.

Yun-Peng Chu is Professor of Industrial Economics, National Central University and Director of Sun Yat-Sen Institute for Social Sciences and Philosophy, Academia Sinica, Taiwan. He obtained his Ph.D. in Economics from the University of Maryland. He previously held the position of Commissioner, Fair Trade Commission, Executive Yuan, Taipei, Taiwan.

Yun-Peng Chu is currently Research Fellow and Director of the Institute for Social Sciences and Philosophy in Academia Sinica, Taiwan. He is also Professor of Industrial Economics at National Central University, and Adjunct Professor of Economics at National Taiwan University. Professor Chu has served as Commissioner of Taiwan's Fair Trade Commission from 1992 to 1996. His research interests include economic development, income distribution, industrial economics, and multi-sector modeling. He has published in journals such as the American Economic Review, Journal of Development Economics and Asian Economic Journal. He has been the co-editor of three books published by Routledge and Edward Elgar, and has contributed papers to these and other edited volumes.

Ryokichi Hirono is currently Professor Emeritus of Economics at Seikei University, Tokyo, and Vice-Chairman of the International Management Association of Japan. He is also Visiting Professor at Saitama University, Waseda University, and Sophia University. He has been a consultant to the United Nations Development Program, the International Labour Organisation, the Asian Development Bank, the Development Assistance Committee of the OECD and the United Nations Conference on Trade and Development, among others. Professor Hirono serves on the Advisory Council on Official Development Assistance, Ministry of Foreign Affairs; the Central Committee on Environment,

Environment Agency, the Office of the Prime Minister; and on the Advisory Committee on International Education, Ministry of Education. He is also a member of the Committee on Development Planning, the UN Economic and Social Council; as well as the Board of Directors of the Japan-ASEAN Association, Tokyo. He has widely published on issues of Asian and international economic development. Professor Hirono received a Ph.D. in economics from the University of Chicago, USA.

Hojin Kang is Professor of Economics and International Trade, School of Business Administration, Korea University. He obtained his Ph.D. from Seoul National University.

Takashi Kiuchi was formerly the Director of Research of the Long-Term Credit Bank of Japan. He currently serves as an advisor to Shinsei Bank.

Tai-Lok Lui is Associate Professor in Sociology at The Chinese University of Hong Kong. His research interests are the formation of the middle class in Hong Kong, industrial restructuring, and economic sociology. Professor Lui is the author of *Waged Work at Home: The Social Organisation of Industrial Outwork in Hong Kong (1994)*. His co-authored publications include *City-States in the Global Economy: Industrial Restructuring in Hong Kong and Singapore (1997), Dynamics of Social Movement in Hong Kong (forthcoming)* and several book chapters and articles on economic restructuring and urban politics. Professor Lui received his Ph.D. from Oxford University, UK.

Chee-Yuen Ng is Chief Researcher at the International Development Research Institute, Foundation for Advanced Studies on International Development, a think-tank of the Japanese Ministry of Foreign Affairs. He has been a visiting senior fellow at the Centre for Management of Innovation and Technopreneurship at the National University of Singapore, and a visiting Professor at the Graduate Institute of Policy Studies, Tokyo. He was also previously Senior Fellow at the Institute of Southeast Asian Studies in Singapore and Director of Bureau of Economic Cooperation, ASEAN Secretariat, Jakarta. Dr Ng has published articles and books on the subject of international development cooperation for sustained growth, equity and human development in

Southeast Asia. He has coordinated projects and symposia on environment and economic development in Southeast Asia, on human resource development, and management and marketization in the ASEAN region. Dr Ng received his Ph.D. in economics at La Trobe University in Australia.

Poh-Kam Wong is currently Associate Professor at the Faculty of Business Administration, National University of Singapore, where he is also the director of the Centre for Management of Innovation and Technopreneurship and the deputy director of the Graduate School of Business. He has been a consultant to The World Bank, the Asian Development Bank, UNDP, ILO, and government agencies in Malaysia and Singapore. His current research interests include Economics and Management of Technological Innovation, Technology Strategies of East Asian Firms, National Science and Technology Policy, and National Information Infrastructure Policy. Professor Wong received his Ph.D. in regional planning at the Massachusetts Institute of Technology, USA. He was a Fulbright Visiting Scholar at the University of California, Berkeley in 1984–85, and a recipient of the Oshikawa Fellowship from the Asian Productivity Organisation, Tokyo in 1989–90.

1

Rethinking the Development Paradigm: Lessons from Japan and the Four Asian NIEs

Poh-Kam Wong & Chee-Yuen Ng

I. INTRODUCTION

This overview chapter of the book seeks to provide a critical re-examination of the relevance and usefulness of the prevailing minimalist state, free market paradigm (MSFMP) for the development of late-industrializing countries by interpreting and integrating the analytical findings of the individual country chapters in the book on the development experience of Japan and the four Asian NIEs (South Korea, Taiwan, Hong Kong and Singapore). We believe that such a re-examination, particularly in the light of the recent East Asian financial crisis, is most timely in enabling us to draw the right lessons from the development experience of these five East Asian countries, not only for the future economic recovery of these countries, but also for other developing economies in and outside the East Asia region as well. Based on this re-examination, we propose an alternative *Transitional Developmental State Paradigm* that we believe is more appropriate for adoption by developing countries.

While recognizing that markets are generally superior to state intervention, and hence the general desirability of moving towards deregulation and market liberalization, the paradigm highlights the fact that private market institutions may not emerge naturally, and thus may require an active role of the state especially in the initial development phase of developing countries, to overcome coordination failures, and to develop the missing market institutions needed for competitive markets to develop subsequently. Thus, rather than a dogmatic adherence to the *minimalist state, free market paradigm* regardless of the stages of economic development, our alternative paradigm supports an active role of the state especially in the early stage of development to overcome market failures, and cautions against hasty, indiscriminate dismantling of state involvement before the necessary market institutions have been established.

At the same time, the paradigm also cautions against the danger of state institutional inertia or dysfunction, whereby state institutions and policies are often perpetuated beyond their usefulness and hence become obstacles to further development of private market institutions. Thus, unlike the prevailing *Developmental State* approach, our paradigm recognizes the limits of state intervention as an economy becomes more advanced, and advocates a progressive reduction of the role of the state as well as a pro-active approach to overcome the in-built inertia in state institutions and policies to perpetuate themselves beyond their period of usefulness. In particular, the paradigm recognizes from the diverse development strategies of the East Asian NIEs that there may be a variety of developmental state models that developing countries can adopt; what specific roles that the state should play depend on a concrete analysis of the initial factor endowments and socio-political pre-conditions of the countries concerned; there is no single developmental state model that is applicable to all. Besides creating the enabling conditions for market institutions to emerge, the state also needs to play the role of forging a social contract among the different social classes in society to ensure that the adjustment costs of market liberalization are borne equitably.

II. OVERVIEW OF THE DEVELOPMENT PARADIGM DEBATE

The rapid growth of many East Asian economies from the 1960s to the mid-1990s had received much attention in the economic development literature, culminating in the by now famous term the East Asian Miracle (EAM) as adopted by the World Bank for their 1993 report on the East Asian development experience. While many explanations have been offered for the success of these so-called High Performance Economies (HPEs) (another term coined by the World Bank), the fundamental debate that has been provoked centered on the role of the state in economic development in general and industrial development in particular.

On one extreme end, the minimalist state, free-market neo-classical school of thought maintains that the East Asian development experience in no way challenges their laissez faire paradigm; rather, they assert that the very exceptional economic performances of East Asia are actually the results of the working of free-market principles. In essence, the basic neoclassical economics argument is that the high growth performance of East Asian countries can be explained by a core of common factors such as high savings rate, high investment in human capital, prudent macroeconomic policy, political stability and protection of property rights, and openness to world trade and investment. Beyond getting these "fundamentals right", this "minimalist state, free market" paradigm (MSFMP) downplays the role of other forms of state intervention, arguing either that such interventions were absent, or where they have been significant, the results have been generally more failures than successes. The underlying assumption is that markets will naturally emerge if the state gets out of the way through liberalization. While acknowledging that there may be instances of market failure, the report generally cautions against state intervention as it may lead to "state failure" that outweighs the market failure it is designed to cure. In particular, the report is generally critical of industrial policy designed to promote the development of particular industries. In this interpretation, then, the exceptional performance of East Asia is interpreted as vindicating the minimalist state, free market paradigm, rather than challenging it. East Asia's success has been in spite of, rather than because of, state interventionist policies beyond the minimum necessary.

On the other end of the spectrum are those who argue that the East Asian development experience demonstrated the need for strong state intervention to promote rapid economic development. Drawing upon the earlier work of Myrdal and Gerschenkeron, proponents of this "developmental state" paradigm (e.g. Amsden,1989; Wade,1990; Chang,1994; Rodrik, 1995) argue that it was significant state interventions that were largely responsible for the backward, late-industrializing East Asian economies to catch up rapidly with the advanced economies. While acknowledging that strong state interventions of the wrong kind can have very negative consequences, they argue that the East Asian states had by and large intervened successfully (despite some mistakes here and there). In this interpretation, the better performance of East Asia can been attributed to strong state interventions of the right kind.

The MSFMP became increasingly dominant in the thinking of the World Bank through the 1980s as expressed in the series of annual development reports produced during the period. The 1993 World Bank EAM report can be interpreted as a slight departure from this tradition in that it sought for the first time to reconcile the MSFMP view and the developmental state views. The attempt was a limited one in that the EAM basically sided with the existing MSFM paradigm while making some concessions to the developmental state paradigm. It does so by introducing the idea of "market-friendly" state intervention, broadly interpreted to mean state interventions that involve little distortion of the market or that somehow improve the working of the market.

This "market friendly" state-intervention paradigm appears to enjoy a brief spell of popularity despite the many criticisms of the study methodologies and interpretations of the World Bank EAM report (see e.g. Rodrik, 1994; Wade, 1994; Amsden, 1995). A number of additional work [e.g. Leipziger (ed.), 1997; Campos and Root, 1996; ADB, 1997] seek to extend the basic arguments of the World Bank EAM further, e.g. by pointing to the high emphasis on equitable distribution of benefits ("shared growth") in East Asian countries as a factor conducive to their high economic growth, and by elaborating on the specific forms of market-friendly interventions that appeared to have beneficial effects. However, significant doubts about the usefulness of the EAM interpretation of East Asian development continue to be expressed by Japanese development scholars and ODA policy makers [see e.g. Yanagihara, 1997; Ohno and Ohno (eds.), 1998], who opposed it on both methodological and normative ground. The main differences between the Japanese view and the neoclassical view about development are aptly summarized in Table 1.1 [reproduced from Ohno and Ohno (eds.), 1998]. An attempt to reconcile the Japanese approach with the neoclassical approach is that of Aoki, Kim and Fujiwara (eds.) (1997), who introduced the "market enhancing" view of the state.

What appears to have ended the popularity of this "market friendly" view of East Asian Development is not so much the continuing criticisms such as the above, but the sudden breakout of the East Asian regional

TABLE 1.1 Comparison of Neoclassical and Japanese Approach to Development and Transition Strategies

	Neoclassical approach	*Japanese approach*
Highest priority	Financial and macroeconomic (fiscal and BOP deficits, money, inflation, debt)	Real (output, employment, industrial structure)
Time scope	Short-term (solving problems as they arise)	Long-term (long-term targets and annual plans)
Basic attitude toward market	*Laissez-faire*; Minimal government intervention	Active support by government
Speed of systemic transition	As quickly as possible	Will take long time even with maximum effort

SOURCE: Ohno & Ohno (1998).

financial crisis in mid-1997 which had since engulfed much of East Asia over the next two years. Economic growth collapsed in much of the East Asian region, with nearly all the previously touted HPEs sliding into recession by early or late 1998 (see Annex Table A).

The terms of debate about the role of the state in East Asia changed dramatically with the changing fortune of the region. Suddenly, the East Asian Miracle has become the East Asian Mirage or East Asian Myth. Rather than trying to accommodate some positive role for the state in contributing to the rapid growth of the region, many proponents of the prevailing MSFM paradigm are now asserting instead that much of the rapid East Asian growth may have actually been artificially induced through perverse state interventions of the crony-capitalism sort (see e.g. Wolf, 1998; Economist, 1998). In this about turn, state interventions that were once seen as market-friendly (e.g. deliberation councils, performance-based contest for state finance, relatively efficient bureaucracy) are now seen as either severely suppressing market signals by substituting non-transparent, government-business relationships for free market competition, or as blatant forms of corruption practices. Although such state-crony capitalism may be pro-growth initially, it is alleged that the resulting growth is not sustainable. Hence the onset of the financial crisis is interpreted as merely the result of these economies collapsing under too much state intervention excesses accumulated over the years.

In calling into question the "quality" of the high East Asian growth in the past, these proponents readily refer to the argument, forcefully articulated earlier by Krugman(1994), that the East Asian Miracle has been a myth, since the growth has been attained essentially "through sweats rather than brains". Based on empirical work by Young (1992, 1993) and Lau (1993) utilizing neoclassical production function estimation methodology, Krugman(1994) argued that the high GDP growth performances of the East Asian NIEs are nothing remarkable, since they could be accounted for by expansion of inputs, with little or no productivity growth through technical progress (i.e. total factor productivity (TFP) is a negligible source of growth in these economies). Krugman therefore concludes that the historically high but "TFP-less" growth cannot be sustained in the future (analogy to the unsustainable growth of Russia is drawn). By implications, the paper also seems to suggest that whatever distinctive institutional or cultural factors these economies have developed could not have been superior to those of the advanced Western nations, since they resulted in only input-driven growth, whereas the latter have produced consistently high TFP growth. Thus, while EAM sees useful lessons from the high East Asian economic growth experience for other developing economies (in terms of how they "get the fundamentals right"), Krugman's argument casts doubt even on that, thus preparing the ground for a revisionist, crony-capitalist interpretation of past East Asian development.

Through the vantage point of this latest crony-capitalism interpretation of East Asian development model, the MSFM paradigm suggests that the way out of the current financial crisis for the East Asia region is to move away from such inefficient state interventions by reducing the role of the state, and to further open up the economy so that free market competition will prevail. There is little doubt that such reasoning has informed IMF's insistence on the adoption of significant liberalization and deregulation policies by Korea and Indonesia as a pre-condition for financial assistance.

The continued weakness of the Japan economy since the bursting of the asset bubble in the early-1990s provided further ammunition to the MSFM paradigm. The Japanese model of development has of course been an outstanding exception to the prescriptions of the MSFM paradigm. For a long time, the rapid ascendancy of Japan into the rank of advanced industrial nation has been difficult to explain using the MSFM paradigm, given that the Japanese model of development has involved a significant degree of state intervention. However, the inability of Japan to sustain her economic growth since the early 1990s has enabled the paradigm to assert more vigorously why even the Japanese model is ultimately not sustainable. From the perspective of MSFMP, although the problems of Japan are not the same as much of the developing East Asian economies, nonetheless, they can be traced to inefficient state interventions in the past, and hence serve as convincing signs that they violated the basic principles of MSFMP.

With the US economy resurgent on the one hand, and most of East Asia engulfed in a severe financial crisis coupled with continuing weakness of Japan on the other, the MSFM paradigm has become the dominant paradigm for thinking about development. Add to it the continuing structural weakness of many of the European countries (their recent higher growths notwithstanding), it is easy to understand why there has been an increasing claim of superiority of the American model of capitalist institutions. Free-market economics proponents (as typified by the *Economist* magazine) argue that the poor economic performance of Japan and other advanced industrial economies in recent years are the cumulative results of years of too much state interventions in the labor and capital markets when compared to the US. They therefore advocate that the only way for these economies to improve their competitiveness is to ditch their old state interventionist policies, and related social institutions, in favour of the free-market institutions of the US.

In the US, the political counterpart of the ascendancy of the free-market enterprise ideology is the argument that the Western model of parliamentary democracy and emphasis on individual freedom is an essential part of the free market enterprise system. The US establishment is particularly keen that the East Asian economies adopt not only free-market liberalization policies but also the political institutions of the West. Hence Vice-President Al Gore's call in the APEC meeting in Kuala Lumpur in 1998 for "political reform" to go hand in hand with economic liberalization.

In summary, it appears that the minimalist state, free market paradigm continues to prevail, indeed becomes more dominant, as an explanatory framework for why East Asia grew so fast earlier, and why it is in such deep crisis now. Developmental state proponents appear to have been put on the defensive by the recent poor economic performance of Japan and most other East Asian countries.

III. OUR APPROACH TO RE-EXAMINING THE EAST ASIAN DEVELOPMENT EXPERIENCE

The main aim of this study is to re-examine the East Asian development experience in the light of the above debates about development paradigms. Our basic approach is one of comparative analysis, in which the specific development experiences of Japan and the four Asian NIEs are compared, with a focus on the role of the state. While a study of this nature obviously builds upon the existing literature (see the extensive Bibliography compiled as part of this project), we believe that there are five distinctive elements in our study approach.

1. Differentiating the NIEs from Other East Asian HPEs

To begin with, we believe that much can be learned from distinguishing the experience of the four Asian NIEs from other high-growth economies like Malaysia, Indonesia and Thailand. In the East Asian Miracle (EAM) report of the World Bank and in much of the subsequent literature on East Asian development (e.g. Campos and Root, 1996; ADB, 1996; Leipziger, 1997), these four NIEs are generally lumped together with Thailand, Malaysia, Indonesia and China as part of the grouping of high-growth East Asian countries [termed High Performance Economies (HPEs) in EAM]. We intentionally choose to focus on these four more advanced NIEs because their economic development performance in general and industrial development performance in particular have been substantially better than the other East Asian tigers.

2. Understanding the Diversity of Development Approaches Among the NIEs Themselves

While some of the fundamental factors as emphasized by EAM and others — high savings rate, high propensity to invest in education, and export orientation — probably do contribute to the higher performance of the NIEs, we are more struck by the remarkable diversity of development approaches among the NIEs themselves. In particular, we examine the diverse differences in historical circumstances and newly evolving geo-political environments, and the possible effects these have on the different institutional and policy approaches to development adopted in the four countries concerned. We combine our understanding of these differences (and their underlying causes) with the common factors already identified by EAM as well as other factors (e.g. geographic proximity to Japan) to derive new insights on why and how the four NIEs succeeded in rapid economic growth through distinctly different models of development. Thus, rather than talking about a single East Asian Miracle, our analysis suggests four different models to relatively successful economic development in East Asia. Furthermore, we provide insights on the historical and geo-political factors that may have influenced the NIEs to have adopted such widely different approaches.

3. Different Pathways to Technological Learning and Upgrading

The NIEs, with the possible exception of Hong Kong after the 1970s, are most markedly successful in industrial development. Not only was there rapid industrial growth, but there has been significant productivity enhancement and technological upgrading as well. While much of the existing literature on East Asian industrial development policies generally emphasized trade policies and policies of "picking winners" through controlling credit allocation and influencing industry entry/ exit, we choose to focus instead on technological capability development as a common underlying theme in understanding the industrial development process in late industrializing economies. We interpret technological learning and upgrading in the broader sense of including all forms of productivity-enhancing mechanisms, i.e. we include not just the adoption of new technologies and the commercialization of new technological innovations, but also the institutional innovation and organizational learning associated with raising productivity. Based on this broader interpretation, we argue that much of the differences in development approaches adopted by the four NIEs can be understood as reflecting different generic pathways to technological learning and upgrading by late-industrializing countries.

4. Industry-Specific Case Studies of the Working of Industrial Policies

To gain further insights into the interaction between policies, institutions and the development process, we seek to go beyond comparative analysis at the macro-economy level to look at the development of specific industries. In particular, we intentionally choose electronics industry as a common industry case study to better understand both the common as well as differentiating factors among the four NIEs. At the same time, we also ask each of the country studies to choose another industry that best characterize another salient aspect of industrial development in their respective countries. Through this industry level comparative analysis, we are able to bring out more concretely the differences or commonality in the working of industrial policies and the institutions involved.

5. Analysis of Institutional Dynamics

Last, but not least, we take a dynamic view of the role of institutions at different stages of the development process. We seek in this study not just to provide a historical explanation of past success, but also to relate our understanding of how the role of the state needs to evolve over different stages of development so as to identify possible institutional rigidities or policy dysfunction, and hence the need for policy and institutional reform. Our analysis suggests that as economies moved from extreme backwardness to industrial take off to eventually reach a more advanced and mature stage, old policies and institutions may no longer apply, even if they have been successful in the past. We also recognize that the external global environment has changed considerably over the years, which may by itself require changes in old policies. Such a prospective analysis of how to sustain the East Asian miracle is particularly relevant in view of the recent financial turmoil and the prolonged economic slowdown of Japan, both of which have been shown to have been caused at least in part by some dysfunctional policies or institutions that have outlived their usefulness.

We believe that such a dynamic institutional approach allows us to examine not only the need for policy reforms in the future development of the NIEs themselves, but also to take a more nuance approach to drawing relevant lessons for other developing countries. Rather than a simple static prescription of the common factors for successful development, we advocate a dynamic interpretation that takes into account the historical and geopolitical specificity of the experience of each of the NIEs, the changed global political-economic and financial/business environment, and the consequences of rapid technological advance.

Overall, a key finding from the five country studies is that some of the policies successfully pursued in the past by these countries may no longer be appropriate in the future. Understanding the sources for such institutional inertia and dysfunction is not only critical for Japan and the NIEs to better define their future reform agenda, but also for other countries to profitably avoid in their own development efforts. Indeed, we believe it is through a judiciously balanced re-assessment of the good and bad experiences of Japan and the four NIEs that the best lessons can be drawn for other developing countries.

IV. DIFFERENTIATING THE NIEs FROM OTHER EAST ASIAN HPEs

While the East Asian HPEs as a regional grouping had indeed achieved significantly higher economic growth rates over the last 4 decades when compared with just about any other regional grouping of countries, a breakdown of the grouping into the four Asian NIEs and the ASEAN-4 "tiger economies" shows that the former had achieved faster aggregate GDP growth than the latter over the period 1960–99 (see Annex Table A). The exception is Hong Kong, which had an average growth rate (6.8%) comparable to that of Thailand (7.1%) and Malaysia (6.4% p.a.).

The difference in economic growth performance between the two groups of economies becomes more obvious when we examine per capita GDP growth, rather than aggregate GDP growth, and after making purchasing price parity adjustments. Table 1.2 highlights the differences in PPP-adjusted per capita GDP growth performance

TABLE 1.2   GDP Per Capita of NIEs and ASEAN Countries, 1965–95

	GDP per capita growth (% p.a.) (PPP adjusted) 1965-95	GDP per capita relative to the US (PPP adjusted)	
		1965	1995
Asian NIEs	*6.6*	*17.3*	*72.2*
Hong Kong	5.6	30.1	98.4
Korea	7.2	9.0	48.8
Singapore	7.2	15.9	85.2
Taiwan	6.2	14.2	56.2
ASEAN-4	*3.9*	*10.0*	*21.2*
Indonesia	4.7	5.2	13.1
Malaysia	4.8	14.3	36.8
Thailand	4.8	9.7	25.6
Philippines	1.2	10.7	9.4

SOURCE: Asian Development Bank (1997).

between the four NIEs and the ASEAN-4 over the 30 years period 1965–95. Basically, the four NIEs have been able to achieve an average per annum growth rate of per capita GDP that is 70% faster than the ASEAN-4 (about 40% faster if Philippines is excluded). Consequently, the ratio of the average GDP per capita of the four NIEs to that of ASEAN-4 has widened from 1.7 times in 1965 to 3.4 times in 1995. Even taking into account the lower population growth in the NIEs vs. the ASEAN-4 since the 1970s, the performance differential remains significant. More recent estimates of PPP adjusted per capita in GNP in 1998 suggest that the gap has further widened to about 4 times in 1998 (see Table 1.3).

Significant difference between the four NIEs and ASEAN-4 also appears to exist when we compare their growth rates of total factor productivity (TFP). There is a great deal of controversy in the literature concerning empirical estimates of TFP of East Asian countries [see e.g. Felipe (1997) for a more detailed review of the empirical evidence], and wide variations exist in the estimated values of TFP reported in different studies as summarized in Table 1.4. Nonetheless, a consistent pattern can be observed from Table 1.4: the TFP estimates for the four NIEs as a group have generally been higher than those for the ASEAN-

TABLE 1.3   Estimates of 1998 PPP-Adjusted GNP Per Capita, Asian
NIEs vs. ASEAN-4

	Per capita Income Estimate US$ (PPP adjusted)	
	1997 (GDP per capita)	1998 (GNP per capita)
Asian NIEs	20,189	20,960
Hong Kong	24,358	22,000
Korea	13,588	12,270
Singapore	23,614	28,620
Taiwan	19,197	na
ASEAN-4	5,464	4,790
Indonesia	3,501	2,790
Malaysia	8,142	6,990
Thailand	6,693	5,840
Philippines	3,521	3,540

SOURCES: International Institute for Management Development, *World Competitiveness Report, 1998;* World Bank, *World Development Report 1999.*

4 in nearly all the studies that cover the two groups (Thailand appears to be an exception in some of the studies).

While the above two indicators pertain to average performance of the economy as a whole, Table 1.5 compares the growth in labor productivity in the manufacturing sector of these eight countries. Again, the NIEs as a group was able to achieve significantly faster industrial productivity growth compared to the ASEAN-4. The laggard among the NIEs is Hong Kong; the contrast would have been stronger if Hong Kong is excluded.

Another indicator of the differences in industrial performance between the NIEs and the ASEAN-4 is the composition of their manufactured exports in terms of broad classification of technological intensity (Table 1.6). With the exception of Hong Kong, the NIEs had higher proportion of their manufactured exports in medium to high tech products when compared to the ASEAN-4. (The seemingly high share of Malaysia was due to the classification of all electronics as falling within the category of medium to high technology.)

The above statistics show clearly that the NIEs as a group has performed substantially better than the other countries included in the

TABLE 1.4 Total Factor Productivity Growth Estimates for Asia NIEs and ASEAN-4 (various sources)

	Korea	Taiwan	Hong Kong	Singapore	Malaysia	Indonesia	Thailand	Philippines
Kim & Lau (1966-90)	1.2	1.2	2.4	1.9	na	na	na	na
Young (1966-90)	1.7	2.6	2.3*	0.2	na	na	na	na
Lindaur & Roemer (1965-90)	4.9	4.9	3.6**	3.6	1.1	2.7	3.3	0.0
World Bank, EAM (1980-89)	3.1	3.8	3.6	1.2	1.1	1.2	2.5	na
Thomas & Wong (1960-90)	2.1	3.6	4.0	2.8	1.9	0.3	2.3	0.8
Hsieh (1966-90)	1.7	3.8	2.8	2.2	na	na	na	na
Manti (1970-90)	1.4	2.1	2.4	1.4	0.4	-0.5	1.6	-0.4
Collins & Bosworth:								
(1960-94)	1.5	2.0	na	1.5	0.9	0.8	1.8	-0.4
(1984-94)	2.1	3.8	na	3.1	1.4	0.9	3.3	-0.9

NOTES: * From 1966–91; ** From 1970–89
SOURCES: Respective authors cited.

TABLE 1.5 Industrial Productivity of NIEs and ASEAN countries, 1980-94

| | Value added/worker in manufacturing sector (US$) | | % growth p.a. 1980–94 |
	1980	1994	
Asian NIEs	9699	42323	11.1
Hong Kong	7840	26436	9.1
Korea	9545	52760	13.0
Singapore	13942	56329	10.5
Taiwan	7470	33766	11.4
ASEAN-4	5447	13335	6.6
Indonesia	3499	6954	5.0
Malaysia	8060	15317	4.7
Thailand	5675	18734	8.9
Philippines	4552	12334	7.4

SOURCE: Calculated from UNIDO(1996).

TABLE 1.6 Share of Medium & High Technology Products in Manufacturing Exports, Asian NIEs vs ASEAN-4

| | Medium & High Tech Products as % of Total Manufacturing Exports | |
	1985	1996
Hong Kong	33.5	42.9
Singapore	46.9	79.4
Korea	32.3	62.3
Taiwan	34.0	61.1
Malaysia	36.5	69.1
Thailand	19.7	49.8
Indonesia	8.7	23.2
Philippines	na	na

SOURCE: Lall (1998).

EAM in terms of industrial and technological performance, and hence strongly suggest the need to explain the development experience of these two groups differently.

V. UNDERSTANDING THE DIVERSITY OF INDUSTRIAL DEVELOPMENT APPROACHES

Among the NIEs

It is tempting to explain the overall superior performance of the NIEs vs the other HPEs in East Asia using the same set of common "fundamental" factors identified in the EAM: perhaps the NIEs just had more of these facilitating factors than the other countries, or had them earlier. It is certainly true that the NIEs on the whole had adopted an outward export orientation earlier than the ASEAN-4. The NIEs had also shifted towards a high savings regime earlier than the ASEAN-4, though not uniformly so. The NIEs may also have started with a higher level of education, and had maintained a higher level of educational attainment among their population since. It is more debatable if the NIEs as a whole had better macroeconomic stability than the ASEAN-4 (e.g. Korea and Taiwan had higher inflation rates than Thailand and Malaysia in the 1970s).

On balance, we have no doubt that some of the fundamental factors as emphasized by EAM and others — high savings rate, high propensity to invest in education, and export orientation — had contributed to the higher performance of the NIEs. However, what we found to be the most important distinguishing feature separating the four NIEs and the ASEAN-4 is the fact that the NIEs embarked on industrial development as a means to economic growth much earlier than the ASEAN-4. Moreover, with the possible exception of Hong Kong since the early 1980s, the NIEs have been able to sustain rapid industrial growth with significant productivity improvement and technological deepening.

Table 1.7 provides several indicators of the level of technological developments in Japan and the four Asian NIEs vs. the ASEAN-4. Clearly, in terms of investment in S&T resources (as measured by R&D expenditure and number of trained scientists and engineers) or investment in utilization of technology (PCs, internet hosts), the NIEs

TABLE 1.7 Indicators of Technological Development, Asian NIEs vs ASEAN-4

	World Competitiveness Report ranking of science & technology, 1999	Scientists & Engineers per million people, 1985-95	Gross Exp. on R&D as % of GDP, 1996	Tertiary Science & Engineering students as % of population, early 1990s	No. of PC per 1,000 population, 1999	Internet hosts per 10,000 population, July, 2000
Japan	2	6,309	3.0	0.46	287	269
USA	1	3,732	2.6[a]	0.73	511	2419.9
Hong Kong	22	na	0.1[b]	0.47	298	182.9
Singapore	12	2,728	1.4	0.56	437	385.7
Korea	28	2,636	2.8	1.34	182	100.1
Taiwan	10	na	1.8	1.09	178	167.1
Malaysia	32	87	0.2[c]	0.15	69	27.6
Thailand	46	119	0.1[c]	0.32	23	8.8
Indonesia	47	na	0.2[c]	0.13	9	1.1
Philippines	33	157	0.2[c]	na	17	2.2

NOTES: [a] – 1997; [b] – 1995; [c] – 1993

SOURCES: World Bank, *World Development Indicators* (WDI) (http://www.worldbank.org/data/wdi2001); Lall (1998); and *World Competitiveness Report 2000*.

are generally at substantially higher level than those of the ASEAN-4, with the possible exception of Hong Kong in terms of R&D intensity. We believe the key to understanding how the NIEs were able to industrialize so fast is to analyze why and how rapid and sustained technological learning and upgrading took place in these economies. Even if one were to accept the most dire analysis of NIE industrialization as being merely expanding the use of inputs — i.e. that their industrial growth has been "TFP-less" (Krugman,1994), it remains remarkable that these economies were able to expand manufacturing production at the pace they did.

1. Manufacturing Upgrading Strategies: Lessons from the East Asian NIEs

Historically, the Asian NIEs shared a common characteristics with many other developing countries in that they were all rather late-industrializing countries in the global economy (Hikino and Amsden,1994). These countries face two common problems in terms of developing high-tech industrial capability: firstly, they were typically distant from the lead user markets in North America, Europe and Japan; secondly, they were also far away from and disconnected to the leading sources of innovation in advanced countries. Despite these disadvantages, however, the Asian NIEs managed to achieve significantly faster high-tech industrial growth over the last three decades than all other developing countries.

More importantly, their manufacturing sector upgrading strategies have been distinctively different from one another. Synthesizing from the findings from the individual country reports for this study as well as other existing literatures (e.g. Hobday, 1994; Ernst 1997, 1998; Wong, 1998), we found that the four countries can be conceptualized to pursue four distinctly different generic routes in upgrading their industrial technological capabilities.

The first generic technological upgrading strategy can be best characterized as one involving technology assimilation/transfer and cooperative R&D promotion through public research institutes (PRIs). Among the NIEs, Taiwan has been most successful in using PRI to promote the diffusion of industrially-relevant technologies. For example, the Industrial Technology Research Institute (ITRI) has been widely credited with helping to create an advanced semiconductor industry cluster in Taiwan through a well-thought out and well-executed strategy of assimilating foreign technology and transferring them to local enterprises through spin-offs (see e.g. Mathews, 1995; Lin, 1994; NRI, 1995). The successful execution of this strategy depended on a number of factors, including careful long-term technology development planning and vision at the top [Electronics Industry Development Project (EIDP)], competent leadership at the helm of ITRI (Dr. Morris Chang), an abundant supply of well-trained engineers, and significant presence of, and strong linkage with, competitive local electronics industries which provided significant markets and customer feedbacks.

Besides such successful spin-offs as UMC and TSMC from PRIs, there are also many examples of PRI-orchestrated R&D consortia in Taiwan These have been promoted in the belief that the many small and medium enterprises in Taiwan would under-invest in new technology development if left on their own. Over the last 15 years, it has been estimated that over 60 such R&D consortia had been established in various industrial sectors in Taiwan. Although the records of these R&D consortia in terms of eventual market commercialization are mixed, it is undeniable that there has been much faster diffusion of product technological capabilities among the participating firms as a result of these consortium programs (e.g. the successful development of the notebook PC industry in Taiwan owes much to the ITRI-orchestrated development consortium). In particular, the significant inroads that Taiwanese firms have made into ODM in recent years are partly facilitated by these R&D consortia.

The second generic route to manufacturing upgrading can be characterized as one involving the deliberate promotion of high-tech conglomerate enterprises of sufficiently large scale. This has been the classic Korean chaebol model of expansion through horizontal diversification in product space and vertical integration in process space. In the early stage of development of "strategic" industries in Korea, the Korean government deliberately encouraged the growth of large-scale chaebols as an instrument to bring about the economy of scale in capital-intensive industries that were deemed "strategic". A variety of policy tools were used (see e.g. Kim, 1993), including subsidized financing, protection of domestic market, incentives for technological learning through capital goods import or turnkey projects vs. DFI, and turning over failing state enterprises to the chaebols.

Although there were notable failures in this heavy industry strategy, several of the big chaebols like Samsung, LG, Hyundai and Daewoo did develop significant technological capabilities in a wide range of export-oriented, capital intensive industries as a result. Where Korea differs from other developing countries in promoting big businesses was in the discipline that the state exercised over these chaebols by penalizing poor performances and rewarding only good ones. This "contest"-based approach (Amsden,1989) enabled a number of high-performing chaebols to quickly establish large scale production, marketing/distribution or R&D economies to compete successfully in several global industries like shipbuilding, automobile, consumer electronics, telecommunications equipment, and semiconductors. The large size of these chaebols enabled them to build global brand and distribution channels, and hence move quickly into OBM in a wide range of consumer products. Deep pockets have also enabled the chaebols to acquire technology capabilities quickly by buying up established companies (recent examples include Maxtor, NCR microelectronics, AST). However, the large size of the chaebols appear to be a source of disadvantage when it comes to competing in technologically dynamic industries like PCs, software, biotechnology and specialty chemicals where scale economies are not important or less critical. Furthermore, indiscriminate and unrelated diversification had often led to over-extension and loss of strategic focus. This conglomeration trend had also become increasingly questioned as a result of political democratization in recent years.

The excessive development of big businesses in Korea had indeed become evident in the light of the recent debt crisis faced by Korea, which exposed the vulnerability of this high financial gearing approach to industrial growth. Nevertheless, this basic approach of "contest-based" resource allocation and the strategy to focus resources to attempt a "big-push" to accelerate the development of selected targeted industries appears to have enabled Korea to enter a wide range of capital-intensive high-tech industries previously dominated by advanced industrialized countries.

The third generic route to manufacturing upgrading, typified by Hong Kong, can be characterized as one of staying within relatively mature industries and product groups, but migrating along the vertical value chain towards marketing, logistics and technical support downstream and product innovation upstream. With little government support for R&D and technological development, Hong Kong manufacturing firms opted not to enter technologically advanced sectors or products involving the early stage of new technology life-cycles. Instead, they sought to achieve cost competitive advantage in relatively mature, less capital-intensive sectors (e.g. textile and garment, watches, electronic toys and games) by redistributing manufacturing operations to China (particularly Shenzhen) and other low-cost regions in South East Asia. At the same time, the Hong Kong base is turned increasingly into the headquarter for product design, marketing, logistics management, technical support and accounting/administration. By focusing on niche markets involving fast fashion changes or short product runs and leveraging on the excellent communications and transport infrastructure of Hong Kong, many Hong Kong manufacturers developed core competencies in managing fast response, dispersed production networks. For example, in textile and garment making, Hong Kong firms have developed sophisticated CAD/CAM design and electronic data interchange capabilities that allow them to quickly turn buyer requirements into design specifications, which are then partitioned into job assignments to different subcontractors, often outside Hong Kong. In reality, this generic route involves substantial de-industrialization of Hong Kong itself, which retains largely the services value-added stages of the manufacturing value chain.

Last, but not least, the industrial development strategy of Singapore can be best characterized as one emphasizing government facilitation of MNC-induced technological learning. Through the Economic Development Board(EDB), the Singapore government has encouraged MNCs to bring in success waves of new technologies to their subsidiary operations in Singapore. Although some have criticized this MNC-led approach as stunting the growth of local firms, research evidence has shown that these MNC operations have spawned a large supporting industry in Singapore and induced substantial technological capability development among many local subcontracting and contract assembly firms (Wong, 1995b). Moreover, active innovative public assistance programs such as the Local Industry Upgrading program (LIUP), programs to promote the adoption of new information and automation technology by SMEs, advanced technical manpower training programs like INTECH, and the early promotion of the ISO9000 certification infrastructure have been shown to have facilitated the technological and management learning process of these supporting industries. Many of these local supporting firms have pursued the process specialist route, and most have since internationalized their operations to the near NIEs like Malaysia and China, not only following the redistribution of their customers to these countries, but diversifying into new buyer markets as well. Regionalization incentives provided by the government have facilitated these overseas venturing.

Moreover, new innovative R&D incentives like Research Incentives Scheme for Companies (RISC) has been introduced by the government to fund integrative process technology capability development efforts in these companies, even though such efforts cannot be neatly packaged into specific R&D projects. A smaller, but increasing, number of companies have also pursued the reverse product life-cycle strategy, moving into new product R&D while leveraging their traditional strengths in low-cost, high-quality manufacturing.

The generic routes described above serve to highlight the dominant routes taken by Taiwan, Korea, Hong Kong and Singapore respectively to upgrading industrial capability development. In reality, it should be recognized, of course, that none of these countries pursue only one route exclusively. For example, the Singapore government has in recent years also started to stress the need to develop high-tech firms of sufficient scale by setting up a government-controlled group, Singapore Technology Group, to spearhead entry into various high-tech industries (e.g. semiconductor wafer fabrication, chip design, aerospace repair and maintenence, systems software) where local entrepreneurs had been found wanting. Many Singapore firms have also adopted the generic upgrading route of Hong Kong by redistributing their manufacturing operations overseas and leveraging Singapore as their regional headquarter hub for product/process development, marketing, logistics and technical support.

The use of public research institute to promote technology diffusion has also been used in Korea, particularly in the early years, as in the case of semiconductor technology acquisition through public research institute like KIET (which was later merged into ETRI) (Mathews, 1995). The considerably larger resources of the big chaebols meant that further direct government involvement in technology transfer was deemed unnecessary once the basic 4M DRAM technology was diffused among Samsung, LG and Hyundai. More recently, the Singapore government has also started to promote R&D consortia as a means to hasten technological capability development of local firms. Involvement with foreign firms or R&D institutions are particularly emphasized to facilitate technology transfer from advanced sources. Examples include the Digital Media Consortium (involving 3 local firms, 3 PRIs, and MIT Media Lab) and cooperative R&D programs in aerospace, data storage and marine technologies.

In highlighting the differences among the East Asian NIEs, we do not intend to belittle the various common state facilitating roles as emphasized by the EAM, such as high investment in education (especially technical education) and infrastructures, export orientation, and macroeconomic stability, etc. have also been of great importance. Indeed, in some sense, these fundamental policies may well represent the pre-conditions for the success of the more specific industrial policies adopted in the different countries.

2. Why the Diversities of Development Strategies?

To understand why the four Asian NIEs adopted such widely different industrial and technological development strategies, it is important to take into account the unique historical social contexts and political circumstances under which these economies first began their industrialization process; as emphasized by Haggard(1988), different developing countries exhibited different "pathways from the periphery" in pursuit of economic development, constrained by the conjuncture of their domestic social contexts, the prevailing external environmental influences, and the outcome of political responses to those domestic contexts and external influences.

Historical contexts

All four countries were former colonies. The city economies of Singapore and Hong Kong were former colonies of Britain; and the other two were colonies of Japan. Both the city economies were unique in the sense that they had no natural resources, but were strategically located with good natural harbors and therefore basically developed by the British to serve their regional interests. Nurtured as entrepot and administrative centers for the British, entrepot trade and auxiliary activities such as banking, transportation, and other infrastructure had been relatively well developed compared to the neighboring region by the early 1950s.

Unlike Hong Kong which remained a British colony, Singapore on gaining independence in 1965 had to quickly develop herself into a nation state in a relatively hostile regional environment (strained political relationship with Malaysia, confrontation with Indonesia). Job creation and national security were of utmost importance to the political leadership at the time. To solve the first problem in the face of no natural resources, no access to the immediate hinterland markets, and absence of any established industrial base, the political leadership had little recourse but to turn to foreign MNCs who could provide the missing "industrial entrepreneurs" with ready markets to export their manufactured goods. To solve the second problem, the state needed to gain direct control over strategic industries such as steel making, shipyards, and seaports. The genesis of two key prongs of Singapore's subsequent development strategies — reliance on MNC investment and state-own enterprises to sustain economic growth — can thus be traced to this historical context that the political leadership found themselves at the start of the country's nationhood.

Taiwan and Korea were both colonies of Japan. Japan's growth model therefore had great influence on the economic thinking of these two economies. However, it was Korea that followed most closely the Japanese growth model particularly during Park Chung Hee's regime. Besides being in the frontline of communist threats, both economies faced the challenge of having to adjust to impending withdrawal of US aid in the 1960s. Both were under the rule of military regimes which needed to win support from a populace not through the ballot box, but through delivery of economic goods and national security. The "siege mentality" underlying both regimes may have also compelled the leadership to develop an early focus on the development of indigenous technological capabilities to support the growth of strategic, defence-related industries.

Despite such similar historical contexts, the developmental path of these two economies diverged significantly. While both regimes exploited the siege mentality, Korea under President Park adopted a much more interventionist approach in order to accelerate economic growth, both to catch up with Japan as well as to bolster security position versus the North. The early success that Park had with using credit rationing to direct investment into manufacturing exports, at a time when banking institutions in the country were primitive, probably laid the foundation for the subsequent system of pursuing industrial policy through state control of bank lending. Meanwhile, the Taiwan leadership, with its mistrust of possible emergence of large local capitalists as possible sources of opposition, focused on promoting the growth of SMEs outside of strategic industries such as steel-making, which was state-owned.

Adaptation to External Influences

In addition to the different unique historical contexts of the four NIEs, it is also important to understand the subsequent changes in external environment that affect the development of these countries. All the four country papers showed that both the US and Japan played significant roles in the development of these economies. First and foremost was the significant US role. Coincidentally or otherwise, US influence and actions in restructuring the Japanese economy over the occupation period set the pace of industrial and economic change in the East Asian region. It is difficult to envisage the pace and scale of sustained post-war long-term economic growth of Japan, if not for the forced agrarian reforms, dissolution of Zaibatsus, rewriting of the constitution' and other contributions such as US security umbrella, aid, technology and market. Likewise in Taiwan and South Korea, US security umbrella and US aid kept these economies from turning into socialist states with their closed economies. Ironically, it was US impending withdrawal of aid that prompted these two economies to take the significant step of opening up through manufactured export-led strategy of economic growth, thereby shortening the necessary but expensive import-substituting strategy. The provision of US security in like fashion provided the political stability for foreign investments in both Hong Kong and Singapore. According to some observers, Hong Kong would have been handed back to China in the 1960s if not for US pressure on the British to do otherwise. In this regard, it can be said that US interest went beyond economics, being heavily influenced by strategic considerations in the "cold-war" geopolitical struggle against the spread of communist influence.

Domestically, all four NIEs with the exception of Hong Kong experienced a sort of siege mentality that made the situation politically feasible to undertake tough belt-tightening measures that built strong foundation for economic growth. The political regimes had to be economically strong to survive. This factor probably added to other factors that made them developmental states. Hong Kong was the exception, precisely because it remained a colony of Britain and hence the political regimes did not face the same pressure.

In addition to the American security umbrella bolstered by economic aids, the expansion of US business interests in general and the growing DFI by US manufacturing firms in particular also contributed significantly to the industrialization of all the four NIEs. Particularly important was the growing outward direct foreign investment by US electronics firms into all four economies from the 1960s, to exploit the low labor cost advantages of these economies, as well as to cope with growing competition by Japanese firms in a wide range of electronics industries. This process of globalization of American production was not evenly distributed worldwide, but concentrated primarily in these East Asian economies, at least in the early stages before their cheap labor supply vanished. As a result, US off-shore production significantly boosted the technological capability and export potential of these economies, ahead of those of other developing countries. Industrialization and rapid economic growth were further enhanced when Japan followed likewise with massive investments in these economies to cope with increasing loss of competitiveness of domestically based manufacturers, particularly after the Plaza Accord of 1985, when the yen appreciated dramatically.

The role played by Japan cannot be underestimated. Japan was and still is a major growth pole for the whole region providing both the demonstration and spillover effects to neighboring economies. President Park Chung Hee, in particular, emulated the Japanese system very closely. The psychology was not only one of "if Japan can so can Korea", but also that this catching-up needs to happen very quickly, given that Korea was once colonized by Japan. Although impossible to quantify, the effect that this national psyche to catch up with Japan had in galvanizing the general populace and in imbuing them with a sense of purposefulness and direction cannot be underestimated in the case of Korea. In the other three NIEs, the influence of Japan was exerted more through demonstration effects, manifested in terms of interest in emulating Japanese management philosophy and practices such as quality control circles, productivity movements and other positive practices. More economically quantifiable are the spillover effects in the form of Japanese investments in offshore production in these economies as a consequence of higher domestic factor costs and other costs such as more stringent environmental laws. As described by Akamatsu's "flying geese" model, the four NIEs were the first in line to benefit significantly from the redistribution of manufacturing production and technologies from Japan to Asia

Industry-Specific Policies

While the above external contexts and domestic political factors shaped the likely development paths pursued by the four NIEs, they do not explain fully how and why industrial development took off so differently in these four countries. To do so require taking account of the specific industrial policies that were adopted in these countries. In this study, all four country research teams were asked to illustrate the specific workings of the industrial and technological development policies in the four countries through the lenses of two major industries. Specifically, we have chosen the electronics industry as a common industry for all four NIEs due to its significant contributions to the growth of all the NIEs. In addition, each of the research teams for the NIEs was asked to identify another industry that best illustrates the role of the state, both positive and negative, in influencing the development of a major industry in the respective economies. In this regard, the automobile industry was chosen in the case of South Korea; the textile industry in the case of Taiwan; the shipbuilding and repair in the case of Singapore; and the garment industry in the case of Hong Kong. We summarize briefly here the findings from the four countries.

Despite receiving little or no encouragement from the British colonial authority, Hong Kong was able to embark on industrialization shortly after the fall of China to the Communists due to the inflows of migrant industrialists and entrepreneurs from Shanghai and other parts of China. These experienced capitalists gave Hong Kong a head start in the textile and garment industry through the establishment of numerous labor-intensive firms. Despite such an early start, however, the Hong Kong paper cited a lack of interest to innovate, as it was too costly and risky for these small enterprises to do so. Instead, focus was given to maintaining low production cost and high degree of flexibility in production, which capitalized on Hong Kong's strength in commercial networks in international subcontracting and production flexibility. Expertise and experience so nurtured did contribute towards Hong Kong's ambition to be a commercially oriented business network center — a trans-shipment center of trading firms and sourcing agents. Unlike Taiwan and Korea, the textile industry in Hong Kong did not result in the development of capital-intensive chemical industries that were facilitated by the increasing demand for man-made fibers. Instead, Hong Kong continued as a center for the manufacture of garments with the textile industry relocated to Southern China.

Likewise in the electronics industry, the SMEs of Hong Kong without R&D support from the state could not go beyond subcontract production for OEMs. The Hong Kong paper cited that Hong Kong is far behind Singapore, not to mention Korea and Taiwan, in the electronics industry because of its failure to upgrade production as well as to catch up with its competitors in the absence of government intervention. Specifically mentioned were the lack of support in R&D, infrastructure and industrial linkages, including the lack of leadership and direction. As a result, Hong Kong firms adopted a strategy of focusing on niche markets and competing on cost, initially through the use of unskilled workers in Hong Kong, and later through outsourcing manufacturing to Mainland China. The strategic gateway position of Hong Kong to the China market allowed Hong Kong to create substantial number of jobs and to achieve substantial economic growth as a trading and business services hub; manufacturing was not necessary as an engine for creating jobs, and indeed, Hong Kong experienced rapid de-industrialization after China opened its door to foreign manufacturing investments in 1978.

In contrast to Hong Kong, Singapore's development strategy relied heavily on attracting manufacturing MNCs to set up operations in Singapore for export markets. With no migrant industrialists and entrepreneurs like in Hong Kong, and with the Malaysian market closed to export from Singapore after political separation in 1965, MNCs with their massive resources and international networks were thought to be the only means by which the government could provide the jobs to cope with the high unemployment at the time. Because of security considerations, the government needed to establish government-owned companies to directly engage in strategic industries such as steel making, shipbuilding, shipping, air and sea-port services, utilities, and ammunition making. To the extent that the government succeeded in making both of these approaches to economic development work, they became the foundations for later economic policies. After the economy had grown rapidly and unemployment was no longer a serious problem by the mid-1970s, the government did have the option to consider other development approaches, but by then, the virtuous cycle of leveraging increasingly more technologically advanced MNC investments had become obvious to the political leadership. Moreover, the success of the strategy had enabled the political leadership to win significant political support from the industrial working class. Local capitalists, who were mainly engaged in trade related services, did not benefit as much from the MNC-leveraging strategy, but they were not a sizable political threat.

With the MNC leveraging strategy dominant, it is not surprising that the role of indigenous firms in the manufacturing industry has largely been negligible until the 1980s, when a sizable number of indigenous supporting industries were able to emerge as subcontractors to the MNCs. Some of these had since grown to become multinational contract manufacturers. While a number of state-controlled high tech enterprises were formed earlier to enter industries deemed strategic by the government, indigenous private high tech start-ups only began to emerge in the mid-1990s after the country had started to expand R&D in the early 1990s.

We have noted earlier that Korea went the large conglomerate (Chaebol) way through credit rationing. Korea like the other three countries is poor in natural resources but highly dependent on imports of intermediate capital and raw materials for its growth. To sustain this process, Korea depended more than the other three on foreign borrowings; and there was also less separation of financial from industrial capital as the Korean government had much greater influence over private investment by means of subsidized loans to targeted industries as part of its industrial policy. Among all four countries, the highest degree of intervention came from the Korean government. The initial push for export-led growth was strongest as credit rationing was based on targeted exports. Expectedly, the expansion of exports has been regarded as the engine of the Korean economy's impressive growth.

On the negative side, however, Korea recorded substantial trade deficits and large amount of external debts in its early industrial growth phase. Korea also experienced the highest rate of inflation among this group of economies. The high inflation rate was caused mainly by excessive expansion of demand associated with rapid expansion of industrial capacity. Negative or low real interest rate caused chronic excess demand for loans. Structural imbalances in the economy occurred through: over investment in heavy industries and under investment in light industries; extensive price distortions and lack of competition due to government control; and a rise in real wages which exceeded productivity improvements. There were a number of measures taken that did not complement but supplant markets. The concentration of economic power in a handful of large family based chaebols which fostered very closed government-business relations eventually led to capture and rent-seeking activities detrimental to the economic health of Korea. The financial crisis that impacted Korea over 1997–99 clearly highlighted the above shortcomings.

In the electronics industry, unlike the two city-states, chaebols and other local firms played a dominant role. From initial protection under the phase of import substitution, the state role has changed to pushing for exports. Currently, the state is playing a more promotional role as Korea entered the technologically dynamic environment. Statistically, the electronics industry has been very successful surging to be the fourth largest producer in the world. On the demand side of technology, the state has helped by creating market through procurement. On the supply side of technology, the state has strengthened public R&D capability and promoting joint research between industry and R&D institutes and between industry and academia. According to the Korean paper, "Government not only set specific export goals and direction, forcing local firms to be competitive in both price and quality in the international market, it also provided incentives. This scheme induced a crisis, compelling local firms to acquire technological capability quickly while providing supports to make the crisis creative rather than destructive".

Taiwan on the hand went the SME way. Partly as a consequence that historically business had been in the hands of native Taiwanese and partly the strong Chinese trait of wishing to be one's own boss. When the KMT relocated to Taiwan, the party had few ties with the local Taiwanese business community. In fact, the KMT government actively tried to check the growth and concentration of large Taiwanese capital as these were seen as threats. It was only in the early 1960s, under US pressure, did economic reforms shifted away from the state-owned sector towards tacit support for private business through more secure property rights and various fiscal and financial incentives. However, the change to export-led growth made the KMT to forge closer relations with the private sector. Increasingly, the interests of both the party and the business sector converged — particularly, in the need for active state involvement for technology upgrading, slower growth in social welfare spending, and the exclusion of organized labor from economic policy-making.

Taiwan's experience in the electronics industry is instructive. Like Singapore and Hong Kong, it was US MNCs seeking a better international division of labor that brought the industry to Taiwan. But it was Taiwan's deliberate effort and ability to cultivate indigenous technology that contributed most to its industrialization effort. According to the Taiwanese paper, industrial and technological market targeting was important to the promotion of local technological capability. While the paper found that industrial targeting did cause some distortions in the economy, it stressed that such a targeting approaching provided invaluable opportunities for learning without which no large local electronics firms could have emerged. Other factors cited include the existence of industrial base for manufacture of parts and components; and local content regulations. In terms of the latter factor, the paper argued that it was useful in forcing MNCs in transferring technology for parts manufacturing and local component sourcing.

On the other hand, the Taiwanese experience on the transfer of technology through formal licensing agreements was less positive as such agreements had the tendency of restricting exports. Another important experience of Taiwan was that at a later stage of industrialization, the lack of investment incentives and inadequate sources of technological innovation from local universities and public research institutions caused many MNCs to leave after Taiwan lost its comparative advantage in low wages. The paper described that only components-producers such as Texas Instrument and Philips, which depended more on process technology innovation than on cheap labor, remained and prospered in Taiwan.

In the case of the semiconductor industry, Taiwan's semiconductor production did not progress beyond the assembly stage and was dominated by MNC assembly operations right up to the end of the 1970s. Taiwan was not able to induce MNCs to set up semiconductor fabrication plants due to the need for large capital commitment and the high risk of technology failure should the host country lack the engineering capability to run the skill-intensive operations. The state came in through the establishment of Electronics Research and Services

Organization (ERSO). This organization in turn established an experimental plant to receive technology from RCA. The plant subsequently spun off to become a private firm named United Microelectronics Company (UMC). UMC and another ERSO spin-off, TSMC, subsequently became the major vehicles for accumulating chip-processing technologies, training local engineers for IC wafer fabrication, and pioneering the growth of the "pure foundry" services model, whereby the Taiwanese firms would become the contract manufacturers that fabricate ICs designed by American and European firms. These developments consequently attracted many overseas Chinese engineers and entrepreneurs in Silicon Valley to set up subsidiaries in Taiwan and other MNCs followed the move, eventually laying the foundation for the development of a vibrant IC-design industry in Taiwan itself.

The study of Taiwan's textile industry is also instructive, by showing how an export oriented strategy, coupled with industrial targeting policy, particularly the policy of targeting the man-made fiber sub-sector, accelerated Taiwan's industrial upgrading process through enhancing backward linkage spill-over effects into chemicals. Initially, the textile industry in Taiwan was highly protected. But limited domestic market combined with the need to earn foreign exchange in order to import capital goods and raw materials forced Taiwan to export. This was facilitated by incentives implemented by the state. Of greater significance is the observation that "the beginning of each kind of new fiber production was associated directly or indirectly with the government". In particular, by targeting the man-made fiber sector, which is much more capital and technology intensive compared to natural fiber, Taiwan was able to establish a strong chemical industry even as she lost competitiveness in the labor-intensive garment sector. As a measure of the importance of textile and chemical industries in Taiwan, these two industries remain among the largest industries today — accounting for more than 35% of employment.

In summary, the industrial case studies provided empirical evidence of the positive roles played by the state in Korea, Taiwan and Singapore, albeit in very different ways. The case study of Hong Kong, in contrast, highlighted why Hong Kong lagged behind the other three NIEs in the development of its electronics industry due to the lack of active government support. Indeed, it is instructive to note that, even though Hong Kong started with a significantly larger and more sophisticated electronics manufacturing base than Singapore in the early 1970s, by 1997, Hong Kong's electronics output was less than 20% that of Singapore, and with a product composition that was significantly lower in technological intensities than Singapore's.

Applicability of East Asian Industrial Policies to Other Countries?

The role of state intervention through industrial policy has been a controversial issue in the development economics literature. On the one hand, various developmental state scholars like Amsden and Wade have argued that industrial policies were critical to the rapid industrialization of Japan, Korea, Taiwan and Singapore. On the other hand, various scholars in the MSFMP tradition have argued either that industrial policies generally don't work at all, or that even if they sometimes work, the fact that there have been many notable failures of industrial policy mean that the risk involved is too high. Other scholars have argued that, empirically, there is no clear-cut case that positive industrial policy intervention has outweighed those with negative consequences (see e.g. Stern *et al.*,1995; Perkins,1994). The failures of the heavy industry program in Korea, the car industry in Taiwan, and the computer industry in Japan have been particularly highlighted by critics of industrial policy. Moreover, they would argue that the case is even worse for other developing countries which lack the institutional capabilities of the state in Japan, Korea, Taiwan and Singapore.

The case of Hong Kong is often cited by scholars of the MSFMP persuasion as a counter-example to suggest that fast economic growth can be achieved without industrial policy intervention. In fact, some of these scholars question the emphasis on industrial and technological development as pursued by Japan and the other three Asian NIEs: the example of Hong Kong is used to suggest that developing economies can grow fast through a laissez-faire policy that neither stresses manufacturing nor services; free market competition will determine which are the profitable sectors to be invested in, and hence which sectors will grow fast.

To the MSFMP policy school, the lessons from Japan and the four Asian NIEs for other developing countries are therefore straightforward: focus on non-sector specific, fundamental macroeconomic policies and eschew "picking the winners" through industrial targeting; adopt market liberalization and deregulate industries as much as possible. While we do not disagree entirely with the importance of market liberalization and competition policy, we draw a different set of policy implications from the experience of Japan and the four East Asian NIEs for other developing countries. Firstly, we believe that the way to move forward is not to discount industrial policy in the aggregate, but to identify with greater precision why certain policies succeeded in certain contexts, and the institutional mechanisms that facilitated such success. Valuable lessons can still be drawn if we take such a fine-grain approach, i.e. the right question in many cases is not whether a policy works, but under what contexts. In particular, rather than a sweeping rejection of the policy of industrial targeting or "picking the winners", we maintain that such a policy is still applicable for late-industrializng countries seeking to embark on the early stage of industrialization.

When a country is far from the technological frontier, the risk of targeting the wrong industries or standardizing on the wrong technological platform is much lower, and may be outweighed by the potential benefits of scale economies and reduction of coordination costs that can result from targeted promotion of certain industries by the state. The key qualifier is that the state must adopt a transparent "performance-based contest" approach to industrial targeting (e.g. export performance) (Amsden,1989), so that the danger of such industrial targeting degenerating into permanent wasteful subsidies is significantly reduced. Yet another facilitating factor is the willingness, and ability, of the state agency concerned to respond to external market forces, and adjust its policies accordingly. The point here is that an industrial policy of promoting a certain industry is more likely to work in the context of a corresponding competition policy, and an institutional capability to respond and learn from external market signals.

Another example of industrial policy pursued by the NIEs (with the exception of Hong Kong) that we believe is still relevant and applicable to other developing countries is that of promoting technological capability development. Our synthesis of the experience of Korea, Taiwan and Singapore from the technological learning perspective strongly suggests that the role of the state has been vitally important in accelerating the development of technological capabilities, albeit in different ways. Indeed, the example of Hong Kong shows that, absent such government role, the pace of technological learning and upgrading has been the slowest among the NIEs. Furthermore, one could argue that S&T policy has been important not just in the rapid technological catch up of the NIEs, but in the earlier industrialization of the by now advanced industrial countries as well.

Besides its over-sweeping rejection of industrial policy, we also believe that the MSFMP position underestimates the extent to which learning from earlier policy failures has enabled the countries concerned to improve their policy design or implementation approach at a later stage and perhaps in a different industry. In the same vein, earlier failures in developing certain industries may also have resulted in the accumulation of technological knowledge and in the development of skills that facilitated the subsequent development of other related industries. Seen in this perspective, the failures of promoted industries had generated spillover benefits that are not captured in the standard approach to cost-benefit analysis of investment projects.

Last, but not least, we believe that state intervention through industrial policies are likely to be necessary in the early industrial development stage of developing countries, where the enabling conditions for free market to operate is absent. As pointed out by Ohno(1998), the state often needs to play the role of creating the market conditions in the first place where none existed. Similarly, Aoki(1997) and others have highlighted the important role of the state in providing the coordination mechanisms to enhance the working of markets when they are not yet well developed, or where market failures are significant.

VI. STATE INSTITUTIONAL DYNAMICS: STRONG GOVERNANCE vs. INSTITUTIONAL INERTIA?

Much of the Developmental State literature on East Asia has stressed strong governance or institutional capability as the major factor that enable the East Asian developmental states to successfully implement state intervention policies. The argument is that, absent such institutional capacity, state failures will be much higher as are indeed commonly observed in many developing countries that sought to pursue interventionist industrial policy.

While confirming the relatively strong role of the state in the early stages of development in the case of Japan and the Asian NIEs with the exception of Hong Kong, the country case studies also highlighted the danger that some of the strong state institutions established in these countries may become dysfunctional over time, leading to potential policy rigidities and institutional inertia that stifle further development of a competitive market economy.

The case of Japan is particularly instructive in this regard. The country paper on Japan has shown clearly that inefficient state intervention has become a major cause for the inability of Japan to get out of the asset bubble since the late 1980s. We see the fundamental problem here as one of institutional inertia: policies and institutions that were once useful at an earlier stage of economic development became dysfunctional at a later stage of development, but were not removed due to institutional inertia. While the prolonged slow growth of the Japanese economy in the 1990s does not invalidate the Japanese industrial policy model in an earlier industrial development stage, they do point to excessive inertia in revising policies and reforming institutions to meet new challenges. For example, while the Japanese educational system has played a major role in meeting the needs of traditional manufacturing industries for highly literate and trainable workers who can work well in group settings, the challenge for Japan in the 1990s and beyond is to produce more specialist professionals as well as more creative talents with greater independent thinking ability. The old educational system of producing generalists to be later trained in specific skills through learning by doing within industries no longer appear to meet the demand for specialist skills well, but it is so entrenched that, despite widespread criticism of the university educational system, little progress towards reforms has been made.

A major contributing factor to institutional inertia in Japan, we believe, is the system of entrenched bureaucracies that manifest significant turf-fighting behavior, and the continuing hostage of state fund allocation based on political electioneering needs rather than to promote investment in more productive public goods such as IT infrastructural development, basic R&D, and educational systems. For example, compared to the US and other large, advanced OECD countries, Japanese public R&D investments are significantly lower.

Korea has similarly experienced major institutional inertia problems in the system of state allocation of credits. Because the banking system had been institutionalized to allocate lending according to state directives, none of the banks had developed the independent capabilities to perform the market function of screening investment projects. While the state may have been able to perform this credit allocation function relatively well in the early development stages when Korea was far from the market and technology frontiers and hence "picking winners" was relatively less risky, such state intervention became woefully inefficient when Korea became more advanced. Moreover, this system of "export contest" for state credit allocation, while facilitating the rapid growth of competitive firms in the early stages, had led to such concentration of power in the beneficiaries of the system — the chaebols — that they were able to flex their influence well beyond the control of the bureaucrats at a later stage.

While the state in Taiwan and Singapore had comparatively wielded less powerful institutions to perform resource allocations and regulatory functions the way that the Japanese MITI and MOF or the Korean EPA did, they too exhibited notable instances of institutional inertia. For example, while the Singaporean government has by and large been willing to reverse wrong policies and remove ineffective management of state own enterprises, they had been somewhat overly conservative and slow in relaxing their control over CPF savings, in deregulating the telecommunications services market, and in liberalizing the financial services markets. In each case, the regulatory policies and institutional frameworks that were implemented had served their intended roles well in the past, and had not become so inefficient that they needed immediate fixing. Thus it was difficult to argue that they should be changed. Ironically, it is the recent financial crisis in the region that accelerated the Singapore government's recognition of the necessity to hasten the pace of deregulation of its financial services sector.

VII. EAST ASIAN DEVELOPMENT MODELS IN THE LIGHT OF THE RECENT REGIONAL FINANCIAL CRISIS

1. From "Market Friendly Policies" to "Crony Capitalism": Interpretation of the Financial Crisis from the MSFM Paradigm

Since the onset of the regional financial crisis in July, 1997, much has been written to the effect that the crisis has proven that the East Asian

Miracle is in reality a mirage. While the impacts of the crisis have been severe on East Asia as a whole, there has of course been significant variations among the different East Asian economies: Thailand, Indonesia, Korea and Malaysia were worst hit; Philippines, Hong Kong and to a smaller extent, Singapore, have also been moderately affected, while the least affected so far have been Taiwan and China. Such differences in impacts notwithstanding, many critics from the MSFMP school have been quick to pronounce a common diagnosis of the vulnerabilities of East Asia: too much state intervention leading to "crony capitalism".

As succinctly summarized by Dean(1999), the crony capitalism argument for the Asian financial crisis can be stated as follows:

> Asian banking systems...are rife with insider lending and government quasi-guarantees...and this led to extreme moral hazard and adverse selection. These factors prompted "Panglossian" valuations of asset values, until, that is, the funds for government subsidization and bailouts simply ran out. At that point the dynamics that had led to overvaluation went into reverse.

This version of the crony capitalism was made popular by Krugman(1998), who presented a formal mathematical model to support the above verbal description. Subsequent popularization of the crony capitalism argument in the western media has become increasingly ideological; in particular, some critics were quick to extend the attack to "Asian value" as nothing but a convenient cover for crony capitalism.

If the financial crisis and economic slowdown of much of developing East Asia have been taken by proponents of the MSFM paradigm of development as vindication of their school of thought, the prolonged slowdown of the Japanese economy since the late 1980s has been cited as yet another vindication by these same proponents of MSFMP. The inability of Japan to get out of its asset bubble since the late 1980s and the consequent inability of Japan to provide the rest of East Asia with the needed stimulus for growth has been argued by many analysts as an important contributing factor to the worsening of the East Asian financial crisis. More importantly, the prolonged economic slowdown in Japan since the late 1980s has been used by the proponents of the MSFM paradigm to cast significant doubt on the viability and sustainability of the Japanese model of economic development. Although the specific causes of Japan's economic slowdown are acknowledged as different from the causes of the financial crisis in other East Asian economies, the MSFMP proponents argue that they share a common root cause: too much state interventions that shackle the working of the free market principle.

From the perspective of MSFMP, the proposed solution to the Asian financial crisis and the prolonged Japanese economic slowdowns is simple: since too much state intervention of the wrong type is the cause, the solution is to minimize state involvement and to liberalize market. In particular, these prescriptions mean the curtailment of government spending and the opening up of domestic market to foreign competition. Among the proponents of the crony capitalism argument was the IMF itself. Indeed, the three key features of the IMF bailout packages for Thailand, Korea and Indonesia — austerity measures, reform of basic domestic institutions and further opening up of the countries to international capital flows — can be seen as following logically from the crony capitalism argument.

2. Interpretations Based on our Five Country Studies

Based on our review of the development experience of the five countries, we developed an alternative interpretation of the lessons of the Asian financial crisis and the prolonged economic slowdown of Japan that is quite different from the MSFMP.

Causes of the Asian Financial Crisis

While the "crony capitalism" explanation of the Asian financial crisis is ideologically convenient to the MSFMP school, the weight of empirical evidence emerging more recently strongly suggest that it is at best a partial explanation, and at worst a cause for deepening and prolonging the crisis itself. As succinctly summarized by McLean(1999), Kumar and Debroy(1999), Sachs and Radelets(1998), Rodrik(1998), among others, the Asian financial crisis can be traced to multiple interacting causes, including the emergence of an asset bubble in several of the affected economies (especially Thailand and Malaysia) leading to large current account deficits, the increasing practice of short term borrowings for long term investment purposes based on the expectation of fixed exchange rate regimes despite persistent and growing trade surpluses, the ensuing financial panic that broke out when such expectations of fixed exchange rate were exposed by hedge fund attacks, and the consequent contagious spreading of the financial panic to other economies in the region.

Underlying these proximate causes, we believe that there are three more fundamental factors at work. The first fundamental factor has been the rapid financial liberalization in the affected economies without adequate supervisory controls being put in place. In particular, the three major economies in the region least affected by the financial crisis — China, India and Taiwan — all had the least open financial market, while the most affected economies — Thailand, Malaysia, Indonesia and Korea — had all recently adopted financial market liberalization without the appropriate controls in place. This observation is indeed consistent with an earlier study by Kaminsky and Reinhart(1995), which found that out of a sample of 25 banking crises that had occurred in recent years, 18 had been preceded by financial market liberalization within the last five years. Thus, contrary to the prescription of the MSFMP school, it is the very countries that follow the liberalization mantra that got into trouble, not the other way round.

The second fundamental underlying factor points to the inherent volatility of the global financial market itself. An increasing number of economists and policy makers have come to recognize that completely free and unregulated capital flows may impose such severe volatility on the financial systems of small economies as to undermine their ability to maintain any reasonably stable environment for pursuing real economic development. To quote Radelet and Sachs(1998): "international financial markets are intrinsically highly unstable; or to put it another way, the East Asian crisis is as much a crisis of Western capitalism as of Asian capitalism"(p.3). Indeed, the recent bailout of the hedge fund company LTCM by Alan Greenspan shows that, even for the largest and most advanced economy of the world, state intervention is deemed necessary to prevent financial turmoil arising from the working of free capital markets. The LTCM bailout case illustrated not only the enormous impacts of global hedge funds, but also the problem of moral hazard arising from asymmetric information and the inherent tendency of over-reaction of capital flights arising from herd instincts behavior. Even prior to the Asian crisis, economists like Stiglitz(1993) have long advocated the need for government intervention in financial markets, especially in the emerging world. As succinctly pointed out by Bhagwati(1998), trade in widgets is not the same as trade in dollars; to him, the MSFMP argument for unfettered flow of capital even for emerging economies is thus seen as ideologically motivated to serve the interest of a Wall Street-Treasury Complex. The third underlying fundamental cause, we believe, has to do with our argument that the ability of developing economies to sustain long term economic growth must ultimately rest on their technological learning efforts and ability. To the extent that there is a fundamental weakness in three of the countries worst affected by the crisis — Malaysia, Thailand and Indonesia — it is their inadequate investment in technological upgrading. Despite the high investment rates in these countries from the mid-1980s (spurred particularly by the appreciation of the Yen and the massive outward DFI by Japan after the Plaza Accord), much of these investments in recent years had gone increasingly into real-estate and other non-productive, consumption-oriented activities, thus contributing to the development of the asset bubble. Despite growing labor shortages, Malaysia and Thailand had not invested sufficiently in education, manpower training and technology development/ absorption activities; instead, they resorted to importation of cheap foreign labor, which eased the pressure on firms to invest in technology to improve competitiveness.

We believe it is this inadequate investment in technological upgrading that has contributed to the gradual erosion of their export competitiveness compared to other emerging market economies since the early 1990s. In particular, the growing export competitiveness of China in the early 1990s (perhaps facilitated by the de facto devaluation of the Yuan in 1994) can be identified as an important factor undermining the export performance of these second-rung NIEs which contributed to their deteriorating balance of payment problems in 1996 and 1997. In light of our focus on the importance of technological learning and upgrading as a source for sustaining rapid economic growth in the long term, the deteriorating competitiveness of these second rung NIEs like Malaysia, Thailand and Indonesia can be predicted from the fact that they had not invested as much into technological learning and upgrading as Taiwan, Korea and Singapore had done at comparable stages of economic development.

In the long run, we can predict that those economies with a deeper industrial and technological capabilities should be less likely to suffer from a crisis arising from any temporary loss of competitiveness, and that they should be able to recover faster and sustain higher long-term economic growth after the crisis. Thus, we would expect the three NIEs of Singapore, Taiwan and Korea to be less affected by the crisis than Hong Kong and the other Asian tigers. That Korea did experience a severe downturn due to the crisis, we suggest, is not due to the competitiveness factor, but to other factors, particularly their rapid financial liberalization without having adequate regulatory controls being established. Because its fundamental competitiveness has not been eroded, Korea should be expected to recover faster than Thailand, Malaysia and Indonesia, as indeed appears to have been the case by the end of 2000. Although Hong Kong also appears to have recovered fairly quickly (although still relatively slower than Korea), the strong continuing growth of China had been an important contributing factor. To the extent that Hong Kong's special gateway role for China will diminish in importance in the future, we believe that its longer term growth prospect will be constrained unless it accelerates technological deepening through state policies in the future.

In summary, our analysis suggests that the causes of the Asian financial crisis are complex and cannot be put down to a simplistic "crony capitalism" argument. Empirically, the country papers have clearly shown that not all state interventions in East Asia are of the crony capitalism type; the image of a Suharto-style patron-client regime in Indonesia prior to the crisis may be ideologically convenient, but it is hardly representative of much of what is going on in other parts of East Asia. The equating of lack of democracy to crony capitalism is also not borne out empirically; the more "democratic" model of Philippines and Thailand does not necessarily imply that they have less crony capitalist practices, nor does it suggest that they are recovering faster and have higher sustainable growth potential in the long run than Korea or Malaysia.

Our analysis also highlights the danger of deregulating and liberalizing too hastily before the necessary enabling conditions and oversight mechanisms are put in place to ensure that the resulting market forces thereby released will be manageable. There is no doubt that the state credit control system of Korea needs to be over-hauled, but the financial market liberalization was adopted too hastily without an oversight system, resulting in the eventual triggering of the debt crisis.

VIII. RE-THINKING THE DEVELOPMENT PARADIGM: TOWARDS AN ALTERNATIVE *TRANSITIONAL DEVELOPMENTAL STATE PARADIGM?*

Our synthesis of the development experience of Japan and the Asian NIEs suggests that the state had played a major role in the development process of these economies, particularly in the early development stages. At the same time, we also found that all these developmental states had experienced varying degrees of institutional inertia — i.e. they appeared to hang on to state institutions and policies that were effective at one time, but which may no longer be useful at a later time. While Japan and Korea appear to exhibit this problem most severely, Taiwan and Singapore also appear to experience similar dilemma, albeit in a less serious manner.

Reflecting on the difficulties that these developmental states faced in the later period of their development, we suggest that they share a common dilemma faced by all developing economies: that of evolving from an initial under-developed stage to that of an advanced, competitive market economy characterized by the presence of efficient competition among highly productive firms under the governance of relatively strong market institutions (see Figure 1.1). While recognizing the desirability of competitive markets in the functioning of advanced economies, it does not follow however that an underdeveloped economy should move towards complete market liberalization immediately. As highlighted in the institutional economics literature, efficiently functioning markets do not emerge automatically everywhere; certain pre-requisite conditions, or institutional frameworks, need to be created before such markets can emerge. While neoclassical economics is right in pointing out that an interventionist state may distort or even suppress markets through over-regulation or misguided policies, institutional economics suggests that markets may fail to function well due to weak state institutions. For example, no market can function where the rule of law completely breaks down, or where trust is totally absent. More generally, markets for certain transactions may be missing or function poorly where the enabling state institution is absent or weak, e.g. where public goods are involved, where transaction costs are high due to uncertainties in property rights, or where coordination failures occur due to information asymmetry.

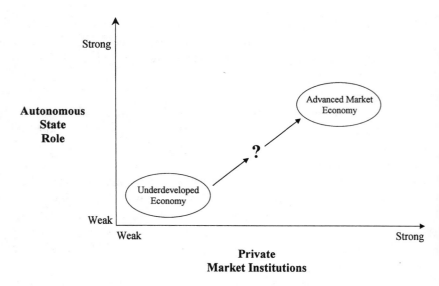

FIGURE 1.1   Co-evaluation of State and Market: The Economic Development Challenge.

While markets can sometimes emerge organically through self-organization among private economic agents, more often than not, the facilitating role of a relatively autonomous state may be necessary, especially in conditions of extreme underdevelopment. Indeed, economic agents will often seek to capture the state to further their own interests. The results of such efforts to capture the state may result in a fracturing of state power, leading to weak or inconsistent policies being pursued by different branches of the state apparatus.

The above analysis thus suggests that the role of the state and that of private market institutions interact and co-evolve dynamically in the economic development process. The role of the state is to create the conditions whereby efficiently functioning markets can operate; in the mean time, however, while markets may still not function well, the state can expedite economic growth by exercising its power to guide resource allocation in certain directions. In so doing, however, there is a danger that the specific state intervention roles may get so entrenched institutionally that they refuse to go away even when the conditions for markets to function efficiently have emerged. In this

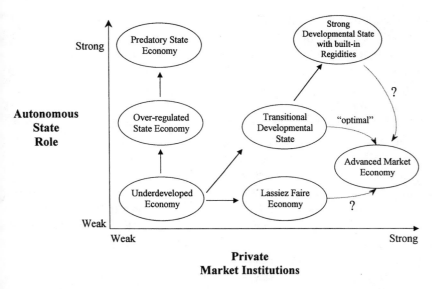

FIGURE 1.2   Pathways in Economic Development.

case, the institutionized state role has become the barrier to the emergence of markets itself.

By examining how the state and market evolve over different development stages, several possible "pathways from the periphery" (Haggard, 1990) towards the advanced competitive market economy model can be discerned (see Figure 1.2). Where autonomous state role is strong, an underdeveloped economy may go down the path of the "over-regulated" state (like India), the "predatory state" (like some African countries), or the "strong developmental state" model like Japan and Korea. Where the state is weak, however, the economy may be stuck in perpetual economic chaos and backwardness due to the absence of minimal enabling institutional conditions (like post-communist Russia), or become fractured by political instabilities and ineffective state institutions (like post-Marcos Philippines).

Is there an "optimal" development path from an underdeveloped economy to that of the advanced, competitive market economy? The experience of Japan and Korea appears to suggest that a relatively strong and autonomous developmental state may facilitate the achievement of rapid economic growth in the early developmental stage, but that this may cause substantial institutional inertia problems in the later development stages. Indeed, an overly strong autonomous developmental state may run the danger of degenerating into a predatory state, operating for the benefit of one interest group at the expense of others, as in the case of Indonesia. In contrast, too weak a state may in the best case slow the process of technological learning (due to the significant market failures resulting in under-investment of R&D, manpower training and supporting infrastructure). In the worst case, it may prevent the emergence of markets altogether, resulting in anarchy and chaos, as is evident in many African economies.

The ideal therefore appears to be a "Transitional Developmental State" that has a sufficient degree of state autonomy to pursue effective state policies in the early development stages, but which is not so strong that it becomes institutionally rigidified and unable to liberalize further to become an advanced, competitive market economy. Our interpretation is that Taiwan and Singapore appear to be closer to this "Transitional Developmental State" model than Korea and Japan, in that the state intervened less strongly as a substitute for market competition, and hence the danger of state institutional inertia appears less serious.

The "lassiez faire" model of Hong Kong may appear to imply the possibility of reaching the advanced competitive market economic condition with even less of a developmental state intervention role than was found in Singapore and Taiwan. However, we believe that Hong Kong is such a special case that it is unlikely to be generalizable to most other developing economies. It is true that the three governance aspects of the British colonial rule which had been widely credited with making the lassiez faire system of Hong Kong work (Weder, 1999) — rule of law, competent bureaucracy and low corruption — can possibly be emulated by other sovereign developing countries. However, two other factors in favour of Hong Kong — the large scale influx of immigrant industrialists and professionals, and the special gateway role to a huge hinterland (China) that confers sizable monopoly rents — are unlikely to be replicable. Even then, Hong Kong had achieved slower economic growth than the other developmental states of Korea, Taiwan and Singapore.

In summary, our interpretation of the experience of Japan and the four Asian NIEs is that neither the minimalist state, free market paradigm nor the strong developmental state model is the most appropriate for developing countries to adopt. The former is likely to be too drastic for most developing countries — the "Big Bang" experience of Russia and the debt crisis of Korea are symptomatic of the problem one may get into by adopting the minimalist state, free market indiscriminately when the enabling conditions for completely free market forces are not yet in place. On the other hand, the latter approach is likely to lead to too strongly entrenched state institutions which would outlive their usefulness, and hence became obstacles to further market liberalization, as can be observed in the case of Indonesia towards the end of Suharto's reign.

Instead of these two extremes, we propose that an alternative development paradigm, that of a Transitional Developmental State Paradigm, should be considered. In this paradigm, developing countries should consider using various forms of state intervention in the early developmental stages to speed up the process of economic growth; in particular, they should focus on using state interventions to overcome market failures in technological learning. However, they should seek to phase out such state interventions later on when they may no longer serve useful functions. In particular, they should reduce the danger of institutional inertia by either subjecting the institutions concerned to regular reviews, limiting their terms of operations at the outset, or planning ahead of time a scheduled process of gradual phase out and reform.

IX. SUSTAINING THE EAST ASIAN MIRACLE BEYOND THE FINANCIAL CRISIS: THE NEED FOR POLICY AND INSTITUTIONAL REFORM IN LINE WITH EVOLVING DEVELOPMENT STAGES AND CHANGING GLOBAL ENVIRONMENT

Based on our review of the development experience of the four Asian NIEs and our interpretation of the causes of the Asian financial crisis, we believe that, in terms of the fundamentals of technological capability, the four Asian NIEs will be able to recover from the financial crisis fairly quickly to their pre-crisis competence level. However, to be able to sustain a high average growth rate over the long-term, the four NIEs will need to continue to have high investment in industrial and technological learning. Rather than seeing high investment as a source for financial crisis as suggested by some quarters, we believe that the four NIEs need to invest even more in basic R&D, information and communications infrastructure, and manpower development in the future, for them to be able to achieve the level of productivity and competitiveness of the advanced countries today. Such sustained investments will require a continuing role of the state. In particular, Hong Kong, which had hitherto been neglecting the development of S&T capabilities, should invest more in public R&D and technical manpower development, besides the recent move towards stock market listing liberalization in the form of GEMS.

In addition to sustained investment in technological learning, the role of the state needs to be constantly reviewed in the four Asian NIEs to identify potential institutional inertia problems. In particular, each of the country papers in this study had identified specific policies and institutions that had become dysfunctional through inertia, and thus were in need of reform.

While it is clear from the country papers that both Japan and the four Asian NIEs will needs to liberalize their domestic markets more rapidly in the future to make their economy more competitive globally, we believe that each of these countries need to ensure that the supervisory system is in place to provide the needed market enabling environment or private institutional coordination mechanisms. Thus, greater liberalization of the listing requirements on stock exchanges should be preceded by the adoption of tighter information disclosure standards. Competition policy such as anti-trust regulation and fair trade rules must also be in place to guard against the emergence of monopolies through unfair competitive means. More generally, improvements in corporate governance will need to be accelerated in all the five countries concerned.

While recommending continuing market liberalization in general, we do not dogmatically advocate that the role of the state be minimized in every instance; instead, every country must carefully weigh the need for state intervention in every case based on the objective conditions being confronted. For example, we believe that the infant industry development argument may still be valid in cases where the particular NIEs are far behind other advanced countries, but have the potential to catch up, e.g. in the case of the biotechnology industry where advanced economies like the US have a very clear technological lead, one can envisage clear roles of public R&D policy in promoting the development of indigenous biotechnology capability in the NIEs.

X. CONCLUDING OBSERVATIONS: LESSONS FROM THE DEVELOPMENT EXPERIENCE OF JAPAN AND THE FOUR EAST ASIAN NIES

In summary, the key lesson we draw from our review of the development experience of Japan and the four Asian NIEs is that there is an important role for the state in the economic development of developing countries, but that this role needs to be pragmatically adapted to the specific context of the countries concerned, and that the role needs to be reduced over time as self-governing market institutions become more established. In place of a dogmatic adherence to the prevailing *Minimalist State Free Market Paradigm* on the one hand and the *Developmental State Paradigm* on the other, we therefore propose the adoption of a *Transitional Developmental State Paradigm*.

The main propositions that we can derive from our study are as follow:

1. There is not one East Asian development model, but at least five distinct ones. The specificity of each of these approaches is shaped by both unique historical contextual factors, as well as interaction with and selective learning from the experience of other countries, especially the more advanced ones that these countries were seeking to catch up with. The multiple pathways to rapid economic growth thus offer a rich menu of alternative development approaches and lessons for other developing countries to selectively imitate and adapt to best suit their own unique contexts.

2. Despite various state failures in the past experience of Japan and the four Asian NIEs, the five East Asian development models offer many examples of positive state roles in promoting industrial development for other developing countries, especially in the early industrial take-off stage.

3. The causes of the recent Asian financial crisis are complex and cannot be put down to a simplistic crony capitalism argument. By and large, while crony capitalist practices may be an important factor in some of the worst affected countries like Indonesia, three other underlying factors — hasty financial market liberalization without proper supervisory controls system being established, inherent volatility of an unregulated global financial system, and inadequate investment in technological learning contributing to

the erosion of export competitiveness and the concomitant development of asset bubble — are likely to be more important. All these three factors suggest an important role for the state, rather than getting the state out of the way. Some of the policies recommended in the name of curbing crony capitalism may have actually worsened the crisis.

4. As the NIEs becomes more advanced, the enabling conditions for free market competition become more favorable, and hence the role of state intervention in general and industrial policy in particular can and should be reduced. However, this does not imply a dogmatic insistence that there is no role for state intervention; rather, each case needs to be reviewed pragmatically. As such, the agenda for policy reforms and the pace for market liberalization need to be different in every country based on their objective conditions, rather than the simplistic MSFMP argument for unfettered liberalization and minimizing the role of the state. In particular, market liberalization may need to be preceded by establishing the enabling supervisory control systems and corporate governance reforms; indeed, the problem in many countries is not over-regulation, but inadequate oversight. State involvement and institutional capacities need to be strengthened, not weakened, to provide adequate oversight, especially for emerging markets.

5. For the NIEs, there is the danger that some of the policies and institutions that worked well at an earlier stage of development may have become dysfunctional at later stages, but are nonetheless perpetuated due to institutional inertia. Such institutional inertia appears to have been an important factor hindering policy reforms in Japan in particular in the 1990s.

6. It is thus not paradoxical to recommend policy changes/institutional reforms in Japan and the four Asian NIEs while at the same time recommending their selective imitations and adaptation by other developing countries. Despite significant changes in the global environment facing other developing countries today vs. what Japan and the four Asian NIEs faced when they achieved their rapid economic take-off, we believe that many of the state intervention policies adopted by Japan and the NIEs in promoting economic development in the earlier years can still be applied, subject to pragmatic adaptation.

In conclusion, despite the recent financial crisis engulfing much of East Asia and the prolonged weakness of the Japanese economy in the last decade, we believe that the development experience of Japan and the four Asian NIEs provides much valuable lessons for other developing countries aspiring to catch up with the industrial west. Indeed, we believe that the recent financial turmoil and economic set-backs encountered by East Asia, far from vindicating the *minimalist state, free market* paradigm, have actually helped sharpened the contrast between what state policies had been positive vs. what had not, and which countries had fared well vs. which had not. As such, they strengthened our conviction in adopting an alternative development paradigm, the *Transitional Developmental State Paradigm*, for adoption by other late-comer nations. From a broader historical perspective, such a paradigm is not only useful in interpreting the past experience of the five East Asian nations seeking to catch up with the advanced industrial west, but also may provide insights on how other advanced late-comer nations are trying to make the transition from developmental states to advanced competitive market economies. In this regard, from a comparative analysis perspective, the experience of countries like Israel, Ireland and Finland, where the state has also historically played an important role especially in facilitating technological learning, will be particularly instructive for the NIEs.

REFERENCES

Aoki, M., Kim, H.K., Fujiwara, M.O. (1997), *The Role of Government in East Asian Economic Development — Comparative Institutional Analysis*, Oxford: Clarendon Press.

Amsden, A.(1989), *Asia's Next Giant: South Korea and Late Industrialization*, Oxford University Press.

Asian Development Bank (1997), *Emerging Asia: Changes and Challenges*, Asian Development Bank

Bhagwati, J. (1998), "The Capital Myth", *Foreign Affairs*, Vol. 77, No. 3, May/June.

Campos, J.E., Root, H.L. (1996), *The Key to the Asian Miracle*, The Brookings Institution.

Economist (1998), "A Survey of East Asian Economies", *The Economist*, March 7, 1998.

Ernst, D., Ganiatsos, T., Mytelka, L. (eds.) (1998), *Technological Capabilities and Export Success in Asia*, Routledge.

Felipe, J. (1997), *Total Factor Productivity Growth in East Asia: A Critical Survey*, EDRC Report Series No. 65, Economics and Development Resource Center, Asian Development Bank.

Haggard, S. (1990), *Pathways from the Periphery: The Politics of Growth in the Newly Industrializing Countries*, Ithaca: Cornell University Press.

Hikino,T., Amsden, A.H. (1994), "Staying behind, stumbling back, sneaking up, soaring ahead: late industrialization in historical perspective", Baumol, W.J., Nelson, R., Wolf, E.N. (eds.), *Convergence of Productivity: Cross National Studies and Historical Evidence*, N.Y.: Oxford University Press.

Hobday, M. (1994), "Export-led Technology Development", *Development and Change*, Vol. 25.

Kim, L. (1993), "National System of Industrial Innovation: Dynamics of Capability Building in Korea", Nelson, R. R. (ed.), *National Innovation Systems: A Comparative Analysis*, Oxford University Press.

Krugman, P. (1994), "The Myth of Asia Miracle", *Foreign Affairs*, 73(6): 62–78.

Krugman, P. (1998), "Will Asia Bounce Back?", *http://web.mit.edu/krugman/www/ suisse.html*.

Kumar, R., Debroy, B. (1999), "The Asian Crisis: An alternate view", Asian Development Bank, Economic and Development Resource Centre: Economic Staff Paper No. 59.

Lau, L.J. (1996), "The Sources of Long-term Economic Growth: Observations from the Experience of Developed and Developing Countries", Landau, R., Taylor, T., Wright, G. (eds.), *The Mosaic of Economic Growth*, Stanford University Press.

Leipziger, D.M. (1997), *Lessons from East Asia*, University of Michigan Press.

Lin, S. (1994), "Government spending and economic growth", *Applied Economics*, 26(1): 83–94.

MacLean, B.K. (1999), "The rise and fall of the 'Crony Capitalism' hypothesis: Causes and Consequences", Working Paper, Department of Economics, Laurentian University, Canada.

Mathews, J.A.(1995), *High-Technology Industrialisation in East Asia: The Case of the Semiconductor Industry in Taiwan and Korea*, Chung-Hua Institution for Economic Research, Tzong-shian Yu.

Ohno, K., Ohno, I.(eds.)(1998), *Japanese Views on Economic Development: Diverse paths to the market*, Routledge.

Perkins, D. (1994), "There Are at Least Three Models of East Asian Development", *World Development* 22(4): 655–61.

Radelet, S., Sachs, J. (1998), "The Onset of the East Asian Financial Crisis", Working Paper, Harvard Institute for International Development.

Rodrick, D. (1994), "Trade Strategy, Investment and Exports: Another Look at East Asia", Working Paper 5339, Cambridge, Mass.: National Bureau of Economic Research.

Rodrick, D. (1995), "Getting intervention right: How S. Korea and Taiwan grew rich", *Economics Policy* (April), pp. 55–107.

Rodrik, D. (1998), "King Kong Meets Godzilla: The World Bank and The East Asian Miracle", *Policy Essay No.11, Overseas Development Council*.

Stern, J.J., Kim, J.H., Perkins, D., Yoo, J.H. (1995), "Industrialization and the State: The Korean Heavy and Chemical Industry Drive", *Harvard Studies in the International Development*, Harvard Institute for International Development.

UNIDO (1999), *International Yearbook of Industrial Statistics 1999*.

Wade, R. (1990), *Governing the Market: Economic Theory and the Role of the Government in East Asian Industrialization,* Princeton, N.J.: Princeton University Press.

Weder, B. (1999), *Model, Myth, or Miracle? Reassessing the role of governments in the East Asian experience*, Tokyo: UNV Press.

Wolf, C. (1988), *Markets or Governments: Choosing between Imperfect Alternatives*, MIT Press.

Wong, P.K. (1995b), "Technology Transfer and Development Inducement by Foreign MNCs: The Experience of Singapore", in K.Y. Jeong and M.H. Kwack (eds.), *Industrial Strategy for Global Competitiveness of Korean Industries*, Seoul: Korea Economic Research Institute.

World Bank(1993), *The East Asian Miracle: Economic Growth and Public Policy*, N.Y.: Oxford University Press.

World Bank (1999), *World Development Report 1999/2000: Entering the 21st Century*, Oxford University Press.

World Economic Forum (1997), *World Competitiveness Report*, Geneva.

Yanagihara, T., Sambommatsu, S. (eds.) (1997), "East Asian development experience: economic system approach and its applicability", papers and proceedings of the symposium held by the Institute of Developing Economies on January 22, 1997 in Tokyo, Tokyo : Institute of Developing Economies, 1997.

Young, A. (1992), "A Tale of Two Cities: Factor Accumulation and Technical Change in Hong Kong and Singapore", *NBER Macroeconomic Annual 1992*, Cambridge, Mass.: MIT Press.

ANNEX TABLE 1A   Real GDP Growth of Japan and the Four Asian NIEs vs. ASEAN-4 (percentages)

	1960-70	1970-80	1980-90	1990-97	1998	1999	1990-99	1960-99
Japan	10.4	4.3	4.0	1.5	−1.1	0.8	1.4	4.9
Asian NIEs:								
Singapore	8.7	9.4	7.1	8.5	0.3	5.9	8.0	8.1
Hong Kong	10.0	6.9	6.9	5.3	−5.3	3.0	3.9	6.8
Korea	8.4	9.6	9.4	7.2	−6.7	10.9	5.7	8.3
Taiwan	9.6	9.7	8.7	6.4	4.6	5.4	6.1	8.6
ASEAN-4:								
Malaysia	6.5	7.9	5.3	8.7	−7.4	5.8	6.3	6.4
Thailand	8.4	7.1	7.6	7.5	−10.8	4.2	4.7	7.1
Indonesia	3.9	7.2	6.1	7.5	−13.1	0.8	4.7	5.3
Philippines	5.1	6.0	1.0	3.3	−0.6	3.3	3.2	3.7

SOURCES: 1960–80: Leipziger; 1980–99: Compiled from World Bank, *World Development Report 2000/01* and ADB, *Asian Development Outlook 2001*; www.economist.com

ANNEX TABLE 1B   Manufacturing Value Add (MVA) by Technology Group and Pavitt Classification of NIEs

	Hong Kong			South Korea			Singapore		
	1984	*1990*	*1994*	*1984*	*1990*	*1995*	*1984*	*1990*	*1995*
Share of MVA by Technology Group (%)									
High-technology industries	12.69	11.43	14.65	8.53	16.91	19.70	17.42	41.75	49.15
Medium-technology industries	34.58	33.17	28.51	54.21	59.05	54.29	63.44	43.39	39.73
Low-technology industries	52.73	55.41	56.83	37.26	24.04	26.01	19.15	14.87	11.12
Total	100.0	100.0	100.0	100.0	100.0	100.0	100.0	100.0	100.0
Share of MVA by Pavitt classification (%)									
Resource-intensive industries	8.05	10.19	15.29	30.81	23.26	18.76	6.73	4.94	10.8
Labor-intensive industries	50.32	46.38	37.93	20.23	11.94	17.10	14.93	11.56	8.7
Scale-intensive industries	18.09	19.71	20.83	31.77	36.76	33.35	28.96	24.09	19.7
Specialized-supplier industries	16.67	13.80	17.48	14.44	23.37	26.95	47.57	51.16	32.0
Science-based industries	6.86	9.91	8.48	2.75	4.67	3.84	1.80	8.25	28.8
Total	100.0	100.0	100.0	100.0	100.0	100.0	100.0	100.0	100.0

SOURCE: Estimated by author from *International Yearbook of Industrial Statistics, 1996*.

2
Rethinking East Asian Industrial Policy — Past Records and Future Prospects

Ha-Joon Chang

I. INTRODUCTION: FROM THE MIRACLE TO THE CRISIS

The debate on the role of industrial policy in East Asian miracle is well known by now. On one side of the debate are the orthodox, that is Neoclassical, economists, who find East Asian-style industrial policy very uncomfortable. With the exception in the case of Japan, they initially denied the very existence of such policy (e.g., Ranis & Fei, 1975; Balassa *et al.*, 1982; Balassa, 1988).[1] However, in response to the growing empirical evidence provided by the heterodox economists against this view (e.g., Sakong & Jones, 1980; Evans & Alizadeh, 1984; Amsden, 1985; Luedde-Neurath, 1986), they grudgingly came to acknowledged their existence by the 1980s. However, they argued that East Asian industrial policy had little impact, either on the ground that it was self-cancelling in the sense that export subsidies cancelled out import protection measures (e.g., the "virtual free trade" argument of Little, 1982 and World Bank, 1987) or on the ground that they were "porous" and allowed the private sector to do what it wanted to do (e.g., the theory of "proscriptive vs. prescriptive" intervention by Bhagwati, 1988).

With further major attacks from the heterodox economists (especially by Amsden, 1989, on Korea, and Wade, 1990, on Taiwan), the orthodox economists responded with the famous "East Asian Miracle Report" (henceforth EAM) by the World Bank. The EAM tried to show that, while theoretically justifiable, industrial policy had few positive impacts, except possibly in Japan. Against this, the heterodox economists who believe in the positive role of industrial policy in East Asia made important methodological and empirical criticisms (see the special symposium in *World Development*, 1994, no. 4; Fishlow *et al.*, 1994; Singh, 1994), to which the authors of the EAM could not properly respond.

Unfortunately, before the debate surrounding the EAM was properly settled, severe financial crises broke out in a number of East and Southeast Asian countries in 1997, pushing the debate on to a new direction, namely, whether industrial policy caused these financial crises. There is now a popular argument, which believes that, far from being a cause of the miracle, industrial policy was responsible for the region's crises. They that the Asian governments, in their attempts to promote their favoured industries, have explicitly and implicitly under-written the investments in them, which naturally encouraged lax management and excessive risk-taking, which in the end led to the crises (e.g., *The Economist*, 15 November 1997; Brittan, 1997).[2]

Given this context, the present paper attempts to contribute to the debate on East Asian industrial policy in three ways. First of all, it will revisit the debate surrounding the EAM, which in our view has not been fully explored (section II). Here, we will devote more efforts to raising issues that were neglected in the EAM debate, rather than to going over the issues that were already debated. Next, we discuss whether industrial policy was responsible for the recent crises in the region (section III). Then we discuss whether the more recent economic, political, and institutional changes (both at the national and international levels) have made the use of industrial policy in East Asia less feasible in the future (section IV). This is followed by concluding remarks (section V).

II. THE DEBATE BEFORE THE RECENT CRISES: THE EAST ASIAN MIRACLE REPORT DEBATE

The EAM distinguished itself from the previous publications by the World Bank and most mainstream economists on the role of industrial policy in East Asia at least in two respects. First of all, it acknowledged the existence of extensive industrial policy in the East Asian countries (except in the case of Japan, the existence of whose interventionist industrial and trade policies was widely acknowledged from the early days). Given that the very existence of industrial policy was a matter of intense debate in the case of Korea and Taiwan even until as late as the late 1980s, this was not an insignificant thing.[3] Secondly, the EAM clearly accepted a number of important theoretical justifications for industrial policy — such as the so-called "Big Push" argument and the existence of learning externalities (see below). This was a big contrast to many earlier mainstream works, which argued that market failures were limited to areas like infrastructure, education, and health, and therefore that there was no reason for governments to intervene in industry in "selective" ways, especially at the sectoral level as in the case of East Asia.

Having abandoned the early mainstream practice of dismissing the issue of industrial policy as theoretically unjustifiable and/or largely absent in the East Asian countries, the EAM resorted to two arguments of more practical vent in order to come up with a negative verdict on the relevance of industrial policy.

First of all, it tried to show empirically that industrial policy, despite its apparent importance, did not make much difference either to the production structure or the productivity performance of the East Asian countries. Secondly, it argued that, whatever its contribution to the development of some East Asian countries may have been, industrial policy cannot be adopted by other developing countries because they face very different domestic and international conditions from the ones that the East Asian countries faced earlier. The latter countries lack, it was argued, firstly, the domestic institutions needed for the effective implementation of East-Asian-style industrial policy (especially a competent bureaucracy), and, secondly, the kind of "permissive" international trading environment that the East Asian countries enjoyed during the time when they actively used such policy (that is, between the 1950s and the 1970s), especially following the then imminent conclusion of the Uruguay Round of the GATT talks (which got concluded in 1994).

In the rest of this section, we critically examine the three aspects of the EAM's verdict on industrial policy that we mentioned above — its (partial) theoretical acceptance of industrial policy (section II.1), its empirical refutation of the success of the policy in East Asia (section II.2), and the practical objections that it raises to the transferability of the policy to other countries (section II.3) — and bring out some issues that we think were inadequately dealt with in the earlier debate.

1. Can Industrial Policy be Theoretically Justified?

As we have repeatedly mentioned, the EAM acknowledged some important justifications for industrial policy, unlike the previous orthodox publications on the subject (see pp. 90–93, and pp. 293–94). First of all, the need to coordinate complementary investments, in the presence of significant scale economies and capital market imperfections, was acknowledged — this is the well-known "Big Push" argument. Secondly, the role that the state can play as the organiser of domestic firms into implicit cartels in their negotiations with foreign firms or governments was recognised. Thirdly, the importance of learning externalities was emphasised.

However, in the same breath, the EAM dismissed another important theoretical justification for industrial policy, namely, infant industry promotion, on the ground that its success is not guaranteed. I find this refutation rather peculiar, since all the other theoretical justifications for industrial policy that the EAM accepted do not guarantee success in practice either. But apart from this rather obvious point, I do not think there is much added value in my elaborating on the theoretical arguments that have already been accepted by the EAM. Therefore, I wish to discuss a few other theoretical justifications for industrial policy which were more or less ignored by the EAM (and in fact by many of its critics) and discuss their implications.

Coordination of Competing Investments

The first of the under-explored justifications for industrial policy is the need to coordinate investments not simply between complementary projects but between competing projects — what is known as "managed competition" (Amsden & Singh, 1994). This issue was actually the central point of contention in the industrial policy debate of the early 1980s surrounding the Japanese experience, but was curiously ignored by the EAM.

The logic here is that oligopolistic competition that characterises many modern industries with significant scale economy often leads to excess capacity, unless there is a coordination of investment activities across competing firms. Excess capacity leads to price war, which damages the profits of the firms concerned and may force them to scrap some of their assets. It can also lead to bankruptcy.

Needless to say, asset scrapping and bankruptcy are useful and costless ways of re-arranging property rights in a world without transaction costs and "specific assets" (the term is due to Williamson, 1985), but we are *not* living in such a world. This means that the specific assets involved in this process have to be scrapped or re-allocated to alternative uses that can create much less value out of the assets concerned, thus incurring a social cost. If the emergence of excess capacity can be prevented through the *ex ante* coordination of competing investments, such social cost may be reduced (for more detailed arguments, see Chang, 1994, ch. 3; also see Telser, 1987, and Amsden & Singh, 1994).

Many mainstream economists have argued that excess capacity is a non-issue, especially for small economies that are price-takers, because what cannot be consumed in the domestic market can always be exported. However, this is often not a viable option, at least in the short-run (and it is the short run that counts here). First of all, at least since the late 1970s, many industries have been suffering from chronic over-capacity on the world scale.[4] Moreover, real-world markets are often segmented along the lines of quality, design, and geography, and therefore the "world market" may not be as big as it seems, given that it takes time and resources to break into new market segments. In addition, some small economies have deliberately built capacities which are far beyond its domestic markets and have become price-makers, rather than price-takers, even on the world scale. For example, Korea, despite being a relatively small economy, is the world's first or second largest producer of ships (depending on the year) and the third largest producer of micro-chips (the largest if we take memory chips only), and therefore what the country produces does have an important impact on world prices. Indeed, this is why the end to the practice of coordination among competing investments became such a problem in Korea recently (see section III for more details).

Given these considerations, there is a clear theoretical justification for coordinating competing investments. And, indeed, such coordination has been one of a key components in the industrial policy regimes of the East Asian countries. Their governments were very concerned for "excessive competition" or "wasteful competition" and attempted to minimise duplicative investments through mechanisms such as industrial licensing and investment cartels (see Chang, 1993, for further details).[5] By ignoring this important issue, the EAM ended up neglecting a huge chunk of industrial policy in East Asia.

Further Thoughts on Scale Economy

The EAM certainly gave a clear recognition to the importance of scale economy, when it talked about the need to coordinate complementary investments. However, this is not the only way in which scale economy can justify industrial policy.

First of all, scale economy has an important implication for the cost competitiveness of a country's industry. Economists may have traditionally debated on whether the social cost from monopoly is 1% or 2% of total output, but in industries with significant scale economy, choosing a sub-optimal scale of capacity can often mean 30–50% differences in unit costs. For this reason, the East Asian governments have used measures such as industrial licensing, government procurement, export requirements, and subsidies in order to ensure that factories would be built at scales which are not too much below (and hopefully above) the minimum efficient scale. Of course, this invited criticisms on anti-trust grounds, but their attitude has been that monopolistic firms producing at optimal scale is much less of a drag on the economy than "competitive" firms all producing at sub-optimal scales.

Secondly, scale economy also has a hitherto-ignored link with luxury consumption control (for a more detailed discussion, see Chang, 1997a). The well-known practice of luxury consumption control in East Asian countries — most notoriously, but by no means exclusively or even mainly, through import control — has often been interpreted as no more than a thinly-disguised protectionist ploy or as a manifestation of the paternalistic desire to impose what the government see as a "sound consumption pattern" (the phrase was explicitly used in, for example, the 4th Five Year Plan document of Korea, 1977, p. 27). However, there were much more than this to these controls. First of all, it was thought important to restrict conspicuous consumption for the purpose of reducing class conflicts, especially given the (real and imagined) presence of Communist threat. Secondly, there was the desire to maximise the investible surplus by repressing luxury consumption out of profit. Thirdly, and most relevantly to our discussion here, restrictions on the consumption of luxury varieties in industries like passenger car industry, where consumer demand for variety is important, was regarded as important in enabling the producers to attain the maximum possible scale in production.[6]

To sum up, while the EAM acknowledged the crucial role of scale economy in necessitating the coordination of complementary investments, it did not explore its role beyond this. However, while it may sound less fancy than coordinating complementary investments, ensuring the achievement of scale economy in key industries was in practice thus maintaining low cost was probably a much more important aspect of East Asian industrial policy than the former.

"Protective" Industrial Policy, Social Insurance, and Structural Change

Another aspect of industrial policy that has received little recognition in the East Asian context is its "protective" role. It is widely believed that what distinguishes industrial policy in East Asia is that it concentrated on "picking winners", rather than "protecting losers" as it was often the case in other countries. There is certainly a large element of truth in such view. However, protective industrial policies were also widespread in East Asia, if less so than in other countries. Therefore, we need to go deeper if we are to understand why protective industrial policy in East Asia did not end up blocking structural change as in some other countries.

We argue that there were two functions that the protective industrial policies in East Asia served. The first was the more short-term-oriented one of providing "social insurance" to firms which are in a temporary difficulty but cannot borrow their way out of it due to capital market imperfections.[7] Like the policy of coordinating competing investments, the practice can be justified in terms of asset specificity. The logic here is that it will be socially inefficient to scrap specific assets in the face of a temporary setback, if the net present values of their future income streams are larger than the costs of supports needed to keep them employed in their current uses. The best example of such policy is the famous Japanese practice of sanctioning (but closely supervising and disciplining) "recession cartels" in industries deemed to be in a temporary difficulty (see Dore, 1986, and Chang, 1994, ch. 3, for more details).

The second, and probably more important, function was the more long-term-oriented one of promoting structural change. When an industry is in need of a large-scale adjustment, those who had made specific (human and physical, or even relational) investments in the industry face the situation where their next best option is a total scrapping of their assets and therefore a drastic reduction in their income. Unless there is a mechanism that entitles them to some minimum income during the transition period, when they run down their existing assets and re-tool themselves (e.g., purchasing new equipment, retraining of workers), they will have an incentive to resist the change by political means. In such a situation, protective industrial policies can accelerate, rather than slow down, structural change by reducing the political resistance to the change, if they also provide incentives for (physical and mental) re-tooling (for a more detailed argument, see Chang & Rowthorn, 1995).[8]

In Japan, "cartels for structurally-depressed industries" (or SDI cartels) were granted to declining industries in return for their efforts to phase out obsolete capacities and upgrade their technologies (Dore, 1986, provides a fascinating study of this experience; also see Renshaw, 1986). During the late 1980s, some of the declining industries in Korea, such as textile, received temporary supports (e.g., subsidies for equipment upgrading, exemption from anti-trust law) through the rationalization programs sanctioned by the Industrial Development Law, in return for achieving certain targets regarding technology upgrading (see Chang, 1993, for details).

What distinguishes these protective industrial policies from similar policies in other countries is that they were "forward-looking" in the sense that they made it explicit that the aim of the protection was not preserving the industries concerned but phasing them out in an orderly manner or to technologically upgrading them. Perhaps more importantly, they also had well-specified performance targets for the beneficiaries, thus preventing the policies from turning into "nursing homes" for declining industries. In other words, because of the way they were designed and implemented, protective industrial policies in East Asia promoted, rather than hindered, structural change.

To summarize, the EAM, by concentrating on "developmental" industrial policy, ignored "protective" industrial policy. Such industrial policy is often regarded as blocking structural change and therefore not justifiable, but it has played a positive role in East Asia in two ways. Firstly, it provided a social insurance to producers who are experiencing a temporary difficulty but cannot borrow their way out of it due to capital market imperfections. Secondly, and more importantly, it promoted structural change by easing the difficulties involved in moving "specific" resources out of the declining sectors or in upgrading them. Such policy was perhaps not the most important aspect of East Asian industrial policy, but was by no means an unimportant aspect.

2. Empirical Evidence

The essence of the EAM's empirical verdict on the role of industrial policy in East Asia can be summarized, at the risk of some simplification, as the following: there is no evidence that the industries promoted by industrial policy had higher output growth or more rapid productivity growth than the other industries.

The detailed methodologies and the data used in this study have been already been subject to a range of criticisms, including the problems inherent in the definition and the measurement of total factor productivity (see Lall, 1994; Kwon, 1994; Rodrik, 1994; and Singh, 1994, among others; also see Chang, 1995, appendix). As they are mostly of technical (which of course does not mean "trivial") nature, the summary of which may take up quite a big space, here I want to do no more than raising a couple of methodological points that had not been adequately dealt with in the earlier debate.

The EAM tries to test the effects of industrial policy by trying to correlate the extent of government support for an industry (however measured) and its performance. The difficulty with this is that, as far as externality constitutes a major justification for industrial policy, it is by definition very difficult (if not entirely impossible) to measure its effects at the sectoral level (the 2-digit level in this case), as its effects will spill over into other sectors. As Joe Stiglitz neatly summed it up in the workshop where the earlier version of the paper was presented, if we can accurately measure the effects of such policy, we probably did not need it in the first place.

The EAM does acknowledge this problem but justifies its sectoral approach on the ground that spillover effects are mostly confined to "closely related sectors, often sectors that would be identified with a two-digit classification" (p. 326). The problem with this conclusion is that it is based on one study on the pattern of spillovers of R&D in industrial economies. Apart from the fact that it is dangerous to draw such a strong conclusion from a single study, it is not clear how relevant such a study is to the understanding the role of industrial policy in developing economies. For developing economies, where R&D plays at best a minor role, more important forms of spillover effects may lie in such things as the formation of a skilled labor force and the increase in generalized engineering capability. Given this, the result of the study on R&D spillover that the EAM cites has only limited relevance, even if it were representative of the developed country situation (for more details, see Chang, 1995, appendix).

Another problem with the empirical study presented in the EAM is that it suffers from a serious "identification problem". It has been already pointed out by Lall (1994) that the EAM classifies the industries at the 2-digit level, which is too coarse a classification to identify the activities that were promoted. Typically, industrial promotion was targeted at a much finer level, sometimes even involving supports defined at the firm level. We can also say that such classification is at the same time too fine, because some major components of industrial policy, such as export promotion, was conducted at a much broader and cross-sectoral level.[9] However, there is a more fundamental dimension to this "identification problem", which is that the EAM did not bother to find out which industries, at whatever levels of classification, were *actually* promoted.

The statistical work conducted in the EAM is based on the notion that the East Asian governments promoted industries that had higher value-added or higher capital-intensity. However, the problem is that the choice of industries to be promoted in these countries was never made on simple criteria like "capital intensity" or "value-added component". Rather, the choice reflected a whole set of considerations, including, to name just a few, international market conditions, the availability of relevant domestic technological capabilities, and the net foreign exchange implication of promoting the industry concerned.

For example, the Korean textile industry, which the EAM regards as the quintessential "non-promoted" industry (p. 316), in fact received a lot of promotional supports even *after* the government launched its (in)famous Heavy and Chemical industrialization program in 1973 — it even had a special promotional law made for it in 1979. This was because of the industry's critical role as the main supplier of foreign exchanges (it was the largest export industry well into the 1980s), which were necessary for the country to import capital equipments and buy technology licenses that were needed for the "infant" industries. Given this, the fact that the Korean textile industry was, according to the EAM, unusually large by international standards is a proof *not* of the failure of Korean industrial policy, as the EAM argues, but of its success (for more details, see Chang, 1995, appendix).

In other words, the EAM has classified industries into the promoted ones and the ones that were not, according to what they *thought* the industrial policy practice was in the East Asian countries, rather than according to what actually *was* the practice in these countries. Such disregard as to what was actually going on in the countries concerned is quite similar to its failure in the theoretical section to consider (if only to disapprove) some key justifications for industrial policy used in these countries (e.g., coordination of competing investments, policy measures to attain scale economy, and the use of "protective" industrial policy — see above).

Paying attention to these hitherto-ignored aspects of industrial policy makes our empirical tests more difficult. Traditionally, many studies have used indicators such as subsidies and tariffs in order to measure the extent of industrial policy in an industry. However, recognising these additional aspects means that we also need to take into account less quantifiable things like the costs saved from coordination of competing investments and from measures to achieve scale economy, or the benefits from the acceleration of structural change that protective industrial policy may accord (which will be even more difficult to measure, as they are likely to spill over into the rest of the economy).

3. The Question of Replicability

One important line of argument employed by the EAM against industrial policy was that in order to be successful the policy requires certain conditions, which most developing countries of today do not meet. Two kinds of arguments were made along this line. First of all, it was argued that, in order to make industrial policy work even to the (allegedly) limited extent that it worked in East Asia, a country needs certain institutions, especially a highly capable bureaucracy. Secondly, it was pointed out that industrial policy is not feasible any more, because the new international trading regime that emerged out of the Uruguay Round of the GATT talks has made the tools of industrial policy that the Northeast Asian countries had used "illegal". How persuasive are these arguments?

Institutional Capability

The EAM argues that successful management of industrial policy, as one of what it calls "selective" policies that go beyond the "fundamentals", requires unusual institutional capabilities that can rarely be found in developing countries. The report argues that effective implementation of "contests" among the recipients of state supports, which are necessary for a successful industrial policy, requires "the competence, insulation, and relative lack of corruptibility of the public administrations in Japan and Korea" (p. 102).[10] From this, the report concludes that the more market-oriented economies of Southeast Asia (Thailand, Malaysia, and Indonesia) provide a better role model for other developing countries, as their success proves that there is a lot of mileage that countries with poor administrative (and other institutional) capabilities can derive from concentrating on (the relatively administratively less demanding task of) achieving the "fundamentals" (macroeconomic stability, human resource development, agricultural development, among others).[11]

The problem with this argument is not so much that anyone seriously doubts whether an effective conduct of selective industrial policy (or for that matter, any policy) requires a bureaucracy that has the competence and the political influence to impose "hard budget constraints" on the recipients of state support according to relatively transparent rules. This proposition is in fact what many critics of the World Bank had repeatedly emphasized. So at that level there is really no dispute.

The problem is that the EAM is implicitly assuming that, the more "selective" a policy is, the more difficult it is to administer and thus more institutional "props" (such as a good bureaucracy) it needs — or, to put it differently, the closer an economic system is to the *laissez faire* ideal, the easier it become to run it. Is this true?

First of all, well-functioning markets require institutional prerequisites as much as well-functioning policies require them, although of different kinds — developed contract law, an efficient capital market, and an effective dispute settlement mechanism, to name just a few — because, without these institutions, market exchange becomes very costly (Chang, 1997b). A successful modern free-market economy will also require highly capable *private sector bureaucracies* that can successfully manage large and complex firms. The enormous difficulties that many developing and transition economies are having in constructing the basic institutions of the market economy and the private sector bureaucratic capabilities are clear testimonies to the fact that more market-oriented economic systems are *not necessarily* easier to construct and run than more interventionist systems.

Secondly, in the same vein, it is not clear to me at all whether industrial policy necessarily requires a more capable bureaucracy than what the EAM calls the "fundamental" policies (e.g., achieving macroeconomic stability, developing agriculture). This will, for one thing, depend on the nature and the scale of the policies concerned. For example, is promoting a small number of relatively unsophisticated industries necessarily more difficult than, say, administering a large-scale primary educational program? For another example, running a good macroeconomic policy in the face of a large (positive or negative) external shock is often a lot more difficult than running selective industrial policy (as the East Asian economies are finding to their chagrin these days). The point is *not* that industrial policy is necessarily more (or less) difficult to run than other policies, but that we cannot make a categorical statement about the ease or the difficulty of a particular type of policy without looking at the particular case at hand.

Thirdly, it is not clear whether the capable bureaucracies in Northeast Asia (or what the pre-EAM debate called East Asia) were the products of "highly unusual historical and institutional circumstances" (p. 366). At first sight, this seems more than reasonable. We all know that the Northeast Asian countries have behind them at least thousand (and more, in the case of Chinese-speaking countries) years of history of meritocratic bureaucracy, and this surely must prove that these countries are highly unusual — or does it?

Let us start answering this question by first thinking about Singapore. Is it really the Confucian tradition that has made its bureaucracy what it is? Many would agree that the principles that lie behind the Singaporean bureaucracy seem more British than Confucian (e.g., matching public sector salaries to comparable private sector salaries). Taiwan provides another interesting counter to the above argument. When its bureaucracy was running mainland China before 1949, it already had the longest tradition of meritocracy and competitive recruitment in the world, but that did not prevent it from being one of the least competent and the most corrupt bureaucracies in the world at the time. Did Korea always have an exceptionally competent bureaucracy? The Korean bureaucracy was also notorious for its incompetence and nepotism in the 1950s (Cheng *et al.*, 1998), and it was sending its bureaucrats for training to countries like Pakistan and the Philippines even until the late 1960s. It was only through continuous efforts at civil service reform, and *not* as a result of history and tradition, that Korea managed to create a competent and relatively clean bureaucracy — this is a point that even the EAM gave a side glance (Box 4.4).

The point is *not* that history and tradition does not matter, but that capabilities (and the institutions that embody them) can be built and destroyed a lot more easily than it is assumed in the EAM (and by many other people). It is true that the process of capability building often takes time, but this is not the same as saying that countries which do not have high capability should never try "difficult" policies (such as industrial policy). Such capability can be, and has often been, built rather quickly, not least because there is also "learning-by-doing" in administration as in production. Institutions are, in other words, subject to imitation and innovation, as are technologies (Westney, 1987). Indeed, the World Bank itself has later come around to accept, although still not wholeheartedly, the line of criticism that we deployed above, as we can see from its 1997 annual report that emphasised the need for state capability building (World Bank, 1997).

Changing International Trading Environment

The EAM cites the birth of the new international trading regime, following the conclusion of the Uruguay Round of the GATT talks and the birth of the World Trade Organization (WTO), is a severe constraint on the use of the kinds of interventionist trade and industrial policy measures used by the Northeast Asian countries (pp. 25, 365). While it accepts that there is some room for manoeuvre[12], its verdict on the effect of the WTO regime on developing country policy autonomy seems overly pessimistic (see Akyuz *et al.*, 1998 and Amsden, 2000, for further details).

To begin with, we should not exaggerate the additional constraints on trade and industrial policies that the WTO regime has brought about by talking as if everything was allowed under the pre-Uruguay-Round regime. The old regime also had a large number of restrictions on the range of acceptable policy instruments, and therefore the Northeast Asian countries had to exercise a lot of ingenuity in choosing the means of industrial policy and diplomatic skills to iron out problems with their trading partners.

Secondly, it should not be forgotten that the WTO regime is still an evolving system. We still do not fully know, several years after the launch of the WTO, how the abstract principles stated in its charter are exactly going to be translated into practice. Given the legalistic nature of the WTO regime, its exact characteristics will be determined only with the accumulation of precedents over time, because, as any other legal system, its principles are stated in fairly general terms and therefore need to be actively "interpreted".

Thirdly, we need to point out that the restrictions on the use of subsidies in the WTO regime are not as binding as they are portrayed to be in the EAM and elsewhere. For one thing, there are subsidies which are perfectly legal (the so-called "non-actionable" subsidies) — these include "non-specific" subsidies and certain types of "specific" subsidies (those for basic R&D, agriculture, disadvantaged regions, and equipment upgrading to meet higher environmental standards). There are also subsidies which are "actionable" (e.g., the trading partner can impose countervailing duties) although not prohibited. However, in this case, the complaining country has to prove that the subsidy concerned has caused a "material damage", which is not easy especially when it concerns developing countries with tiny market shares. The only subsidies which are prohibited outright are subsidies that require their recipients to meet certain export targets or to use domestic goods instead of imported goods. However, the poorest countries (defined roughly as countries with less than $1,000 per capita income) are in fact exempt from even this.

Fourthly, as in the pre-WTO regime, countries are allowed under the WTO regime to raise tariffs or introduce quantitative restrictions when they have balance of payments problems. Given that practically almost all of them are in a permanent balance of payments crisis, this provides a significant room for manoeuvre for the developing countries. Indeed, it was actually almost invariably on this ground, rather than under the infant industry provision of the GATT, that the East Asian countries imposed tariffs and quantitative restrictions that they used for infant industry promotion (Akyuz et al., 1998, p. 31). Of course, these measures are supposed to be commensurate to the scale of the balance of payments problem, which means that there is a clear restriction on the total magnitude of measures that can be used. However, the WTO expressly allows the individual countries to choose *where* to impose these measures (i.e., how they define "non-essential imports"), so there is actually a significant room for selectivity in the use of these measures, which is after all what the debate is about.

To summarise, it is true that the WTO regime has put greater restrictions than before on the range of trade and industrial policy tools that are acceptable. However, the restrictions are by no means as wide-ranging and severe as the EAM suggests, and there is non-negligible room for manoeuvre for developing countries, especially the poorest ones which are given some special exemptions. Given that the pre-WTO world trading regime was by no means permissive, it seems doubtful whether the birth of the new international trading regime makes the past industrial policy practices in East Asia as irrelevant for other developing countries as they are argued to be.

III. THE EAST ASIAN CRISIS (AND THE JAPANESE RECESSION) AND INDUSTRIAL POLICY

The debate on East Asian industrial policy recently took a new turn following the continued recession in Japan and the economic crises in a number of other countries in the region.[13]

As we already pointed out in a number of places, many mainstream economists have until recently tried hard to deny the very existence of industrial policy in East Asia. Even many of those mainstream economists who acknowledged its existence (including, especially, the authors of the EAM) were basically arguing that it made few, if any, differences to the economies concerned. With the recent economic troubles in the region, however, many of those who denied the existence or the effectiveness of industrial policy in East Asia have made an intellectual U-turn, and argued that industrial policy was widespread and "effective" in the region — although effective in the negative sense of creating inefficiencies and encouraging excessive risk-taking (for a more comprehensive critique of this argument, see Chang, 2000).

Before we discuss the role of industrial policy in the East Asian crisis, we need to put this crisis into perspective. The point is that, while the scale of crisis was truly mind-boggling, it is by no means the case that the whole region is falling apart. Taiwan and Singapore have done quite well over the last 3 years (although Taiwan is experiencing problems these days due mainly to political reasons). As for Japan, the problem seems more to be in perception than in reality (although this is not to say that therefore the recession can be ignored). True, during the 1990s, the country has been in the longest recession in its postwar history, but even then its performance was by no means a disaster. During the 1990s, the Japanese per capita GDP growth rate, at 1.4%, was only a fraction lower than that of the USA (1.6%), which is supposed to have entered a new "Golden Age", and superior to those of Switzerland (−0.4%), Sweden (0.8%), Canada (0.8%), Italy (1.1%), and France (1.3%) (data from the World Bank and the *Financial Times*). Also, according to the data from the *Economist* published in April 1999, in terms of productivity growth rate (that is, the rate of growth of GDP per worker), the US, at 0.9%, was behind Japan, which was at 1.2%, between 1989 and 1998.

The main difficulty with the argument that industrial policy was behind the Asian crisis is that it is in fact mostly the more market-oriented Southeast Asian countries and Hong Kong, rather than the industrial-policy states of Northeast Asia, that are in crisis. In the Japanese case, there is a widespread agreement that the recent economic problem was caused by poor macroeconomic policy, rather than industrial policy. Despite their industrial policy practices, Taiwan and Singapore are not experiencing crises. Of course, the inclusion of Korea, a well-known practitioner of industrial policy, in the list of crisis countries complicates things, but we begin to see a consistent pattern when we note that the Korean industrial policy was actually largely dismantled by the mid-1990s. Let us elaborate on this line of argument.

To begin with, let us look at the Southeast Asian countries. While the EAM certainly under-estimated the role that industrial policy played in these countries — it played an important role in developing some natural-resource-related industries (e.g., see Jomo & Rock, 1998) — it is undeniable that industrial policy was not the key element in the policy regimes of the Southeast Asian countries. Thailand and Indonesia have had little industrial policy, except in agricultural processing industries in the case of Thailand and in a few "prestige" projects (e.g., aircraft) in the case of Indonesia. Malaysia has had a more systematic industrial policy, but it can hardly be described as the dominant factor in the country's policy regime in the way that it was in the Northeast Asian countries. Indeed, during the last decade or so, many observers of the Southeast Asian countries have argued that the absence of industrial policy is precisely why they were finding it increasingly difficult to upgrade their industry and export structures. In short, industrial policy could not have been a major factor behind the crises in the Southeast Asian economies, because there was, simply, little of it around. Indeed, it was the real estate investments that had nothing to do with industrial policy, rather than industrial investments, that led the Southeast Asian bubbles (see Henderson, 1999, for more details).

Then how about Korea? Isn't it one of the archetypal industrial-policy states and therefore a case proving the defects of industrial policy? The fact that the over-investments that caused the country's crisis was mostly in industries, rather than in real estate development as in the case of Southeast Asia, also seems to corroborate this argument.

However, contrary to the popular perception, industrial policy was largely absent in Korea in the build-up to the current crisis. Slowly from the late 1980s, but very rapidly from 1993 with the inauguration of the Kim Young Sam administration, the Korean government dismantled industrial policy, except for R&D supports in some high-technology industries (see Chang, 1998b, for further details). Therefore, it is difficult to blame the Korean crisis on industrial policy as it was not around any more in any meaningful way.

In fact, we can go even further and argue that it was actually the *demise* of industrial policy, rather than its continuation, that was one major factor behind the current crisis in Korea (see Chang *et al.*, 1998, and Chang, 1999 for further details). Most importantly, the end to the policy of investment coordination among competing firms (see sub-section II.2) allowed the proliferation of duplicative investments in the key industries, which in turn led to some key bankruptcies that shook international investors' confidence and thus contributing to the crisis.

To summarize, contrary to the popular perception, the recent economic problems in East Asia do *not* show us that industrial policy was a major drag on the economies of the region. Above all, given the fact that there was little industrial policy around in the crisis countries (including Korea, which largely dismantled such policy by the mid-1990s), it seems highly implausible to argue that such policy was responsible for the crisis. On the contrary, it can even be argued that it was the absence of such policy that contributed to the crisis at least in some of the countries concerned.

IV. THE FUTURE OF INDUSTRIAL POLICY IN EAST ASIA

Is there future for industrial policy in East Asia? To some, this question may sound pointless, given the wide-ranging liberalization measures that have been instituted following the recent crisis, and also given, at least for the moment, the conversion of most governments in the region to the liberal cause.

However, formal laws and rules cannot fully determine the working of an economic system — after all, it was out of the very American formal institutional structures that the Occupation Authorities imposed after the Second World War that the "idiosyncratic" Japanese and German economic systems had developed. Moreover, policy needs and fashions change, and therefore it is not certain for how long the governments in the region will maintain their current policy stances. Therefore, I think it is still useful to explore the more structural economic and political trends to reflect on whether the governments in the region can use an activist industrial policy in the future, should their political commitments and vision change.

1. Economic Maturity

It has been popular during the last decade or so among the researchers of the more advanced East Asian economies (Japan, Korea, and Taiwan) to argue that the attainment of economic maturity in these economies has made industrial policy almost impossible to implement. There are two variants to this argument — one based on the problem of complexity, and the other based on the problem of uncertainty.

The complexity argument is that, with economic development, economies become more complex, and therefore it becomes more difficult to administer centrally. This argument is accepted as a truism by almost everyone, but I am not so sure whether I agree with it.

It is true that, other things being equal, a more complex problem increases the informational requirements of its successful policy solution, and therefore is more difficult to manage centrally. But the problem is that other things are *not* equal.

First of all, a more mature economy is likely to have a better administrative capability, if only because its bureaucracy will have had more

opportunity to engage in "learning-by-doing". As we pointed out in
sub-section II.3, it is not only in production activities where learning-
by-doing exists. The implication is that even a relatively "simple" policy
will be difficult to administer for developing country bureaucracies
with low capability, while more advanced economies have bureaucracies which can deal with quite complex policies with ease.

Secondly, a more developed economy is typically better organized
into larger and better-managed units (e.g., large modern corporations,
producer associations, community organizations). This means that it is
easier to implement a given policy in a more mature economy, as the
latter is likely to have more effective "intermediate" enforcement
mechanisms. Indeed, this was precisely one of the factors that Marx
and his followers (including the anti-socialist Schumpeter) thought
would make socialism increasingly feasible with economic development. The point can also be made from the opposite end. It is well
known that industrial policies are typically very difficult to implement
in industries where firms are very small and are not organised into
industry or regional associations.

In short, a more mature economy typically (if not always) has more
complex tasks at hand, but at the same time it typically has better
capabilities (both at the governmental level and at the social level) to
manage those tasks. Therefore, it is not clear whether centralized coordination through industrial policy becomes necessarily more difficult
with economic development and maturity.

A related, but slightly different, line of argument is based on the
problem of uncertainty, rather than complexity. The argument is that,
when a country reaches the frontier of technological development, it
becomes much more uncertain what the government should be doing
to help the industry. I find this argument more compelling than the one
based on complexity that we have just examined.

However, it is one thing to say that industrial policy becomes more
difficult in "frontier" industries, and it is another to say that this makes
industrial policy impossible in a mature economy. For one thing, most
of the justifications of industrial policy that we reviewed above should
hold for frontier industries too. Indeed, some of these justifications
may become even stronger with economic maturity (e.g., learning
externalities). Moreover, even in a frontier industry with genuine uncertainty about its future, there is no reason why an intelligent
bureaucracy in close consultation with the private sector should not be

able to identify the broad trends and provide support for certain types of productivity-enhancing activities. The best examples of the successful use of industrial policy in the frontier industries is provided by the experience of Japan during the 1980s and the early 1990s (e.g., see Okimoto, 1989; Fransman, 1990 and Weiss, 1995, for some examples).

Now, I must point out that this argument, which is very sensible in the context of some frontier industries in the most advanced economies, has been, unfortunately, liberally applied to situations which do not deserve it. Even in the most advanced countries like Japan, there are many industries that are still in a catch-up position. When it comes to economies like Korea and Taiwan, the argument is unconvincing. Despite what the locals, especially the Koreans, like to think, these economies are still good 2–3 decades behind Japan in almost all industries. Therefore, if industrial policy worked well in Japan as late as the late 1980s and the early 1990s, it should work for Korea and Taiwan in the early decades of the new millennium, if not necessarily beyond. It is needless to say that the argument is basically irrelevant when it comes to the Southeast Asian economies.

To sum up, the first variety of the "maturity" argument — namely, the complexity argument — does not seem compelling to me. As economies mature, policy implementation capability increases both at the governmental and at the "intermediate" levels, and therefore it is not clear whether they necessarily become more difficult to manage centrally. The second variety — namely, the uncertainty argument — is more convincing, but its applicability is pretty limited — it applies basically only to Japan among the East Asian countries. Moreover, even with an overall economic maturity, a country will still have a lot of industries where the technological capability has not reached the world's frontier. And even in those industries at the frontier, the more sensible solution is often not the abandonment of industrial policy but the modification in its form, as the Japanese experience since the 1980s show.

2. Democratization

It has long been argued that interventionist industrial policy requires strong states which can over-ride sectional interests. Therefore, it is often believed, increasing democratization of the East Asian countries during the last decade or so should make such policy politically less acceptable and therefore less feasible. This is argument is used especially in relation to countries like Korea and Taiwan, which have recently gone through a substantial degree of democratization.

However, it is not clear to me whether industrial policy is incompatible with a democratic polity. Countries like France, Japan, Austria, Norway, and Finland, whose democratic credentials and consensus-orientation in politics during the postwar period no one will dispute, have all successfully used industrial policy in one way or another. In fact, one can go one step further and even argue that, if there is a democratic consensus on it (as it had been in the above-mentioned countries), industrial policy can be even more effectively implemented, given that every policy requires for its long-term success some degree of consent by those who are going to be affected by it (see Weiss, 1998, ch. 2, for a similar argument).

In my view, what seems to be creating the impression that democracy and industrial policy are mutually incompatible is the fact that industrial policy in Taiwan, and especially Korea, has lost its political legitimacy in the eyes of the population because of its past association with dictatorship. However, there is no inherent reason why industrial policy cannot re-gain its legitimacy even in these countries, if a democratic political consensus can be built around it. It may be true that at least in Korea there is no chance of that happening in the near future. However, this is an argument which is based on an assessment of the present political situation in the country, and therefore has to be distinguished from the argument that industrial policy is inherently incompatible with democracy.

To summarize, the association between industrial policy and authoritarianism in the minds of the observers of certain East Asian countries is understandable, but this association is a product of history, rather than the manifestation of some underlying law. If we applied the same logic to the experience of the 19th century Britain, USA, or some European countries, we would have probably concluded that a free market policy was incompatible with democracy, which is indeed what most Liberals of the time thought to be the case (on the earlier view on the relationship between democracy and liberalism, see Bobbio, 1990; also see Polanyi, 1957).

3. Changing Balance of Power between the Government and the Private Sector

Throughout their economic development, but especially more recently, the East Asian countries have witnessed the rise of large private sector industrial and financial corporations, and their increasing internationalisation. This has prompted many people to argue that industrial policy that restricts private sector interests will not be possible any more, as the private sector firms now have enormous political influence, given the weight that they have in the economy and also given their ability to veto government policy by "exiting" from the domestic economy.

Undoubtedly, corporations which have become economically and politically more powerful and have more freedom to move around the world certainly would be, other things being equal, better able to resist government policies that sacrifice their individual interests for the sake of national goals. And indeed in Korea, the giant conglomerates (the *chaebols*) have aggressively campaigned during the 1990s to convince the population that the government should abandon its industrial policy and financial regulations.[14]

However, we need to be careful in jumping from such observation to the conclusion that economic development means the rise of the private sector, which, when combined with globalization, makes industrial policy impossible.[15]

The problem here is that it is not clear whether there is an inevitable association between economic development, the rise of the private sector, and the demise of industrial policy. For one thing, the experience of Taiwan shows that economic development need not lead to the emergence of a powerful private sector, as the process of corporate development is as much a political process as an economic process — in the Taiwanese case, the government deliberately restricted the rise of large private sector firms for political reasons (Fields, 1995). The Japanese experience is also consistent with such observation. The Japanese corporations had already become very powerful and internationally mobile during the 1970s and the 1980s, but Japan had great success with industrial policy during that period, because these firms saw benefits in industrial policy and cooperated with the government for its success.

Moreover, it needs to be pointed out that the extent of internation-alization of even the largest corporations in East Asia (with some exceptions from Japan) is still limited. Telling from the experiences of other countries with longer history of internationalized business, the chance that they will turn into truly "transnational" corporations with-out a "home base" in the foreseeable future is low. When we also note that globalization is a trend that can be, and was (in the aftermath of the Great Depression), reversed, it is not clear whether the current process of globalization will continue until it makes industrial policy impossible.[16]

So, in the end the argument that industrial policy has become less feasible in East Asian countries because their economic development has led to the growth in the power of the private sector, which naturally resist industrial policy, is problematic. It may fit the Korean example rather well, but as a general proposition, it is rather suspect. This is because there is no direct causal link between economic development and the rise of the private sector (recall the Taiwanese counter-exam-ple), on the one hand, and between the rise of the private sector (including its internationalization) and the demise of industrial policy (recall the Japanese counter-example), on the other hand.

V. CONCLUSION

In this paper, we examined some key debates surrounding industrial policy in East Asia, in relation both to its past records and to future prospects. What conclusions can we draw from this exercise?

First, at the theoretical level there are more theoretical justifications for industrial policy than acknowledged by the EAM, and we need to explore these issues deeper. This is important, especially given that those justifications (e.g., coordination of competing investments, scale economy) were probably more important in the actual formation of industrial policy in the East Asian countries than the ones acknowl-edged by the EAM (e.g., "Big Push", formation of implicit cartels in international negotiations).

Secondly, we need to think much harder to find the ways to test the true effects of industrial policy. Apart from the detailed methodologi-cal criticisms that have already been made of the tests conducted on the issue in the EAM, there remain some issues that we need to resolve in future research. For example, how should we deal with the problem of externalities? Whether and how do we, for another example, quantify the effects of policies like the achievement of scale economy through licensing policy, the prevention of a price war through the encouragement of a recession cartel, or the acceleration of technological change in the long run through the use of "protective" industrial policy in the short run? These are only some of the questions that need to be discussed further before we come up with an empirical conclusion.

Thirdly, the "capability" argument used by the EAM is not without its merits, but has important limitations. First of all, it is not clear why industrial policy regardless of its scale and sophistication requires an exceptionally competent bureaucracy. And, secondly, bureaucratic capability is something that can be accumulated through deliberate efforts and learning-by-doing. It should be also added that, it is not as if more market-oriented systems do not require high institutional capabilities, as we can see in the difficulties that many transitional and developing economies are currently experiencing in establishing a "free market system". They just need different types of capabilities

Fourthly, the argument against the feasibility of East Asian-style industrial policy in the post-WTO era, which was also emphasized by the EAM, draws an overly pessimistic conclusion without looking at the full array of possibilities that exist for policy manoeuvre.

Fifthly, as for the argument that attribute the recent recession in Japan and the crises in other East Asian countries to industrial policy, it should be pointed out that it is actually the countries which did not have (e.g., Southeast Asia, Hong Kong) or ditched (e.g., Korea) industrial policy that are in crisis.

Lastly, as for things like economic maturity, democratization, and the rise of the private sector power, which are frequently cited as reasons why industrial policy will not be feasible any more even in the countries that have successfully used it, we argue that they presuppose causal links which are not robust and are not really backed by empirical evidence.

The debate on the role of industrial policy in East Asia is hardly over. If it seems to be over, it is only because there are many mainstream economists who want to close the debate that has proved most awkward to them. Of course, in the current environment where industrial policy is regarded at best as an irrelevant relic of the past or at worst as the main cause of the recent economic troubles in the region, it is difficult to keep the debate alive, let alone extending it. However, a more careful re-assessment of the past records and the future prospects of industrial policy in East Asia will not only be important for the countries in the region but also for the more general debate on development policy. Given the total failure of the currently dominant policy regime to generate economic growth (never mind income equality) in most developing countries, a serious re-thinking of the (now-declining) East Asian model will be necessary.

NOTES

1. Important works that emphasized the positive contribution of Japanese industrial policy include Magaziner & Hout (1980), Johnson (1982), and Reich (1982). In the opposite camp, Schultze (1983) and Badaracco & Yoffie (1983) were influential. Reviews of this debate can be found in: Johnson (ed.) (1984), introduction; Thompson (ed.), 1989; and Chang (1994), ch. 3.
2. This argument is best summed up in the following passage from *The Economist*: "Most of the financial mess is of Asia's own making, and nowhere is this clearer than in South Korea. For years, the government has treated the banks as tools of state industrial policy, ordering them to make loans to uncreditworthy companies and industries" (15 November 1997).
3. For example, as late as 1988, the famous mainstream trade economist Bela Balassa was arguing that "apart from the promotion of shipbuilding and steel, [the role of the state in Korea] has been to create a modern infrastructure, to provide a stable incentive system, and to ensure that government bureaucracy will help rather than hinder exports" (Balassa, 1988, S.286).
4. Of course, this does not mean that new entries cannot or do not happen. The East Asian producers have been quite good at gaining market shares in some industries with chronic over-capacity problem. However, successful entry into these industries will be much more difficult than that into other industries.
5. When duplicative investments emerged for whatever reason (e.g., government's failure to take timely action, non-compliance by the firms), the East Asian governments tried to minimize excess capacity by encouraging, and sometimes forcing, mergers or recession cartels. There were of course national differences. The Japanese government preferred to use recession cartels, while the Korean government periodically resorted to forced mergers. Examples of the latter include the so-called "industrial restructuring program" of the early 1980s (which affected industries such as automobile, naval diesel engine, copper smelting, power-generating equipment, heavy electrical machinery, and electronic switching system) and the so-called "Big Deal" program following the 1997 crisis (which affected industries such as semiconductor, automobile, power-generating equipment, naval diesel engine, aircraft, petrochemical, petroleum refining, and railway carriage).

6. The cost inefficiency that results from the presence of excessive product variety is widely recognized in, for example, the South African car industry, and for that matter in the same industry of one East Asian country, namely, Taiwan (where about 10 producers each produce several thousand cars in an industry where the minimum efficient scale is believed to be around 300,000 units per year).

7. I thank Joe Stiglitz for highlighting this dimension of protective industrial policy, which was only implicit in the earlier version of the paper.

8. Different countries have dealt with this problem in different ways. Many European economies have used unemployment insurance to soften the blow of structural change on the owners of specific human skills and *ad hoc* subsidies to do the same for the owners of specific physical equipment. More proactively, the Scandinavian countries combined such system with the "active labor market policy", which provided re-training and relocation subsidies to the workers. As we shall see, the East Asian countries used protective industrial policy in order to deal with this problem.

9. The EAM distinguishes industrial policy as a separate category from export promotion policy. However, this is not right because export promotion policy was a key element in the industrial policy regimes of the East Asian countries. New industries that the government wanted to promote almost invariably needed to have access to foreign exchanges in order to buy the new technologies and the equipments that embody them, and knowing this, the government saw export success as a prerequisite of industrial upgrading. Also see Rodrik (1994).

10. The EAM also cites "the pragmatism and flexibility of governments" as another condition, but this subsequently plays a much less important role in the argument.

11. The list of "fundamentals" in the EAM keeps changing, because it does not really have a good theory of which area of policy is more important and why. However, these three items are almost always included in the list.

12. For example, the EAM does recognize that there is a time provision of up to 8 years for the developing countries to bring their trade policies in line with those practised in advanced countries (p. 365). It also acknowledges that there are other means than subsidies or export-directed credit programs that may be used in order to promote export (p. 25).

13. For further discussions of the East Asian crisis, see Radelet & Sachs (1998), Stiglitz (1998), Furman & Stiglitz (1998), Singh (1999), and Chang (2000).

14. In 1996, the Korea Federation of Industries, the association of the *chaebols* prepared a report arguing for the abolition of all government ministries except the ministries of defence and foreign affairs and for the consequent reduction of government staff by 90%. The report had to be officially withdrawn because it was unfortunately leaked in advance by a careless reporter and created a popular uproar. While the chance of such proposal being taken seriously was non-existent even in Korea that was then (and still is to a large extent) in the grip of an anti-statist reaction, but the incident is illustrative of the aggressiveness that the *chaebols* were showing in pushing for greater business freedom in the recent period.

15. For a comprehensive critique of the argument that globalization makes industrial policy impossible, see Weiss (1998). Chang (1998a) makes a similar argument more specifically in relation to the rise of transnational corporations.

16. The world economy was almost as globalized in the late 19th and the early 20th centuries as it is now on many indicators, and on some indicators even more. For example, international labor mobility was much higher then and international policy uniformity was much greater then — especially given the Gold Standard and the lack of tariff autonomy in all countries except the strongest (even Japan did not have tariff autonomy until 1899). See Bairoch & Kozul-Wright (1996) for the historical evidence.

REFERENCES

Akyuz, Y., H-J. Chang and R. Kozul-Wright. "New Perspectives on East Asian Development". *Journal of Development Studies* 34, no. 6 (1998): 4–36.

Amsden, A. "The State and Taiwan's Economic Development". In *Bringing the State Back In*, edited by P. Evans, D. Rueschemeyer and T. Skocpol. Cambridge: Cambridge University Press, 1985.

Amsden, A. *Asia's Next Giant*. New York: Oxford University Press, 1989.

_____. "Industrialisation under New WTO Law". Paper presented at the UNCTAD X meeting, 12–19 February 2000, Bangkok.

Amsden, A. and A. Singh. "The Optimal Degree of Competition and Dynamic Efficiency in Japan and Korea". *European Economic Review* 38, nos. 3/4 (1994): 941–51.

Badaracco, J. and D. Yoffie. "Industrial Policy: It Can't Happen Here". *Harvard Business Review* 61, no. 6 (1983): 97–105.

Bairoch, P. and R. Kozul-Wright. "Globalisation Myths: Some Historical Reflections on Integration, Industrialisation and Growth in the World Economy". UNCTAD Discussion Paper, no. 113. Geneva: United Nations Conference on Trade and Development (UNCTAD), 1996.

Balassa, B. "Development Strategies and Economic Performance". In *Development Strategies in Semi-Industrial Economies*, edited by B. Balassa *et al.* Baltimore: The Johns Hopkins University Press, 1982.

_____. "The Lessons of East Asian Development: An Overview". *Economic Development and Cultural Change* 36, no. 3, Supplement (1988): S273–S290.

Bhagwati, J. *Protectionism*. Cambridge, Mass.: The MIT Press, 1988.

Bobbio, N. *Liberalism and Democracy*. London: Verso, 1990.

Chang, H-J. "The Political Economy of Industrial Policy in Korea". *Cambridge Journal of Economics* 17, no. 2 (1993): 131–57.

_____. *The Political Economy of Industrial Policy*. London and Basingstoke: Macmillan, 1994.

_____. "Explaining 'Flexible Rigidities' in East Asia". In *The Flexible Economy*, edited by T. Killick. London: Routledge, 1995.

_____. "Luxury Consumption Control and Industrialisation in East Asia". Mimeo. Background paper prepared for *Trade and Development Report 1997*, UNCTAD. Geneva: United Nations Conference on Trade and Development (UNCTAD), 1997a.

Chang, H-J. "The Economics and Politics of Regulation". *Cambridge Journal of Economics* 21, no. 6 (1997b): 703–28.

_____. "Transnational Corporations and Strategic Industrial Policy". In *Transnational Corporations and the World Economy*, edited by R. Kozul-Wright and R.E. Rowthorn. London and Basingstoke: Macmillan Press, 1998a.

_____. "Korea: The Misunderstood Crisis". *World Development* 26, no. 8 (1998b): 1555–61.

_____. "The Hazard of Moral Hazard – Untangling the Asian Crisis". *World Development* 28, no. 4 (2000): 775–88.

Chang, H-J., H-J Park and C.G. Yoo. "Interpreting the Korean Crisis: Financial Liberalisation, Industrial Policy, and Corporate Governance". *Cambridge Journal of Economics* 22, no. 6 (1998): 735–46.

Chang, H-J. and R. Rowthorn. "Role of the State in Economic Change: Entrepreneurship and Conflict Management". In *Role of the State in Economic Change*, edited by H-J. Chang and R. Rowthorn. Oxford: Oxford University Press, 1995.

Cheng, T., S. Haggard and D. Kang. "Institutions, Economic Policy, and Growth in the Republic of Korea and Taiwan Province of China". *Journal of Development Studies* 34, no. 6 (1998): 87–111.

Dore, R. *Flexible Rigidities: Industrial Policy and Structural Adjustment in the Japanese Economy 1970-80*. London: The Athlone Press, 1986.

Evans, D. and P. Alizadeh. "Trade, Industrialisation, and the Visible Hand". *Journal of Development Studies* 21, no. 1 (1984).

Evans, P. *Embedded Autonomy - States and Industrial Transformation*. Princeton: Princeton University Press, 1995.

Fields, K. *Enterprise and State in Taiwan and Korea*. Ithaca, New York: Cornell University Press, 1995.

Fishlow, A., C. Gwin, S. Haggard, D. Rodrik and R. Wade. *Miracle or Design? Lessons from the East Asian Experience*, Washington, D.C.: Overseas Development Council, 1994.

Fransman, M. *The Market and Beyond: Information Technology in Japan*. Cambridge: Cambridge University Press, 1990.

Furman, J. & J. Stiglitz. "Economic Crises: Evidence and Insights from East Asia". Paper presented at the Brookings Panel on Economic Activity, 3–4 September 1998, Washington, D.C.

Henderson, J. "Uneven Crises: Institutional Foundations of East Asian Economic Turmoil". *Economy and Society* 28, no. 3 (1999).

Johnson, C. *MITI and the Japanese Miracle*. Stanford: Stanford University Press, 1982.

Johnson, C., ed. *The Industrial Policy Debate*. San Francisco: Institute for Contemporary Studies, 1984.

Jomo, S.K. and M. Rock. "Economic Diversification and Primary Commodity Processing in the Second-tier South-East Asian Newly Industrialising Countries". UNCTAD Discussion Paper, no. 136. Geneva: United Nations Conference on Trade and Development (UNCTAD).

Jones, L. and I. Sakong. *Government, Business and Entrepreneurship in Economic Development: The Korean Case*. Cambridge, Massachusetts: Harvard University Press, 1980.

Kwon, J. "The East Asia Challenge to Neoclassical Orthodoxy". *World Development* 22, no. 4 (1994): 635–44.

Lall, S. "Does the Bell Toll for Industrial Policy?" *World Development* 22, no. 4 (1994): 645–54.

Little, I. *Economic Development*. New York: Basic Books, 1982.

Luedde-Neurath, R. *Import Controls and Export-Oriented Development; A Reassessment of the South Korean Case*. Boulder and London: Westview Press, 1986.

Magaziner, I. and T. Hout. *Japanese Industrial Policy*. London: Policy Studies Institute, 1980.

Okimoto, D. *Between MITI and the Market: Japanese Industrial Policy for High Technology*. Stanford: Stanford University, 1989.

Polanyi, K. *The Great Transformation*. Boston: Beacon Press, 1957.

Radelet, S. and J. Sachs. "The East Asian Financial Crisis: Diagnosis, Remedies and Prospects". *Brookings Paper on Economic Activity*, no. 1 (1998): 1–90.

Ranis, G. and J. Fei. "A Model of Growth and Employment in the Open Dualistic Economy: The Cases of Korea and Taiwan". In *Employment, Income Distribution, and Development*, edited by F. Stewart. London: Frank Cass, 1975.

Reich, R. "Why the US Needs an Industrial Policy". *Harvard Business Review* 60, no. 1 (1982): 74–81.

Renshaw, G. *Adjustment and Economic Performance in Industrialised Countries: A Synthesis*. Geneva: International labor Office (ILO), 1986.

Rodrik, D. "King Kong Meets Godzilla". In *Miracle or Design? - Lessons from the East Asian Experience*, edited by A. Fishlow *et al.* Washington, D.C.: Overseas Development Council, 1994.

Schultze, C. "Industrial Policy: A Dissent". *The Brookings Review* 2, no. 1 (1983): 3–12.

Singh, A. "'Openness' and the 'Market-friendly' Approach to Development: Learning the Right Lessons from Development Experience". *World Development* 22, no. 12 (1994): 1811–23.

Singh, A. "Asian Capitalism" and the Financial Crisis. In *Global Instability — The Political Economy of World Economic Governance*, edited by J. Michie and J. Grieve Smith. London: Routledge, 1999.

Stiglitz, J. "Sound Finance and Sustainable Development in Asia". Keynote address to the Asia Development Forum, jointly organised by the World Bank and the Asian Development Bank, 9–12 March 1998, Manila, the Philippines.

Telser, L. *A Theory of Efficient Cooperation and Competition*. Cambridge: Cambridge University Press, 1987.

Thompson, G., ed. *Industrial Policy: US and UK Debates*, London: Routledge, 1989.

Wade, R. *Governing the Market*. Princeton: Princeton University Press, 1990.

Weiss, L. *The Myth of the Powerless State*. Cambridge: Polity Press, 1998.

Westney, E. *Imitation and Innovation: The Transfer of Western Organisational Patterns to Meiji Japan*. Cambridge: Cambridge University Press, 1987.

Williamson, O. *The Economic Institutions of Capitalism*. New York: The Free Press, 1985.

World Bank. *The East Asian Miracle*. New York: Oxford University Press, 1993.

World Bank. *World Development Report 1997*. Oxford: Oxford University Press, 1997.

3

Economic Growth and Restructuring in Post-war Japan — Contributions of Industrial and Technology Policies

Ryokichi Hirono

I. INTRODUCTION

The East Asian Miracle was most frequently referred to in economic and development literature in the 1990s, pointing to the so-called miraculously high rates of economic growth sustained over the last 30–year period (1965–95) by East Asian countries such as the Asian Newly Industrializing Economies (ANIEs) and several countries of the Association of Southeast Asian Nations (ASEAN).[1] The "Economic Miracle" when used in the 1960s, however, was the term applied to the Federal Republic of Germany and Japan when these two war-torn economies had made a miraculous recovery to attain the highest growth rates ever experienced in their own modern economic history and as compared with the other industrial countries. Looking ahead, the 21st century was then called the Japan Century by some serious futurologists.[2]

Even during the 1970s and the 1980s the same two countries, together with the United States, were called upon at the annual summit meetings of the Group of Seven (G7) to serve as the locomotives to propel the world trade and economy, which had become less buoyant, following the 1973/74 and 1979/80 energy crises. As late as the early 1990s many economic and political observers around the world referred to the coming 21st century as the Asia-Pacific century, based on a commonly shared belief that the high rates of economic growth during the years 1965–95 would be sustained in the region well into the next century.

In the midst of these world acclaims the governments, industry and people alike in East Asian countries, including Japan, began to slowly recognize the growing importance of their economies in the world and seek ways and means by which they could fulfil their roles expected by the rest of the world community. The formation of the Asia-Pacific Economic Co-operation (APEC) in 1989, the ASEAN Regional Forum (ARF) in 1990 and the Asia-Europe Meeting (ASEM) in 1996 in succession during the first half of the 1990s, with the aim of promoting freer trade and investment and security arrangements at the regional and global levels, attests to this keener sense of global responsibility as recognized by these East Asian countries, as much as their realistic response to the growing sentiment of regionalism prevailing in North America and Western Europe as exemplified respectively by the birth of the North American Free Trade Agreement (NAFTA) in 1993 and the European Union (EU) in 1994.

As is well known, improvement in total factor productivity, together with the expansion of productive inputs such as land, labor and capital, lies at the base of any economic growth and industrial expansion. The rapid economic growth and manufacturing development in post-war Japan have been made possible in the main by a steady expansion of the labor force and a rapid increase in per worker productivity. The latter in turn has been realized through a steady and fast expansion in capital investment, persistent inflows of technological innovations in engineering and management practices, continued structural changes in the national economy and individual industry sectors and government policy measures accelerating these changes in input and output markets.

It is equally well understood that the moderation in the annual rate of manufacturing growth since the two energy crises and Japan's stagnation since the mid-1980s have been brought about mainly by two factors. First, the rapid appreciation of the Japanese yen *vis-à-vis* the U.S. dollar and the other currencies linked to the U.S. dollar has compelled Japanese firms, particularly those in the manufacturing sector, to invest and create jobs overseas rather than at home in order to maintain their competitiveness in the world market. Second, many changes have taken place in the very factors affecting the rate of total factor productivity increases in the Japanese economy, which in turn are influenced by numerous interacting factors not only in the economic but also socio-cultural arenas, and not only at the corporate but also national levels. Both factors emerged as an inevitable result of Japan's economic success, but also partly reflected the failure of the government in dealing swiftly with both internal and external changes taking place in the economic, political and social environments. It is these successes and failures of the Japanese government policies that would be the main focus of this chapter.

The purpose of this chapter, therefore, is threefold: (1) to review the process of the overall economic growth, manufacturing expansion and structural changes in post-war Japan; (2) to re-examine the productivity performance in some selected industries, including electronics, and analyze the major factors favourably or adversely affecting that performance at the national and plant/firm levels; and (3) to critically evaluate the impact and contributions of government policies, particularly in technology, with a view to making suggestions on possible options in technology policies and priorities for sustaining productivity improvement in the Japanese industry and economy during the 21st century. By so doing, the chapter would critically examine the changing role of the state in the process of economic development and industrialization of Japan, with some reflections on the East Asian development paradigm.

Because of the enormity of the changes in the domestic and external economic environments experienced by Japan during the last half of the 20th century, the post-war period has been divided in this chapter into four distinct phases: the economic reconstruction period, 1945–54; the high-growth period, 1955–73; the adjustment period, 1974–85; and the bubble and post-bubble period, 1986–99. The special circumstances of the immediate post-war period, together with the limitation of the length of the chapter, however, unfortunately do not allow a full-length discussion of the most distant phase, 1945–54. The discussion of the intervening high-growth period 1955–73 might be beneficial to the policymakers in those countries of East Asia that had enjoyed a rapid economic growth up to 1996 and who would like to see it continued into the first decade of the 21st century, after recovering from the current financial and economic crises that started in mid-1997. It is self-evident, however, that the possible implications of enormous changes in the external economic environment represented by the process of globalization during the 1980s and 1990s would have to be taken into account.

Nevertheless, it would be more useful to the policy-makers in developing countries in general and East Asian countries and the ANIEs in particular to focus our discussion on more recent phases, such as the period 1974–99, to discern from the Japanese development experiences what to learn and what to avoid. As argued later in the chapter, during this critical phase many Japanese firms individually had successfully undergone drastic changes at home and abroad to remain competitive in the increasingly globalized world market, while many others which had been long protected and regulated by the Japanese government — farming, banking, insurance and small businesses in particular — had unfortunately not rationalized their corporate strategies, structures and management to the extent necessary. Also, the Japanese government, living in the glory of the successful economic performance of the 1960s and 1970s, unfortunately has become one of the major factors constraining the Japanese private sector dynamism and individual initiatives and leading the country from the land of the rising sun into the land of sunset. The chapter, however, entertains a hope that once the essential reforms in policies and institutions have been undertaken, the land of sunset will re-emerge as the land of the rising sun, though with enormous sufferings in the meantime among many segments of the population, firms, industries and economy which will be, as already are, prolonged to the extent that those reforms get delayed.

There are growing uncertainties now in the international economic arena caused by the recent currency-cum-economic crises in East Asian countries and the ongoing trend towards another bubble in the U.S. economy. In addition, a growing burden of non-performing assets in the financial sector to the tune of an estimated 100 trillion yen, or 20% of Japan's GDP, an overly cautious consumer behaviour producing on the average a savings rate of 20% of the household's disposable income and a sheer political indecision under conflicting pressures of the vested interests to deal squarely with the economic downswing and structural reforms in many sectors have certainly reinforced the recent difficulties in reversing the declining rates of economic growth and import expansion in Japan. Such developments have had a serious impact not only on East Asian economies but also on the rest of the world economy closely interlinked under globalization. As discussed later, it was only sometime after the installation of the Obuchi administration in 1998 that some economic recovery has begun, attaining positive growth rates in the first and second quarters of 1999.

However, according to the most recent forecasting done by the Japan Economic Research Centre, one of the most authoritative institutions publishing quarterly economic forecasts in Japan, the Japanese economy will now be expected to stagnate once again from the annual growth rate of 0.4% in fiscal 1999 to 0.1% in fiscal 2000 in real terms. Given the annual rate of labor force expansion at around 1%, unemployment 1999–2000 will possibly rise from 5.1% to 5.8%.[3] It is also expected that labor productivity will decline in the economy as a whole during the coming few years, though there will continue to be large variations in productivity change among different industries, different corporations and different regions as well as different sectors within the same industry, pushing many into the category of the so-called structurally declining industries.[4] This chapter hopes to clarify some of these major developments in the Japanese economy during the coming decade by looking at long-term trends observed in various economic, technological and social factors and government policies in particular that will be affecting productivity performance in various industries, including electronics, which happens to be the industry studied in common by all writers on country economics for effective comparison on policies and their impact.

II. JAPAN'S POST-WAR ECONOMIC PERFORMANCE

1. Rapid Growth during the 1960s and Early 1970s

Beginning in the mid-1950s Japan's economic growth showed a steady climb, rising from 8.9% during the 1955–60 period through 10.0% during the 1960–65 years to 12.1% during the 1965–70 period in terms of the average annual growth rate of real GNP. Even during the first half of the 1970s, when the world economy was going through international monetary instability and the energy crisis, Japan's real GNP grew much more rapidly than other Organization for Economic Co-operation and Development (OECD) countries, reaching a similarly high rate as achieved in the latter part of the 1950s (Table 3.1). During the entire decade of 1963–73, the Japanese economy grew at an average annual rate of 10.2%, over twice as high as that for most of the OECD member countries, resulting in a steady rise from 3.8% in 1955 to 11.0% in 1970 for Japan's share in the aggregate GNP of the six major OECD countries (Table 3.3).

While a number of domestic and external factors could be singled out as having been responsible for the sustained high rate of economic

TABLE 3.1 Gross Domestic Products of Major Industrial Countries in the World Economy, 1950–97 (in US$ Billion)

Country	1950	1960	1970	1980	1990	1995	1997
Canada	39.90	73.80	253.40	263.19	570.15	568.93	603.09
France	60.10	142.90	651.90	664.60	1,190.78	1,536.09	1396.54
Germany	72.10	184.50	819.10	—	1,488.21	2,415.76	2,100.11
Italy	37.20	107.50	394.00	449.91	1,090.75	1,086.93	1,145.37
Japan	11.00	43.10	203.70	1,059.25	2,942.90	5,108.54	4,201.64
United Kingdom	71.40	106.50	522.90	537.38	975.15	1,105.82	1,271.71
United States	506.70	1,011.60	2,587.10	2,709.00	5,392.20	6,952.02	7,745.71
Industrial countries (A)	944.00	2,083.10	5,993.40	7,777.00	16,239.00	22,485.55	22,321.97
Developing countries (B)	182.70	389.00	1,334.30	3,017.43	3,334.26	5,393.14	5,909.68
World (C)	1,100.00	2,472.10	7,327.70	11,815.00	22,856.00	27,846.24	28,157.01
A/C	0.86	0.84	0.82	0.66	0.70	0.81	0.79
B/C	0.14	0.16	0.18	0.26	0.15	0.19	0.21

NOTES:

1. All figures are in billions of current U.S. dollars.

2. The figures for industrial countries since 1990 include those for high-income developing countries; previously they were classified under developing countries.

3. The figures for the world from 1950 to 1970 exclude those for centrally planned economies, and their figures for 1995 and 1997 are included under those for developing countries.

The figures for industrial countries include those for high-income developing countries; previously they were classified under developing countries.

SOURCES: Miyazaki, Okumura and Morita, *Kindai Kokusai Keizai Yoran* [Commentary on the international economy in the modem era] (1981); World Bank, *World Development Report 1972,1992, 1995* and *1998/99* (New York, various years); and Economic Planning Agency, Japan, *2000 Nen no Nihon* [Japan in the year 2000], (Tokyo:GPO, 1982).

TABLE 3.2 Average Annual Growth Rates of Real GNP in Six Major Industrial Countries, 1955–98 (in percentages)

	1955–60	1960–65	1965–70	1970–75	1975–80	1980–85	1980–90	1990–98
France	5.0	5.8	5.8	3.9	5.2	5.8	2.4	1.5
W. Germany	6.6	5.0	4.8	2.2	4.5	4.7	2.2	1.6
Italy	5.6	5.3	5.9	3.8	3.7	5.1	2.4	1.2
Japan	8.9	10.0	12.1	6.8	7.4	6.6	4.0	1.3
United Kingdom	2.7	3.4	2.4	2.3	2.2	3.0	3.2	2.2
United States	2.2	4.8	3.3	2.5	3.3	2.2	2.9	2.9
Major industrial countries*	4.3		4.9		3.1		2.9	1.8

NOTES:

1. The figures for France, Italy and the United Kingdom for the entire period and those for the other countries for the period 1980–98 are GDP growth rates.

2. *The annual average growth rates for the major industrial countries are respectively for 1951–60, 1961–70, 1971–80, 1981–90 and 1991–98, expressed in constant 1980 U.S. dollars.

SOURCES: OECD, *National Accounts of OECD Countries, 1955–75* (Paris); World Bank, *World Development Report 1998/99*, Table 11, pp. 210–11, and *1999/2000*, Table 11, pp. 250–51 (New York, 1999, 2000); and United Nations secretariat, *Historical Estimates of Gross World Product, Population and Labour Force, 1950–95* (New York, May 1995).

TABLE 3.3   Shares of the Six Major OECD Countries as Percentages of the Total GNP[1]

Country	1955	1960	1965	1970	1980	1997	1998[2]
France	7.8	7.4	8.0	8.6	10.4	7.8	24,940
Germany	7.3	8.5	9.4	9.9	15.6	11.8	25,850
Italy	3.7	4.1	4.7	5.2	7.0	6.4	20,250
Japan	3.8	5.1	7.1	11.0	16.5	23.5	32,380
United Kingdom	8.6	8.7	8.3	6.9	8.4	7.1	21,400
United States	64.5	61.6	58.3	53.9	42.2	43.4	29,340

NOTES:
1. Converted into U.S. dollars at the exchange rates for the respective years.
2. Per capita GNP in U.S. dollars.
SOURCES: OECD, Interfutures' Final Report, *Facing the Future: Mastering the Probable and Managing the Unpredictable* (Paris, 1979) Table 19, p. 69, and World Bank, *World Development Report, 1998/99*, Tables 1 and 12, pp. 190–91 and pp. 212–13, and *1999/2000*, Table 1, pp. 230–31 (New York, 1999, 2000).

growth during the post-war period 1945–73, and whereas the emphasis may vary among different people as to the relative importance of economic over institutional factors, there seems to be a broad agreement on a number of factors as key contributors to Japan's successful economic performance. These factors are: (1) continued political stability; (2) an abundant supply of well-educated, well-trained and well-disciplined labor force; (3) a high level of savings propensity among the households; (4) competitive spirit of major economic actors; (5) high-growth economic policies of the government; (6) relatively clean and efficient bureaucracy; and (7) favorable international economic environments. It is to be reminded that with the exception of the last factor which is external to Japan, all the factors singled out above are internal factors, and as such there were relevant government policies and measures, including technology policies, that had either shaped or facilitated to shape those factors.

Post-war Japan, afflicted with a heavy wartime destruction of physical assets, including industrial plants, machinery and equipment as well as transport facilities, fortunately inherited a vast number of well-educated and well-disciplined workers and was able to mobilize them for its economic reconstruction immediately after the war and for its rapid economic expansion beginning in the mid-1950s. Already in 1945 nearly 100% of the children 6–12 years old were enrolled in primary schools, about 28% of those 13–18 years old in secondary schools and roughly 5% in tertiary schools. By 1960 those enrolled in the different levels of schools reached 100, 74 and 10% of the respective age groups, and in 1975 hit the marks of 100, 92 and 25% respectively. While an expanding supply of better educated labor force was in response to the rising demand for such a workforce caused by rapid economic growth and technological changes introduced in post-war Japan, various government policies had helped such an expansion. Immediately after the war the Japanese government extended compulsory education from six years for primary school to nine years for the six-year primary and the three-year junior high school. It also expanded secondary and tertiary education by setting up a large number of government-run senior high schools and universities, in addition to a mushrooming growth of privately run institutions. Successive governments heavily subsidized both government and private schools at all levels, thus making it possible to keep tuition fees low, though lower for the former than the latter. Subsidies covered not only textbooks and personnel and administration costs incurred, but also the costs of school buildings and equipment, including research and education laboratories and computer facilities. There was also an extensive coverage of college and university students under government and private scholarship and fellowship programs on both grant and loan bases, favoring students in science and engineering streams at the undergraduate and graduate levels. The government also provided tax incentives to encourage employers to provide in-service training programmers for skill and technology upgrading.

Brought up under socio-cultural environments where diligence, dedication and hard work were given priority, Japanese workers had traditionally been highly disciplined and industrious. The prevailing excess supply of labor, as exemplified by a relatively high rate of unemployment and a relatively low rate of job openings over job seekers up to the mid-1960s, reinforced these characteristics observed among the Japanese work-force (Table 3.4). Furthermore, the traditional employment practices separating the workforce into two distinct groups, permanent and temporary employees, and favoring the former over the latter in terms of wage rates, fringe benefits and other conditions of employment, made it easier for employers to discipline their workers effectively. The paternalistic attitude prevailing among employers

TABLE 3.4   Labour Market: Demand and Supply Fluctuations in Post-war Japan

Year	Labour Force (A) (1,000)	Unemployment (B) (1,000)	B/A (%)	Job Openings/Job Seekers Age Group			
				Average[1]	15–19	35–44[2]	60–64[3]
1955	41,560	680	1.6	0.28	—	—	—
1960	45110	750	1.7	0.59	—	—	—
1965	47,870	570	1.2	0.64	1.57	0.57	0.05
1970	51,530	590	1.1	1.47	6.07	2.45	0.15
1975	53,230	1,000	1.9	0.65	2.78	0.80	0.08
1980	56,500	1,140	2.0	0.77	2.60	0.97	0.16
1985	59,630	1,560	2.6	0.67	1.64	0.90	0.10
1990	63,840	1,340	2.1	1.51	4.32	2.28	0.25
1995	66,660	2,100	3.2	0.63	1.83	1.04	0.10
1996	67,110	2,250	3.4	—	—	—	—

NOTES:
1. The figures for 1955 are the monthly averages for all the job applications and job openings, whereas those for the period since 1960 exclude new school leavers.
2. The figures for 1965 and 1970 are for the age group 36–40.
3. The figures for 1965 and 1970 are for the age group 56 and over.
SOURCES: Bureau of Statistics, Office of the Prime Minister, *Japan Statistical Yearbook 1961, 1977* and *1998* (Tokyo, 1961, 1977, 1998).

towards their permanent employees contributed further to creating a sense of loyalty among the latter to their employers. Even here the government's hand was visible in that it provided a legal framework under which employers and unions would co-operate in enhancing output and productivity by setting up labor-management consultation councils, while restraining wage increases by allowing enterprise unions to bargain collectively with employers rather than industrial and craft unions which had been traditionally considered as the militant workers' stronghold in Western countries.

A High Level of Savings Propensity among the Households

Household savings as a percentage of disposable income averaged 16–20% during the two decades 1954–73, rising steadily over the years in response to higher levels of income. An overwhelming majority of these household savings were channelled into the banking and life insurance institutions, which in turn financed investment projects in the private and public sectors. As a result, expenditures on gross fixed capital formation accounted for roughly one-quarter of Japan's gross national expenditures during the 1950s and often exceeded one-third during the 1960s (Table 3.5). Large doses of capital investment in the private and public sectors year after year thus contributed to the steady expansion of both productive capacity and economic infrastructure and an incessant improvement in the national level of productivity in nearly all sectors of the national economy.

Among the most plausible explanations for the continued high rates of savings among the Japanese households even at the time of a relatively low personal income level are the persistence of the traditional concept of savings as a virtue of life as well as the traditional pattern of personal consumption, the societal need for a continued reliance upon household savings under conditions of relatively poor social security benefits after retirement, the social pressures on postponing personal consumption for residential investment under the high cost of real estate and housing construction, and a national craze for providing children with better educational opportunities as part of their career preparation and climbing up the social ladder. It is also agreed that the traditional practice of a sizeable bonus paid twice or thrice a year by private and public sector enterprises and national and local government departments contributed to higher rates of household savings, as most households would put aside a large share of the bonuses paid to purchase high-priced consumer durables at a later time and/or for repayment on their real estate and housing loans.

Small-saver schemes and other tax incentives instituted by the government to encourage household savings also helped to bring about high rates of domestic savings in post-war Japan. Under the small-saver schemes, since each individual was allowed to save up to 3 million yen in banks, another 3 million yen in national government bonds and another 3 million yen in postal savings accounts for which he would pay no income taxes on the interests earned, the average household consisting of the parents and two children would be able to save up to 36 million yen without paying any income taxes on its interest earnings. Furthermore, any savings beyond this amount were subject to only a fixed percentage point tax on all the interest earnings without

TABLE 3.5 Japan: Average Monthly Disposable Income (A); Saving Propensity (B) among Households and the Composition of Household Savings by Form; and Gross Fixed Capital Formation (GFCF) as Percentage of Gross National Expenditure (GNE) (C), 1955–96

Year	A1 (yen)	B	b1	b2	b3 (%)	b4	b5	GNE (billion yen)	GFCF (billion yen)	C (%)
1955	25,896	9.0	—	—	—	—	—	8,865.0	1,778.0	20.1
1960	37,708	16.0	—	—	—	—	—	16,207.0	5,048.0	31.1
1965	59,557	17.0	15.5	30.7	21.8	26.5	5.5	32,813.0	9,916.0	30.2
1970	103,634	20.3	14.6	36.8	22.5	21.1	4.9	188,323.0	58,687.0	31.1
1975	215,509	23.0	14.1	45.2	19.6	16.7	4.4	234,459.0	68,580.0	29.3
1980	305,549	22.1	9.0	49.1	19.6	16.7	5.5	290,551.0	85,630.0	29.5
1985	373,693	22.5	7.2	46.6	23.5	17.9	4.9	342,950.0	91,323.0	26.6
1990	440,539	24.7	7.2	42.2	28.9	18.7	3.9	429,986.0	136,685.0	31.8
1995	482,174	27.5	8.1	45.1	31.1	11.3	4.3	461,456.0	136,737.0	29.6
1996	488,437	28.0	8.2	44.6	32.4	10.5	4.2	483,295.0	150,659.3	31.2

NOTES:

1. All figures are for worker households, and those for column A are in current prices.

2. All figures are for households: b1 stands for demand deposits; b2 for time deposits; b3 for life insurance; b4 for securities including bonds and shares; and b5 for savings with non-financial institutions.

3. GNE and GFCF figures for the years 1955–65 are in current market prices and those for the rest are in calendar year 1990 market prices.

SOURCES: Computed from data in Bureau of Statistics, Office of the Prime Minister, *Japan Statistical Yearbook 1961, 1977 and 1998* (Tokyo, 1961, 1977, 1998); and JERC, *Quarterly Economic Forecasts* no. 99 (December 1997).

any progressive taxation, thus inducing people to save in banking and non-banking financial institutions rather than corporate bonds and stocks. Later the interest earnings from housing savings accounts up to a certain ceiling came under tax exemption, encouraging people to save for residential investment. As an extension to all these savings incentives, corporations were provided tax incentives which allowed them to make tax deductible all the interest paid on loans from banking and non-banking institutions for long-term plant and equipment investment purposes.

Competitive Spirit of Major Economic Actors

While an abundant supply of well-educated and well-disciplined labor force and a high level of savings propensity among the households laid the necessary foundation for the high rate of economic growth and investment expansion achieved during the post-war period, they alone were not sufficient unless accompanied and activated by major economic actors endowed with highly competitive spirit. A series of economic, political and social democratization programs drafted by the Allied Powers occupying post-war Japan and enforced by the Japanese government provided a climate in which major economic actors were allowed to give a free play to their competitive spirit.

Younger-generation business managers, suddenly elevated to the top executive positions after the purging of wartime industrialists and financiers and confronted by intense competition for corporate survival as a result of the Zaibatsu dissolution under chaotic economic conditions, had to go all out reorganize their production and distribution facilities and install technological innovations to expand and modernize production and other corporate activities and reduce their costs of production and operations. The anti-monopoly legislation and administration, though weakened over time as exemplified in the government approval of the so-called "repression cartels", provided a public policy and institutional framework in which effective competition was encouraged. In fact, concentration ratios went down in many industries, reflecting the entry of many more firms into the production mainstreams with enlarged output capacity and resulting in steady price reductions, particularly in the consumer durables and producer goods sectors.

Contrary to the situation in pre-war Japan, the workers in all sectors of the economy, including national and local government services,

TABLE 3.6   Trade Unions, Union Membership and Labour Disputes

Year	Trade unions	Membership (1,000)	Unionization rate (%)	No. of Disputes	No. of Workers in Disputes (1,000)
1945	509	381	3.2	256	165
1950	29,144	5,774	46.2	1,487	2,348
1955	32,012	6,166	37.8	1,345	3,748
1960	41,561	7,516	33.8	2,222	6,953
1965	52,879	10,070	34.6	3,051	8,975
1970	60,954	11,481	35.0	4,551	9,137
1975	69,333	12,473	34.4	8,435	10,261
1980	72,693	12,241	30.8	4,376	5,456
1985	74,499	12,319	28.9	4,826	3,249
1990	72,202	12,193	25.2	2,071	2,026
1995	70,839	12,495	23.8	1,200	1,207
1996	70,699	12,331	23.2	1,240	1,183

NOTE: As applied to regular workers.
SOURCES: Bureau of Statistics, Office of the Prime Minister, *Japan Statistical Yearbook 1961, 1977* and *1998* (Tokyo, 1961, 1977, 1998).

were encouraged by the post-war Occupation Forces to form their trade unions to bargain collectively with their management on wages and other conditions of employment and, if necessary, to take industrial actions in an effort to make economic gains for themselves (Table 3.6). Confronted by the rapid upsurge in union organizations and membership and threatened by their stronger bargaining position, employers were under constant pressure to raise corporate productivity to reasonably satisfy union demands for higher wages and improved working conditions, including a shorter workweek. Otherwise, employers had to face work stoppages which they could not afford under the highly competitive product markets and the increasingly sellers' labor market in the late 1960s and early 1970s. Had it not been for such trade union pressures, protected and precipitated by labor legislations during the 1950s and by the high rates of economic growth during the 1960s, the innovative spirit — particularly among industrial employers — would not have been sustained at the high level that it was.

Also, it is important to note that the expansion of the domestic consumer market was made possible by rapidly rising employment and wage earnings among Japanese workers, enabling employers to expand their production facilities to gain economy of scale and lower the cost of production per unit of output. With one-third to one-half of the labor force engaged in the primary sectors and with one-fourth to one-fifth of the GNP originating from agriculture, farmers were one of the major economic actors, particularly during the late 1940s and the 1950s. Liberated under a series of land reform programs, farmers took a great initiative in making their farmland more productive, intensifying the use of the crop rotation system, fertilizers and insecticides and introducing high-yielding varieties and improved agricultural machinery and equipment. A variety of agricultural assistance, including farm price support programs of one kind or another for rice, barley and other farm products, contributed to further stabilization and improvement in the level of farm income, which in turn meant an expanding domestic market for industrial commodities, including consumer durables. With industrialization and urbanization spreading all over the country, however, there emerged a continuing out-migration of labor from agriculture and other primary sectors to secondary and tertiary sectors, drastically changing the distribution of employment and GNP by industry throughout the post-war period (Table 3.7).

TABLE 3.7   Changing Employment Structure of Japan, 1950–97

Year	Total (1,000)	Primary Sector (1,000)	(%)	Secondary Sector (1,000)	(%)	Manufacturing (1,000)	(%)	Tertiary Sector (1,000)	(%)
1950	35,700	17,283	48.4	7,812	21.9	5,690	15.9	10,605	29.7
1955	39,267	16,111	41.0	9,220	23.5	6,902	17.6	13,930	35.5
1960	44,700	14,240	31.9	12,762	28.6	9,545	21.4	16,717	37.4
1965	47,300	11,420	24.1	14,780	31.2	11,500	24.3	21,100	44.6
1970	50,940	9,060	17.8	17,710	34.8	13,770	27.0	24,170	47.4
1975	52,230	6,770	13.0	18,250	34.9	13,460	25.8	27,210	52.1
1980	55,360	5,880	10.6	19,150	34.6	13,670	24.7	30,330	54.8
1985	58,070	5,180	8.9	19,830	34.1	14,530	25.0	33,060	56.9
1990	62,490	4,570	7.3	20,930	33.5	15,050	24.1	36,990	59.2
1995	64,570	3,730	5.8	21,190	32.8	14,560	22.5	39,650	61.4
1997	65,570	3,570	5.4	21,270	32.4	14,420	22.0	40,730	62.1

SOURCES: Bureau of Statistics, Office of the Prime Minister, *Nihon Tokei Nenkan* [Japan Statistical Yearbook] *1961, 1971, 1981, 1991* and *1998* (Tokyo, 1961, 1971, 1981, 1991, 1998).

High-Growth Policies Uninterrupted Under Continued Political Stability and Undertaken by Relatively Clean and Efficient Bureaucracy

Devastated by the war and reduced to half of the pre-war GNP and one-third of the pre-war industrial production, Japan emerged as a single-track-minded nation preoccupied with the fastest possible economic reconstruction immediately after the war and rapid economic growth after the Korean War. Throughout the 1950s and 1960s all the monetary, fiscal and specific policy measures legally permissible to the government were mobilized, and, if not legal, were legalized to increase national output, modernize production facilities and expand exports and foreign exchange earnings, often at the expense of workers' wage earnings and working conditions, including long hours of work particularly in small and medium industries, and at the cost of consumer welfare.

These policy measures were intended: (1) to ensure a continued supply of energy and raw materials required for expanded production at home; (2) to facilitate the inflow of advanced foreign technology and management expertise at a reasonable cost; (3) to improve the level of domestic absorptive capacity towards an effective utilization and development of new scientific knowledge and technology; (4) to expand and improve the economic and social infrastructures, including transport, communications and power network to reduce the cost of production and distribution per unit of output and throughput; and (5) to enable banking and other financial institutions to assist manufacturing and other corporations to expand capital investment.

In view of the technical requirements of higher capital coefficients in nearly all the industrial sectors, the high-growth economic policies of the government, to be effectively implemented, called for an ever-increasing amount of capital resources mobilized at home and abroad.

Policy instruments such as accelerated depreciation allowances, low-interest loan and subsidy programs, tax and import duty exemptions and reductions, administrative guidance and the Central Bank assistance and guidance in commercial banking operations were effectively and discriminatingly utilized to accelerate and redirect capital investment flows consistent with high rates of economic growth and in favour of those export industries and strategic industries with high potentials for productivity improvement and high income elasticity of demand.

In the meantime various kinds and magnitude of social costs, including natural and urban environmental deterioration and various respiratory diseases associated with a high rate of economic expansion and unbridled industrial development, were not considered serious and little efforts were made to rectify them until late in the 1960s when it became totally unbearable to all residents in metropolitan areas and industrial centres such as Keihin (Tokyo-Yokohama), Chubu (Nagoya-Yokkaichi), Hanshin (Osaka-Kobe) and Kitakyushu (northern part of Kyushu Island).

As often said about developing countries, it is one thing to draft a long-range economic development plan incorporating a high-growth strategy and completely another to be able to effectively implement the plan and achieve the planned growth rate. Fortunately for Japan, however, during the period 1950–73 nearly all the planned growth rates were overshot, necessitating annual recalculations and modifications in various subordinate growth targets in respective development plans. The fulfillment and overshooting of planned growth targets were made possible, aside from the favourable international economic environments discussed below, in a large measure by continued political stability observed in post-war Japan under the Liberal Democratic Party (LDP) regime. The LDP members in Parliament and the government bureaucracy assisting them, though often fiercely criticized by socialist and other parties, were for the most part hand in hand in translating the high-growth strategy into concrete policy measures and achieved both overall and sectoral growth targets. Such remarkable economic performance in turn contributed to the continued reign of the LDP over three decades, with a strong support given by industrialists, financial groups, farmers and the middle-class component of the population who benefited from the high-growth performance.

As regards major economic policy thrusts, there was a steady shift from economic reconstruction during the late 1940s and the early 1950s to trade expansion policies during the late 1950s and the 1960s. As announced by the Japanese government in its Economic White Paper in 1956, the post-war period was coming to an end with the rapid economic reconstruction during the early 1950s partly aided by the Korean War boom of 1950–52, and the government began to reorient its economic policy focus from preoccupation with domestic issues to integrating the Japanese economy with the rest of the world.

The Export-Import Bank of Japan was created as early as in 1950 to assist Japanese trading houses and manufacturers in financing their imports and exports by giving them greater access to medium- and long-term loans at easier terms. The Japan Export Trade Promotion Organization was established in 1954 to assist Japanese exporters explore and expand their overseas markets, together with providing them various financial and tax incentives. Import restrictions were also relaxed in the mid-1950s to help Japanese manufacturers acquire advanced technologies from overseas and ease and enhance their access to stable sources of raw materials and intermediate inputs at reasonable cost. Trade insurance schemes were introduced and implemented by the Japanese government itself in view of the high risks involved to help reduce the commercial and non-commercial risks facing Japanese exporters and importers as well. In 1952 the Corporate Rationalization Promotion Law was also enacted to provide tax exemption and accelerated depreciation on imported equipment and technology for the purpose of technological improvement. To enhance the Japanese industry's competitiveness in the international market, there were also a series of industry rationalization and promotion programs announced by the Ministry of International Trade and Industry (MITI) during the latter part of the 1950s for basic industries, such as iron and steel, electric power and transport machinery including vessels, as well as for new industries such as electronics, petrochemical and synthetic rubber.

The decade of the 1960s began with the Income-Doubling Program which mobilized all the domestic resources — financial, technological and manpower — to attain high rates of economic growth and reorient the traditional patterns of production in favour of those sectors with greater demand and technological potentials. Also, in line with repeated calls for across-the-board 50% cut in import tariffs (the so-called Kennedy Round of multilateral trade negotiations) by President Kennedy of the United States, the Japanese government, beginning in 1961, announced a series of import-liberalization measures in spite of strong resistance from export manufacturers and exposed them to import competition from overseas, which in fact helped enormously to strengthen their competitiveness in the international market. Japan's import-liberalization process was accelerated with its admission into the OECD in April 1964. It is no exaggeration to say that had it not been for such import-liberalization measures during the 1960s, the Japanese manufacturing industries would not have been able to become competitive so soon as they actually did. They would, of course, have become much more competitive if the Japanese government had accommodated the international pressures for a steady appreciation of the Japanese yen *vis-à-vis* the U.S. dollar during the late 1960s as their European counterparts did, as discussed later.

As revealed later, however, the same successful regime of a close nexus between the LDP, the central government bureaucracy, the large-scale industrialist and financial groups and the agricultural co-operatives, when prolonged too long, became excessively entrenched and interwoven, and acted as the conservative and constraining forces that have slowed down the pace of economic deregulation, liberalization and opening up to the globalized world markets of goods, services and finance and that have eventually repressed the private sector dynamism and individual initiatives at home so prevalent during the immediate post-war years.

Favourable International Economic Environments

Aside from the various domestic factors mentioned above, a steady expansion of the world economy and trade made possible under the Bretton Woods regime of fixed exchange rates and the General Agreement on Tariffs and Trade (GATT) trade regime accelerated Japan's economic growth during the 1950s and the 1960s. Governments of the major industrial countries were willing to pursue under the GATT and the OECD agreements the external economic policies promoting trade and capital liberalization, lowering tariff and non-tariff barriers and decontrolling foreign trade and exchange transactions. Under the Bretton Woods regime, competitive devaluation of major currencies prevalent before World War II was prevented and a relative stability of the international monetary system was maintained. Those countries facing repeated bouts of fundamental disequilibria, however, were allowed to vary their foreign exchange rates and those countries confronted by short-term balance of payments difficulties were given various International Monetary Fund (IMF) relief measures, including compensatory financing and tranche. In addition, the United States, then the sole major industrial country well equipped with finance, technology and management know-how and a large domestic market, was willing and ready to share its economic resources and market with the rest of the non-socialist world for economic, political and security reasons.

In pursuing its high-growth policies, Japan took full advantage of those favourable international economic environments. Free from the heavy burden of costly military build-up, it made every effort to channel domestic and foreign financial resources into fixed capital formation, accelerate the inflow of foreign technology and management know-how, expand exports and maintain a stable supply of energy and other mineral resources from abroad at reasonable prices. During the two decades up to the energy crisis in 1973–74, Japan attained among major industrial countries one of the highest, if not the highest, rates of export growth, resulting in a steady increase in the merchandise export as a percentage of its gross national expenditure (GNE), that is, from 6.5 to 13% between 1950 and 1975 (Table 3.8). In particular, exports expanded more rapidly during recessions when the domestic market grew less, thereby contributing to higher rates of economic growth than otherwise. The maintenance throughout the 1960s of the undervalued Japanese yen *vis-à-vis* the U.S. dollar and other major currencies tied to the latter accelerated Japan's exports while restraining its imports, and created a steady increase in its trade surplus, thus allowing Japan to adopt expansionary policy measures without straining its balance of payments position.

The Japanese government's policy of maintaining the undervalued yen came under fierce attacks by the United States and a few other industrial countries that began to run trade deficits *vis-à-vis* Japan since the mid-1960s. Exasperated by the reluctance of Japan to appreciate the yen relative to the U.S. dollar, then President Nixon announced the New Economic Policy which forced Japan to revalue its currency upward by devaluing the U.S. dollar through delinking from gold, in addition to the import surcharge of 10%, a cut in foreign aid program by 10% and the tax credit to all U.S. corporations for their domestic investment in the U.S. economy. In spite of the Smithsonian Multilateral Currency Realignment in December 1971, which raised the exchange rate of the yen from 360 to 308 per U.S. dollar, Japan continued to increase its trade surplus not only bilaterally with the United States but also multilaterally, until moderated by the imposition of the floating exchange rate regime in February 1973 and interrupted by the energy crisis of 1973–74. As discussed later, it was not until the Plaza Accord in October 1985, when the Japanese yen *vis-à-vis* U.S. dollar was upvalued from the bottom of 260 during the Reagan administration's high-interest policy to 214 and once again sharply to 128 in 1988 during the height of Japan's low-interest policy, that a rising trend for the Japanese trade surplus began to decelerate.

TABLE 3.8   Average Annual Growth Rates of Exports and Exports as Percentages of GNE for Six Major Industrial Countries[1]

Country	Average Annual Growth Rates of Exports					Exports as Percentage of GNE				
	1950–60	1960–70	1970–80	1980–90	1990–98	1960	1970	1975	1980	1998
France	6.4	7.6	11.7	3.7	4.1	15.0	16.0	20.0	22.0	24.0
W. Germany	16.6	12.6	15.1	4.6	2.8	19.0	21.0	25.0	—	27.0
Italy	10.5	13.4	2.7	4.1	7.5	15.0	19.0	25.0	22.0	27.0
Japan	15.9	17.2	14.3	4.5	3.9	11.0	11.0	13.0	14.0	9.5
United Kingdom	4.8	3.0	0.6	3.9	5.5	21.0	23.0	27.0	27.0	29.0
United States	5.1	5.7	5.6	4.7	8.1	5.0	6.0	9.0	10.0	12.0

NOTE: 1. Growth rates of exports are in real terms, whereas exports as percentage of GNE are calculated on the basis of current market prices.

SOURCES: United Nations, *U.N. Yearbook of Statistics 1977* (New York, 1977); and World Bank, *World Development Report 1978, 1998/99* and *1999/2000* (New York, 1978, 1999, 2000).

Japan's rapid export expansion resulted mainly from its internal capacity to reorient its industrial production in response to changing patterns of overseas demand as well as changing relative factor prices at home. Among the high-growth export items were found those products of the heavy and chemical industry sectors which tended to be more capital-intensive and among the low-growth export items those products of the light industry sectors which tended to be more labour-intensive (Table 3.9) Not only were capital-intensive production processes more amenable to improving physical productivity than labor-intensive ones, but also those products of the heavy and chemical industry sectors enjoyed higher rates of demand expansion resulting from further industrialization in the developing world and continued economic growth in the industrial world. They had higher income elasticities of demand than their labor-intensive, light industry counterparts. With further advances in Japan's industrialization, its import structure by major commodity groups also underwent significant changes during the period 1955–73 (Table 3.10).

The United States was by far the major supplier of foreign capital, technology and management know-how to the rest of the world during the period 1950–73. Though varying from year to year, roughly two-thirds of the foreign direct investment inflows were from the United States, and over two-thirds of the foreign portfolio investment, corporate bonds and bank loans were raised in that country. Furthermore, U.S.-based transnational corporations supplied nearly two-thirds of the foreign technology imported by Japan, with those based in West Germany, Switzerland, the United Kingdom and France trailing as minor technology suppliers (Table 3.11). Out of the 6,766 contracts concluded during the period 1950–75 for the importation of foreign technology, 6,527 were in the field of manufacturing and the annual amount of corporate royalties paid by the Japanese manufacturing industry totalled as high as 164.9 billion yen in 1975. Of this amount, 38.2 billion yen was paid by the electrical machinery industry, 35.7 billion yen by the transportation machinery industry, and 26.9 billion yen by the chemical industry (Table 3.12).

Much of the foreign technology imported during the earlier period had been developed for commercialization prior to World War II, and those transnational corporations in the United States and European countries were quite willing to supply it overseas as they had little to gain from withholding it from the expanding international technology

TABLE 3.9 Changing Export Structure of Japan by Major Commodity Groups, 1950–97 (in percentages)

Commodity Group	1950	1955	1960	1965	1970	1975	1980	1985	1990	1995	1997
Heavy and chemical industry products	33	38	44	62	72	83	85	87	87	88	87
Metals and metal products	21	19	14	20	20	19	16	11	7	7	6
Iron and steel	6	13	10	15	15	18	12	8	4	4	4
Machinery	10	14	25	35	46	57	64	72	75	75	74
Vessels	—	4	7	9	7	—	—	—	—	—	na
Chemical products	2	5	5	7	6	7	5	4	6	7	7
Light industry products	59	52	48	32	23	15	13	13	12	11	12
Textile products	47	37	30	19	13	6	5	4	3	2	2
Non-metallic minerals	3	5	4	3	2	1	1	1	1	1	1
Others	10	10	13	10	9	7	7	8	9	8	9
Raw materials and fuels	2	4	2	2	1	1	0	—	0	0	0
Foodstuff	6	6	6	5	3	1	1	1	1	1	0
Total (billion yen)	300	700	1,500	3,320	6,954	16,545	29,382	41,956	41,457	41,531	50,938

SOURCES: Bureau of Statistics, Office of the Prime Minister, *Japan Statistical Yearbook 1961, 1971, 1981, 1991* and *1998* (Tokyo, 1961, 1971, 1981, 1991, 1998).

TABLE 3.10 Changing Import Structure of Japan by Major Commodity Groups, 1950–97 (in percentages)

Commodity Groups	1950	1955	1960	1965	1970	1975	1980	1985	1990	1995	1997
Food and direct consumer goods	33.6	25.3	12.2	21.5	16.1	17.1	11.5	13.1	14.8	15.0	13.5
Industrial materials and supplies	48.3	82.8	65.6	67.4	68.3	72.0	77.1	70.0	54.3	43.5	43.3
Crude materials	42.0	47.4	58.5	34.7	32.1	17.5	15.4	12.3	11.1	8.8	7.6
Mineral fuels	3.7	8.3	13.5	19.9	20.7	44.3	49.8	43.1	23.9	15.9	15.4
Industrial chemicals	—	—	—	5.0	5.2	3.5	4.3	6.1	6.7	7.1	6.6
Metals	—	—	—	4.8	6.5	2.5	3.8	4.3	5.9	5.0	4.3
Textiles	—	—	—	0.5	1.0	1.1	1.0	1.2	1.5	1.4	1.4
Capital goods	18.1(1)	11.8(1)	20.5(2)	8.8	11.7	6.6	6.5	8.9	14.0	20.5	24.0
General machinery	—	—	—	5.5	6.7	3.6	2.7	3.6	6.0	8.3	9.8
Electrical machinery	—	—	—	1.3	2.4	1.6	1.8	2.8	4.9	9.1	10.2
Transportation equipment	—	—	1.4	1.5	1.9	3.9	1.3	1.7	2.2	1.6	2.0
Consumer non-durables	—	—	—	0.6	1.3	1.7	1.9	2.6	6.0	8.8	8.1
Textile products	—	—	—	0.0	0.6	1.1	1.3	1.7	4.0	5.9	5.2
Consumer durables	—	—	—	1.3	1.9	1.9	1.7	2.3	8.7	9.3	8.6
Household equipment	—	—	—	0.1	0.1	0.1	0.1	0.2	0.3	0.4	0.3
Household electric appliances	—	—	—	0.0	0.1	0.2	0.1	0.1	0.5	1.2	1.1
Passenger cars	0.2	0.3	0.2	0.3	0.3	0.4	0.3	0.4	2.6	3.0	2.3
Toys and musical instruments	—	—	—	0.4	0.7	0.5	0.4	0.6	0.9	1.2	1.2
Other goods	0.0	0.1	0.2	0.4	0.8	0.6	1.3	3.2	3.1	2.8	2.3
Total (in billions of yen)	348	890	1,617	2,941	6,797	17,170	31,995	31,085	33,855	31,549	40,956

NOTES: Because of rounding, percentage figures may not total 100.

SOURCE: Bureau of Statistics, Office of the Prime Minister, *Japan Statistical Yearbook 1978* and *1997* (Tokyo, 1978, 1997).

Fiscal Year		France	Germany	Italy	Netherlands	Switzerland	United. Kingdom	United States	Total
1950	A								2.6
	B	0	0	0	0	5	0	21	27 (76)
1955	A								20
	B	4	9	0	1	2	3	44	71 (184)
1960	A								95
	B	5	45	8	7	18	10	200	327 (588)
1965	A								166
	B	21	55	8	22	31	39	265	472 (958)
1970	A								433
	B	73	189	29	23	73	108	745	1,330 (1,768)
1975	A	7.1	21.2	4.5	1	8.9	11.6	106.7	169
	B	144	154	42	36	57	116	689	1,403 (1,836)
1980	A	11	21	1	6	16	20	154	240
	B	228	230	na	na	na	159	1092	1,860 (2,142)
1985	A	7	18	2	16	16	15	209	293
	B	198	199	79	48	82	166	1430	2436
1990	A	23	27	2.4	20	15	10	255	372
	B	158	201	60	86	106	185	2,119	3,211
1995	A	18.9	19.4	na	23.4	20.5	12.1	277.6	391.7
	B	134	144	41	73	91	1,099	1,981	3,901

NOTES:

1. A denotes the annual amount of royalty payments on all types of technology imports, while B figures show the number of new licence contracts for technology imported, classified as vital, with those B figures in parentheses showing both vital and non-vital contracts for the years between 1950 and 1980.

2. A figures for the years between 1950 and 1970 are in US$ million.

SOURCES: Bureau of Statistics, Office of the Prime Minister, *Japan Statistical Yearbook 1981 and 1998* (Tokyo, 1981, 1998); and Science and Technology Agency, *Indicators of Science and Technology 1961, 1965, 1969, 1976 and 1996*, and *Analysis of Foreign Technology Imports 1977 and 1997* (Tokyo, various years).

TABLE 3.12 Japan's Technology Imports by Sector, 1950–95

Year	Number of Cases			Amount of Payment (billion yen)						
	All Industries	Construction	Manufacturing	All Industries	Construction	Manufacturing	Chemical	Electrical Machinery	Transport Machinery	Telecom and Public Utilities
1950	76	0	76	0.948	—	0.146	0.048	0.036	0.063	—
1955	184	1	183	7.199	0.012	7.079	3.003	1.553	1.571	—
1960	588	0	588	34.818	0.093	3.725	5.647	6.792	5.197	0.134
1965	958	10	948	—	—	—	—	—	—	—
1970	1,768	14	1,754	156.6	—	—	—	—	—	—
1975	1,836	27	1,809	169.1	3.1	164.9	26.9	38.2	35.7	-
1980	2,142	—	—	239.5	2.7	233.2	39.3	61.7	40.3	0.5
1985	2,436	—	—	293.2	3.5	288.6	37.4	84.2	59.7	0.9
1990	3,211	28	3,117	371.9	1.8	368.3	54.0	159.9	52.3	1.2
1995	3,901	23	3,854	391.7	1.3	388.3	66.2	199.7	32.5	2.0

NOTE: The figures for royalty payments for transport machinery for the years 1950-60 include those for general machinery.

SOURCES: Bureau of Statistics, Office of the Prime Minister, *Japan Statistical Yearbook 1981 and 1998* (Tokyo, 1981, 1998); Science and Technology Agency, *Indicators of Science and Technology 1961, 1965, 1969, 1976 and 1996*, and *Analysis of Foreign Technology Imports 1977 and 1997* (Tokyo, various years).

TABLE 3.13 Japan's Technology Exports by Sector, 1955–95

Year	Number of Cases			Amount of Payment (billion yen)						
	All Industries	Construction	Manufacturing	All Industries	Construction	Manufacturing	Chemical	Electrical Machinery	Transport Machinery	Telecom and Public Utilities
1955	8	2	6	0.316	0.075	0.241	0.013	0.014	0.154	—
1960	48	7	38	0.810	0.039	0.771	0.187	0.072	0.053	—
1965	na	na	na	6.000	na	na	na	na	na	na
1970	na	na	na	21.24	na	na	na	na	na	na
1975	2,811	209	2,565	66.6	5.5	58.9	21.5	7.3	6.3	na
1980	4,103	110	3,947	159.6	25.4	133.3	31.9	23.0	21.8	0.1
1985	5,885	384	5,449	234.2	26.5	205.6	38.2	59.5	32.4	1.6
1990	7,163	286	6,821	339.4	16.9	320.7	58.2	97.0	92.0	0.8
1995	9,073	115	8,881	562.1	3.1	556.4	72.1	215.0	164.0	0.1

SOURCES: Bureau of Statistics, Office of the Prime Minister, *Japan Statistical Yearbook 1981* and *1998* (Tokyo, 1981, 1998); Science and Technology Agency, *Indicators of Science and Technology, 1961, 1965, 1969, 1976* and *1996* (Tokyo, various years).

market. It was only since the beginning of the 1970s that transnational corporations overseas became increasingly reluctant to provide their newly developed technologies unless done on a cross-licensing arrangement, for fear that such technology transfer should create strong competitors, as they had experienced with Japanese corporations throughout the late 1960s. Here again it was the internal capacity of those Japanese corporations importing foreign technology to tailor it to their own domestic needs and requirements and even improve the design and quality, which enabled Japanese industry to earn worldwide fame for high quality and consumer satisfaction.

The period 1945–73 presented a resource-poor Japan with a favourable international economic environment in that a steady increase in the availability of energy and other mineral resources was observed, with the consequence of assured supply at relatively reasonable cost. With the exception of aluminium, nickel and petroleum for which Japan had long been wholly dependent upon imports, Japan's imports as a percentage of its total consumption increased for most of the major raw materials in line with the continued expansion of its industrial production and GNP during the 1960s. For copper, the percentage rose from 51 to 76% during the period 1960–70, for zinc from 26 to 55%, for iron ore from 68 to 88%, for coking coal from 36 to 76%, and for natural gas from 0 to 38%, and all the figures continued to rise into the 1970s. With the exception of lead, the rate of increase in Japan's consumption of major mineral resources exceeded that of any other industrial country during the 1960s. By 1971, Japan thus accounted for 10.8% of the total consumption of petroleum in the non-socialist world, 11.3% of that of aluminium and 14.6% of that of copper.[5] Also, per unit of GNP, Japan's consumption of petroleum and other mineral resources was the highest among the major industrial countries, reflecting the great importance of the mineral-processing and energy-intensive industries in the Japanese economy.

Favourable international economic environments also allowed Japanese corporations to invest heavily in the exploration and production of energy and other mineral resources overseas. Out of the total investment of US$68 billion during the period 1951–73, US$23 billion or 33.5% went into the mining sector, by far the largest single sector for Japanese investment overseas. Such investment projects overseas were undertaken to ensure a constant supply of energy and other mineral resources at reasonable prices for the expanding industries at home. As late as even in 1976, such mining investment projects were responsible for only 9.6% of the total lead imports, 10.1% of the total bauxite imports, 14.4% of the total zinc imports and as little as 8.8% of the total crude oil imports, though constituting 62.3% of the total copper imports. The low figures for various mineral imports, except copper, under Japanese financing in the 1960s represented the late start observed among Japanese corporations in the exploration and development of energy and other mineral resources overseas. Towards the end of the 1960s, however, there was a growing pressure from resources-supplying countries for processing energy and other mineral resources instead of exporting them in raw form as part of their industrialization programs to achieve higher employment, value added per worker and per capita national income.

2. Growth Slowdown during the Post-Energy Crises, 1973–85

Growth and Distribution

Unlike the period 1945–73, 1973–85 was the period during which the Japanese economy, confronted with a number of structural issues at home and abroad, had to shift from a high-growth path to what was then called a stable-growth phase and undergo structural reforms to attain a soft-landing. While the government succeeded in attaining macroeconomic stabilization, as discussed later in more detail, in the face of all kinds of turbulence on the international economic scene, the real growth of GDP slowly moved downward annually from 4.9% in 1975–80 to 3.9% during the first half of the 1980s. The government failed to institute the structural reforms required to put the Japanese economy on a long-term stable-growth basis, resulting in the bubble economy during the latter half of the 1980s, the inevitable burst of the bubble during the first half of the 1990s and the prolonged recession during the latter half, as discussed later.

The turbulence on the international economic scene which hit the 1970s included the destabilization of the international monetary system precipitated by the New Economic Policy (NEP) of President Nixon in August 1971; the commodity boom of 1971–73; the world food crisis of 1972–74; the energy crises of 1973–74 and 1979–80; and the global adoption of the floating exchange rate system in February 1973. All these developments precipitated domestic inflationary pressures not only in Japan but elsewhere. Higher import prices for foodstuff and industrial raw materials were translated into higher wholesale prices under the administered pricing policies of oligopolistic firms and publicly regulated pricing system prevailing in many sectors of the Japanese economy. Higher wholesale prices were in turn translated into higher consumer prices, partly reflecting further wage increases in the inefficient distribution sector unable to absorb the higher costs through productivity improvement. Consumer prices had thus begun to edge up already in 1972, rising by 16.1% in one single year of 1973, generating nation-wide pressures for wage increases for both organized and unorganized labor under the conditions of full employment.

The sudden, quadruple price increases for crude oil in the fall of 1973 and through the winter of 1974 by the concerted efforts of the governments of the Organization of Petroleum Exporting Countries (OPEC) further fueled the inflationary pressures at home and abroad. Import, wholesale and consumer price indexes all shot up, triggering rounds of cost-push inflationary pressures, as shown in Table 3.14. There was also a recessional pressure building up in the Japanese economy because of the need to keep Japan's balance of payments position from further deterioration in the face of rapidly rising monetary values of crude oil imports essential to maintaining an adequate or moderate economic growth in the short and intermediate runs.

Bringing to a halt the steady weakening and erosion of the Japanese yen *vis-à-vis* the U.S. dollar, which began to show up in the foreign exchange market as a result of the energy crisis, was also crucial to a continued fight against the inflationary pressures in the economy, as such erosion would increase the import prices of energy and other raw materials and contribute further to rising production costs and higher price levels through the cost-push mechanism.

A vast decline in the growth of domestic demand was partially compensated for by a high rate of export expansion maintained throughout the post-energy crisis period, resulting in continued favourable basic balances and reverting to the appreciation of the Japanese yen relative to the U.S. dollar even to the point of hitting the peak of 178.5 yen to US$1 on the Tokyo market on 26 October 1978. By this time, however, a drastic change began to emerge in the international capital market where constant shifts in the high-volume liquidity made

Year		Total	Manufacturing	Food	Textiles	Machinery[1]	Machinery[2]	CP Products	ArP Products	Utilities	Scrap
1955	W[3]	44.9	—	32.7	62.5	117.6	90.3	26.0	31.6	30.3	—
	I[3]	55.1	—	44.0	84.1	—	—	30.6	—	—	—
	C[3]	18.2	25.9	19.7	19.6	62.2	—	—	15.5	26.7	—
1960	W[3]	46.1	—	32.8	55.7	122.5	87.6	27.0	34.0	31.9	95.6
	I[3]	46.6	—	68.8	69.1	85.2	—	28.1	—	—	—
	C[3]	19.1	26.5	20.6	19.1	63.5	—	—	16.5	30.1	—
1965	W	24.5	48.5	27.0	55.3	108.6	84.7	24.7	37.5	32.3	82.8
	I	23.0	—	72.4	68.5	91.0	—	25.8	—	—	—
	C	24.9	32.0	43.8	23.7	67.3	—	—	24.9	35.1	—
1970	W	52.4	53.2	42.9	63.9	107.1	81.0	24.3	50.1	32.3	105.0
	I	49.6	n.a.	80.8	65.0	94.0	—	24.2	—	—	—
	C	32.3	38.8	33.5	30.6	68.0	—	—	35.5	44.6	—
1975	W	80.0	80.6	68.8	83.7	127.6	103.9	63.8	81.8	60.6	116.1
	I	103.6	—	178.3	94.9	105.6	—	102.5	88.0	—	57.2
	C	55.3	66.2	61.7	55.0	109.9	—	—	60.4	59.8	—
1980	W	104.8	104.5	87.1	103.0	129.8	106.1	126.0	101.8	109.7	162.1
	I	159.8	—	167.2	121.3	117.1	—	196.3	107.4	—	107.1
	C	76.3	84.5	77.1	71.8	119.1	—	—	81.9	96.8	—
1985	W	105.3	101.5	97.9	105.3	123.3	107.0	134.8	102.8	124.4	119.8
	I	152.2	—	135.1	113.8	136.8	—	200.4	90.0	—	78.7
	C	87.4	94.1	88.4	83.5	121.6	—	—	92.2	111.4	—
1990	W	100.0	100.0	100.0	100.0	100.0	100.0	100.0	100.0	100.0	100.0
	I	100.0	—	100.0	100.0	100.0	—	100.0	100.0	—	100.0
	C	93.5	96.7	92.6	95.1	111.5	—	—	98.3	95.7	—
1995	W	96.1	96.1	104.9	93.7	87.3	98.1	87.5	89.3	98.7	70.9
	I	72.9	—	81.5	79.8	99.6	—	57.5	113.0	—	101.1
	C	100.0	100.0	100.0	100.0	100.0	—	—	100.0	100.0	—
1996	W	95.3	95.4	104.9	94.8	84.3	96.5	92.6	90.2	96.4	66.6
	I	79.9	—	89.9	82.3	88.9	—	72.9	113.6	—	90.9
	C	100.1	99.0	99.7	100.8	95.8	—	—	100.2	99.0	—

NOTES:

1. The wholesale prices for machinery are for electrical machinery, while its import prices are for general machinery.
2. The wholesale price figures for the machinery are for transportation machinery.
3. The date for the wholesale, import and consumer prices for all the industrial sectors were computed by the author.

SOURCE: Bureau of Statistics, Office of the Prime Minister, *Japan Statistical Yearbook 1961, 1977* and *1998* (Tokyo, 1961, 1977, 1998).

available by the surging petro-dollar and pension funds through the multinational banking system, running after small variations in interest rates and speculative moves, began to influence major currencies' exchange rates more, thus enormously increasing their volatility. This was unlike the pre-1973 period when the macroeconomic fundamentals acted as the dominant determinant of exchange rate adjustment.

The slowdown in the annual rate of economic growth and the overall stagflationary climate in the Japanese economy since the 1973–74 energy crisis were most dramatically reflected in the rising level of unemployment and underemployment resulting mainly from continued displacement of part-time and temporary workers earlier and even of regular workers later in a large number of firms in the manufacturing sector. As shown in Table 3.4, the number of unemployed workers rose from 680,000 in 1973 to one million in 1975 and continued to rise, doubling in 1985 from 1973. Reflecting the growing number of displaced workers and possibly unplaced workers, the number of job seekers has risen, exceeding that of job openings ever since 1974.

The slowdown in growth has also affected the annual rate of wage increases across industries, as shown in Table 3.15. In many firms not only restrained increases but also reductions have been observed for bonus payment since the mid-1970s, partly reflecting the management initiative of channeling profits into retained reserves in the face of more intense competition and reduced profitability resulting from business downturns. Underlying the new trend in bonus payment has been a shift in target priority among trade union leaders from high wage and bonus increases to employment stability, reflecting the changing sentiment among their rank-and-file membership.

To summarize the developments during 1973–85, in spite of the fact that Japan sustained into this period, though at a slower pace, the remarkably high rates of economic growth for 1955–73, and that in the early 1980s Japan became the world's No. 2 richest country in terms of per capita GDP, the Japanese people, because of government policy failures, were not able to sufficiently enjoy the fruits of their hard labor in their day-to-day lives in the form of shorter working hours, longer and flexible holidays, lower food prices, better-quality and lower-cost housing conditions, safer and less noisy streets, improved urban amenities and environments, an easier and lower-cost access to higher-quality child and old-age care centres, better public education, better public health facilities and services, less crowded commuting train and bus

TABLE 3.15 Average Monthly Cash Earnings for Regular Workers in Japanese Industry, 1955–96 (in thousands of yen)

Year	All Industries	Mining	Construction	Manufacturing	Utilities	Transport & Communications	Trade	Finance	Real Estate	Services
1955	21.9	19.3	15.5	20.9	23.0	23.0	22.1	31.2	—	—
	9.6	8.4	7.2	8.2	13.7	13.7	10.2	14.9	—	—
1960	29	27	23	29	38	30	29	41	35	—
	12	12	10	11	22	17	13	20	14	—
1965	47	44	43	44	62	50	46	68	58	—
	22	18	19	20	36	30	23	32	25	—
1970	83	80	75	84	109	87	76	111	105	—
	40	35	33	37	63	55	41	52	46	—
1975	192	195	164	185	250	201	177	268	204	220
	106	91	81	85	148	132	98	128	104	138
1980	284	273	243	280	352	282	260	408	304	317
	162	133	121	120	191	191	132	195	150	194
1985	347	327	295	347	442	342	309	512	368	376
	177	171	148	143	241	226	139	243	171	227
1990	408	359	370	410	532	409	364	611	464	423
	202	188	185	167	286	245	156	294	228	252
1995	448	395	411	449	604	457	396	677	492	464
	227	240	222	189	321	267	169	310	240	280
1996	452	404	420	456	613	445	403	684	479	466
	230	237	226	196	342	245	169	315	236	281

NOTE: The figures in the upper row are for male workers, while those in the lower are for females.
SOURCE: Bureau of Statistics, Office of the Prime Minister, *Japan Statistical Yearbook 1961, 1977 and 1998* (Tokyo, 1961, 1977, 1998).

services and a better social security system, including pension programs. It reflected government policy priorities still placed in the
investment for economic growth and structural changes to maintain the
competitiveness of Japanese export industries at the expense of a steady
improvement in the economic and social well-being of the people. In
other words, the basic framework of Japanese economic policy during
this period was still built upon the traditional post-war approach to
development, that is, preference of producers' over consumers' interests, investment over consumption and exports over domestic demand
expansion.

Successes and Failures in Government Policy

As in other countries, there were both remarkable successes and mis-
erable failures in the economic and industrial policies undertaken by
the Japanese government during this period. As discussed later, the
government partially succeeded in restructuring the Japanese economy
by making it less energy-intensive through accelerated changes in
industrial structures and successive developments of energy- and raw
materials-saving technology in many industrial sectors. This contributed to retaining and at times improving the competitiveness of the
Japanese export industries, such as iron and steel, petrochemicals and
automobiles. The energy-saving technology and less energy-intensive
economic structure had a favourable spillover effect on the environment, specifically less CO_2 emission per unit of GDP in Japan, as
compared with other industrial countries.

Nevertheless, the government did fail in restructuring the Japanese
economy by not instituting structural reforms essential in the age of
advancing globalization, such as deregulation, decontrol and enhancing competition in domestic industries, including agriculture,
construction, banking and non-banking financial institutions and information and telecommunications services; liberalization of trade and
incoming investment; decontrol of foreign exchange transactions; and
decentralization of public administration and taxation. In all these efforts
Japan was once again a late starter as compared with the United States,
the United Kingdom, Canada and New Zealand, as it had been in
industrialization a century and a half ago. All these government policy
failures resulted in the weakening of the basic structure of the Japanese
industries and economy, the distortion and greater inefficiency of

resources allocation among different industries, sectors and regions in favour of protecting the sunset industries and those with less comparative advantage in the world market and enhancing the social rigidities in the name of establishing an egalitarian society.

Thus, it is no exaggeration to conclude that the major policy failures of the Japanese government during the period 1973–85 were no less than a prelude to yet another series of government policy failures in the latter half of the 1980s and throughout the 1990s, that the seed of the latter had already been sown in the preceding period and that the same factor contributed to the government policy failures on both occasions. To put it bluntly, the Japanese government was then and has since been unable to adjust to the changing needs and requirements at home and abroad in an age of advancing globalization and deal squarely with them by implementing right policy packages at the right time and at the right speed because of the entrenched nexus among politicians or policymakers, bureaucracy and the vested business interests including, agricultural co-operatives.

In dealing simultaneously with the inflationary and recessional (stagflationary) attacks on the Japanese economy precipitated by the energy crisis, the Japanese government essentially took two major policy thrusts: one was a mixture of monetary and fiscal policy measures and another technology policy to kill the two birds (inflationary and recessional pressures) with one stone. In order to cope with the mounting inflationary pressures in the national economy, the Bank of Japan (BOJ), though too little and too late as usual, raised its rediscount rate successively from 4.25% on 2 April 1973 to 9.0% in December.[6] As part of the anti-inflationary policy package, the BOJ also restrained an increase in money supply at an annual rate of 27.6% during the third quarter of 1973. It was only during the first quarter of 1975 when money supply expansion was scaled down to 7.6% on an annual basis. Such high rates of monetary expansion were partly caused by a rapid inflow of foreign currencies, particularly U.S. dollars in exchange for the undervalued Japanese yen immediately after Nixon's NEP announcement in August 1971 and even after the Smithsonian Multilateral Currency Realignment in December 1971.

The incremental tight-money policy, together with drastic cuts in fiscal spending in 1973 and 1974 consecutively, as shown in Table 3.16, while successful in reducing inflation but overshooting the target, brought down Japan's real GDP growth rate from 10.4% in 1972 to

TABLE 3.16 Japan: Average Annual Changes in GNE by Major Components, 1965–98 (in percentages)

Component	1965–70	1970	1973	1974	1975	1970–75	1980	1985	1986	1990	1995	1998
A	8.9	8.1	6.9	2.2	3.9	5.6	0.2	3.4	3.4	4.4	2.1	-1.1
B	14.7	9.4	12.1	-16.4	12.8	5.3	-10.1	2.6	7.8	4.8	-6.5	-13.7
C	21.5	10.3	16.4	-9.7	-4.4	1.0	5.7	12.1	4.4	10.9	5.2	-11.3
D	—	104.3	45.6	-43.0	-92.1	—	-3.9	127.4	-34.4	-869.4	1,023.3	-554.5
E	5.4	5.7	4.2	4.8	5.8	5.2	1.4	1.7	4.5	1.5	3.3	0.7
F	12.1	17.1	-6.6	0.7	3.6	6.6	-0.5	-6.6	3.6	4.9	0.6	-0.3
G	—	-147.0	-50.1	-197.8	79.1	—	-860.1	96.6	72.5	164.0	-172.5	-166.5
H	16.1	15.9	8.1	23.7	4.1	11.3	18.2	6.4	-5.4	6.9	5.4	-2.3
I	16.1	18.7	25.8	3.2	-7.2	6.6	-1.7	-0.9	0.6	7.9	14.2	-7.5
GNE	11.3	10.2	6.5	0.0	3.2	4.7	3.7	5.2	2.6	5.1	1.5	-2.7

NOTES: 1. In 1970 prices for 1970–74; 1975 prices for 1975–80; 1985 prices for 1985–89; and in 1990 prices for the rest.

2. A — private final consumption
   B — private residential investment
   C — private plant and equipment investment
   D — private inventory investment
   E — government final consumption
   F — government fixed capital formation
   G — government inventory investment
   H — exports
   I — imports.

SOURCES: JERC, *Quarterly Economic Forecasts* 12/1972, 12/1982, 12/1992, 12/1998 and 9/1999 (Tokyo, various years).

6.5% in 1973 and 0.0% in 1974, thus creating confusion and uncertainty in the minds of investors and consumers alike.

This was a prime example of the adverse impact upon the general well-being of the public and the Japanese economy as a whole of the government's wrong foreign exchange rate policy that ignored the market in favor of a particular vested interest group — the export industry sector. This sector thrived in the short and intermediate run with the undervalued yen, delaying the structural reforms essential to its long-run survival and competitiveness on the world market. The government should have allowed more rapid, flexible and market-friendly upward adjustments of the yen's exchange rate in response to changes in the real sector at home and abroad, and provided Japanese consumers a greater purchasing power with which to import goods and services required, thus contributing on the one hand to domestic aggregate demand expansion and on the other to more intense competition at home which should have stimulated the development of new technologies and products. In other words, by protecting a wrong specie of tree, the Japanese government helped to retard forest development to the extent of possibly even destroying the entire forest in the long run.

Unfortunately this foreign exchange rate policy adopted in the late 1960s and pronounced at the time of the international monetary crisis in the early 1970s was a beginning of the road to a series of wrong and distorted policy interventions by the government and the BOJ in the wrong direction, at the wrong time, in the wrong sequence and at the wrong speed, that is, the notorious "too little and too late" policy interventions. The government should have recognized that such policy interventions would not work and be would inimical to the long-run national interest of Japan in an increasingly globalized world economy where the deregulated and liberalized market, and not the government in spite of its apparent authority and might, would determine relative prices of all goods and services, including foreign exchange rates.

On the trade and industrial policy side, the Japanese government should have also liberalized imports of agricultural and forestry products, petrol and other refined petroleum products, rather than maintaining the traditional policy of "agricultural self-sufficiency and protection" and "refining crude oil at home". The government should have also deregulated the domestic distribution industry so that the Japanese consumers would gain the full benefits from the upvalued exchange rate of the Japanese yen through lower consumer prices of imported products. Furthermore, deregulation and effective competition policies should have been introduced in a large number of sub-sectors of the manufacturing industry, and in all the non-manufacturing sectors of the national economy, including banking, construction, insurance, transportation, communications and various services, so that they could accelerate technological and management innovations to remain competitive in the world market.

While different interpretations and pros and cons arguments had then been made, it is the firm conclusion of the author that the MITI's defeat in the mid-1970s in trying through an auto merger enactment to bulldoze the merger of the existing automobile manufacturing companies into a few in the name of making them competitive in the world market was a decided victory not only for the individual auto manufacturers struggling to get into the expanding world auto market as latecomers but also more importantly for Japan's competition policy which alone has since the 1950s made it possible for Japanese industry to become increasingly competitive in the world market through technological innovations and new product developments. If the MITI's merger policy had been successfully introduced in the Japanese auto industry, Japan would not have such a highly competitive auto industry as we have seen since the mid-1970s. In this connection, it would have been far more desirable for promoting the international regime of freer trade and effective competition in favour of the world consumers' well-being, if the MITI had not bulldozed through with the involuntary Voluntary Export Restraints (VERs) program which the ministry actually imposed on the Japanese auto industry in its dealing with the U.S. Government.

The introduction of these trade liberalization, industry deregulation and competition policy measures would have been much easier during the rapid economic growth of 1960s and even the 1970s than during the 1980s and 1990s. It is important to note that the adverse impact of such wrong government policies has become even more serious and visible today than ten or 20 years ago, as the Japanese economy growing negatively in recent years is now saddled and burdened with uncompetitive industries, including agriculture, construction, banking, insurance, transportation, communications and some services that have been draining not only the Japanese government's dwindling treasure chest but also the precious savings of the Japanese public in the form of endless subsidies and other budgetary support at the expense of the social safety net provision to the poor, the elderly and those others who really need such support.

Not all the government policies, however, went wrong during this period of vast economic adjustments and restructuring. The government policy of raising crude oil and refined oil prices in response to rising prices of imported crude oil forced many manufacturing industries, power and transport industries to seek energy-saving technology, while compelling the aluminium and other energy-intensive industries to shift their processing factories to those countries with cheap power and resources. The government policy of providing tax incentives and low-interest loans assisted the iron and steel, cement and automobile industries to develop new energy-saving technologies which were highly competitive in the world market. In fact, the automobile trade dispute between the United States and Japan which became intensified during the latter part of the 1970s was a result of the Japanese auto industry successful in installing small, low-cost energy-saving engines far superior to those by the U.S. counterparts.

Also, the government policy of promoting research and development in strategic industries through tax and financial incentives during the latter part of the 1970s also paid dividends in the rapid emergence of high-technology industries in electronics, telecommunications and personal computer manufacturing industries in the early part of the 1980s. However, the MITI's program of promoting large-scale computers through research co-operatives and associations among competing firms failed, as no firm was willing to take leadership in such "joint" efforts on the understanding that the new technology invented by such efforts would have to be shared by all those competing firms associated with the co-operatives.

As seen in Table 3.17, of all plant and equipment investment by Japanese private sector enterprises, rising from 149,943 billion yen during the period 1971–75 to 209,595 billion yen during the years 1981–85, the fixed investment in the high-technology industries — comprising general and electrical machinery manufacturing sectors — rose most sharply from 6.3% to 12.5% of the total between the two periods, rising annually from 3.9% during the earlier period to 18.2% during the latter period. Also, fixed investment in the information and telecommunications sectors — consisting of finance, insurance, transport, telecommunications and services — rose sharply from 18.7% to

Table 3.17   Japan: Changing Composition of Plant and Equipment Investment by Industry Groups, 1966–90 (in percentages)

Sector	1966–70	1971–75	1976–80	1981–85	1986–90
Primary industries	12.2	12.3	15.3	9	7.5
Manufacturing					
Materials	23.4	19.9	14.8	14.9	11.9
Processing	25.3	22.8	20.9	24.2	23.6
Mining and construction	5.2	6.2	6.2	4.6	3.2
Tertiary industries	33.9	38.8	42.8	47.3	53.8
All industries (billions yen)	97,332	149,943	166,737	209,595	258,686
High technology and					
related sectors	8.1	6.3	6.8	12.5	14.6
Software and information					
related sectors	17.4	18.7	19.3	22.5	34.6

NOTES: 1. Primary industries cover agriculture, forestry and fishery.
   2. Materials sector covers textiles, paper and pulp, chemical, primary metals and metal products.
   3. Processing sector covers food processing and all classifications of machinery.
   4. Tertiary industries cover construction.
   5. High-technology and related sectors include all classifications of machinery.
   6. Software and information-related sectors include finance, insurance, transportation and communications and business services.

SOURCES: Economic Planning Agency, *National Accounts Summary, 1972, 1982* and *1992* (Tokyo, 1972, 1982, 1992).

22.5% of the total between the same two periods, representing an annual growth rate of 10.5% during 1971–75 and 8.0% during 1981–85.

Looking at the proportion of the total fixed investment in high-technology plant and equipment by industry breakdown, it is interesting to observe that of all the manufacturing and non-manufacturing industries in 1985, the electrical machinery industry took the lead by registering 72.4%, followed by the leasing industry at 60%, general machinery at 42.8%, chemicals at 40.3% and non-ferrous metals at 34.7% (Table 3.18). The growth rate of the high-technology fixed investment during the 1983–85 period, however, showed the non-ferrous metals industry as the top runner at 201.9%, followed by iron and steel at 189.4%, electrical machinery at 102.8%, glass and

TABLE 3.18 Japan: Plant and Equipment Investment — High-Technology Types (A) and All Types (B), 1983–85

	Investment in High Technology Type Equipment (A)				Growth Rate (%)		A/B (%)	
	1983	%	1985	%	B	A	1983	1985
All industries	2,579.2	100.0	3,755.3	100.0	17.2	45.6	18.2	24.2
Manufacturing	1,375.8	53.3	2,535.4	67.5	26.4	84.3	23.6	34.3
Materials	343.8	13.3	576.0	15.3	8.4	67.5	14.5	22.5
Chemical	250.0	9.7	375.0	10.0	16.6	50.0	31.2	40.3
Ceramics	30.6	1.2	57.0	1.5	40.3	86.3	14.7	19.8
Iron and steel	8.5	0.3	24.6	0.7	-2.4	189.4	0.9	3.6
Non-ferrous	26.7	1.0	80.6	2.1	25.9	201.9	14.2	34.7
Processing	1,032.0	40.0	1,959.4	52.2	41.2	89.9	33.1	44.0
General machinery	116.0	4.5	189.0	5.0	40.1	62.9	36.6	42.8
Electrical machinery	670.0	26.0	1,359.0	36.2	76.8	102.8	66.9	72.4
Automobiles	116.2	4.5	187.7	5.0	20.9	61.5	12.9	17.3
Non-manufacturing	1,203.4	46.7	1,219.9	32.4	10.0	1.4	15.4	15.0
Leasing	1,195.0	46.3	1,155.9	30.8	-3.3	-3.3	65.1	60.0

NOTES: 1. All figures are for fiscal year.

2. Investment figures for A are in billions of yen.

SOURCE: Samuki Toshio, "Kenkyuu ga Setsubi wo Yobu Jidai" [R & D calls for increased fixed investment], JERC Research Bulletin, No. 518 (15 August 1986), p. 26.

ceramics at 86.3%, general machinery at 62.9% and automobiles at 61.5%. While these fixed investments were made by private sector enterprises in order to remain competitive in the domestic and international markets, there is no doubt that the government policies promoting high technology through government-owned research institutes and fiscal and financial incentives encouraged them to invest heavily in such sectors.

Underlying Social Changes

Coming back to the underlying factors contributing to Japan's decline in economic growth since the early 1970s, it reflected not only the impact of the crude oil and natural gas price increases and the Japanese government's excessively tight money and fiscal policies on Japanese industry, particularly manufacturing, but also the structural changes underlying Japanese industry and society in general. Long after overcoming the inflationary pressures and the energy crisis in the middle of the 1970s, the Japanese economy showed a much lower growth throughout the rest of the 1970s and the 1980s, ranging from 1.2% at the lowest to 6.0% at the highest peak, unlike the average of more than 10% growth between 1955 and 1973. While all the gross national expenditure items suffered a long-run decline in their respective growth rates between 1973 and 1985, with minor exceptions, it reflected a growing gap between production volumes resulting from rapid expansion in productive capacity and the slow growth in demand that had been observed since 1970. It also reflected tremendous changes in the composition of private investment and consumption, moving on the one hand, as shown in Tables 3.17 and 3.18, from the high capital-intensive heavy and chemical industries, the champions of the 1960s and the early 1970s, to the technology- and skill-intensive sectors such as automobiles, electrical machinery, including consumer and industrial electronics, and precision machinery manufacturing, and on the other hand from the goods to services sectors.

Behind a continued expansion in the household income there was a subtle shift taking place in the structure of the domestic demand in Japan. A decline in the annual growth rate of household consumption expenditures from double digits to single digits between the early 1970s and the 1980s partly reflected a declining trend in household income growth and partly a decided shift in consumer behavior in

TABLE 3.19   Trends in Domestic Consumption Expenditures for Japanese Households

Components	1972	1973	1974	1975	1976	1977	1978	1979
Durables	23.8	15.7	−9.6	2.6	14.1	2.0	16.1	10.7
Semi-durables	12.9	3.5	2.2	3.3	6.2	0.8	1.7	2.1
Non-durables	8.4	6.3	2.0	4.7	3.1	3.7	0.9	1.7
Services	9.5	6.3	4.8	3.8	3.7	5.5	8.1	8.9
Total	10.5	6.6	2.3	4.0	4.5	4.0	5.3	5.8

NOTE: Annual rates of increase in percentages, in 1970 prices.
SOURCE: Economic Planning Agency, "Annual Report on National Accounts", in JERC Quarterly Economic Forecasts, no. 43, (December 1979).

favor of services rather than goods, particularly durables, an 180-degree turnaround since the 1950s and 1960s. As shown in Table 3.19, the most dramatic decline in the annual growth of private consumption expenditures during the period 1975–85 was exhibited for durables, falling from an annual rate of 8.11% during 1975–80 to 6.2% during 1980–85. As compared with durables, the private consumption expenditures for semi-durables, non-durables and services declined at slower rates, respectively from 3.6, 2.6 and 4.6% annually during the latter half of the 1970s to 3.3, 2.2 and 4.2% during the first half of the 1980s.

3. Advancing Globalization and Changing Political and Social Priorities since 1985

Changes at Home and Abroad

The period since the mid-1980s has seen enormous changes at home and abroad, far beyond those changes observed during the preceding three decades, 1955–85. On the external side, there was the Plaza Accord of October 1985, following which the yen appreciated by nearly 50% vis-à-vis the U.S. dollar, from 214 to 124 between 1985 and 1992. There was also the worldwide bubble sky-rocketing the prices of shares and real estate during the late 1980s, followed by the bursting of the bubble during the early 1990s. A rapid enlargement of the highly liquid international capital market accompanied by new varieties of financial market instruments based on information and telecommunication technology increased the volatility of foreign exchange rate changes. There was a renewed effort in the international community to promote further liberalization of trade in goods and services including agricultural products and services, as seen in the creation of the World Trade Organization (WTO) in 1994. Also there was a remarkable expansion of foreign direct investment in industrial countries and some developing countries, particularly in East Asia and Latin America. All these have affected Japanese economic growth and restructuring enormously.

On the domestic scene, both the size of the bubble during the late 1980s and the depth of the bubble burst during the first half of the 1990s were far greater in Japan as compared with other industrial countries, with all the implications for the Japanese economy, as discussed later. There has also been increasing concern over the de-industrialization of Japan as a result of a disproportionately large outflow of Japanese manufacturing investment precipitated by the rapid and huge appreciation of the Japanese yen, with an adverse impact on the labor market and competitiveness of Japanese industries at home. The ageing of the population with its implications for industrial restructuring and productivity changes has become a key concern among policymakers, along with its impact on the social security system, including health insurance and pension programs. Changes in social values and priorities have been steadily observed among Japanese from different walks of life, affecting the rate and the direction of economic growth through their impact upon the patterns of personal consumption, corporate behaviour and resources allocation at the local and national levels. They have also exerted persistent changes in the degree, direction and depth of Japan's involvement in international economic, political and social activities.

All these changes both at home and abroad have increased the importance of productivity improvement and technological innovations to sustain the necessary structural changes and economic growth consistent with employment stability and the economic, social and environmental wellbeing of the people in Japan. Hence the rising importance of government policies and institutions affecting productivity and technology advances. As discussed later, however, a complex layer and a heavy load of industrial regulations and the protectionist mindset prevailing in most of the non-manufacturing sectors, including agriculture, construction, finance, insurance, transportation, communications and services, interacted to negatively impact economic growth and restructuring throughout this period, in spite of some remarkable advances in manufacturing technology as seen in the electronics and various machinery sectors. These conservative, if not regressive, and anti-growth features of the Japanese economic, political and social institutions have in fact retarded the out-migration of the brainpower and financial resources in lower-productivity and highly regulated sectors, including government services, to those more productive growth sectors, thus constraining productivity improvement at the national level, which is crucially needed in the age of globalization and global competition.

Acceleration of Globalization Generating Regionalization and Rising Frictions

As a result of trade and capital liberalization around the world, international trade and investment has been expanding far faster than the growth of the world's GDP. This is particularly conspicuous in the Asia-Pacific region where real economic growth prior to 1997 exceeded 8% on the average even since the mid-1980s (Table 3.20), and where as of 1992, intra-regional trade constituted 46.8% of total trade, signifying an ever closer interdependence among the economies of the region (Table 3.21). The increasing intra-regional trade has also signified an enormous expansion of direct investment by Asian-based multinational corporations in the region, pointing to a rapid progress in the intra-corporate division of production and trade.

On the international monetary side, the famous Plaza Accord in October 1985 and the currency turbulence thereafter realigned the exchange rates of major currencies, in particular appreciating the Japanese yen from 260 to 214 *vis-à-vis* the U.S. dollar between February and October 1985, from 214 to 124 between 1985 and 1992, and from 124 to 98 between 1992 and 1995 (80 in April 1995). This drastically weakened the price competitiveness of Japanese industry *vis-à-vis* the United States and other competitors whose currencies were tied to the U.S. dollar. Now reflecting a wide gap between the U.S. and the Japanese economic growth and rediscount rates, the Japanese yen swung back to 120 per U.S. dollar in January 1999 and 102–103 in December

TABLE 3.20 Economic Growth Performance of East Asia, 1970–2001 (in US$ billion, 1990 prices)

Country / Subregions	Real GDP						Real GDP Average Annual Growth Rate (%)								
	1970	1980	1990	1997	2001	Share (%)	1960–70	1970–80	1980–90	1990–97	1997	1998	1999	1990–2001	Adjusted
Hong Kong	15	37	70	171	178	0.4	8.7	9.4	6.9	5.3	5.2	-4.9	-1.0	5.5	1.3
South Korea	46	100	244	443	446	1.6	9.1	8.2	9.5	7.2	5.5	-5.2	0.3	7.0	0.8
Singapore	7	18	35	98	99	0.2	8.7	9.0	6.6	8.5	7.8	0.7	1.0	6.1	0.8
Taiwan	29	74	155	303	305	1.0	9.7	9.7	7.7	6.5	6.8	5.1	4.8	6.3	1.2
Asian NIEs	97	229	505	1,013	1,028	3.2	—	8.9	8.2	—	—	—	—	6.5	1.2
Indonesia	29	83	107	215	211	0.7	3.0	8.0	6.1	7.5	4.6	-14.3	-5.0	6.8	-1.0
Malaysia	11	24	42	98	98	0.3	—	8.0	5.2	8.7	7.8	-6.2	-0.1	7	0.0
Philippines	21	38	44	83	92	0.2	4.9	6.1	1.6	3.3	5.1	0.0	2.6	3.1	1.2
Thailand	20	38	80	157	160	0.6	8.0	6.8	7.8	7.5	-0.4	-7.7	-0.2	8.0	1.2
ASEAN Four	81	162	274	553	561	1.8	—	7.2	5.4	—	—	—	—	6.7	0.8
China	115	231	525	825	880	2.8	—	5.6	8.7	11.9	8.8	7.2	7.0	8.2	7.2
Vietnam	7	8	14	25	31	0.1	—	1.4	6.1	8.6	8.8	5.7	4.6	7.8	6.7
Japan	1,283	1,957	2,940	4,202	4,220	14.0	11.1	4.5	4.2	1.4	0.9	-1.8	1.0	1.7	1.0
East Asia	155	327	642	2,378	2,533	8.0	—	—	7.1	6.7	5.5	0.1	3.1	—	—
South Asia	172	236	399	440	474	1.5	—	—	5.3	4.8	5.1	5.3	—	—	—
West Asia	394	873	858	816	778	2.5	—	—	-2.2	2.6	5.9	4.0	—	—	—
Africa	257	383	456	484	392	1.3	—	—	1.9	1.7	3.0	3.3	—	—	—
Latin America	584	999	1,086	1,617	1,773	5.7	—	—	1.0	3.4	5.4	3.3	—	—	—
Eastern Europe	285	502	541	—	—	—	—	—	—	—	—	—	—	—	—
Former USSR	887	1,444	1,900	—	—	—	—	—	—	—	—	—	—	—	—
European Union (15)	2,563	4,085	5,473	7,604	8,489	27.2	—	—	—	—	—	—	—	—	—
United States	3,256	4,276	5,522	7,391	8,092	28.0	3.9	2.9	2.6	1.6	2.5	2.8	—	2.3	1.9
World	12,680	17,637	23,004	28,157	31,189	100.0	4.9	3.4	2.7	2.3	3.3	2.5	—	2.8	2.3

NOTE: Forecasts for the years 1990–2001 in the United Nations Project Link have been adjusted downward due to the recent Asian financial and economic crises.

SOURCES: International Monetary Fund (IMF), International Financial Statistics (Washington, D.C., relevant years); Asian Development Bank (ADB), Key Indicators of Developing Asian and Pacific Countries 1998, vol. XXIX (Manila, 1998); United Nations, Project Link World Economic and Social Survey 1998 (New York, 1998); World Bank, World Development Report 1998/99 (New York, 1999); and Japan External Trade Organisation (JETRO), White Paper on International Trade 1999 (Tokyo, 1999).

TABLE 3.21 Inter- and Intra-regional Trade by Destination, 1981–92 (in percentages)

From/To	Japan		Asian NIEs		ASEAN		China		East Asia		Americas		European Community (EC 12)	
	1981	1992	1981	1992	1981	1992	1981	1992	1981	1992	1981	1992	1981	1992
Japan	—	—	13.7	21.4	7.1	8.1	3.4	3.5	24.1	33	29	1.7	13.1	18.5
Asian NIEs	10.6	9.1	10.1	14.6	10.4	7.8	2.5	11.2	33.5	42.8	28.5	27	13.7	14.6
ASEAN	32.7	21.1	17.8	22.7	3.7	4.4	0.8	2.5	54.9	50.6	18.2	21.6	11.6	16.1
China	24.4	14.5	28.1	52.1	3.5	2.8	—	—	56.1	69.4	6.5	11.7	10.2	10.3
East Asia	10.2	8.4	15.1	24.1	7.8	7.7	2.7	6.6	35.7	46.8	27.1	28.1	13	16.5
Americas	8.4	8.8	4.9	8.3	1.9	2.4	1.5	1.5	16.7	21.1	35.5	43.3	20.5	18.5
European Community (EC 12)	1	1.8	1.2	2.4	0.9	1.1	0.4	0.6	3.5	5.9	8.2	7.8	53	61.4
World	6.8	19.5	4.8	8.8	2.1	2.9	0.9	2.3	14.6	19.5	17.5	19.4	32.9	39.9

SOURCE: Pacific Economic Co-operation Conference (PECC), Pacific Economic Outlook 1994 (Washington, D.C.: PECC, 1994).

1999 after reaching 146 yen in September 1998, nearly the same level as in the mid-1990s, bringing again to Japan ever-larger trade and current account surpluses (Table 3.22).

The Plaza Accord contributed a great deal to the rapid rise in Japan's manufactured imports, particularly from Asian countries. It was also partly responsible for the great rush of Japanese corporations, small and large, investing overseas for offshore production both for import substitution and as exporting bases to the rest of the world market. On an annual basis, Japanese direct investment overseas increased on average from US$5 billion during the first half of the 1980s to US$35 billion during the latter half, though declining in the 1990s as a result of the bubble burst. Even today, however, roughly two-fifths of Japanese direct investment goes to North America, another one-fifth to East Asia, one-fifth to Western Europe and the rest to South Asia and Latin America as well as Oceania (Table 3.23). If confined to the manufacturing sector, more than 50% of Japanese direct investment overseas has been destined to Asia and the Japanese direct investment, in terms of both annual flows and stocks, has retained the top ranking in many countries of East Asia (Table 3.24). There has also been a rapid increase in the number of Japanese tourists abroad during this period, peaking to over 18 million people in 1997, the majority of whom went to Asia.

In addition, the establishment of the NAFTA and the EU during the first half of the 1990s has prompted closer consultation among East Asian countries. ASEAN increased its membership from six to ten countries; APEC supplemented its annual meetings among foreign ministers with those among ministers of finance and environment and among the heads of state; and ASEAN brought the heads of state of China, Japan and the Republic of Korea into consultation with their heads of state every year. These heads of state meetings, followed up by meetings of senior officials and economic and environment ministers, have contributed to closer trade, investment, aid and environmental co-operation among the countries of this region, as well as closer consultations in macroeconomic policies and implementation. The ASEM has now been added to the existing consultation and co-operation mechanisms, bringing the EU closer to East Asia. As a result of these regional efforts, there is today a greater flow of information and a greater sense of co-operation among the countries in the region, which

TABLE 3.22   Japan's Economic Growth, Current Account Balances and Foreign Exchange Rate Fluctuations of the Yen, 1985–99

Fiscal Year	GDP Growth Rate (%)	Current Account Balance (US$ billion)	Foreign Exchange Rate (yen/US$)
1985	4.1		200.6
1986	3.2	85.8	160.1
1987	5.0	87.0	122.0
1988	6.0	79.6	126.0
1989	4.7	57.0	143.0
1990	5.3	35.9	135.0
1991	3.0	68.2	
1992	0.4	112.6	124.8
1993	0.5	131.6	107.8
1994	0.6	130.3	99.4
1995	2.8	111.0	96.5
1996	3.2	65.9	112.7
1997	–0.6	114.6	122.7
1998	0.1	136.7	133.6
1999	–0.5	151.1	132.3

SOURCE: JERC, Quarterly Economic Forecasts, relevant issues (Tokyo, various years).

has proven to be quite helpful to those countries afflicted with the East Asian financial and economic crises since mid-1997.

The rapid pace of economic globalization has been producing friction in many countries, particularly in East Asia. The process of globalization, precipitated by increased trade, investment, services and information flows between nations, has been demanding in the name of "global standards" deeper and a broader range of economic, business, political and social reforms in the East Asian countries including China, Laos, Myanmar and Vietnam, countries with different political systems, let alone cultural values. It is well known that the inter-governmental organizations and in particular the IMF, the World Bank and the WTO have been pushing hard for the adoption of "global standards" by all their member countries. Since the mid-1980s the Bretton Woods institutions such as the IMF and the World Bank have been negotiating structural adjustment programs (SAPs) containing a cer-

TABLE 3.23 Japanese Direct Investment Overseas by Region and Selected Host Country, 1951–97 (in US$ million)

Region/Country	1951–75	1980	1985	1990	1995	6/1/1997	1951–96	Percentage
Africa	284	139	172	551	379	184	8,507	1.5
Liberia	—	110	159	531	s307	41	7,108	1.3
South Africa	—	—	—	—	57	130	299	0.1
Asia	1,881	1,186	1,435	7,054	12,264	6,690	100,094	17.8
China	—	—	100	349	4,473	1,158	15,712	2.8
Hong Kong	—	156	131	1,785	1,125	394	16,493	2.9
Indonesia	—	529	408	1,105	1,596	1,677	20,991	3.7
Malaysia	—	146	79	725	573	307	7,501	1.3
Philippines	—	78	61	258	718	293	4,094	0.7
South Korea	—	35	134	284	445	129	6,129	1.1
Singapore	—	140	339	840	1,152	700	11,80s3	2.1
Taiwan	—	—	114	446	457	277	4,975	0.9
Thailand	—	—	48	1,154	1,224	1,133	9,811	1.7
East Asia	—	—	1,414	6,946	11,763	6,067	—	—
Asian NIEs	—	378	718	3,355	3,179	1,500	—	—
ASEAN Four	—	786	597	3,243	4,110	3,409	—	—
India	—	—	—	30	127	171	809	0.1
Pakistan	—	—	—	9	42	42	304	0.1
Sri Lanka	—	—	—	—	59	260	233	0.0
Vietnam	—	—	—	—	197	143	754	0.1
Others	—	—	20	69	76	4	486	0.1
Europe	971	578	1,930	14,294	8,470	3,248	105,709	18.8
Belgium	—	—	84	367	358	52	3,661	0.7
France	—	—	67	1,257	1,524	369	8,418	1.5

TABLE 3.23 *(cont'd)*

Region/Country	1951–75	1980	1985	1990	1995	6/1/1997	1951–96	Percentage
Germany	—	110	172	1,242	547	389	9,179	1.6
Ireland	—	—	81	49	340	525	2,378	0.4
Italy	—	—	32	217	120	69	2,026	0.4
Netherlands	—	—	613	2,744	1,509	800	22,055	3.9
Spain	—	—	91	320	51	19	3,337	0.6
Switzerland	—	—	60	666	100	10	3,333	0.6
United Kingdom	—	186	375	6,806	3,445	899	40,712	7.2
Latin America	917	588	2,616	3,628	3,877	3,624	63,471	11.3
Middle East	530	158	45	27	148	135	5,123	0.9
North America	1,817	1,596	5,495	27,192	22,761	9,053	248,473	44.2
United States	—	1,484	5,395	26,128	22,193	8,925	238,628	42.4
Canada	—	112	100	1,064	568	128	9,845	1.8
Oceania	463	448	525	4,166	2,795	567	30,942	5.5
Australia	—	431	468	3,669	2,635	515	27,323	4.9
New Zealand	—	—	23	231	94	28	1,519	0.3
World	6,876	4,693	12,2s17	56,911	50,694	23,501	562,320	100.0

NOTES: 1. All figures for 1997 were published in Japanese yen, which were converted into U.S. dollars on the basis of the Bank of Japan interbank rate averages.
2. The figures for 1995 and 1997 do not include direct investments totalling less than 100 million yen, which were included prior to 1995.

SOURCES: Japan External Trade Organization (JETRO), White Paper on Direct Investment Overseas 1972, 1982, 1992 and 1998 (Tokyo, various years); and Export-Import Bank of Japan (Eximbank), Journal of Research Institute for International Investment and Development, 1998 (Tokyo, 1998).

TABLE 3.24 Japanese Direct Investment Overseas by Sector, 1951–95 (in US$ million)

Sector	1951-70	1971-75	1976-80	1981-85	1990	1951-93	1995
Manufacturing	928 (25.9)	4,109 (33.2)	7,536 (36.7)	11,825 (25.1)	15,486 (27.2)	115,112 (27.2)	18,236 (36.8)
Food	51 (1.4)	237 (1.9)	298 (1.5)	505 (1.1)	820 (1.4)	6,123 (1.4)	811 (1.6)
Textiles	189 (5.3)	827 (6.7)	621 (3.0)	445 (0.9)	796 (1.4)	5,540 (1.3)	1,008 (2.0)
Wood and pulp	212 (5.9)	298 (2.4)	249 (1.2)	362 (0.8)	314 (0.6)	4,057 (1.0)	351 (0.7)
Chemicals	50 (1.4)	725 (5.9)	1,852 (9.0)	1,356 (2.9)	2,292 (4.0)	16,300 (3.9)	2,079 (4.2)
Metals	138 (3.9)	644 (5.2)	1,839 (9.0)	2,571 (5.5)	1,047 (1.8)	12,794 (3.0)	1,498 (3.0)
Machinery	68 (1.9)	332 (2.7)	495 (2.4)	1,077 (2.3)	1,454 (2.6)	11,491 (2.7)	1,810 (3.7)
Electrical machinery	73 (2.0)	450 (3.6)	1,057 (5.1)	2,166 (4.6)	5,684 (10.0)	27,235 (6.4)	5,190 (10.5)
Transportation equipment	87 (2.4)	273 (2.2)	619 (3.0)	2,383 (5.1)	1,872 (3.3)	15,007 (3.6)	1,939 (3.9)
Miscellaneous	61 (1.7)	325 (2.6)	508 (2.5)	947 (2.0)	1,207 (2.1)	16,565 (3.9)	3,549 (7.2)
Non-manufacturing	2,249 (62.9)	7,502 (60.7)	12,270 (59.7)	34,318 (72.8)	40,621 (71.4)	300,293 (71.1)	30,395 (61.3)
Mining	804 (22.5)	3,058 (24.7)	3,207 (15.6)	4,683 (9.9)	1,328 (2.3)	19,758 (4.7)	1,034 (2.1)
Trade	381 (10.7)	1,825 (14.8)	3,202 (15.6)	7,269 (15.4)	6,156 (10.8)	45,364 (10.7)	5,149 (10.4)
Finance and insurance	318 (8.9)	981 (7.9)	1,127 (5.5)	8,433 (17.9)	8,047 (14.1)	81,271 (19.2)	5,272 (10.6)
Services	49 (1.4)	424 (3.4)	920 (4.5)	3,292 (9.0)	11,292 (19.8)	50,152 (11.9)	10,350 (20.9)
Real estate	578 (16.2)	871 (7.0)	2,965 (14.4)	2,533 (5.4)	11,107 (19.5)	65,966 (15.6)	5,813 (10.7)
Total	3,577 (100.0)	12,365 (100.0)	20,554 (100.0)	47,151 (100.0)	56,911 (100.0)	422,555 (100.0)	49,568 (100.0)

NOTE: Figures in parentheses indicate percentages.
SOURCES: Ministry of Finance, Japan, *Monthly Statistics on Money and Finance, December 1971, 1981, 1991* and *1997* (Tokyo, various years).

tain set of economic conditionalities, "the global standard of market economies", with those developing countries receiving financial assistance. The GATT in the 1980s and the WTO in the 1990s have reinforced these efforts by the Bretton Woods institutions through the promotion of further trade and investment liberalization in developing countries. It is equally well known that the United States, as the biggest shareholder of these multilateral institutions, has been a key player, if not the key player, behind their tireless efforts in favour of these "global standards".

Globalization and the Changing Role of the State

The central issue here has been on the role of the state in economic development under a market-economy system. To be more exact, the role of the state at different stages of economic and social development under diverse market-economy systems. The SAPs by Bretton Woods institutions and similar programs by other international organizations dominated by Western countries tend to project a Western type of market-economy system and minimize the role of the state in economic development. They promote small government, leaving all investment, production, distribution and consumption decisions in the private sector to the market forces as well as the implementation of public sector investment decisions. All in the name of achieving "greater efficiency in resources allocation" and therefore resulting in "greater well-being of the people". On the other hand, semi-industrial and developing countries that have set their national goals on catching up with industrial countries within the shortest period of time have affirmed the positive role of the state to intervene in the marketplace and orient their economic and institutional resources in favor of strategic sectors considered essential to the satisfaction of the basic human needs and strategic industries expected to grow fastest in exports and productivity. Resisting the Western concept of the market-economy system, they have insisted not only on the legitimacy of diverse models of market-economy system, but also on the effectiveness of their own models of development.

According to this view therefore, no "global standards" should be imposed on all countries with regard to economic management. Rather, there should be many national standards governing the different market economies and a set of internationally agreed upon standards that should govern international economic transactions, whether in trade, investment and technology development. While it is true that the process of economic globalization has fostered the trend towards the unification of industrial standards and the need to adopt some internationally agreed upon standards in international economic management, the imposition on the rest of the world of a national standard and/or institution for domestic economic management specific to a particular civilization such as the Western one, or to a particular country, such as the United States, will continue to be difficult, if not impossible, despite its economic, political and military superpower position.

In recent years, however, the Bretton Woods institutions have gone further, to impose on sub-Saharan African and East Asian countries under economic crisis a series of political conditionalities. This is, to undergo political and social reforms consistent with the "global standards of Western democracies" which can be nearly equated with American standards. The WTO has also been linking trade with human rights and environment issues *à la* Americana. Many developing countries, including those in East Asia however, have increasingly voiced concern with this concept of "global standards" based upon the prevailing social values, norms and institutions of the Western countries. One of the most controversial issues is the acceptability of human rights, individual freedom and democratic institutions as interpreted by Western countries. The political conditionalities imposed by these multilateral institutions in the name of promoting "good governance" in developing countries, though prohibited in their respective Charters, except for the charter that founded the European Bank for Reconstruction and Development (EBRD), have been producing some social unrest and political instability in host countries and straining the relationships between them and these multilateral institutions.[7]

The Bubble, the Bubble Burst and the Prolonged Recession: Salient Examples of Government Policy Failures of Too Little and Too Late

Unlike the developing countries of sub-Saharan Africa and East Asia, Japan has been pressured bilaterally since the mid-1980s by the governments of the United States and the European Community (EC), precipitated by their mounting bilateral trade deficits *vis-à-vis* Japan, to undergo structural reforms similar to those now being advanced by the IMF in the East Asian countries confronted with financial and economic crises. In 1984, just one year before the Plaza Accord, the U.S. trade deficit totalled US$107.4 billion, the highest ever in U.S. history. Its trade deficit with Japan also skyrocketed to US$34 billion, in addition to nearly US$20 billion with the ANIEs. As part of the solution to this, the United States intensified its demand for Japan's further aggregate domestic demand expansion, deregulation and market opening, in addition to the appreciation of the Japanese yen *vis-à-vis* the U.S. dollar. Because of enormous political difficulties in deregulation and market opening, which represented nothing but the lack of political leadership, Japan took an easier way out through an easy-money policy and the appreciation of the Japanese yen, as shown in the earlier policy failures during the 1960s and 1970s.

Confronted with the possible adverse impact of the Plaza Accord of October 1985 on the export and export-led economic growth of Japan, and pressured by the United States and the EC to expand the domestic demand leading possibly to import expansion, the Japanese government compelled the BOJ to take an easy-money policy, reducing its rediscount rate four times in 1986 by as much as 2 percentage points. The government hesitated, which it should not have done, to take expansionary fiscal policy measures lest they should, while certainly increasing imports and correcting the huge trade surplus, raise the domestic interest rate in Japan through crowding-out and reverse the capital flows hitherto observed between Japan and the United States, thus sharply appreciating further the value of the Japanese yen *vis-à-vis* the U.S. dollar, with implications for the re-emergence of Japan's economic downturn and export drive to the United States, the worst scenario in the United States-Japan relations. It was not until September 1986 (additional 3,600-billion-yen fiscal package) and May 1987 (additional 6,000-billion-yen fiscal spending) that the government resorted to fiscal spending policy measures. The former was too little and the latter too late, however, as the Japanese economy was already on an upward trend beginning in November 1986. This was once more a prime example of the Japanese government's "too little and too late" fiscal policy intervention.

The BOJ also failed to raise its rediscount rate in spite of the steady economic recovery from late 1986 because of the political agenda in 1987 that required further economic expansion. The Black Monday global stock market crash, triggered by that of the United States in

TABLE 3.25   Trends in Asset Values Relative to GDP and Interest Rates in Japan, 1981–92

Fiscal Year	Ratio of Asset Value to GDP		Ratio to GDP x Interest Rate (%)	
	Stocks	Land	Stocks	Land
1981	0.308	0.490	2.572	4.089
1982	0.333	0.495	2.747	4.082
1983	0.374	0.488	2.885	3.760
1984	0.451	0.487	3.232	3.494
1985	0.522	0.543	3.177	3.308
1986	0.680	0.829	3.498	4.260
1987	0.850	1.269	4.166	6.217
1988	1.045	1.403	5.184	6.961
1989	1.308	1.292	7.362	7.272
1990	1.101	1.192	7.611	8.235
1991	0.815	1.103	4.475	6.058
1992	0.614	0.885	3.400	4.900

NOTES: Stock values are the total market values of issues listed on the first section of the Tokyo Stock Exchange. Land values are the total posted prices for residential land in Tokyo, based on the Economic Planning Agency's Economic Account Statistics for the years through 1990 and on the National Land Agency's appraisal data for 1991-92. Interest rates are the rates of return on long-term government bonds. Land values are as of mid-year and the other figures are annual averages.
SOURCE: Yoshikazu Kato *et al.*, *The Japanese Economy in the 1990s: Problems and Prognoses* (Tokyo: Foreign Press Centre of Japan, 1993).

October 1987, further delayed the BOJ's decision to shift to a tighter money policy, resulting in the rediscount rate staying at 2.5% until May 1989, the lowest rate in Japanese monetary history since the Meiji Restoration of 1868. During these years the Japanese banking and non-banking financial institutions were heavily involved in providing loans to investors in shares and real estate markets, contributing to enormous asset price appreciation far beyond the level justified by macroeconomic fundamentals (Table 3.25). It may be appropriate, therefore, to conclude that the Japanese government's political indecision and sole reliance on the easy-money policy, which probably would not have happened if the BOJ had been independent from the Ministry of Finance, unequivocally contributed to the bubble in the late 1980s.

The bursting of the bubble was triggered by the BOJ's shift from an easy-money to a tighter money policy in May 1989. The BOJ's policy shift reflected a correct response not only to a resurgence of the Japanese economic expansion as exhibited in the rising labor shortages, rapid increases in wages and possible cost-push inflationary pressures, but also to the continued appreciation of real estate and financial asset prices and the resulting widening wealth and income gaps between those haves and have-nots. Further increases in the BOJ's rediscount rate were introduced to stem the inflationary pressures resulting from the Gulf War and increases in crude-oil prices beginning in mid-1990.

But led by an overriding preoccupation with reduction in annual budget deficits and in the deficit bonds outstanding on the one hand and the possible continuation of asset price inflation on the other, the Japanese government and the BOJ did not take necessary steps immediately to prevent the Japanese economy from sliding into recession in 1991. It was not until April 1992 when the BOJ reduced its rediscount rate from 5.3% in 1991 to 3.75% and not until March 1993 that it was reduced down to 2.5%. The BOJ bank rate remained high until October 1993 when it was finally reduced to 1.75%. Here again the story of the BOJ's "too little and too late" policy intervention was repeated, further aggravating the bubble burst and recessional trend till today.

In fact, it was too much to expect that monetary policy alone could solve the problem of the bursting of the bubble. Its solution required not only a mix of monetary and fiscal policy, but more importantly structural changes throughout the Japanese economy, finance and politics. These have been resisted because of the possible adverse impact on the vested interests in Japanese industrial, political and administration circles and because of inertia on the part of the conservative people. The recent political decisions during the fall of 1998 by the Obuchi administration to rescue the Japanese economy from further crumbling into depression by resorting to a huge amount of fiscal deficit spending, while necessary and essential in the short run, clearly indicate the priority placed on anti-recessional policies rather than on the structural changes essential for the intermediate and long-term wellbeing of the Japanese economy. While distinctions must be clearly made in government policy packages between those that deal with the bursting of the bubble, which would have been essential and inevitable, and those that deal with the recession, which should have been redressed urgently to minimize, if not to prevent, its adverse impact, both actions are urgently required.

Sources of Growth Decline

The growth of the Japanese economy had decelerated, as shown in Table 3.16, from 5.1% in 1990 down to 1.5% in 1995 and negative 2.7% in 1998. There is no prospect of its returning to a desirable growth rate such as a positive 2% before the turn of this century, in spite of the economic stimulus packages announced successively by the Hashimoto and Obuchi administrations in 1997–99. While the growth of the real GDP has been decelerating ever since the bursting of the bubble, the most dramatic growth decline has been observed for private final consumption, from 4.4% in 1990 to negative 1.1% in 1998 (Table 3.16). Since the share of private final consumption as a percentage of real GDP has been ranging between 58 and 60% during the 1990s, the long-term declining growth of private final consumption has been critical in bringing down the overall economic growth in Japan.

This is a great contrast to the preceding period 1973–85, let alone the years 1955–73 when investment by private and public sectors were the main engine of economic growth, further generating virtuous circle of increased income, consumption and investment. It is to be understood, of course, that both the residential investment and plant and equipment investment by private sector corporations have remained significant in determining the overall economic growth of Japan, as they constituted during the same period 4–6% and 18–20% of real GDP respectively, though varying enormously between different years. In terms of contribution to real GDP, both government consumption and investment expenditures have been equally significant as private fixed investment and exports.

As the decade of the 1990s progressed further, private final consumption expenditures were hard hit by the dismal prospects of increasing unemployment and underemployment, declining wage increases and bonus payments and a continued process of corporate restructuring. The rise of the national consumption tax from 3 to 5% in April 1997 and the heavier burden placed on patients in national health insurance programs have precipitated the downward trend in personal consumption. With the rapid ageing of the population and continued recessional pressures in the economy, people are increasingly concerned with the imminent prospects of increased social security premiums and reduced pension, unemployment, disability and health insurance benefits. Hence the visible increases in marginal propensity to save, when the contrary is urgently required. There was much doubt on how effective the granting of nearly 470 billion yen, agreed upon in November 1998 between the LDP and the Komeito, in coupons to the Japanese elderly families and those whose incomes were below a specified level and with children below 16 years of age, would turn out to be to stimulate the sagging personal consumption among the Japanese public. After one year of the grant operation, various statistical data today on personal consumption and other components of the Japanese economy indicate that the Japanese public are still rather uncertain about their own future, because of the continuing prospects of growing unemployment and pension cuts. Voices have been raised louder and louder everyday for personal and corporate income tax reductions to stimulate personal consumption, which the Japanese government has had to include in its budget for fiscal 1999 and now repeat in the new budget proposal made in December 1999 for fiscal 2000.

There have also been some long-term changes that are social rather than economic in nature that have affected the declining growth of private final consumption among the Japanese people. It has been said that the most outstanding among the social values and priorities associated with the Japanese during the 1950s and the 1960s were a keen sense of self-discipline and hard work, the spirit of dedication and loyalty to the group, and a strong desire for a higher standard of living. The erosion of these social values and priorities, however, has begun to take place under the conditions of full employment, rapid growth in wage earnings and other incomes, fast corporate expansion, incessant urbanization of the countryside and remote villages and constant proliferation and improvement in social security and welfare benefits at the local and national levels. The erosion of traditional values and priorities has been more prevalent and deeper among younger generations and the better off.

Corporations and various other organizations requiring the spirit of dedication and loyalty and hard work among their employees have been incorporating modifications and new ideas to adapt their institutional arrangements to the changing values and requirements among their employees and in the wider society, all in an effort to sustain and/or improve organizational efficiency and productivity. They have long abandoned their initial ambition to slow down, if not stop, the erosion process. It has yet to be seen if the erosion process might be slowed down under the current situation of sustained stagflation involving high unemployment, low growth in wage earnings, slow corporate expansion, local and nation-wide reassessment of welfare schemes and burden sharing, and greater socio-political uncertainties. It is doubtful, however, if the traditional values and priorities will in the 21st century regain the same degree of social prevalence and acceptance as in the past.

The widely held belief during the three decades following World War II that the objective of the highest possible economic growth in the nation would override all other policy objectives, let alone social objectives, was steadily displaced during the 1980s. This was caused not only because of substantial success in achieving the growth objective, but also because of a variety of rising social dislocations and environmental pollution consequent to the very success and the way the success had been brought about in economic growth and restructuring.

Furthermore, in this reorienting the social values and priorities among the Japanese people, an important role has been played by the increasing economic interdependence among nations. Not only was economic growth *per se* questioned at home and abroad, but also the need to come to grips with the dire reality came to be distinctly recognized, so that with an increasing degree of economic interdependence among nations there was no justification for any country, particularly a major power, to pursue growth objectives at the expense of the well-being of other national economies on this increasingly smaller planet. The rising social cost associated with industrial adjustment in Japan during the 1970s and 1980s has become an effective reminder of the need to keep Japan's rapid export growth to a reasonable level. There is a growing awareness among the people that the objective of achieving economic growth consistent with the environment, justice and equity must be pursued not only within Japan but also at the global level. Japan as one of the major economic powers is expected to play an important role in pursuing economic growth consistent with the environment and human development at home and abroad.

While these changing personal consumption, social values and priorities were important sources of growth decline in the 1990s, it must be emphasized, as clearly stated earlier, that the successive failures of the Japanese government in restoring public confidence in the resilience of the Japanese economy and the stability of the financial system at home have been the key to the consistent decline in Japan's economic growth in recent years. In fact, the ability of Japanese industry to innovate new technologies and products has neither declined over time nor been a major source of growth decline. One could safely say that the Japanese economic debacle has been observed not because of, but in spite of, Japanese industry's technological capability.

III. STRUCTURAL CHANGES: OUTPUT, EMPLOYMENT AND PRODUCTIVITY

1. Changing Industrial Structure

Japan's economic growth both in the three decades of high growth following the end of the World War II and in the recent decade of low growth has been accompanied by perceptible changes in the economic structure, with economic resources moving from primary to secondary and tertiary sectors. Equally significant changes occurred in the structure of manufacturing industries, moving from labor-intensive to capital-intensive and then to technology- and skill-intensive sectors. The manufacturing industries expanded rapidly both in absolute terms and as a percentage of real output during the first three decades, and have subsequently declined since the mid-1980s, for example from 28.3% in 1985 to an estimated 23.7% in 1996. The materials sector, consisting of the textiles, chemicals and metals industries, has also followed the same trend, registering a relative decline from 24.0% to 21.8% during the same period. The processing sector, consisting of general machinery, electrical machinery and transportation machinery, has remained more or less the same as a percentage of total real output, moving from 46.3% to 47.1% (Table 3.26). Of the non-manufacturing output, which increased as a percentage of the total real output from 71.7% to 76.3% during the period 1985–96, the expansion in construction and services industries has been most conspicuous, rising respectively from 7.9 and 8.5% to 11.2% and 12.8%.

In this section a few manufacturing sectors have been singled out for detailed discussion on the basis of their importance to the Japanese economy in terms of output, employment and technological development. The iron and steel and petrochemical industries represented Japanese industrial development during the 1960s and 1970s, while transportation (for example, automobiles and shipbuilding) and electrical machinery (for example, electrical home appliance and heavy

TABLE 3.26 Changing Structure of the Japanese Economy 1955–96 (in billion yen, at current market prices)

Industry	1955	1960	1965	1970	1975	1985	1990	1995	1996
Primary sector	1,587.0	2,094.5	3,100.3	4,462.8	8,165.9	10,214	10,921	9,325	—
Secondary sector	2,972.8	6,830.7	13,602.3	32,622.7	57,336.0	95,632	122,341	120,314	—
Manufacturing	2,356.0	5,527.6	10,746.6	26,339.7	37,749.4	90,523	119,028	117,204	119,304
Food and beverage	588.9	930.8	1,479.2	1,958.8	3,610.9	6,542	8,001	9,286	9,190
Textile products	236.6	448.2	708.4	1,505.2	1,761.9	3,011	3,109	1,795	1,739
Clothing	48.9	78.3	178.8	385.5	576.6	1,701	2,191	2,438	2,292
Wood and wood products	79.1	129.9	250.7	704.4	598.0	1,375	1,664	1,527	1,533
Furniture and fixtures	33.8	69.2	171.7	405.3	471.5	1,205	1,757	1,556	1,591
Pulp and paper	83.3	159.0	316.2	745.5	1,243.7	2,290	3,081	3,227	3,280
Printing and publishing	120.3	175.9	412.2	1,062.3	1,810.2	4,552	6,360	6,735	6,903
Leather and leather products	6.4	11.0	1,024.4	122.6	116.2	382	475	384	368
Rubber and rubber products	31.3	71.1	134.4	317.4	559.1	1,195	1,630	1,535	1,567
Chemical products	208.5	439.5	952.7	2,492.3	4,057.0	7,956	11,272	11,984	11,902
Coal and petroleum products	66.5	269.1	570.6	265.0	737.3	3,961	4,693	5,547	5,356
Ceramics and clay products	93.6	218.6	456.2	1,169.4	1,817.4	3,936	5,093	4,965	5,005
Iron and steel	158.4	517.6	682.5	1,693.4	2,833.3	5,188	6,209	4,969	4,921
Nonferrous metals	46.0	95.0	147.8	654.4	926.9	1,566	2,110	1,967	2,092
Fabricated metal products	78.0	248.1	697.4	1,595.0	1,808.7	5,523	8,055	7,970	8,110
General machinery	132.5	572.3	1,129.1	2,900.5	3,876.1	10,002	13,602	12,131	12,769
Electrical equipment	102.7	440.2	825.8	2,925.0	4,247.2	14,863	20,085	19,643	20,165
Transportation machinery	161.9	446.8	1,080.0	2,332.1	4,626.8	9,774	12,582	12,494	13,398
Precision machinery	43.6	92.1	219.2	388.2	703.0	1,834	2,021	1,673	1,738
Miscellaneous	35.7	114.9	309.3	949.7	1,367.5	1,698	2,336	2,289	2,220
Construction	425.5	1,040.1	2,473.9	5,661.8	13,494.9	25,381	43,428	49,693	—
Tertiary sector	4014.2	7,760.2	16,757.7	38,901.8	88,377.9	189,192	258,464	303,598	—
Total	8985.4	16,928.3	33,813.3	73,659.7	148,955.3	320,419	435,154	482,930	503,068

SOURCES: Economic Planning Agency, "Annual Report on National Accounts", in JERC, *Shows Roku Junen no Nihon Keizai* [Japanese

electrical equipment) spearheaded it during the 1970s and 1980s. In the 1990s the consumer and industrial electronics industry, including computers and telecommunications dominated the industrial scene not only in Japan but also in other industrial countries. In the 21st century, however, biotechnology and life sciences, along with information technology, seem to be emerging as the most promising in Japan and other industrial countries. Because of the limitations of this chapter, only the heavy and chemical industries will be discussed, particularly focusing on the materials sector (the iron and steel and petrochemical industries) and the fabrication sector (the electrical machinery and electronics industries).

This section will analyze the development of these industries in terms of employment, output and productivity, identify some of the major issues they have encountered, and discuss the role of the state particularly in technology development in these industries. In addition to output and productivity, the fundamental factors contributing to industry competitiveness in the world market, impacts on employment or employment adjustments are crucial in formulating industrial policies in industrial countries such as Japan where workers — organized or unorganized — small businesses and their family members have significant political clout as voters in national and local elections. The next section will deal mainly with alternative policy recommendations for further development of a particular industry, that is, the electronics industry in an increasingly interdependent world economy.

2. Materials Sector

Strategic Role of the Materials Sector during the 1960s and 1970s

In all the economic development plans formulated from the 1950s to the 1970s, the iron and steel and petrochemical industries were given a strategic role for three reasons. First, these industries would provide basic industrial raw materials required by expanding industries with high income elasticities of demand. Secondly, they would, by requiring highly capital-intensive technology and production processes, be most amenable to constant improvement in physical productivity through a larger volume of capital input and the associated economy of scale.

Thirdly, the kind and level of production technology required in these basic materials industries were such that the nation had ample supply of technical and engineering manpower necessary for their rapid expansion and there was also better possibility of improving physical productivity through constant management efforts in technological change.

Under the first rationalization program for the iron and steel industry during 1951–55 and the second during 1956–60, the investment and output in the industry achieved remarkable growth, followed by equally high rates of expansion during the 1960s, though they experienced substantial fluctuations in response to overall economic conditions. In fact, these rationalization programs during the 1950s were a necessary follow-up as a result of the stretching of the productive capacity of the industry under the priority production program during the late 1940s when every government assistance was given under acute shortage of industrial raw materials and foreign exchange to the iron and steel industry — together with the coal mining, electric power generation and distribution, fertilizer and shipbuilding industries — to accelerate the pace and reinforce the basic foundation of economic reconstruction after World War II.

The petrochemical industry was one of the fastest growing industries in post-war Japan during the late 1950s through the early 1970s. The growth of the industry coincided with, and closely followed, the substitution of coal by petroleum as the major source of energy, beginning in the mid-1950s. Many technologies, new to post-war Japan, that had been developed abroad during the pre-war days were imported by the growing petrochemical industry to turn out new products for the equally fast-growing synthetic and chemical textiles; plastic products and chemical fertilizer manufacturing plants. These new industrial raw materials manufactured by the petrochemical industry utilizing low-cost crude oil rapidly pushed existing materials such as natural fibres, including cotton, wooden and metal products and organic fertilizers out of the market on account of cost and quality competitiveness, and steadily found their new uses through constant inflows of technological innovations in both production processes and end-products. In the National Income Doubling program starting in 1961, the petrochemical industry was chosen as one of the priority industries to be encouraged by the central government to make the downstream and allied industries more competitive in the international market and provide a large amount of employment opportunities in those related sectors using petrochemical products as industrial raw materials.

The rapid pace of plant and equipment investment in the iron and steel and petrochemical industries during the 1960s and the 1970s introduced a drastic change in the structure of output and a significant change in the structure of employment in Japanese industry. As shown earlier in Table 3.26, the value added of the total manufacturing production at current market prices rose from 2,356 billion to 26,339 billion yen, or by more than 1,100% between fiscal 1955 and 1970. During the same period, the value added of the iron and steel industry rose from 158.4 billion to 1,693 billion yen and that of the chemical industry from 208.5 billion to 2,942 billion yen, with the coal and petroleum products industry rising from a mere 66.5 billion to 265 billion yen.

In terms of the annual average rate of increases for the value added, the iron and steel industry grew very rapidly at 26.8% between 1955 and 1960, quite slowly at 5.7% during the following five-year period and regained its growth rate partially at 17.3% during the 1965–70 period. In contrast to this, the chemical industry exhibited more or less constant growth rates at 16.1, 16.7 and 18.7% during the three respective five-year periods. The coal and petroleum products industry, rising sharply at 32.3% during the 1955–60 period, halved its annual growth rates during the subsequent five-year periods at 16.2 and 17.4% respectively. The annual growth rates of the value added for the manufacturing sector as a whole showed few changes during the three five-year periods, at 18.6, 14.2 and 18.3% respectively. As a result, the importance of the iron and steel industry in the total manufacturing value added rose from 6.7 to 9.4% between 1955 and 1960, declining to 6.4% in 1965 and 6.1% in 1970. In contrast, the importance of the chemical industry fell from 8.8 to 8.0% between 1955 and 1960, but rose to 8.9% in 1965 and further to 9.0% after five years. There was a rapid rise in the importance of the coal and petroleum products industry from a mere 2.8% to 4.9% between 1955 and 1960, and further to 5.3 and 5.1% in 1965 and 1970 respectively.

Sources of Output Expansion in the Materials Sector

The rapid rise in the value added of the iron and steel industry and the petrochemical industry between 1955 and 1970 was made possible partly by the equally rapid rise in the amount of capital investment, partly by the much slower increase in the number of workers employed and more importantly by the technological innovations introduced in the respective industries.

With the fast expansion of capital investment, the number of persons engaged in both the iron and steel industry and the petrochemical industry increased significantly between 1955 and 1970 (Table 3.27). In 1955 the total number of persons engaged in the production of iron and steel stood at 262,000, reaching 771,000 in 1970, whereas that for the chemical industry increased during the same period from 422,000 to 626,000 persons and for the coal and petroleum products industry from 35,000 to 52,000 persons. As compared with the enormous expansion in the output, the increase in employment was quite modest in the three respective industries, signifying a tremendous rise in productivity per person employed during the 15–year period. This pattern of employment growth relative to output expansion was observed in other heavy industries, while nearly the reverse was true in food and tobacco, clothing, lumber, furniture and other light goods industries. As a result, the importance of the heavy and chemical industries in the total manufacturing employment rose only slightly, particularly in the processing sectors such as iron and steel, chemical and coal and petroleum products, unlike the importance of these industries in the total manufacturing production and value added.

With the rapid rise in the productivity of the iron and steel industry translated into increased price and quality competitiveness in the international market, the structure of Japanese manufactured exports made a dramatic shift during 1955 to the 1980s from a light-goods orientation to the heavy and chemical products orientation. As shown earlier in Table 3.9, in 1955 the heavy and chemical products as percentage of total exports constituted only 38.0% but rose to 82.2% in 1974, while iron and steel exports increased from 12.9 to 19.4% and those of chemical products from 5.1 to 7.3% during the same period. In the iron and steel and chemical sectors the Japanese became one of the strongest competitors in the world market, not only expanding their exports in volume and earnings but also enlarging their market shares steadily, leading to frequent outcries abroad for orderly marketing, including involuntary voluntary export restraints and protectionist measures for domestic industries, particularly in those industrial countries losing their international competitiveness for various reasons.

	1955	1960	1965	1970	1975	1985	1990	1995	1996
Primary sector	16,111	14,240	11,738	10,060	7,354	5,180	4,570	3,730	3,570
Secondary sector	9,220	12,762	15,242	17,651	18,098	19,830	20,930	21,190	21,270
Manufacturing	6,902	9,545	11,507	13,442	13,236	10,890	11,173	10,371	10,103
Food, beverage and tobacco	812	906	1,106	1,072	1,153	1,017	1,090	1,136	1,129
Textile products	1,259	1,393	1,444	1,397	1,124	609	531	265	248
Clothing	284	408	571	727	860	540	578	594	555
Wood and wood products	503	563	561	548	478	276	253	212	207
Furniture and fixtures	253	290	340	359	357	222	231	204	206
Pulp and paper	215	315	368	362	358	275	284	269	264
Printing and publishing	331	408	540	598	645	515	554	542	534
Leather and leather products	86	100	133	134	140	77	79	62	60
Rubber and rubber products	83	158	171	212	199	165	172	152	148
Chemical products	422	506	595	626	627	396	401	392	389
Coal and petroleum products	35	41	43	52	63	420	469	483	473
Ceramics and clay products	347	475	537	631	636	465	459	429	418
Iron and steel	262	424	695	771	250	388	338	297	285
Non-ferrous metals	66	106	799	502		163	170	161	158
Fabricated metal products	397	676	946	1,312	1,250	787	847	817	797
General machinery	414	725	930	1,174	1,123	1,124	1,192	1,087	1,089
Electrical equipment	309	692	934	1,397	1,328	1,825	1,940	1,750	1,703
Transportation equipment	371	553	702	961	1,058	962	943	914	909
Precision machinery	112	180	236	308	312	262	251	198	188
Miscellaneous	301	549	656	776	749	261	260	235	224
Construction	1,783	2,679	3,403	3,993	4,729	5,300	5,880	6,630	6,700
Tertiary sector	13,930	16,717	20,653	24,325	27,689	33,060	36,990	39,650	40,730
Total	39,261	43,719	47,633	52,042	53,141	58,070	62,490	64,570	65,570

NOTE: In thousands of persons engaged as self-employed, family workers and wage and salary workers.
SOURCE: Bureau of Statistics, Office of the Prime Minister, *Japan Statistical Yearbook 1961, 1977 and 1998* (Tokyo, 1961, 1977, 1998).

In expanding output and improving productivity, there was a constant upgrading of the product mix in both iron and steel and chemicals industries. For example, in 1950 nearly a quarter of the total value of output in the chemical industry came from the production of ammonia and allied products, and nearly one-fifth of the total was from edible oil and fat production. In 1970 ammonia and related products constituted only 3.8% of the total value of output, while edible oil and fat production contributed only 6.7% of the total. Instead, plastics and resin, which comprised only 2.7% of the total value in 1950, constituted 15.8% of the total value of output in 1970. Petrochemical products comprising only 1.4% of the total value in 1950, became in 20 years the most important single product category in the chemical industry, constituting 28.6% of the total value of the industry output (Table 3.28). It is important to note, however, that in the expanding chemical industry there was also an absolute increase in the production of those less technology-intensive and less value-added products such as ammonia and edible oil and fat products during the two decades. It is interesting to observe in the 1980s and 1990s an absolute decline in the value of output for these products in response to increasing import competition, particularly from developing countries rich in their respective raw materials.

Massive Changes in the Materials Sector during the 1980s and 1990s

The technological competitiveness of the Japanese iron and steel industry, which led the world from the 1960s to the mid-1980s, had been derived from the installation of oxygen blast furnaces and continuous strip mills and the locational advantage of large-scale production units built on the seashore and reclaimed land which allowed an easy access for imports of raw materials and energy resources and exports of semi-finished and finished products as well as the use of large-sized specialized vessels carrying iron ore and bituminous coal. These technological advantages of the Japanese steel mills, however, have disappeared since the mid-1980s with the introduction of cost-competitive electric furnaces using iron scraps in many industrial countries and with the adoption of the Japanese technological advantages at lower cost in many advanced developing countries such as India, Brazil and Algeria.

TABLE 3.28 Changing Structure of the Japanese Chemical Industry by Major Commodity Group, 1950–96
(in percentages)

Commodity Group	1950	1955	1960	1965	1970	1985	1990	1995	1996
Ammonia and ammonia products	23.9	20.5	9.0	7.1	3.8	0.8	0.4	0.3	0.3
Calcium carbide	7.7	5.5	4.9	3.3	1.4	0.2	0.1	0.1	0.1
Compound fertilizers	—	—	4.8	4.8	2.8	3.1	1.5	1.2	1.1
Sulphuric acid	6.0	5.5	3.6	2.5	1.5	0.7	0.6	0.4	0.4
Soda and soda products	6.0	5.8	5.5	5.0	4.0	2.4	1.8	1.6	1.6
Tar products	3.0	2.3	2.4	1.4	2.9	0.5	0.1	0.1	0.1
Synthetic dyestuff	2.9	2.7	2.2	2.0	1.5	1.4	1.0	0.7	0.7
Plastics and resins	2.7	5.5	11.7	13.3	15.8	22.3	18.6	15.9	16.2
Petrochemical products	1.4	1.5	6.2	18.8	28.6	33.8	27.5	28.3	29.1
Photographic films	2.0	2.9	2.5	2.8	3.1	4.8	4.1	3.5	3.4
Oil and fat products	16.8	10.9	9.4	8.6	6.7	3.6	2.9	2.5	2.5
Paints	5.2	5.0	6.2	5.5	5.2	10.1	7.6	6.6	6.8
Printing ink	1.5	1.5	1.7	1.8	1.5	3.5	2.5	2.6	2.7

SOURCES: Bureau of Statistics, Office of the Prime Minister, *Japan Statistical Yearbook 1962, 1987* and *1998* (Tokyo, 1962, 1987, 1998).

By 1990 nearly 40% of crude steel in the United States came to be produced by these small-scale steel mills using electric furnaces, as compared with roughly 20% in 1975. While the corresponding figures today are still smaller for Japan and the EU countries than the United States, these small mills are already dominating the markets in the industrial countries in the production of steel bars for concrete blocks and of ordinary steel wires for the construction industry, with large-scale blast-furnace mills now concentrating on high-grade special steel and steel slabs, sheets and plates for the automobile and other manufacturing industries. The installation of continuous strip mills for sheet slabs using German technology by U.S. New Core, Inc. in 1989 has revolutionalized the iron and steel industry, making it much less capital-intensive than traditional blast-furnace technology, and threatening the latter into oblivion even in the steel sheet market. For example, it is calculated that an investment of US$800 is required per ton of output per year for blast-furnace steel mills with an annual production capacity of 3.5 million net tons, while only US$400 is required for small-scale mills with an annual capacity of 1 million tons, using electric furnaces and the German sheet-slab technology.

While the iron and steel industry is now planning to expand its global investment in more cost-competitive compact strip mills utilizing electric furnaces and sheet-slab technology, some technological constraints will still have to be overcome in producing thinner sheet slabs and improving the product quality. Research and development for innovative technology in meeting the rising market demand for thinner and higher-grade sheet slabs has been intensified in large-scale blast-furnace steel mills in Japan and abroad so as compete with compact strip mills which are engaged in similar research and development to stay competitive in the expanding world market. Japanese blast-furnace steel mills are now said to be capable of producing 1-mm-thick steel sheets, as compared to the U.S. New Core's 1.7-mm sheets.

Because of the severe environmental regulations in industrial countries that compel manufacturers of machinery, including automobiles and electrical equipment, to recycle their products, it is quite realistic to predict a rapid rise in the quantity of iron scrap entering the market. This will enable compact strip mills to reduce their costs of production further and become more competitive with blast-furnace mills, if they could discover new technology that separates non-ferrous metals, such as copper and tin, from the recycled steel products at competitive cost.

So far such technology has yet to be developed and the current technology of mixing the highly pure direct reduction iron into the electric furnace is still far from being competitive with blast-furnace steel sheets in purity required by automobile and electrical machinery manufacturers. As a result, small-scale electric-furnace strip mills have captured only a very small percentage of the sheet steel market in Japan. Their biggest competitors are imported hot coils rather than large-scale blast furnace mills. Also, many electric-furnace steel producers in Japan are subsidiaries of large-scale blast-furnace steel mills, and thus are not in a position to compete directly with the latter.

It is expected that with the rapid growth of electric-furnace steel mills around the world and improved technology, competition in the international market for iron and steel, particularly higher-grade steel sheets and plates, will become increasingly intense, challenging the Japanese iron and steel industry to expand the production capacity of compact electric-furnace strip mills and further improve their technology in order to upgrade their product quality. The need for higher-grade steel sheets and plates by electric-furnace steel mills and the growing environmental concern in industrial countries have been raising the market demand for direct reduction iron, roughly 70% of which is now being supplied by Midrex, Inc., a wholly owned subsidiary of a Japanese steel producer Kobe Steel, using either pellet or sponge iron now produced mainly in Venezuela and Malaysia. To produce pellet, now in short supply, at a lower cost, new technological innovations are being experimented in a pilot plant at Kobe Steel, New Core and Rulugi of Germany. Once the technological constraints of pellet and natural gas, essential to competitive production of sponge iron and direct reduction iron, are lifted by new competitive technology, the iron and steel industry of Japan currently predominated by blast-furnace producers will have to undergo a dramatic transformation in their business strategy from the traditional emphasis on economies of scale to the new priority of product differentiation.

Further Technological Upgrading and Government Support for the 21st Century

The Japanese iron and steel industry will probably continue, as in the past, to be noted for producing the high-quality products in response to demand for such quality by major steel users such as electrical equipment, shipbuilding and automobile manufacturing industries that have so far gained competitiveness in the world market on the basis of not only price but more importantly quality assurance. A well-known system of close technical collaboration established in the 1980s between the iron and steel producers and their users to ensure high-quality products will continue to be functional. And increasing global competition will reinforce, rather than reduce, the market requirements for higher grade steel products, as seen in the past, providing domestic iron and steel producers a competitive edge over foreign competitors. Interspatial atom-free steel, commonly known as IF steel, is a good example of the Japanese steel manufacturers' high-quality product, containing the minimal level of carbon, which they are now supplying to nearly 100% of the world's market totalling over 10 million tons, will be replicated by other equally innovative technology in the 21st century.

Since the mid-1980s Japan's iron and steel industry, like other major manufacturing industries, has fiercely sought instrumentation innovation based on sensor, simulation and system technologies, on the conviction that production technology based on economies of scale is no longer tenable in the new global market. These innovations for controlling the production process have enabled the industry to improve energy efficiency and reduce defect ratios enormously. Vast improvements in measuring instruments have made it possible for the industry to measure those temperatures and surface and inner pressures in furnaces that had in the past been considered impossible and more importantly measure them with a high degree of accuracy and precision. Advances in computer technology as reflected in the higher speed of computation and the lower cost of electronic computers and software have also enabled the industry to apply simulation models much more efficiently and effectively. Such innovations in instrumentation technology will also be enhanced by yet another stream of new technologies. Furthermore, innovations in metal physics, such as the transformation from optical to electronic microscopes and from chemical analysis to nuclear analysis, have in the past enabled the iron and steel industry to identify and control the changes in the micro-organism of iron and steel in the production process. It is expected that the organizational control mechanism thus improved will be applicable to other industries and contribute enormously to product-quality improvement.

It is clear from the above that the essence of strengthening the competitiveness of Japanese industry, including the iron and steel, will lie in integrating new scientific knowledge and technological know-how into production processes as well as into intermediate parts and components and final products so that they will become knowledge industries rather than merely fabrication industries. This will involve a closer partnership among private industry, academia and government, with the government providing industry with tax and financial incentives as well as institutional arrangements and infrastructure, including the adequate provision of well-educated, well-trained and well-disciplined manpower in every category of skills and technology.

3. Machinery Sector

Changing Output and Employment Mix during the 1970s and 1980s

While the importance of the heavy and chemical industries in total manufacturing output, value added and employment grew steadily over the 1950s through the early 1980s, the process of technological deepening was continuously observed on two major fronts within the sector. One was a rapid rise in the importance of the machinery industry in the total economy in terms of output, value added, employment and export, with a tremendous spillover effect upon the wholesale and retail sectors. Another was a constant change in product mix in most of the machinery industry from less to more technology-intensive products, from numerically to digitally controlled, from large and heavy to small and lightweight and from low to higher value-added products.

The machinery industry, composed of general machinery, electrical equipment and machinery, transportation equipment and precision machinery manufacturing, had a value added of 440 .7 billion yen and employed 1,206,000 persons in 1955. In the same year the machinery constituted 13.7% of total exports. In 1970 the value added, employment and exports of the machinery industry rose respectively to 832.3 billion yen, 3,840,000 persons and 46.3% of total exports; respectively, a rise of 1.9 times, 3.2 times and 3.4 times from the 1955 figures (Tables 3.9, 3.26 and 3.27). The rapid expansion of the machinery industry was a result of the fast expansion of plant and equipment investment, durable goods consumption, public investment in physical infrastructure and the demand overseas for consumer and producer goods manufactured in Japan.

Whether in terms of output or employment, the expansion of the electrical equipment and machinery manufacturing industry was by far the fastest in the machinery group, and it was most remarkably represented by transistor radios, television receivers and tape-recorders and their related products, together with home electrical appliances such as washing machines, refrigerators and air-conditioners. The growth of this industry reflected — apart from the so-called demonstration effect of more advanced lifestyles from overseas, particularly the United States — on the one hand steady changes in the consumption pattern among individual households associated with a rising level of personal income, and on the other ceaseless efforts on the part of manufacturers to develop new technology and new products at lower cost and to develop new, expanding markets around the world. Similar explanations could be made for the fast expansion of the general machinery industry manufacturing industrial plants and equipment, including lathes and other fabrication equipment and measuring instruments; the transportation equipment industry manufacturing motor vehicles and vessels; and the precision machinery industry producing cameras and other optical goods. Between these machinery industries and electronics, the newest and fastest-growing sub-sector of the electrical equipment and machinery industry, there was a broad range of interactions, increasing further the demand for the latter products at home and abroad.

The rapid growth of the general machinery industry resulted mainly from the fast expansion in plant and equipment investment in the manufacturing and other sectors during the 1960s to the mid-1980s, feeding these rapidly growing sectors with technologically improved, and often lower-priced, and diversified tools, equipment and machinery required in increasingly competitive situations at home and abroad. The modernization of general machinery manufacturing had reached by the late 1960s a level of sophistication sufficiently competitive in the international market so that the industry became increasingly export-oriented. Declining growth in plant and equipment investment in the Japanese manufacturing industries at home also accelerated the export orientation of the general machinery industry, particularly since the mid-1970s.

Technological deepening by way of shifting the product mix from less to more technology-intensive and from low to higher value-added products took place in the machinery industry, as elsewhere, in response to higher household income, changing consumption patterns and growing competition in product markets at home and abroad, as well as changing relative prices of labor to capital and among various inputs. A good example of such technological deepening has been observed in the electrical equipment and machinery industry over three decades. The output of radios, which had a constant expansion during the 1950s and 1960s, began to decline absolutely during the 1970s, in spite of a continued growth in their exports. Nearly the same trend had been observed in the production of black-and-white television sets during the same period. On the other hand, the production of electronic desk calculators and colour television sets saw a rapid expansion during the 1970s and 1980s (Table 3.29). In particular, the electronics industry has in recent years been increasing its product mix with new varieties of consumer electronics products such as cordless telephones, facsimiles, mobile telephones, video tape-recorders, video cameras, digital audio disk players, personal computers and peripheral equipment for household use (Table 3.30). There seems to be no end to the new product list for high-quality consumer electronics products, as the industry has been, and will continue to be, confronted with ever increasing competition at home and abroad, as well as with increasingly sophisticated consumer demand.

Technology Import through Licensing Arrangements

Throughout the 1950s to the 1980s, the importation of advanced foreign technology from the United States and some European countries was instrumental in the rapid growth of the machinery industry. This was especially in the communications, electronics and transportation equipment; the precision machinery; and the specialized and general industrial machinery sub-sectors. In many sub-sectors, however, the importation of advanced foreign technology was promoted by way of licensing agreements between Japanese manufacturing firms and foreign licensors rather than in the form of direct investment, whether wholly owned or jointly owned, by foreign companies with such technological capability.

Japanese foreign technology imports were characterized by three major factors. First, it was the long-held policy of the Japanese government since the Meiji Restoration to discourage foreign ownership of productive assets in Japan for fear that it would eventually lead to economic colonialism by Western countries. This policy of encouraging technology unbundling explains why incoming foreign direct

TABLE 3.29 Japan: Production of Selected Old-Variety Electrical Home Appliances and Consumer Electronics Products, 1950–96 (in thousand pieces)

Products	1950	1955	1960	1965	1970	1975	1985	1990	1995	1996
Electric irons	253	1,223	2,790	2,680	3,766	2,779	—	—	—	—
Electric fans	119	515	1,866	2,813	6,789	4,323	—	—	—	—
Radio receivers	287	1,823	12,851	23,915	34,640	16,364	—	—	—	—
Car radio receivers	0	0	121	1,548	6,210	6,103	—	—	—	—
Black-and-white television sets	0	137	3,578	4,060	6,089	3,153	—	—	—	—
Colour television set	0	0	0	98	6,399	7,472	—	15,132	9,022	7,568
Magnetic recorders	0	0	477	4,954	21,391	26,078	51,195	25,565	12,984	10,620
Console and radio/phono combination	0	0	0	1,188	3,212	2,364	—	—	—	—
Amplifiers for hi-fi	0	0	159	220	1,686	2,997	2,705	3,356	2,137	1,394
Record players	—	—	104	202	712	2,660	—	—	—	—
Speaker systems for hi-fi	0	0	94	133	1,032	2,777	—	—	—	—
Electronic desk calculators	0	0	0	4	1,423	29,882	—	—	—	—
Electric washing machines	2.328	461	1,529	2,235	4,349	3,174	5,092	5,576	4,876	5,006
Electric refrigerators	4.996	31	904	2,313	2,631	3,473	5,354	5,048	5,013	5,163
Vacuum cleaners	0	0	847	1,435	3,526	3,661	5,995	6,851	6,595	6,708
Telephones	393	510	1,311	2,149	3,682	3,631	8,326	15,710	12,779	11,290
Dry batteries (in millions)	75	102	293	970	1,479	1,450	2,967	4,113	4,716	4,523
Facsimiles	0	0	1,445	2,713	7,665	22,163	866	4,350	5,747	5,634
Semiconductor devices (in millions)	0	0	206	722	3,716	4,574	38,283	59,495	68,239	63,259
Integrated circuits (in millions)	0	0	0	0	136	330	9,350	16,054	22,953	21,665

SOURCES: Bureau of Statistics, Office of the Prime Minister, *Japan Statistical Yearbook 1961, 1977 and 1998* (Tokyo, 1961, 1977, 1998).

TABLE 3.30   Japan: Production of New-Variety Consumer Electronics Products, 1985–96 (in thousand pieces)

Products	1985	1990	1995	1996
Cordless telephones	0	7,113	7,359	6,350
Microwave ovens	7,909	4,673	3,174	3,407
Electric rice cookers	6,459	7,690	6,962	6,483
Facsimiles	866	4,350	5,747	5,634
Mobile phones	0	0	8,197	18,414
Video tape recorders	30,581	31,640	16,115	12,725
Video cameras	2,574	8,803	8,658	8,830
Radio cassette players	21,784	4,692	1,765	936
Digital audio disk players	4,135	9,139	13,184	12,775
Magnetic tapes (in millions)	1,686	3,201	2,107	2,088
Magnetic video recording tapes (in millions)	1,307	2,560	1,582	1,629
Floppy disks (in millions)	230	1,240	68,239	63,259
Computers	2,026	3,292	22,955	21,665
Personal computers	1,924	3,018	6,382	8,942
Peripheral equipment	15,867	45,752	67,831	62,689
Magnetic disk equipment	631	5,075	16,688	14,039
Flexible disk equipment	7,662	24,240	14,738	12,077
Input-output devices	7,480	16,224	20,896	24,519
Printers	5,582	13,146	16,036	18,457
Display units	1,851	2,894	4,655	5,873
Alkaline batteries (in millions)	236	626	1,179	1,051

SOURCES: Bureau of Statistics, Office of the Prime Minister, *Japan Statistical Yearbook 1977* and *1998* (Tokyo, 1977, 1998).

investment has been much rarer in pre-war and post-war Japan as compared to many East Asian countries. Reflecting this policy on foreign collaboration, the government assisted Japanese industrial corporations in locating advanced technology abroad and even in negotiating licensing agreements with foreign licensors. Foreign exchange allocations were also made available on a preferred basis to Japanese licensees importing advanced technology. In this connection, Japanese licensees importing foreign technology to expand their exports were given top priority, including tax and financial incentives.

Secondly, Japanese industrial enterprises firmly believed that it would be more economical to purchase foreign technology and pay royalties under licensing agreements than to develop new technology through their own research and development efforts. This business policy was particularly relevant to those companies trying to catch up as quickly as possible with their Western competitors in terms of product quality and cost of production and become efficient competitors in the world market where product cycles were rather short. Thirdly, Japanese industrial corporations had been blessed with relatively well-educated and well-trained engineers and technicians who could quickly master advanced foreign technology, adapt it to specific requirements in Japan, and even develop new technology from these imports.[8]

Technology imports through licensing arrangements, however, have become increasingly difficult in recent years unless accompanied by the licensee's exports to the licensor of equally advanced technology in return, that is, a cross-licensing arrangement, or unless packaged with foreign capital participation either as a wholly owned or jointly owned enterprise operating in Japan. Foreign corporations that have previously exported their technology have learnt through their past experiences that Japanese corporations importing such technology grow to be competitive and oftentimes begin to outsell their products in the international market. While instances of Japanese corporations exporting advanced technology have grown in number since the 1980s, the slow expansion of research and development expenditures has in effect restrained cross-licensing agreements between them and foreign corporations not only in the machinery industry, but also in other sectors of the economy. It is vital, as argued later, that the Japanese government assists Japanese industrial corporations to accelerate their research and development in order to come up with original and innovative technologies that will be marketable in the global market.

4. Electronics Industry

Technological Developments

Unlike in the United States where technological innovations in the manufacturing sector have been closely related to, and often accelerated by, national defence requirements, the innovations in the electronics industry in post-war Japan have invariably resulted on the one hand from changing demand on the part of consumers seeking greater convenience whether in weight or size, better designs, multiple functions and cheaper prices and on the other from the constant efforts on the part of the private manufacturers to meet those changing consumer demand. The consumer-producer interactions through the market have been most intense in the electronics industry because of both effective import competition and fierce competitive pressures at home under the highly liberal competition policy of the government for the manufacturing industries since the early 1970s unparalleled in agriculture, construction, finance and various service sectors.

The growth of the electronics industry, accelerated essentially by private sector efforts for commercialization, higher productivity, quality improvement and research and development in fabrication and process technology, has been most conspicuous since the mid-1970s. The electronics industry, hiring 1.1 million workers or roughly 9% of the total manufacturing employment, has today become the biggest employer; by far bigger than the materials sector such as the iron and steel (308,000 workers) and chemical industries (398,000 workers) that have long been considered to be strategic industries. Employment in the electronics industry has now surpassed that of the automobile manufacturing industry (789,000 workers) that has for so long dominated the export scene and has been often the source of bilateral trade disputes between Japan and the United States. This industry has also come to constitute the largest share of Japan's trade surpluses year after year since the late 1970s, eventually, as discussed later, resulting in the conclusion of the United States-Japan agreement on semi-conductors in 1992.

The centrepiece of the electronics revolution, comparable to the agricultural revolution ten centuries ago and the industrial revolution in the 18th–19th centuries, is digitalization, the technology converting voices, characters, pictures and data into digital information made accessible to computer input, accumulation, transmission and processing. The constant improvement in semiconductor technology and the enormous advances made in networking through telecommunications, by reducing the cost of data production, accumulation, processing and transmission, enlarging data-loading capacity as well as increasing data transmission speed and improving its quality, have contributed enormously to the electronics revolution in the 20th century.

Compared with the Electronic Numerical Integrator and Computer (ENIAC) manufactured in the United States in 1945, the notebook personal computer today is only 1/15,000 the weight, requires 1/13,000 of the electricity and processes data at the speed 10,000 times faster.

The scaling down of integrated circuits in semiconductor technology still continues, ever improving memory capacity and data-processing speed and reducing their cost. For several years now, data-processing speed has been quadrupling every three years. With constant application of electronics technology, the electronics industry has revolutionalized not only the whole machinery sector, whether in general, construction, electrical, transportation or precision equipment manufacturing, but also the non-manufacturing sector such as retail and wholesale trade, finance, insurance and business, medical and education services.

Globalization Pressuring Changes in Japan's Industrial Policies

Under increasing global competition and the information and telecommunications revolution, there will continue to be an expanding market for semiconductors and a broad range of machinery products incorporating electronic devices in the world, including Japan. The question, however, is how far the competitiveness of the Japanese electronics industry in the world will continue. There are some arguments that at least in electronic hardware it will remain for some time, with constant improvement and investment expansion in the plant and equipment and the research and development required for the production of upgraded semiconductors as well as the availability of high-quality engineers and technical manpower and related technologies. However, there is also a looming possibility that the technological innovations for increasing the capacity of integrated circuits may not be sustained indefinitely in the future, mainly due to the possible constraint of further improvements in photolithography now used in the production process and the time-consuming nature of research in the development and application of X-ray and electronic beam methods. It is also well understood that because it is overly concerned with technological improvement in hardware and neglects similar improvement in software, the Japanese electronics industry has been losing its competitiveness *vis-à-vis* their competitors in the United States.

As is known the world over, the Japanese government took a long time not only to realize the importance of software in the development of the computer industry and the growth of the electronics industry, but also to come to grips with the fact that software development is by itself an industry with the potential of producing much higher value-added than the hardware computer industry. There was strong resistance on the part of government bureaucracy against undertaking further deregulation of the information industry to accelerate development and application of software.

The basic reason for such resistance lay in the nature of the software industry, which consists of three major areas of activity, that is, the development of programs to activate computers, such as basic and application software, the development of software for screen game play and the development of the Internet. The government feared that giving a free reign to the software industry would drive some existing industries, such as newspapers, printing and publishing, radio and television broadcasting and even part of the banking business out of market, and thus disrupt the orderly restructuring of the information industry market, the cornerstone of Japanese industrial policies. It also feared that such competition would result in a loss of jobs for a large number of blue- and white-collar workers, thus creating enormous labor and social adjustment problems in Japan, which had already turned into a low-growth economy.

The rapid rise of the software industry was also interpreted as weakening the authority of the government bureaucracy overseeing the existing industries by making useless the traditional industrial boundaries. It was also feared as having the potential to further intensify inter-ministerial rivalry, particularly between the Ministry of Post and Telecommunications (MOPAT) and the MITI, the last thing that the government bureaucracy would want. The software industry was thus considered as contrary and a challenge to the very concept and objectives of the traditional industrial policies formulated and implemented by the government.

By giving all kinds of excuses, the Japanese government resisted the rapid growth of the software industry and tried its best to subordinate it to hardware computer and electronics industries. It was only after sustaining for some time strong foreign pressures for deregulation and liberalization of the information and telecommunications sectors at home, as seen in the United States-Japan bilateral talks on Structural Impediments Initiative, and the privatization of the telecommunications industry as exemplified in that of Nippon Telephone and Telegraph (NTT), that the software industry began to grow in all directions, giving rise to a series of new industries that have become quite significant in the rapidly changing industrial scene of Japan. Once the software industry was acknowledged as essential, not only to the computer and electronics industries but to practically all sectors using such software to stay competitive in the world market, and once the social benefits of the software industry was found to outweigh tis social cost, the Japanese government turned 180 degrees to support the industry to become more mature as quickly as possible, providing policy, legal and institutional environments conducive to such development.

In spite of the government policies mentioned earlier, it has been the intensified global competition since the mid-1980s that has precipitated the use of computers in Japanese industries and the growth of software industry, together with electronic mails, the Internet and electronic banking and purchases since the mid-1990s. With enormous price reductions in computer hardware, computers are now found in more households. Only ten years ago there were only a few thousand Internet users in Japan; this number has now increased to over 17 million. The software industry has even begun to make inroads in those industries that are essentially regional or local in nature and not subject to global competition, such as medical, educational, restaurant and personal services. This has occurred in response to rising competitive pressures seeking greater efficiency in resources allocation and greater business opportunities in local communities. It also reflects increasing competition among software producers and service providers to obtain a greater share of the market and enhance their profits.

It is important to note, however, that in spite of the growth in the software industry there has been in recent years an interruption in the growth of the electronics industry, which has exhibited a constant output expansion since the late 1950s except in 1971 due to the Nixon shock; in 1975 due to the energy crisis; in 1986 due to the Plaza Accord; in 1992–93 due to the bursting of the bubble and export stagnation; and in 1994–95 due to rapid import expansion of electronic components and finished products partly caused by the rapid revaluation of the Japanese yen to less than 100 to the U.S. dollar. One of the major factors contributing to the growth interruption has been structural in nature, the emigration of Japanese consumer electronics firms resulting from the rapid appreciation of the Japanese yen triggered by the Plaza Accord. Imports of consumer electronics products as a percentage of their domestic consumption reached 26% in 1995, rising from 13% only five years before, in 1990. The emigration of Japanese electronics industry, however, is a result of economic globalization and the intense global competition taking place since the 1980s, resulting from further deregulation at the national level consistent with international trade and capital liberalization.

Rising Importance of Software Development

The recent trend of the Japanese electronics industry shown above clearly indicates that the industry growth at home, if dependent largely as in the past upon technological innovations in hardware production oriented towards cost reduction, will no longer be possible under global competition. In the future it will increasingly depend upon the availability and application of competitive software oriented towards higher value-added in sectors with high growth potential. The future growth of the Japanese electronics industry will require, among others not only an improvement of hardware production technology and a reduction in its cost of production, but also the imposition of *de facto* standards in the world's electronics industry, the building of the information superhighway, the mobilization of financial resources at reasonable cost, including the minimization of foreign exchange risk and the promotion of industry and corporate restructuring, including corporate rationalization, acquisitions, mergers, consolidations and tie-ups.

This will require further efforts on the part of the Japanese, particularly the MITI, the Ministry of Finance (MOF), the MOPAT, the Ministry of Construction (MOC) and the Ministry of Transportation (MOT), to further deregulate the industries under the ministries' supervision and encourage effective competition at home and abroad in all these sectors. These ministries must limit themselves to industrial policy formulation, monitoring and evaluation, and not involve themselves in the micro-management of private sector industry, let alone at the firm level which they have so often done in the past. They must leave all investment and production decisions, including technology development, to the private sector enterprises, which should know far better than the government ministries, given that their own survival and growth in the face of fierce global competition is at stake.

It will also require the redirection of public investment programs that have hitherto been rather rigid in terms of the allocation of government loan and investment resources among a few selected ministries, such as the MOC, MOT, MOF and MOPAT, in favour of the comprehensive development of software technology. For this purpose a drastic reorientation will be required from the Japanese government's traditional "specific industrial policy" of promoting the electronics industry only and in particular hardware production technology and investment with all kinds of fiscal and financial incentives and institutional arrangements. Rather, it needs to adopt a new "comprehensive industrial policy" which links the development of the electronics industry with that of all related industries and economic and social infrastructures. This means, however, that the MITI must work much more closely with various other ministries, such as the MOF, MOPAT, MOC, MOT, Ministry of labor and Ministry of Education, in drawing up its industrial policy packages and co-ordinate with them in the implementation of its own development strategy.

It is important to note in this connection that the administrative reform proposals initiated and deliberated by the Hashimoto administration since 1996 and finally approved in November 1998 by the Obuchi administration contain the establishment of an all-powerful Economic and Fiscal Policy Council (EFPC) in the Office of the Prime Minister in January 2001. The EFPC will be empowered to make all decisions concerning the basic direction of the economic, fiscal and industrial policies that would determine budgetary allocation among the ministries.

Under these circumstances the new "comprehensive industrial policy" in the 21st century will no longer be the MITI's but will definitely be the Japanese government's policy, with the various programs and components of the policy formulated by the new EFPC and implemented in an integrated manner by a consortium of these relevant ministries. It will be a new institutional arrangement, a radical departure from the traditional bureaucratic practices in the Japanese government, and the implementation of such new arrangements will therefore require strong political leadership on the part of the Prime Minister and other relevant ministers, with solid support of the Parliament. It is welcome in this connection that the administrative reform proposals, though far less than desirable and far inferior to those hoped for, would lead to the strengthening of the Prime Minister's authority and the reorganization of the current 13 ministries with nine agencies into the new 12 ministries with one agency to start in the year 2001.

It is sincerely hoped that the new bureaucratic structure of the Japanese government will be implemented at the earliest possible date rather than waiting for the year 2001, as such a structure is urgently needed for the effective formulation and implementation of the comprehensive industrial policy packages, not only for electronics industry but for all the other major industries in Japan. It is also sincerely hoped that in spite of some obvious worries over the actions taken by the LDP to form a coalition government with the Liberal Party headed by Ozawa in January 1999 and subsequently with the Komeito headed by Kanzaki in September 1999, the administrative reform and marketization processes will be accelerated by the new Obuchi administration in collaboration with Ozawa and Kanzaki, who seem to have had a long and strong commitment to "cheap government" and the supremacy of the marketplace and the Parliament over the bureaucracy that, with the exception of World War II and the immediate post-war Occupation period, has in effect controlled the government of Japan since the Meiji Restoration of 1868.

NOTES

1. Here East Asia refers to the region covering both Northeast and Southeast Asia, consisting of all the member countries of ASEAN, Cambodia, China (including Taiwan), Mongolia, the Republic of Korea and Japan. The term Asia-Pacific region covers both East Asia and the South Pacific countries such as Australia, New Zealand and many island states.

2. According to several surveys taken, the Japanese never felt easy with the term "Japan Century" and detected some strategic implications of the terminology as expounded mainly by American futurologists.

3. For a detailed discussion, see JERC, December, 1999.

4. Structurally declining industries are designated by the Ministry of International Trade and Industry (MITI) on the basis of their monthly surveys on the plant capacity under-utilization, the new order received for machinery and equipment and the annual rate of output expansion. Once designated as structurally declining, all the firms are eligible to apply for employment subsidies that are predetermined in favor of smaller firms based on the amount of paid-up capital and the number of employees.

5. For more details see JERC (1981).

6. The BOJ raised its rediscount rate five times between April 1973 and December 1973; from 4 to 5% on 2nd April 1973, 5.5% on 30th May, 6% on 2nd July, 7% on 29 August, and 9% on 22 December 1973. The high interest rate remained unchanged until 16 April 1975, when it fell to 8.5%. Faced with the high-growth fever, the BOJ reluctantly adopted a tight money policy. The BOJ should have done this earlier and with higher increases.

7. For a more detailed discussion on this issue, please see Hirono (1999b).

8. For a more detailed discussion see Ryokichi Hirono, Ng Chee Yuen and Robert Siy Jr., eds., *Technology and Skills in ASEAN: An Overview.* Singapore: Institute of Southeast Asian Studies, 1986.

REFERENCES

Asian Development Bank (ADB). *Asian Development Outlook, 1988* and *1998.* Manila: ADB, 1988, 1998.

_____. *Emerging Asia: Changes and Challenges.* Manila: ADB, 1997.

Calder, K. *Strategic Capitalism.* Princeton: Princeton University Press, 1993.

Export-Import Bank of Japan. *Journal of Research Institute for International Investment and Development* 24, no. 4. Tokyo: EXIM/RIIID, 1998.

Government of Japan, Bureau of Statistics, Office of the Prime Minister. *Japan Statistical Yearbook 1957, 1967, 1977, 1987* and *1998.* Tokyo: Government Printing Office, various years.

Griffith-Jones, S. *et al.* "The East Asian Financial Crisis: A Reflection of the Causes, Consequences and Policy Implications". IDS Discussion Paper 367. Brighton: IDS, 1998.

Hirono, R. "Innovation in Japan". *Seikei University Journal of Economic and Business Studies* 9, no. 1 (1978).

_____. *Factors Which Hinder or Help Productivity Improvement: Japan Report.* Tokyo: Asian Productivity Organization, 1981.

_____. *Seshin Kougyoukoku no kouzou henka to koyou.* [Structural changes and employment in industrial countries]. Tokyo: Koyou Shokugyou Sougou Kenkyuujo, 1984.

_____, ed. *Macro-Micro Linkage for Technological Innovation in Asia.* Tokyo: APO, 1985.

_____. "Globalisation, Competition and Development Cooperation in the 21st Century: A Japanese Perspective". *SUJEBS* 27, no. 2 (1997).

_____. "Changing Japanese Policies for the Economic Development of East Asia in the Postwar Period". *SUJEBS* 29, no. 2 (1999a).

_____. "Globalisation and Its Impact on Human Security". In *Best Practices and Lessons Learned Towards Sustainable Human Development and Human Security*, edited by R. Hirono *et al.* Tokyo: International Management Association of Japan, 1999b.

Hirooka, Y. "Sekyuu Kagaku: Fukakachi Seisan Kouritsu wo Takameru Gijutsu Kaihatsu wo" [Petrochemical industry: Wanted technological innovations for higher value added and productive efficiency]. *[JERC Research Bulletin]*, nos. 775 and 776 (1 and 15 May 1997).

Inoue, R. *et al. Higashi Ajia No Sangyou Seisaku [Industrial policies in East Asia].* Tokyo: Nihon Boueki Shinkoukai (JETRO), 1990.

Itou, Motoshige *et al. Sangyou Saisaku No Keizai Bunseki [Economic analysis of industrial policy].* Tokyo: Tokyo University Press, 1988.

Japan Economic Research Centre (JERC). *Nisen nen no sekai no nakano nihon.* [Japan in the world in the year 2000]. Tokyo: JERC, 1981.

_____. *Shihanki keizai yosoku 1980–1998* [Quarterly Economic Forecasts 1980–1998]. Tokyo: JERC, December 1999.

Johnson, C. *MITI and the Japanese Miracle: The Growth of Industrial Policy 1925–1975.* Stanford: Stanford University Press, 1982.

Kakazu, H. and T. Yoshida. *Ajia gata kaihatsu no kadai to tenbou* [Major issues and prospects of the Asian-type development]. Nagoya: Nagoya University Press, 1997.

Kanamori, H. "Heisei Fkyou no Genin to Kongo no Keiki" [Causes of the Heisei depression and Japan's business climate in the future]. *JERC Research Bulletin,* no. 807 (1 September 1998).

Kanbayashi, T. "Jouhou Tsuushin: Shakai Keizai Kouzou Henkaku no Saranaru Suishin wo Mezashite" [Information and telecommunications: Toward further reforms in economic and social structures]. *JERC Research Bulletin,* no. 778 (15 June 1997).

Kano, Y. *et al. The Japanese Economy in the 1990s: Problems and Prognoses.* Tokyo: Foreign Press Centre of Japan, 1993.

Komiya, R. *et al. Nihon no sangyou seisaku* [Japanese industrial policy]. Tokyo: Tokyo University Press, 1984.

Kuninori, M. "Setsubi Toushi Doukou" [Recent trends in plant and equipment investment]. *JERC Research Bulletin,* no. 812 (15 November 1998).

Miyazawa, K. *Sangyou no keizai seisaku* [Economic policy for industrial development]. Tokyo: Touyou Keizai Shinpousha, 1986.

Mori, K. "Jouhou Kaden: Dejitaruka Jidai ni Sekai he Hasshin" [Information and consumer electronics: Looking ahead in the digital age]. *JERC Research Bulletin,* no. 783 (1 September 1997).

Nakamura, S. *Sangyou seisaku: Sengo 30 nen no kaiko to tenbou* [The industrial policy: Recollection of the 30–year experiences after the war and its future prospect]. Tokyo: Keizai Seisaku Gakkai, 1985.

Ng, C.Y., R. Hirono and Y.S. Robert, Jr., eds. *Technology and Skills in ASEAN: An Overview.* Singapore: Institute of Southeast Asian Studies, 1986.

Ng, C.Y., R. Hirono and A. Narongchai, eds. *Industrial Restructuring in ASEAN and Japan: An Overview.* Singapore: ISEAS, 1987.

Nomura Research Institute (NRI). *Nihon no yuusen kadai* [Priority issues for Japan]. Tokyo: NRI, 1990–98.

Okimoto, D. *Tsuusanshou to haiteku sangyou* [The Ministry of International Trade and Industry and the high-technology industry]. Tokyo: Simul Press, 1991.

Ono, G. *Jissenteki sangyou seisaku ron* [Practical industrial policy]. Tokyo: Tsuushou Sangyou Chousakai, 1992.

Patrick, H. *Japan's High Technology Industries: Lessons and Limitations of Industrial Policy.* Madison: University of Wisconsin Press, 1989.

Sangyou, G.K., ed. *Boueki jiyuuka to kokusai kyouryoku* [Trade liberalization and international co-operation]. Tokyo: Sangyou Gijutsu Kaigi, 1992.

Sanuki, T. "Kenkyuu ga Setsubi wo Yobu Jidai" [The age of research-induced plant and equipment investment]. *JERC Research Bulletin,* no. 518 (15 August 1986).

Sato, M. "Tekkou: Hai teku Gijutsu Kushi shi Chishiki Sangyouka heno Dappi wo" [Iron and steel: A way ahead toward high-technology and knowledge-intensive industry]. *JERC Research Bulletin*, no. 770 (15 February 1997).

Small and Medium Industry Research Association, Japan. *Chuushou kougyou ni okeru gijutsu shinpo no jittai* [Technological progress in small and medium industry]. Tokyo: Toyo Keizai Shinposha, 1960.

_____. *Koudo seichou katei ni okeru chuushou kigyou no kouzou henka* [Structural changes in small and medium industry under high economic growth]. Tokyo: Toyo Keizai Shinpousha, 1962.

Suzuki, Y. "Erekutoronikkus: 21 Seiki no Riidingu Sangyou he Mukatte" [Electronics: Toward a leading industry in the 21st century]. *JERC Research Bulletin*, nos. 775 and 776 (1 and 15 May 1997).

United Nations Development Programme. *Human Development Report 1998*. New York: Oxford University Press, 1998.

World Bank. *World Development Report 1968, 1988 and 1998/99*. New York: Oxford University Press, 1968, 1988, 1999.

Yamada, K. and A. Kuchiki. "Lessons from Japan: Industrial Policy Approach and East Asian Trial". In *Economic and Social Development Issues in the 21st Century*, edited by L. Emmerij. Washington, D.C.: Inter-American Development Bank, 1997.

Yamamoto, T. "Nihon no Kikai Sangyou no Ajia Tenkai Joukyou" [Japanese Machinery Industry in Asia]. *JERC Research Bulletin*, no. 718 (15 December 1994).

Yamamura, K. and Y. Yasuba, eds. *The Political Economy of Japan*. Stanford: Stanford University Press, 1987.

4

A Broken Social Contract: Dynamics of the Thrust Towards Restructuring Japan

Takashi Kiuchi

I. INTRODUCTION

There has never been a time during the post-war period like today when opinion leaders agree unanimously that Japan is at a historic crossroad. It appears that the nation is soul searching to question its past economic, social and political heritage. True, the economy was shaken a couple of times in the past, for example, by the oil shock of 1973 and the yen's sharp appreciation that began in 1985. In retrospect, however, these appear rather minor events when compared with the recent crushing economic misfortunes. The disastrous defeat of the Liberal Democratic Party (LDP) in the 1998 Upper House election witnessed once again unequivocally an end of the post-war domination by the LDP in Japanese politics. Socially, baby-boomers who were born right after World War II are approaching their last phase of their working career and getting seriously worried over their life after retirement in an aging society.

How should we interpret this sense of need for a big change? We all know that economic, social and political factors are intrinsically interacting with each other. This chapter is basically a humble exercise by an economist to examine how this interaction has been working in Japan and, in so doing, to demonstrate the inevitability of restructuring its society in the future. Unfortunately, it is almost unavoidable for an economist to focus somewhat upon economic analyses of the society and politics, rather than social and political analyses of the economy. Nevertheless, it is hoped that the analysis is a worthwhile exercise to deepen understanding of Japanese society in transition.

One has to become immediately aware that cause and effect chains cannot always be readily identified. It is particularly so when social changes take place only gradually while economic and political events often occur dramatically. This chapter will try to show, first, how Japanese society was restructured right after the war and how it nourished economic growth and social stability. Then it examines how economic success and other independent factors — economic and social ones alike — began to erode the basis of economic growth and social stability. Finally, this chapter investigates how politics has been and is trying to cope with changes in the nation's economic and social structure.

II. POST-WAR SOCIAL CONTRACT

Let me begin with how Japanese society was restructured right after the war. The lessons that Japan learned, rightly or wrongly, from the war were essentially these. The first was that a war could ruin the nation and bring the people inexcusable misery. The élite's political expansionism abroad was grossly misplaced. At the same time, it was impressed on the people that Japan's industrial power and economic wealth were indeed far behind those of the West.

Against this background, a set of new national aspirations emerged. One of them was the pursuit of economic reconstruction and development that utilizes domestic resources as much as possible. Another was a creation of "democratic society" or the introduction of a decision-making mechanism based upon consensus-building to weaken privileged leadership. The nation was convinced that an unchallenged domination of their decisions resulted in a grotesque misguiding of the nation in the pre-war period.

It is probably fair to state that the post-war society was organized based upon institutions or bureaucracies that emphasize the bottom-up decision-making approach. Moreover, business institutions or producing units of the society were chosen as principal agents, which represent individuals collectively and interact with each other within a corporatist society. In other words, non-producing institutions such as religion, neighbourhood clubs, consumer unions, etc. were grossly under-represented in the nation's decision-making process. The other side of the same coin was that trade associations acquired powerful voices in the country's political process.

Government was also rebuilt to reflect these new propositions. First, it was given a role of co-ordinating the nation's industrial development. Accordingly, the Ministry of Finance, which allocates scarce fiscal resources, and the Ministry of Industry and Trade, which formulates industrial policies, acquired greater prominence, replacing the pre-war Home Office. Secondly, a variety of devices were installed to make the nation immune to any dictatorship by delegating to bureaucracies more power to forge collective decisions. The parliamentary cabinet system was one such machinery. In addition, a number of councils and advisory committees were set up to foster intimate consultation between the government and industries.

It is important to note here that this post-war Japanese system achieved incredible success in diffusing capital-labour confrontation, which seems to be one of the fundamental problems inherent to capitalism. This enabled most of the institutions in Japanese society to devote their energies single-mindedly to their business development. Without this, an extremely successful high growth in the first two or three decades after the war could not have been possible. For instance, Japanese industries lost only 43 days due to labor strikes and other disputes in 1996 while U.S. counterparts lost as many as 4,889 days.

The post-war system worked beautifully in two ways. At a micro-level, a pre-war top-down management style was abandoned in private sector business institutions and, also to some extent, in government agencies. Instead, the so-called Japanese management system was adopted. It is worthwhile noting that this is a relatively recent creation in the nation's history. As is widely known, the system incorporates a couple of distinctive features, which have characterized Japanese institutions to date. They are life employment, hierarchy of salary and authority based upon seniority, and career development through rotation.

From an economic point of view, this management system had its distinctive merits. It cultivates a good team spirit. An emphasis on team accountability encouraged employers and employees to invest aggressively in the development of skills and experiences. Accordingly, it contributed to an incremental but steady enhancement of the institution's collective efficiency.

Moreover, it should be noted that the system has a kind of social virtue. It gave people a strong sense of belonging to communities, that is, employer institutions. A blurred distinction among top management, white and blue collars generated an environment in which any employee could enjoy due appreciation of his peers. As a result, Japanese institutions accomplished a high degree of trust among their members. As a consequence, one of the spectacular achievements of the Japanese system was to make every working place pleasurable or at least rewarding for any level of employee.

At the same time, offices as well as factories functioned as a kind of mutual surveillance mechanism, which kept members from slipping away as dropouts or outcasts. Hence it is not surprising that Japan is known for its exceptionally low crime rates. All these were conducive to an enviable social stability that prevailed in post-war Japanese society. Some historians observed that Japan is the first nation in Asia which succeeded in extending a chain of trust beyond blood to develop larger business institutions as effective vehicles towards industrialization.

The Japanese system was also instrumental in securing social stability at a macro-level. In fact, one of the major social tensions in the early period of the high growth era was the one between the two contrasting sectors of the economy. The first was an industrializing sector as represented by the manufacturing sector and its big businesses. The second were the traditional sectors that typically comprised the non-manufacturing sector and its small businesses, the self-employed, farmers and fishermen. Incidentally, small businesses that are contract part-makers and distributors for big manufacturers are also included in the second group, as they were perceived as a target for potential exploitation. Peter F. Drucker was quite correct to diagnose Japanese industrial policy as a disguised social policy.

In reality, this conflict among a variety of sectors in the economy was skilfully mitigated in the nation's political process. It can be labelled as a kind of implicit grand-coalition-like pact between the ruling LDP and protesting Socialists. In other words, a macro-level labor-capital confrontation was pre-empted by a carefully crafted co-operative mechanism that worked among producing institutions. To be more precise, promotion of targeted industries, which are mostly in the industrializing manufacturing sector, was well balanced by protection for declining industries, which are mostly traditional sectors. Newly acquired wealth of urban areas was transferred back into poor rural farming areas through fiscal measures. This also advanced social and political stability. In this connection, a Japanese equivalent of the former left in the West were the Socialists who represented interests of small businesses, on top of workers, and forced the LDP to introduce various correcting measures for the dual economy. On the other hand, Japan's old right was a part of the LDP that pursued industrialization at any cost.

III. DEMOGRAPHIC AND SOCIAL TIME BOMBS

In spite of outstanding economic success, there have been a variety of developments in the last 10 or 20 years, which indicate that the Japanese system began to wear out. This institutional fatigue is largely attributable to several time bombs. They are combinations of inflated promises, economic affluence and demographic and environmental changes, which were necessitated by economic transformation of the nation.

Let me focus here upon demographic and other social changes. The shortcomings of the Japanese system will be discussed later. Major agents of these changes seem to be mass education, urbanization and a corresponding decline of agriculture-based rural communities, disintegration of big families, ensuring the advancement of women, an aging population, globalization and IT and other technological development.

To begin with, the mass education system broke down a pre-war monopoly of expertise by the establishment and people no longer placed blind faith in their leaders. True, the post-war reform opened up an unprecedented range of educational opportunities for the larger populace. In fact, a desire of typical Japanese parents soon after the war was to let their children go to good schools in order to secure rewarding jobs, which were not readily available for their parents in the old days.

As a result, the number of those going to higher education rose continuously. In the 1990s, the proportions of those going to high school and university reached 95 and 40% respectively, a huge jump from 40 and 10% in the early 1950s. Japan has become one of the most educated nations in the world. Without any doubt, it contributed greatly to economic growth. It was widely accepted that the Japanese education system is good at enhancing basic skills for the masses, even if it is not so good at producing innovative leaders. Nevertheless, diligent, educated and skilled workers were exactly what the economy needed in its catching-up process with the West.

In spite of its obvious merits, it is suspected that the introduction of the mass education system bred some inevitable over-expectation that could not be sustained for long. People have recently begun to look at educational institutions somewhat critically. They recognize that a college diploma is no longer a ticket to a safe and comfortable life. Some signs of disillusionment are visible. A couple of episodes illustrate this point.

Firstly, university attendance ratios which have stagnated for some years are now slowly dropping. Clearly people have begun to question if the return on investment on higher education is justifiable. Secondly, an increasing number of young people have begun to study at vocational schools (computer, accounting and others) while they attend university. Apparently, they do not believe that a university education alone will guarantee them decent jobs. Professional and other vocational schools now number more than 3,500 and enrol close to one million.

What is implied here is that Japanese society has become an extremely competitive place for people to live in. They have to face performance competitions throughout schools and the work-place. To put it simply, the mass education system resulted in an over-qualification problem for those educated. The stresses are increasingly evident. In elementary and secondary schools, it is reported that violence or other disturbances by rebellious pupils are spreading alarmingly. Juvenile delinquency has been markedly on the rise. The number of arrests doubled from 200,000 in the early 1960s to 400,000 in the mid-1980s.

Let us now turn to urbanization and its impact. This has been progressing on a colossal scale and reshaped the Japanese social fabric beyond recognition. Modern industries are located largely in metropolitan areas and have siphoned off countless numbers of workers from the rural areas, where farming, fishery and forestry had been the mainstay of their lives. In this process, a great many people found themselves uprooted from their native rural communities. Statistics show that the number of urbanites rose from 40% in early 1950s to 65% in the mid-1990s as a proportion of the nation's total population. Furthermore, urban concentration was compounded in a way in which bigger towns attract more people from smaller towns. At present, more than ten million people live in metropolitan Tokyo. It should be remembered, however, that greater Tokyo is the residence of 25 million or a quarter of the entire population of the nation. Japan today is a highly urbanized nation in which Tokyo commands an acknowledged position of the centre, economically as well as socially.

Accordingly, an increasing number of people represent a layer of nuclear families and have become residents in unfamiliar new towns or more recently in complexes of apartment buildings in metropolitan areas. During the 1960-90 period, there was a decrease in the number of multi-generation families from 31 to 17%. Liberated from the inhibiting confinement of old communities, people opted to remain anonymous in lonely crowds in the new settings. In other words, their involvement in social institutions was reduced to a bare minimum. True, during the high growth period, working lives were rewarding enough for them to ignore the merits of belonging to social institutions. However, when the era of low growth arrived, urbanites began to complain bitterly that their interests were not adequately catered for. Urban decay and congestion problems, environmental degradation, lack of social facilities and infrastructure, and absence of consumer protection are all sources of their discontent.

Another social change deserving close observation is the advancement of women in society. It seems that women are basically beneficiaries of the above-described social changes. Firstly, they were freed from the scrutiny of parents-in-law and from other social constraints that characterized the old communities, and increasingly chose not to conform to the traditional role of the subordinate and devoted wife. The mass education system helped women to acquire qualifications for jobs. Women often outperformed men academically and received encouragement from this fact.

True, Japanese businesses were fairly discriminating until quite recently against hiring women as career employees. Hence many women are still frustrated by the difficulty of moving into managerial posts. Typically they have to endure clerical occupations. However, the chronic acute labor shortages in the boom years enabled women to find more attractive jobs, albeit gradually. In any event, it is amazing to find that the worker participation ratio of women around 50 years old has reached one of the highest in the industrialized world at some 70%.

However, the advancement of women into the work-place did not come without its social costs. An aging population is one notable such consequences. As women realized that marriage and child-bearing could be insurmountable obstacles that hamper their working careers, they delayed the age of marriage and, in turn, came to have fewer children. The consolidated reproduction rate decreased from 2.14% in 1974 to 1.39% in 1997. It implies that the entire population is bound to decrease fairly rapidly in the future. Men were somewhat perplexed by women's changing attitude but could not do anything about it. This trend eroded the distribution of labor that was assumed as a norm between the husband, who is supposed to earn a living by devoting his entire energy to company life, and the wife, who is expected to look after the home and care for the children. The divorce rate has been creeping up in recent years.

Furthermore, social tensions arise, as the work rules of business institutions are found to be rigid and impose extra hardships upon working women. It became apparent that the social infrastructure, such as daycare centres and maternity leave, is hopelessly lacking. Men and women have not yet come to terms with the reality of the new age. It suggests strongly that the economy remains poorly equipped to take advantage of women's ability. As a matter of fact, women often choose non-Japanese employers.

Apart from there being fewer children and smaller families, the aging population is also accelerated by ever-longer life expectancy. In 1997, Japanese life expectancy stood at 83 years for women and 77 years for men. This was a spectacular jump from 73 for women and 68 for men in 1965. Economic affluence and progress in medical treatment are clearly contributing factors. Nonetheless, this extension of life expectancy was beyond anybody's anticipation. Accordingly, society has come to confront an entirely different challenge: caring for an increasing number of elderly. The existing social institutions are simply inadequate for this task. Elders often reside in rural areas while children live in big towns. Even if elders live close to their children, working women do not have the time to care for their parents, who can no longer rely on family support.

Finally, economic affluence began to generate a diversity of aspirations, especially among the younger generation. For the first time in post-war history, youth have begun to question if a higher income is the only legitimate purpose of life. They turn more towards a so-called quality of life or self-fulfilment and often turn their back on being incorporated submissively into the Japanese system. For example, they frequently prefer to work as "freeters" (permanent part-time workers) and consider careers at the established institutions as enslavement. Surprising the popularity of the Japanese Peace Corps in recent years indicates that younger people are not lazy but have a keen desire to be rewarded spiritually rather than materially. Incidentally, society came to appreciate the merits of their cause when their participation in NGOs proved to be immensely helpful in the rescue operations right after the Kobe earthquake.

IV. GLOBALIZATION AND THE DIGITAL REVOLUTION

Globalization and the digital revolution are not necessarily unique to Japan, since other industrialized nations are also profoundly affected. Nonetheless, these changes imposed extra stress upon the Japanese system. Broadly speaking, globalization and the digital revolution seem to have marked a new stage of international competition, by enabling information, money and other managerial resources to move swiftly as well as inexpensively around the globe. It gives multinational businesses far more room to develop a very flexible cross-border division of labour. Accordingly, these changes work forcefully to equalize any price differentials that remained between domestic and international markets. Yes, trade liberalization had similar impacts, but it was rather limited to tradable goods or manufactured merchandise. What is new about the on-going changes is the far-reaching nature that affects prices of non-tradables such as wages, interest rates, utility costs and prices of services. In short, it has become increasingly difficult to shield the domestic system from the global market discipline.

In retrospect, the yen's sharp appreciation in the mid-1980s was a watershed when Japanese manufacturing businesses made a historic turn in their strategy from pursuit of domestic efficiency towards globalization. Faced with the incessant climb of domestic wages, it became apparent that rationalization would no longer ensure international competitiveness. Instead manufacturers had to embark upon massive direct investment programmes to set up production capacities abroad. In recent years, Japanese multinationals have invested as much as 30-50% abroad out of their total capital spending budgets.

This globalization of Japanese businesses led to a striking shift in the industrial policy debates regarding "democratic" governing of the nation under the post-war system. To put it briefly, it exposed a serious divide between the manufacturing and service sectors. The former represents big businesses, which are typically headquartered in Tokyo and other large metropolitan areas, favour deregulation as a catalyst for innovation and are determined to survive in the global market-place to compete against or team up with non-Japanese multinationals. The latter manifests typically small businesses, which are often rooted in the small communities, oppose deregulation and are devoted to preserving the Japanese system that protects them from any external shocks. Interestingly enough, employees in both camps support their respective employers almost unanimously.

In the past, manufacturing big businesses appreciated social and political stability that enabled them to concentrate on modernization of their operations. However, they began to resent the high costs of social stability, which now handicaps their competitiveness. Many observers have pointed out that Japan became an exceptionally high service cost economy, which also raises unduly the already high living costs for urban dwellers. Some claim that the "small guys" as a group somehow formed a united front with unbeatable political might and the support of powerful vested interest groups so as to preserve a complex of regulations which allow them to price their services dearly at the expense of the "big guys". To illustrate this point, the Economic Planning Agency (EPA) confirms that living costs in Tokyo are considerably higher than in other major world cities, for example, 52% higher than New York, 50% higher than London and 43% higher than Paris in 1994.

In this connection, public works projects became a target of criticism. By the 1980s, this had been transformed into a monstrous instrument to transfer income from metropolitan areas to the rest of the nation. In other words, the purpose was shifted cunningly from the original purpose of infrastructure development towards reduction of the regional income disparities. It means that public works projects are now frequently a waste of money. One such absurd example is the four huge bridges that connect Shikoku Island with the nation's main island. No one dares defend the economics of these bridges. Toll revenues are unlikely to recover their construction cost in the foreseeable future. It is very indicative that public works projects as a proportion of GDP are exceptionally high at 6% in Japan while they are normally 3–4% in other industrialized economies.

In addition, the digital revolution has elevated the level of globalization even further. Information flies effortlessly beyond the national borders. Likewise, together with liberalization of capital flows, money now moves almost instantly. This combination is essentially bringing the service sector to the forefront of global competition. It is not so much confined to the financial service industry. For example, e-commerce seems to have given birth to a number of virtual retailers that can reach people easily in any corner of the world. The digital revolution also spreads the distribution of labor to many different locations. Contracting out of software development for the Operating System

(OS) by Microsoft to India shows that labor can now cross national borders virtually. Moreover, the industrial structure is undergoing profound changes — new ventures are replacing big businesses as the front-runners in the so-called new economy.

Indeed, the digital revolution is shaking the Japanese system and its industrial structure. First, highly regulated service industries such as financial services, retailing, communications, transportation and other business services are thrust into an intensely competitive international market-place. It was found that regulatory arbitrage neutralizes domestic regulations such that the paternal guardianship of the government ceases to function. In other words, the carefully crafted mechanism to preserve deep pockets in the nation's service sector that is a stable source of employment in bad economic years, is being destroyed. In particular, small businesses suffer as their traditional turf is being encroached upon by big businesses equipped with networking abilities. When we compare small businesses in the mid-1990s with those in the early 1970s, new entry firms decreased from 7 to 4%, while the number closing down increased from 4 to 5%. This illustrates the seriousness of the situation in which small businesses found themselves. The most notable example of this is found in the retail industry where deregulation enabled big businesses to expand chain operations at the expense of the small "papas and mamas" stores.

Big businesses, too, are facing an unexpected new challenge. The digital revolution seems also to have reshaped office work in a fundamental way. It tends to polarize white collar workers into the professional and managerial group at one end and the clerical and technicians group at the other end. It may still be meaningful to keep the former group under the life-employment practice. However, outsourcing is often more economical for the latter group, whom some critics call "gray collar" workers. Yet the Japanese management system seems unable to cope with this problem. Moreover, ventures are a kind of operation which the Japanese management system can seldom accommodate.

Finally, the digital revolution and the ensuing intensification of globalization are now reaching into the domain of public enterprises in Japan. The distinction between infrastructure and private businesses is no longer clear-cut. This necessitates a rethinking of appropriate roles for the government in a new economy. Obviously the post-war Japanese system has not yet acquired any new criteria to redefine the place of the public sector.

V. BUBBLE YEARS AND BROKEN PROMISES

The post-war Japanese system prospered during the high growth era. However, a fatal shortcoming of the system is that it does not function well in a matured economy that grows sluggishly. First, it became increasingly difficult to maintain an ideal pyramid-shape structure in its management. The Japanese management system constantly produces an ever-increasing number of senior members qualified for posts of higher responsibility. Without rapid expansion, an institution cannot afford to promote these senior staff to the posts that they deserve. Under the life-employment practice, institutions cannot throw redundant employees out into the street. It may well be said that the Japanese management system inherently lacks an exit strategy.

Secondly, when lower growth makes it impossible for businesses to recruit a large number of fresh graduates every year, the average labor cost rises incessantly as employees advance in seniority. This prevents cost competitiveness. In this respect, it is probably fair to claim that the 1980s were the decade during which the Japanese system and its inertia lapsed subtly from an asset into a liability of the economy. There is no hard evidence to prove this. However, one statistic is very suggestive. In an average Japanese business institution, wage payment to staff aged 40 or higher was around 50% as a proportion of the total labor costs in early 1960s, but it exceeded 60% at the end of the 1970s. In the mid-1990s, the ratio reached as high as 70%. Correspondingly, the workers' share in the total value added continued to rise at the expense of return on capital that was reduced to a historical low.

In fact, circumstantial evidence is plentiful to suggest institutional fatigue. Job assignments given to individuals were progressively diminished in terms of scope and authority. The focus was frequently on damage control of past failures rather than forward-looking new ventures, and occasionally on keeping unprofitable business lines alive. This downsizing of an individual's responsibility could be labelled as a kind of "title inflation". Incidentally, the number of subordinates that division managers oversee in big businesses has been dramatically reduced from 48 to 29 in the last 20 years. Management began to emphasize rigorous performance assessment, while employees were assigned to narrowly defined specific tasks irrespective of whether the task utilized one's ability or not. All this turned out to be deeply demoralizing. Work-places thus became unbearably discomforting and in some cases were considered an insult for employees. One admirable virtue of the Japanese system was lost.

The author is a great believer of the generation theory, which claims that baby boomers tend to dominate the social and political agenda of the time for any nation. Indeed, baby boomers are unfortunate in the sense that they cannot escape from the pressures of their population boom throughout their entire life. In post-war Japan, most of the nation's urgent problems have been their problems. They have experienced rigorous competition to enter good schools, and have suffered agonizing job hunting, housing shortages, etc. They are now faced with an aging population.

To be more precise, the narrowly defined post-war baby boom was the period 1947–49, during which approximately 2.6 million were born each year. If one includes the period of 1945–51, the total births reached 16 million, which comprises as high as 19% of the current working age population. It is in great contrast to find that new births in recent years are fewer than 1.2 million. The baby boomers are now in the age category between 48 and 54 years. They were at the centre of the student revolt movement in the very early 1970s.

In this connection, the burden of institutional fatigue weighs heavily upon baby boomers. As they reach middle age, most of them find themselves locked in the old system, being unable any longer to explore new career paths. They find their experience hardly marketable, because their skills are often too company-specific, rather than generic, and narrow in scope due to excessive fragmentation of the management system. It is no surprise to detect an air of despair among those who lost their jobs in a wave of on-going corporate restructuring. In recent years, dismissal of workers at the age of 50 or higher due to managerial reasons has been around 3% of total dismissals, which is noticeably higher than the 1% for younger workers.

To put it differently, baby boomers are looking back at the post-war social contract with bitter resentment. In short, they feel betrayed by the system. When they were recruited many years ago, they were told that they would have to endure the first 20 years by working like slaves with inadequate pay. Higher posts with sufficient remuneration were programmed to be made available only years later. Instead, what has been awaiting them is corporate restructuring aimed at reducing wage payment mercilessly either through wage cut or dismissal by persuasion. Top management now emphasizes performance-based rewards and the self-reliance of employees. Employers have begun to blame blind devotion to an institution as excessive dependence. To sum it up, their dream turned out to be a broken promise.

To make matters worse, baby boomers cannot find comfort outside their jobs. To begin with, they had devoted so much of their life to their employer institutions that their social life appears non-existent. They are typically men who return home customarily late at night. This makes their wives feel deserted and frustrated. Some of the wives have been forced in recent years to work at menial tasks to compensate for their husbands' insufficient salaries. Wives regard this as a serious breach of a kind of pact, which they accepted at the time of marriage. It can be said that their devotion to home is also met with broken promises. The unity of the family is severely shaken. The divorce rate has also been creeping up recently.

At the same time, children do not respect parents as much as in the past. Young people were raised in an affluent society and do not have a fear of unemployment. They seek a better quality of life and are less patient to accomplish whatever goals they set for their lives. They may even have spent some years abroad while their fathers took on overseas assignments. Therefore, they are often affected by Western culture and even despise their fathers as the company's excessively domesticated servants. They value self-fulfilment and are less willing to sacrifice their aspirations to care for their parents. In other words, baby boomers realize that they would not be able to depend upon their children when they grow old and need extensive care. Moreover, their pension fund and elderly care insurance now appear grossly inadequate and they became a serious political issue in the 1999 autumn session of the National Diet. Their lives after retirement are likely to be dispiriting rather than comfortable. It is not surprising to detect that suicides by baby boomers have been sharply on the rise in recent years.

Did the Japanese economic failure that resulted from the bubble that burst and the deep recession highlight the underlying social and political conflicts? The answer is a definite yes. Society becomes intolerable when people realize that their employer institutions no longer provide them with economic stability and progress. It is probably appropriate to conclude that the bubble years were the period during which a phantom economic boom helped businesses over-stretch their conventional management system, accumulating potential problems that were destined to crash sooner or later. In a way, the bubble years converted a chronic disease into an acute illness that needs surgery.

In other words, it was very unfortunate that the bubble boom put all this institutional fatigue out of sight for a while. Many institutions even aggravated the situation by upgrading their anticipation for future growth and adding to their existing over-commitment to future obligations: generous wage hikes and heavy capital investment. For example, the persistent labor shortage gave them an excuse to recruit staff even more aggressively. These measures are now backfiring.

Moreover, the bubble boom generated over-confidence. A symptomatic phenomenon was the so-called Japanese arrogance. Japanese executives reinforced their belief in Japanese-style management and government-business partnerships, while they looked down on the United States for its social divide and inefficiency, and on the rest of Asia for their lack of vigilance and skills, for instance. This blind trust in the Japanese system may well be labelled as a Japanese equivalent of the new right in the West. Of course, the Japanese new right is almost dead now that the boom has gone.

The role of the public sector or government bureaucracy cannot be overlooked. This is the sector of the economy that is the least responsive to the global market discipline. They can preserve the Japanese management system far more easily than the private sector. In fact, the government created new artificial demands for their services one after another. One of the motivations behind this is their desire to ensure jobs for retired civil servants. In any event, the public sector, not only government agencies but also public and quasi-public enterprises, inflated themselves into a grotesque monster group to occupy a vast area of services in the nation's economy. A quick look at, say, the banking industry, is illustrative enough. The Postal Savings Institute is by far the nation's biggest deposit-taking institution. The Housing Financial Corporation dominates the housing loan market. Japan Development Bank crowds out private sector banks to lend aggressively at concessional terms to blue chip business institutions. It may not be so much an exaggeration to say that the public sector is beginning to choke off private sector dynamism. *Keidanren* calculated that the public sector, including public enterprises, comprised as much as 46% of the nation's GDP in 1994. In any event, there is no doubt that the public sector is one serious cause of the high service cost economy.

Incidentally, it is worthwhile noting that the younger generation seems to be coping with the digital revolution far better than the baby boomers. They have been raised by game machines and animation software and have acquired high computer literacy. While some of them are regarded as a new breed of outcasts who loiter around fashionable streets without firm career prospects, others are intelligent, adventurous and individualistic in their professional orientation. In addition, they communicate easily with foreigners.

In this respect, we are perhaps witnessing a first wave of internet-related ventures, which capitalize on these young talents. Mr Masayoshi Son of Softbank, Mr Kazuhiko Nishi of Ascii, Microsoft and several other computer star ventures have been providing them with the ideal training ground. It now seems that a critical mass of young venturists is taking shape and becoming a Japanese version of Silicon Valley in Tokyo, although the scale and depth are far smaller. Without this development, one could not explain the boom in over-the-counter (OTC) stock market trading, which is a definite bright spot in the weak recovery of 1999.

Yet there is still much skepticism. Several things are cited as obstacles. Japan does not have constructive partnerships between universities and enterprises. It also lacks infrastructure such as taxation, stock market listing procedures, accounting rules, legal framework for appropriate investment vehicles, and venture capital expertise that is essential for the growth of new enterprises. The government does not manage Research and Development (R&D) expenditures in such a way as to promote new ventures. Heavy regulation regarding communications and distribution works against innovation. Big businesses are inexperienced in working together with ventures.

All this is a handicap to enterprise in Japan. However, one cannot ignore the fact that the younger generation is ready to take on the challenges. It remains to be seen how far these developments will grow and become pervasive enough so as to reshape Japanese industries in the coming years. It will also be interesting to see how these ventures will make their voices heard in the political process.

VI. COLLAPSE OF 1955 REGIME

Another critically important component of any society is politics. This section examines how politics has been trying to accommodate changing national aspirations of the time. The emphasis is placed on associating parties' realignment with underlying restructuring of their constituencies, which represent different economic stakes.

When the post-war social contract became a nation's firm consensus in the 1950s, a period of turbulent and chaotic politics came to an end and stabilized. Political scientists call what emerged as "the 1955 regime". Under this regime, the political landscape was as follows: the pro-growth LDP represented the production units of society while the pro-egalitarian Socialists spoke out for labor and small businesses. It can also be said that the LDP was a friend of manufacturing big businesses as an agent of modernization and the Socialists cared for the sector of the society that was left out. Communists attracted anti-establishment believers on the fringe of the nation's political spectrum.

The LDP dominated politics almost all the time, while the Socialists remained a distinct minority. In 1960, for instance, the LDP enjoyed an absolute majority in the Lower House, occupying 63% of its seats. On the other hand, the Socialists secured 31%, while the Communists kept only 2%. Notwithstanding, the LDP did not perform many of the policy-making functions, which were rather delegated in wholesale fashion to the government bureaucracy. The LDP supported policies that were proposed by the bureaucracy, whenever the policies were likely to help economic growth and industrial development. The war experience convinced the public at large that endowment of excessive power on political leaders and the accompanying political interference in economic management resulted in the Japanese failure in the pre-war era. Accordingly, the importance of the bureaucracy was generally accepted based upon the assumption that the institution is more trustworthy than individual heroes.

However, the domination of the LDP did not mean that the Socialists were ignored. On the contrary, as described earlier, the LDP and Socialists entered into a kind of grand coalition in which they both negotiated how the post-war social contract should be applied to specific cases. Promotion of big modern industrial sectors and protection of traditional sectors were thus carefully balanced. Consequently, the nature of the dual economy in Japan was preserved for a sustained period of time for the sake of social stability. In fact, whenever the LDP were perceived to be diverting from the social contract and forcing their will on the Socialists, the public at large would express their rage and cast protest votes to punish the LDP harshly in subsequent national elections.

It is probably worthwhile noting that the LDP itself operated as just another typical Japanese institution. In other words, the Japanese management system prevailed. The seniority principle was respected so that a politician would have to survive more than a quarter of a century before he could be a serious contender for the nation's premiership. The only political drama was a kind of political game played by various factions to seek posts. LDP leaders basically share the same ideology and are thus unable to launch bold and unique policy initiatives. This is why Japanese political reporting concentrated so much on power struggles among strongmen and confused non-Japanese observers who wanted to identify policy disputes.

It is vital to appreciate subtle but continuous changes in the constituency basis, as economic growth altered the wealth distribution of the nation. The LDP's miraculous success in holding onto power was attributable to its efforts to accommodate the new rich of the time politically. The shift from the old rich, or blue chip big businesses such as banks, trading houses, textile-makers, utilities, steel manufacturers, ship-builders and electric machinery makers, was completed by the birth of Keiseikai. Its founder was the disgraced late Prime Minister Kakuei Tanaka. His group became the largest faction within the LDP with their firm grip on public works projects, which was continuously beefed up to cater for rural Japan. And this was probably the beginning of the perpetuation of pork barrel politics in post-war Japan.

As time went by, institutional fatigue of the Japanese system also began to affect politics. This was exemplified by a sequence of events. The first was the rise of Komei, which succeeded in gaining the support of small people in metropolitan areas, while the Socialists cornered themselves more and more into the rural areas. The second was the break-up of the Socialists — the right-wing spin-off as Democratic Socialists had support from moderate private sector labor unions, while the remaining mainstream Socialists relied more on militant public sector unions. Nonetheless, the Democratic Socialists could never muster a critical mass of political might to alter the nation's political equation, probably because of its failure to lure white-collar and gray-collar workers, while blue-collar workers diminished in number. Incidentally, urban Komei supporters included these gray-collar workers, who felt alienated from the nation's politics, although the party's religious background kept it from reaching out to the rest of the public.

The old political divide became obsolete by the late 1980s. The marginalization of the Socialists was revealing. Of course, the end of the Cold War was a factor. The collapse of the Soviet Union discredited a communist ideology beyond salvation and worked against any leftist party. However, this does not explain the complete picture. The real failure of the Socialists was their inability to expand their constituency bases beyond hawkish (public sector) labor unions, agricultural co-operatives and rural chambers of commerce (a nest of small businesses). In particular, the Socialists lost support significantly when they sided with militant labor unions at national railway strikes in the late 1970s. On this dispute, the union became a public enemy due to its arrogance and unrealistic demands. Subsequently, the Socialists could not block the-then-PM Nakasone's move to privatize the Japan Railway System. This privatization is still cheered as a remarkable success and critics call it a precursor of the structural reform of the nation's economy, which is now about to take place. Socialist supporters as a proportion of the total electorate diminished continuously from approximately 20% in the early 1960s, 10% in the mid-1970s and 5% in the mid-1980s.

At the same time, the LDP has lost its dominance. It was indeed indicative that a coalition government began as a result of the LDP break-up in 1993, which gave birth to the Hosokawa cabinet or the first non-LDP cabinet in many years. The fatal shortcoming of the LDP was its inability to reach out beyond producing institutions of the society. It means that, just like the Socialists, the LDP could not organize ef-fectively the white-collar middle class, women and other urbanites. One public opinion survey found that people who supported a party decreased from 67% in 1990 to 44% in 1995, while people who did not support any party increased from 20 to 43% during the same period. This illustrated a loss of confidence by the public at large in political parties. Correspondingly, it became extremely difficult to secure a stable majority in the National Diet after the mid-1970s.

The change is also vividly shown in the fact that the turnout for general elections has long been on a downward trend. For instance, the turnout for the Upper House election has declined markedly from 70 to 45% in the last decade. It is even noted that the turnout by young people in their 20s seems as low as 20% in the Tokyo metropolitan area. This assured that the LDP remained in power; those who were alienated from direct involvement in politics simply tolerated it. How-ever, when the LDP mismanaged the economy or when some scandal erupted, suddenly there was a mass of protest votes to deprive the LDP of an absolute majority in the National Diet. In other words, a high turnout was always bad news for the party, as represented by the fact that a relatively high turnout of 55% resulted in a disastrous defeat of the LDP in the 1998 Upper House election.

VII. POLITICAL REALIGNMENT IN SLOW PROGRESS

The political landscape is changing but restructuring of political constituencies remains an unfinished task. The basic challenge is to capture
urbanites, who feel excluded from the political process and who have
become a vast pool of swinging votes in the recent elections. To put
it differently, the political parties are required to present a fresh social
contract, which can accommodate the reality of a globalized economy
and, at the same time, provide the demoralized baby boomers with
renewed hope.

In any event, votes for the LDP have been on a continuous decline.
Many LDP leaders are frustrated by its loss of appeal to grass-roots
people. Despite this, the LDP could not offer a new platform that lures
them. One reason is over-bureaucratization of the LDP itself. Old bosses
become obstacles for younger generations to launch bold new agendas.
Another misgiving is marginalization of the Socialists. Without a clear
ideological rival, the LDP has lost its political identity. The LDP has
begun to look like a coalition of contradicting elements. It has included
hawks and doves, élitists and populists, big and small government
advocates, internationalists and nationalists, pro-growth and pro-egali-
tarians, etc. It may not be exaggerating to call the LDP an ideological
zoo. The only common denominator appears to be realism.

The LDP itself has begun to re-examine its rationale. It should be
noted again that an age of coalition government began when the LDP
broke up in 1993. Mr Ichiro Ozawa was an heir apparent of Keiseikai
but he decided to break with his boss, Mr Noboru Takeshita. His departure from the LDP put an end to Mr Kiichi Miyazawa's tenure and
kicked the LDP out of power for the first time in four decades. Mr
Ozawa formed a cabinet to make Mr Morihiro Hosokawa PM in an
alliance with non-LDP parties. Thus, an age of coalition began.

For a while, Mr Ozawa held on to power while he changed his
coalition partners skilfully. But it was very difficult to continue to do
so when political fragmentation progressed. When the Socialists deserted him for the LDP, the latter resumed its ruling power with the
Socialists in 1994. After the Socialists defected again, PM Obuchi was
currently trying to broaden a ruling coalition to include Mr Ozawa's
Liberals and Komei. The principal opposition party is now Mr Yukio
Hatoyama's Democrats, which is in substance an amalgam of LDP

defectors, Socialists defectors and Democratic Socialists. Mr Hatoyama himself began his political career with the LDP.

Currently in the Lower House, the LDP has 53% of the seats or an absolute majority while 19% is held by the Democrats, 10% by Komei, 8% by Liberals, 5% by Communists and 3% by Social Democrats (renamed Socialist). However, in the Upper House, the LDP has only 42% while 22% is held by Democrats, 10% by Komei, 23% by Communists, 6% by Social Democrats and 5% by Liberals. This means that, with the exception of the budget, any important legislation needs some coalition support for its passage in the Upper House.

These frequent changes of coalition illustrate that the nation has been doing some soul searching. It is likely for on-going political fragmentation to stay at least for a while. It means that no political groups have yet succeeded in articulating a clear new political ideology. However, there are a couple of positive changes that have already been accomplished.

One significant improvement is the return of politicians to the driving seat replacing civil servants in the business of governing the nation. Politicians finally stood up to their task for the first time last year in the midst of the economic and financial crisis, and proposed and passed a series of legislations on their initiatives. The second encouraging sign is the rise of young politicians who have come to influence the policy-making processes based upon their professional expertise. As a result, the substance of policy debates is becoming far more visible than before.

Another aspect of the on-going political contest is which party would be the most effective agent for structural reform. One may remember that PM Hosokawa invoked high expectations in this regard and became Washington's favourite. His supporter and strongman, Mr Ozawa, has long been regarded as a reformist believer. However, PM Hosokawa's tenure was suddenly interrupted by public uproar against a consumption tax hike proposal. Soon after that, the Socialist defected and the cabinet collapsed.

This episode shows two things. Firstly, the Japanese political system has a strong inertia to preserve the status quo. The parliamentary system does not give the Prime Minister the authority and power to embark upon any bold initiative. The Upper House and Lower House often offset each other's moves. It should be reminded that the underlying basic design was to prevent too much concentration of power upon a selected group of political élite. Notwithstanding, the wholesale restructuring of society requires a strong leadership. Unfortunately, consensus builds up only slowly. This necessitates a gradual approach. Or consensus can be reached only when crisis arrives. I believe that it arrived in 1998.

People are after all ambivalent in many respects, until they are exposed to clear policy options available and foresee resultant outcomes. One revealing fact is the rising popularity of Obuchi. Sometimes, strong ideology, as represented by Mr Ozawa, alarms people rather than exalts them — they prefer a realist like PM Obuchi, who delivers immediate comforts.

PM Obuchi is indeed an interesting leader. He appears to be an old-fashioned politician and far from being a reformist. But he proved to excel in several tasks. First, he single-mindedly pursued a recovery and almost succeeded. In this process, he mobilized conventional means very forcefully. Second, he reigned over bureaucracy tactically. Third, he demonstrated a keen sense of public opinion in his agenda setting. However, he is not without his shortcomings either. He is not eloquent in his view of the nation's future. He cannot present a persuasive new ideology and spell out clear strategies to achieve it. People are kept uncertain as to where he will lead the nation. One cannot ignore the possibility that people may choose another leader once a recovery is secured and the restructuring of the society becomes recognized as the most pressing task of the day.

One interpretation is that the reform process has become irreversible by now because PM Obuchi incorporated so many measures that necessitate corresponding changes in regulation and rules so that they will feed on their own in the coming years. One such example is the recent corporate restructuring legislation, which was launched to make it easier for businesses to restructure their company organizations through merger, divestiture and other means. It will alter the investment environment profoundly and help foster new ventures in the future.

At this point in time, however, people are drifting among competing and often-contradicting visions for the future. Among other things, normal state vs. internationally low-profile state, self-defence vs. pacifist, caring government vs. minimalist government, regional communalism vs. strong central government, free market advocates vs. interventionists, élitist vs. populist leadership, etc. Political leaders are also responsible for this confusion. Every party still has an uneasy combination of conflicting elements within itself and has not yet succeeded in presenting any consistent vision for the future. Similarly, no party has accomplished the task of incorporating alienated urbanites well into the nation's political process.

VIII. CLOSING REMARKS

It is apparent that the nation needs a restructuring of its economy, society and politics. Unfortunately, it seems a bit too early to show with some confidence what a new social contract might look like, what kind of shape the new economic system would take, and how political realignment would evolve. It remains to be seen where on-going restructuring will lead the nation. However, there are several requirements which the new society must fulfil.

The first is to let the economy acquire an ability to make a flexible resource re-allocation in terms of human and capital resources. It is far more practical to limit life-employment practice to a selected group of employees. It is hoped that the anxiety of potential unemployment be reduced by developing a critical mass of mobility in the labor market, which assures workers of their marketability. In other words, industrial policies should be replaced by issue-oriented policies like employment and education policies.

The second is to diminish the role of the public sector in the economy to make the best use of private sector dynamism. This is especially important when new growth areas associated with information technology (IT) development is revolving around the traditional public sector that is currently highly regulated. The devices should be introduced to let some rigorous discipline work on bureaucracy. It is suspected that deregulation is occasionally a misleading conceptualization. Sometimes market enhancing regulatory restructuring appears to be a more appropriate terminology. In addition, more emphasis should be placed upon privatization.

The third is to maximize the potential of small businesses by delegating more powers to independent and local government agencies so that they can function more harmoniously with a new breed of small businesses. These changes are aimed at nourishing the process of transformation of small businesses from impoverished inefficient operators in traditional areas into innovative entrepreneurs experimenting on novel modes of businesses.

The fourth is to foster development of non-employer institutions such as professional societies and institutions. The era of total devotion by employees to their working place is gone. However, people in any economy need peers' reliable support. Otherwise, they lose trust in the society as well as motivation to make long-term commitment towards self-exploration. As such anchor institutions, professional societies are worthwhile commanding new attention.

The fifth is to help the growth of non-economic civil society institutions. The desirability of non-employer economic institutions holds true also for them. In other words, it is necessary to modify the situation in which people's aspirations are pursued only through consultation among producing units of the society. People's aspirations are more diverse now. There are some developments recently towards this direction. In the fields of official development assistance (ODA) and environmental protection, many NGOs have mushroomed and are becoming legitimate partners for the government in the policy-making process. For instance, taxation should be further improved to allow NGOs to flourish.

The sixth is completion of the political realignment and clarification of public choices available to determine our fate in the future. It seems that it can be done only by fostering of civic society organizations and by incorporating them in the political process. Otherwise, it appears almost impossible for political parties to capture the hearts of urbanites and cater for their aspirations properly. Incidentally, there is an interesting debate regarding the final shape of political realignment. One school envisions rivalry between two large parties as found in the United States and the United Kingdom. Another school foresees a continuation of coalition politics, in which three large parties, say, right ideologist, left ideologist and pragmatist, are potential partners to form a coalition at any given time. Only time will tell which prediction turns out to be true.

Finally, the Japanese people detest it if modification of the Japanese system means a total surrender to an American system. In this respect, it appears that Japan shares many concerns with the so-called third way approach that seems to be emerging in Europe. The point is to develop non-business institutions to hit some appropriate balance between economic dynamism and social stability. In so doing, the nation has to make efforts to preserve mutual trust and social capital as a basis of healthy economy and society.

5

Rethinking the Development Paradigm: Lessons from Taiwan — The Optimal Degree of State Intervention

Yun-Peng Chu, Tain-Jy Chen and Been-Lon Chen

I. PARADIGM OF DEVELOPMENT: THE HISTORICAL PERSPECTIVE

1. Japan

The rise of capitalism in the West, as described in North (1973) and North (1990, 1991) and many other works, has been attributed to the virtuous interaction between businessmen and the state, with the former taking the lead. It is noted in D.C. North and T.R. North that associations of merchants would typically introduce experimental institutions designed to reduce transaction costs. If the results were successful, merchants would then push the state to enact new laws or revise existing laws, which could then be effectively enforced, to provide a legal foundation for these new institutions. The reduced transaction costs then made possible the expansion of trade and the scale of production, generating further need for new institutions, thereby repeating the process. Trade and commerce boomed as a result.

It was a revolution from below. Throughout the late Middle Ages and the advent of the modern era, the influence of the merchant class increased, while that of the aristocracy waned. In this way the expansion of maritime trade — that of the market economy — the industrial revolution, the proliferation of capitalist institutions and the establishment of democracy, were the many facets of the same process. Such an understanding of the process of industrialization gives rise to the "free-market, minimalist state" paradigm for economic development which, as pointed out by Ohno, rests on two assumptions: (1) markets will emerge naturally and (2) they will develop hand in hand with the arrival of liberal democracy. In reality, the experience of the developing countries, or even of the latecomers among the developed countries such as Germany, shows otherwise. The Anglo-Saxon model that was characteristic of the forerunners of the industrial revolution was not followed by the latecomers, for an obvious reason: namely that the industrial revolution in the latter countries was more a deliberate effort to catch up with the forerunners than a spontaneous evolution.

In Europe, the deliberate catching-up process was already apparent (see for example, Polanyi 1944). Outside Europe, it was even more so. In Asia, around the 1850s, the previously stable order was almost totally destroyed by the advent of Western forces. China was forced open, as was Japan, followed by the other Asian economies. The arrival of the West meant more than simply the arrival of gunboats. It meant the arrival of a civilization that was thought superior to the existing Eastern ones. The survival of the countries and their civilizations were thought to be at stake. In short, it was a crisis of a scale rarely seen in the history of these nations.

In Japan, the first Asian country to later become developed, the response was a consolidation of the state. The Meiji Restoration of 1868 was essentially a nationalist movement to effect the concentration of power at the top, in order to save Japan from being ruined by foreigners (see for example, Yoshihara 1994). The state took the lead in setting up the hardware and software of military-force-oriented industrialization, as well as of the establishment of the market economy, in an effort to emulate and to catch up with the West.

In the process, private enterprises were part of the state-led efforts. Big businesses were protected and given privileges by the state; in return, they followed the directions given by the state, which was governed by a coalition of officials who understood the West better than the populace and were determined to westernize Japan quickly in order to save it. It was a "revolution" from the top.

Led by the state, the social-ranking system was abolished in 1869; the first telegraphic service was in operation in 1870; the first postal service was inaugurated in 1871; compulsory education was introduced in 1872 and the first railway service was opened in the same year; the Bank of Japan was established in 1882; by 1886 the paper-money system was established; by 1890 commerce laws (allowing joint-stock companies) were enacted; by 1890 banking regulations had been set up and became effective in 1893; in 1887 the stock exchange was established, and subsequently strengthened in 1891; the gold standard was adopted in 1897. Tariff autonomy was partially restored in 1899 and fully restored by 1911.

In 1889 a Constitution was promulgated and the first general election was held in the following year. But according to many scholars (for example, Nobuo 1990), those were not really acts of democratization. It was an effort, again from the top, to gear the entire population towards rapid industrialization, under strong leadership of the state, as before. The Taisho democracy movement actually ended in failure. Japan became more oriented towards the concentration of power. It was the era of "absolutist, nationalist militarism", an idea as alien to the rise of democracy based on individual rights as one could possibly imagine.

After World War II, even though the large *zaibatsu* prominent in the previous nationalist-capitalist regime were largely dissolved and a Western style of Parliamentary democracy established, the Japanese model was still very different from the *laissez-faire-cum*-liberal-democratic paradigm. The state was heavily involved in directing industrial development, in credit rationing and in the overseas expansion of Japanese enterprises. Political competition of the Western style was more apparent than real, at least during the 1960s and 1970s.

2. Taiwan before World War II

In Taiwan, another "model" of successful development, the story has been more complicated. Nevertheless, it is doubtful that the *laissez-faire-cum*-liberal-democratic paradigm can be said to be characteristic of its history of economic development, at least in the early stages. In the later half of the 19th century, after Taiwan was ruled by the Ching Dynasty and one of its ports was forced open along with several others in China, trade in tea boomed. Foreign trading companies controlled the export trade and the manufacturing of the choicer varieties, while local merchants and producers were involved in the plantation, in the transportation and in some manufacturing. It can be said that the commercialization of tea expanded at a rapid rate without much state involvement. But it is equally clear that commercialization of the tea industry was not by itself able to initiate sustainable economic growth island-wide.

The first effort to improve inland transportation as well as other infrastructure for military and commercial purposes was made by a Ching official, Liu Ming-Chuan, who was the governor of Taiwan in 1887–91. This effort had limited success both because governor Liu lacked an able and corruption-free staff and because his tenure as governor was not sufficiently long. After Taiwan became a colony of Japan in 1895, economic growth really picked up. Reynolds (1982) marks that year as the point of take-off of Taiwan's economy. The tea trade continued, joined later by sugar and rice. In the later years of the Japanese colonization, the fertilizer and textiles industries were also established. It has been estimated that the national product grew at an average rate of 45% per decade during 1903–40 (Ho 1978, p. 26). Even though the average Taiwanese family was still quite poor, given that a substantial part of the surplus was siphoned off to Japan, the quality of life became much better than before Japanese rule.

As in Japan, the development in Taiwan under Japanese rule was largely state-led. It was the state that established the various capitalist institutions. Law and order were maintained by the establishment of courts and police forces. Land ownership was clarified through a series of land surveys, land reforms and establishment of a registration system. Measurements were unified and regulated. A central bank under the name of Bank of Taiwan was established in 1899. In name it was a joint venture of different sources of Japanese private capital; in practice it was created through the mobilization and heavy subsidization by the government. The bank then issued currency, first silver-based then gold-based, which gradually became the standard unit of exchange. By 1911–14 the same monetary law as in Japan was enforced in Taiwan (see for example, Davidson 1903; and Yanaihara 1929).

In 1900 the Taiwan Sugar Making Company was established by Japanese capital (mainly Mitsui), again under heavy government subsidy and mobilization. Thereafter, other private firms followed, all supplementing the state policy of modernizing the sugar-making industry. The government coerced the farmers to sell their lands to sugar companies, provided these companies monopsony rights, and saw to the establishment of a cartel association.

Yanaihara (1929) summarizes the nature of state-led efforts to favour the growth of Japanese capital, to wipe out or weaken non-

Japanese foreign commercial power, and to promote economic development as follows:

1. Infrastructure: law and order, land surveys, monetary reform and the measurement system.
2. National capital: the railway, which became a state enterprise in 1899 after private efforts failed; harbors; and forestry.
3. State subsidization: the total subsidy for sugar during 1900–25 was estimated at 24.7 million yen. It is worth noting that the six largest sugar manufacturers made up 94% of all registered capital around 1925. The authorities also subsidized the Bank of Taiwan, Taiwan Power (half state, half private) and later a giant irrigation project in southern Taiwan.
4. Personnel: numerous retired officials worked for the private sector.
5. Mobilization of private capital: private capitalists were mobilized and encouraged to start new businesses in Taiwan. Taiwanese capitalists were also encouraged but became merely the suppliers of fund; the real managing power belonged to the Japanese.

In the process, monopolies were frequently granted or created. For example, in 1899 the camphor trade was monopolized by the government, which then entrusted Mitsui to do the actual trading. The same story applies for opium, salt, tobacco and wine.

So in Taiwan throughout the period of Japanese colonization, a revolution from the top occurred just as in Japan during the same period. It was the state that designed strategies, implemented capitalist institutions and mobilized private capital. The result was impressive. Exports of rice to Japan constituted 12% of Japan's total rice consumption by the end of the 19th century, while those of sugar comprised two-thirds by 1925. There were trade surpluses in most of the later years of colonization, signifying net capital outflows.

3. Post-war Taiwan

Immediately after the War, Taiwan was returned to China and ruled by the Nationalist government, which confiscated all Japanese capital, state and private. Because Japanese capital dominated all sectors except rice farming, the extent of state ownership was pervasive. The state became the biggest capital owner as well as the biggest landlord. Because of the civil war and internal uprising, Taiwan was under *de facto* military rule until 1949. Then the Nationalist government retreated to Taiwan and dug in. In the 1950s, aside from continuing military strengthening, attention was paid to the reconstruction of infrastructure damaged during the war and to economic development. Because of the authoritarian power of the state and its extensive involvement in industry and commerce, it was again the leading and dominant force in shaping the direction of the economy. But there are important differences between Japan and Taiwan in the ways the state handled the economy. While before the war the state took *de facto* control of the economy directly or indirectly through its agent, big business, after the war although in the beginning the state itself was an economic giant, it gradually encouraged private enterprises, which it did not control, to participate in economic development.

Through consecutive development plans, various policies were taken. Table 5.1 lists chronologically economic policies in ten different categories considered by Li (1995) to be of vital importance. This table reveals the following:

1. During most of the 1950s, centralized control was imposed as the government tried to stabilize the economic situation following the chaotic inflation in 1949–50, when the Nationalist government retreated to Taiwan from its military defeat in mainland China. That was why the Economic Stabilization Board was established (Table 5.1G., 1952). Even though interest rate was maintained at high levels (Table 5.1B., 1949), domestic saving was insufficient, as was foreign exchange, and Taiwan had to rely on U.S. aid (Table 5.1B., International Capital Movement, 1950) to make ends meet. During this period the military threat from Communist China was imminent, so resources had to be spent on defence. Industrialization was encouraged through import substitution — behind high tariff walls (Table 5.1A., External Trade, 1951).

2. In the 1950s, agriculture was one of the major focuses of reform. A genuine and extensive land reform was carried out in 1952. Public land and land from landlords, who were forced to sell their land to the government, were distributed to tenants on a very large scale. In the process, the distribution of land ownership became more equal. In addition, the government gave stocks of public

enterprises as compensation to the landlords, who were encouraged to involve themselves in industrialization through such privatized public enterprises (Table 5.1C., 1954). So the tone was set: even though the government controlled the majority of the resources at the time, it was ready to encourage the private sector to take an important role in the process of economic development. Such an announcement (Table 5.1G., 1952) was made very early, perhaps at the suggestion of the U.S. aid representatives in Taipei. Direct investment by foreign nationals was also welcome, as indicated by the promulgation of relevant laws (Table 5.1B., International Capital Movement, 1955).

3. Towards the end of the 1950s, an important shift in policy occurred, perhaps also at the suggestion of U.S. representatives (Wade 1990). In 1958–59 the multiple foreign exchange rates were unified and the restrictive import quota and foreign exchange control systems discontinued (Table 5.1B., Foreign Exchange Rate, 1958 and 1960). In 1959 the Nineteen-point Economic and Fiscal Reform was adopted (Table 5.1A., Domestic, 1959), as the government intended to formally change its development strategy from import substitution to export expansion, and from state dominance to active private involvement (see Jacoby 1966; Wade 1990; and Li 1995). Concurrent with and as a follow-up to the reform, the Statute for Encouragement of (Private) Investment was promulgated (Table 5.1A., Domestic, 1960), the Economic Stabilization Board was disbanded and the Council for U.S. Aid was first expanded (Table 5.1G., 1958), then reorganized into a planning agency (Table 5.1G., 1963). Export-led industrialization was also the main focus of the Third Four-Year Plan (Table 5.1G., 1961).

4. Although the 1960s and early 1970s saw tremendous growth of private, export-oriented enterprises, the government was still active. It established the stock exchange in 1962 (Table 5.1A., Domestic, 1962) and the bond market in 1974 (Table 5.1A., Domestic, 1974), began establishing export processing zones in 1966 (Table 5.1A., External Trade, 1966), more actively promoted foreign direct investment inflow (Table 5.1B., International Capital Movement, 1965), and set up an Industry Bureau under the Ministry of Economic Affairs in 1970 to better plan and implement industrial development policies (Table 5.1G., 1970). On the technology front, it established a defence-oriented research institute in 1965 (Table 5.1F., 1965), a

committee to promote applied technology in 1966 (Table 5.1F., 1966), an agency to promote basic research in 1967 (Table 5.1F., 1967), and a research institute to promote industrial technology in 1973 (Table 5.1F., 1973). With regard to human capital, it extended compulsory education from six to nine years in 1968 (Table 5.1E., 1968) and promoted vocational education and manpower training in 1970 (Table 5.1E., 1970). The government was also able to maintain the good "fundamentals" as emphasized in World Bank (1993). It turned the government budget deficit into surplus (Table 5.1A., Domestic, 1961 and 1964), further rationalized the tax system (Table 5.1A., Domestic, 1969), and maintained price stability (Table 5.1B., Interest Rate, 1961–71).

5. From 1973–74 to 1980–81 the world experienced two oil-price shocks. Taiwan was also a victim of stagflation during both crises. To offset the decline in export demand, the government embarked on large-scale infrastructure-building public investments (Table 5.1D., 1973 and 1978; and Table 5.1B., International Capital Movements, 1973). To maintain competitiveness, it continued its efforts to enhance science and technology by investing in the related manpower (Table 5.1F., 1975), formulating science and technology development programs (Table 5.1F., 1979), setting up an agency to promote the information industry (Table 5.1F., 1979), and establishing the now famous Hsinchu Science-Based Industrial Park (Table 5.1F., 1979). There was also during this period a moderate softening of import controls (Table 5.1A., External Trade, 1971) and that of controls on the foreign exchange rate (Table 5.1B., Foreign Exchange Rate, 1973 and 1978), mainly as a result of external pressure or changes in external conditions.

6. Since the mid-1980s Taiwan has implemented important liberalization policies. In 1985 regulation on interest rates was removed (Table 5.1B., Interest Rate, 1985); in 1987 foreign exchange transactions by domestic residents were deregulated (Table 5.1B., Foreign Exchange Rate, 1987); and throughout the 1980s tariffs were further reduced, with the top rate lowered to 50% by 1988 (Table 5.1A., External Trade, 1983–88). The first policy was very likely a genuine move towards liberalization. The second and third measures were more probably the results of pressure than of subjective intention. Still, the government was active in many other ways. It rationalized the tax system by adopting the value-added

TABLE 5.1 Economic Policies in Taiwan, 1949–92

A. Fiscal, Trade and Financial Policies

Domestic
1955	Consolidated income tax introduced
1959	Nineteen-point Economic and Fiscal Reform
1960	Statute for Encouragement of Investment
1961	Budge deficit under control
1962	Stock exchange established
1964	Budget surplus realized
1969	Tax Reform Commission established
1974	Bond market established
1982	Small budget deficit
1983	Introduction of Bill for Value-added Tax
1986	Implementation of value-added tax
1987	Calling rate raised on government bond issuance
1987	Tax Reform Commission established
1988	Amendment of Land Tax Law
1990	Statute for the encouragement of private infrastructure

External Trade
1951	Tariff protection and import controls
1956	Customs duty rebate on exports
1966	Export-processing zones established
1971	Liberalization of import controls
1971	Tariff rate adjustments within 50% authorized by law
1983	Further tariff reductions
1983	Further liberalization of import controls
1986	New customs valuation system introduced
1987	Extensive tariff reduction. Top rate reduced from 67.5% to 58%
1988	Further tariff reduction. Top rate reduced to 50%
1990	Foreign Trade Law drafted

B. Monetary and Foreign Exchange Policies

Interest Rate
1949	High interest rate policy
1961-71	Price stability
1972	Combating inflation with high interest rates
1974	Bond market established
1976	Money market established
1980	Interest rate liberalization
1985	Interest rate regulations discontinued
1985	Prime rate system introduced
1985	Issuing of beneficiary certificate approved

(cont'd overleaf)

TABLE 5.1 *(cont'd)*

B. Monetary and Foreign Exchange Policies

Interest Rate
1986   Structure of interest rates on deposits simplified residents to freely hold and use foreign exchange
1987   Insurance market opened to U.S. companies
1987   Bank credit rating system established free price negotiation
1988   Restrictions relaxed on establishment of security brokerage and trading firms
1989   Bank Law revised to allow the entry of new private banks
1989   Interest rate restrictions relaxed
1991   Promoting privatization of state-owned financial institutions
1991   Opening of 15 new private banks
1992   Insurance law revised

Foreign Exchange Rate
1958   Foreign exchange reform
1958   Import foreign exchange quota system discontinued
1960   Unitary exchange rate
1973   Appreciation of NT dollar 1st in 1973 and 1978
1978   Floating exchange rate introduced
1983   Rationalization of foreign exchange regulations
1986   Appreciation of NT dollar
1986   Amendment of foreign exchange regulations
1987   Relaxing foreign exchange controls and allowing
1986   Structure of interest rates on deposits simplified residents to freely hold and use foreign exchange
1989   Establishing a new exchange rate system based on free price negotiation

International Capital Movement
1950   Inflow of U.S. aid
1955   Statute for Investment by Foreign Nationals
1965   Termination of U.S. aid
1965   Inflow of private foreign investment and loans
1973   Raising of substantial loans to support large infrastructure and heavy industries projects
1983   Liberalization of capital market
1983   Statute for International Financial Activities enacted
1990   Allowing foreign institutional investors to directly invest in local stock market

TABLE 5.1 *(cont'd)*

C. *Government Enterprises and National Construction*

1954	Transfer of four major government enterprises (cement, paper, agriculture & mining) to private ownership
1973	Ten major development projects
1978	Twelve new development projects
1981	Evaluation of government enterprises
1984	Fourteen major infrastructure projects
1987	Listing of public enterprise shares on stock market
1990	Public Construction Supervisory Board set up
1991	Statute for the Privatization of State-owned Enterprises revised
1991	China Petrochemical Corporation issues shares on stock market
1992	China Steel Corporation issues shares on stock market

D. *Agricultural Policy*

1949	Rice-Fertilizer Barter Program
1952	First land reform
1952	Land-to-the-Tiller Program
1970	Mechanization of farming
1973	Rice-Fertilizer Barter Program discontinued
1973	Statute for Agricultural Development
1974	Price guarantee of rice
1981	Second land reform
1981	Promotion of joint management, contract farming and enlargement of average farm size
1984	First Six-Year Program for cultivation of non-rice crops (1984–89)
1988	Guidelines for the Implementation Of Accelerated Rural Development promulgated
1990	Second Six-Year Program to convert rice fields to cultivation of non-rice crops (1990–95)
1991	Integrated Agricultural Adjustment Program (1991–97)

E. *Manpower and Labour Policies*

1960	Employment and dismissal of labourers regulated
1968	Compulsory education extended to nine years
1968	Family planning officially encouraged
1969	Guidelines of Population Policy promulgated
1970	Promotion of vocational education and manpower training
1981	Employment and Vocational Training Administration established
1981	Technical manpower training in co-operation with foreign enterprises
1985	Labour Standards Law
1986	Council of Labour Affairs established under Executive Yuan

(cont'd overleaf)

TABLE 5.1 *(cont'd)*

E. Manpower and Labour Policies

1987	Employment Services Act drafted
1987	Population Policy Guidelines and Program for the Promotion of Population Policies implemented
1987	Law for the Settlement of Labor Disputes revised
1988	Integration of technical and vocational education systems
1988	Regulations governing universities and colleges revised
1990	New Family Planning Program implemented
1991	Third-Stage Working Program for Strengthening Vocational Training (1991–97) implemented
1991	Labor Standards Law revised
1991	Labor Insurance Act revised
1991	Labor Inspection Law revised
1992	Employment Services Act promulgated
1992	Five-Year Programme for Development and Improvement of Adult Education (1992–96)

F. Development of Science and Technology

1965	Chung Shan Institute of Science and Technology set up
1966	Committee for R & D on Applied Technology set up
1967	National Science Council set up
1973	Industrial Technology Research Institute set up
1975	Development of high-calibre manpower in natural science and engineering
1979	Science & Technology Development Program Formulated
1979	Institute for Information Industry set up
1979	Hsinchu Science-Based Industrial Park set up
1980	Strengthening defense research and development
1981	Promotion of R & D
1981	Academia Sinica first Five-Year Plan approved
1982	Amendment of Trademark and Patent Laws
1983	Synchrocyclotron Radiation Project established
1983	Programme for strengthening the education, training and recruitment of high-level science & technology personnel formulated
1984	Defense Science and Technology (S & T) Development Program announced
1985	Academia Sinica second Five-Year Plan approved
1986	Ten-Year Science and Technology Development Plan (1986–95)
1990	Statute for Industrial Upgrading announced
1991	Third Five-Year Plan of Academia Sinica (1991–96) approved
1991	Ten emerging industries and eight key technologies selected for development
1992	Long-Term Science and Technology Development Plan (1991–2002) implemented
1992	Mid-Term Science and Technology Development Plan (1991–96) implemented

TABLE 5.1 *(cont'd)*

G. *Economic Development Planning*

1952	First Four-Year Economic Development Plan (1953–56)
1952	Economic Stabilization Board (ESB) set up
1952	Policy of assigning to private sector principal role in industrial development reaffirmed
1957	Second Four-Year Economic Development Plan (1957–60)
1958	ESB disbanded and Council for U.S. Aid (CUSA) expanded
1961	Third Four-Year Economic Development Plan (1961–64)
1963	Reorganization of CUSA into Council for International Economic Co-operation and Development (CIECD)
1965	Fourth Four-Year Economic Development Plan (1965–68)
1969	Fifth Four-Year Economic Development Plan (1969–72)
1970	Industry Bureau established
1973	Sixth Four-Year Economic Development Plan (1973–76)
1973	Reorganization of CIECD into Economic Planning Council (EPC)
1976	Six-Year Economic Development Plan (1976–81)
1977	Reorganization of EPC into Council for Economic Planning and Development (CEPD)
1980	Ten-Year projection announced (CEPD) 1980–89
1982	Reverting to a new Four-Year Economic Development Plan (1982–85)
1986	Ninth Medium-Term Economic Development Plan (1986–89)
1986	Perspectives of the Taiwan economy up to the year 2000
1990	Tenth Medium-Term Economic Development Plan (1990–95)
1991	Six-Year National Development Plan for Taiwan (1991–96)

SOURCE: Li (1995), revised by authors.

tax (Table 5.1A., Domestic, 1983 and 1986), established a bank credit rating system in 1987 (Table 5.1B., Interest Rate, 1987), embarked on 14 major infrastructure projects (Table 5.1C., 1984) and reinforced R&D-related measures (Table 5.1F., 1980–86). The government also strengthened labor protection laws and institutions (Table 5.1F., 1985 and 1986). There was, however, a major government failure during this period. During 1986–87 when the government tried to prevent the New Taiwan (NT) dollar from appreciating, it intervened by purchasing a large amount of U.S. dollars but did not sterilize the operation adequately; as a result, the money supply soared. Imports became cheaper as the NT dollar appreciated after intervention failed, so general commodity prices remained stable or even fell. The excess liquidity found its way first to the stock market, then to the real estate market, thus creating gigantic asset price inflation, namely a bubble, which will be discussed in more detail below.

7. Beginning in the late 1980s and the 1990s, liberalization proceeded at a much greater speed. In 1988 new brokerage firms were allowed to be set up (Table 5.1B., Interest Rate, 1988); in 1991 15 new private banks were allowed to enter the banking market (Table 5.1B., Interest Rate, 1989 and 1991); in 1990 efforts were made to encourage private enterprises to engage in public infrastructure construction (Table 5.1A., Domestic, 1990), and foreign institutional investors were allowed to invest directly in the local stock market (Table 5.1B., 1990). Also in 1990 the across-the-board tax-holidays for new investment were replaced by selective incentives: only new investment on automation, research and development, and pollution prevention enjoy such holidays, as stated in the newly enacted Statute for Industrial Upgrading (Table 5.1F., 1990). During 1991–92 efforts were made to privatize major public enterprises (Table 5.1C., 1991–92). The government still took an active role in technology upgrading. In 1991 for example, it planned to promote the development of ten emerging industries and eight key technologies (Table 5.1F., 1991). It also expanded the Scientific Industrial Park to other parts of Taiwan. But the trend was clear. The role the government played became less of an athlete, and more of a referee, or sometimes a coach. There was no indication that the government planned the transition in advance, although it did not resist the political pressure once it had begun. The transition was consistent with intensive democratization during this period and the concurrent rise of the influence of big private enterprises in national policies.

So we have seen above that the government took an active role in almost every stage of Taiwan's development. The role changed a great a deal in the 1990s, but before that the government was an athlete, a coach and a referee, all at the same time in many cases. In the 1950s and 1960s it protected (in some cases created) domestic manufacturers (see the classic Formosa Plastic story to be described elsewhere in this volume) and helped them to expand their sales to the international markets. In the 1970s and 1980s the government again took an active role to ward off the threats posed by the two oil-price crises and the NT dollar appreciation crisis.

Many scholars attribute Taiwan's successful post-war development to involvement of private enterprise. That may be true. But as is clear from above discussion, as well as from the cases of the man-made fibre and electronics industries to be discussed later, it was the state that provided the protective shelter in the beginning, took measures to reduce or remove the risks associated with industrial pioneering, and offered various institutional preferences (for example, tax rebates) and conveniences (for example, export-processing zones), not to mention the fact that it supplied the basic services of maintaining law and order, maintained a non-inflationary environment (see entries in Table 5.1A. on government budgets and Table 5.1B. on interest rates), constructed and maintained adequate infrastructure (see entries on national construction in Table 5.1C.), and invested in human capital improvement (see entries on manpower policies in Table 5.1E.). It is very doubtful that the economy would have grown as rapidly as it did in the absence of these policies.

Sometimes the government even had to "install" markets, as shown by the experience of establishing the stock market (with centralized trading), the bond market, and the money market in 1962, 1974 and 1976 respectively (see Table 5.1A. and 5.1B.). In the establishment of the capital market, for example, it first enacted laws and regulations, and then mobilized state-owned financial concerns to invest in and establish the Taiwan Stock Exchange. Unlike the Champagne Fair described in North (1991), these markets were the creation of the state, which was clearly emulating the capitalist institutions existing in the developed countries.

Such a view of the state is consistent with those of Fei, Ranis and Kuo (1979), Ranis (1979), Kuo, Ranis and Fei (1981), Kuo (1983,1997), Amsden (1985), Gold (1986), Wade (1990), Weiss (1994), Li (1995) and Chen (1996). Table 5.2 gives a conceptual framework of state successes *versus* failures. It is clear that for basic public goods, lack of or inappropriate state efforts can undermine economic development. This part of state activities is often seen by the neoclassical economists as a necessary evil. In World Bank (1993) it is emphasized that the government of most East Asian countries has been able to register a high score on these items.

It is in the area of higher-order public goods that the World Bank report may have understated or failed to give due attention to the contributions made by East Asian governments. This is not to say that

TABLE 5.2 Taiwan: Government Economic Successes and Failures

Successes		Failures
On Basic Public Goods		*Failures*
1. Infrastructure construction and maintenance	1.	Insufficient or excessive infrastructure
2. General law and order, including protection of private property	2.	Lack of law and order
3. Stable macroeconomic environment, including fiscal and monetary disciplines	3.	Lack of fiscal and monetary disciplines leading to unstable macroeconomic environment
4. Human capital improvement	4.	Insufficient or excessive or wrongly placed human capital investment
5. Redistributive policies to balance efficiency with equity	5.	Absence of redistributive measures in face of excessive inequality and/or prevalence of poverty, or excessive redistributive policies leading to chaos
	6.	Risk associated with unstable government policies due to frequent transfers or changes in ideas/personnel

TABLE 5.2 *(cont'd)*

Successes	Failures
On Public Goods of Higher Orders	
6. Starting or subsidizing risky but worthy projects that cannot emerge under imperfect capital markets	7. Starting or subsidizing unworthy projects due to lack of knowledge or corruption
7. Co-ordinating or mobilizing groups of private enterprises to engage in joint ventures which may not emerge otherwise due to their size, riskiness (themselves results of imperfect capital markets) and/or transaction costs involved in private negotiations	8. Government involvement in co-ordinating or mobilizing private enterprises to participate in joint ventures can result in wrong or excessive investment or may undermine private efforts that would otherwise have succeeded
8. Protecting infant industries to allow learning and realization of scale economies without which they cannot compete with imports	9. Protected industries never learn or achieve scale economy but become vested and influential interests
9. Establishing those capitalist institutions which are otherwise not forthcoming and which need to operate under state-enforced regulations	10. Establishing capitalist institutions prematurely
10. Subsidizing or itself undertaking activities that have positive spill-overs	11. Subsidizing activities that do not really have spillover effects
	12. Public enterprises or R&D institutions are inefficient and wasteful

these governments never make mistakes. Taiwan's government is no exception. It gives lengthy protection to and has spent large sums of money on the automobile industry which to date is not able to compete in the global market. Many of its public enterprises are inefficiently run, etc. And, as indicated above, it created a bubble by intervening in the foreign exchange market. But by and large, it seems that the effect of state successes has overwhelmed that of failures on higher-order public goods.

However, it is important to point out that the probability of net success is itself a function of other factors. These factors change over time, that is, they evolve over different stages of development of the society, and therefore so will the probability of net success. As the probability changes, so will the optimal role of the state. Some of these factors, such as the nature of the government's decision-making process, will be analyzed below. Suffice it to mention here that many scholars in Taiwan now think that while the state still has to fulfil its duty of providing basic public goods, the quality of which has deteriorated over the years, the time has come for the state to refrain from being directly involved in the production of goods and services, and to reorient its policies towards the establishment of fair rules of competition and towards such public goods as environmental protection, which has been ignored in the past. Such a view of the subjective optimal role of the state is consistent with the objective reality in Taiwan — as indicated above, when private enterprises became more influential along with intensive democratization, they demanded a greater role in the economy. There will be more discussion on this later.

II. INDUSTRIAL POLICIES, PRODUCT CYCLES AND TECHNOLOGICAL CAPABILITIES

As is clear from Mizaki (1995), international factors have been important in shaping the development of East Asian economies. The flying geese paradigm and the multiplex catching-up process, first proposed by Akamatsu (1935, 1962), then elaborated by Kojima, Yamazawa, Watanabe and others, are useful conceptual tools to understand the linkage effects among different industries in different countries over different periods of time (or stages of development). Had the flying geese phenomenon been automatic, there would be no role for the state or its industrial policies. This is, of course, hardly the case. Some industries in some countries catch up with those in the leading countries, while others lag behind. The factors contributing to the difference in performance can be identified by a thorough analysis of different sectors in different countries over time.

In a single-country study like this one, such an analysis is not possible. What is available is the experience of different industries over time, based on which many studies are undertaken. Although their importance varies over time and across industries, industrial policies have generally been found to be significantly important in shaping the pattern and speed of industrial development (see for example, Amsden 1985; Wade 1990; and Hsiao 1994). For non-industry-specific industrial policies in Taiwan, according to Hsu (1996), the inauguration of the Statute for the Encouragement of Investment (1960–90, Statute for Industrial Upgrading thereafter) has been the most important. The effects of two policy packages included in the statute are discussed: tax reduction and industrial land use policy.

The impact of business tax reduction for investment is gauged to be positive though not substantial for the period of the 1960s and 1970s, when Taiwan's industrial growth was at its fastest. After the second energy crisis, additional tax reduction for investment was implemented (in 1981), and studies have found effects of larger magnitudes. As for the land use policy, the freedom (1960–80) to convert farm land into industrial land (even when scattered or isolated) has had a major effect on reducing the cost of investment, particularly if the factory is located in the countryside. Even though the effects of these formal non-industry-specific policies do not appear overwhelming, it is important to note the general attitude of the government towards investment. Whenever investment slowed down, it would be widely discussed in the press and within the government, which would then take action deemed necessary to remedy the situation. In some instances, the government would carry out new investment in industry by itself. In the early 1970s, for example, when Taiwan was in a severe recession as result of the first oil crisis, the government deliberately inaugurated large infrastructure and industrial investment projects, summarily called the Ten Major Development Projects to maintain an adequate rate of overall investment when private investment was sluggish (see Table 5.1C.).

It is correctly pointed out in Li (1995) that many government policies were not based on well-thought-out plans prepared far in advance.

Many were simply the government's responses to practical problems, crises, difficulties, etc., at the time they arrived, anticipated or not. An important example is the shift from import substitution to export promotion. The shift was put into effect both because the domestic market had been saturated for many products and because the United States was going to terminate its aid to the island and Taiwan had to earn hard currency by itself.

If this has been the case for non-industry-specific policies, it has been even more so for industry-specific ones. This study is not meant to discuss all the industries in detail (Hsiao 1994, contains a good discussion of a number of different industries), but it will provide an in-depth investigation of two industries, electronics and man-made fibre, appearing appearing in later chapters. Details will not be presented here, but the important findings can be noted, and we will begin with the man-made fibre industry. The development of the textile industry in the 1950s and 1960s gave rise to that of the man-made fibre industry later. The following are the related important policies adopted and the concurrent industrial developments:

1. High tariffs on textiles for import substitution (1949–65); production of textiles rose substantially.
2. As the production of man-made textiles increased, the demand for man-made fibre rose. To import-substitute (remember Taiwan was in severe trade deficit and U.S. aid was about to be terminated, see for example, Yin 1963), the government set up in 1957 publicly owned (later privatized) China Man-Made Fibre Corporation, a joint venture between Taiwan and Teijrin of Japan, to produce rayon.
3. Inauguration of the Third Four-Year Plan (1961–64) for export promotion; export of textiles rose sharply. The demand for man-made textiles rose faster than for cotton textiles; the former accounted for more than half of exports by 1968.
4. Under the pressure of Long-Term Agreement, and also to import-substitute, the state-sponsored China Man-Made Fibre Corporation set up a new company to produce nylon in 1962 (under licensing agreements with Chemtex of the United States and Zimmer of West Germany), and another (a joint venture with Teijrin of Japan) to produce polyester in 1964.

5. A private PVC-producing company, which in the beginning (in 1957) was also a creation of the government in its efforts to mobilize private entrepreneurs, began making acrylic in 1967 (signing a licensing agreement with Japan's Asahi in 1968).
6. Numerous private investments, mostly under licensing agreements with foreign firms to acquire technology, then took place after that.
7. Taiwan's production and then exports of man-made fibre boomed. By 1986 Taiwan had become the world's third largest producer of man-made fibre, after the United States and Japan. In 1989 Taiwan's output surpassed Japan's and became the second largest.

The story of the electronics industry is summarized as follows (see also Chen 1992):

1. In the 1950s, under import protection, Taiwan began producing radios for the domestic market.
2. Experience from making radios gave rise to exports of transistor radios, which began in the early 1960s. Exports rose to 2 million sets by 1966.
3. The government set up television broadcasting in 1962; a domestic market for television sets emerged. Local firms began production under licensing agreement or joint venture with Japanese firms. Segregated from the local-market-oriented firms was a group of multinationals, mostly U.S.-based, which came to Taiwan in the 1960s and produced television sets exclusively for exports. By 1973, exports reached 3.8 million units (of monochrome sets).
4. State-owned television station began broadcasting programs in colour in 1969. Local-market-oriented firms began production of colour television sets, as did multinationals producing for export. The former joined the export drive later. By 1978 total production reached 1.3 million sets, the majority of which was exported.
5. General Instrument of the United States established a wholly-owned subsidiary in Taiwan in 1964 to produce electronic parts. Local content regulations were imposed by the government in 1965 in order to nurture a local parts industry for electronic products (including televisions). Such regulations forced Japanese televsion-set makers to transfer parts manufacturing technology to their local

partners in Taiwan. Other local firms emulating technology from multinational firms from other countries (for the lower-end products) or acquiring them through licensing (for the higher-end products) also entered the market. The government itself engineered a joint venture between major local television-set manufacturers and RCA to embark on CRT production in 1971. Production of this and other electronic parts expanded, for both the home and export markets. In the home market many parts were re-exported after assembling, of course. (Such a solid parts industry laid the foundation for the production of calculators in 1972 and digital watches in 1975. Experience in designing and manufacturing digital products in turn laid the foundation for the transition to personal computers and parts in the 1980s and 1990s.)

6. In 1976 the state-owned Electronics Research and Services Organization (ERSO) acquired from RCA the technology to produce complementary metal oxide semiconductor chips through a joint project, which later spun off to become a private firm, the now famous United Microelectronics Corporation (UMC), in 1980. Before that, most operations in both local and multinational firms were limited to the assembly and testing of integrated circuits (ICs).

7. The establishment of IC-design houses began in the 1980s, again in association with the (former) staff of ERSO. Before long many investors joined in. There was a derived demand for foundry services. The government set up the now famous Taiwan Semiconductor Manufacturing Co. (TSMC), inviting Royal Philips Electronics ("Philips" in short) to take 27.5% of the shares, to provide such services. ERSO acquired the static random access ram technology from Philips and it then spun off around 200 personnel to join TSMC. Other investors later joined.

8. By the 1990s, Taiwan had developed an electronics industry (including personal computers and parts) that was among the largest in the world.

From the history of the two industries, it can be seen that product-specific industrial policies played an important role in the development of both industries. They took the form of (1) import protection, (2) the imposition of such regulations as local content requirement, and (3) the setting up or engineering, by the state, of joint ventures of manufacturing plants and research institutions. There was no given formula, and the timing and approach depended on which point in the course of development of specific products Taiwan was on at the time.

Success is not always guaranteed. The government took similar steps — import protection, attempts to engineer joint ventures, local content requirements, subsidization of research and development — for the development of the automobile industry. However, until today this industry cannot compete in the international market. Most, if not all, of the firms were set up to overcome the tariff/quota barriers to imports.

Nor is heavy state intervention always necessary. For the bicycle industry, for example, although there was import protection in the beginning, that was about all the government did (in terms of industry-specific policies). In the early 1960s even though overall policies had shifted from import substitution to export promotion, bicycle exports remained almost non-existent. It was in the late 1960s, when the U.S. market expanded quickly and Japan's rising wages prevented it from providing cheap bicycles in large quantities, that orders began to be shifted to Taiwan. Once they began, the industry boomed. By the mid-1980s, Taiwan had become the world's largest exporter of bicycles.

In conclusion, when they are working at their best, industrial policies are actions taken by the government to correct or remedy various kinds of market failures (to create various kinds of public goods). There could be a strong demand for such actions when (1) the industry is in its infancy, (2) a great deal of risk is involved, (3) a great deal of capital is needed, and (4) further development requires considerable efforts on research and development. The government can also play a key role in enhancing the technological capability of the economy by setting up publicly owned research institutions which would acquire foreign technology through licensing or joint-venture arrangements. Industry-specific policies can fail. This is likely to be the case if dependence on the domestic market is perpetuated. Local firms can become vested interests and hold the government hostage. After a period of protection if local firms have yet to become competitive, the government could be in a dilemma: if it gives up import protection, local firms which it has nurtured for such a long time, spending money and effort, will very likely fail immediately. If, on the other hand, protection is continued, then the lack of discipline provides even less incentive for the firms to become efficient. For products that do not require numerous technologies that are difficult to emulate through reverse engineering and other available means, industry-specific policies are not always needed, except for the initial import protection. Many products in the light manufacturing sector belong to this category. So industrial policies are not always necessary, as noted above.

The optimal type and extent of intervention in the form of industrial policies may differ across countries. Factors on both demand and supply sides are both important. The demand side has been elaborated above: it really depends on the stage of development and life cycles of the products. The supply side has a lot to do with the quality of civil servants and the nature of the collective decision-making process, to which we now turn.

III. THE POLITICAL ECONOMY OF DEVELOPMENT

The nature of the collective decision-making process depends on the pattern of the political regime, which varies from one country to another and is very much path-dependent. The Anglo-Saxon model works optimally by having a periodically elected government, which during its rule is answerable to a legislative body. The protection of basic human rights, including minority rights, is set down in various laws and enforced by a judiciary system. Such a regime, under ideal circumstances, would either find or mould a consensus among the majority of the population, whose collective wills are carried out by the government, while at the same time the possible abuse of majority power is prevented by the law, and the possible abuse of executive power is preventable or remediable through the enforcement of laws by the court, by the legislative procedure, and by periodic elections.

There are those who believe that Asian cultures are fundamentally different from Western cultures, which are based on the foundation of liberal democracy (see for example, Huntington 1996). So the forms of democracy that emerge in Asia will be different from the models understood and implemented in the West. There are also those who believe that both liberal democracy and freely operating market economy reflect human nature better than any other system, so in the long run there will be an ultimate convergence of political and economic institutions in all human societies (see for example, Fukuyama 1992).

While the viewpoints of the two schools are apparently paradoxical, by deeper reasoning the difference is not as important as it sounds.

Even if there will be an ultimate convergence, there could be little doubt from the experience of mankind that institutions in most societies evolve over time in a path-dependent manner. The actual paths taken will, in general, be different. Also, when democracy and a freely operating market economy do appear, there is ample variety within the two broad concepts across countries, and there is no guarantee the two institutions will be sustained whenever they emerge. In effect, political scientists often talk about the "consolidation" of democracy, which could be fragile unless well "consolidated".

So the more interesting and important part, as far as an understanding of the Asian experience is concerned, is the pattern of the evolution of institutions. In questioning the culture-deterministic views of many scholars before him, Diamond (forthcoming, chapter 5) recently argued that political culture or attitude is itself often a dependent variable: it can change according to people's experience with various institutions. This is a powerful concept. At any point in time, the political institution is given (*the status quo*). It then changes due to the interplay of power among the élites, between the élites and forces external to the country, and between the élites and the masses. The interplay is affected by people's mind or attitude, which is itself affected by the outcome of the last round of the game. We will analyze and conceptualize the Taiwan situation after the war along this line of thinking.

Throughout Taiwan's history, external powers have played an important part. Immediately after the war, Taiwan was returned to China from Japan. The Nationalists first sent to rule the island inherited the assets and the political and economic power left by the Japanese, both public and private, as indicated above. They also had serious clashes with the local population, particularly the élites, many of whom were alienated. When the entire Nationalist government retreated to Taiwan, which became its last stronghold following its defeat in the mainland by the Communists, it was faced with the following realities: (1) a strong and imminent enemy across the Taiwan Strait, (2) aid was arriving from the United States, whose military and economic advisors were stationed in Taiwan, particularly after the eruption of the Korean War, (3) hostility among many of the Taiwanese élites towards the regime, and (4) the fact that it commanded an army that was large and obedient enough to quell any serious attempts to challenge its power at home.

It is clear from the "Political Event Matrix" in Fei and Chu (1996), which records chronologically the process of democratization in

Taiwan, that in the 1950s and 1960s rule was very much authoritarian. There were no real elections at the central government level. County and sub-county level elections were held periodically but there was no serious challenge to power as most of the politicians at the local level were more interested in local economic privileges than in the sharing of political power. Oddly enough the government actively preached democracy, which was taught in schools. The government rationalized the situation by arguing that it was a special time of military crisis and of the taking over of the mainland by the Communists. Full democracy would be granted once the mainland was recovered.

The authoritarian Nationalist government put technocrats in charge of the economy. Several historians argue that many of these people in executive positions performed their duties well. The existence of a team in the government that is competent and fairly clean, is an important variable in the supply function of state services. Some states are extremely understaffed, corrupt, or both. When either of these conditions is absent, it is probably socially sub-optimal for the state to actively intervene in the economy, other things including the stage of development, being equal. Given any demand conditions, the socially optimal intervention in the economy should be greater, if there is a greater supply of competent and special-interest-independent state services. This is because when such a supply exists, the possibility of state intervention resulting in state successes as defined earlier exceeds that of state action resulting in failures.

Entering the 1970s and 1980s, Taiwan's authoritarianism gradually waned. At least two conditions made possible the movement towards democratization in Taiwan: (1) the existing members of the Legislature who were elected before 1949 were aging and passing away, while it became increasingly apparent that the Nationalist recovery of the mainland was not forthcoming in the foreseeable future; (2) the military threat from mainland China no longer appeared imminent; and (3) there had emerged a private sector that commanded a substantial amount of resources which the opposition power (mainly the alienated local élites) could tap. So first partial then across-the-board legislative re-elections were held, and the opposition became active and visible.

As democratization proceeded, and as these new institutions were perceived to have rendered greater political and media freedom at tolerable expenses of stability and orderliness, people's attitude towards democracy also changed. As is clear from the works of Diamond (forthcoming, cited earlier) and others, the popular support for democracy became greater over time and by the early 1990s it became dominant. This is why many of these scholars argue that democracy has been to a large extent "consolidated" in Taiwan.

This has also been the period when the private sector overgrew the state sector by a larger margin than in the 1950s and 1960s. Many of the capitalist institutions, previously established and nurtured by the state, now were operating in a mature manner, including the capital market. This lessened the demand for state interventions to correct capital market failures. But other demands emerged. Strong capitalist institutions need effective regulation: as traffic gets heavier, so does the demand for policemen to regulate traffic (and for frequent revisions of regulations that are no longer appropriate). Also, for some products (in their relevant cycles) and for some activities, there could still be demand for state intervention (subsidies and taxes to correct external economies and diseconomies).

So on the demand side, it cannot be said that state services are no longer needed. It is better to say that a different kind of services is demanded. On the supply side, although there does not seem to be a shortage of competent personnel, there have emerged two concerns. One is the time required to make a collective decision; it is generally longer under democracy, for many reasons not to be explored here. The other is the activity of special interest groups, as forcefully argued in Olson (1982), and not to be explored here either. From the viewpoint of the supply side (that is, holding demand fixed), both concerns cast doubt on the optimality of maintaining a level of state intervention as high as in the past. This view is consistent with the analysis given earlier.

IV. TAIWAN AND THE ASIAN CRISIS

The Asian financial crisis can be read differently by different people. To some, the crisis has been a confirmation of their long-held belief that the so-called Asian miracle was merely a facade. The fundamentals of the Asian economies have been weak for a long time, reflecting the accumulated results of years of economic mismanagement and corruption, inefficiency in resource allocation, and insufficient human resource investment. Consequently there was no way that growth could have been sustained.

To others, the crisis was not inevitable, but rather it was the unfortunate marriage of weak domestic financial institutions with large amounts of foreign short-term capital inflow in recent years, that caused the problem. According to this school of thought, the fundamentals have generally been good and things were moving in the right direction before the 1990s. But the authorities (particularly among the Association of Southeast Asian Nations [ASEAN] countries) opened up the capital account without first establishing the capability to deal with capital flows, nor undertaking a house-cleaning of their financial sector. So when foreign short-term capital arrived in the mid-1990s, the monetary authorities did not know what to do, and the financial sector directed these funds towards the chasing of stocks, real estates and other speculative investments, thus in the process creating a bubble. The planning and development authorities in these countries probably fuelled the problem by embarking on showcase, white-elephant type of investments, which did not look so expensive given the continuous inflow of foreign capital. When there emerged signs of the bursting of the bubble, and of larger-than-expected current account deficits, some foreign capital began to evacuate. This led to panic withdrawal of all short-term foreign capital, thus creating a financial crisis.

Because the crisis is still with us, it is too early to give the verdict as to which of the two competing hypotheses can be rejected. It is also possible that there are elements of truth in both. But whichever of the two may be correct, there are important lessons to learn from the crisis. In what follows, we will discuss these lessons and refer to the Taiwanese experience wherever appropriate.

1. The Creation of Bubbles

Regardless of whether the fundamentals were strong or weak, it is clear that prior to the outbreak of the crisis, there were bubbles occurring in Thailand, Indonesia and Malaysia (and to a lesser extent in the Philippines). In all of these economies, the beginning of a sharp rise in short-term capital inflow coincided with one in domestic credits (in 1988 for Thailand, in 1989 for Malaysia and the Philippines, and in 1990 for Indonesia, see Bhattacharya et al., 1998). The latter in turn fuelled the rapid rise in asset prices. Real estate capital values rose sharply during 1990–91, 1988–91, 1988–92, and 1988–96 in Thailand,

Indonesia, Malaysia and the Philippines respectively, followed by construction booms (*ibid.*). Stock prices rose sharply from the late 1980s to record highs in 1993 for Thailand, in 1993 (first peak) and 1997 (second peak) for Indonesia, and in 1993 (first peak) and 1996 (second peak) for Malaysia and the Philippines (*ibid.*). These were clearly unsustainable in the long run; and so when worries emerged, all short-term foreign capital fled.

Taiwan, in spite of its reputedly sound financial management, had had bitter experience in this area as well. In the mid to late 1980s, perhaps as a result of the sharply weakening NT dollar at the time, Taiwan's exports expanded so quickly that its current account surplus amounted to about one-fifth of GNP. As its foreign reserves piled up, scholars and analysts both in Taiwan and abroad (and also foreign government officials) criticized the Taiwanese authorities for under-valuing its currency and under-investment in public infrastructure.

As such "talking up" of the NT dollar continued, there came the speculative movement of capital inflow. It was not unlike the situation the ASEAN countries faced in the mid-1990s, except that in Taiwan's case such funds entered the country for expected quick profits from the predicted appreciation of the local currency. In the case of the ASEAN countries, these funds entered for expected quick profits based on the predicted high growth rates in these emerging markets.

The Central Bank tried to stop the local currency from appreciating but the efforts were unsuccessful, as indicated earlier. At that time capital-account currency convertibility was still highly restricted. Because there was still a sizable black market with premiums on ex-change rates, the authorities figured erroneously that by liberalizing the capital accounts, many domestic residents would purchase U.S. dollars and therefore ease the pressure in the foreign exchange market. When they actually allowed much higher convertibility, completely contrary to the expectation of the authorities, there emerged a massive inflow of capital, making a defence against appreciation impossible. The authorities finally gave in, and the NT dollar sharply appreciated (Chu 1994).

That was fine. Unfortunately, it was not the whole story. The inflow of foreign portfolio investment was largely purchased by the Central Bank in its efforts to intervene, and so became a component in the monetary base. The government sterilized these flows but not suffi-ciently. The result was a rapid monetary expansion and the creation of a bubble in Taiwan's real estate and stock markets in the late 1980s (see Chu 1994 and 1998 for details).

The bubble burst in the stock market in 1990, with the Taiex Index falling from 11983.46 in early 1990 to 2912.16 by October that year. Prices of residential real estate in the Taipei area, which rose sharply during 1987–89, began to show decreases, though milder than in other areas, from 1990. The effects of that monumental fall in stock prices are over, but those of the depressed real estate market are being felt even today.

Because of the prolonged recession in the properties market, and also because of the slow-down in Taiwan's growth due to the Asian financial crisis, more and more companies have recently been in trouble. Large cheques of U-Land Group (with lines of business in real estate, airline and electronics) bounced on 1 October 1999. The event was preceded by cheque bouncing on 29 July and 28 October 1998 by An Feng steel group (steel and real estate), followed by incidents with the Luo Chieh Construction group (real estate and food-processing), Chinese Automobile Company (import car dealer, owing banks NT$40-50 billion, default in stocks transactions; belonging to Panvest Group, which is also involved in real estate, electronics, convenience stores and leasing; see *United Daily News*, 3 November 1998), and New Magnitude Group (real estate, construction, electronics, steel, owing banks NT$15.4 billion; see *United Evening News*, 3 November 1998). Adding to this list was the incident involving the Central Bills and Finance Corporation (closely related to New Magnitude Group, which owns 3.96% of its shares and has commercial papers of group enterprises endorsed by this bills company, totalling NT$1 billion, from *China Daily News*, 3 November 1998). This company endorsed a total of NT$23 billion of commercial papers out of an equity of NT$2.7 billion (from *United Daily News*, 2 and 5 November 1998). The Company was coercively seized by banks (Hua Nan Commercial, First Commercial, Taiwan Small and Medium Business), designated by the Ministry of Finance, on 4 November 1998.

Hung Fu Bills Finance Company (endorsing a total of NT$29 billion of commercial papers out of an equity of NT$3.75 billion — from *United Daily News*, 6 November 1998 — and belonging to the Hung Fu group, which is involved in real estate, securities brokerage, stocks financing and banking, and is headed by Cheng-Chung Chen, Taipei City Council Member and Kuomingtang Whip — from *Economic Daily*

News, 6 November 1998) was also hit on 5 November 1998 because its creditor banks lowered their credit lines. On 9 November 1998 four institutions — International Bills Finance, International Commercial Bank of China, Overseas Chinese Bank and Shanghai Commercial Bank — negotiated a purchase of 51% of ownership, and their staff are now in the troubled institution for supervision and auditing (*China Daily News*, 10 November 1998).

In response to these incidents, the Premier announced a Five-Point Easing Plan calling for financial institutions to extend the maturity of short-term lending to enterprises by six months (*Economic Daily News*, 5 November 1998). Meanwhile, the Central Bank announced on 5 November 1998 that it would take NT$30 billion out of the deposits (at the Central Bank) by the Postal Savings to provide emergency loans to small- and medium-sized enterprises (SMEs) in trouble, through the Task Force to Assist Enterprises in Need of Fund set up by the Ministry of Finance (*United Daily News*, 6 November 1998). The Ministry of Finance also announced on 7 November that bad loans directly resulting from such extension would not be counted as such in its evaluation of banks' performance (*China Daily News*, 8 November 1998).

Meanwhile the bad loan ratios at the credit departments of the farmers' and fishermen's associations and at credit cooperatives, the weakest spots in Taiwan's financial system, constituting about 11% of all loans, also rose. The ratio for the former rose to an alarming 12% in the second quarter of 1999, mainly a consequence of the depressed real estate market as well as the accumulated result of mismanagement related to local politics (Chu 1998). Fortunately however, the bad loan ratios at the major banks have been small — between 3 and 6%. So the bursting of the bubble in Taiwan has not been as serious as that in the other Asian countries (see Chu 1998 for a comparison between Taiwan and Japan). Nevertheless, it is important to realize how vital it is to avoid similar situations from happening again.

2. The Nature of State Intervention in Industrial Development

In Taiwan, as noted earlier, the state took an active role in most economic affairs. Although the role has been changing towards less intervention during the last decade, the government has not shied away from taking actions when it felt it was necessary. Its involvement in introducing new technologies to the computer-related industries (such as IC design) described earlier is an example.

However, also as argued earlier, the government seldom carried out interventions step by step, persistently following well-thought-out master plans designed at the initial stage. In most cases it followed a "do-and-see" approach, a learning by doing attitude. And most cases were subject to market tests: spontaneous follow-up investments by private enterprises in the man-made fibre development for example, were always the key to subsequent expansions. Also, as noted earlier, in that industry the first product the government chose to develop (in 1957), rayon, turned out not to be the leading product. Rather, it was polyester, which the government finally chose to develop in 1964, that later dominated Taiwan's man-made fibre industry. This was the choice of the market, not government officials with perfect foresight in the late 1950s.

Another example was the building up of the petroleum industry through the publicly owned China Petroleum Corporation. When it was assigned to undertake second-stage import substitution in the 1970s, the prices of its products were basically set according to international levels. Otherwise the downstream users, who exported the majority of the products in the international market, could not compete with exporters from other countries. This would to a certain extent impose constraints on the costs of production.

Although the petroleum industry in South Korea was equally subject to international competitive pressure, in terms of other aspects, especially with respect to the choice of products and industrial organization, the government in South Korea appears to have adopted a much more dominant position. According to many accounts, once the government decided what products to develop, it would do so through dominant intervention in private enterprises chosen to carry out its plans. The government gave easy credits, protected domestic markets, and even intervened in the actual operations of the companies, in order to have the targets met (see for example, Scitovsky 1986). In the case of the man-made fibre industry, as in many others, the government limited market entry (and therefore domestic competition) in order to let its chosen companies achieve scale economies and enjoy domestic market power (see for example, Kim 1991; and Kim and Ma 1997).

So compared to the Taiwan model of "illustrative intervention", the South Korean model of "directive intervention" has been much more strict. It was more effective in achieving rapid results. However, should the government make mistakes or lose its independence, the result could be devastating. This again reminds us of the points made earlier, about the supply factors of government intervention. The higher the competence and the more independent from special interests the government team is, the more likely government intervention will result in the successes instead of the failures described in Table 5.2. Most importantly, these supply factors are not invariant with time and regime. Even in Taiwan, where bureaucrats are of high quality compared to many other semi-industrialized countries, generally speaking, a more intimate relationship can be observed between politicians and business, particularly big business. Kuo and Tsai (1998) assert that this is a general phenomenon among East Asian economies, and a major reason for the current financial crisis.

3. Government and the Financial Sector

In Taiwan, as iterated in Chu (1998), the financial sector is governed by the Ministry of Finance and the Central Bank. As powerful agencies inside the Cabinet, they are independent of the Ministry of Economics Affairs, which is responsible for industrial development, and the Council for Economic Planning and Development, responsible for overall development. Moreover, until early 1999, all the major banks in Taiwan were public, and their employees had public servant status. If they made bad loans they could be prosecuted for negligence or fraud, which are criminal offenses for civil servants. So in general banks have been very conservative, and have actually been nicknamed "pawnshops" because of this.

This is why the banks in Taiwan, when they did err, tended to err in the direction of ultra-conservatism (with the exception of the credit departments of farmers' and fishermen's associations and credit co-operatives, as noted earlier). After January 1999, although three major commercial banks were privatized, the move was more technical than real. The government is still the biggest shareholder. Even though their employees are no longer civil servants, which would help, the general atmosphere of conservatism remains within the management at the major banks.

While the financial sector is generally independent of development agencies, it is not at all independent of its supervisors. In effect, the

Ministry of Finance and the Central Bank have tried very hard to regulate and supervise the banks and other financial institutions. The Bank for International Settlements (BIS) requirements are strictly enforced. All new financial products of the banking, securities, mutual fund and insurance sectors have to be approved before being marketed; the setting up of branch offices inside or outside Taiwan has also to be approved beforehand; etc.

The authorities have also been very cautious in opening up the market. The move to allow residents to sell and purchase foreign currencies was made, as explained earlier, not as a natural step in the master plan of financial liberalization, but rather under extraordinary circumstances. The authorities resisted for years after agreeing to open the banking sector to new entrants in 1991. When they did, they set the threshold very high: a minimum paid-up capital of NT$10 billion. In the end 16 new banks were approved, the majority of whom are doing well today.[1] With regard to foreign portfolio capital, the authorities were also very cautious. There were heated debates on the timing and extent of opening up the stock market to foreign mutual funds. To date, foreign portfolio investment is allowed up to only one-third of the total market value of listed stocks; this has not been binding however, because actual foreign investment constitutes less than 4% of the total.

When encountering market disturbances, the monetary and financial authorities have been very swift and decisive in taking actions. During the NT dollar appreciation episode, not only did they impose strict limits on banks' foreign exchange exposure, they also required the banks to report all orders (to purchase NT dollars) exceeding a certain amount to the Central Bank, so the authorities could check the background of the persons or companies making the transactions. They closed the forward market for many months in 1987. And they staged quite a few "account auditing" raids on the foreign banks in Taiwan suspected of large-scale speculations.

During the stock market and real estate boom in the late 1980s, when the government realized that too much money was flowing into these two markets, they again imposed restrictions. For the real estate market, limits were set on the percentage of loan exposure, and in 1989 a Seven-Point selective credit control was promulgated, aimed at curbing speculative transactions (see Chu 1998 for details). Although during the boom the percentage of loans going to the construction industry (an important part of the real estate sector) increased by much more than that going to manufacturing, relative to its contribution to GDP (Table 5.3), it would probably have gone further, if not for these restrictive measures.

For the stock market the tax on capital gains was re-activated in September 1990. It directly contributed to the burst of the bubble in the stock market. In hindsight, the authorities probably did not foresee such a gigantic fall (the market value shrank by about three-quarters in two months), or else they would not have done it. But it was obvious they wanted to do something about the ballooning stock market.

Conversely, if the stock market fell to levels that were judged "unreasonable" by the authorities, they ordered government-controlled funds (such as retirement funds) to purchase stocks; if that was not enough, they persuaded financial institutions to do the same. The scheme was activated in late 1990, when the bubble burst, and again in 1995, when mainland China trained its missiles at targets across from and near Taiwan.

In October 1997 Taiwan was faced with speculative attacks on its currency. After spending about US$10 billion defending the local currency and witnessing the stock market taking a nose dive as funds were pulled out of that market to be converted into U.S. dollars, the authorities finally gave in. The NT dollar depreciated sharply after that. It seems that the government had learned not to fight against fundamental market forces. But it did more than that. At the height of defending the NT dollar, it barred domestic financial institutions from trading in the non-deliverable forward (NDF) market. It also required all banks to report all of their large foreign exchange purchasing orders before actual transaction. Administrative intrusion was direct and obvious.

The government has also been active in dealing with bank runs and other types of crisis in the financial market. Many such cases happened during the two oil-price crises, and during the early 1990s when the effects of the stock market crash were severe. In most cases of serious wrongdoing by the existing management, the government would replace management personnel, sometimes by force. The institution was then transferred to new ownership, merged with other healthy institutions or dissolved. In most cases depositors were protected, in the sense that after the take-over, the new owner/management would honour existing deposits. Thus there could be some kind of moral hazard (Akerlof and Romer 1993), especially for the depositors, who did not

TABLE 5.3   Taiwan: Sectoral Shares in Loans and GDP, Manufacturing *vs* Construction (in percentages unless otherwise noted)

Year	Manufacturing			Construction		
	Share in Loans (A)	Share in GDP (B)	C=A/B (ratio)	Share in Loans (D)	Share in GDP (E)	F=D/E (ratio)
1978	51.35	35.6	1.44	1.93	6.1	0.32
1979	49.90	35.9	1.39	1.80	6.2	0.29
1980	48.87	36.0	1.36	1.71	6.3	0.27
1981	47.37	35.6	1.33	1.90	5.7	0.33
1982	44.07	35.2	1.25	2.08	5.0	0.42
1983	40.96	35.9	1.14	2.25	4.6	0.49
1984	38.80	37.5	1.03	2.22	4.3	0.52
1985	35.19	37.6	0.94	2.47	4.1	0.60
1986	31.13	39.4	0.79	2.74	3.8	0.72
1987	28.14	38.9	0.72	3.49	3.9	0.89
1988	25.81	37.2	0.69	4.43	4.2	1.05
1989	23.80	34.6	0.69	3.73	4.5	0.83
1990	23.21	33.3	0.70	4.02	4.7	0.86
1991	23.39	33.3	0.70	5.56	4.7	1.18
1992	22.31	31.7	0.70	7.02	5.0	1.40
1993	21.00	30.5	0.69	8.19	5.3	1.55
1994	19.17	29.0	0.66	7.97	5.3	1.50
1995	19.44	28.1	0.69	6.38	5.2	1.23
1996	17.80	27.9	0.64	5.19	4.8	1.08
1997	17.34	27.7	0.63	4.80	4.4	1.09

NOTE: Loans refer to all loans made by banks. Shares in GDP are evaluated at market prices.

SOURCES: Data are from Central Bank, Taiwan, *Monthly Financial Statistics* (January 1993, January 1995 and September 1998); and Council for Economic Planning and Development (CEPD), Taiwan, *Taiwan Statistical Data Book, 1998.*

care and in most cases did not know if their banks were insured by the Deposit Insurance Company or not.

So the government's handling of the financial sector has been very different from its handling of other sectors. Here the intervention and supervision have been in most cases pervasive, swift and decisive, and recently have become more so. In the real sector bankruptcies of companies in most cases were not seen by the authorities as threats to the entire economy. But in the financial sector bank runs, even on a tiny credit department of a farmers' association, were taken seriously, for fear of the chain reactions they might cause.

With such pervasive intervention and supervision, one can imagine how much competence and independence of special interests the officials must possess in order to get the job done. For the former, the dominance of public financial institutions has played an important role. Most of these institutions are properly (and conservatively) managed, and the staff are well trained (both in school and on the job). The staff of these banks are like a large (in numbers), reliable and well-trained army at the government's command. In the case of the swift take-over of the Central Bills and Finance Corporation referred to earlier, on the evening of 3 November 1998 the Ministry of Finance sent about a dozen staff from Hua Nan Commercial Bank, which is still controlled by the government although it was technically privatized in January 1999 (that is, with government ownership below 50%), to audit accounts at the bills finance company but encountered resistance (*United Daily News*, 4 November 1998). So on the next day the Ministry of Finance ordered a united task force composed of the staff of Hua Nan Commercial Bank, the First Commercial Bank, and Taiwan Small and Medium Business Bank (the latter two are also *de facto* controlled by the government) to take over the entire company at 8:30 in the morning with a police escort (*United Daily News*, 5 November 1998). The government could not have acted so effectively without such staff support.

With respect to the political economy side, the bureaucrats involved have generally been clean, despite the fact that potential gains from corruption would have been huge, given the vast power the authorities have and the extensiveness of their intervention. While cases of such corruption are not unheard of, they have been rare in Taiwan. However, while the bureaucrats who carried out the policies might have been clean, there has been increasing doubt as to whether the very policies chosen have been made independent of politics. As explained earlier, as Taiwan gradually entered the era of democracy, so has it entered the arena of political playing such as log-rolling, pork barrels, and the like. These are unavoidable in mature democracies, not to mention emerging ones.

It has been reported that the bills finance companies were a strange creation in Taiwan, unique in the world. These companies issue, sell and endorse commercial papers of enterprises, and that is all. In most other economies such services are the business of commercial banks. But in Taiwan, in 1995, under pressure from elected legislators, the authorities reluctantly opened up the market to 13 new entrants with only a rudimentary regulatory provision. In addition, banks were later allowed to enter this market as well. In order to achieve sales targets amidst fierce competition, the bills finance companies, especially the new ones, have not been prudent in their management of endorsement. This contributed to their growing risks (*China Daily News*, 9 November 1998).

So the sequence, the timing and the scope of financial liberalization have been affected by politics. The sudden establishment of so many new financial institutions has been reported to result in over-banking (*ibid.*) The value of transactions in the money market for example, reached NT$70 trillion in 1997, the largest in Asia (*United Daily News*, 5 November 1998). Meanwhile, according to the newly established Taiwan Ratings Corporation, which was created from the government's efforts, only seven of the existing 16 bills companies have applied for a rating, and only two of these seven belong to class A (*China Daily News*, 5 November 1998).

What happened to most of the business groups in trouble was that they expanded too fast, often into territories new to them, and they were highly leveraged (does this sound similar to the experience of the ASEAN countries?). Most of them borrowed large amounts of money through bills finance companies or from banks which held their stocks as collateral. Loans from the latter were normally set at 70% of market value of the stocks. As their regular business was not making much money, many of them ventured into the stock market, sometimes to raise the prices of their own stocks in order to sell them at higher prices. As they held more of these stocks at higher prices, they got more fund from the banks or from the money market. If the scheme succeeded, they would make a lot of money. If the scheme failed, perhaps as a chain reaction to other crises, and the prices of their stocks began to fall "prematurely", they would be in big trouble, because when prices fall by 30%, the banks sell the collateral, contributing to a further fall in stock prices. Before long they had to default in stock transactions or they write bad cheques, or both (*United Daily News*, 6 November 1998).

The handling of individual crisis cases has also recently drawn criticism from the media. Some of the rescue operations were said to be politically motivated. Although the authenticity of such reports remains to be verified, in emerging (and even mature) democracies these things are bound to occur, as analyzed earlier. Again, this is not a case against democratization and for authoritarianism (remember Marcos in the Philippines), but it is a case against the adequacy of the supply factors of government intervention. Admittedly, as the financial sector gets bigger, more complicated and changes ever faster, the demand for government services also rises. There is, therefore, a need to balance the two.

V. CONCLUDING REMARKS

The socially optimal level of state intervention depends on demand and supply factors, both of which in turn depend on the history of the evolution of institutions of a society as well as the level of its development. When a society is at an earlier stage of development, the demand for state actions is usually high, because of the non-existence of a mature capital market, the infancy stage many products are in, as well as other kinds of possible market failures, as listed in Table 5.2. If the state has itself been a much larger economic force than the private sector to begin with, the demand is stronger, because the latter is not resourceful enough to be a viable substitute for the state. On the supply side competence and independence (of special interests) of state personnel are most important. The lack of either one of these qualities is more likely to result in state failures than successes as defined in Table 5.2. So with the demand side held fixed, the socially optimal level of state intervention should be lower, if the state lacks either or both of these two characteristics.

From the 1950s to the 1970s the extent of state intervention in Taiwan was strong. The state was itself a massive economic power. It also implemented numerous economy-wide and industry-specific policies. The former set of policies are listed in Table 5.1, which included, among others, the construction and maintenance of infrastructure, establishment of various markets, including capital and money markets, and continuous improvements in education.

As for the industry-specific policies, while there have been failures, the electronics and man-made fibre industries, to be explored in full detail in later chapters, saw extensive state interventions in (1) initial import protection; (2) setting up of state enterprises or engineering of joint ventures (among private enterprises, between private and state enterprises and/or with foreign companies) to begin manufacturing of new products; and (3) the operation of state research and development institutions which imported foreign technology and then transferred it to domestic firms. These interventions seem to have been pivotal in the development of both industries.

The high level of state intervention from the 1950s to the 1970s might have been socially optimal. On the demand side, many of the capitalist institutions needed to be established, many products were still in their infancy and the private sector was still small. On the supply side, state services appeared to be competent and independent relative to most developing countries.

Entering the 1980s and 1990s, many markets had become mature, and the private sector had grown in size. This lessened the demand for state interventions to correct market failures, particularly in the real sectors. Also, when the government did intervene, it became increasingly illustrative as well as learning-by-doing in nature. That is, the intervention would result in a critical mass only if the private sector voluntarily followed up. The private sector was, of course, driven by the market. So at least indirectly, the illustrative interventions were subject to the tests of the market. In the man-made fibre case, to be explained in more details elsewhere, the first product the government promoted in as early as 1957 was rayon. But instead it was polyester which later turned out to be the leading product, and the development of that product was the last one pursued by the government, in as late as 1964. Had the government insisted on developing rayon at the expense of other fibres, it is doubtful whether the man-made fibre industry would have developed as successfully as it did.

In terms of industrial organization the number of firms is usually larger than in, say, South Korea, due to unlimited access in most cases in the real sectors. Competition among domestic producers has been keen, again in contrast to the case in South Korea. Sometimes competitive investment led to over-supply, particularly during the recession years. When this happened, the government sometimes intervened to forge mergers and acquisitions. The illustrative and learning-by-doing nature of intervention as well as the prevalence of domestic competition were probably important factors contributing to the promotion of successful government intervention and to the avoidance of government failures. These may also have contributed to Taiwan's resilience to the adverse effects of the Asian crisis.

On the financial front, the demand for intervention has been stronger. These included taking liberalizing measures in proper sequence, tighter supervision of the financial sector as it was liberalized, and swifter handling of financial crises wherever and whenever they occurred, as clearly illustrated in the past experience of the Taiwanese authorities with regard to financial emergencies. The inability to meet these demands may be fatal to the economy, as the recent Asian financial crisis has shown.

So far the government in Taiwan has been able to meet these demands in most cases. In spite of the mishandling of speculative money which went to the real estate and stock markets in the late 1980s to create a bubble, the government was later able to curb credit expansion to these two markets by selective credit controls, to stabilize the stock market when it overshot, to closely supervise the operations of financial institutions (sometimes to the point of being accused of over-regulation), to put out fires in the financial sector by taking over troubled institutions swiftly and decisively while protecting the depositors, and to take cautious steps towards liberalization. The financial authorities accomplished all these with a large, reliable and well-trained corps of staff at their command in the government-controlled financial institutions, which still dominate the market today.

Can such performance continue in the future? Can the supply factors which are vital to successful government intervention be maintained? Will the nature of decision-making and the quality of civil servants change over time? We do not yet have definitive answers, but will note the following:

First, democratization in recent years has proceeded more intensively than ever before: in 1987 the martial law was lifted, and people's rights to hold meetings, stage demonstrations and form political parties were formally resumed; in 1988 the ban on new newspapers was lifted; in 1991 and 1992 respectively, general elections of the National Assembly and Legislature were held. In 1996 the first direct election of the President occurred (see Fei and Chu 1996). While occasionally there have been riots in the streets, chaos, and fist-fighting in the Legislature, it has been perceived that greater political and media freedom could be earned at tolerable expenses of stability and orderliness. Perhaps as a learned response, according to many studies, the popular support for democracy appeared to increase, and by the early 1990s it appeared to have become dominant. Democracy has thus been "consolidated".

The change has implications for the supply side of state intervention. Although there does not seem to be a shortage of competent personnel, there have emerged concerns about the time required to make a collective decision and the influence of special-interest groups. While these concerns have not persuaded people to return to the previous authoritarian rule, they do cast doubt on the socially optimal level of state intervention remaining as high as it has been in the past.

The evolution of policies in these late decades did go in the direction of less state intervention and greater market freedom for the real sectors in Taiwan. There were a series of import tariff reductions in the 1980s and 1990s. Beginning in 1991, the policy of privatizing public enterprises has been inaugurated and enforced. In recent years the government has also decided to deregulate and open up to new entrants the petroleum, electric power and telecommunications markets. Whether these measures of liberalization, deregulation, and privatization reflect a healthy move towards social optimality, or if they have been inadequate, excessive, or not adequately supplemented by the necessary re-regulation, is an interesting subject for future study, when more data on their effects becomes available.

The evolution of policies in the financial sector has followed the direction of liberalization but is still under tight government regulation and intervention. Both represent mixed blessings. Liberalization has led to more competition, but it might also have led to over-banking and higher risks, particularly when some of the liberalization measures were forced upon the bureaucrats, who advised against the scope of such measures from their professional knowledge, by the politicians. Tighter government controls means more swift and decisive rescue/ seizure operations, which may have been necessary to avoid a meltdown, but at the same time there are doubts as to whether the choice of targets in the rescue operations and the terms of ownership transfer arranged are free from political considerations. Here, there is stronger demand, which is for greater intervention, but a possible deterioration in the supply factors, which is for less intervention. Again, it remains to be seen whether the measures taken, particularly in the recent episodes of financial emergencies, are socially optimal.

Secondly, as in many other countries, there could be inertia in the system which delays necessary reforms. In the private sector changes take place rapidly, driven by market forces. During the late 1980s and in the 1990s, as indicated earlier, Taiwan's traditional low-skill, labour-intensive industries suffered tremendously from the appreciation of the currency as well as from rising labor and land costs. Many went under. An equally large number shifted their production overseas. Those that remained upgraded their technology. The result was impressive: the share of capital- and/or technology-intensive products in total exports rose sharply (see for example, Council for Economic Planning and Development, *Taiwan Statistical Data Book, 1998*, p. 206) during the period.

No equal adjustment on the side of the public sector has been seen. There had been progress. In some cases new government agencies such as the Environmental Protection Administration, Public Construction Commission and Fair Trade (anti-trust) Commission were established to tackle new problems. In other cases old organizations went through major changes: the "old guards" in the old congress were forced to retire and replaced by new, elected members; major state enterprises such as China Steel became private; and the Telecommunication Bureau was divided into two parts, one for business which was later privatized, and the other for supervision. But important areas of inertia remain:

1. The responsibility of financial supervision falls under at least three organizations: the Central Bank, the Ministry of Finance and the Central Deposit Insurance Corporation. For years there have been talks of unifying the authorities but so far it has not been achieved. It has been reported that one of the main reasons was the existence of a salary differential.
2. Many of the financial institutions at the village level are in a serious condition but the government has avoided confronting the problems. As time passes, and as Taiwan's real estate market remains stagnant, many of these will go under, eventually at larger costs to the government.
3. It has been known for some years that inadequate supervision of cross-holding of stocks among related enterprises can create problems (the South Korean situation during the Asian financial crisis

has been a case in point). But the government has still not taken action. The Ministry of Economic Affairs holds that cross-holding should be allowed and that it is the responsibility of the Ministry of Finance to supervise it properly. The latter agency maintains that supervision should come from the former, which is the competent authority of company laws.

4. The process of privatization can be slowed down or aborted due to opposition from the employees. The Postal Bureau, for an important example, was to be privatized, but recently it has become unclear whether it will be. One of the reported reasons was that the employees were uncertain whether the assets of the Bureau were sufficient to meet the expected payment of retirement benefits. The government also encountered difficulties when it tried to privatize loading services at the harbours.

5. Real estate development is a big sector in Taiwan's economy but there is no specific government agency functioning as its competent authority. There are no specific regulations on the sale of newly constructed residential houses or apartments, and until very recently, none on the transaction of existing ones. As a result numerous problems, frauds, and disputes with consumers emerged. Overbuilding was a recent problem and has become one of the primary concerns of the government.

6. Co-ordination of technology development between the academic community and the business sector has been poor. The incentive system existing in academic institutions does not encourage empirical, own-country-specific studies. As a result, the work done by most academicians has little to do with the actual needs of the firms in the country.

So there are different kinds of inertia in the system. In some cases a new authority needs to be established from the existing decentralized system, but has not been created. In others old authorities who should make way for changes fail to leave the scene. Inertia is usually not the result of ignorance on the part of the authorities but of political impasse. As such, it is precisely what Mancur Olson (1982) calls "social sclerosis". It is the prisoners' dilemma situation: the (stable) Nash equilibrium among political forces is Pareto sub-optimal. The disease can be found in every society, and, according to Olson (1982) and North (1991), its severity determines whether an economy can grow sustainably or not. If this argument is correct, the disease should not be characteristic of East Asia, at least prior to the financial crisis. It is even less likely that Taiwan has suffered a great deal from the problem compared to the other economies. However, the fact that such problems still exist in Taiwan, as shown above, is a very clear indication that it is really a problem of degree.

The issue of government intervention is also a problem of degree. We have reiterated time and again, that in each stage of economic development, and probably pertaining to each specific problem, there are demands for and the supply of government intervention. The two sets of factors can be thought of as determining the socially optimal degree of intervention. When the government is competent and clean, and commands a large amount of resources (the supply factors), and when the market system is still in its infant stage (the demand factors), the optimal degree of intervention would be higher, and vice versa.

It can be hypothesized that a nation's growth is more sustainable if the actual degree of government intervention in that nation is closer to the optimal degree. As argued above, it is very likely that the actual degree of intervention by the Taiwanese government has not been far away from the optimal level in most cases during the different stages of development. In addition, it is fairly clear that, in spite of the fact that both demand and supply factors are likely to change over time, and so does the socially optimal degree of intervention, the latter is bound to be much bigger and more sophisticated than the simple slogan of *laissez-faire* in most if not all of the developing countries, including newly industrializing economies like Taiwan.

NOTE

1. Unfortunately, due to political factors, such prudence has increasingly been challenged. The example of the opening up of the bills finance market will be discussed below.

REFERENCES

Akamatsu, K. "Trade of Woolen Products in Japan" (in Japanese). *Studies of Commerce and Economy* 13 (1935): 129–212.

_____. "A Historical Pattern of Economic Growth in Developing Countries". *The Developing Economies* (1962): 1–25.

Akerlof, G. and P. Romer. "Looting: The Economic Underworld of Bankruptcy for Profit". *Brookings Papers on Economic Activity* (1993): 1–75.

Amsden, A. "The State and Taiwan's Economic Development". In *Bringing the State Back in*, edited by P. Evans, D. Rueschemeyer and T. Skocpol. Cambridge, Cambridgeshire: Cambridge University Press, 1985.

Bhattacharya, A., S. Claessens, S. Ghosh, L. Hernandeq and P. Alba. "Volatility and Contagion in a Financially Integrated World: Lessons from East Asia's Recent Experience". Paper presented at the PAFTAD conference on Asia-Pacific Financial Liberalization and Reform, May 1998, Chiangmai, Thailand.

Central Bank, Taiwan. *Monthly Financial Statistics*, various issues. Taipei, various years.

Chan, V.L., B.L. Chen and K.N. Cheung. "External Economies in Taiwan's Manufacturing Industries". *Contemporary Economic Policy* 13 (1995): 118–30.

Chen, B.L. "Picking Winners and Industrialization in Taiwan". *Journal of International Trade and Economic Development* 5 (1996): 137–59.

Chen, P.C. and Y.P. Chu. "The Present State and Prospect of the Taiwan Economy: Structural Adjustment and Its Implication for Changes in the Pattern of International Division of Labour". Paper presented at the conference of the East Asian Economic Association, 1994, in Taipei.

Chen, T.J. "Technical Change and Technical Adaptation of Multinational Firms: The Case of Taiwan's Electronics Industry". *Economic Development and Cultural Change* (1992): 867–81.

Chu, Y.P. "Taiwan's External Imbalance and Structural Adjustment: A General Equilibrium Analysis". *Asian Economic Journal* 8 (1994): 85–114.

_____. "Taiwan and Asia: Towards the Establishment of an Asian Monetary Stabilization Mechanism". Paper presented at the Workshop on Trends and Issues in East Asia, 1998, sponsored by the Foundation for Advanced Studies on International Development, Tokyo.

Council for Economic Planning and Development (CEPD), Taiwan. "Current Economic Situation" (in Chinese). Report submitted to the Executive Yuan, Taiwan, August 1998.

_____. *Taiwan Statistical Data Book, 1998*. Taipei: CEPD, 1998.

Davidson, J. *The Island of Formosa: Past and Present*. New York: McMillan, 1903.

Diamond, L. *Developing Democracy: Toward Consolidation*. Baltimore: Johns Hopkins University Press, forthcoming.

Dollar, D. "Outward-oriented Developing Economies Do Grow Rapidly". *Economic Development and Cultural Change* (1992): 523–44.

Fei, J.C.H., G. Ranis and S.W.Y. Kuo. *Growth with Equity: The Taiwan Case*. London: Oxford University Press.

Fei, J.C.H. and Y.P. Chu. "Economic Liberalization and Political Democratization in Taiwan". Paper presented at the Ta-Chung Liu Memorial Conference, 1996, Cornell University.

Fukuyama, F. *The End of History and the Last Man*. New York: Free Press, 1992.

Gold, T. B. *State and Society in the Taiwan Miracle*. New York: M. E. Sharpe, 1986.

Ho, S.P.S. *Economic Development of Taiwan, 1860-1970*. New Haven: Yale University Press, 1978.

Hsiao, F.H. *Industrial Policies and Industrial Development in Taiwan* (in Chinese). Taipei: Far-East, 1994.

Hsu, S.K. "Contribution of Taiwan's Industrial Policy: 1960-90" (in Chinese). Institute of Economics, Academia Sinica, Discussion Paper no. 8502, 1996.

Huntington, Samuel P. *The Clash of Civilizations and the Remaking of World Order.* New York: Simon & Schuster, 1996.

Jacoby, N.H. *U.S. Aid to Taiwan*. New York: Praeger, 1966.

Ka, C.M. (1993). *Markets, Social Network, and the Production Organization of Small-Scale Industry in Taiwan: The Garment Industries in Wufenpu* (in Chinese). Taipei: Institute of Ethnology, Academia Sinica, 1993.

Kawai, M. "Evolving Patterns of Asia-Pacific Financial Flows". Paper presented at the PAFTAD conference on Asia-Pacific Financial Liberalization and Reform, May 1998, in Chiangmai, Thailand.

Kim, J.H. "Korea: Market Adjustment in Declining Industries, Government Assistance in Troubled Industries". In *The Political Economy of the New Asian Industrialism*, edited by H. Patrick. Ithaca: Cornell University Press, 1991.

Kim, H.K. and J. Ma. "The Role of Government in Acquiring Technological Capability: The Case of the Petrochemical Industry in East Asia". *The Role of Government in East Asian Economic Development*, edited by M. Aoki, H.K. Kim and M. Okuno-Fujiwara. Oxford: Clarendon Press, 1997.

Krugman, P. "The Myth of Asia's Miracle". *Foreign Affairs* (November-December 1994), pp. 62–78.

Kuo, C.T. and T.J. Tsai. "Differential Impact of the Exchange Crisis on Taiwan, Japan and South Korea: A Politico-Institutional Explanation". Paper presented at the conference on the East Asian Economic Crisis: One Year After, 1998, in Taipei, organized by the ASEAN Institute of Strategic and International Studies and the Institute of International Relations, Taiwan.

Kuo, S.W.Y., G. Ranis and J.C.H. Fei. *The Taiwan Success Story: Rapid Growth with Improved Distribution in the R.O.C., 1952–1979*. Boulder: Westview Press, 1981.

Kuo, S.W.Y. *The Taiwan Economy in Transition*. Boulder: Westview Press, 1983.

———. *Economic Policies: The Taiwan Experience, 1945–1995*. Taipei: Hwa-Tai, 1997.

Lau, L. *Models of Development: A Comparative Study of Economic Growth in South Korea and Taiwan*. San Francisco: ICS Press, 1990.

Li, K.T. *The Evolution of Policy Behind Taiwan's Development Success*. Singapore: World Scientific, 1995.

Lin, C.Y. *Industrialization in Taiwan*. New York: Praeger, 1973.

Medhi, K. "Growth, Transformation and Crises in the Thai Economy and Their Welfare Implications". Paper presented at the conference on Growth, Poverty and Income Inequality in the Asia-Pacific Region, 1998, in Sydney, organized by the School of Economics, University of New South Wales.

Mizaki, M. "Growth and Structural Change in Asian Countries". *Asian Economic Journal* 9 (1995): 113–36.

Nobuo, K. *Modern Political History of Japan*, (Chinese translation by Chi-Chien Zhou, Wen-Ho Lu *et al.*), vols. 2 and 3. Taipei: Guei-Guan, 1990.

North, D.C. *Institutions, Institutional Change and Economic Performance.* Cambridge: Cambridge University Press, 1990.

_____. "Institutions". *Journal of Economic Perspectives* 5 (1991): 97–112.

North, Thomas, R. *The Rise of the Western World: A New Economic History.* Cambridge: Cambridge University Press, 1973.

Olson, M. *The Rise and Decline of Nations.* New Haven: Yale University Press, 1982.

Polanyi, K. *The Great Transformation.* Boston: Beacon Press, 1944.

Ranis, G. "Industrial Development". In *Economic Growth and Structural Change in Taiwan,* edited by Walter Galenson, pp. 206–63. Ithaca: Cornell University Press.

Reynolds, L. *Economic Growth of the Third World.* New Haven: Yale University Press, 1982.

Sachs, J. "The IMF and the Asian Flu". *The American Prospect,* March-April 1998, pp. 16–21.

Schive, C. *Taiwan's Economic Role in East Asia.* Washington, D.C.: Center for Strategic and International Studies, 1995.

Scitovsky, T. "Economic Development in Taiwan and South Korea". In *Models of Development: A Comparative Study of Economic Growth in South Korea and Taiwan,* edited by L. Lau and L. Klein. San Francisco: ICS Press, 1986.

Shieh, G.S. *Boss Island: The Subcontracting Network and Micro-Entrepreneurship in Taiwan's Development.* New York: Peter-Lang, 1992.

Wade, R. *Governing the Market: Economic Theory and the Role of Government in East Asian Industrialization,* Princetonm N.J.: Princeton University Press, 1990.

Weiss, L. "Government-Business Relations in East Asia: The Changing Basis of State Capacity". Taipei: Chung-hua Institution for Economic Research, Occasional Paper Series no. 9407, 1994.

World Bank *The East Asian Miracle.* New York: Oxford University Press, 1993.

Yanaihara, T. *Taiwan under Imperialism.* Tokyo: Iwanami Shoten, 1929. Chinese translation by H.W. Chou; published by Pamir, Taipei, 1929.

Yin, K. Y. *My View of Taiwan's Economy* (in Chinese). Taipei: Council on U.S. Aid, 1963.

Yoshihara, K. *Japanese Economic Development.* Kuala Lumpur: Oxford University Press, 1994.

6

The Development of Taiwan's Electronics Industry

Tain-Jy Chen, Been-Lon Chen and Yun-Peng Chu

I. INTRODUCTION

The development of Taiwan's electronics industry illustrates an industrial development strategy shaped by international market forces but which goes beyond the principle of the international division of labour. The electronics industry was brought to Taiwan by multinational firms seeking an international division of labor. Taiwan took full advantage of the presence of multinational firms in order to gain production experience and to accumulate skills. Moreover, the government created an environment designed to maximize the possibility of local participation in the industry to facilitate technology diffusion. It also established public research organizations for the purpose of acquiring the relevant technologies necessary for industry upgrading.

The principle of comparative advantage may give rise to economic activity as long as government policies are not designed to negate the natural process of industrial relocation emanating from advanced countries. But an industry will not be born and grow automatically unless indigenous technology can be cultivated. The key to the development of Taiwan's electronics industry lies in the efforts of the private and public sectors towards technology acquisition and diffusion. Local industry in Taiwan is so structured that it is conducive to technology diffusion and the government has played an instrumental role in technology acquisition.

In the following section we make an historical review of the development of the electronics industry in Taiwan. In section III we discuss the development of the consumer electronics sector in particular, with a focus on television receivers. The consumer electronics sector is characterized by segmented markets in which foreign subsidiaries dominate the export market and indigenous and joint-venture firms dominate the domestic market. Market segmentation entails distortions in resource allocation but it also provides ample opportunities for learning. Although the television receiver industry declined in the 1980s, production experience gained and the technology diffused in the process gave birth to a self-sustained electronics parts sector which endured after the withdrawal of multinational television set manufacturers.

In sections IV and V, we discuss the personal computer and semiconductor sectors, whose roots can be traced back to the electronic parts production of the 1960s. The experience of these sectors illustrates that local production by multinational firms can provide only limited impetus to technology diffusion. The role of the government in facilitating technology diffusion is clearly critical. Some conclusions are drawn in section VI.

II. HISTORICAL REVIEW

Generally speaking, the electronics industry was brought to Taiwan by multinational firms. Before 1960, there were only a small number of indigenous firms engaging in the assembly of vacuum-tube radios for domestic sales. Assembly of transistor radios started in 1961 by indigenous firms but was boosted by subcontracting orders placed by Japanese general trading companies. The industry quickly turned from an inward-looking business orientation to embrace an export-oriented strategy. Production of transistor radios grew at a double-digit rate from its inauguration until 1968, when total output reached 4 million sets (Chu, 1975, p. 117).

Starting from the mid-1960s, black-and-white television receivers came to occupy the central stage of Taiwan's electronics industry, through the production of joint ventures or wholly-owned foreign subsidiaries. Joint-venture firms were mostly domestic-market oriented whereas wholly-owned foreign subsidiaries were aiming at the export markets. Growth of the television industry was remarkable where export expansion was the main driver of the growth. Total production of television receivers, mostly monochrome, was only 66,260 sets in 1966, but grew to 1,254,125 sets in 1970, a 20-fold increase in a short span of five years.

Colour television receivers were subsequently introduced to Taiwan in 1969 and became a rapidly growing sector in the 1970s. Also joining the electronics industry scene in the 1970s were cassette tape recorders and video tape recorders. Multinational firms consistently played a dominant role in the evolution of the industry. They introduced new products to Taiwan, placed subcontracting orders and assumed the market service roles. Technologies were transferred from multinational companies to local subsidiaries and indigenous subcontractors. The development of the electronics industry in Taiwan followed the classical product cycle model. By the end of the 1970s Taiwan had become a major offshore production center of the world's low-end consumer electronics.

The industry entered a new era in the 1980s as consumer electronics gave way to computer-related products. Personal computer was introduced in the late 1970s and Taiwan quickly jumped on the bandwagon of this booming industry with its unique approach to production. Like its predecessors in the electronics industry, computer production was dominated by multinational firms in the beginning. Multinational firms, notably those based in the United States, used Taiwan as an offshore assembly and export platform. These multinational firms were soon overwhelmed by the emergence of a large number of small, yet nimble indigenous producers, however. Indigenous firms, while small and limited in technology capability, specialized in a small niche of the product array. Through a flexible production network, they were able to provide a wide spectrum of products, either being integrated into a system or standing alone as discrete products, at competitive costs.

The key difference between computer products and conventional consumer electronics is that Taiwanese firms found a unique way to standardize and separate the products. Transforming computer parts into stand-alone devices, Taiwanese firms were able to specialize and gain expertise in a small niche in which they excelled. Although most indigenous firms continued to serve in the international subcontracting markets, their bargaining power was greatly enhanced through refined specialization.

Aiding the transformation in production structure was the enhancement of indigenous technological capabilities. Production experience in the 1960s and 1970s had provided ample room for learning. Although technology gained in the process was made obsolete by rising labor costs in the 1980s, indigenous electronics firms transformed these technological capabilities for application in computer-related products. For example, the capability to design and manufacture television receivers was transformed and applied to computer monitors.

Further augmenting the indigenous technological capabilities were the government-sponsored research institutes which acquired technology from abroad and diffused it throughout the domestic industry. The role of public research institutes was most evident in the development of Taiwan's semiconductor industry which came into being after the booming computer industry had generated a stable demand for upstream integrated circuits (IC) products. The details of the government-aided development of the semiconductor industry will be presented in section V.

Table 6.1 lists the growth profile of the electronics industry in Taiwan between 1971 and 1995. It can be seen that in 1971 the number of electronics firms was only 624, many of which were foreign-invested ventures. Total employment in the electronics industry was 85,953 persons, accounting for 7.2% of the total manufacturing jobs. Foreign-invested firms, whose total number was about 100 in 1971, provided about 40,000 jobs out of the above total (Chu, 1975). Indigenous firms, mostly small-sized, played only marginal roles in the industry at the time.

TABLE 6.1   Taiwan: Growth of Electronics Industry 1971–95
(in million NT, except exports which are in million U.S. dollars)

Year	No. of Firms	Total Output	Value Added	Employment (workers)	Total Wages	Total Fixed Assets	Total Export
1971	624	19,562	4,517	85,953	1,893	—	169
1981	2,121	182,524	50,172	225,367	24,178	—	3,100
1991	5,449	626,684	167,787	309,297	90,662	310,929	13,722
1995	4,876	—	523,201	333,578	—	519,595	26,157

NOTE: Percentage growth p.a. in value added — 1971–81: 27.2%; 1981–91: 12.8%; 1991–95: 32.9%.
SOURCE: Total export data from Council for Economic Planning and Development (CEPD), Taiwan, *Taiwan Statistical Databook;* other data from *Census of Industry and Commerce.*

TABLE 6.2   Taiwan: Share of Electronics Industry in Total Manufacturing (in percentages)

	1971	1981	1991	1995
Output	8.1	8.9	12.7	—
Value Added	10.9	9.3	10.4	20.1
Employment	7.2	10.3	11.6	15.4
Export	8.2	13.7	18.1	23.4

SOURCES: Same as Table 6.1.

Value added of the industry grew rapidly between 1971 and 1981 when the consumer electronics sector went through its thriving decade. From 1981 to 1991, value added of the electronics industry grew by about three times in nominal value, in which production of consumer electronics was stagnant and computer-related products accounted for most of the growth. From 1991 to 1995, rapid growth in terms of value added was resumed as it grew by another three times. Computer and semiconductor products were the main driver of the growth.

Table 6.2 lists the share of the electronics industry in total manufacturing, measured in various dimensions. In terms of value-added, the share of the industry stood at 10.9% in 1971 and declined to 9.3% in 1981 before it recovered to 10.4% in 1991. The decline between 1971 and 1981 was partly due to the heavy- and chemical-industry drive pursued by the government during the decade, and partly due to a statistical mismatch as the electronics industry was more narrowly defined in later years. Between 1991 and 1995, the share of the electronics industry in terms of value added quickly moved up from 10.4% to 20.1% as the conventional, low-technology industries were dormant whereas the high-technology information industry flourished.

In terms of employment, the share of the electronics industry showed a steady upward trend. Its share stood at 7.2% in 1971 and steadily climbed to 11.6% in 1991 and further to 15.4% in 1995. In 1981 and 1991 the share of employment in the electronics industry was comparable to the share of value added, but in 1995 the share of value added clearly surpassed the share of employment. This suggests that labor productivity in the electronics industry improved in relation to the rest of the economy.

TABLE 6.3   Taiwan: Productivity of Electronics Industry *vs* All Manufacturing (in NT $1,000 per worker)

	1971	1981	1991	1995
Value added/worker electronics industry	53	223	542	1,568
Value added/worker all manufacturing	34	244	604	1,202

SOURCES: Same as Table 6.1.

The share of exports accounted for by electronics products also showed a steady upward trend. In fact, export share has exceeded the share of value added since 1981, indicating that the electronics industry has been more export-oriented than the average industry in the economy. The industry has had an export focus since its inauguration in Taiwan.

One reason for the electronics industry thriving and continuously evolving despite rising labor costs in recent years is the improvement in productivity. Table 6.3 lists the labor productivity of the electronics industry in various years. The improvement in labor productivity over time is evident from the table. Compared to the labor productivity of the manufacturing sector as a whole, the electronics industry lagged behind the average in 1981 and 1991, however. This was due to the labour-intensive nature of the industry at the time. labor productivity of the electronics industry surpassed the manufacturing average in 1995 as the share of the semiconductor sector in the electronics industry increased.

The composition of the electronics industry shifted markedly throughout the years. Table 6.4 separates the electronics industry into four sectors. Unfortunately, due to changes in sectoral classification, the data are not strictly comparable over time. For example, in 1971 radio and television receivers were classified as telecommunications equipment. This boosted the share of the telecommunications sector to 74.0% of the electronics industry at the time. The same products were classified as consumer electronics in 1981, allowing that sector to account for the lion's share of the industry's output.

The real difference between 1971 and 1981 is the growth of the electronics components sector which came to account for 20.4% of the industry's output in 1981. The size of the components sector was relatively small in 1971 and hence was neglected in statistical classification. The share of the components sector grew further between 1981 and

TABLE 6.4 Taiwan: Sectoral Composition of Electronics Industry (in percentages)

Subsector	1971	1981	1991	1995
Computers and peripherals	0	0	40.1	27.3
Telecommunication equipment	74.0	8.2	8.6	6.2
Consumer and other industrial electronics	26.0	71.4	13.4	12.6
Electronic componemts	0	20.4	37.8	54.0
Total	100.0	100.0	100.0	100.0

NOTES:
1. Percentage is based on value of output, except for 1995 which is based on value-added.
2. Computers and Peripherals were not listed as a subsector in 1971 and 1981. Such products did not exist in 1971 and might have a minimum value in 1981 when they were included in the category of other industrial electronics.
3. Electronic components include semiconductor products. No value in this subsector is provided in the 1971 statistics.

SOURCES: Same as Table 6.1.

1991 to record a 37.8% share in 1991. But the most dramatic change of the electronics industry in the decade of 1981–91 was the emergence of personal computers and computer peripherals. The production of these products was miniscule in 1981 and was recorded under the "other industrial electronics" category. The share of personal computers and computer peripherals rose to 40.1% in 1991, marking a dramatic transformation of the industry. Even more dramatic changes were witnessed in 1991–95 as the components sector surpassed all the other sectors of the industry to claim a stunning 54.0% share of the value added in the industry. This signalled the rise of the semiconductor sector to the central stage of the industry scene.

In Table 6.5, we further identify the key products of the electronics industry. The table reinforces the notion that the electronics industry in Taiwan has been subject to continuous destructions and reconstructions. Products were introduced and abandoned at a rapid pace, in line with the country's comparative advantage. In 1971 the total production of television receivers was 1,887,571 sets (Chu, 1975), mostly black and white. In 1976 production of black-and-white television receivers started to decline and colour television receivers followed suit after some time. Computer products started to emerge in the 1980s. In 1981

TABLE 6.5   Taiwan: Composition of Electronics Industry by Key Products (quantity in sets; value in NT$ million)

		Computer Systems	Computer Terminals	Colour Television Sets	Black & White Television Sets	Video Tape Recorders
1976	Quantity	—	—	518,644	3,282,404	—
	Value	—	—	7,157	8,347	—
1981	Quantity	828	62,680	1,625,870	5,248,493	—
	Value	80	62	18,358	12,891	—
1991	Quantity	2,927,714	1,830,747	2,467,235	1,537,721	773,334
	Value	51,824	10,591	15,524	1,646	5,912
1995	Quantity	6,966,897	874,257	1,337,448	358,884	847,085
	Value	130,370	5,161	11,839	345	5,217

SOURCES: Ministry of Economic Affairs, *Monthly Statistics on Industrial Output*, various issues.

the most important item of all computer products was the computer terminal, the output of which was merely 62,680 units. Most of these products were consignment orders made by Taiwanese subsidiaries for their multinational parents. Output for the whole spectrum of computer products increased sharply during 1981–91, including terminals and other peripherals. Along with the surge in computer production was the emerging role played by indigenous firms.

In spite of its changing product composition, Taiwan's electronics industry was consistently dominated by small and medium-sized firms. Table 6.6 lists the structure of industry concentration. It can be seen that the electronics industry was dominated by small firms employing less than 100 workers. In 1981 small firms accounted for 84% of the total number of firms in the industry. The share of small firms further increased to 88% in 1995. In contrast, large firms with employment of 500 or more accounted for only 4.3% of the number of firms in the industry in 1981 and their share decreased to only 2.0% in 1991. In fact, the number of large firms did not increase much during the 1981-91 period while small start-ups swarmed the industry. The share of large firms in terms of industry output has increased significantly in recent years, however, indicating an increasing market power. This is a manifestation of the advantage of globalized production, in which large firms are more successful than their small counterparts.

TABLE 6.6   Taiwan: Concentration Structure of Electronics Industry
(number of firms)

Size Distribution by Employment	1971	1981	1991	1995
<50		1,578	4,522	4,308
50–99		209	438	
100–199		135	216	250
200–499		107	161	318
500–999		54	63	
1000 and above		38	47	
Total		2,121	5,447	4,876

SOURCES: Same as Table 6.1.

III. DEVELOPMENT OF THE CONSUMER ELECTRONICS INDUSTRY

The history of Taiwan's electronics industry can be traced back to 1948 when some local merchants began assembling radios using imported vacuum tubes and other electronic parts. The quality of locally assembled radios was naturally mediocre. The government moved swiftly to protect this budding industry by putting radios under import licensing control in 1950. Domestic sales expanded under protection and small assembly shops operated by local merchants soon turned into large-scale factories. Less sophisticated parts also began to be manufactured locally (IDIC, 1968).

Taking advantage of their experience in assembling vacuum-tube radios, Taiwanese firms quickly jumped on the bandwagon of transistor radios manufacturing when these products were mature. The first transistor radio plant was established in 1961 and in the following year it successfully exported 30,000 units of the new products (IDIC, 1968). This was the turning point for Taiwan's electronics industry because a new market frontier had been discovered. At that time, Taiwan had just overhauled the orientation of its economic policy from import substitution to export promotion. Blessed with low wages, Taiwan attracted a large number of consignment orders to manufacture transistor radios for export. Japanese trading firms were the major source of the consignment orders. By 1966 Taiwan's exports of transistor radios had exceeded 2 million sets, mostly destined for the U.S. market. This experience established Taiwan's reputation as a good site for assembling electronic products.

Taiwan's electronics industry expanded through the introduction of television. With technical assistance from Japan, the Taiwanese government started television broadcasting in 1962. Concomitant with television broadcasting, local manufacturing of monochrome television sets sprang up. This was 16 years behind the United States, which invented the television and started formal production in 1946, and nine years behind Japan which started television set production in 1953 (Levy, 1981, p. 190, Table 5–5). Local firms obtained technology from Japan through technology licensing or joint-venture arrangements. The major Japanese electronics firms like Matsushita, Sanyo, Sharp, and Toshiba formed joint ventures with local entrepreneurs while Sony and Mitsubishi licensed technology to local firms without taking equity shares. All of them were geared to serve the local market.

Segregated from local and joint-venture firms was a group of multinational firms engaged in television-set production exclusively for export. Led by Philco in 1965, a series of direct investments in Taiwan were made by American firms, including Admiral (in 1966), RCA (in 1967), Motorola (in 1970) and Zenith (in 1971). These firms either established bonded factories or chose to locate in export-processing zones. They were allowed to import components and parts duty-free but were required to export all finished products. This facility allowed American multinational firms to take advantage of Taiwan's low wages to combat increased imports of Japanese television receivers into the U.S. market. American multinationals in Taiwan specialized in small-screen sets and re-exported them to the United States under the parent firm's brand names (Levy, 1981, pp.261–67). U.S. investments in Taiwan were encouraged by a provision of the U.S. Trade Law (Section 807) which allowed duty-free re-entry of U.S. components and parts embodied in final products that were assembled overseas. Taiwan was one of the two major overseas platforms through which American multinationals took advantage of this "offshore assembly provision", the other popular site being Mexico. Given the proximity of Mexico to the United States, Taiwan had to use its advantage in low wages to attract investors. Wage rates in Taiwan in the late 1960s were about half of those in Mexico.

Taiwan's reputation as a competitive site for television-set assembly also attracted multinational firms from other countries. Hitachi and Orion of Japan, Philips of the Netherlands and Grundig of Germany also established bonded factory operations in the early 1970s. Likewise they exported all finished products, mainly to the U.S. market. By the early 1970s, Taiwan had become a major exporter of television sets in the world. In 1973, for instance, Taiwan exported a total of 3.8 million units of monochrome television sets, on top of a local consumption of 373,000 units (Schive and Yeh, 1980). Exports had been the lifeline of Taiwan's television-set industry.

With ample experience in monochrome television-set production, Taiwan had little difficulty making the transition to the age of colour TV. Like the inauguration of monochrome television broadcasting, the beginning of colour television broadcasting in 1969 by state-owned television stations was accompanied by the launch of the local production of colour television receivers. Although Taiwan was far behind the United States. and Japan in initiating colour television production, it was running virtually neck-and-neck with European countries in entry into this new field. For example, the United Kingdom, France and Germany started the production of colour television receivers in 1967 and Italy started it in 1969 (Levy, 1981, p.191, Table 5–5). Domestic demand provided an initial boost to local production, but it was again the export market that paved the way for rapid growth of the local industry. In 1978 domestic production of colour television receivers exceeded 1.3 million, of which only 486,000 were sold to domestic consumers; the rest were exported (Schive and Yeh, 1980). Multinational firms remained the major players in the export drive, but indigenous and joint-venture firms which used to target the domestic market in the monochrome television age also began to venture into the export market. Exports from Taiwan put enough pressure on domestic U.S. producers to prompt the U.S. government to negotiate an "orderly marketing arrangement" with the Taiwan government in 1979 as a means of restraining the number of colour television receivers imported into the United States from Taiwan.

Although the growth in the assembly of radios and television sets was phenomenal, Taiwan's electronics industry would not have performed as well had it not had a solid foundation in the manufacturing of parts and components. Multinational firms played the role of catalyst in the parts and components sector, but it was the small indigenous firms that constituted the core of the industry and drove the growth. The first major multinational firm to be involved in Taiwan's electronic parts industry was General Instrument (GI) of the United States. GI established a fully-owned subsidiary in suburban Taipei in 1964 to operate the first-ever bonded factory in Taiwan. The plant was designated for the production of electronic parts such as transistors, tuners, deflection yokes, capacitors, etc. for shipment back to the parent company. Following GI's model, Philco's and RCA's operations in Taiwan also started with components production before they moved into television-set assembly.

Local firms which copied technologies from multinational firms or licensed technology from them strove to get into exports in addition to serving the domestic market. Although the quality of their products was inferior, they targeted latecomers in the television industry such as Southeast Asia, the Middle East and Latin America as their market focus and excelled at niche products with ultra-low prices. Exports enabled them to realize scale economies which improved production efficiency. Moreover, making money from exports enabled them to invest in new-vintage equipment in which more sophisticated technology was embodied.

A solid parts industry laid the foundation for Taiwan's successful entry into the production of calculators in 1972 and digital watches in 1975. Experience in the design and manufacturing of these primitive digital products in turn laid the foundation for the transition to the field of personal computers which blossomed in the 1980s.

1. Market Segmentation

The Taiwanese government has adopted a two-tiered policy towards the consumer electronics industry. On the one hand, consumer electronics products that were produced domestically were put under licensing controls, while on the other, various fiscal incentives and promotion measures were instituted to promote the export of electronics products from Taiwan. One group of firms targeted the domestic market while the other group targeted the export market. The two markets were segmented and there was little cross-hauling between the two groups of firms.

In the case of television receivers, the domestic market was dominated by indigenous firms licensing technology from Japan and joint-venture firms formed between indigenous enterprises and Japanese multinationals. The export market was dominated by American multinationals. Japanese multinational firms usually took a minority equity position in the joint ventures while the American multinationals preferred wholly-owned subsidiaries.

Products destined for the domestic market benefited from import controls and high tariffs. Free importation of television sets was not allowed until 1986. Lai (1972) has estimated that the effective rate of protection for monochrome television sets is 128%, while that for colour television sets is as high as 170%. These figures might be over-estimated, however, because the author did not take into account the effect of local content regulations which substantially increased the costs of components and parts. Only products destined for domestic sales were subject to local content regulations; exported products were exempted. The local content ratio was adjusted from time to time commensurate with the status of the local electronics parts industry.

Television sets aimed at the export market, meanwhile, were assembled in bonded factories or export processing zones. Components and parts used in assembly could be imported free of duty but no domestic sales were allowed for the final products. The export industry was therefore immune from the trade regime governing the domestic market. The two markets were effectively segregated.

Segmentation in the final products market also extended to the parts market. American parts makers like GI, TRW and Texas Instrument exported all their products. Being free from local content regulations and enticed by the "offshore assembly provisions" of the U.S. Trade Law, most American assembly operations in Taiwan used American-made components and parts. Local American parts makers were largely unconnected with American assembly operations. A survey in 1970 indicated that of the monochrome television sets exported to the United States from Taiwan, 89.58% of the components and parts were of American origin. Most of these television sets were produced by American subsidiaries in Taiwan. In comparison, of the colour television sets exported to the United States from Taiwan, only 60.46% of the contents were of American origin. This is because Japanese subsidiaries in Taiwan accounted for a sizable portion of these exports and they preferred Japan-made components and parts (Lai, 1972, p.21).

In contrast, bounded by local content regulations, Japanese electronics giants brought their suppliers to Taiwan to produce the needed components and parts. These suppliers usually entered into joint ventures with indigenous firms. In addition to serving the local market, their products were also exported. Parts makers producing exclusively for the local market were rare. Indigenous television-set assemblers who licensed technology from Japan also sought technology support from their licensors for parts production. This led to another round of technology licensing agreements. Independent local parts makers also obtained technology mostly from Japan.

Under the segmented market structure multinational firms oriented towards exports tended to be the largest. They were followed by joint-venture firms which had a mixed market orientation, and indigenous firms were the smallest. Among export-oriented multinationals, the American subsidiaries were larger than their Japanese counterparts. A survey conducted in 1975 (Chu, 1975), for instance, indicated that the average employment of American subsidiaries was 1,546 persons, while that of Japanese subsidiaries was 841 persons. An average of 445 persons were employed by joint-venture firms, and 116 by pure indigenous firms. American subsidiaries also topped all groups in terms of capitalization. In fact, at the time of the survey American capital accounted for 52% of investment in Taiwan's electronics industry. Pure indigenous firms were typically small and engaged in parts production.

In the case of colour television-set assembly, fully-owned foreign subsidiaries exported their entire production whereas joint-venture and indigenous firms targeted the local market. Fully-owned foreign subsidiaries used imported components and parts more than other firms. As shown in Table 6.7 joint-venture and indigenous firms had a higher local content ratio than fully-owned foreign subsidiaries. Foreign-owned subsidiaries were also shown to be less active in research and development activities and instead relied on parent firms for the provision of technology (Schive and Yeh, 1980, pp. 281–82). Due to a lack of localized technology and the ability to innovate, most American television-set assemblers exited Taiwan in the 1990s when rising local wages made the offshore assembly activities in Taiwan uncompetitive. Zenith withdrew from Taiwan in 1991, followed by RCA in 1992. Japanese television-set maker Orion also left the island in 1992 (Hattori and Sato, 1996, p. 204). Parts producers like GI, Texas Instruments and Philips however, continued to innovate and have prospered in Taiwan. Joint-venture television-set manufacturers like Matsushita, Sanyo and Toshiba restructured themselves and have survived the changing operating environment.

TABLE 6.7   Taiwan: Export Ratios and Local Content Ratios of Colour Television-set Assembly Firms (in percentages)

	Export Ratio 1976	Local Content Ratio		
		Start	1975	1978
Foreign subsidiaries	100.0	8	25	33
Joint ventures	2.24	20	58	60
Indigenous firms	1.32	25	47	71

SOURCE: Schive and Yeh (1980), p. 269, Table 5; p.279, Table 13.

A study of foreign subsidiaries and joint-venture firms in Taiwan's electronics industry (Chen and Tang, 1986) revealed that export-oriented firms use more labor intensive technology, employ a larger proportion of unskilled labor, and accomplish a lower percentage of value-added as compared to domestic-market oriented firms. However, both groups are shown to increase their value-added percentage over time. Localization also takes the form of de-skilling and capital-intensity reduction (Chen, 1992).

American multinationals are found to localize more swiftly than Japan-based multinationals. According to the survey on all multinationals in Taiwan's electronics industry, American multinationals exported 96.8% of their products in 1975 compared to the 72.5% of Japanese multinationals. But the export ratio of American multinationals was reduced to only 78.4% in 1989, while Japanese multinationals only increased their export ratio slightly to 75.9%. The swift re-orientation of American multinationals is partly attributable to the exodus of the 100% exporters which dominated the American group in the early years and partly attributable to the re-orientation of existing firms towards the local market. American multinationals are also shown to have increased their purchase of locally made components and parts more substantially than their Japanese counterparts (see Table 6.8).

There is little evidence to suggest that the production experience gained in import substitution paved the way for export-oriented production. When Philco inaugurated television-set production in 1965 exclusively for export, Taiwan had had only one or two years of television-set manufacturing experience behind it. Philco was apparently attracted by Taiwan's performance in assembling transistor

TABLE 6.8   Taiwan: Export Ratios and Use of Local Materials by American and Japanese Multinationals in Electronics Industry (in percentages)

	Export Ratio		Local Material Percentage	
	American	Japanese	American	Japanese
1975	96.8	72.5	33.9	36.9
1980	92.8	77.6	32.4	34.6
1985	89.7	78.1	36.6	42.1
1989	78.4	75.9	48.6	41.2

SOURCE: Chen and Wang (1994).

radios rather than its shallower experience in television production. Had Taiwan not created a segregated local market for indigenous and joint-venture firms to produce television sets, the only difference would have probably been the absence of several local electronics giants that we see today, such as Tatung and Sampo. The real success of Taiwan's electronics industry lies with its broad production experience based on exports. It should not be disregarded that Taiwan granted GI a licence to operate a bonded factory in 1965 with 100% foreign ownership. It was approved at a time when dependency theory dominated economic thinking and when there was ample sentiment opposed to multinationals' exploitation of local labour. The monthly wage for local operators in electronics firms was only about NT$20 in 1965. In fact, exporting from Taiwan was an American defence strategy designed to counter the competition from Japanese exports.

The segmented markets for television sets eventually converged in the 1980s when the government allowed a fraction of the products made in the bonded factories to be sold locally after some tax adjustments. However, the crossing of market lines had begun earlier in the parts industry. Supported mainly by Japanese technology and niche markets in developing countries, local parts makers gradually improved their quality. Competitive pressure eventually made American subsidiaries switch parts supply from parent firms to local producers. The proportion of locally procured materials increased drastically among American subsidiaries during the 1980s. As indicated in Table 6.8, in 1975 American multinationals purchased 33.9% of needed materials from local suppliers in comparison to the 36.9% of their Japanese counterparts. The local procurement ratio of the American multinationals increased to 48.6% in 1989, surpassing the 41.2% recorded by the Japanese multinationals in the same year.

The existence of parts makers whose survival partially depended on the local market was essential to the localization of American firms. In fact, when Arthur D. Little Co. (ADL) evaluated the prospects of Taiwan's electronics industry in 1974 on behalf of the Taiwanese government, it considered Taiwan to be more competitive than Singapore and Hong Kong in the electronics industry because of Taiwan's superior components manufacturing capability (ADL 1974). Local content regulation was instrumental in establishing the local parts industry, although the eventual success of the industry was due to growth in the export market.

2. Local Content Regulations

Local content regulations were instituted by the government in 1965 with the aim of nurturing the local parts industry for electronics and machinery products. The initial local content ratio imposed on monochrome television sets was 50%. It was raised to 60% in 1966. After the indigenous producer of cathode ray tubes (CRT), Chung-Hua Picture Tube, inaugurated production in 1970, the local content ratio for monochrome television sets was raised to 70% in 1972. Since CRT constituted about one-third of the cost of a television set, a local content ratio of 70% was unattainable without using locally produced CRTs. As locally made CRTs became widely adopted by local producers, the local content ratio was raised further to 80% in 1973 and eventually to 90% in 1974. By then, virtually all components could be sourced locally. The local content requirement for monochrome television sets was phased out in 1983 by which time it had apparently become redundant.

A local content regulation was also imposed on colour television sets in 1970 at an initial ratio of 40%. It was gradually raised to 50% and then to 60%. The 60% ratio left some room for the use of imported colour CRTs. The local content requirement on colour television sets was phased out in 1986 when the entire trade regime in Taiwan was greatly liberalized. Local content regulations were useful in forcing

Japanese television-set makers to transfer parts manufacturing technology to their local partners or to local parts makers. Major Japanese television-set assembly firms also encouraged their parts suppliers in the *keiretsu* networks to form joint ventures with indigenous parts makers.

In general, the government was pragmatic in imposing local content requirements. The target was set at a level which was attainable through reasonable efforts, and was gradually raised in line with the progress of the local parts industry. When a bottle-neck arose blocking the achievement of a higher level of local content, the government would even take the initiative to create local parts suppliers. This happened with CRTs, and later with compressors used in air conditioners.

Take CRT as an example. The first firm to produce CRT in Taiwan was Clinton of the United States, which began investing in Taiwan in 1969. Philips followed in 1971. Both established fully owned subsidiaries to produce monochrome tubes. To ensure local participation in this critical industry, the government engineered, in 1971, a joint venture between major local television-set manufacturers and RCA to embark on CRT production. Named Chung-Hua Picture Tube, the joint venture was intended to serve the local market. The initial production volume was merely 50,000 units. Lack of scale and technical sophistication led to losses. Continued losses prompted RCA to abandon the joint venture in 1976. Local partners however, held on and turned to Toshiba (Japan) for technological assistance. Successive expansions enlarged the production capacity of Chung-Hua to 3 million units in 1980, which was by this time finally producing competitive products. Aiding the expansion were exports to the Southeast Asian countries of Thailand, Indonesia and Malaysia. By 1980 locally produced monochrome CRTs had completely replaced imported ones in domestic-oriented television sets in Taiwan. Total production of CRTs in 1980 reached nearly 10 million units, with about half exported to the United States, Europe and Southeast Asia, while the other half was consumed locally.

3. Technology Acquisition and Diffusion

The United States and Japan were the major sources of technology for Taiwanese consumer electronics firms. Taiwanese firms acquired technology in two ways: licensing and emulation. Among all manufacturing industries, technology licensing has been most active in the electronics industry. From 1952 to 1979 there were 337 cases of technology licensing agreements between local electronics firms (including subsidiaries of multinational firms) and foreign technology providers. Among them, 236 cases were contracted with Japanese firms, 80 with American firms and 18 with European firms.

Local licensees and foreign licensors may be independent or joint-venture partners. A technology licensing agreement may also be accompanied by a licence to use the licensor's brand. In the case of local licensees being independent of foreign licensors, 22.22% of these local firms also license brands from licensors. In the case of local licensees being joint-venture partners or subsidiaries of foreign licensors, 45.24% of these local firms also license brands from the licensors (Investment Commission, 1980, p. 15). Brand licensing is usually confined to the domestic market. Licensees are not allowed to use the licensors' brands for export. Sometimes the licensees are even prohibited from engaging in any exports.

It is also common for technology licensors to supply components and parts to licensees. This is necessary because part of the technology is embodied in components and parts. The method may also be a bargaining ploy whereby technology licensors use components and parts to extract rent from the licensees, in addition to normal royalties stated in the formal licensing agreements. Licensing agreements, which entail transfer of foreign exchange, had been subject to government approval until recently. A survey by the Investment Commission (1980) showed that independent licensees purchased 21.82% of their components and parts from foreign technology licensors while joint-venture or subsidiary licensees purchased 35.81%. The higher ratio of the latter group indicates that shifting rent through the components trade is indeed practised.

One important reason for local Taiwanese firms to preferring Japanese technology is the local entrepreneurs' familiarity with the Japanese language. Taiwan was a Japanese colony from 1895 to 1945. Most local entrepreneurs received Japanese education in their youth. The language barrier has been shown to be a serious obstacle to technology transfer (Branson, 1970). Another reason for the popularity of Japanese technology in Taiwan is that Japanese technology could be adapted to smaller-scale and more labour-intensive production and hence is more suitable for Taiwan's manufacturing environment. In the absence of a language barrier, local small firms widely adopted Japanese technology to develop their product niche. Operating mostly in the parts industry, these small firms grew and multiplied to become the backbone of Taiwan's electronics industry.

It is often difficult to transfer technology intact because of locational differences. Some adaptation is usually necessary to make transferred technology operational. Technology licensees need to expend resources on learning and adaptation (Teece, 1977). A survey by the Investment Commission (1980, p. 35, Table 5.2) indicated that on average, local licensees in the electronics industry expended 27.42% of their R&D expenditure on product improvement and another 26.11% on process improvement. In general pure indigenous and joint-venture firms are more active than foreign subsidiaries in R&D. Casual observations indicate that local joint-venture partners sometimes modify the technology transferred from partners to the extent that it amounts to an innovation and can be exported elsewhere. For example, Taiwan Matsushita improved the remote-control device of television receivers and consequently exported the technology to its parent company and its subsidiary in Australia (Investment Commission, 1980, p. 36).

One drawback of obtaining technology through formal licensing agreements is the export restrictions which may be imposed by the licensors. A survey by the Taiwan government (Liu, 1985) showed that out of 73 technology licensing contracts with Japanese firms in the electronics industry, exports were prohibited in four cases. In another five cases an export trade could only be conducted by the licensors on behalf of the licensees. The export restrictions clause is generally limited to contracts involving joint-venture partners, however.

But even with export restraints in place during the licensing period, the licensees can regain their right to export after the contract expires. The average technology licensing period in the electronics industry lasts about six years. The Investment Commission (1980) surveyed 114 licensing contracts agreed upon between 1970 and 1979, and found that only 32 contracts were renewed after expiration. Most licensees showed reasonable satisfaction with the technology transfer. The renewal cases mostly involved joint-venture partners and the licensing contracts between them were likely to serve the purpose of transfer pricing in addition to technology transfer.

Even without a formal technology licensing agreement, the presence of foreign firms may still facilitate technology diffusion through emulation by local firms. This may be the most important channel through which fully-owned foreign subsidiaries have contributed to technology development in Taiwan. Emulation is sometimes made possible by the turnover of skilled workers from foreign subsidiaries. For example, Taiwan developed a competitive light emitting diode (LED) industry in the 1980s. Skilled ex-workers from Texas Instruments, which introduced LEDs to Taiwan, provided the initial technology to local LED producers. Texas Instruments commenced production in Taiwan in 1970, and the first indigenous LED manufacturer, Liteon, was established in 1975 with former Texas Instruments engineers supporting the company. Likewise, Taiwan's production of diode rectifiers also benefited from the technology spillovers of multinational firms. The major technology source for diode rectifiers was GI, which came to Taiwan in 1964. The first domestic diode rectifier producer, Li-Cheng Electronics, was established in 1976 with support from ex-GI engineers (Chien, 1988, p. 49).

Of course, ex-engineers of multinational firms can only provide the initial technology impetus to start operations. Innovation and catching-up with new technology have to come from independent R&D efforts or subsequent technology licensing. Both Li-Cheng and Liteon expended extensively on R&D and were eventually capable of transferring their own technology to Southeast Asia in the 1980s.

It is interesting to note that technology diffusion tends to stay within a small region surrounding the original source of technology. In the case of LEDs, for example, Liteon and other indigenous firms relying on the derivative technology of Texas Instruments all located in the city of Chung-Ho and its adjacent town Pan-Chiao. Chung-Ho has been the plant site of Texas Instruments since its arrival in Taiwan. Local networks of skilled workers originating from Texas Instruments serve these emulating indigenous firms (Chien, 1988, p. 41, Table 4–2). Emulation seems to be limited to relatively unsophisticated technology, however. For example, indigenous firms have not been able to make significant inroads into the manufacturing of transistors despite stringent local content regulations. GI started transistor assembly in 1965, Philco followed in 1966 and Hitachi (Japan) in 1967. The first indigenous attempt to produce transistors came many years later with

Wan-Peng Co. in 1973. Drawing technological assistance from locally trained engineers without much industrial expertise, Wang-Peng engaged in transistor production without the benefit of foreign technology. It succeeded in some niche products (such as small signal transistors) but never made it into the mainstream. Despite local content requirements, most of the time imports supplied more than 90% of the domestic demand for transistors. Local production of transistors was dominated by multinational firms which were export oriented and segregated from the local market.

The lesson of transistor production suggests that there is a limit to natural technology spillover. Some technology gaps may need to be bridged by indigenous research initiatives and at such times the government may have to provide the push. In the next section we present the case of the semiconductor sector in which we will see a more proactive role played by the government in promoting technology development in integrated circuits (ICs). Taiwan's IC industry proved to be much more successful than the transistor industry.

IV. DEVELOPMENT OF THE PERSONAL COMPUTER INDUSTRY

Taiwan's personal computer (PC) industry began in the late 1970s as some Taiwanese companies started assembling PC kits for domestic sales, using imported microprocessors from Intel, Zilog, Texas Instruments, etc. The industry was subsequently boosted by a boom of electronic games on the Taiwan market. During this boom local game-parlour operators imported game machines from Japan and contracted local electronics firms to replicate them in mass volume through direct copying or redesign. Electronics firms imported microprocessors from the United States and designed the circuit boards which constituted the core operating units of the machines. The electronic game boom gave the initial impetus to Taiwan's PC industry, whereby some primitive design capabilities were established. For example, Taiwanese firms disassembled the programmable logic arrays (PLA) built inside the Japanese game machines through reverse engineering and redesigned them for local production. Some of these locally redesigned circuit boards were even exported to Hong Kong (Chou, 1996, pp. 80–82). The electronic game boom came to a sudden end when the government surprised the industry by banning electronic games in 1982, claiming that many of them involved gambling. Electronics firms which were left with a large inventory of microprocessors scrambled for outlets. They found that these microprocessors were also used in Apple II computers and started to make unauthorized clones of Apple II for resale. This was the beginning of Taiwan's export of personal computers. The Apple II clone was a hit on the U.S. market as it substantially undercut the price of genuine Apple computers with comparable quality. The Taiwanese government was forced to crack down on such illegal clones in 1982–83 under the pressure from Apple and the U.S. government. But the industry resurrected itself by producing IBM clones as IBM was willing to license the relevant technology, primarily BIOS technology, to Taiwanese manufacturers.

In the early 1980s the PC industry in Taiwan was dominated by American multinational firms. Companies like Atari and Wang were producing PC-related products for export to the U.S. market to take advantage of Taiwan's low-cost labor and engineers. But local companies quickly seized the opportunities to join the market by serving as subcontractors and OEM producers for multinational firms.

Using its dense production networks developed since the 1960s, Taiwan competed successfully in the PC industry by separating the production of computers into small segments in which small firms developed their niche and prevailed. As a result of refined division of labour, there were hundreds of specialized producers in the fields of mother boards, keyboards, monitors, mice, add-on cards, and so on. Each product was sold separately to system producers for integration, or was combined with other products to form a sub-system for re-sale in the international markets.

Many of Taiwan's small PC component suppliers had previous experience in producing consumer electronics and components (Dedrick and Kraemer 1998, p. 147). For example, when the television industry declined in the mid-1980s and many multinational firms withdrew from Taiwan, the engineers released from the television industry were immediately absorbed into the computer monitor industry. The design and manufacturing capabilities transferred from the television industry quickly made Taiwan the world's number-one producer of monitors. Local CRT manufacturer, Chung-Hua Picture Tube, also adapted itself from making television tubes to monitor tubes. Capitalizing on the booming monitor industry, Chung-Hua Picture Tube has become the world's largest CRT manufacturer, surpassing such international giants as Hitachi and Philips. Among local firms that made the transition from making television receivers to computer monitors were local companies like Tatung and Sampo, as well as multinational firms like Philips and Matsushita. Local companies served as subcontractors for system producers such as IBM and Compaq. Their anonymity, while a fatal deficiency in their endeavours to become a world-class producer of consumer electronics such as television receivers, made them perfect partners for world-renowned systems producers which source components and parts globally to minimize costs.

A strong and interwoven network of component producers constitutes the core competence of Taiwan's PC industry. For example, mother boards are supported by high-quality printed circuit boards (PCB) whose production was originally to serve the production of television receivers, telephone receivers, calculators and other electronic devices. Switching power supply (SPS) is supported by a strong transformer industry whose root can also be traced back to television receiver production. In addition to the design and manufacturing capabilities developed during the previous experience of making consumer electronics, Taiwan's PC industry was aided by technology and skills acquired from overseas. Through contact with Taiwan's overseas engineers and technicians working in the Silicon Valley of the United States, Taiwan's PC industry was able to access frontier technologies in the industry. Through repatriation of these overseas engineers, the industry was able to acquire scarce skills which were critical to the development of these key technologies. For example, there are more than 30 chipset makers in Taiwan, most of which are spin-offs from the U.S. firm, Chips & Technologies (Dedrick and Kraemer, 1988, p. 159). Taiwan is the world's leading producer of scanners and mice, of which all the major companies were established by engineers who had worked in Silicon Valley.

The industry was further supported by the state-run research laboratory named Electronics Research and Service Organization (ERSO). ERSO undertook R&D projects to develop technologies pertinent to computer hardware. For example, ERSO developed IBM's BIOS technology through reverse engineering and transferred it to local firms in 1983, enabling them to produce computers compatible with IBM XT (Chou, 1996, p. 112). This was how the production of IBM-compatible computers started in Taiwan. With the technology alrealy dispersed,

IBM was forced to accept a nominal licensing fee from Taiwanese PC manufacturers employing the BIOS technology to which IBM claimed a patent right. Later on ERSO also helped the industry acquire the technology to manufacture notebook computers, which were heretofore monopolized by the Japanese producers. By pooling more than 40 local PC makers in a research consortium, ERSO successfully developed the prototype technology which was subsequently shared by the members of the consortium. Although cut-throat competition among the consortium members, coupled with a recession in the PC industry in the early 1990s, led to massive failures in Taiwan's PC industry, the surviving PC makers soon captured the largest market share of the world's notebook computers.

In addition to providing technology, ERSO was instrumental in training and seasoning engineers to support Taiwan's PC industry. Funded by the government on a project-by-project basis, ERSO usually recruited a group of young engineers from domestic sources and a few veteran engineers from all over the world to undertake a research project. The project usually lasted for three to five years. When the project ended, some engineers would be lured away by private companies interested in the technologies that they had acquired or the skills that they had possessed. The other engineers would be retained to lead research teams on subsequent projects. Sometimes the whole research team was spun off to form a new company which was to engage in the manufacturing of the products developed by the research project. It is said that the majority of veteran engineers in Taiwan's PC industry have their roots in ERSO or Silicon Valley.

In addition to indigenous technology accumulated from the previous production experience and that acquired through government-sponsored R&D, Taiwan's PC industry obtained critical technology from multinational firms. This is achieved mainly through linkages to multinational firms with which Taiwanese manufacturers form a strategic relationship. For example, up to now the revolution of PC has been brought about by Intel through the introduction of new-generation microprocessors in its central processing unit (CPU). A close relationship with Intel would enable Taiwanese firms to access the information regarding the newest CPU and allow them to introduce new-generation products a step ahead of their competitors. This strategic relationship is built upon the trust that early access to the critical information by small Taiwanese producers, while useful for Intel in evaluating the performances of its new CPU, does not present a threat to upset the balance that Intel wishes to maintain among the world's major system producers.

Taiwan also took advantage of its manufacturing capabilities to form strategic alliances with multinational firms in an attempt to acquire critical technology. For example, through the arrangement of ERSO, Taiwan's major PC manufacturers formed the Power-PC Alliance with Apple, IBM and Motorola in an effort to promote Power-PC computers to counter the monopoly power of Intel. Under the alliance Apple, IBM and Motorola agreed to establish a research and support centre in Taipei to support the consortium members. Although in the end the alliance failed to present a credible challenge to Intel, it strengthened Taiwan's linkages to multinational firms. For example, a member of the consortium, Umax, was licensed by Apple to produce Power-PC computers based on the Macintosh operating system, the first such licence ever awarded by Apple.

V. DEVELOPMENT OF THE SEMICONDUCTOR INDUSTRY

As with consumer electronics, Taiwan's semiconductor industry started with multinational firms. The industry was inaugurated by Philco of the United States, which started assembling ICs in 1967 in Taiwan's first export-processing zone in Kaohsiung (Chien, 1988, p. 13, Table 1–2). Similar foreign direct investments (FDI) were made around the same time by Fairchild and Motorola in South Korea, and Texas Instruments, National Semiconductor, and Fairchild in Singapore, all aspiring to take advantage of the international division of labor (Henderson, 1989, p. 51).

Philco's path-breaking operation in Taiwan was followed by Philips in 1969, Texas Instrument in 1970, RCA in 1971, as well as other multinational firms in later years (Hsiao, 1995). All foreign-owned operations were concentrated in assembly and testing, however. There was little incentive for multinational firms to set up fabrication lines in Taiwan because such operations entailed a large capital commitment and a high risk of technology failure if the host country lacked the engineering capability to run the skill-intensive operations. Nonetheless, the IC-assembly operations of multinational firms in Taiwan were imitated by some local concerns, which set up much smaller-scale operations. In 1980 assembly operations still dominated Taiwan's IC industry, accounting for 97.13% of the total output of the semiconductor industry in Taiwan, which was then valued at NT$7.5 billion, with the remaining 2.87% attributed to chip fabrication at a government-owned foundry. Among the 12 assembly firms, nine were owned by multinationals (ITRI, 1987, p. 58). Needless to say, virtually all assembled products were exported.

Despite showing reluctance to upgrade their operations in Taiwan, multinational firms have been instrumental in transferring technology to the local industry. In 1976 RCA began one of its ventures to transfer complementary metal oxide semiconductor (CMOS) chip technology to ERSO. RCA provided ERSO staff with training in chip processing, design engineering and other operation-related know-how (Hobday, 1995, p.111). ERSO established an experimental plant to receive the technology from RCA. The plant subsequently spun off to become a private firm named United Microelectronics Co. (UMC) in 1980. UMC was the major vehicle for accumulating chip-processing technology, training local engineers and providing foundry services that laid the foundation for Taiwan's IC-design houses.

In 1982 the first IC-design house, Syntek, was established in Taiwan. Led by the former manager of the IC-Design Department of ERSO, Kuo-Chao Wang, and his colleagues, Syntek was supported by indigenous capital and ERSO technology (Lin, 1987, p. 38). A design house is a knowledge-based operation with a minimum requirement of capital. The crucial infrastructure for a viable IC-design industry is the availability of a foundry service that can turn blueprints into products. Moreover, the foundries must work with the design houses closely enough that designers and fabricators can interact to improve product design and fabrication technology.

Syntek was soon followed by other local and foreign design houses. Two American design houses owned by overseas Chinese engineers and entrepreneurs in Silicon Valley, Vitelic and Mosel, set up subsidiaries in Taiwan in 1984 and 1987 respectively. Both specialized in memory chip technology which was complementary to Taiwan's expertise in logic IC. In addition to working with UMC and ERSO for new product development, both Mosel and Vitelic also formed strategic alliances with Japanese semiconductor manufacturer Oki. Using Mosel's and Vitelic's designs, Oki fabricated DRAM chips, some of which bore its own brand name while the others bore the designers' brand name. The alliance enabled the two design houses to accumulate skills within their firms while improving their design capabilities in preparation for launching their own fabrication facilities.

The rich endowment of local engineers on the island of Taiwan itself and the seemingly undepletable supply of Taiwanese engineers in advanced countries, particularly in the Silicon Valley of the United States, attracted a flock of multinational firms, including Fairchild, Motorola, Texas Instrument, Philips and NEC, to set up IC-design houses in Taiwan in the mid-1980s. Philips and Motorola had co-operation programs with ERSO in the area of technology exchange and personnel training (Lin, 1987, p. 39).

The design house boom created a shortage of foundry services, since UMC was the only supplier, and it was reluctant to devote too much of its capacity to such services. In 1987 the Taiwanese government took the initiative to establish the Taiwan Semiconductor Manufacturing Co. (TSMC) to specialize in foundry services. Philips responded to the government's solicitation by taking a substantial share (27.5%) of the company's equity. The joint venture culminated Philips' localization process and integrated Philips into Taiwan's industrial networks. Through this joint venture, Philips transferred its static random access ram (SRAM) technology to ERSO and ERSO, in turn, spun off around 200 personnel, mostly engineers, to join TSMC (Hobday, 1995, p. 110).

Specializing in foundry services without its own products, TSMC's approach to the international semiconductor market proved to be successful. It gained business not only from local IC-design houses but also from overseas designers. Even top manufacturers in the IC industry sought TSMC's fabrication support to supplement their capacity to maintain product variety. TSMC's quick and stunning success encouraged UMC to embark on its first major expansion by investing NT$6 billion to establish its second fabrication line, mainly devoted to the production of SRAM with design technology provided by Mosel. Mosel also provided SRAM technology to Winbond, which was established in 1988 by a leading local wire and cable company (Walsin). By the end of 1990 there were eight IC manufacturing firms in Taiwan, all locally owned, except for TSMC, in which Philips had a minority share (*Semiconductor Industry Yearbook* 1991, pp. 32–34). Fabrication generated NT$12 billion worth of IC products, accounting for 31.5% of overall IC production in Taiwan, which was valued at NT$39.4 billion in 1990 (*Semiconductor Industry Yearbook* 1991, p. 46, Table 4.2). Assembly and testing, which were virtually monopolized by multinational firms, still dominated the Taiwan IC industry at that time, with NT$27.4 billion worth of output. The largest assembly firms were, in order, Philips, Texas Instrument, Motorola and General Electric (formerly RCA). All were wholly owned foreign firms whose products were destined for the export market. Multinational firms seemed to be segregated from local fabrication and concentrated on assembling products for their parent companies.

This segregation line was first broken by Philips when it entered TSMC as a joint-venture partner. Philips was followed by Texas Instruments, which was incidentally, the second largest IC exporter in Taiwan, after Philips, when it formed a joint venture with a local computer manufacturer, Acer, in 1989. The Texas Instruments-Acer joint venture established Taiwan's first fabrication line for the mass production of DRAMs. Although Texas Instruments only contributed about 26% of the capital for the joint venture, it transferred its 4M DRAM technology to the new firm and thus brought Taiwan's IC industry into the mainstream. Texas Instruments' long presence in Taiwan yielded an apparent bonus for the joint venture. The new firm was managed by senior Taiwanese managers from the local Texas Instruments subsidiary in co-operation with other managers dispatched from Acer. There was no need for expatriate managers from the parent company.

As can be seen from the cases of TSMC and Texas Instruments-Acer, multinational firms were not keen on establishing wholly owned subsidiaries to manufacture ICs in Taiwan. It is noteworthy that both Philips and Texas Instruments insisted on a wholly owned corporate structure when they invested in offshore assembly operations in the 1970s. They were keen on managerial control through expatriates to ensure the quality of products which were destined for international markets. But in the case of semiconductor manufacturing, they were not concerned about control of the joint venture and chose a minority ownership position. For them, the Taiwan joint venture was part of the portfolio of their global investment map for risk diversification. The Taiwanese partners had to provide most of the ingredients for the joint venture, including capital and skilled manpower. The contribution of multinational firms was mainly in the area of technology.

The cases of TSMC and Texas Instruments-Acer are indicative of a successful joint-venture formula for the high-technology age. Their success pointed the way for other joint ventures. In 1995 Mitsubishi of Japan formed a joint venture with the Umax-Elite group of Taiwan, which specializes in computer peripherals, mainly mother boards and scanners. The joint venture, named PowerChip, set out to establish a fabrication plant capable of processing 20-cm (8-inch) wafers into memory chips. Mitsubishi was to provide the chip technology but took only a minority equity share in the joint venture.

1. Technology Acquisition and Skill Accumulation

In the development of Taiwan's IC industry, skill accumulation and reproduction is an essential mechanism driving industrial growth, and government-sponsored research institutes also play a crucial role in this process. A typical mode of skill accumulation and reproduction goes like this: a government-sponsored research agency, for example ERSO, acquires or develops technology through R&D projects, and then spins off engineers involved in the projects to support business operations based on the newly acquired technology. The spin-off may be a deliberate plan of the government or simply a profit-seeking move undertaken by the engineers involved in the projects (San, 1993). Successive ERSO projects develop new technology that augments the capabilities of the industry and strengthens the infrastructure underlying its operations. Strengthened infrastructure attracts investment from all directions, which in turn produces synergy effect furthering technology deepening. The virtuous cycle rolls on and the industry expands along the way.

Skill accumulation in Taiwan's semiconductor industry began with the establishment of a semiconductor laboratory at Chiao-Tung University, located in Hsinchu, in 1964. The laboratory trained many engineers who were to form the backbone of Taiwan's semiconductor industry (Lin, 1987, p. 25). In 1980 the government chose to set up its first science-based industrial park in Hsinchu partly because of its proximity to the laboratory.

Large-scale accumulation of skills for industrial application did not begin until the establishment of ERSO in 1974, however. ERSO was also located in Hsinchu, near Chiao-Tung University. Its initial mission was to establish an experimental IC fabrication plant in order to acquire IC manufacturing technology from abroad and transfer it to local firms. Assisted by a group of veteran semiconductor specialists recruited from the United States, ERSO decided to acquire complementary metal oxide semiconductor (CMOS) technology from RCA as its admission ticket to the world's semiconductor industry.

ERSO began the construction of the experimental plant in 1976 and started sending engineers to RCA for training in 1977. Between 1977 and 1979, ERSO sent a total of 295 engineers to acquire technology knowledge from RCA, with the training time accumulating to a total of 363 man-months (ITRI, 1987, p. 11). After the RCA project was completed in 1979, ERSO produced its first spin-off company, UMC, to establish Taiwan's first commercial fabrication line for IC chips. UMC gathered 60% of its initial capital from the private sector in Taiwan, with the remaining 40% provided by the government. The deputy director of ERSO, Robert Hsin-chen Tsao, was called upon to head the new firm, with 14 other ERSO colleagues following him into major management positions. ERSO also provided training for employees of the new firm, totalling 262 man-months (Lin, 1987, p. 36). The 7-micron metal gate CMOS technology acquired from RCA was transferred to UMC to be applied to the production of logic ICs used in watches, calculators, ROMs, telephones, melody chips, etc.

Once the fabrication lines were established, ERSO moved to develop photomask technology and to promote IC-design houses. In 1978 ERSO contracted with International Material Research (IMR) of the United States to transfer photomask manufacturing technology. After the technology transfer, ERSO began producing photomask working plates with master masks provided by RCA. In 1980, ERSO further purchased a full line of photomask-manufacturing equipment from Electromask Co. of the United States, which also transferred the related technology to operate the equipment. Starting from 1981, then, ERSO was able to manufacture photomasks on its own without sourcing from RCA, and began servicing local customers. This greatly shortened the time needed to introduce new IC products into the market (Lin, 1987, pp. 39–40).

To promote IC-design houses, ERSO acquired computer-aided design (CAD) technology from abroad and operated a Common Design Service Centre to promote local design technology. ERSO established its first spin-off design house, Syntek, in 1982. Three engineers left ERSO to serve the company, taking the positions of president, R&D

manager and chief engineer. In 1983 seven ERSO engineers joined other investors to form another design house named Holtek. Both Syntek and Holtek were successful businesses and Holtek went on to establish its own fabrication plant in 1988. Other design houses entered the market in later years, including those established by multinational firms. Except for Fairchild, Texas Instruments, NEC and locally owned Acer Design, all local design houses benefited from ERSO's technology spillover, either through hiring ex-ERSO engineers or through formal technology transfer agreements (Lin, 1987, pp. 38–39).

With the photomask-manufacturing capability and design houses in place, ERSO moved to deepen Taiwan's chip fabrication technology. ERSO undertook a four-year project, called the VLSI (very large-scale integrated circuits) project, beginning in 1983, to upgrade chip manufacturing technology to the 2-micron level. Unlike the project to transfer technology from RCA, which provided a package of technologies including all the ingredients needed for IC design and fabrication, the VLSI project emphasized in-house research, with ERSO's own experimental plant, UMC, local design houses and downstream users called upon to participate in the project (ITRI, 1987, p. 24). The consortium not only created synergy effect in technology advancement but also facilitated technology diffusion in the course of research.

When the VLSI project ended in 1987, ERSO launched TSMC, joining forces with Philips. ERSO again transferred personnel to TSMC, along with technology. ERSO also announced that its experimental fabrication plant would cease all commercial operations from then on. Some of ERSO's senior engineers left to form Winbond Semiconductor which became one of the most successful chip manufacturers of the 1990s, rivaling UMC and TSMC. In 1988 ERSO spun off its photomask operations to form a photomask manufacturing firm, Taiwan Photomask. This completed the vertical integration of Taiwan's semiconductor industry. By 1990 the industry was able to fabricate 1.2-micron chips on 15-cm (6-inch) wafers. The major remaining vacuum in the industry was the capacity to produce DRAM, and that was quickly filled by the Texas Instruments-Acer joint venture formed in the same year. Taiwan's technology, however, still lagged behind the world's leading-edge technology by roughly one generation, that is, three to five years (Lu, 1995).

ERSO therefore undertook yet another aggressive project, this time aimed at breaking the 1-micron barrier in chip manufacturing in

TABLE 6.9   Milestones in IC Technology Development in Taiwan

* 64K DRAM	1.5 micron
World leaders :	1980
ERSO in 1980 :	5 micron
Taiwan achieved 1.5 micron by 1986	
Gap :	6 years
* 256K DRAM	1.2 micron
World leaders :	1983
ERSO in 1983 :	3.5 micron
Taiwan achieved 1.2 micron by 1988	
Gap :	5 years
* 1M DRAM	1.0 micron
World leaders :	1986
ERSO in 1986 :	1.5 micron
Taiwan achieved 1.0 micron by 1990	
Gap :	4 years
* 4M DRAM	0.8 micron
World leaders :	1990
ERSO in 1990 :	1.0 micron
Taiwan achieved 0.8 micron by 1991	
Gap :	1–2 years
* 16M DRAM	0.5 micron
World leaders :	1992/93
ERSO in 1992 :	0.7 micron
Taiwan achieved 0.5 micron in 1994	
Gap :	1 year

SOURCE: Mathews (1995).

Taiwan. The project, appropriately named the Submicron Project, was inaugurated in 1990. DRAM and SRAM were designated as the vehicle devices to carry the technology. Device design was contracted to a newly formed design house operated by a group of veteran memory chip designers who had returned from the United States. The contractor was also responsible for training ERSO designers in related design technology. The project proceeded rapidly. In 1992 ERSO completed construction of its clean room, capable of processing 20-cm (8-inch) wafers. It successively developed the capability to process 4M-bit

DRAM (at the 0.7-micron level) and SRAM (at the 0.5-micron level) and transferred the technology to UMC and TSMC, who soon established their own 8-inch wafer fabrication lines for commercial production. By the end of the project, 16M-bit DRAM was also being produced, with samples tested and certified by several users (Lu, 1995). ERSO wasted no time in producing its latest spin-off in 1995, capitalizing on the facilities installed for the Submicron Project, and technology developed accordingly. The leader of the Submicron Project, Chi-yuan Lu, was appointed president of the new company, which was named Vanguard Semiconductor.

By the time Vanguard joined the élite group of Taiwan's semiconductor industry, it was not monopolizing the 20-cm (8-inch) wafer fabrication capacity, as UMC and TSMC had already commenced such operations with the technology transferred from ERSO during the course of the Submicron Project. When that project ended in 1995, Taiwan's technology gap with respect to front runners in the IC industry was shortened to about a quarter of one generation, or approximately one year (Lu, 1995). The breakthrough in submicron technology, aided by a surging demand for memory chips in the world market, fuelled an investment rush in the semiconductor industry. By October 1995 at least 14 firms had announced plans to join the league of 20-cm (8-inch) wafer fabricators, with proposed investment exceeding NT$414 billion (*Commonwealth*, 1 October 1995).

Looking back at the technology catch-up process, the progress made by Taiwan's IC industry is remarkable indeed. Table 6.9 documents the milestones of this catch-up process. In 1980 ERSO developed Taiwan's first chip of 64K DRAM with 5-micron technology while the world's leaders were on 1M DRAM with 1.5 micron technology. The technology gap was then approximately six years. ERSO developed 256K DRAM in 1983 and 1M DRAM in 1986 to close the technology gap to approximately four years. By the end of the Submicron Project in 1994, ERSO had achieved 0.5-micron-level technology to produce 16M DRAM, reducing the gap with the world leaders to only one year. The history of Taiwan's semiconductor industry reveals the importance of skill accumulation and reproduction. At all times the government-sponsored research institutes sought to diffuse technology as widely as possible. Technology was treated like a semi-public good once it was acquired. This did not reduce the incentive to innovate because the technology was not frontier technology. Furthermore, it was mainly design and processing technology that could be employed to develop new products as the transferees saw fit. Since the semiconductor industry has clustered around the Hsinchu Science-Based Industrial Park, skills spread around the area and new engineers are continually being absorbed into the pool. Because of the speedy multiplication of firms, the industry also employs a very young cohort of workers. Veteran engineers are a rare species and are dispersed throughout different firms. The first generation of ERSO engineers who were trained in the RCA project are today mostly presidents and vice-presidents of major semiconductor firms.

VI. CONCLUSIONS

Taiwan's experience in the electronics industry indicates that three major forces are at work in the development of an industry, namely international linkages, local conditions and government policy. International linkages are critical in bringing new products and new technologies. It was the Japanese trading firms that brought the radio-assembly business to Taiwan and it was the American multinationals that made Taiwan one of the major offshore assembly sites for television sets. Japanese linkages were instrumental in Taiwan's acquisition and diffusion of technologies pertinent to electronic parts. American linkages were instrumental in Taiwan's skill accumulation in IC design and processing technologies.

Local conditions underlie Taiwan's comparative advantage. In the early years it was low-cost labor that attracted multinational firms to Taiwan. In later years it was indigenous technology and local skills that attracted foreign investment. The case of the semiconductor industry clearly indicates that low-cost labor only attracts the low-skill segment of the IC industry, namely assembly and packaging. Indigenous technology is crucial to the development of the core of the IC industry, namely design and fabrication. The lesson of Taiwan's electronics industry points out the importance of creating an investment climate which is conducive to maximum technology diffusion and skill accumulation. A local presence of multinational firms offers a potential opportunity for technology diffusion, but there is no guarantee that this will actually take place. More importantly, technology diffused from multinational firms may be fragmented and non-operational because of some missing links. Sometimes it is up to the government to locate these missing links and to make up for them with direct involvement in research.

The policy of the Taiwanese government towards the electronics industry has been to maximize local participation in the industry to create maximum exposure to new technology. A dichotomized market structure allows indigenous firms to operate in the domestic market and subsidiaries of multinational firms to focus on the export market. The co-existence of local-market-oriented and export-oriented firms creates a wide spectrum of demand for parts and components. This encourages both local and multinational firms to find their niches in the industry. The technology gap between foreign and indigenous firms creates the learning opportunities. In Taiwan, such learning led to technology deepening, resulting in the increased integration of local industries. Even multinational firms have been engulfed by the integration process and become increasingly localized.

REFERENCES

Arthur D. Little (ADL). "The Electronics Industry in Taiwan". *Industry of Free China* 42, no.1 (1974): 21–34.

Branson, J. "Technology Transfer through the International Firm". *American Economic Review* 60 (1970): 435–40.

Chen, T.J. "Technical Change and Technical Adaptation of Multinational Firms: The Case of Taiwan's Electronics Industry". *Economic Development and Cultural Change* (1992): 867–81.

Chen, T.J. and D.P. Tang. "The Production Characteristics of Multinational Firms and the Effects of Tax Incentives". *Journal of Development Economics* 24 (1986): 119–29.

Chen, T.J. and W.T. Wang. "Wai T&U Ch'ang Shang Te Pen Tu Hua: Mei Jih Den Tzu Ch'ang Te Pi Chiao Yen Chiu" [Localization of foreign firms: A comparative study of American cover], 1994.

Chien, J. C. *Den Tze Ling Tso Chien Yeh Fa Chan Ch'e Lieh Yen Chiu Pao Kao* [Development strategy of the electronic components industry]. Project Report. Taipei: Taiwan Institute for Economic Research, 1988.

Chou, C. H. *Shi Cheng-Rong Te Den Nou Chuan Chi* [Legends of Stan Shih]. Taipei: Lien-Ching Press, 1996.

Chu, C.H. "Taiwan Chih Den Chih Kung Yeh" [Taiwan's electronics industry]. *Bank of Taiwan Quarterly* 26, no. 1 (1975): 112–30.

Dedrick, J. and K. Kraemer. *Asia's Computer Challenge*. New York: Oxford University Press, 1998.

Hattori, T. and Y. Sato. *Kankoku Taiwan no Hatten Mekanizumu* [The development mechanism in Korea and Taiwan]. Tokyo: Institute of Developing Economies, 1996.

Henderson, J. *The Globalization of High Technology Production*. London: Routledge, 1989.

Hobday, M. *Innovation in East Asia: The Challenge to Japan*. Vermont: Edward Elgar, 1995.

Hsiao, F.H. "Tsung Shih Chang Ching Ju Chang Ai Tan Tao Tai Wan Kao Ko Chi Chan Yeh Fa Chan Tse Lueh — Chi Ti Tien Lu Chan Yeh Chih Ko An Yeh Chiu" [A study on industrial development policy from the viewpoint of entry barriers — the case of the IC industry]. *Industry of Free China*, March 1995, pp. 7–29.

IDIC (Industrial Development and Investment Center) (1968), "The Electronics Industry in Taiwan", *Industry of Free China*, vol. 29, no. 3, pp. 32–44.

Investment Commission. *Wo-Kuo Den Tze Den Chih Chih Tsao Yeh Chih Su Ho Tso Chen Kuo Tiao Ch'a Pao Kao* [Survey report on technology co-operation programs in the electronics industry]. Taipei: Investment Commission, Ministry of Economic Affairs, 1980.

Industrial Technology Research Institute (ITRI). "Chi Ti Tien Lu Chuan An Chi Hua Tui Chan Yeh Ying Hsiang Chih Chui Tsung Yu Fen Hsi" [An assessment of government R&D projects on the development of the IC Industry]. Project Report. Taipei: ITRI, 1987.

Lai, V.S. "Tai-wan Den Tze Kung Yeh Chih Yen Chiu" [Taiwan's Electronics Industry]. Masters thesis, National Taiwan University, 1972.

Levy, J. "Diffusion of Technology and Patterns of International Trade: The Case of Television Receivers", Ph.D. thesis, Yale University, 1981.

Lin, H.M. "Ai Fa Chung Kuo Chia Hsin Hsing Chan Yeh Fa Chan Kuo Cheng Chih Yeh Chiu — Wo Kuo IC Kung Yeh Shih Li Tan Tao" [Newly emerged industries in developing countries — the case of Taiwan's IC industry], Masters thesis, Graduate Institute of Business, National Taiwan University, 1987.

Lin, R. F. "Tai-wan Den Chih Kung Yeh Chung Chih Chao Wai Chih," [Foreign capital in Taiwan's electronics industry]. *Bank of Taiwan Quarterly*, 22, no. 4 (1971): 172–78.

Liu, T.Y. "Jih Shang:Lai Hua Tou Tzu Tui Wo Kuo Ching Chi Chi Yin Shiang" [Economic impacts of Japanese investment in Taiwan]. Taipei: Project Report to Research and Development Council, Executive Yuan, 1985.

Lu, C.Y. " Wo Kuo Tzu Wei Mi Pan Tao Ti Chi Shu Fa Chan Chi Chan Wang" [The development of submicron semiconductor technology in Taiwan and future perspectives]. Unpublished manuscript, 1995.

Mathews, J. *High-Technology Industrialization in East Asia: The Case of the Semiconductor Industry in Taiwan and Korea*. Taipei: Chung-Hua Institution for Economic Research, 1995.

San, G. " National Systems Supporting Technical Advance in Industry: the Case of Taiwan". In *National Innovation Systems*, edited by R. Nelson. New York: Oxford University Press, 1993.

Schive, C. and R.S. Yeh. "Direct Foreign Investment and Taiwan's TV Industry". *Economic Essays* 9, no. 2 (1980): 261–91.

Teece, D. "Technology Transfer by Multinational Firms: The Resources Costs of Transferring Technological Know-How". *Economic Journal* 87 (1977): 242–61.

Wu, Y.P. "Ko Hsueh Yuan Chu Chi Ti Tien Lu Chan Yeh Hsien Kuang Fen Hsi Chi Wei Lai Fa Chan Mu Piao Yu Tse Lueh" [Analysis of the current status of the IC industry in the Hsinchu Science-Based Industrial Park and future perspectives]. Hsinchu Science-Based Industrial Park Administration, 1994.

7

The Role of Textiles and Man-made Fibre in the Process of Industrialization: The Case of Taiwan

Been-Lon Chen, Tain-Jy Chen and Yun-Peng Chu

I. INTRODUCTION

The four Asian tigers' success in industrialization and economic development attracts much interest from economists and policy-makers. Among these economies the experiences of both South Korea and Taiwan convey greater implications for problems faced by developing economies during the period of economic development. Much existing literature was devoted to the economic transition and evolution of these two economies, mainly treating both as comparison and as case studies.[1] From a prolonged perspective, the dominant feature of growth and development is the contribution of science and technology. This characteristic is shared by mature economies of virtually all kinds, even though countries may undergo varied phases due to varying initial conditions, cultures and behaviors over time. An important aspect leading to the success of economic development is the adoption of suitable science and technology. Specifically, if a developing economy is able to adopt proper technology, it can take off and can moreover industrialize gradually and sustain growth. That is, to pick the winners or the potentially productive industries. There have been a few theoretical papers on policies in this direction.[2]

The textiles and apparel industry has played an vital role in the history of industrialization. When Britain established the modern factory system in textiles in the late 18th century, the result was the Industrial Revolution and Britain's gradual industrialization and prosperity.[3] Since then, the early stages of industrialization in many developed countries have been strongly related to the establishment and improvement of their own textiles industry. One reason that the textiles industry is able to play such a function is attributed to both the technological properties of textiles and the structure of demography in a developing economy. As the fabrication of textiles is the most labour-intensive among major industries in the early stages of economic development,[4] and as a developing country typically possesses surplus unskilled labor, the making of fabrics provides the most striking example of the combination of extensive division of labor and the use of surplus rural and suburban laborers. The development of textiles technology thus makes possible the transition from agriculture to textiles manufacturing. For this reason the exceptional role of textiles features strongly in the early stages of industrialization.

In Taiwan and South Korea, the development of a modern textiles industry started after World War II and focused mainly on cotton textiles and apparel at the beginning. The production and export of cotton textiles and apparel increased very quickly during the late 1950s and the early 1960s. This threatened not only exports but also the domestic markets of countries in North America and Western Europe. This threat compelled developed countries to negotiate a trading arrangement with less-developed cotton-textiles exporting countries and to regulate the expansion of trade in cotton textiles. The Long-Term Arrangement (LTA) was then established through the General Agreement on Tariffs and Trade (GATT) in 1962 and has been in operation since then. Taiwan and South Korea were therefore forced to switch to textiles of other kinds such as wool, silk and artificial fabrics in particular. Nevertheless, this forced change expanded the production and exports of man-made textiles and apparel, which surpassed those of cotton textiles in the late 1960s. The growth and development of man-made textiles in turn assisted the growth of many other manufacturing industries, especially the chemical industry. For this reason the role of man-made textiles/apparel was critical to the industrialization of Taiwan and South Korea, especially during the early stages. The first objective of this chapter is to document the role of textiles and apparel in Taiwan's industrialization.

The production of artificial fabrics needs raw material called man-made fibre. The manufacturing of man-made fabrics in Taiwan and South Korea led to the manufacturing of man-made fibre in a manner of backward linkages. As a consequence of the creation of a man-made fibre industry, Taiwan became the world's fourth largest producer of man-made fibre by 1984 and the second largest in 1989, second to only the United States, while Korea became the sixth largest by 1984.[5] This rapid expansion of man-made fibre then led to the growth and development of the chemical industry, which became the largest industry in the manufacturing sectors of both economies by the mid-1980s.[6] Unlike the textiles/apparel industry which is labor-intensive, the artificial fibre industry is not only capital-intensive but also technology-intensive. A less developed economy in general has no such technology and moreover lacks the capability to conduct innovation. The technology therefore must be imported and adopted from leading developed countries, according to the product cycle theory of North-South trade (Vernon 1966; Grossman and Helpman 1991).

The theory of North-South trade emphasizes the comparative advantages of the north and the south. It ignores the issue of how a production technology can be imported successfully by developing countries. Different from commodity trading, importation of production technology is much more difficult as it involves not only an *object good* but also an *idea good*, using the terminologies of Romer (1993, 1994). Technology importation calls for more than buying a machine and flipping a switch. Elements of technology adoption include, among others, adoptions of processes and procedures, quality control, raw-material control, production scheduling, production management and after-sales services. There is, however, no acceptable and satisfactory theory *a priori* concerning how to successfully import a technology. A successful case of technology adoption is thus valuable in providing a useful experience. Little attention has been paid to this issue although factors affecting technological capability and technological change in the Third World have been investigated.[7] It follows that no study has been devoted to this point. The second objective of this chapter thus attempts to document the experience of how Taiwan adopted successfully the technology of man-made fibre.

Many newly rapid-growing East Asian latecomers (for example Thailand, Indonesia and China) are now expanding, relying especially upon their cotton textiles industries. These economies may sooner or later switch to producing artificial textiles, and then to the development of their own man-made fibre and chemical industries. The different experiences and strategies of adopting synthetic fibre technology in both Taiwan as well as South Korea can guide and instruct these latecomers. The successful adoption of man-made fibre technology is important, as the establishment of this industry renders successful a transition and progression in industrialization from a more traditional labor-intensive textiles/apparel sector to more modern capital- and technology-intensive chemical and other sectors.[8] This study therefore contributes in at least two aspects: (1) it provides a constructive example of successful man-made fibre technology importation; and (2) it sheds light on the transition of industrialization in developing economies.

This chapter is organized as follows. In the next section we start by verifying the fact that Taiwan became industrialized during the three and a half decades from 1952 to 1987. As this process of industrialization was found closely associated with the manufacturing sector, we then discuss disaggregated two-digit level of manufacturing industries. We find that the growth of textiles and apparel was the most vital to the process of industrialization. In section III, we investigate the sources of development and growth of textiles and apparel and their contribution to the growth of other industries, especially the chemical industry. Section IV documents the expansion of man-made fibre industries, while section V investigates the sources and forms of technology adoption. In section VI we conclude and comment on the recent East Asian financial crisis.

II. INDUSTRIALIZATION

Industrialization, if an economy begins to take off, is a process during which the share of employment in the modern or industrialized sector increases whereas that of the agricultural or traditional sector declines; as a result, the productivity per capita increases in the industrialized sector.[9] During the period between 1952 and 1987, Taiwan's industrialization evolved just as described above. Below, we describe the process of industrialization and then point out the unique role of textiles and apparel by studying disaggregated two-digit industries in manufacturing.

Taiwan started the process of industrialization in the early 1950s, when in 1952 the agricultural sector accounted for as high as 58.0% of aggregate employment, whereas the industrial sector accounted for only 15.0%. By the end of 1987, however, the corresponding figures

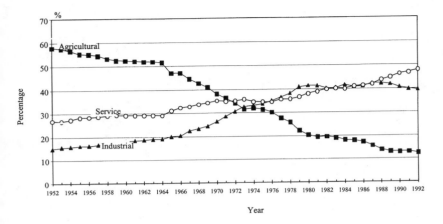

FIGURE 7.1   Taiwan: Employment Share by Industry.
NOTE: Mining is included in the agricultural sector.
SOURCE: Calculated based on CEPD, *Taiwan Statistical Data Book* (*TSDB*)
(1993), Table 2-9b.

became 5.7% and 42.3% respectively. This significant transformation of Clark (1940) scheme is illustrated in Figure 7.1 in which we see a spectacular role reversal occurring between the agricultural and industrial sectors, with the employment share of the industrial sector increasing progressively while that of the agricultural sector decreased. As a result of industrialization, the value added per unit of employment in the industrial sector increased. In Figure 7.2 we demonstrate the shares of GDP for the three fundamental sectors. According to this Kuznets (1957) scheme, the GDP share of the agricultural sector diminished progressively from 1953, whereas the share of the service sector showed no trend.

As a consequence of industrialization, the GNP per capita increased from US$196 in 1952 to more than US$5,000 in 1987 and more than US$10,000 in 1992 (TSDB 1996, Table 1-1a), over which period the average rate of real economic growth per year was more than 8% (TSDB 1996, Table 3-1a). During industrialization the industrial and the manufacturing sectors moved in tandem, as manufacturing had the largest share of employment and value added in the industrial sector (above 80% and above 70% respectively). The question is

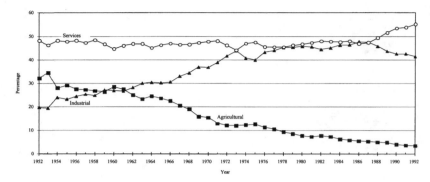

FIGURE 7.2   Taiwan: GDP Share by Sector.
SOURCE: Calculated based on CEPD, *TSDB* (1993), Table 3-11b.

which industries mainly caused the manufacturing sector to grow so
rapidly in the three and a half decades. To answer this question, we
need to conduct the research at a disaggregated (two-digit) level of
manufacturing. We first scrutinize the evolution of employment and
then examine the resulting evolution of value added. We will find that
the textiles and apparel industry was important at all stages before the
late 1980s whereas the chemical industry was vital at later stages.

For labor input we concentrate on the employees on payroll as this
is the only source of data for labor input available at the two-digit level.
Figure 7.3 illustrates employment as a share of manufacturing in food,
textiles/apparel, beverage/tobacco, chemical and electrical industries.
These five industries were chosen because they were large in terms of
both the number of employees and value of production either at the
earlier stages or at later stages. According to Figure 7.3, the food industry was the largest from 1952 to 1959, and was still large before
1972, accounting for above 20% on average. This result is obvious
given the fact that the food industry, of which the major components
were sugar and canned pineapple in the 1950s and 1960s, was closely
related to agriculture and the agricultural sector was large before 1972.
This share has, however, declined greatly since that time, and accounted
for less than 8% in 1973 and much less later. The most important
feature in Figure 7.3 is that the textiles/apparel industry was invariably
large from 1952 on. Its share became the largest after 1960 except for
two years, the peak being 26.49% in 1975 and the average 21.44%.

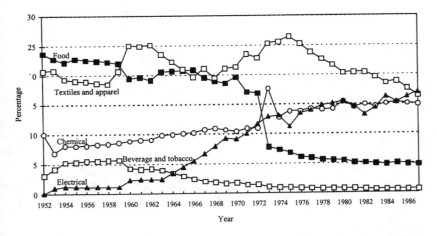

FIGURE 7.3 Taiwan: Employment Share of Five Major Two-digit Industries Over Manufacturing as a Whole.

SOURCES: Calculated based on —

1952–61:	CEPD, *Industry of Free China* 19, no. 1
1962–63:	*Taiwan Reconstruction Statistics*, no. 9
1964–65:	by construction
1966:	*General Report on the Third Industrial Commercial Census of Taiwan, ROC*, no. 3 (1968)
1967:	Ministry of Economic Affairs, Taiwan, *The ROC Report on Industrial and Commercial Surveys*, no. 1 (1968)
1968-72:	Department of Statistics, Ministry of Economic Affairs, Taiwan, *"Taiwan Industrial Production Statistics"*, no. 48
1973:	Directorate General of Budget, Accounting and Statistics, Taiwan, *"Monthly Bulletin of Labour Statistics"*, no. 135
1974, 1975–87:	*Monthly Bulletin of Earning and Productivity Statistics*, nos. 230 and 236

As for the remaining three industries, the share of the beverage/tobacco industry was small from the very beginning, with a maximum of 5.73% in 1959. The share of the chemical industry was less than 10% at the early stages, and that of electrical industry was even less than 5% before 1965, but these two industries gained shares progressively; they were about the same size after 1973 and in the meantime approached that of textiles/apparel. The chemical and textiles industries have recently been the two largest industries, having accounted for more than 35% of employment on average since 1973.

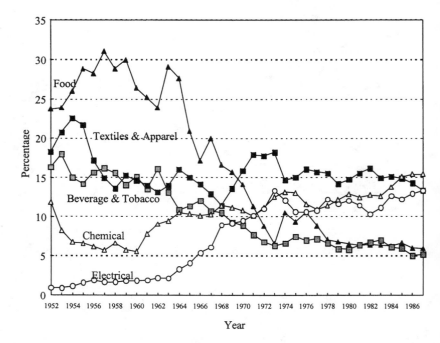

FIGURE 7.4   Taiwan: GDP Share of Five Major Two-digit Industries Over Manufacturing Sector as a Whole.

SOURCE: Calculated based on EPS databank, except for the chemical industry from 1952 to 1980, which is calculated based on *National Income, Taiwan District, ROC,* 1993, Table 1 in part 2 of this chapter.

We now analyze the resulting GDP shares of the five major two-digit industries as a fraction of manufacturing (Figure 7.4). Of the three largest industries at the earlier stages, the food industry was again the largest in the early phase; although once about 30%, this share declined quickly. In reality, the development of the food industry was spurred by the need to supply Taiwan's domestic market that was recovering from World War II. The GDP share of textiles/apparel had the same share as that of beverage/tobacco from 1956 to 1963, after which it became larger. The share of beverage/tobacco was large at the early stages; it fluctuated around 15% between 1952 and 1963, after which period its share decreased. For beverage and tobacco, the share was large at the earlier stages because they were state-owned monopolies whose profits accounted for more than 20% of total government revenue in most years before 1970; its annual average share of total government revenue between 1952 and 1970 was as high as 21.15% (*Yearbook of Tax Statistics of ROC* 1976, Table 1). Finally, for the two remaining industries, the shares of the chemical and electrical industries were small at the early stages. At the later stages, the GDP shares of the textiles/apparel, chemical and electrical industries were the largest. The share of the textiles/apparel industry was the largest starting from 1970 except for the last three years under inquiry and accounted for above 15% on average. The shares of chemical and electrical industries showed an upward trend and competed for the title of second largest industry between 1970 and 1980. The title was held by the chemical industry after 1980. After 1985, the chemical industry surpassed the textiles and apparel to become the largest. The shares of food and beverage/tobacco were small, below 7% after 1979.[10]

III. SOURCES OF GROWTH IN TEXTILES/APPAREL INDUSTRY AND ITS LINKAGES TO CHEMICAL INDUSTRY

In this section we investigate the main sources of growth in the textiles/apparel industry and its linkages to the growth of other manufacturing industries. The main sources are the government policies of trade openness and the world trade boom. The linkages between the textiles/apparel and chemical industries are formed through the textiles industry's demand for the raw materials produced in the chemical industry.[11]

1. Trade Policies and World Trade

Like many other developing economies after World War II, Taiwan was confronted by the need to expand its consumer goods industries in order to meet its domestic demand. This demand was intensified further by a sudden enlargement of its domestic market due to both the vast number of immigrants from mainland China and the heavy military requirement after 1949. This situation naturally led to the development of such nondurable consumer goods industries as food, beverage/tobacco, textiles/apparel and others.

The development and growth of the textiles and apparel industry in Taiwan was subsequently enhanced by the policy of import substitution: the replacement of imports by domestic production. The policy of import substitution was originally based upon the argument of infant industry aimed to increase employment growth and to establish domestic industry. After World War II the larger enterprises producing sugar and important intermediate products were retained by the government and their rehabilitation was facilitated through the extension of low-cost loans from state-owned banks and U.S. aid. In contrast, numerous small enterprises producing consumer goods like textiles and apparel enjoyed no such assistance in the initial post-war years. The policy of import substitution beginning in June 1949 salvaged these infant industries from extinction. Under the policy of import substitution exchange controls, import licensing, protective tariffs and multiple exchange rates were used in combination. High protective tariff rates imposed on textiles were noticeable. Table 7.1 lists these tariff rates for selected years before 1965. The tariff for rayon, for instance, was 100% in 1949 and 45% in 1965. Overall, tariff rates on textiles were large before 1965. The adoption of such an import-substitution policy enhanced the growth of the textiles/apparel industry in the decade after 1949. Table 7.2 lists the employment as a share in manufacturing for the textiles/apparel and food industries for selected years before 1960. There we see the expansion of the textiles/apparel industry from less than 8% before 1950 to more than 20% after and the contraction of the food industry from above 30% before 1950 to about 20% after. Hence import substitution led to the development and growth of the textiles/apparel industry in the 1950s.

Taiwan faced other problems in the late 1950s. With textiles/apparel in terms of employment being as large as 20%, the import-substitution policy was unable to sustain the growth of the industry. One reason was that the domestic market in Taiwan was limited. Moreover, Taiwan, an economy scarce in resources, had to import capital goods and raw materials in order to establish domestic industries, the import of which amounted to more than 90% of total imports (TSDB 1989, Table 11-9). Although there was U.S. aid, it could cover only a small fraction of import.[12] Indeed, during the 1950s Taiwan had a serious trade deficit; the average trade deficit-GDP ratio was 5.24% per year between 1952 and 1960 [*TSDB*, 1989,

TABLE 7.1   Taiwan: Changes in Tariff Rates for Components in Textiles/Apparel Industry (in percentages, for selected years)

	September 1949	1955	1959	1965
Raw cotton	10	10	12.5	12.5
Cotton yarn	5	17	25	25
Cotton piece goods, gray	20–30	40	42.5	42.5
Cotton piece goods, bleached and dyed	20–30	40	45	45
Wool	75–100	85	25.35	12.5–35
Woollen yarn	22.5	90	65	65
Woollen velvets plushes	40	100	85	85
Man-made fibres — rayon	100	140	86	45
Man-made fibres — other	100	140	50	45
Yarn spun from rayon staple	100	140	100	50
Yarn spun from other man-made fibres	100	140	80	50

NOTE: This table shows only the basic tariff rates. The actual rate of import duties includes surtax, harbor charges and other charges.
SOURCE: Ching-yuan Lin (1973), Table A-9.

TABLE 7.2   Taiwan: Evolution of Employment Share of Textiles/ Apparel and Food Industries in Manufacturing Sector (in percentages, for selected years before 1960)

Year	1947	1950	1952	1954	1956	1958	1960
Textiles/apparel	5.46	7.85	20.73	19.33	18.98	18.54	25.02
Food	35.72	36.11	23.73	22.23	22.61	22.28	19.49

SOURCES: For 1947 and 1950, the figures are calculated based on CEPD, *Industry of Free China* 2, no. 1; for others, see Figure 7.3.

Tables 3-1a and 11-4]. Taiwan thus needed to export to earn foreign exchange in order to import capital goods and raw materials. Prior to 1960, Taiwan's exports were related to agricultural and processed agricultural products. The two largest items were sugar and rice; exports of sugar accounted for more than half of total exports before 1958, whereas exports of sugar and rice together accounted for about three-fourths of total export before 1958, and half by 1960 (*TSDB*

1989, Table 11.12a). As a result of its weak exports, Taiwan had a serious trade deficit throughout the 1950s.

Facing these difficulties, the government took actions in the late 1950s and early 1960s. In the Third Four-Year Economic Plan (1961–64) policies to encourage export, especially textiles, were formally proposed and adopted. In the later phases of the Economic Plans this strategy was reinforced. Tax benefits, tariff rebates, low-interest loans and other measures were designed and executed. Another incentive to stimulate exports was the establishment of export-processing zones in January 1965; many privileges were given to manufacturing enterprises in such zones under the requirement that all their finished products were exported.

The import-substitution policy was adopted by many developing countries after World War II. However, few of these countries succeeded if this policy was maintained for long. India was an example of this failure. India started this policy in 1951 in order to protect small textiles enterprises and thus to increase employment of this industry. Since 1948–50, India's cotton textiles exports amounted to more than 11% of the world trade in cotton textiles. This share has declined progressively since 1951 although it remains an important source of foreign exchange.[13] The reason for failure was later realized to be that protection of an industry using import substitution distorted resource allocations and thus reduced efficiency; hence this effect outweighed the benefit of employment growth. In a case where international trade can bring new goods into an economy, the efficiency loss is much larger (see for example, Romer 1994). India's cotton textiles, therefore, could not compete in the world market. Taiwan was fortunate to switch to export-promotion policies earlier.

This export-promotion strategy employed in Taiwan proved successful during the following decades. This success was amplified by the favourable world environment, as international trade was good in this period. World trade grew only 5.2% on average per year in U.S. dollar value between 1954 and 1959, but grew by an average 8.2% per year between 1960 and 1967 and by 22.6% per year between 1968 and 1974 (IMF, various issues). The trade of the late 1960s and early 1970s was even more pronounced in the textiles and apparel markets. Between 1968 and 1974, the U.S. dollar value of textiles trade increased by 18.9% per year, whilst the apparel trade increased 21.6% per year (UN 1969).

TABLE 7.3   Taiwan: Exports of Textiles and Apparel as a Percentage of Total Exports, 1952–70 (in percentages)

	1952	1954	1956	1958	1952–59	1960	1962	1964	1966	1968	1970	1960–70
Textiles/apparel	0.75	1.10	3.89	3.26	3.07	14.16	20.15	14.59	17.79	25.67	31.71	20.29

SOURCE: Calculated based on CEPD, *TSDB* (1989), Table 11-12a.

As a consequence of the export-promotion policy and world trade boom, the U.S. dollar value of Taiwan's exports increased from an average of 10.48% per year between 1952 and 1960, to an average of 25.33% per year between 1960 and 1970 and to an even larger magnitude thereafter (*TSDB* 1989, Table 11-4). The export of manufacturing products other than food expanded, and the most noticeable product was textiles and apparel. In Table 7.3 we present exports of textiles and apparel as a percentage of total exports between 1952 and 1970. The average share of textiles and apparel in total exports increased from 3.07% per year between 1952 and 1959 to 20.29% between 1960 and 1970. To demonstrate more specifically how exports of textiles and apparel increased relative to those of other industries, we also illustrate in Figure 7.5 the composition of exports for major industries as a percentage of total exports after 1961. According to the figure, although exports of food remained dominant before 1966, they declined dramatically. The two export items which were initially most important (sugar and rice) declined swiftly, whereas exports of textiles and apparel increased rapidly. In fact, exports of textiles and apparel reached their peak in 1971.

In removing import substitution, what policy makers feared most was decreasing employment in the protected industries. For this reason India insisted on this policy, but a similar condition failed to occur in Taiwan. Eliminating import substitution and adopting export promotion did not decrease employment in the textiles and apparel industry; rather it increased after 1960, as is evident in Figure 7.3. The export-promotion strategy led Taiwan to enjoy a decade of the highest rate of real economic growth: from 1961 to 1970, Taiwan's average real economic growth was as high as 9.66% per year (*TSDB* 1989,

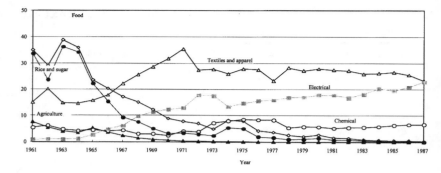

FIGURE 7.5   Taiwan: Export of Major Industries as a Percentage of Total Exports.

SOURCE: Calculated based on CEPD, *TSDB* (1989), Tables 11-12 (1961–79) and 11-13 (1978–87), except for rice and sugar which comes solely from Table 11-12.

Table 3-1a); and Taiwan started to achieve trade surplus after 1970 (*TSDB* 1989, Table 11-4). Hence Taiwan had a greater domestic supply of capital to facilitate investment.

Such a promising result based on of the policy of export expansion should not be surprising, although it is difficult to estimate and test the evidence in regressions for a single economy.[14] The positive effect of exports on economic growth was, however, documented in recent regressions by Dollar (1992), Chen (1998) and others, using cross-country data. The basic theory and mechanism supporting the positive effect of trade openness is as follows. First, according to Romer (1990) and Grossman and Helpman (1991), the benefit of trade lies not only in increasing the extent of the market, but also in expanding the number of specialized inputs. Second, firms competing against foreign suppliers in world markets tend to learn more about production scheduling, sales promotion and after-sales services in remote locations (Lau and Wan, 1991). Third, there exists useful knowledge of many types not embodied in material input, such as production engineering and information about altering product patterns, that are likely to be transferred as a result of expanded trade (Pack, 1992). All these arguments indicated a positive relationship between trade openness and economic growth.

2. Chemical Industry

The production of artificial fabrics needs raw material called man-made fibre. The restriction of cotton textiles export under the LTA turned out to help the production and development of artificial fibre in Taiwan. This in turn affected the growth of Taiwan's petrochemical industry. The petrochemical industry involves four stages of production. From upper stream downward, the first stage includes the production of basic materials of chemical products, the second involves manufacture of intermediates, thirdly production of polymers and finally manufacture of end products. The chemical industry in Taiwan developed basically in a direction of backward integration.[15] The domestic manufacture of man-made fibre began after the development of artificial fabrics had been developed to a certain degree. When the production of these fibres grew, the production and progress of chemical intermediates was initiated; the latter in turn induced the development of basic chemical materials. Hence the development of the textiles industry assisted the growth of the chemical industry. Partly for this reason, the chemical industry in Taiwan grew rapidly after the late 1960s, as evidenced in Figure 7.3 in which the chemical industry gained a large share of employment after 1967.

As many chemical products were produced in Taiwan to supply the domestic manufacture of textiles and apparel, an implication was that fewer chemical products were exported even when a large portion of textiles and apparels was exported. Table 7.4 documents such evidence in terms of the ratio of exports to output value between 1952 and 1987. Textiles and apparel were exported on average at 25.93% per year before 1966 after the policy of export promotion was adopted in 1960; they were exported on average more than 55% per year after 1967 when the man-made fibre of a fourth kind (polyacrylonitrile) began to be produced, and much more later. However, a smaller proportion of chemical products produced was exported and it was on average less than 18% per year for the period under inquiry. An implication was hence that a large percentage of chemical products was produced solely for domestic use, of which textiles/apparel was an important target. Because of this relation between textiles/apparel and chemicals, Taiwan's exports of textiles and apparel was unaffected by the LTA and continued to grow. As Taiwan started early to produce and export artificial fabrics, it gained a certain share of the world market and its exports remained enormous even when the Multifibre Arrangement (MFA) was established in 1974 to restrain exports of textiles and apparel, including artificial fabrics, evident from the remaining large ratio of export to output of textiles and apparel after 1974 in Table 7.4.

It has become popular recently to employ a production with externality in many theoretical analyses, following the works of Romer (1986) and Lucas (1988). The mechanism for including externality in production is to generate sustainable economic growth, and a production with externality is not a theoretical curiosity. In fact, it has been documented that there existed external economies among two-digit manufacturing industries (Caballero and Lyons 1989, 1990; Chan et al. 1995). The backward integration argument according to which the chemical industry in Taiwan developed, indicated a relation between textiles/apparel and chemicals; namely the rate of growth of output value of textiles/apparel externally affected that of chemicals. Accordingly, we assume that production of chemicals is homogeneous of degree one with respect to capital and labor and is externally affected by the growth of textiles and apparel. By making this assumption, we do not rule out the possibility that there is also a repercussion of chemicals on textiles prevailing in annual data as there could be supply-driven externalities as well.[16]

To verify the externality relation of textiles on the production of chemicals using annual data, we denote by $\dot{Y_c}/Y_c\,1$ and K_c the growth rate of output values per capita of chemicals and that of capital input per capita of chemicals respectively and by $\dot{Y_t}/Y_t\,2$ the growth rate of output value of textiles and apparel; we then run a linear regression of $\dot{Y_c}/Y_c\,3$ against K_c and $\dot{Y_t}/Y_t\,4$. We are aware of the possibility of simultaneity bias when using this simple estimation method; a better way is to use an instrumental variable of gt or other estimation methods. We are also aware of the biases due to the situation where there are important variables not included in this regression. Nevertheless, to provide preliminary evidence, we employ this estimation method. The regression yields the following equation.

$$1962\text{-}87:\quad \dot{Y_c}/Y_c\,5 = -0.076 + 0.919\ K_c + 0.642\ \dot{Y_t}/Y_t\,6$$
$$(-1.245)\quad (7.069)\quad\ (2.681)\quad R_2 = 0.6866$$

where the numbers in parentheses are *t*-values.

TABLE 7.4   Taiwan: Average Exports of Textiles/Apparel and Chemicals as Percentages of Value of Production per Year, 1952–87 (in percentages)

	1952–58	1959–66	1967–73	1974–80	1981–87
Textiles/apparel	1.56	25.93	55.88	58.74	73.72
Chemicals	11.33	12.82	10.95	17.46	12.30

SOURCES: Data for export are from CEPD, *Taiwan Statistical Data Book* (1989), Table 11-12 (1952–77), and Table 11-13 (1978–87). Data for value of production are from CEPD, *Industry of Free China* 11, no. 2 (1952–56), 19, no. 1 (1957–60), 33, no. 1 (1961–64), 45, no. 1 (1965–70) and 53, no. 1 (1971–75); and from *Annual Statistics of ROC*, 1984 (1976), 1986 (1977–80) and 1990 (1985–87).

It is obvious that the coefficients of K_c and $\dot{Y}_t/Y_t$ 7 both differ from zero statistically significantly. As R^2 is not large enough, there are variables omitted as noted. Nevertheless, this regression indicates that, given the inputs of chemicals, the production of chemicals was externally reinforced by that of textiles. The estimated coefficient of $\dot{Y}_t/Y_t$ 8 is 0.642 after controlling K_c. We conjecture that when an instrumental variable of $\dot{Y}_t/Y_t$ 9 is used and when other important variables affecting production of chemicals are included, the positive externality of textiles on the production of chemicals still holds and is stronger than the externality of textiles on any industry in manufacturing. As textiles and chemicals account for more than 35% of employment (Figure 7.3) and about 30% of value added (Figure 7.4) in manufacturing, their relation is important to industrialization in Taiwan.

IV. EXPANSION OF MAN-MADE FIBRE INDUSTRIES IN TAIWAN

Having illustrated that textiles/apparel led to the development of chemicals in Taiwan, we are ready to document the growth and expansion in the production of man-made fibre through which textiles and chemicals are related. Two principal items of textiles/apparel exports in Taiwan are cotton and man-made fibre. At the early stages, exports of textiles/apparel were mainly in terms of cotton, whereas at the later stages man-made textiles/apparel accounted for a larger share. Table 7.5 documents the exports of cotton textiles, man-made textiles and their relative share.[17] According to the table, both items increased very quickly, with cotton textiles increasing 663 times whereas man-made textiles leaped 16,907 times between 1958 and 1987. During the early stages exports of cotton textiles dominated; the share of man-made textiles exports relative to cotton and man-made textiles as a whole was less than 20% by 1961. In the later stages however, man-made textiles dominated: it accounted for more than 50% by 1968 and 80% by 1980.

How did the growth and expansion in production and exports of man-made textiles affect the domestic production of artificial fibre? A simple answer is that it was through the derived demand for inputs. Specifically, the manufacturing of man-made textiles needs man-made fibre as an input. Man-made fibre falls broadly into two categories; one is cellulosic fibre in which rayon is the major product, and the other is non-cellulosic fibre in which nylon, polyester and polyacrylonitrile are three major items. Although the manufacturing of man-made textiles in Taiwan started shortly after World War II, at the beginning the raw material was wholly imported. As the domestic production of man-made yarn and fabrics increased, the demand for this fibre in the domestic market led to its establishment and development. In 1957 Taiwan started producing rayon, in 1964 nylon and polyester, and in 1967 acrylic. In a sense, man-made fibre was developed basically in a direction of backward integration. With the rapid expansion in the production and exports of man-made textiles/apparel after 1968 (see Table 7.5) and therefore its induced demand for man-made fibre, the production of man-made fibre was consequently promptly boosted. Table 7.6 registers the production of the four major kinds of man-made fibre after their creation. As can be seen, the production of each kind of man-made fibre expanded swiftly in the 20-year period between 1967 and 1987. The production as a whole increased more than 72-fold during this period, while the production of polyester expanded even faster.

Given the rapid growth and progress in the production of man-made fibre in Taiwan, what was its share in the world markets? Table 7.7 documents the evidence for ten major countries. According to the table, Taiwan accounted for only 0.82% of world production in 1970. By 1978 the production of man-made fibre in Taiwan accounted for a

TABLE 7.5 Taiwan: Exports of Cotton and Man-made Textiles (in NT$ million, for selected years)

	1958	1961	1964	1967	1968	1971	1976	1980	1985	1987
Cotton (A)	43	883	1,341	2,580	2,707	5,278	16,188	23,988	23,549	28,498
Man-made (B)	11	184	726	2,108	3,682	18,119	64,640	116,816	170,160	185,972
B/(A+B) (%)	20.3	17.72	35.1	44.97	57.63	77.46	79.97	82.96	87.84	86.71

SOURCE: Calculated based on Inspectorate General of Customs, Taiwan, *Annual Report of the Trade of China* (various years).

TABLE 7.6 Taiwan: Production of Four Kinds of Man-made Fibre (in 1,000 tons, for selected years)

	1957	1961	1965	1967	1971	1973	1975	1978	1984	1987	1990	1994
Rayon	0.8	10	19	24	33	50	49	73	128	120	162	149
Nylon	0	0	0.8	8	32	41	63	90	128	174	188	270
Polyester	0	0	0.6	2	27	57	136	291	612	1,076	1,290	1,905
Acrylic	0	0	0	0.1	11	28	35	83	131	141	134	155
Total	0.8	10	20.4	34.1	103	178	283	537	998	1,511	1,774	2,479

SOURCES: Calculated based on CEPD, *Industry of Free China* 19, no. 3:30, no.4:50, no. 3:59, no. 6:69, no. 5:79, no.3 and 84, no.5.

TABLE 7.7 Share of World Man-made Fibre Manufacturing for Major Countries (in percentages, for selected years)

	1970	1973	1975	1978	1979	1981	1984	1986	1989	1992
United States	26.20	28.82	27.01	27.18	27.95	25.80	21.77	20.27	19.12	17.56
Japan	17.87	15.56	13.38	13.22	12.65	12.27	11.80	10.61	9.35	9.33
West Germany	8.68	8.51	6.95	6.28	6.21	6.18	5.72	5.45	5.11	5.24
Soviet Union	7.66	7.34	9.24	8.32	7.95	8.62	8.83	8.53	8.24	5.22
United Kingdom	7.23	6.35	5.34	4.42	3.34	2.19	2.46	1.69	1.32	1.38
Italy	4.81	4.40	3.53	3.30	3.31	3.53	3.75	3.81	3.29	3.42
France	3.80	3.56	2.79	2.83	2.13	1.18	1.47	1.19	0.87	0.59
China	0.63	—	1.51	2.10	2.33	3.63	5.31	6.26	8.07	9.88
Taiwan	0.82	1.60	2.75	4.02	3.93	4.89	6.72	8.56	9.44	12.00
South Korea	0.61	1.09	2.64	3.41	3.59	4.54	5.13	5.55	6.81	8.03

NOTE: = means not available.

SOURCES: Calculated based on Japanese Chemical Fibre Association, *Man-Made Fibre Handbook* (various years).

4.02% share globally and surpassed that of France and Italy, becoming the sixth largest producer in the world. Taiwan then overtook a major producing country once every few years: surpassing the United Kingdom in 1979, West Germany in 1984, the Soviet Union in 1986 and finally Japan in 1989. Since then, Taiwan has become the second largest producer of man-made fibre, second only to the U.S., and its global share reached 12% in 1992. Among the four kinds of man-made fibre, polyester and nylon have many applications and are therefore the most important. Table 7.8 documents the world share of polyester manufacturing for five major countries, whereas Table 7.9 documents the share of nylon for six major countries. As can be observed from the tables, Taiwan was the largest polyester supplier by 1992 and the third largest nylon producer by 1993.

TABLE 7.8 Share of World Polyester Manufacturing for Five Major Countries (in percentages, for selected years)

	1975	1980	1985	1992	1993
United States	40.45	35.29	23.31	16.37	15.76
Japan	13.25	12.21	10.03	7.57	6.99
West Germany	10.42	6.20	4.91	3.73	3.47
Taiwan	4.43	6.82	11.57	16.56	17.08
Korea	0.52	5.41	7.83	10.39	11.26

SOURCES: Same as Table 7.7.

TABLE 7.9 Share of World Nylon Manufacturing for Six Major Countries (in percentages, for selected years)

	1974	1980	1985	1990	1991	1992	1993
United States	37.06	33.97	30.85	32.22	31.91	31.12	33.02
Japan	11.30	10.09	9.16	7.71	7.74	7.19	6.57
West Germany	8.11	6.38	6.07	5.93	5.55	5.55	5.59
Russia	5.06	9.32	10.96	10.57	10.04	8.62	8.49
Taiwan	1.76	3.46	4.03	5.10	6.19	6.70	6.65
South Korea	1.54	3.46	4.02	5.42	6.10	6.41	6.49

SOURCES: Same as Table 7.7.

The development of the man-made fibre in Taiwan was slow in the beginning. The China Man-Made Fibre Corporation was established in 1957 and remained the only firm in the man-made fibre industry until 1962. This may be partially because of the fact that cotton textiles and apparel was the major profitable industry. A more important reason may be that man-made fibre needed more capital and involved more sophisticated technology, therefore containing larger risks. The stagnation in the development of this new industry, together with the pressure of the LTA, forced the government to direct the state-owned China Man-Made Fibre Corporation to invest in United Nylon and Hualon in 1962. Nevertheless, private enterprises did not enter this business immediately after the establishment of these two additional public firms. It was not until 1966 when two private firms, Ko Hua and Liang Yu, joined the production of nylon that the turning point occurred. After that, Taiwan witnessed a surge of new firms in this industry. We summarize below how the new entrants joined and how they introduced technology.

1. *Rayon.* China Man-Made Fibre Corporation was the only producer of rayon before 1967. Its daily capacity was 5 tons initially and was expanded to 10 tons per day in 1960. Its annual output increased from 800 tons in 1957 to 2,800 tons in 1967. In 1967 Formosa Chemicals and Fibre Corporation, a firm of the Formosa Plastics group, joined the industry through a licensing agreement with Maurer of Switzerland, with a production capacity of 45 tons per day. It began production in 1968. Confronted with strong competition from the new Formosa Chemical and Fibre Corporation, China Man-Made Corporation later expanded to a daily capacity of 40 tons in 1969. In light of this, Formosa Chemicals and Fibre Corporation subsequently expanded its daily capacity to 140 tons per day in 1973, increasing from 70 tons per day in 1970, 90 tons in 1971 and 120 tons in 1972. The rayon production in Taiwan was then expanded to 49,000 tons in 1975 and 78,000 tons in 1980. Its production in 1993 was 131,000 tons (see Table 7.6).

2. *Nylon.* Two years after the production of nylon by United Nylon Corporation, Ko Hua and Liang Yu were induced to join the industry in 1966. Ko Hua adopted technology from Zimmer of West Germany, whereas Liang Yu imported technology from Dow of the United States, both through licensing agreements. All these three firms built a daily capacity of 20 tons at the beginning. In 1967 Formosa Chemicals and

Fibre started production of nylon through licensing agreements with Zimmer of West Germany. Jang Dah Nylon and Bao Chen joined the industry in 1968, whereas Dah Ming and Tai Ping Yang participated in 1969. Ming Bon and Jen Dar entered in 1972 and 1973 respectively, whereas Hsing Chung, Ta Hsing, Yeong Jinn and Chung Hsing appeared in 1974. These 14 firms constituted the nylon industry in Taiwan by 1980. Licensing agreements were the only way to acquire technology for all these firms. Moreover, most of the technology came from Europe, especially West Germany; the United States was the second source, and Japan was the source for only firm, namely Jang Dah Nylon. Taiwan's nylon industry expanded rapidly after 1975. Its annual output increased from 63,000 tons in 1975 to 243,000 tons in 1993, increasing fourfold in less than 20 years (see Table 7.6). Taiwan's world share was 6.65% in 1993, after the United States and Soviet Union (see Table 7.7).

3. *Polyester.* Polyester is the most important man-made fibre as it can be blended with cotton, wool or rayon and has many applications. The annual production capacity of the first polyester manufacturer, Hualon, was only 3,300 tons per year. Three years later, Nan Ya Plastics, a firm of the Formosa Plastics group, entered the industry by introducing technology from Zimmer of West Germany through licensing agreements. Its annual production capacity, 14,000 tons at inception, expanded to 50,000 tons in 1974. One year after the entrance of Nan Ya Plastics, three firms joined; they were Ko Hua, Hung Chou Chemical and Yu-Ho Fibre. They all used technology from either West Germany or Switzerland through licensing agreements. In 1969 four firms came in, among which were two big firms, Far Eastern Textiles and Shinkong Synthetic Fibre. The annual capacity of Far Eastern Textiles was initially 13,500 tons but later expanded to a total of 58,000 tons in 1975, whereas that of Shinkong Synthetic Fibre was 3,700 tons in 1969, which increased to 30,000 tons in 1975. In the 1970s 11 more firms participated (see Table 7.10). This brought the total number of firms in the polyester industry to 20 by 1976. As there were so many firms entering polyester manufacturing, it is no wonder that the production of polyester in Taiwan increased very rapidly after 1977. Indeed, the production of polyester in Taiwan was expanded from 213,000 tons in 1977 to 1,753,000 tons in 1993, an average annual growth rate of about 50 per cent. With such a high speed of expansion, it comes at no

surprise that Taiwan became the world's largest supplier of polyester by 1992, surpassing traditional world large suppliers such as the United States, Japan and West Germany.

4. *Acrylic.* Acrylic is a kind of man-made wool. Soon after Formosa Plastics introduced acrylic production in 1968, it expanded to a daily capacity of 20 tons in 1969. In 1970 another firm, Tong-Hwa Synthetic Fibre, entered the industry using technology from Mitsubishi Rayon of Japan through joint venture. Its daily production capacity was 15 tons. Faced with this new competition, Formosa Plastics then planned an expansion of its capacity. By 1976, Formosa Plastics had reached a daily production capacity of 155 tons. Tong-Hwa Synthetic Fibre also expanded its daily production to 25 tons in 1972, and subsequently to 95 tons in 1977. In 1976 Tung Ho Spinning joined the industry, employing technology from ICI of the United Kingdom. This industry then grew steadily, with its annual output increasing from 63,000 tons in 1977 to 131,000 tons in 1993.

It is obvious from the above evidence that Taiwan has already become a very important world man-made fibre supplier. Taiwan had no production of man-made fibre before 1957, but it has made itself a world giant producer in 30 years. How was Taiwan able to import and adopt such technology successfully? Where were its sources of technology? The next section conducts this analysis. As will be seen, Taiwan underwent a catching-up process.

V. TECHNOLOGY ADOPTION: A CATCHING-UP PROCESS[18]

Long before the LTA came into effect, the government in Taiwan perceived the creation of a rayon-making plant as part of a plan to diversify the textiles industry away from cotton fibre by 1954. Authorized by the government, the state-owned Central Trust Bank of China brought together an American artificial fibre engineering consultant company, Von Kohorn, as well as several local private and public textiles companies. The project was started through importing machinery and licensing agreements with Von Kohorn. The resulting corporation was called China Man-Made Fibre Corporation. At the inception of production in early 1957, however, this firm faced various operational and technical difficulties. In late 1957 this company switched to a joint venture with Teijrin of Japan, a man-made fibre and chemical giant, and the aforementioned difficulties were then overcome. The establishment of China Man-Made Fibre Corporation was important not just as the start of the new industry, but also because it set the pattern for foreign partners participating in other kinds of man-made fibre production and other sectors throughout the 1960s and 1970s, with the government taking the lead in bringing together foreign companies and local producers to fill gaps in the production structure. Other joint ventures of this kind included Taiwan Cement, Hsing-Chu Glass, Naphtha Cracker, China Steel, China Shipbuilding, United Microelectronics Corporation and Taiwan Semiconductor Manufacturing Corporation.

Under the pressure of LTA, in 1962 the government once again ordered China Man-Made Fibre Corporation, together with China Development Corporation, a state-owned financing agency, to create another company to make nylon. This new company was United Nylon Corporation. The technology was also imported from developed countries, coming through licensing agreements this time rather than joint ownership. The licensing agreements were with Chemtex of the United States and Zimmer of West Germany. United Nylon Corporation started manufacturing in 1964. At the same time China Man-Made Fibre Corporation also started a joint venture with its Japanese partner in rayon, Teijrin, to establish a new firm to produce the third kind of man-made fibre, polyester. This investment venture organized a company called Hualon which started production also in 1964. In a word, the government had an important role in the initiation of rayon, nylon and polyester fibre.

The only possible exception in initiating production of man-made fibre is that of acrylic. Taiwan's first PVC producer, Formosa Plastics (Tairylan Plant), started making acrylic with the technology from its own research and development in 1967. Since the inception of production, however, it had never reached its quality and quantity targets. Formosa Plastics then turned to a licensing agreement with Japan's Asahi in 1968 and the problems were solved. Since Formosa Plastics was originally initiated by the government, the start of acrylic fibre production was therefore indirectly related to the state as well.[19]

All four kinds of man-made fibre had therefore been initiated in Taiwan by 1968, and the beginning of each kind of new fibre production was associated directly or indirectly with the government. Many enterprises later then joined the industry to get a share of the market once the new industry was introduced. By 1970, 21 companies had emerged and by 1976, there were 38. Table 7.10 lists the names of these 38 firms, the sources of technology and the country from which the technology was imported, as well as the form and year of importation. Several characteristics emerge from the table and are discussed as follows.

1. *European countries and engineering firms dominating the sources*. Taiwan's technology of man-made fibre came mainly from West Germany, whereas Japanese technology played only a minor part. This is puzzling as Taiwan was colonized by and geographically close to Japan. This indicates that other factors may partially explain why this was so. The attitude towards ownership is one of these other factors. The fact that many entrepreneurs in textiles and apparel emigrated from mainland China is another factor. It is well known that Taiwan's entrepreneurs like to be their own boss (Shieh, 1992), whereas Japanese firms prefer joint ventures to gain some ownership. Taiwanese entrepreneurs would therefore not go into joint ventures with Japanese firms unless there were no alternatives. As for the immigrant entrepreneurs from mainland China who were in the textiles and apparel business, they came especially from Ching-Dao and Shanghai, where the modern textiles and apparel industry had been developed before World War II. These two cities had been colonized by Germany and other Western countries. Since these immigrant entrepreneurs invested in many firms in the Taiwanese man-made fibre industry, their connections with Western countries built up in Ching-Dao and Shanghai provided a channel for procuring technology.

Two sources of technology were available: one through manufacturing firms and the other through engineering consultant firms. Von Kohorn, Zimmer and Inventa were all old and famous engineering consultant firms, whereas Dow, ICI, Teijrin, Toray and Mitsubishi Rayon were large manufacturing firms. Technology in Taiwan was mainly adopted from engineering consultant firms. Two primary suppliers of technology in Taiwan were Zimmer of West Germany and Inventa of Switzerland, according to Table 7.10, both of which were engineering consultant firms. In only a few cases was technology in Taiwan adopted from large manufacturing firms. As noted, Taiwan's entrepreneurs prefer to retain ownership. Moreover, many entrepreneurs immigrated from

Ching-Dao and Shanghai. When they searched for technology, their business connections with European entrepreneurs made them target European firms first. They selected engineering consultant firms, thereby obtaining the technology that they needed without losing control of their firms. Since West Germany had many famous engineering consultant firms, this fact also partly explains why West Germany was a more important source of technology for Taiwan than Japan or the United States.

2. *Forms of technology adoption.* There are many channels of technology importation, including joint ventures (direct foreign investment), licensing agreements, production cooperation, original equipment manufacturing (OEM) and other informal accumulation of non-proprietary information. There are many factors determining the type of technology adoption. The important elements include: (1) domestic savings, (2) attitude towards ownership by foreign firms and (3) the bargaining power of foreign *vis-à-vis* local firms. Most channels of technology importation in Taiwan were in the form of licensing agreements. According to Table 7.10, only four out of the 38 firms listed engaged in joint ventures. Two of these four firms, China Man-Made Fibre and Hualon, were established when Taiwan had no production in rayon and polyester respectively. Before the introduction of man-made fibre, Taiwan's major manufacturing was in textiles with small average firm size and labor-intensive, less sophisticated technology being used. The creation of man-made fibre manufacturing, however, required intensive capital as well as more advanced and complicated technology. These small textiles firms did not accumulate enough capital, technology and management know-how. Moreover, starting a new industry is a risky business even with the assistance of the government. The difficulties that China Man-Made Fibre Corporation faced at the outset in its licensing agreements with von Kohorn were an example. Joint ventures not only provided technology but also shared the risks. In this circumstance the bargaining power of the domestic firms was modest. These firms were therefore obligated to employ joint ventures as a channel of technology adoption. Once an industry was established, the bargaining power of domestic firms became stronger. Together with the facts that Taiwanese preferred sole ownership and that Taiwan's savings rate was high,[20] this made licensing agreements the most popular form of technology adoption.

TABLE 7.10 Sources of Technology of Man-made Fibre Manufacturing in Taiwan by 1976

Product	Name of Firm	Source of Technology	Country of Source	Form of Importation	Year of Importation
Rayon	China Man-Made Fibre	Von Kohorn/Teijrin	U.S./Japan	Licensing/ Joint venture	1954/1957
	Formosa Chemicals and Fibre	Maurer	Switzerland	Licensing	1967
Nylon	United Nylon[1]	Chemtex/Zimmer	U.S./W. Germany	Licensing	1962
	Ko Hua[1]	Zimmer	W. Germany	Licensing	1966
	Liang Yu	Dow	U.S.	Licensing	1966
	Formosa Chemicals and Fibre	Zimmer	W. Germany	Licensing	1967
	Bao Chen[1]	Zimmer	W. Germany	Licensing	1968
	Jang Dah Nylon[2]	Toray	Japan	Licensing	1968
	Dah Ming	Inventa/Luigi	Switzerland/W. Germany	Licensing	1969
	Tai Ping Yang[2]	Zimmer	W. Germany	Licensing	1969
	Ming Bon	Didier/Zimmer	W. Germany/W. Germany	Licensing	1972
	Jen Dar	Chemtex	U.S.	Licensing	1973
	Hsing Chung	Zimmer	W. Germany	Licensing	1974
	Ta Hsing	Chemtex	U.S.	Licensing	1974
	Yeong Jinn	Karl Fisher	U.S.	Licensing	1974
	Chung Hsing	Chemtex	U.S.	Licensing	1974
Polyester	Hualon[1]	Teijrin	Japan	Joint venture	1964
	Nan Ya Plastics	Zimmer	W. Germany	Licensing	1967
	Ko Hua[1]	Inventa	Switzerland	Licensing	1968
	Hung Chou Chemical	Holchst	W. Germany	Licensing	1968
	Yu-Ho Fibre	Didier	W. Germany	Licensing	1968

TABLE 7.10 (Cont'd)

Product	Name of Firm	Source of Technology	Country of Source	Form of Importation	Year of Importation
	Far Eastern Textiles	Inventa/Luigi	Switzerland/W. Germany	Licensing	1969
	Shinkong Synthetic Fibre	Toray	Japan	Joint venture	1969
	Dah Ming	Inventa	Switzerland	Licensing	1969
	Tai Ping Yang[2]	Zimmer	W. Germany	Licensing	1969
	Tung-Yun	Chemtex/ICI	U.S./U.K.	Licensing	1972
	Tuntex	ICI	U.K.	Licensing	1972
	Tainan Spinning	Zimmer/Inventa	W.Germany/Switzerland	Licensing	1973
	Hsing Hsing[1]	Inventa	Switzerland	Licensing	1973
	Shi Dai	Inventa	Switzerland	Licensing	1973
	Ta Chin	Inventa	Switzerland	Licensing	1973
	Ta Shin Textiles	Inventa	Switzerland	Licensing	1973
	Tung Ho Spinning	Zimmer/ICI	W. Germany/U.K.	Licensing	1973
	Ta Jiuh	Zimmer	W. Germany	Licensing	1974
	Chung Hsing	Inventa	Switzerland	Licensing	1976
	Ho Jong	Luigi/Inventa	W. Germany/Switzerland	Licensing	1976
Acrylic	Formosa Plastics	Formosa Plastics /Asahi	Taiwan/Japan	R&D/	1967/
				Licensing	1968
	Tong-Hwa Synthetic Fibre	Mitsubishi Rayon	Japan	Joint venture	1970
	Tung Ho Spinning	ICI	U.K.	Licensing	1976

NOTES: 1. They merged to become Hualon in 1977.
2. They were purchased by Fu-Point Synthetic Corporation in 1983.

SOURCES: Taiwan Institute for Economic Research, *Annual Report of Textiles Industry* (various years).

3. *Firm size and state intervention.* There were as many as 38 firms making man-made fibre in Taiwan by 1977, whereas the number of comparable firms was much smaller in South Korea, slightly more than a dozen (Tran, 1988). As South Korea's population was twice that of Taiwan's, firm size in Taiwan tended to be much smaller than that in South Korea.

This is partially related to different political factors. In Taiwan an anti-big-entrepreneur philosophy ran deep in the minds of economic bureaucrats.[21] In contrast, in South Korea a powerful nationalism that arose after 35 years of harsh Japanese colonialism supported the notion of the whole South Korean people as a team against the rest of the world.[22] Combined with entry restrictions, this political factor made South Korea's firms large in size.

The government in Taiwan intervened in the development of man-made fibre. In general, the Taiwanese government intervened in the new field mainly through setting up a public enterprise for each kind of fibre as an initiative. As most firms in Taiwan were small or medium in size, the government started a public enterprise or arranged for a private firm to start the business, and then induced private firms to participate in the industry by providing a market with stable prices and by moderately protecting the domestic market from foreign competition through selective tariff policies. By doing so, the state aimed to send signals to private enterprises that there were indeed not only risks but also opportunities in this industry. In contrast, South Korean firms were large. In South Korea the government provided immense support in the form of subsidized credit as well as growth and entry protection. Moreover, the South Korean government even promoted the expansion of existing firms using many policies. The existence of large conglomerates was not seen as a threat to the regime as it was in Taiwan. The state and big businesses usually became a coalition in which the state specified performance requirements for the firms[23] and guided the market, and in return provided massive assistance using financial, tax, exchange rate and tariff instruments. The conglomerates emerged as South Korea's champions through such a coalition.

As a result of the different types of government intervention in Taiwan *vis-à-vis* South Korea, the market structure became different. Taiwan's business groups were small and loosely integrated, whereas South Korea's business groups were large and highly central (for example, Hamilton *et al.*, 1987). Entry barriers in the man-made fibre industry were high in South Korea and thereby only a smaller number of large firms were able to enter, whereas the opposite occurred in Taiwan. The difference in market structure led to the following results. Taiwan's small firms made them nimble, becoming quite sensitive and responsive to international opportunities and profit margins; Taiwan's numerous niche-seeking firms therefore needed less firm-specific help, but had relatively more demand for stable prices and real exchange rate.[24] On the other hand, South Korea's few large firms helped to sustain a relatively well-developed policy network between the state and these firms, allowing the government to target its industry-specific policies at a smaller number of firms, each capable of a substantial response. Consequently, the availability of massive assistance encouraged South Korean big firms, for example, to adopt the high-risk strategy of competing head-on with U.S. and Japanese firms under their own brand names (Wade, 1990, p. 322).[25]

The man-made fibre industry in Taiwan grew rapidly after 1966 when private enterprises began to join in. The total production of man-made fibre was 34,000 tons in 1967, which increased to 178,000 tons by the time of the first oil shock. Because the world's production was large, Taiwan's world share was not high during this period, being only 1.6% in 1973 (see Table 7.7). The first oil shock hit this industry seriously, however. The numerous entrants into and rapid expansion of the man-made fibre industry before the first oil shock followed by insufficient demand during this oil shock led to losses and difficulties in many firms. In response, many firms either stopped operation or were forced to reduce production temporarily.[26] Some firms were merged.[27] The government also instituted policies to stabilize the domestic prices and subsidize the purchase of domestic man-made fibre. Due to these responses from private firms and the government, the industry was able to recover rapidly and grow steadily when the first oil shock was over. By 1980 the production of man-made fibre had reached 635,000 tons, and its world share was 4.46%, becoming the fifth largest world supplier. Witnessing the growth of man-made fibre and other chemical fibre, the government directed state-owned Chinese Petroleum Corporation to invest in upstream firms to provide raw materials such as caprolactum (CPL) for nylon (for example, Chung-Tai Chemical in 1976), dimethyl terepgthalate (PTA) for polyester (for example, Chinese American Chemical in 1979) and acrylonitrile monomer (AN) for acrylic (for example, Chinese Petroleum and Chemical Corporation in 1976), and to invest in even upper-stream firms (for example, Naphtha Cracker). This subsequently established the vertically integrated chemical industry in Taiwan, which has been the largest in manufacturing since 1985, according to Table 7.4. It is thus obvious that the chemical industry in Taiwan developed in backward integration, for which man-made fibre played a critical role.

The above discussion is about the initiation and development of the man-made fibre industry in the early stages. In the process of economic development, the initiation and development in the early stages are very important. With a successful first step, a chance is provided for a new industry to grow. As our above analysis reveals, in the initiation of many new fields in the process of industrialization and economic development, the government in Taiwan has consistently played a vital role. The state typically began with the establishment of public enterprises in new industries, and then either handed the factories over to selected private entrepreneurs or ran them as public enterprises. This intervention is used to attract private enterprises to join in. The underlying reasons may be that there is a lack of capital in a developing economy. But, more importantly, there is an inadequate supply of entrepreneurs looking out for new production methods or new ideas in the developing economy, incapable of or unwilling to take the risks of introducing them.[28] Government initiation or intervention is necessary in taking or reducing the risks of departing from existing or traditional production methods. Once the entrepreneurship is started, it is self-sustaining. The creation of the man-made fibre industry was an example, and Taiwan's strategy proved effective and successful.

In the 1980, new entrants in Taiwan's man-made fibre industry no longer relied on imported technology. The first successful cases occurred in 1985 when Chi Yuan (now Cheng Chi) and Fu Jiuh produced nylon and acrylic respectively using technology based on their own R&D. The same also applied to Acelon and Chain Yarn which manufactured nylon based on their own R&D in 1988, and Acelon also produced polyester later based on its own R&D. In the 1990s some firms started to export whole plants of man-made fibre, including technology. Two of the examples were Tuntex, which exported a whole plant of polyester to Indonesia in 1991, and Nan Ya Plastics which exported several plants of polyester to the United States also in 1991. Viewing this evidence, we may say that Taiwan's technology in man-made fibre has already caught up with that of the developed world.

VI. CONCLUDING REMARKS

In this chapter we document the role of textiles and man-made fibre in the process of industrialization in Taiwan. We find that textiles played a critical role in the early stages of development. The man-made fibre industry then became significant as it made possible a transition from the labour-intensive textiles industry to a capital- and technology-intensive industry. In developing these two industries, the government played a vital role in several aspects: from initiating an industry and granting tax and financial benefits and import-substitution protection at the earlier stages, to providing export-promotion encouragement at the later stages. Most of the policies proved successful and as a result these two industries expanded swiftly.

Finally, we comment on the recent financial crisis which occurred in East Asia. The crisis started from the middle of 1997. Countries in East Asia, including Indonesia, South Korea, Malaysia, Philippines and Thailand were affected. The financial troubles have ignited lively debates on the wisdom of closing shaky banks. The International Monetary Fund (IMF) has pursued that policy seriously, making bank intervention and closures a part of its conditionality in the affected countries. Others, however, have charged the policy with producing runs on healthy banks and creating an unnecessarily large credit crunch. The prescription thus clearly depends on one's assessment of the crisis.

Although analysts have proposed various reasons as to how the crisis occurred, liquidity seemed to be the key problem. These countries in fact had very good macroeconomic performances. Along with Taiwan, we list in Table 7.11 some basic data for these countries before the financial crisis. In general, except for the Philippines, these countries had high real GDP growth rates, high savings and investment in GDP, and low inflation rates. Some of these countries even outperformed Taiwan during this period. Moreover, most of these countries had a government budget surplus, and if a country had a deficit, its share in GDP was very small. In a word, these countries pursued cautious fiscal policies.

Given these good macroeconomic accomplishments, how did the crisis happen? The key factor is that these countries accumulated too

TABLE 7.11 Basic Macroeconomic Data for Selected Countries Before Financial Crisis (in percentages)

	Real GDP Growth		Inflation		Savings/GDP		Investment/GDP		Government Budget Surplus/GDP	
	1991–96 Average	1996	1991–96 Average	1996	1991–96 Average	1996	1991–96 Average	1996	1991–96 Average	1996
Indonesia	7.24	7.82	1.92	-0.40	28.4	30.6	32.93	32.66	0.82	1.16
South Korea	7.42	7.13	0.97	6.70	35.4	33.9	36.64	36.78	-0.16	0.07
Malaysia	8.65	8.58	4.67	4.40	34.6	40.6	41.4	42.24	0.35	1.72
Philippines	2.74	5.48	12.97	13.80	19.1	22.7	26.27	23.91	-0.105	0.03
Taiwan	6.15	5.70	3.05	3.10	27.39	25.11	22.64	20.93	4.05	2.24
Thailand	7.98	5.50	5.63	7.40	28.6	31.5	46.71	41.07	0.28	0.23

SOURCES: For Taiwan, CEPD, *Taiwan Statistical Data Book* (various years); for other countries, IMF, *International Financial Statistics Yearbook* (various years).

TABLE 7.12   Some Statistics of Accumulated External Debt for Selected Countries (in percentages)

	Indonesia	South Korea	Malaysia	Philippine	Taiwan	Thailand
Total external debt/international reserves						
June 1990	220.80	106.1	21.7	318.5	0.13	59.1
June 1994	173.0	161.0	25.2	40.5	0.11	99.2
June 1997	170.4	206.0	61.2	84.8	0.12	145.3
Short-term debt/long-term debt						
June 1990	51.60	66.45	25.66	33.34	—	60.18
June 1994	61.10	72.53	59.12	44.17	—	74.29
June 1997	59.02	67.85	56.45	58.75	—	65.68

SOURCES: For Taiwan, Central Bank of China, Taiwan, *Financial Statistics Monthly* (various years); for others, IMF, *Financial Statistics Yearbook* (various years).

much debt. In past years these countries aimed to expand very quickly and thereby invested too much. As evidence of this, except for the Philippines, the share of investment in GDP was over 30% in these countries, and it was even above 40% for Malaysia and Thailand as illustrated in Table 7.11. As their savings rates were not so high, the consequence was that external borrowing became an important source of capital accumulation. As Table 7.12 shows, the ratios of total external debt to international reserve were high in these countries. In particular, the short-term debt accounted for more than half of the external debt. The accumulation of so much external debt comes as no surprise given the large investment rates in these countries.

The large investment rate was also induced by other factors. In these countries the financial sector was liberalized during this period. Deregulation coupled with explicit or implicit guarantees on banks and inadequate oversight then generated a serious moral hazard problem, resulting in overlending and excessive risk-taking in these countries. The skyrocketing prices of stocks and real estate in the late 1980s and the first half of the 1990s were examples of the results of overlending and excessive risk-taking. It has been documented that financial liberalization preceded the banking crisis (Kaminsky and Reinhart 1996). Ignited by the international financial attacks, the public was led to speculate and became panicky. The financial crisis then easily occurred.

As few studies have been made on the relationship between financial liberalization and economic growth, it is too early to make assessments. A lesson that can nevertheless be learned from the crisis is that external debt, especially short-term debt, should be managed with more care. Policies discouraging reliance on short-term debt are necessary although they is not easy due to cost minimization of the borrowers and imperfect information or monitoring of the creditors. Moreover, the financial sector may be liberalized gradually rather all at once, as an immediate deregulation can generate instability and thus hurt economic growth. The government definitely has a big role to play in this regard.

NOTES

1. For comparison of economic transition between South Korea and Taiwan, see Lau (1990), among others. For the case study of South Korea, see Kim and Roemer (1979); Taiwan, Galenson (1979).

2. See, for example, Lucas (1988), Krugman (1991), Matsuyama (1991) and Chen and Shimomura (1998).

3. For readers interested in the history of the textiles industry in the Industrial Revolution, see Chapman (1972).

4. Coleman (1973) presents the same argument.

5. Documentation will be made in Table 7.7

6. The sources are CEPD, *Taiwan Statistical Data Book* for Taiwan and *Major Statistics of Korean Survey* for South Korea.

7. See, for example, Fransman and King (1984).

8. The share of chemicals in total manufacturing has been used as an indicator of industrial depth in production. For example, see Wade (1990, chapter 2).

9. A stylized model of this kind can be found in Matsuyama (1991) and Chen and Shimomura (1998).

10. The GDP share of the food industry was less than 7% after 1979, and that of beverage/tobacco was less than 7% after 1972.

11. This section draws on Chen (1996).

12. U.S. aid started in 1952 and ended in 1968.

13. For and analysis and review of India's export of cotton textiles, see Nayyar (1973).

14. This is so because, in time-series data of a single country, both the insufficient number of observations and the little variation of trade openness over time make regressions difficult.

15. One of the important reasons for this backward integration of chemicals is large capital- and technology-intensities for the upstream industries, and developing economies generally lack capital and technology in their early stages of development.

16. There are theoretically several sources of externalities in production, but so far few works have been successful in distinguishing them empirically. The work by Bartelsman *et al.* (1994) which distinguishes between consumer- and supplier-driven externalities, represents one of the few successful works, but more needs to be done.

17. Only exports of cotton and man-made textile are illustrated here because no data are available for apparel which distinguish between cotton and man-made fibre.

18. Part of the discussion in this section draws on Chen and Hsu (1997).

19. The government decided to develop PVC production and Y. C. Wang was then chosen in 1957 to establish the firm. This company was Formosa Plastics and it later grew to become the largest Taiwanese conglomerate in manufacturing.

20. The gross savings in GDP were above 20% by 1965 and almost 30% by 1970 in Taiwan (CEPD, *Taiwan Statistical Data Book*); it was higher than the 14.09% and 18.80% for the corresponding years respectively in Korea (Bank of Korea, *Economic Statistics Yearbook*).

21. This philosophy has been carried down since the founding of modern China, specified in the book *Three Principles of the People*, written by its founding father, Dr Sun Yat-Sen.

22. See Amsden (1989) and the Korean authors cited therein for this point.

23. Well-known requirements include performance of production and exports, for example.

24. This is probably one of the reasons why the computer industry and machinery industry in Taiwan outperformed those of South Korea after the mid-1980s.

25. For example, the exports of South Korean automobiles under their own brands expanded rapidly after the late 1980s.

26. Tai Ping Yang, Jen Dar and Dah Ming stopped operation. Tai Ping Yang and Jen Dar were later purchased by Fu-Point, whereas Dah Ming was rented by Hualon.

27. Bao-Chen, Ko Hua, Hsing Hsing and United Nylon were merged with Hualon.

28. See Lewis (1955) for a similar argument. For a modern theoretical formulation of this argument, see Baland and Francois (1996).

REFERENCES

Amsden, A.H. *Asia's Next Giant: South Korea and Late Industrialization.* New York: Oxford University Press, 1989.

Bartelsman, E.J, R.J. Caballero and R. Lyons. "Consumer- and supplier-driven externalities". *American Economic Review* 84, no. 4 (1994): 1075–84.

Caballero, R.J. and R.K. Lyons. "The role of external economies in U.S. manufacturing". NBER Working Paper no. 3033, 1989.

_____. "Internal versus external economies in European industry". *European Economic Review* 34 (1990): 805–70.

Central Bank of China, Taiwan. *Financial Statistics Monthly*, various issues. Taipei, various years.

Chan, V.L., B.L. Chen and K.N. Cheung. "External economies in Taiwan's manufacturing industries". *Contemporary Economic Policy* 13 (1995): 118–30.

Chapman, S. D. *The Cotton Industry in the Industrial Revolution.* London: The Macmillan Press, 1972.

Chen, B.L. "Limited diffusion of technology, learning incentives and a low level of industrialization". *Journal of Economic Development* 19, no. 2 (1994): 253–72.

_____. "Picking winners and industrialization in Taiwan". *Journal of International Trade and Economic Development* 5, no. 2 (1996): 137–59.

_____. "Openness and economic growth: evidence of East Asia and Latin America". Mimeographed. Taipei: Institute of Economics, Academia Sinica, 1998.

Chen, B.L. and M. Hsu. "Technology adopton and industrialization: different experiences of man-made fibre in Taiwan and Korea". Mimeographed. Institute of Economics, Academia Sinica, 1997.

Chen, B.L. and K. Shimomura. "Self-fulfilling expectations and economic growth: a model of technology adoption and industrialization". *International Economic Review* 39, no. 1 (1998): 151–70.

Clark, C. *The Conditions of Economic Progress.* London: Macmillan, 1940.

Coleman, D. C. "Textile growth". In *Textile History and Economic History: Essays in Honor of Miss Julia de Lacy Mann*, edited by N.B. Harte and K.G. Ponting. Manchester: Manchester University Press, 1973.

Council for Economic Planning and Development (CEPD), Taiwan. *Taiwan Statistical Data Book (TSDB)*, various issues. Taipei, various years.

_____. *Industry of Free China*, various issues. Taipei, various years.

Dollar, D. "Outward-oriented developing economies really do grow rapidly: evidence from 95 LDCs, 1976-1985". *Economic Development and Culture Change* (1992), pp. 523–44.

Fransman, M. and K. King, eds. *Technological Capability in the Third World.* London: Macmillan, 1984.

Galenson, W., ed. *Economic Growth and Structural Change in Taiwan.* Ithaca: Cornell University Press, 1979.

Grossman, G. and E. Helpman. *Innovation and Growth in the Global Economy.* Cambridge, Mass.: MIT Press, 1991.

Inspectorate General of Customs, Taiwan. *Annual Report of the Trade of China*, various issues. Taipei, various years.

International Monetary Fund (IMF). *Direction of Trade Statistics Yearbook*, various issues. Washington, D.C., various years.

_____. *International Financial Statistics Yearbook*, various issues. Washington, D.C., various years.

Japanese Chemical Fibre Association. *Man-Made Fibre Handbook*, various issues. Tokyo, various years.

Kaminsky, G. and C. Reinhart. "The twin crisis: the causes of banking and balance of payments problem". *International Finance Working Paper no. 544*, Board of Governors of the Federal Reserve Bank, 1996.

Kim, K. S. and M. Roemer. *Growth and Structural Transformation: Studies in the Modernization of the Republic of Korea, 1945-1975*. Cambridge, Mass.: Harvard University Press, 1979.

Krugman, P. "History versus expectations". *Quarterly Journal of Economics* 106 (May 1991): 651–67.

Kuznets, S. "Quantitative aspects of the economic growth of nations: II. Industrial distribution of national product and labor force". *Economic Development and Cultural Change* 5 (1957): supplement.

Lau, M.L. and H.Y. Wan. "The theory of growth and technology transfer: experience from the East Asian economies". *Seoul Journal of Economics* 4 (1991): 109–22.

Lau, L. J., ed. *Models of Development: A Comparative Study of Economic Growth in South Korea and Taiwan*. San Francisco: ICS Press, 1990.

Lin, C.Y. *Industrialization in Taiwan, 1946–72*. New York: Praeger Publisher, 1973.

Lord, P. R. *Economics, Science, and Technology of Yarn Production*. Manchester: Merrow, 1981.

Lord, P.R. and M.F. Mohamed. *Weaving: Conversion of Yarn to Fabric*. Durham: Merrow, 1976.

Lucas, R.J. "On the mechanics of economic development". *Journal of Monetary Economics* (1988), pp. 3–42.

Matsuyama, K. "Increasing return, industrialization, and indeterminacy of equilibrium". *Quarterly Journal of Economics* 106 (1991): 617–50.

Nayyar, D. "An analysis of the stagnation in India's cotton textile exports during the sixties". *Oxford Bulletin Economics and Statistics* 35, no. 1 (1973): 1–19.

Pack, H. *Productivity, Technology, and Industrial Development*. New York: Oxford University Press, 1987.

_____. "Technology gap between industrial and developing countries: are there dividends for latecomers?" *Proceedings of the World Bank Annual Conference on Development Economics*. Washington, D.C.: World Bank, 1992.

Romer, P. "Increasing returns and long-run growth". *Journal of Political Economy* 94, no. 5 (1986): 1002–38.

_____. "Endogenous technical change". *Journal of Political Economy* 98 (1990): S72–102.

_____. "Two strategies for economic development: using ideas". *Proceedings of the World Bank Annual Conference on Development Economics*, pp. 63-91. Washington, D.C.: World Bank, 1993.

_____. "New goods and old goods, and the welfare costs of trade restrictions". *Journal of Development Economics* (1994).

Shieh, G.S. *Boss Island: the Subcontracting Network and Micro-Entrepreneurship in Taiwan's Development*. New York: Peter Lang, 1992.

Taiwan Institute for Economic Research. *Annual Report of Textile Industry*, various issues. Taipei, various years.

Tran, V.T. "Foreign capital and technology in the process of catching up by the developing countries: the experience of the synthetic fibre industry in the Republic of Korea". *Developing Economies* 26, no. 4 (1988): 386–402.

United Nations (UN). *Yearbook of International Trade Statistics 1969*. New York, 1969.

Vernon, R. "International investment and international trade in the product cycle". *Quarterly Journal of Economics* 80 (1966): 190–207.

Wade, R. *Governing the Market*. Princeton: Princeton University Press, 1990

World Bank. *World Development Report*. New York: Oxford Univesity Press, 1987, 1988.

8

The Development Experience of South Korea — The Role of Public Policy

Hojin Kang

I. INTRODUCTION

Like other Asian newly industrialized countries (NICs), South Korea (hereafter "Korea") has achieved very rapid industrialization over the last three decades. Korea's economic success stands as proof that one country can rise from being one of the poorest in the world and ascend to be a member of the Organization for Economic Co-operation and Development (OECD) in just one generation. Economic prospects seemed dismal in the early 1960s. Growth was slow. Korea had very low rates of saving and investment, and depended heavily upon other countries, especially the United States, for aid and capital. Korea was in the past the third highest aid-receiving country in the world after Vietnam and Israel. At the time external assessments of economic prospects were typically very pessimistic relative to those for Latin America and Africa. In the early 1960s the Korean government initiated significant policy changes. Then, the economy started to surge and Korea became one of the fastest growing countries in the world. A question naturally arises: what changes in policy brought about this dynamic process?

Related to this question is the debate on what policy measures contributed to East Asia's success. Policy measures that have been suggested can be divided into two groups. The first comprises policies that have played a positive role in both capital accumulation and productivity gains. These include stable macroeconomic policy and the promotion of education. The policies in the second group have been more interventionistic ones. Trade policy, more specifically outward-looking development strategy, is often cited as a central element of the region's success. Most controversial are the different types of selective intervention that have been pursued to varying degrees over the years by governments in the region.

It is generally accepted that state intervention has permeated and affected all other contributing factors, and is thus a factor of overriding importance in Korean economic development. Evidence of intervention in Korea can be found in every field of economic activity. Such state intervention raises a host of thorny questions as to why and how the government has intervened, and what are the consequences of the intervention. This issue has become more important in the light of current developments in the Korean economy that was forced to rely on the stand-by credit from the International Monetary Fund (IMF) to get relief from the foreign exchange crisis in December 1997.

In the next sections we are going to review some of the salient features of Korean economic growth, how the economic development strategy evolved over time, and the extent of government intervention in some key areas such as industrial policy, technological capability development, co-ordination of economic activities. Then, we review the development of Korea's financial crisis of 1997-98 and the public policy issues it raises with regard to the role of government in the economic development of Korea, followed by the conclusion.

II. AN OVERVIEW OF KOREAN ECONOMIC GROWTH

This section presents an overview of Korean economic development for the period of accelerated growth beginning in 1962. This overview is intended to provide some background knowledge on the overall picture, patterns and salient features of the country's growth before we discuss the role of government in this development process.

1. Growth and Structural Change

Since the early 1960s, the Korean economy has recorded sustained high economic growth, interrupted only in 1980 when output temporarily declined. Korea's real GNP grew at an average annual rate of 8.5% or about 15-fold increment over the three decades from 1962 to 1995, much higher than the average growth rate of about 4% for the preceding period (1953–62). The country's per capita GNP, which had grown only 1% a year prior to 1962, also increased rapidly thereafter. Per capita GNP rose about 8.5 times in real terms during the period between 1962 and 1995 (in 1990 constant prices), and reached US$10,000 in 1995. This rapid growth of per capita GNP was, of course, largely attributable to the rapid growth of output, but was also facilitated by the gradual decline in the population growth rate from about 2.5% in the 1960s to around 1% in the recent decade after the mid-1980s.

This sustained high rate of growth transformed a traditional agrarian economy of Korea into a dynamic industrial one. The long-range growth is usually characterized by an uneven growth of various sectors, particularly by a higher growth of the industrial sector relative to the primary sector. Evidence for this can be seen in the rapid industrialization of the advanced countries during the 18th and 19th centuries. The high economic growth of Korea over the last three decades was accompanied by rapid industrialization. Despite the steady growth of the primary sector at an average annual rate of about 3%, the share of agriculture in GNP declined drastically from 44% in 1963 to 7% in 1995. The primary reason was the rapid growth of the manufacturing and services sectors. The manufacturing sector, which had grown at an average annual rate of 11% in the post-war reconstruction period grew by about 14% per annum during the period 1962–95, leading the growth of the overall economy. As a result, the share of manufacturing in GNP more than doubled from 12% in 1962 to about 27% in 1995. Its share peaked at 32% in 1988 and showed a gradual decline thereafter, as was also seen in other advanced countries. In contrast, the primary sector (including mining) grew at an average annual rate of only about 3% during the 1962 to 1995 period. That sector's share in GNP thus declined from about 44% in 1962 to 7% in 1995. On the other hand, a combined share of the social overhead, construction and other service sectors in GNP showed a continuous rise from 44% to about 66% during the same period, mainly reflecting the rapid rise of the share of the social overhead and construction sector in GNP.

2. Outward-Looking Development

Korea's high growth was ignited by the expansion of exports and sustained by the rapid growth of export industries. The rapid growth of the Korean economy actually began with the rapid growth of exports following the shift in the industrialization strategy in the early 1960s. The country's merchandise exports, which were small and stagnant in the 1950s, started to increase very rapidly from the early 1960s. The exports amounted to only US$55 million in 1962, but increased to US$15.1 billion by 1979, showing an average annual rate of increase of 39 per cent. Between 1979 and 1995, they increased at an average annual rate of about 14% despite a gradual deceleration in recent years. Due to this rapid growth in exports, the ratio of exports to GNP also rose substantially from 2% in 1962 to about 28% in 1995. The nominal value of merchandise exports in 1995 reached US$125.1 billion, which is roughly equivalent to 2.4% of the world's export volume; it was only 0.1% in 1965.

The rapid growth of exports was made possible by a significant progress in the diversification of export products. In the early 1960s the greater part of Korean exports consisted of primary products — tungsten, iron ore, fish, raw silk, etc. — while manufactured exports constituted only a small fraction of the total. After 1962, however general machinery, footwear, plastic products and petroleum products.

Korea relied heavily on imports, particularly raw materials, crude oil, agricultural products and intermediate capital goods. Imports increased from US$500 million in 1963 to US$135 billion in 1995, a 19% annual growth over that period. Imports as a percentage of GNP increased from 16% in 1963 to 42% in 1995. As a result of rapid growth in both exports and imports, Korea has become the world's 12th largest trading nation. Korea has recorded substantial trade deficits each year, except during 1986-89 when low oil prices, low international interest rates and a favorable exchange rate yielded substantial surpluses.

3. High Investment and Savings

The rapid growth and structural change that took place in Korea were made possible to a great extent by a rapid rise in capital formation.

Investment rose rapidly after 1962 and particularly during the late 1970s. Gross domestic investment, which had been less than 13% of GNP in 1962, increased to 36% in 1979 and maintained roughly a similar level until the mid-1990s. Throughout the period 1963–95, the share of private investment increased remarkably, and since 1970 it has been steady at about 85% of annual investment. Government investment has been relatively low and constant, but it has played a pivotal role in the sectoral allocation of overall investment. The government has greatly influenced private investment by means of subsidized loans to targeted industries and firms as part of its industrial policy.

With a high rate investment, the capital coefficient has increased significantly. The capital-output ratio (net non-residential fixed assets and inventory stocks, excluding land and consumer durable, divided by GNP) had gradually declined up to 1970, and thereafter it had increased up to 1990. As economic development began to take off, income grew faster than capital, thus reducing the capital-output ratio. However, as labor supply became scarce in the mid-1970s, the capital-output ratio started to increase, indicating that the country's production activities had become increasingly more capital-intensive over the period. For instance the incremental capital-output ratio (ICOR) for manufacturing, which was only 1.1 in the first decade (1964–73) increased to 2.4 in the second decade (1974–83) and then to 3.1 in the last decade (1984–93). The ICOR for the whole economy increased in the same pattern from 1.6 in the first decade to 3.4 in the second decade and then to 3.8 by the last decade.

The sustained accumulation of physical capital would not have been possible without a significant increase in domestic savings. As the income level continued to increase, gross domestic savings gradually increased from 3% of GNP in 1962 to 27% in 1979 and then to 36% by 1995. Since the mid-1980s Korea's savings rate has been one of the highest in the world, with its major part accounted for by private savings.

This increase in domestic savings did not, however, prevent a substantial rise in per capita consumption level over the last three decades. Per capita private consumption expenditures showed a six-fold increase, rising at an average annual rate of nearly 6% over that period.

The continuous rapid rise in per capita consumption level was accompanied by a significant change in the average consumption pattern of individual households over the last three decades. The household expenditures for food, beverages and tobacco, clothing and footwear showed a relative decline in their share of total private consumption expenditures over the same period. In contrast the shares of furniture, furnishing, household equipment; operations, medical care and health expenses; transport and communications; recreation and entertainment; and education and cultural services showed gradual increases over the same period.

4. The Growth of Employment

Korea is one of the most densely populated countries in the world and lacks economically important natural resources. Therefore, efficient mobilization of the country's abundant human resources has played a critical role in its economic development over the last three decades.

In 1963 over 60% of the country's economically active population were living in rural areas and about 64% of those employed were engaged in agriculture and fishery. The official unemployment rate stood at 8.2% in 1963. Although official labor statistics indicate that the rural unemployment rate was around 3% in 1963, it seems that there existed a high level of disguised unemployment or underemployment. In the urban sector the unemployment rate was as high as 16% in that year.

Demand for labor has grown with Korea's rapid economic growth. Employment rose from 7.6 million in 1963 to 20.4 million in 1995, a 3.1% annual growth. As the focus of industrial policy shifted in the late 1970s towards heavy and chemical industries, the absorption of labor declined because of the high-capital technological intensity of these industries. Thus, the growth of employment slowed down after the 1980s. But the national unemployment rate that was 8.2% in 1963 continually declined to 3.8% in 1979 and to 2.0% by 1995. The high growth of employment was propelled by a rapid increase in non-farm employment. From 1963 to 1995 non-farm employment increased at an average annual rate of 6%, while farm employment declined by 1.7% a year. The rapid industrialization made a rapid growth of non-farm employment possible. The rapid increase in non-farm employment has accompanied a significant change in the structure of employment. The non-farm employment, which accounted for 36% of total national employment in 1963, surpassed farm employment after 1974. The absolute level of farm employment actually showed a decline beginning in 1977. Its share in total employment continued to decline to 13.7% in 1995. Manufacturing employment rose from 8% of total national employment in 1963 to about 28% in the late 1980s but thereafter showed a gradual decline to reach 23% by 1995.

This structural change in employment caused by the rapid expansion of employment in the non-farm sector helped to raise the average income per person employed, which had generally been lower in the farm sector than in the urban sector as reflected in the difference in labor productivity between the two sectors. This high growth of employment was also accompanied by rapid increases in labor productivity and real wages. During 1964–94, productivity of labor measured by value added per employed person rose by 4.2% a year across all industries and by 7.1% a year in manufacturing industries. Rapid increases in labor productivity, combined with employment growing faster than the population, resulted in rapid increase in per capita GNP.

The rapid growth of GNP and the expansion of employment in the non-traditional sectors would not have been possible without an increased investment in education. Korea's traditional emphasis on education contributed to growth, by enhancing the average labor productivity for the economy as a whole. The country actually increased its investment in education continuously to meet the popular demand for various levels of education. As a result, the average level of schooling for the working-age population rose significantly between 1960 and 1995. This increase in the average education level of the working-age population enabled the country to accommodate the rapid growth in non-farm employment without experiencing any real shortage of engineers, managers and other skilled workers until the mid-1990s.

5. High Level of Income Equality

Despite the growth-first strategy, distribution of income in Korea was among the least unequal in the developing world. Statistical measures show that income distribution did not change significantly over the period 1965–90. For instance, the Gini coefficient started at 0.34 in 1965, one of the lowest among developing countries, rose to 0.39 in 1975, and gradually declined to 0.31 in 1993. This pattern of income distribution held true for both urban and rural households.

6. Salient Features of Korean Economic Growth (1963-95)

The preceding overview reveals some of the salient features of Korea's economic growth over the last three decades. First of all, this period is characterized by sustained high growth. During this period the Korean economy recorded an annual average growth rate of 8.5%, making it one of the fastest growing countries in the world. This pace of growth was substantially faster in Korea's own historical experience since the average growth rate for the preceding period (1953–62) was about 4%.

The high growth of the Korean economy is associated with a rapid expansion of exports. Exports initially represented a modest share of GNP. As the rapid export growth was leading the economic growth, the ratio of exports to GNP rose substantially from 2% in 1962 to about 28% in 1995. The expansion of exports is regarded as the engine of the Korean economy's impressive growth. The sustained rapid rise in income and exports over more than three decades began with significant policy changes in the early 1960s. It is considered to be primarily the result of the adoption of an export-oriented industrialization strategy in the first half of the 1960s, although it was certainly helped by other factors, such as domestic political stability and a favorable international environment, especially in the 1960s and the early 1970s. Thus, the initiation of such policy changes and the effective implementation of those policies are one of the important contributing factors of economic development.

Another related characteristic during this rapid industrialization is a high investment rate. The rapid growth and structural change that took place during this period were made possible to a great extent by a rapid rise in capital formation. Gross domestic investment grew at an average annual rate of 22% in the 1960s and the investment share of GNP, which had been less than 13% of GNP in 1962, increased to 36% in 1979 and maintained roughly a similar level until the mid-1990s.

This combination of high growth with high investment is a focal point of many studies on high Asian growth. Many studies report that the extraordinary growth of East Asia has been driven by factor accumulation, while gains in TFP (total factor productivity) have been rather modest. According to Professor Krugman, while Asian economies have recorded spectacular economic growth over the past several decades, it is neither mysterious nor miraculous. It has been achieved in large part simply through the rapid accumulation of physical and human capital. Therefore, the search for lessons from high Asian growth along this approach would focus on the magnitude and persistence of capital accumulation, not on productivity gains. Then one of the important lessons of the Korean experience is to explain how countries can achieve and sustain high rates of investment and savings without lowering the level of TFP as has happened in other regions. The sustained high level of investment record of Korea has been impressive, and government policies may well have been a key contributor to this accomplishment. What was the role of the government in the successful mobilization of resources?

High investment, high savings and export promotion are the characteristics most often cited as central elements in the economic development of Korea. As a matter of fact, they are common traits among the Asian NICs and Japan. These countries are poor in natural resources and densely populated. They share a Confucian tradition. Their people are highly educated and saving rates are high. Exports have served as the engine for increased growth. However, Korean economic growth has many distinctive features as well as similarities. For example, Korea has recorded substantial trade deficits most of the period and consequently accumulated a large amount of external debt, unlike other Asian NICs and Japan. Korea has suffered from chronic deficits in current account balance of payments and is one of the top four largest debtor nations in the world. Thus, Korea has often had to worry about the debt-servicing problem and finally asked for an IMF bailout in 1997. What government policies created and maintained an economic environment that induces such balance of payments deficits over the years?

Over the last three decades Korea had the highest inflation rates among the Asian NICs. High economic growth in Japan and other Asian NICs was accompanied by very gradual inflation, but in the case of Korea both wholesale and consumer prices rose sharply and fluctuated widely. This was especially so when the economy was hit by oil-price hikes, poor harvests, changes in government and other shocks. Price stability was finally achieved in Korea from 1982. Until then the Korean economy could be described as having "high growth with high and highly fluctuating inflation". Korean economic growth then was "inflationary growth" — Korean economy had grown at high real rates despite high rates of inflation. The high inflation was caused mainly by the excessive expansion of demand associated with rapid expansion of industrial capacity. What were the policy objectives behind this pattern of high growth that allowed high rates of inflation? How did the Korean government manage to achieve price stability from the early 1980s?

Another distinguishing feature of the Korean economy is that the industrial structure is dominated by large industrial conglomerates, the *chaebol*, while small businesses predominate in Taiwan. The concentration of economic power in a handful of large, family based *chaebols* aroused various economic and non-economic arguments against it and has been a subject of hot debate in Korea. Many people, including government officials, tend to agree that controlling the excessive concentration of economic power is one of the most important tasks for the future economic growth of Korea. However, it is also true that the Korean government intentionally created large firms and *chaebol*. What were the policies that created *chaebol* and helped them to grow?

Out of the various factors contributing to Korea's rapid economic development over the last three decades, economic policy is a critical factor. State intervention has permeated and affected all the other contributing factors, and it is thus a factor of overriding importance. Evidence of intervention in Korea can be found in every field of economic activity. Such state intervention raises a host of thorny questions as to why and how the government has intervened, and whether the intervention has, in effect, contributed to economic development. This issue has become more important in the light of current developments in the Korean economy that was forced to rely on the stand-by credit from IMF to get relief from the foreign exchange crisis in December 1997.

In the next section we are going to take a look at how the economic development strategy has evolved over time in Korea. Although Korea's rapid growth depended largely on export expansion, it should be noted that import substitution was not neglected during the last three decades. Import substitution was promoted on a very selective basis in the 1960s and the early 1970s. But beginning in 1973 it was pushed to an expanded scale by the implementation of an ambitious govern-

TABLE 8.1 Major Economic Indicators of Korea, 1963–95

	1963	1970	1980	1990	1995
Population (million)	27	32	38	43	45
GNP per capita (US$)	100	252	1,589	5,659	10,076
GNP (US$ billion)	2.3	8	61	242	452
Gross saving rate (%)	8.7	18.0	23.1	36.0	36.2
Gross investment rate (%)	13.5	24.3	32.0	37.1	37.5
Share of GNP (%)					
Agriculture	43.5	26.5	14.9	8.7	6.6
Manufacturing and mining	11.6	22.4	31.0	29.8	27.2
Services	44.9	51.1	54.1	61.5	66.2
Share of employment (%)					
Agriculture	63.1	50.4	34.0	17.5	12.5
Manufacturing and mining	8.7	14.3	22.5	27.6	23.6
Services	35.4	35.3	43.5	54.9	63.9
Unemployment rate (%)	8.2	4.4	5.2	2.4	2.0
Exchange rate (won/US$)	130	317	660	716	775
Exports (US$ billion)	0.09	0.9	17.2	63.1	123
Imports (US$ billion)	0.50	1.8	21.6	65.1	128
Trade balance (US$ billion)	–0.41	–0.9	–4.3	–2.0	–4.7
Exports/GNP (%)	2.9	9.8	28.3	25.1	27.2
Imports/GNP (%)	13.7	20.0	35.4	25.9	29.4

	1963–69	1970–79	1980–89	1990–95	1963–95
Average annual economic growth (%)	9.8	9.7	8.3	7.8	8.9
Gross saving rate (%)	11.7	22.2	30.2	35.6	24.8
Gross investment rate (%)	18.9	27.9	30.4	37.0	31.4
Inflation (CPI) — average annual rate(%)	15.8	15.2	8.4	6.6	11.7
Average population growth (%)	2.5	1.8	1.2	0.9	1.6

ment plan for the promotion of heavy and chemical industries (1973–81). One characteristic of the Korean economy is its adaptability. It has been quite responsive to changes in the external economic environment and quick to exploit the opportunities that came after the initial crisis. Then, we are going to review government intervention in some of the fields that are closely related to the issues raised here.

III. EVOLUTION OF ECONOMIC DEVELOPMENT STRATEGY

1. Post-war Reconstruction and Import Substitution (1953–61)

The Korean War reduced to ashes many production facilities, houses and infrastructure, and forced the Korean people to rebuild the economy from scratch. The period between 1953 and 1961 was one of slow recovery of the war-ravaged economy.

The economic activity in the 1950s that contributed to development focused on light manufacturing sector of non-durable consumer goods industries, particularly textiles, and especially spinning and weaving. Economic policy focused on import substitution and massive investments in education. Trade policy was thus inward-looking with imports controlled by high tariffs, various quantitative restrictions, a complex system of multiple exchange rates, and an over-valued exchange rate.

Under all these protective measures the consumer goods industries demonstrated healthy growth, although the limits of the domestic market dampened their growth in the late 1950s. By 1957 textiles had achieved enough import substitution to induce the government to prohibit their import. Industry in general experienced a recession during the period from 1958 to 1961, and the textiles industry in particular showed a real decrease in production.

As late as 1961 economic conditions in Korea were similar to those of any resource-poor, low-income developing country today. Korea, already overpopulated, was experiencing an annual population growth of nearly 3%, and there was widespread unemployment and underemployment. Per capita GNP in 1961 was a meagre US$82, and the level of domestic savings was almost negligible. The nation has run chronic balance of payments deficits ever since its independence in 1948.

The emphasis on import substitution might not have been a wise choice in hindsight although it was a natural choice at that time as other less developed countries (LDCs) underwent similar phases of industrialization, including other Asian tigers such as Taiwan. But private and public investment in education turned out to pay off handsomely in terms of producing a well-educated labor force that would provide the backbone of the labour-intensive industries in the early 1960s.

2. Outward-Looking Development Strategy (1962–72)

The assumption of power by President Park Chung Hee in a military coup in May 1961 opened a new page in Korea's political and economic history. Economic growth and modernization became an ideology, under the auspices of which the military government launched large-scale industrial development programs. After the military coup of 1961, Park was relatively successful in rationalizing his military authoritarian rule by effectively using the threat from North Korea and the exigency of rapid industrialization. For him, rapid industrialization was essential not only for national development, but also for national security. The government emphasis on rapid industrialization created a unique pattern of industrialization, often known as state-led or government-directed industrialization, with an accompanying high level of administrative efficiency.

Park believed that military authoritarian rule was necessary to lead the people out of starvation and poverty. He argued, "In order to ensure efforts to improve the living conditions of the people in Asia, even undemocratic emergency measures may be necessary." For Park, economic development was top priority because it was an undeniable fact that the people of Asia were suffering more from poverty than from oppressive political conditions. He believed that the Asian people wanted to first achieve relative economic prosperity and build a more equitable political system afterward. The implications of his long-term strategy were far-reaching, affecting both political and economic life greatly throughout the entire Park era.

Park chose an outward-looking development strategy, turning away from then ongoing inward-looking development strategies based on import substitution. Supported by state initiatives, Korea's now well-known development process of export-led light industrialization began to take shape during this period. Because of its poor natural resource endowment and small domestic market, Korea chose an outward-looking development strategy emphasizing trade when launching the First Five-Year Economic Development Plan in 1962. Policy makers reckoned that Korea's industrial stage had already passed the "easy phase" of import substitution, which denotes an industrial phase where substitution of non-durable consumer goods is relatively satisfactory. They thought it was desirable for Korea to produce simple light manufactures for export utilizing its cheap labor force. For a nation with a long inward-looking tradition, the adoption of the outward-looking strategy was indeed very remarkable, and it is truly to the credit of the political leadership at that time that such a strategy was adopted. President Park's strong commitment to economic development was translated into action by the state's reorganization of bureaucratic initiations. These institutions had a mandate to facilitate economic growth, and to organize the new emerging relationship between state and business. They also formulated and implemented export-oriented policies in the following years.

The essence of the outward-looking strategy adopted in the early 1960s was to promote labor-intensive manufacturing exports in which Korea had a comparative advantage. In order to implement this strategy, the government made fundamental changes in institutional arrangements and institutional innovations to mobilize both internal and external resources. To mobilize domestic savings, the government allowed commercial banks to raise interest rates on deposits from 12% to as high as 26.4%. For three years in a row after 1965, the year when interest rates were raised, savings deposits in Korean banks nearly doubled each year. To minimize the adverse effect of inflation, the government proceeded to eliminate chronic budgetary deficits by revamping the tax administration. In order to encourage the inflow of foreign savings to make up for the insufficiency of domestic savings, in 1966 the government enacted a comprehensive Foreign Capital Promotion Act whereby the government underwrote the risk borne by foreign investors.

In order to promote exports, the government readjusted the exchange rate. In 1964 the multiple exchange rate system was replaced by a unified exchange rate system and the Korean won was devalued by nearly 100%, thus eliminating a bias against the export sector. In addition the government made available short-term export financing and allowed tariff rebates on materials imported for export production. Furthermore, customs procedures were simplified. These measures enabled Korean exporters to conduct their business as if they were operating under a free trade regime.

With regard to import policy, two major changes were made. As a first step towards liberalizing imports, a shift was made from a "positive list" system of import controls to a "negative list" system. Second, the government no longer rigidly adhered to the policy of self-sufficiency in the supply of major grains and for the first time allowed importation of these grains in large quantities.

The result of the outward-looking strategy was phenomenal success. The annual growth of exports in real terms between 1961–71 was more than 36%, and, propelled by growth in exports, real GNP grew at an annual rate of 8.7%.

There were several factors working for the outward-looking development strategy that yielded such a spectacular performance. For one thing, Korea was fortunate to be endowed with a well-educated population. Korea had a large pool of highly trained managerial manpower. It also had many dynamic entrepreneurs who had the energy and spirit to exploit new opportunities.

The international economic environment was extremely favourable, too. Throughout the 1960s world trade volume was expanding nearly 8% per annum, major industrial nations were still abiding by the original General Agreement on Tariffs and Trade (GATT) rules and regulations, and the world had not yet experienced the oil crisis of the 1970s.

3. Heavy and Chemical Industries Promotion (1973–79)

In the early 1970s the Korean government began to modify its outward-looking development strategy by emphasizing import substitution, particularly in heavy and chemical industries and in agriculture. In order to implement this shift in strategy, the government intervened extensively with the working of the market mechanism. Several international and domestic developments that occurred at that time prompted this shift in government policy.

One of the external catalysts of the Heavy and Chemical Industries (HCI) plan was the change in U.S. behavior towards Korea. In 1971 the Nixon administration reduced the U.S. troop level in Korea by one third. The decision was seen as the first of several moves toward the eventual withdrawal of all U.S. troops from Korea. This led Korea to develop its own defence industry. Carter's 1976 presidential campaign promise to carry out total U.S. troop withdrawal only reinforced Korea's resolve in this direction.

Other factors in the international environment put additional pressure on Korea. The sudden breakdown of the Bretton Woods monetary system in 1971 was highly significant for yet another reason. The protectionist trend in the industrial world accelerated. Many industrial countries were unwilling to undertake structural adjustments, exacerbating the fluctuations of exchange rates and balance of payments.

Facing growing protectionism, Korea was forced to do two things: diversify trading partners and restructure the commodity composition of its exports in favor of more sophisticated, high value-added industrial goods. In the early 1970s light industry exports began to sag, thus highlighting the need to develop new exportable products. At the same time export-oriented economic policies resulted in an unbalanced industrial structure. The export-promotion consideration along with the desire to develop defence industries led to efforts to accelerate the growth of heavy and chemical industries, including iron and steel, nonferrous metals, shipbuilding, machinery, electronics and petrochemicals to a degree perhaps unjustified by Korea's factor endowment.

The worldwide commodity boom of 1972–73 and the quadrupling of oil prices in 1973–74 also affected Korea greatly. Higher prices for imported grains meant further pressure on the balance of payments position which in turn lent support to the argument that Korea should develop its own agriculture and achieve self-sufficiency in major food grains. The quadrupling of oil prices in 1973–74 forced Korea to respond to an alarming deterioration in its balance of payments in an unprecedented fashion.

Major Policy Shifts

The major policy adjustments to effect all these changes fell into three categories: (1) efforts to accelerate the development of heavy and chemical industries; (2) efforts to diversify trade; and (3) efforts to increase domestic production of major food grains.

The government instituted a policy to develop the heavy and chemical industries to correct the imbalance in the manufacturing sector caused by a growth policy that favoured light industry. The development of heavy and chemical industries was already an important priority in the Third Five-Year Plan (1972–76), and because of the new political and economic environment noted above, the development of these industries was given added emphasis. The Heavy and Chemical Industries Development Plan, announced in 1973, called for an accelerated schedule to develop technologically sophisticated industries to meet defence needs and also to upgrade the composition of exports. Six industrial sectors — steel, machinery, automobiles, electronics, shipbuilding and petrochemicals — benefited greatly from generous government assistance.

Financial support from the government was crucial to the development of HCI. In order to channel capital to the strategic sectors, the Korean government adopted two basic approaches: (1) inducing a vast inflow of foreign capital and (2) mobilizing domestic savings and allocating this capital through so-called "policy loans".

Despite huge support from the state, the private sector was not interested in investing much at first. However, the ongoing inducement policy assured private firms of limited risk and provided a golden opportunity for expansion. The actual interest rates were negative and government procurement was enormous. During this time *chaebol* groups participating in the HCI program enjoyed subsidized credit, monopoly or oligopoly market positions and, in some sectors, guaranteed sales through government procurement.

Unfortunately, the plan was drawn up on the assumption that world trade would continue to expand at a very rapid rate. On the grounds that the heavy and chemical industry projects had long gestation periods, the loans were granted at very low nominal interest rates that in most cases turned out to be negative in real terms. This, together with the over-optimistic assumption regarding world trade prospects, led to unwise and excessive investment, particularly in the fields of power generation, electrical equipment and diesel engines. In addition, the low interest rates caused a chronic excess demand for loans, which stimulated the expansion of the domestic money supply. Furthermore, the low interest rate policy limited the ability of banks to offer interest rates high enough to attract savings. This impeded the normal growth of the financial sector of the economy.

To diversify trade and to circumvent quotas and other non-tariff barriers, Korea developed new exports and diversified export markets geographically. New product success was most noticeable in electronics, steel and ships. However, efforts to improve the quality of light manufactured exports such as textiles, footwear and leather goods were inadequate due to the lack of funds available for these industries.

The efforts to achieve geographic diversification of exports were directed initially to all regions, but they achieved only very limited success in Latin American and African markets. Greater success was, however, achieved in the Middle East and Europe. The share of commodity exports to the Middle East rose from 1.8% in 1973 to 11.7%

in 1976, and those to Europe from 11.8% to 17.5%. In the Middle East, Korea sold goods as well as construction services. Gross earnings from construction contracts won in the region by the end of 1978 totalled almost US$14 billion.

Despite the invaluable experience gained by Korean workers and firms from participating in large development projects, the immediate consequences of the Middle East ventures were a mixed blessing. The departure of a large number of skilled workers to the region pushed up domestic wages. This, together with the growing demand for skilled workers in heavy industries, widened the wage differential between skilled and unskilled workers, a development hardly desirable from the point of view of income distribution in the short run. In addition, the rather sudden improvement in the balance of payments due to the remittance of earnings from the Middle East expanded the domestic money supply that aggravated inflation.

The government policy responses to these two developments were not considered wise. In order to narrow the wage differential, the government pressured employers to pay higher wages for unskilled workers, a move that caused the average wage to increase faster than labor productivity. The increase in the domestic money supply and its consequences could have been dealt with by such policy measures as currency revaluation or rapid import liberalization. But for a nation that had long been accustomed to external payments deficits, such measures were either unthinkable or difficult to implement in time. Thus, the government tended to fight inflationary pressures with price controls.

When the Third Five-Year Plan was being formulated, the growing gap between rural and urban incomes became a major social concern. This social concern, combined with a deteriorating balance of payments position due to the international commodity boom, led to the adoption of a policy on agriculture which aimed at self-sufficiency in major food grains, particularly rice and barley. In order to achieve the twin objectives of improving rural income and ensuring self-sufficiency in food grains, the government adopted a grain-price support programme. In the initial phase the program was highly successful, particularly in increasing rice yield per acre and also in reducing the urban-rural income disparity.

One thing to note is that the Saemaul Movement, a comprehensive rural community development program implemented jointly by the government and the people, was rather successful. Under the Saemaul

Movement the government provided basic equipment and materials for farm road construction, rural electrification, running water and other social projects while people in the rural areas provided the necessary labor. In addition, the government helped the farmers to remodel their houses, subsidized fertilizer and other farm inputs, and provided free agricultural technical services. As a result of these comprehensive efforts, not only was the average rural household income raised but also living conditions were greatly improved.

Consequences

The three major policy thrusts just examined contributed to the high annual average growth of 10.8% between 1972 and 1978. Growth was particularly pronounced during the 1976-78 period when the average annual growth rate reached 11.2%. The heavy and chemical industries grew tremendously, which brought about advances in the industrial structure. These policy thrusts also contributed to the upgrading of the export structure. The share of heavy and chemical industrial products in total exports rose from 21.3% in 1972 to 34.7% in 1978.

This high growth and the structural changes were accompanied by a high degree of inflation. Between 1972 and 1979 the average annual rate of inflation measured in wholesale prices was nearly 18% as opposed to about 12% between 1962 and 1971. In addition, the high growth and the structural changes contributed to some structural imbalances in the economy, the most obvious of which were: (1) over-investment in heavy industries and under-investment in light industries; (2) extensive price distortions and lack of competition due to government controls; and (3) a rise in real wages which exceeded productivity improvement. These imbalances eventually weakened export competitiveness, thus slowing down the overall growth of the economy and at the same time aggravating inequalities in the distribution of income.

The inflation-led growth in Korea during this period also resulted in a high debt-equity ratio in the heavy and chemical sector by the end of the 1970s. As a consequence of easy access to bank loans, large enterprises in the strategic sector were accustomed to borrowing both domestic and external credit. Many firms made over-ambitious investment, exceeding domestic market capacity. Some large-scale projects were subject to chronic cost escalation, and were difficult to complete due to the shortage of funds. These structural problems of the late 1970s also prompted serious political agitation from various parts of society.

IV. GROWTH WITH PRICE STABILITY AND LIBERALIZATION (1980-)

1. Price Stability

Inflationary pressure, which gradually abated in the early 1970s, rose again in 1978. In 1979 consumer prices rose 18.3%, while wholesale prices rose 18.8%. By 1979 it became clear to many policymakers that structural imbalances in the economy were the real cause of the high inflation the country was suffering from. The inflation had an adverse effect on income distribution by causing a more rapid rise in the prices of daily necessities on which the low-income group spent relatively more than others. By discouraging investment in productive assets, this inflation was also jeopardizing the long-term growth prospects of the economy. In April 1979 the government announced a stabilization program that had a far-reaching goal. The goal was nothing less than restructuring the whole economy so as to enable the nation to make full use of its potential for continued high growth.

The 1979 stabilization program had three major components. To control excessive liquidity, the government set lower targets for the growth rate of the money supply and also proposed a fundamental reform of the banking sector. To deal with over-investment in the heavy and chemical industries and under-investment in the light industries, the government temporarily suspended all new projects in the heavy and chemical industries and realigned credit priorities in favour of light industries. To eliminate price distortions and promote competition, the government decontrolled prices on many items and stepped up import liberalization efforts.

The success of the policies was quite limited, due to drastic changes in both the external and domestic environments. First, within three months of the program's launch, the Organization of Petroleum Exporting Countries (OPEC) began to raise oil prices, which in the course of the succeeding twelve months nearly doubled Korea's oil import bill. This naturally meant an additional burden on Korea's balance of payments, and made it impossible to continue with the efforts to liberalize imports. Second, after the assassination of President Park on 26 October 1979, the nation began to experience many political difficulties, and by the spring of 1980 these difficulties had reached crisis proportions.

When the dust had settled, power had been appropriated by General Chun Doo Hwan. General Chun assumed the presidency in August 1980. He immediately began to undertake radical economic reforms. The reforms were motivated to achieve three related goals: (1) price stability, (2) continued high growth and (3) improvement in income distribution. The strategy that the new government had chosen to achieve these objectives was to promote competition in all sectors of the economy and liberalize its external economic policies in every direction. More emphasis was placed on reliance of the market mechanism and aggressive exploitation of Korea's comparative advantage.

Under this new policy direction the government sought to redress economic distortions created by the channelling of a disproportionate share of national resources into heavy industries in the 1970s. The new regime wanted to prove that it could bring political and economic stability and correct the negative effects of President Park's economic policies, such as high inflation, high concentration of economic power and excessive investment in HCI.

One result of these economic stabilization measures was that the consumer price increase, which had reached 28.8% in 1980, stabilized to single digits and dropped to 7.1% in 1982 and 2.3% in 1984. Wholesale prices, which had risen to 39.0% in 1980, rose only 0.2% in 1983. In 1986 the Consumer Price Index itself declined compared to the previous year.

2. Change of Industrial Policy — Anti-trust and Fair Trade

The Chun regime adopted a new industrial strategy to solve the structural problems of the past regime and earn the support of society. Selective industrial promotion laws, oriented towards "picking winners" in heavy industries, were criticized under the new regime and curbing the concentration of economic power became a pronounced policy goal. The *chaebol*'s increasing economic power gave rise to monopolistic abuses such as creating scarcities, price gouging and predatory behaviour in the domestic market. In response, the government shifted its policy on *chaebol* from promotion in the 1960s and 1970s to the regulation of their growth in the 1980s by adopting a policy of economic democratization. The Fair Trade Act of 1980, along the lines of American anti-trust legislation, included, among other things, the prohibition of unfair cartel practices and mutual investment among the *chaebol*'s affiliated companies, a ceiling on investment by and credit to large *chaebol*, and restrictions on their vertical and horizontal integration.

However, the *chaebol* continued to grow, with economic concentration increasing further until the mid-1980s and declining slightly thereafter. Although the anti-trust policy made a small dent in the mid-1980s, the economic power of the *chaebol* and their collusion with political power were so strong that the government could not implement some announced policy programs, showing a significant gap between what it intended to do and what it actually could do. In addition, the government bailed out insolvent enterprises to mitigate their impact on downstream sectors, so as not to tarnish the credibility of *chaebol* in the international market. As a result some of them, anticipating a government rescue, expanded well beyond their evident financial capability and some postponed adjustments to market change. In many cases the government was under pressure to accept economic reality rather than fulfil economic justice.

Then, facing accelerating globalization in the 1990s, the government once again shifted its policy on *chaebol* from regulation to liberalization by revising the Anti-trust and Fair Trade Act. Restrictions on the credit controls of the 30 largest *chaebol* were lifted, provided that their firms reduced internal ownership to less than 20%, raised their capital-to-asset ratio above 20%, and offered more than 69% of their shares to the public. Such a liberalization policy was designed to enable *chaebol* to compete freely in the expanding global market.

In short, after promoting the formation and growth of *chaebol* during the first two decades and attempting unsuccessfully to regulate them in the 1980s, the government decided to limit protection and intervention and rely more on market mechanisms. *Chaebol* have been and will continue to be the dominant factor in Korea's industrialization and globalization.

3. Change of Industrial Policy — SME Promotion

A major government mistake in the 1960s and 1970s was neglecting to encourage balanced growth between large firms and small firms. It was in the late 1970s that the government belatedly realized the importance of small and medium-sized enterprises (SMEs) in healthy economic growth. The government began promoting SMEs, particularly technology-based small firms, to remedy the imbalance between the large- and small-business sectors. The government established sanctuaries for SMEs, designating 205 business territories where neither large corporations nor their affiliates could intrude. The Compulsory Lending Ratio program stipulates that the nationwide commercial banks should extend more than 35% of total loans and that regional banks offer more than 80% of their total loans to SMEs.

4. Change of Industrial Policy — Functional Incentives

State intervention became less selective but more functionally based. The focus of industrial policy shifted from the promotion of strategic sectors to promotion of innovation-related activities. In the 1960s and 1970s special incentives — tax concessions, customs rebates, access to foreign exchange and other forms of protection or enhancement — were granted to strategic industries to make them competitive at a world level. In contrast, the government abolished all industry-specific promotion acts introduced in the 1960s and 1970s and instead legislated a new Industrial Promotion Act in 1986 that tied all incentives to special industrial activities such as research and development (R&D) and human resource development. In the late 1980s, however, the government again designated several high-technology industries, including information technology and aircraft, for support, but its role in these industries was much more limited than that in the labour-intensive industries in the previous two decades.

5. Trade Liberalization

In drastic contrast to the government's export-targeting system, the situation room and heavy export-subsidy programs in the 1960s, Korea's export trade was significantly liberalized during the 1970s. Most of the *ad hoc* incentive measures used in the 1960s were abolished, and Korea's export trade was almost completely liberalized by 1982. The ratio of net export subsidies to the exchange rate dropped, for instance, from 36.6 in 1963 to 6.7 in 1970 to 0.4 in 1982. In other words although export-oriented industrialization continued in the 1980s and

1990s, Korean firms were able to compete in the international market without government subsidies during these decades.

Import policies were also liberalized in the 1980s. The government promulgated the Tariff Reform Act in 1984, which was aimed to phase in general reductions in tariff levels. As a result, the import liberalization ratio — defined as the ration of the number of unrestricted items to the total — rose from 51% in 1973 to 95.2% by 1988 and to 98.6% in 1994. The government also brought down the average tariff rate from 26.7% in 1984 to 7.9% by 1994. Nontariff barriers such as delay in custom clearance and tax examination of foreign car purchasers were also largely eliminated in recent years. As a result, import increased, for instance, by 20.1% in 1989 compared with a 2.8% increase in exports, forcing Korean firms to compete, with little government assistance, against multinational firms not only in the export market but also in the domestic market.

6. Import Substitution

The economy recovered its competitiveness and productivity. As domestic prices were stabilized and productivity improved rapidly, Korea's international competitiveness was greatly strengthened. The double-digit economic growth in the middle of the 1980s was led by the exports of and further investments in the heavy and chemical industries and coincided with the beginning of the secondary import-substitution phase. The successful establishment of most of the heavy and chemical industries now allowed the substitution of domestic supply for hitherto imported industrial intermediate inputs. Thus users of petrochemical products could now rely on the domestic producers for a stable supply of intermediate inputs even in the midst of worldwide shortage and thus continue to expand their exports. Likewise, the steel industry played a key role in sustaining the competitiveness of Korea's manufacturing exports by serving domestic industrial activities even during a worldwide shortage of steel. From 1986 to 1989, further boosted by favourable external conditions known to Koreans as the three lows — low oil price, weak dollar and low global interest rates — the economy achieved a high annual growth rate of 12–13%. The balance of payments that had always been in the red moved into the black.

7. Financial Liberalization

In contrast to its monopoly of the financial sector in the 1960s and 1970s, the government has also taken major steps to liberalize the financial market. For example, the government reduced the regulation of non-bank financial intermediaries, many of which had long been controlled by *chaebol*, resulting in a significant rise in their share of total deposit liabilities in the 1980s. The denationalization of commercial banks led to a shift of significant share from government hands to the *chaebol*. The conversion of local short-term financing firms to either merchant banks or commercial banks in 1990 marked another important step forward in restructuring the financial sector, thus allowing for increased participation by private firms.

Nevertheless, direct state intervention during this period did not decrease, despite the government's frequent assertions of "liberalization" and "deregulation" in its policy approaches. Privatization of government-owned banks was nominal, with banks still operating as *de facto* arms of the government's industrial policies and lending primarily to well-established industrial groups favoured by the government. In the 1980s the available financial resources of Korean banks were still concentrated in very limited sectors in accordance with government-set priorities. Official interest rates, which would have soared if decontrolled, remained artificially low. The protection of the local market from foreign financial institutions resulted in gross inefficiencies; Korean banks were loaded with non-performing loans.

V. THE ROLE OF GOVERNMENT IN THE ECONOMIC DEVELOPMENT OF KOREA

Broadly speaking, the crucial role of government policy in economic development is unquestionable. The recent debate about Asia's growth "miracle" has made popular the view that, to grow, countries need merely to invest: in equipment, in roads, in human capital as East Asian NICs accumulated lots of capital. This leaves one crucial question unanswered: under what conditions will the right sort and right amount of investments happen? Establishing those conditions is the task of economic policy. Olson (1996) argues that the great differences in the wealth of nations are mainly due to differences in the quality of their institutions and economic policies. A country's institutions and economic policies are decisive for its economic performances. Neither differences in access to the world's stock of productive knowledge or its capital markets, nor differences in the ratio of population to land or natural resources can explain the large differences in per capita income across countries. The individuals and firms in underdeveloped countries may display rationality, and often great ingenuity and perseverance, in eking out a living in extraordinarily difficult conditions, but these individual achievements do not generate anything remotely resembling a socially efficient outcome. The big gains in overall efficiency of the economy, that is economic growth, cannot be obtained through uncoordinated individual actions. They can only be obtained through the efficient co-operation of many millions of specialized workers and other inputs: in other words, they can only be attained if a vast array of gains from specialization and trade are realized. This kind of intricate social co-operation that emerges when there is a sophisticated array of markets requires appropriate institutions and economic policies.

There are two views on the role of the state in the economic development of East Asian countries. According to one view, they have been successful because they adopted an outward-oriented development strategy. Too often, this has been presented as the primary, if not the sole reason for the success of these economies. Implied in this view is a prescription that the role of the state be limited to establishing a stable and neutral incentive structure. Another view is that the state has played a far more active and direct role in promoting economic development than suggested by an outward-oriented development strategy.

As far as Korea is concerned, however, it is generally accepted that the government played a decisive role in the country's successful economic development during the last 30 years. At least in the early stages of industrial development, the government did much more than merely adopt an outward-oriented development strategy that created a favourable economic environment for private enterprises. The government single-mindedly pursued investment and growth from the early 1960s in Korea and has played an active role in promoting economic development by working closely with private enterprises. The government, under strong military leadership, channelled scarce capital into particular industries, promoted risk-taking, provided temporary protection to encourage the entry of domestic rivals and facilitated construction of large-scale manufacturing units. It also helped firms to acquire foreign technology and encouraged exports, all of which are necessary conditions for achieving this stage. Without the state taking the lead in investment to create and upgrade production factors, Korea might not have been able to reach this level. To influence the pattern of resource allocation in order to accelerate the pace of industrial development, the government has deployed a wide range of policy instruments, including administrative guidance, credit subsidies, tax incentives, public enterprises to produce the intermediate goods needed by private industry downstream, tariff protection and the socialization of investment risk. Evidence of intervention in Korea can be found in every field of economic activity. In this section we are going to review how the government has intervened in the sectoral allocation of resources, technology capability development, the coordination of economic activities, and factor markets.

1. Industrial Policy

There is no doubt that Korea pursued an active industrial policy, at least through the 1970s. In its efforts to create conditions for industrial growth and to ensure the transition from one stage to the next, the government used a complex web of direct and indirect policy instruments to achieve its policy goals and discipline business, thus affecting sectoral allocation of resources. This is very pronounced in the ambitious export-oriented industrialization in the 1960s and the promotion of heavy and chemical industries in the 1970s. The government promoted exports in the 1960s and 1970s, and heavy and chemical industries in the 1970s by pushing the private sector into crises to reach imposed targets while providing incentives to make the crises creative rather than destructive.

Export Promotion

In the export-led industrialization of Korea the volume of exports has grown rapidly and the composition of exports has changed significantly over a short period. Over three decades the composition of exports changed radically, from simple manufactured goods to heavy goods and electronics. This rapid increase in volume and upgrading in commodity composition of exports is not just a market outcome of industrialization, but the result of government promotion. The Korean government made exports a life-or-death struggle in order to achieve its economic growth goal. It designated so-called strategic industries for export promotion. Thirteen items, including silk, cotton, radios and electrical goods, were targeted as exports in 1965, and this list was later expanded.

Targeted industries received a wide array of incentives, such as direct tax incentives, subsidies and policy loans. The government borrowed heavily from abroad and channelled the funds into export-oriented investment at below-market interest rates. Firms were granted unrestricted and tariff-free access to imported intermediate inputs and automatic access to bank loans for working capital for all export activities, even when the domestic money supply was being tightened. These firms also had unrestricted access to foreign capital goods and were encouraged to integrate vertically in order to sustain international competitiveness. These incentives operated automatically and constituted the crux of the Korean system of export promotion. Furthermore, the rationing of longer-term bank loans was used as a carrot to draw firms to new paths of exporting, encouraging diversification and increased exports. Exporters also benefited from a variety of tariff exemptions, accelerated depreciation, exemptions from value-added taxes, and duty-free imports of raw materials and spare parts. Tax holidays and reduced rates on public utilities further boosted corporate profitability. Assignment of lucrative import licences was linked to export performance. These direct and indirect subsidies were large enough to cancel out the adverse effect of temporary currency overvaluation in the late 1960s.

In addition to these financial incentives, the Korean government utilized direct, administrative measures to promote exports. For example, it created the Korea Trade Promotion Corporation (KOTRA) which, with its extensive overseas network, became an effective instrument for promoting exports.

What was perhaps unique to Korea was the Monthly Export Promotion Conference, established in December 1962, which became one of the most important administrative support mechanisms for exports. The meeting was attended by President Park Chung Hee, the Minister of the Economic Planning Board, the Minister of Trade and Industry, the director of the KOTRA, the chairman of the Korea Traders Association, and other public officials and private experts concerned with trade. The progress of exports and the performance of exporting firms were routinely reported at these meetings, and almost every month the

President made the practice of awarding successful businessmen with medals and citations.

At the meetings with the President businessmen were asked to present their problems and opportunities, especially the problems that they faced in dealing with government offices. These meetings thus served not only as a forum in which the President could hector businessmen to increase exports but also as a place where they could frankly inform the president of various problems, including bureaucratic red tape, that they encountered in their attempts to achieve export targets.

Another administrative measure used for export promotion was the export-targeting system adopted in early 1962. It was initially used to establish an annual target for total exports. But by the second half of the 1960s, the system had become more elaborate with annual targets set for major commodity groups and destinations. Targets for major commodity groups were given to the Korean embassies in the respective countries or regions for implementation. A "situation room" was installed inside the Ministry of Trade and Industry to monitor export performance, comparing it with the annual targets. The status of export performance was then reported at the Monthly Export Promotion Conference, which the President regularly attended.

Targets for export values were set for each commodity and export activity was closely monitored by the government. Achievement in exporting was rewarded with further incentives. Credit could be withheld to discipline firms that consistently missed their export targets, which were set by firms themselves with government guidance. A link between subsidies and exports in Korea gave government intervention a unique character. Almost all governments in developing countries offer the private sector a battery of incentives to stimulate industrial activity. But few governments monitor and control the outcome of subsidies, which is the function the export-targeting system in Korea.

State control of credit and intense pressures to export gave unique characteristics to Korea's industrialization. Credit control was the major device to discipline firms to invest in productive activities, eschew capital flight and earn foreign exchange. Exporting, rather than a competitive market structure or competing against imports, stimulated efficiency and allowed scale economies to be realized as industrialization progressed from light to heavy industries.

Tariffs were also used as a major policy tool. Korea's tariff system was characterized by dualism. Imported intermediate inputs could be obtained duty-free but industries targeted for development were granted tariff protection. They were then pressured to begin exporting at once.

Promotion of Heavy and Chemical Industries

Another target of industrial policy was the promotion of heavy and chemical industries in the 1970s. It began formally in June 1973 with the promulgation of the Heavy and Chemical Industries (HCI) Promotion Plan. According to the plan, six industries — steel, non-ferrous metal, machinery (including automobiles), shipbuilding, electronics and chemicals — were to be promoted at a total investment amounting to US$9.6 billion between 1973 and 1981. These were targeted to become future leading industries with their share of commodity exports expected to be more than 50% by 1980.

In early 1972 there was virtually no Korean firm that possessed the technical or financial resources necessary for starting any of the heavy and chemical industries. Furthermore, given large-scale economies and high risks inherent in such industries, not many firms, including the *chaebol*, were willing to invest in these industries. Implementing the plan thus required the government to hand-pick suitable firms, offering them various incentives.

The HCI program is a clear case of close co-operation between the state and the private sector in preparing the economy for changing international conditions and comparative advantage. By the late 1960s Korea began to face import restrictions on its light manufacturing exports in the United States and other developed countries. It also began to face challenges from China and the developing countries in Southeast Asia in the world markets for light manufactured goods.

The selection of the heavy and chemical industries for the next phase of industrial development was a natural step for the top policy makers as they were fully aware of the fact that Japan had earlier taken the same path of industrial development with great success. Furthermore, the experience in helping the light manufacturing industries to become internationally competitive gave them confidence in the country's ability to establish heavy and chemical industries as the next leading export industries.

In order to provide a market for the newly established industries, the government re-instituted import restrictions and rolled back tax exemptions on the import of certain intermediate goods and capital equipment. It also granted higher investment tax credits to businesses that purchased domestically produced machines.

A major package of tax incentives for investment in the heavy and chemical industries was provided in the Tax Exemption and Reduction Law of 1975. It included tax holidays, investment tax credits, and accelerated depreciation for the firms investing in the designated industries. These tax incentives had the effect of lowering the tax rate on the marginal return to capital by 10 to 15 percentage points, making the tax rate about a quarter lower than otherwise.

The government also began to invest heavily in the infrastructure relating to the heavy and chemical industries: large-scale industrial parks were constructed; educational and training systems were overhauled to produce engineers and skilled workers; and research institutes were established to develop the necessary technology.

Separate industrial complexes were established throughout the country: Pohang for steel; Kunsan for non-ferrous metal; Kumi for electronics; Changwon for machinery; Ulsan, Ok-po and Chukdo for shipbuilding; and Ulsan and Yeochon for chemicals.

The educational system was also revised to increase the supply of skilled manpower. Thus, between 1973 and 1980 the enrolment capacity of science and engineering colleges expanded from 26,000 to 58,000 and the total enrolment in technical high schools doubled while that in technical junior colleges increased more than fivefold.

Six research institutes were established for science and technology, especially for the machinery, chemistry and electronics sectors, with a corresponding increase in R&D expenditures financed by the government.

What was perhaps most important among all these promotional measures was the financial policy. The government was directly involved in mobilizing and allocating financial resources for the targeted industries, and it did so by controlling much of the credit system and giving preferential credit to these industries.

To finance the new projects the government established the National Investment Fund created with the funds contributed by the government and financial institutions. These funds were not, however, sufficient for the entire HCI program, and as an additional measure the government required a portion of commercial bank loans to be allocated to the heavy and chemical industry projects. As a result, the firms engaged in the HCI program received loans with a longer than usual period for repayment and at a rate 25% lower than that for other industries.

An effect of all these promotion measures was the creation of excess capacities in the heavy and chemical industries by 1979. The severe world recession following the second oil shock, combined with a tight monetary policy at home, worsened the problem, requiring subsequent restructuring of the industries by the government. It can be said, however, that it was this excess capacity in human as well as non-human capital that laid the foundation for the export boom in the heavy and chemical industries that began in 1983.

2. Technological Capability Development and Government

During the successful economic development over the last four decades, the rapid increase in industrial output and exports in Korea was accomplished not by simple augmentation of existing lines of activities but by significant changes in the configuration of production and exports. In the 1950s Korea was a resource-poor, low-income agrarian country with no significant exports and depended on imports of both raw materials and most manufactured goods. In the mid-1960s Korea began to export textiles, apparel, toys, wigs, plywood and other labour-intensive products. Ten years later ships, steel, consumer electronics and construction services challenged established suppliers from industrially advanced countries. By the mid-1980s computers, semiconductor memory chips, videocassette recorders, electronic switching systems, automobiles, industrial plants and other technology-intensive products were added to the list of Korea's major export items. This upgrading of commodity structure of exports and industrial output would not have been possible without the accumulation of technological capability over time.

Over the years the Korean government has adopted an array of policy instruments designed to facilitate technological learning in industry and strengthen the international competitiveness of the economy. On the demand side of technological learning, the government sanctioned the private firms to accommodate technologically challenging, government-imposed projects and overly ambitious export goals and to accomplish them within the planned time frame, inducing a series of challenging crises for the private sector. These crises pushed the private sector into something of a life-or-death struggle and forced them to exert all efforts towards accelerating technological learning. But at the same time, the government provided the necessary support through various incentives to make the crises creative rather than destructive.

We are going to focus here on the role of the government in the supply side of technological learning. Specifically, we will focus our attention on the following questions: (1) how did the government policy affect the channel of technology transfer from abroad? (2) what was the role of government in technology diffusion? (3) what were the mechanisms through which the government tried to develop indigenous R&D? (4) how did the government encourage R&D activities?

The Korean government's policy decisively affected the channel of technology transfer from abroad. Lacking technological capability at the outset of its economic development, Korea had to rely on foreign technology imports. However, Korea's policies on foreign licences were quite restrictive in the 1960s. In the case of manufacturing general guidelines issued in 1968 gave priority to technology that promoted exports, developed intermediate products for capital goods industries or brought a diffusion effect to other sectors. The guidelines also set a ceiling for royalties at 3% and duration at five years. This restrictive policy on licensing strengthened local licensees' bargaining power on generally available mature technology, leading to lower prices for technology than would otherwise have been the case. The 1970s, however, saw a significant change in government policy. In an attempt to attract sophisticated technology in response to the changing international environment, restrictions on foreign licensing were relaxed in 1970 and 1978, allowing, for one, a higher royalty rate. As a result, royalty payments for foreign licences increased significantly in the 1970s and 1980s.

One distinguishing characteristic of Korean economic development is that the size of foreign direct investment (FDI) and its proportion to total external borrowing were significantly lower than in other NICs. In the 1960s the FDI policy was quite free, permitting any form of *bona fide* foreign capital, including fully owned subsidiaries. But few foreign investments were made during the 1960s, primarily due to questions about Korea's political stability and its uncertain economic outlook. The government reversed its FDI policy in the 1970s, tightening its control. Joint ventures received higher priority than wholly owned subsidiaries. A general guideline was adopted setting three criteria: first, competition with domestic firms was seldom allowed in both domestic and international markets; second, export requirements were forced on FDI; and third, foreign participation ratios were basically limited to 50%. Korea was one of the few countries with restrictive regulations on FDI when technology was not a critical element and necessary mature technology could be easily acquired through mechanisms other than foreign licensing and FDI, for example, reverse-engineering. This reflects Korea's explicit policy of promoting its independence from multinationals in management control. Under this restrictive policy environment, not many multinationals were keen to invest in Korea. As a result, unlike other NICs, FDI had a minimal effect on the Korean economy.

Korea promoted technology transfer in the early years through the procurement of turnkey plants and capital goods. The rapid growth of the Korean economy required commensurate growth in investment for production facilities. However, government policy had been biased in favour of the importation of turnkey plants and foreign capital goods as a way to strengthen international competitiveness of industries using capital goods. Various instruments deployed in the 1960s played an important role in lubricating the inflow of foreign capital goods to Korea. For example, the slight over-valuation of the local currency, tariff exemptions on imported capital goods and the financing of purchases by suppliers' credits, which carried low rates of interest relative to those on the domestic market, all worked to increase the attractiveness of capital goods imports. Among NICs, the proportion of capital goods import to total technology transfer was highest in Korea, suggesting that Korea had acquired more technology from advanced countries through the importation of capital goods than through any other means. This massive import of foreign capital goods became a major source of learning through reverse-engineering by Korean firms.

In short, Korea imported foreign capital in the form of foreign loans. Such a policy, designed to maintain Korea's management independence from foreign multinationals, restricted FDI but promoted technology transfer through other means such as capital goods imports in the early years. It was effective in forcing Korean firms to take the initiative and a central role in learning, that is, acquiring, assimilating and improving imported technology, rather than relying entirely on foreign sources.

After two decades of restrictive policy towards FDI and foreign licensing, Korea liberalized its technology transfer policies in the 1980s and 1990s. As Korea's upgrading of industrial output continued, it needed progressively more sophisticated foreign technology to sustain its international competitiveness in high value-added industries.

In upgrading the overall technological capability of the economy, the effective diffusion of imported technology across firms within an industry and across industries within an economy is as important as the acquisition of foreign technology. In 1962 the government established a scientific and technological centre as a linking mechanism for disseminating technical information, but its use by industry was quite limited in the early years because mature products were easily imitated through reverse-engineering without the need to consult technical literature. In 1966 the government established a public research institute as a diffusion agent. But Korean researchers, mostly from the academic fields or R&D centres in advanced countries, lacked the manufacturing know-how that was in greatest demand during the early years and failed to serve as diffusion agents. The most important diffusion agents the government unintentionally created were the government enterprises established in the 1950s and 1960s. Engineers who accumulated modern production experience in state-owned fertilizer and machinery plants later left to head engineering and production departments in private enterprises.

Only in the 1980s did the Korean government introduce an extensive network of government, public and non-profit (private) technical support systems to promote technology diffusion within the economy.

Korean firms acquired and assimilated foreign technology primarily through imitative engineering in the 1960s and 1970s, when relevant technology was readily available in a machine-embodied form and learning by doing was relatively easy. Consequently, none of the policy instruments to stimulate the country's own R&D were effective.

As Korea underwent structural transformation and entered progressively more technology-intensive industries, the government focused more attention on indigenous R&D activities, primarily through two major mechanisms: direct R&D investment and indirect incentive packages. The government's direct investment was to develop the science and technology infrastructure and to promote R&D at universities and government R&D institutes (GRIs). Its indirect incentive packages, including preferential finance and tax concessions, were aimed at stimulating increased industry R&D.

Anticipating increasing demands for science and technology, the government established the Korea Institute of Science and Technology (KIST) in 1966 as an integrated technical centre to support the industry's technological learning. As Korea's first multidisciplinary research institute, KIST covered a broad spectrum of activities in applied research, ranging from project feasibility studies to R&D for new products and processes. KIST spent a large proportion of the nation's total R&D expenditure in its early years.

The government also created two science centres. Seoul Science Park started in 1966 with three R&D institutes and three economic research institutes, but it failed to attract private R&D centres to the vicinity. Two of the three R&D institutes have been relocated. In contrast, Taedok Science Town, established in 1978 in an area 200 kilometres south of Seoul, boasts 14 GRIs and three tertiary educational institutions and has attracted more than 11 corporate R&D laboratories. It became the first high-technology valley in the country. But despite more than 20 years of existence, it has neither built a reputation for attracting world-class scientists, as Tsukuba has in Japan, nor become a bustling industrial park with technology-based SMEs, as Hsinchu has in Taiwan.

The Korean government's attempts to promote university R&D activities began in the mid-1970s. Frustrated in its efforts to reform the undergraduate teaching-oriented tradition in education, the government conceived a dual system: since almost all universities under the Ministry of Education were essentially teaching oriented, the Ministry of Science and Technology founded a research-oriented graduate school of applied science and engineering, the Korea Advanced Institute of Science, offering both master's and Ph.D. programs, adding another in 1995. These schools draw the most highly qualified entrants by offering extraordinary incentives for students. These schools produce almost half of all Ph.D.s in science and engineering in Korea.

The government also enacted the Basic Research Promotion Law in 1989, explicitly targeting basic research as one of the nation's top technological priorities. Emulating the U.S. experience, in 1989 the government introduced a scheme to organize science research centres and engineering research centres in the nation's universities.

Given the inadequacy of university research, GRIs have served as the backbone of advanced R&D in Korea. The government has made these institutes the major instruments in its direct R&D investment through various technology development projects. They have been the recipients of more than 90% of the research grants awarded by the government in new technology areas. GRIs undertake most of these projects in conjunction with private firms.

The government offered various tax incentives and preferential financing for R&D activities in the 1960s and 1970s. During the 1970s the preferential financing did not stimulate private R&D investment as much as the government desired. The interest rate for R&D loans was one of the highest, reflecting the low priority of R&D in government policies. At the same time these mechanisms were largely ignored by industry owing to the absence of a clearly felt need to invest in R&D and the relatively easy means of acquiring and assimilating foreign technology then available from many sources. Only in the early 1980s did preferential R&D loans become the most important means for financing private R&D activities. Preferential financing accounted for more than 90% of total corporate R&D financing funded by the government. In contrast, direct R&D investment by the government through NRPs and IGTDPs accounted for only 4% of the total and direct investment through venture capital firms accounted for 1.7% of the total.

Public financing, mostly in the form of preferential loans, accounted for 64% of the nation's total R&D expenditure in manufacturing in 1987. In short, the government played a major role in funding corporate R&D in Korea, primarily through allocation of preferential financing. The impact of this financing should be interpreted with caution because, with rates of preferential loans ranging between 6.5% and 15 per cent, they conferred little advantage over financing terms available for the importation of plants and capital goods, which was an alternative means of acquiring technology.

Tax incentives are another indirect mechanism to make funds available for corporate R&D. In Korea tax incentives may be classified into five categories, according to objectives to be served. Most important are tax incentives aimed at promoting corporate R&D investment, reduced tariffs on import of R&D equipment and supplies, deduction of annual non-capital R&D expenditures and human resource development costs from taxable income and exemption from real estate tax on R&D-related properties. The incentives also include a tax reduction scheme through the Technology Development Reserve Fund, whereby an enterprise can set aside up to 3% (4% for high-technology industries) of sales in any one year to be used for its R&D work in the following three years. Other tax incentives are aimed at reducing the cost of acquiring foreign technology, promoting technology-based small firms, reducing the cost of commercializing locally generated technology, reducing the cost of introducing new products and promoting the venture-capital industry.

In addition, the government introduced various indirect support programmes. It has launched various programs to induce the private sector to establish formal R&D laboratories. These include tax incentives and preferential financing for setting up new laboratories and exemption from military service obligation for key R&D personnel. Realizing the importance of new technology venture firms, the government introduced in 1992 the Spin-off Support program to encourage researchers in GRIs to spin off and establish new technology-based small firms. Financial, managerial and technical assistance is offered to such prospective technical entrepreneurs.

Facing the imperative to shift to higher value technology-intensive products, R&D investment has increased faster than GNP in Korea, raising the share of R&D expenditure in GNP from 0.38% in 1970 to 2.61% in 1994. There also has been significant structural change in R&D investment. The government played a major role in R&D activities in the early years, when the private sector faltered in R&D investment despite the government's encouragement. More recently, the private sector has assumed an increasingly large role in the country's R&D efforts in response partly to increasing international competition and partly to a policy environment supportive of private R&D activities. For example, while the private sector accounted for only 2% of the nation's total R&D expenditure in 1962, the figure had risen to 84% by 1994. The number of corporate R&D laboratories increased from one in 1970 to 2,272 in 1995, reflecting the seriousness with which Korean firms pursued high-technology development.

3. Government and Co-ordination of Economic Activities — Economic Planning and Command

Economic Planning

One of the most conspicuous characteristics of the industrialization of Korea is the strong government and its orchestrating role. When Park Chung Hee seized power in 1961, he was single-minded in his goal to industrialize Korea and transform its subsistence agricultural economy into an industrialized one in spite of the odds against it. Toward this end, he created a highly centralized, strong government to plan and implement ambitious economic development programmes. Then, with a small group of competent economists to advise him, he made all important decisions himself. As a former army general, he was literally a field commanding general of Korea's industrialization drive. A strong leadership commitment to development and the successful implementation of development plans were important contributing factors to Korea's economic development.

Many people believe that the achievement of high economic growth since the early 1960s has been mainly the work of planning and that the "visible hand" of government intervention in the operation of the market system has been constant and extensive. The Korean government has actively and extensively intervened in the economy since the beginning of its rapid growth in the early 1960s. It was the government, not market forces, which controlled the direction and pace of industrialization until the late 1980s. The government steered the wheel and supplied the fuel. It set ambitious goals and directed the private sector with sticks and carrots, and private firms functioned as engines.

Effective formal economic planning in Korea started with the First Five-Year Economic Development Plan (FYP) (1962–66) since President Park Chung Hee's new military government drafted the First FYP in 1961 and implemented it. Korea has completed six five-year planning cycles since then. The objectives of Korea's successive five-year plans have changed over time with the rise in income, shifts in economic structure, and changes in economic issues and priorities. The main objectives of the First FYP were to build a foundation for self-sustaining growth. These were closely related to the establishment of an economic and legal framework. The major contents of the fiscal and financial policies as stated in the First FYP were largely an enumeration of reform measures concerning various policy systems, that is, the tax, budget and monetary systems, financial markets and foreign exchange systems. As stated in the economic development plan, the government reformed various policy measures to stabilize prices and to facilitate sound economic growth from 1965. The major reforms included financial reform assuring positive and realistic interest rates in September 1965, exchange rate reform normalizing highly over-valued exchange rates in March 1965, trade reform allowing generous importation of parts and machinery to be used for the production of export goods in 1964, and fiscal reform stabilizing government expenditures in 1965. The consecutive five-year economic plans from 1962 have provided clear and consistent signals to economic players both at home and abroad.

Decision Making in Planning

The most important characteristic of the decision-making machinery involved in formulating and implementing economic plans and policies in Korea is that it is headed by the President and as such is a nation-wide apparatus. If necessary, this apparatus can mobilize any institution or policy instrument in Korea to help formulate or implement plans or policies. And the apparatus has been managed by leaders who were fully committed to economic development. Presidents such as Park and Chun threw the full commitment of their administrations behind economic development.

Economic decision-making has been overwhelmingly a top-down process under the Park regime. Korea's economic decision-making process was very close to a General Headquarters (GHQ) style, in which the President himself made all major decisions and settled policy disputes among his senior officials. Many critics complained that Korean economic policy in the 1960s was managed by command. The influence of politicians and political parties was rather small as Park's approach to managing the economy relied on using a handful of capable technocrats and bureaucrats. The hierarchical order in the policy-making process is from the President to the Deputy Prime Minister, who heads the Economic Planning Board (EPB), and then to the head of the relevant ministry.

The EPB has played a central role in preparing and implementing Korea's various economic plans and policies ever since it was established in 1961. The Minister of the EPB was given the concurrent title of Deputy Prime Minister and authorized to control co-ordinate, and adjudicate among other ministries on economic matters. The EPB has been quite successful in its planning function since it has had strong support from the President, obtained the participation of important decision makers in the preparation and implementation of economic plans, and was able to control and co-ordinate the decisions of various economic ministries through its control of the national budget.

Implementation

One of the most important characteristics of Korea's style of plan implementation is its extensive use of both incentive and disincentive mechanisms. Particularly during the period when highly centralized and growth-oriented development strategy was pursued by the government of President Park, the government made extensive use of discretionary authority in manipulating incentives such as subsidies, tax differentials and loans, and in using command procedures such as tax differentials, loans and the termination of infrastructure services. Whenever incentive procedures were not effective the government was quick to employ disincentive mechanisms or command procedures to secure compliance by private firms. Some of the disincentive mechanisms often used were tax audits, suspension of bank credit and disconnection of infrastructure services. Because of these strong disincentives, Korean firms soon learned that the best way to survive and prosper was to comply with the government's directives.

Co-ordination by Command

Korean government did not hesitate to use command to co-ordinate economic activities in the 1960s and 1970s. Command type of co-ordination was used to promote exports, to ease financial burdens on private firms and to suppress inflationary pressure. The Korean government made exports a life-or-death struggle in order to achieve economic growth goals. It instituted the export-targeting system in the 1960s as a regular instrument to assess industrial success. Annual targets were assigned to major commodity groups, which were allocated to related industrial associations. They were also assigned by destinations, which were allocated to the Korean embassies in the respective countries. The Ministry of Trade and Industry maintained a situation room to monitor export performance. If a firm did not respond as expected to particular goals or programs, its tax returns were subject to careful examination, its application for bank credit was studiously ignored or its outstanding bank loans were not renewed. Government agencies often showed no hesitation in resorting to command backed by compulsion. It usually did not take long for a Korean firm to learn that it would be better to get along by going along.

In 1971 the government introduced a maxi-devaluation of its currency of 12% to stimulate exports. The immediate effect was a sharp increase in the domestic currency (won) cost of debt financing. This created severe short-term financial problems for firms that had borrowed abroad. Rather than allowing troubled enterprises to go bankrupt, the government took an extraordinary step to bail them out. The bailout was specified in a Presidential Emergency Decree announced on 3 August 1972. The 3 August Decree had two immediate objectives: to revive economic activity by stimulating investment demand to relieve the interest burden of overextended firms. To stimulate investment, the government reduced overall interest rates of banking institutions. The time deposit rate was lowered from 17.4% to 12.6% and the rate on loans up to one year fell from 19% to 15.5%. To alleviate the interest burden of overextended companies, the government redistributed income from lenders to borrowers in the unofficial capital market, or curb market. As of 2 August 1972 all loan agreements between licensed business firms and lenders in the curb market were nullified and replaced by new agreements, which carried far more lenient terms. This was a measure not to complement but supplant the working of the financial market.

The 3 August Decree also called for an across-the-board price freeze, while informal price controls had been in effect throughout the 1960s. After the freeze was lifted, less blanket controls over prices remained in effect until 1975; this time their declared purpose was to restrain monopoly power. The price controls in effect for the remainder of the 1970s gave the government discretionary power over the prices of a wide range of commodities that allegedly affected the lives of the people. Firms were prohibited from exceeding price ceilings, which were determined by the EPB on the basis of firms' costs plus a mark-up. Apart from agriculture, price controls covered commodities such as steel, petrochemicals, cement, kraft paper, synthetic fibres, pharmaceuticals as well as consumer durables such as television sets and cars. The prices of electricity and oil were designed to subsidize firms at the expense of households. The price of gas for non-commercial use was more than three times higher than in the United States while the price of diesel fuel was only one-third as great. By international standards, electricity for households was expensive but for firms it was unusually cheap.

The price stability in the 1980s was achieved by a combination of market mechanism and a direction of political leadership. The "growth at any cost" strategy of the Park regime had been replaced by "stability at any cost" under Chun in the early 1980s. With his firm leadership commitment, the bureaucracy worked hard to achieve this goal. Korea quickly succeeded in taming inflation. Wholesale and consumer prices on a year-end basis reached 42.3% and 38.2% respectively in 1980.

These rates were brought down to 11.3% and 13.8% in the following year, and were further reduced to 2.4% and 4.7% in 1982. This Korean type of stabilization policy, which was directed by political leadership, was in theory far removed from liberal economic policy. The so-called "liberalization" measures of this period were almost the opposite of Western-style *laissez-faire* or liberal economic policy.

The relative degree of importance of the government and the private sector has changed substantially since the first plan. During the early planning periods the government played the dominant role since the market system was not well developed. As the urban-industrial sector expanded, market activities and the function of the market system began to modernize. As a consequence, the function of the private sector market system expanded greatly relative to that of the government. Since the fifth plan (1982–86), particular emphasis has been put on enhancing free competition. There is no doubt that in an increasingly complex economy such as Korea's in the 1980s, the impersonal rule of law is preferable to the personal rule of men. As economic liberals emphasize, non-discretionary measures — rather than discretionary measures — should be relied on as much as possible. Such thinking has become popular among Korean businessmen since President Park's death in 1979 and has been accepted by policy makers as a more desirable approach to implementation. This has been one of the important changes in the liberalization of economic management from the early 1980s, representing a major shift towards a more pure market-directed system and the readjustment of government functions.

4. Government Intervention in the Factor Market

Financial Reform and Incentive Systems

One of the most conspicuous institutional changes in the early 1960s was a fundamental reorganization of the financial system, with new financial institutions beginning to play a more vital role in Korea's industrialization process. Such changes also contributed to the emergence of Korea's unique industry structure. Under the Law for Dealing with Illicit Wealth Accumulation promulgated in 1961, all commercial banks became, in essence, the property of the state and were placed under the direct control of the Ministry of Finance. The Bank of Korea (BOK), the central bank established by the Bank of Korea Act of 1950, had its charter amended in 1962. This amendment strengthened government control over the BOK's monetary policy, ended the previous autonomy of the BOK and placed it under the control of the Monetary Board, which was chaired by the Minister of Finance.

During this period a series of specialized banks were reorganized or established to provide financial support for the development of "strategically important" industrial sectors. For example, the Korean Development Bank was reorganized in 1962 and authorized to make long-term loans for government-promoted projects, particularly in infrastructure development and targeted industries. In 1967 the Korean Exchange Bank was established to attract foreign currency that would be utilized to facilitate the financing of Korea's expanding export sector. In order to ensure that loan funds were utilized as intended, loan proceeds were transferred to a credit-control account in the name of the borrower, only to be withdrawn when documentation assuring the "proper" use of the funds was produced.

The central pillar of the Park regime's strategy of rapid industrialization was credit control. Although private firms were free in theory to borrow abroad, in practice they could only do so with government approval. Raising capital abroad was contingent on loan guarantees, which the government gave only to loans which it approved. Private ownership of domestic banking institutions was altogether prohibited.

State control over the allocation of credit was the principal mechanism to induce the private sector to develop state-targeted industries. Credit for developing targeted strategic sectors was offered at interest rates between 4% and 14%, while credit to finance non-targeted projects was either unavailable or at rates exceeding 20 to 25%. In real terms interest charges for targeted projects were usually negative. This preferential allocation of credit eliminated the high level of risk for entrepreneurs engaged in a state-designated industry, while providing the state a high degree of microeconomic control over sectoral development. The close alliance between state and private enterprises was born under this financial allocation system.

Government control of credit differentiated Korean and Japanese development. The Japanese *zaibatsu* owned their own banks whereas the Korean *chaebol* did not. Thus, direction of the economy under the Park regime was more centralized than in Japan because power over the purse was more centralized.

The initiative to borrow could be taken by either the government or the private sector. In the latter case the first hurdle was project approval by the EPB, the bureaucracy responsible for targeting specific sectors for development. If the private applicant had political connections and a project that complemented the EPB's own aims, credit would be arranged by the Ministry of Finance. If the government took the initiative, it would identify a private firm to own and manage the project in question. Public enterprise in the manufacturing sector has been rare, limited in the 1970s to steel, oil refining and metals.

The Park regime's labor policy featured a ban on strikes and barriers to free trade union organization. In attempting to create a conducive environment, in which the government's development goals could be achieved without interruption, the Korean government, as the central orchestrator for economic development and export, also emerged as the responsible agency to control labor movements and maintain industrial peace. The government's leading role in repressing labor was a consistent policy through the late 1980s. Although the formal ban on unions had been lifted in the early 1960s, the legal framework in which unions could function was so restrictive that it virtually eliminated the possibility of organizing any genuine independent unions. Furthermore, the government used the Korean Central Intelligence Agency (CIA) to spy on and repress labor as part of a broader economic strategy through the 1970s. As a result, workers became exceedingly docile. A drastic shift towards political democratization in the late 1980s, however, triggered an upsurge in labor unrest for three years.

Many intellectuals, in Korea and abroad, criticized the dreadful negative side of many of the government's practices to suppress labor movements, but it at least provided Korean firms with uninterrupted opportunities, to learn cumulatively and continuously, making undoubtedly significant contributions to rapid industrialization. Such a repressive policy retarded the growth of trade unions and workers taking part in industrial democracy. Scandinavian and German experiences show that industrial democracy supports and encourages innovation.

5. Adverse Consequences of Industrial Policy

The expansion of industrial capacity in Korea was achieved through the expansion of existing firms rather than through the creation of new firms. The government's licensing policy was highly risk averse. The firms that had already proved themselves tended to be the firms that were awarded licences to enter new industries. This was the genesis of the diversified business groups. This pattern has persisted for over two decades and has resulted in the growth of a small number of very large firms and business groups or *chaebol*, causing a large gap between large and small firms. A related pattern is that the market concentration ratio in Korea has been much higher than in either Japan or Taiwan. The Japanese pattern, in contrast, has been based on the growth of both a significant number of very large firms as well as a large number of small firms. The Korean economy was often called a "large firm economy", in contrast to the "small firm economy" of Taiwan or the "bi-polar economy" of Japan.

Exporting firms' free access to imported intermediates had also aggravated the imbalance between large firms and SMEs in Korea. It hurt SMEs that might have produced those intermediate imports with relatively minor-scale economies. This retarded Korea's subcontracting system and was the root of the problem surrounding SMEs that surfaced in the late 1970s. Exporting also helped the growth rate of output more than the current account, necessitating higher foreign credit than otherwise.

The basic policy objective during the Park regime was "exports first" or "nation building through export promotion". Therefore, setting highly ambitious export targets and then exceeding those targets was regarded as the height of achievement for businessmen and public officials in charge of export promotion. Under President Park's government, large Korean firms were assigned annual 'export targets' by officials in the Ministry of Trade and Industry which maintained an "export situation room" to supervise the export behaviour of various firms. The export targets were seen by firms as virtual "orders" or assigned "missions". If they succeeded in fulfilling their export goals, they obtained numerous benefits reserved for exporters, including preferential credit and loans, administrative support and tax and other benefits. Thus, Korean exporters saw the over-fulfilment of their export targets — usually determined jointly with the government — as the keystone of their business strategy.

This type of aggressive export promotion and growth policy necessitated that the economy consistently performed far beyond normal capacity, resulting in the forced expansion of investment and output by businessmen. Overly ambitious investment plans caused the inflationary financing of investment. The excessive investment demand created by this type of policy provided one of the links between the forced export growth strategy and high inflation that persisted until 1982.

VI. FINANCIAL CRISIS IN KOREA, 1997–98 AND PUBLIC POLICY ISSUES

1. Introduction

Korea was on the brink of defaulting on its debts at the end of November 1997, when the country's usable foreign currency reserves plummeted to US$7.3 billion, way below the level sufficient to cover even one month's imports. Consequently, the government had to turn to the IMF to request bail-out loans on 21 November. On 3 December 1997 Korea and the IMF signed an agreement for a financial-aid package totalling US$58.3 billion subject to a broad range of conditionalities, including macroeconomic stabilization and structural reform.

The IMF agreed to provide a total of US$21 billion to be disbursed in 11 instalments over a three-year period from its emergency financing and other facilities. It also secured financial commitment totalling US$36 billion from international organizations such as the World Bank and the Asian Development Bank, and countries such as the United States and Japan, which would serve as a second line of defence. The IMF conditionalities required tight monetary policy, a fiscal surplus, sweeping financial reform, further liberalization of the financial markets and also two conditionalities which were unusual to an IMF program; greater flexibility in the labor market and restructuring of the *chaebol*.

Korea's financial crisis has been as dramatic as it has been unexpected. In fact over a two-month period, from October to December 1997, Korea was reduced from being the world's 11th largest economy to an economy surviving on overnight loans from the international money markets.

This section first looks back upon the series of developments which culminated in the foreign exchange crisis in November and December 1997 and describes policy initiatives undertaken to overcome this crisis and the impact of the financial crisis on the Korean economy in sub-section 3. In sub-section 4 we analyze both the internal and external factors responsible for the financial turmoil in 1997 and discuss public policy issues brought forth by the crisis.

2. Development of the Crisis

Downturn of Business Cycle

Korea rebounded strongly from its slow-down in growth in 1992 and 1993. The economic growth from 1994 to the beginning of 1997 was almost 8% on average per annum. Like the earlier periods of high economic growth, the economy was once again being fuelled by exports. What was different during the 1994–96 period was that the high growth was also spurred by high investment. In many respects this high investment was a positive development as the economy was coming out of a mild contraction during the 1992–93 period, but was also responsible for a sharp increase in the current account deficit and the financial and foreign exchange crisis in which Korea finds itself today. (Why exactly did Korean firms embark upon such an investment spree? There were two major developments: the strengthening of the yen and the financial liberalization and market opening, which increased the availability of low-cost foreign credit.)

Symptoms of the impending financial crisis started to appear when the economy began to slow down in 1996. From a 9% level in 1994-95, the real GDP growth rate slipped to 7.1% in 1996, before falling to 6.2% in the first half of 1997 (Table 8.2). Although these figures might seem to indicate a soft landing, the truth was otherwise. The growth from 1996 onwards resulted from an increase in inventories as firms failed to adjust their production in line with the reduced demand. The consequence was a profit squeeze for the corporate sector; the ROE (return on equity) of manufacturing firms in 1996 fell dramatically to 2.0% as against 11.0% the year before, and deteriorated further to register –4.2% in 1997 (Table 8.3).

Widening of Current Account Deficits and Accumulation of External Debt

In the meantime, despite the slow-down in the economy, the current account deficit had widened from US$8.5 billion in 1995 to US$23 billion in 1996. For the first half of 1997 alone, it stood at US$9.9 billion. The ratio of the current account deficit to GDP rose to 4.7% in 1996 from below 2% in the two preceding years (Table 8.2). This widening current account deficit was brought about by the deceleration

TABLE 8.2   Korea: Key Economic Indicators

	1980–85	1986–91	1992	1993	1994	1995	1996	1997
GDP growth rate (%)	6.3	9.9	5.1	5.8	8.6	8.9	7.1	5.5
Consumer price inflation (%)	10.9	6.1	6.3	4.8	6.2	4.5	4.9	4.5
Current account (%)	−2.7	4.1	−3.9	1	−3.9	−8.5	−23	−8.6
Current account/GDP (%)	−3.8	3	−1.3	0.3	−1	−1.9	−4.7	−1.9
External debt[1] (US$ billion)	46.8	39.1	42.8	43.9	56.9	78.4	157.5	154.4

[1]From 1996, external liabilities.
SOURCE: Bank of Korea.

TABLE 8.3   Korea: Net Income to Stockholders' Equity in Manufacturing, 1990–97 (in percentages)

1990	1991	1992	1993	1994	1995	1996	1997
5.53	5.53	4.33	4.22	7.56	11.03	2.02	−4.21

SOURCE: Bank of Korea.

of export growth due to the fall in the prices of Korea's major export items, especially computer memory chips, coupled with a rapid expansion of imports, most notably of capital goods and consumer goods. The deficit was financed mainly by inflows of foreign capital, which caused a sharp increase in external debt.

Successive Corporate Insolvencies and Increase in Non-performing Loans

From the beginning of 1997 a number of large companies that had been hit by sluggish sales and low profitability finally collapsed under their huge burden of financial costs. The failure of Hanbo Group, the 14th largest conglomerate, on 23 January was followed by the insolvencies of smaller conglomerates, including Sammi, Jinro and Dainong. The biggest blow came with the insolvency on 15 July 1997 of Kia Motors, one of the three largest auto companies and the main company in the eighth largest conglomerate.

The series of large corporate insolvencies inevitably undermined the soundness of financial institutions with large exposure to these con-

TABLE 8.4   Non-performing Loans of Korean Financial Institutions[1]
(in trillion won)

	1996	September 1997[2]	December 1997	March 1998
Commercial banks	12.2 (3.9)	21.9 (6.4)	22.6 (6.0)	28.0 (7.7)
Merchant banking corporations	1.3	3.9 (2.9)		2.2 (4.8)
Total	13.5	25.8		30.2

NOTES: [1]End of period; figures in parentheses indicate ratios to total credit.
[2]October 1997 for merchant banking corporations.

glomerates. Non-performing loans[1] of commercial banks as at the end of 1996 stood at 12.2 trillion won, which was a relatively small 3.9% of total credit. They almost doubled to 21.9 trillion won in the next nine months to September 1997. At the same time merchant banking corporations, whose functions are broadly similar to those of commercial banks, recorded non-performing loans of 3.9 trillion won at the end of October 1997, three times the 1.3 trillion won at the end of 1996. Non-performing loans of the entire financial sector rapidly accumulated, amounting to 56.5 trillion won, equivalent to 13% of nominal GDP at the end of March 1998.

Contagion Effects from Southeast Asia and Downgrading of Sovereign Rating

The Southeast Asian currency crisis that started with the plunge of the Thai baht early in July 1997 quickly spread through the neighbouring Southeast Asian region, notably to Indonesia and Malaysia. This further unsettled foreign investors who had been apprehensively observing the weakening of both companies and financial institutions in Korea. Reflecting this, the leading international credit rating agencies, Standard & Poor (S&P) and Moody's, downgraded Korea's long-term sovereign rating very sharply in October 1997. This caused foreign financial institutions to turn down requests to roll over their loans to Korean banks and led institutional investors to withdraw their portfolio investment from the Korean stock market. The big fall in the Hang Seng Index on 23 October 1997 aggravated Korea's foreign currency liquidity conditions further, by fanning fears as to the future of all the Asian economies.

Inept Government Responses

By the first week of September 1997 six *chaebol,* including Kia, had been placed under a work-out plan or had become insolvent. They accounted for about 10.4% of the total assets of the 30 largest *chaebol,* not a large enough amount to threaten the stability of the economy, but their demise made the economic outlook more pessimistic than otherwise. Yet, the authorities still failed to take any action, ignoring the growing clamour for much-needed financial reform and restructuring of industry and the *chaebol.* By this time the Korean public had by and large become disillusioned with the ineptness of the administration, which became a lame duck government. There seemed to be no end to the bankruptcies, and the economic slow-down had already dragged on for nearly two years. Whatever economic control the government had still held after liberalization was now therefore even further compromised, and with the next presidential election to be held in December 1997 there was no way the administration was going to be able to take any serious action to restore stability to the Korean financial markets. The foreign investors knew this all too well, prompting some of them to begin withdrawing their funds from the Korean stock market and out of Korea in early September 1997.

The behaviour of the government in its management of exchange rate policy in the last three months leading up to the crisis did not help and in fact exacerbated the financial problems. The exchange rate policy was rather inconsistent and unpredictable, suggesting to foreign and domestic investors alike that the government was at a serious loss as to how to deal with the deteriorating financial situation. The won had been under strong depreciatory pressure since the early months of 1997. Time after time throughout the year, the government would publicly state that it would defend the won at a certain level, only to be forced to retreat and attempt defending the won at a new level.

Between June and November 1997 the BOK's reserve holdings fell by US$10 billion. During the same period the central bank sold US$12.2 billion in the spot market and made forward sales amounting to US$7 billion to defend the won. By the end of November, the actual level of usable reserves fell to US$7 billion dollars.

Depletion of International Reserves and Application to the IMF

In November 1997, as the roll-over ratio of short-term external borrowings by domestic financial institutions fell rapidly[2] and it became almost impossible to find other sources of new foreign loans, the demand for foreign currency to redeem foreign debts increased markedly in the Seoul foreign exchange market (Table 8.5). However, the anticipation of the Korean won's depreciation became so widespread that there were few sellers of foreign currency. Although the daily band of exchange fluctuations was widened from ±2.25% to ±10% on 16 November, the foreign exchange market was paralyzed repeatedly because of the still narrow trading band. The Korean won fell to its daily floor against the U.S. dollar as soon as the market opened, and foreign exchange trading had to be suspended.

The BOK had to supply foreign exchange to companies and financial institutions that faced default on their foreign currency obligations within the limits of real demand. However, Korea soon found itself on the brink of national insolvency as the country's usable foreign exchange reserves became severely depleted.

Consequently, the government had to turn to the IMF to request bailout loans on 21 November. On 3 December 1997 Korea and the IMF signed an agreement for a financial aid package totalling US$58.3 billion subject to a broad range of conditionalities including macroeconomic stabilization and structural reform.

The IMF agreed to provide a total of US$21 billion to be disbursed in 11 installments over a three-year period from its emergency financing and other facilities. It also secured financial commitment totalling US$36 billion from international organizations such as the World Bank and the Asian Development Bank, and countries such as the United States, Japan, which would serve as a second line of defence. The IMF conditionalities required tight monetary policy, a fiscal surplus, sweeping financial reform, further liberalization of the financial markets and also two conditionalities which were unusual to an IMF program: greater flexibility in the labor market and restructuring of the *chaebol*.

Contrary to expectations, the swift and successful conclusion of the negotiations did little to allay fears and stabilize the financial markets, including the foreign exchange market. The won/dollar exchange rate continued to depreciate, and interest rates began to soar while the stock

TABLE 8.5 Korea: Trend of Roll-over Ratio, 1997 (in percentages)

January 1997	February	March	April	May	June	July	August	September	October	November	December
115.4	94.2	109.0	94.9	100.6	106.3	89.1	79.2	85.8	86.5	58.8	32.2

price index went into a nosedive. On 16 December the 10% daily fluctuation band of exchange rate was lifted, and a free-floating exchange rate system was introduced. A few days later the 25% interest rate ceiling was also abolished as it had become clear that interest rates had to rise well above that level. Most of the capital controls were also abolished. The limit on aggregate stock ownership by foreigners was raised to 55%, the market for corporate bonds with maturities longer than three years was opened up, and the short-term money market would also be deregulated for foreigners' investment.

The IMF financing package together with the conditionalities did not help change the markets' sentiment because many thought that Korea might not be able to comply with the structural reforms mandated by the IMF and that the extremely tight monetary and fiscal policies required of Korea under the IMF program would depress economic activity so much that they would in the long-run undermine Korea's ability to service its foreign debt. This would clearly defeat the purpose of the IMF program. The roll-over rate at commercial banks fell to about 10%, market interest rates shot up to the dizzying height of 40% and the won/dollar exchange rate continued to depreciate, reaching 1,995 won per dollar on 23 December.

The financial situation was clearly unsustainable, and rumours began to circulate among the foreign investors that Korea might have to declare a debt moratorium. The IMF and the U.S. Treasury clearly had to take stronger measures to stop further haemorrhaging of the Korean economy. On Christmas eve the IMF and the Group of Seven (G-7) countries came up with a US$10 billion emergency financing programme, drawing US$8 billion from the second line of defence. The new package succeeded in turning market sentiment around as it demonstrated the resolve of the IMF and G-7 to rescue Korea from financial collapse. (It would actually seem that a new watershed has been reached as the IMF has clearly served as a lender of last resort in the East Asian financial crisis.)

3. Economic Policy Actions and Economic Consequences

Upon the signing of the financial-aid package on 3 December 1997 the Korean government agreed with the IMF that it would pursue an economic reform program focused on macroeconomic stability and reforms in the financial, corporate, and labor sectors. In the spirit of this agreement, Korea began to take steps to resolve the crisis.

To achieve macroeconomic stability, the BOK has maintained a tight monetary policy stance since December 1997. This was reflected in the big jump in market interest rates right after the agreement with the IMF, although they are now coming back down again. In the public sector a stringent government budget was drawn up with a 3.8% growth rate, which is lower than the growth of nominal GDP. The organization and staff of government agencies are to be slimmed and local government budgets rationalized.

On the exchange rate policy front Korea widened the daily band for exchange rate fluctuation to ±10% from ±2.25% of the market average rate on 20 November and shifted to a free-floating exchange rate system on 16 December. Now the foreign exchange rate can be decided solely by the interplay of market forces.

To enhance confidence in the overall financial system, top priority is being placed on the resolution of unsound financial institutions as promptly as possible. The first to be dealt with among 26 banks were Korea First Bank and Seoul Bank. Their capital was reduced in January 1998, with primary responsibility for their mismanagement being borne by their shareholders. They were then put on a sound footing through recapitalization by the government's subscription with public enterprise stocks. Government-held shares in these two banks would be sold by open bidding to domestic and foreign investors at the earliest possible date. The other 12 banks that failed to meet the Bank for International Settlements' (BIS) 8% capital adequacy ratios at the end of 1997 had submitted rehabilitation plans to the supervisory authority. Reviewing these plans, the government shut down five banks.

As for merchant banking corporations, 14 of them have been already shut down with the business of another two being currently suspended. The remaining 14 merchant banks are supposed to clear off their bad loans through an increase in equity capital. They also will be closed if they fail to do so. The licences of two securities companies and one investment trust company have been revoked, and investigations are now underway to gauge accurately the management status of non-banks such as leasing and life insurance companies.

The Non-performing Asset Resolution Fund, set up in November 1997 to clear bad loans from the books of financial institutions, has already bought at a discount bad loans with a book-value of 16 trillion won. The resources for this were raised by the issue of bonds. The size of the dund will be expanded to 31.5 trillion won to increase its purchases of bad loans.

Furthermore, financial supervision has been strengthened by improving the supervisory system and raising standards for prudential regulation. In April 1998, the Financial Supervisory Commission (FSC) was established in a move to integrate the supervision of the banking, securities and insurance industries. To enhance transparency in the financial sector, statistics on non-performing loans of banks, including substandard loans, are now released every six months. Prudential standards are made stricter by forcing financial institutions to set aside provisions of 100% of loan losses and securities valuation losses.

Meanwhile, to resolve the moral hazard problem as it applies to depositors, the coverage of deposit protection is scheduled to be narrowed. From August 1998, however, only the principal will be guaranteed in the case of deposits of 20 million won or more per person. For deposits of less than 20 million won, payment of the principal and interest at the average rate for time deposits with commercial banks will be guaranteed.

Since the very high leverage of Korean companies and the lack of transparency of their financial statements played a crucial role in causing the crisis, urgent priority in corporate sector reform is being put on achieving a major reduction in corporate indebtedness and bringing accounting standards into line with best international practice.

It is well known that industrial giants in Korea have tended to borrow excessively through cross-payment guarantees among interlinked affiliates. To redress this tendency, all new cross-payment guarantees among companies belonging to the 30 largest conglomerates have been forbidden since April 1998. They would also be obliged to retire all outstanding cross-payment guarantees completely by March 2000. In addition, interest payments on borrowings exceeding a multiple of five times equity capital would no longer be classed as expenses deductible from taxation from the year 2000. Banks are to play a major role in the drive to reduce the high corporate leverage, through agreements between large firms and their main creditor banks on improving the financial structure. In this context, on 18 June 1998 creditor banks announced a list of 55 non-viable firms to be forced into liquidation by withholding new loans to them. The exit of non-viable firms would consistently be pursued in line with market principles.

Regulations related to foreign ownership of real estate are being greatly eased. This will give foreigners national treatment across the full range of economic activities in Korea.

To enhance transparency, the 30 largest conglomerates would have to provide combined financial statements from the fiscal year 1999. This should make it much simpler to obtain an accurate picture of a firm's position. To improve corporate governance, all listed companies are required to ensure that at least one-quarter of the membership of the board of directors is made up of outside directors starting in the fiscal year 1999. The rights of minority shareholders have also been greatly strengthened.

The dismissal of workers as part of rationalization is now allowed, which eases the rigidities of the labor market. Representatives of labor unions accepted a system allowing lay-offs as part of their contribution towards solving the economic crisis in a consensus achieved by a Tripartite Committee made up of labour, management and government. Legislation was subsequently enacted on the basis of the agreements reached. A Second Tripartite Committee has now been inaugurated. It is reviewing the status of the structural reforms in progress and discussing the matters of concern not dealt with by the first committee.

Since Korea applied to the IMF for bail-out credit on 21 November 1997, it has accelerated the speed of capital account liberalization, which had been only fitfully pursued up to then. The ceiling on foreign investment in Korean equities was raised from 26% to 55% in December 1997 and entirely abolished in May 1998, as mentioned earlier. The local bond markets, including those for government and corporate bonds, and the money markets for CP, CDs and RPs also have been completely opened to foreigners. Starting in March 1998 foreign financial institutions have been allowed to establish subsidiaries of banks and securities companies and to set up joint-venture banks.

To raise foreign investors' confidence in government policy, the system of compiling foreign exchange reserves has been changed to reflect the actual status of usable reserves. Figures for usable foreign reserves are released twice a month (for the 15th and the last day of each month) within five business days and those for external liabilities are announced every month.

The government also plans to abolish the Foreign Exchange Management Act and instead pass a new Foreign Exchange Act with the characteristics of a negative system, allowing all transactions except those specifically prohibited. In addition, the Foreign Investment Act is to be revised and retitled the Foreign Investment Promotion Act. The relevant legislative procedures for these are now in progress.

Recent Economic Trends

As may be gathered from what has been discussed so far, Korea has taken wide-ranging measures in order to consolidate the basis for stability, while reforming the overall economic structure and building up the foreign exchange reserves. Gratifyingly, several bright spots have recently emerged: an improvement in the foreign exchange market and the stabilization of interest rates. On the other hand, many dark clouds still remain: the credit crunch in the course of the financial institutions' restructuring, negative GDP growth and rising unemployment.

Up until October 1997 the Korean won had remained around 900 won to the U.S. dollar, but it continued to fall rapidly thereafter. It came as a great shock to policymakers and the public that after the agreement with the IMF for the provision of emergency loans, the speed of depreciation actually accelerated. In the last few days of December 1997 the exchange rate was quoted at 1,960 won, a fall of 50% in two short months. Since the beginning of 1998, though, it has shown a comparatively stable range of movements at around the 1,400 won per dollar level, and the daily range of its fluctuations has narrowed considerably. Since the middle of March 1998 the exchange rate has been moving in a range of some 1,300 to 1,400 won per U.S. dollar. This new-found exchange rate stability is attributable to the following factors: the great improvement in market conditions assisted by the inflow of funds from international financial organizations such as the IMF; the turn of the current account balance to a substantial surplus; the successful conclusion of the restructuring of US$21.8 billion of the banks' short-term debt; and the issue of US$4 billion worth of global sovereign bonds which were well received by the international capital market. As a result, usable foreign exchange reserves, which had plunged to just US$8.9 billion at the end of 1997, returned to their pre-crisis level of US$34.4 billion by the end of May 1998 and rose to US$45 billion at the end of October 1998, which was above the year-end target level of US$41 billion agreed as a condition of the IMF's stand-by agreements.

Market interest rates rose sharply from 13–14% before the crisis to peak at 40% in December 1997, driven by the sharply increased risk of corporate lending and the BOK's increase in its market intervention rate as agreed with the IMF. Since then, though, market interest rates have been easing and they had been hovering around the 17% mark in May 1998 and finally declined to the 10% level at the end of October 1998, lower than prior to the outbreak of the currency crisis.

However, the credit crunch which had deepened in the first half of 1998 has not eased yet. Financial institutions have become reluctant to provide enterprises with funds for fear of incurring fresh non-performing loans. They seem unwilling to assume the heightened credit risk of enterprises in the course of structural adjustment. Their need to maintain acceptable BIS capital adequacy ratios is also a factor. (Deposit money in banks increased by only 11.3 trillion won for the year to May 1998, compared to the increase of 15.4 trillion won during the same five-month period a year earlier.) To make matters worse, the merchant banking corporations, which used to provide corporations with short-term funds, have virtually suspended new lendings to corporations and tended to refuse rolling over loans falling due. In the capital market only a few large blue-chip enterprises are able to issue corporate bonds. As firms' financial difficulties deepened, the percentage of bills dishonoured rose considerably and the number of corporate insolvencies has stayed at a high rate.

The recession is deepening in the real sector due to the reluctance of both consumers to spend and companies to invest. During the first quarter of 1998 the growth rate of GDP registered a negative figure (–3.9%) for the first time in the past 18 years. The second quarter's growth rate slid further to –6.6%. Indicators related to production, consumption and investment all decreased still further. Among them, the manufacturing operation ratio index dropped sharply from 104 in October 1997 to 75.3 in August 1998. The unemployment rate peaked at 7.6% in July 1998 and declined a little to 7.3% in September 1998, which was more than three times the level just before the crisis, which was 2.2%, and the number of the unemployed increased to 1.6 million.

Meanwhile, the current account recorded a surplus of over US$31.5 billion for the first nine months of 1998, which was quite a contrast to a deficit of US$12.1 billion for the same period of 1997. But, this was brought about mainly by the sharp contraction of import bills rather than an increase in exports. There is concern that unless exporters' competitiveness is strengthened, the surplus may not be sustainable.

Consumer prices, although their pace of increase is no longer accelerating, have posted rises of more than 7% year-on-year as of October 1998. This aggravates the difficulties of the general public, already hard hit by unemployment and reduced income.

4. Public Policy Issues of the Financial Crisis

External Debt Management Problem

Korea has recently experienced a rapid increase in its total external debt and predominance of short-term loans. The rapid increase in the speed of accumulation of external debt, particularly that of short-term debt, has played a critical role in Korea's recent financial crisis. Korea, during its industrial development, relied heavily on foreign savings to finance its investment. In the early 1980s Korea was one of the largest debtor countries in the world. The overall debt to GNP ratio declined after 1987 as the Korean economy had recorded a substantial amount of current account surplus, but this ratio started to rise after 1991. In particular, the change in the ratio of debt over GNP increased by 2.5% in 1995 and 4.1% in 1996. These increases were relatively higher than other countries, even though Korea's debt to GNP ratio was still low compared to other developing countries such as Brazil and Argentina.

Table 8.6 shows Korea's gross external debt from 1988 to 1996. Total debt decreased in the late 1980s due to an economic boom, but started to increase at rates higher than 30% as Korea's trade deficit worsened rapidly from 1994. The share of Korea's short-term debt also increased rapidly from 1995, more than doubling from 26% in 1994 to 58% in 1995. The trend shows unmistakable characteristics of Korea's foreign debt: a rapid increase in both the absolute amount and the ratio of debt to output and a predominance of short-term debt, which is not quite healthy. At the same time the foreign exchange reserve situation did not show much preparedness for the structural changes in external debt.

Financial Liberalization with Inadequate Supervision

A natural question arises: what caused such an extraordinary increase in short-term capital inflows and rapid accumulation of external debt? This has a lot to do with financial liberalization.

TABLE 8.6 Korea's Gross External Debt, 1988–96

	1988	1989	1990	1991	1992	1993	1994	1995	1996
Gross debt (US$ billion)	31.2	29.4	31.7	39.1	42.8	43.9	56.9	79.0	104.5
Growth rate (%)	-12.4	-5.8	7.8	17.0	9.5	2.6	29.6	38.8	32.3
Debt/GNP (%)	17.3	13.3	12.6	13.4	14.0	13.3	15.0	17.5	21.6
Share of short-term debt (%)	27.4	29.9	30.9	28.2	27.0	25.9	25.5	57.8	62.2
Foreign exchange reserves (US$ billion)	12.4	15.2	14.8	13.7	17.2	20.3	25.7	32.7	33.2

From the 1960s through the 1980s capital account transactions had been tightly regulated in Korea. Many restrictions on capital movements in and out of the country were put in place to facilitate the government's industrial policy and to minimize the destabilizing effects of short-term capital flows on the economy. All of this began to change in the early 1990s. By this time the effectiveness and viability of Korea's interventionist regime had come into question due to the increasing complexity of the economy. Korea had also come under increasing pressure from developed countries, led by the United States, to liberalize its financial sector, so Korea found itself beset by necessity to pursue liberalization.

Financial deregulation and market opening began in earnest in 1993, immediately after the inauguration of the new administration, and it was accelerated by Korea's accession to the OECD as its 29th member. Although the market deregulation and opening in Korea had been carried out in a gradual and piecemeal manner, it led to a surge in foreign capital inflows during the 1994–97 period, much of which were short-term and speculative.

With the acceleration in financial liberalization, domestic financial institutions were allowed greater freedom in managing their assets and liabilities, in particular in borrowing from international financial markets. On the other hand, Korea was an attractive market for foreign investors. Not only had there been both rapid growth and domestic stability, but the rates of return to capital, adjusted for credit and market risks, had been relatively high. The national budget was generating surpluses. Moreover, its policymakers had maintained the stability of nominal exchange rates relative to the U.S. dollar in order to stabilize real exchange rates and domestic prices. Given these sound economic fundamentals and the region's commitment to liberalization, bond market dealers, fund managers and other institutional investors had seen enormous opportunities to make money. Korea had become an emerging market, where investors sought to be the first to move in and also the first to get out, if need be.

Since foreign capital had predominantly been used to finance investment rather than consumption, the capital inflow tended to induce higher levels of investment. Between 1994 and 1996 net foreign capital inflow amounted to US$52.3 billion, more than three times the total net inflows for the 1990–93 period. Much of the inflows, which consisted of short-term liabilities of domestic financial institutions and firms, were then channelled to finance investment in Korea's major export-oriented industries: electronics, automobiles, iron and steel, shipbuilding and petrochemicals. As a result investment jumped to 38.2% of GDP in 1996 from about 35% three years earlier and resulted in a large increase in the current account deficit, which reached almost 5% of GDP. An increase in the ratio of investment to GDP would push up the growth rate of GDP. The economic growth from 1994 to the beginning of 1997 was almost 8% on average per annum, which was spurred by this high investment. This high investment was also responsible for a sharp increase in the current account deficit and the financial and foreign exchange crisis in which Korea finds itself today.

Next, what caused such a large increase in short-term capital inflows? One factor was economic and another was policy-induced. One reason was the rapid growth in trade volume which required an equal increase in imports and export-related credits. Furthermore, the high interest rate differentials between the domestic and foreign financial markets with expectation of stable foreign exchange rates and the deregulation of trade credits led to a more rapid increase in short-term trade-related credits than the expansion in trade itself. There was another reason for the surge in short-term bank borrowing. Beginning in 1994, the ceiling on foreign currency loans by commercial banks was lifted, but the ceiling on commercial banks' medium- and long-term borrowings from international financial markets was not eased. As a result, commercial banks were forced to raise short-term credits to finance long-term loans at home.

Why did the policymakers let banks and other financial institutions borrow so much from the short-term money markets? Why did they not open the domestic bond market and liberalize long-term external financing? Perhaps they ignored the management of short-term liabilities, because these liabilities do not add to the stock of foreign debts as they mature and are paid off within a year, whereas long-term liabilities do. The Korean authorities have not regulated short-term external credit transactions of banks and financial institutions because these transactions are tied to the international financial services they provide. They may have overlooked the possibilities that short-term loans could not be rolled over continuously and that short-term credit facilities could be abused as means of financing long-term investment.

In retrospect, Korean financial institutions were not adequately prepared for the financial market opening because they had not developed expertise in credit analysis, risk management and due diligence. They had little experience in foreign exchange and securities trading and international banking in general. The supervisory authorities were not monitoring and regulating their international financial activities as much as they should have because they were pressured to overhaul the regulatory system to make it more compatible with the liberalized system. They eliminated and relaxed many restrictions and control measures, but failed to install in their place a new system of prudential regulations needed to safeguard the stability and soundness of the financial institutions.

Although the deterioration in the quality of assets and prevalence of short-term external financing were clearly visible, the supervisory authorities did not order the financial institutions to take corrective measures. They did not do so because, nurtured in the old tradition of direct control and bank examination, they had neither the resources nor experience in monitoring and exercising their regulatory power to maintain the overall soundness and profitability of the financial institutions.

Long relegated to the role of supporting manufacturing industries under the control of government, banks and other financial institutions had become accustomed to accommodating much of the credit needs of the industrial conglomerates without necessarily checking their creditworthiness. In fact, many commercial banks were competing among themselves to win over these *chaebol* as they were regarded as prime customers with little credit risk.

Moral Hazard Caused by Failure to Observe Market Principles

One may raise the question of why Korea's industrial groups were so inflexible and slow in adjusting their investment and output in response to the changes in the internal and external environment. This can be explained by moral hazard problems that were prevalent among almost all the economic actors, including enterprises, financial institutions, workers and depositors.

Large-scale enterprises, especially those belonging to large conglomerates, had enjoyed a high level of government protection in return for playing the role of locomotive for economic growth. Their domestic markets were often protected by import restrictions, and they were supported by low-cost funding from the financial sector. They were

given strong incentives to keep expanding without a careful consideration of the related returns and risks. The principle of too-big-to-fail,
typified by the popular expression "conglomerates will never go broke"
had been considered an unwritten law. In consequence, the debt-equity
ratios of Korean enterprises, especially those of large-scale enterprises,
rose alarmingly. At the end of 1997 the 30 largest Korean conglomerates had an average debt-to-equity ratio of 519 per cent, a sharp contrast
with 154% in the United States, 193% in Japan and 86% in Taiwan.
Weighed down by such abnormal levels of debt, large enterprises
collapsed one after another as the economic downturn became pro-
tracted and a shift of government policy let them go under.

Financial institutions also did not properly comply with market principles, having depended on government control and protection over a
long period. The business style of Korean banks was usually to make
loans to large enterprises and to those who were able to offer collateral
such as real estate, without thoroughly screening their investment plans.
As a result, financial institutions contributed to the crisis by failing to
prevent firms from wasting resources through inefficient and duplicate
investments.

The neglect of market principles was especially serious in the case
of merchant banking corporations which deal with businesses broadly
similar to those of commercial banks. The number of merchant banking corporations increased sharply from only six up until 1993 to 30
by 1996 as all the investment finance companies were allowed to convert
to merchant banks in the course of financial deregulation. With the
belief that the government would not allow financial institutions to
fail, they began to do business boldly in the area of international finance where they had very little experience. Tempted by the lure of
large profits, they borrowed short-term and lent or invested in long-
term deals, mainly to Southeast Asian and other regions' emerging
markets. This led to a serious mismatch in maturities between borrowings and lendings. Under these conditions, they faced a liquidity crisis
almost immediately once they ran into difficulties in borrowing.

In addition, it should be pointed out that workers and depositors paid
no regard to market principles. Unemployment was unfamiliar in Korea
where the notion of lifetime employment was deeply embedded to the
extent that workers had little inclination to boost productivity or promote competitiveness. Depositors purchased high-yielding products
from unsound financial institutions as they believed that all their

deposits were guaranteed implicitly by the government. This worked to undermine the soundness of financial institutions as a whole.

One may also have to point out that this moral hazard appears to have affected the behavior of foreign financial institutions lending to Korean banks and other financial institutions. Since they should and expected to receive national treatment, they also believed that, like domestic depositors, the payment of principal and interest on their loans was guaranteed by the government, although there was no formal arrangement of guarantee to that effect. They also knew that as a group they could put pressure on the Korean government to come forward with the promise of guarantee by threatening a financial and currency crisis through their withdrawal of loans from Korea. Indeed, when some signs of the financial crisis began to appear, this is precisely what they did, and very successfully at that.

Loss of Market Confidence Caused by Lack of Transparency

One view of the current financial crisis is that unless financial market opening is properly managed in emerging market economies with adequate supervision, it could easily lead to a boom and bust cycle during the transition period. At the same time it is equally true that there exist some domestic factors that caused foreign investors to pull out en masse. One of them would be the loss of confidence in the country in the eyes of international investors, a loss primarily due to inadequate transparency.

First, there was a lack of accounting transparency. The figures which international investors consider most important as basic data when lending to domestic financial institutions or investing in stocks were not reliable, making it difficult to grasp the actual status of firms. In particular, the large conglomerates were composed of many seemingly independent companies which were interlinked through a web of affiliations and cross-payment guarantees. Their profits were often overstated by internal transactions among them.

In the case of financial institutions the scale of bad loans was underestimated. Figures for banks' non-performing loans were announced by supervisory authorities, but they were underestimated by excluding substandard loans, that is, credits covered by collateral on which interest payments were at least six months in arrears. Thus, the banks' apparent soundness was based on unreliable figures. Furthermore, the standards for setting aside loan loss provisions were less exacting than the international norm and this resulted in overstatement of banks' profits. No strict examination was carried out on the scale of non-performing loans of the non-bank financial institutions, whose business conditions were no better and often worse than the banks.

On top of all these, policymakers refused to admit the difficulties the Korean economy was facing. Though warnings of the likelihood of a crisis had been circulating among foreigners, Korea denied the possibility, repeatedly citing its strong 6 to 7% GDP growth rate and high savings ratio. In several instances, the authorities concerned insisted on the relevance of the statistics, or were reluctant to disclose them when doubt was cast on the credibility of official figures for foreign exchange reserves and the country's external liabilities. Quite contrary to their intention of avoiding unsettling the markets, they made international investors unduly pessimistic about the prospects for the Korean economy.

The lack of transparency, one of the weakest points of the Korean economy, was nothing new, and had become a tradition during the 30-odd years of rapid growth. Because of the fact that the financial market had been only recently opened up, in the 1990s international investors did not fully recognize the seriousness of the problems. Furthermore, these problems had been downplayed or brushed under the carpet while the economy maintained strong growth during the earlier part of the 1990s. As the lack of transparency became obvious in 1997 with the deepening of the recession, foreign investors showed widespread apprehensions about the safety of their investments. This was one of the biggest factors that led to the loss of confidence in the Korean economy.

It is true that a loss of confidence due to inadequate transparency contributed to the financial crisis. However, as Stiglitz pointed out, it is also true that financial and currency crises have occurred in Scandinavian countries which had highly transparent economic systems.

Inappropriate Policy Responses to the Evolving Problems

Amid the deepening economic difficulties in 1997, the government drafted and implemented various policies designed to overcome them. But these policies were frequently ineffective due to inappropriate timing, and sometimes the markets were given confusing signals because of inconsistencies among them.

A prime example is the foreign exchange policy. The daily fluctuation band of the exchange rate was kept narrow after the market average foreign exchange rate system was adopted in 1990.[3] However, with the widening current account deficit from 1995, pressure for depreciation of the Korean won had accumulated and expectations of additional depreciation were widespread, especially during the summer and autumn of 1997. Therefore, there was no justification for adhering to a narrow daily fluctuation band any longer. But it was kept in place and, as a result, the foreign exchange market was nearly paralyzed in the latter half of November 1997. In hindsight, if the band had been widened earlier, the sudden massive fall in the exchange value of the Korean won towards the end of 1997 could have been avoided through a gradual depreciation.

Another example is the way in which distressed enterprises dealt with. It had been repeatedly declared that troubled enterprises would be dealt with on the basis of the market mechanism. However, not infrequently, the procedures took the form of court mediation or the application of the Bankruptcy Prevention Accord[4], which were not necessarily consistent with market principles. To be more specific, the failure to deal with the problems of Kia, the eighth largest conglomerate, properly at an early stage heightened the confusion and distrust.

Sometimes the policies aimed at enhancing international creditworthiness perversely served to lower the country's credit standing. As mentioned earlier, it was emphasized at every opportunity that the fundamentals of the Korean economy were sound. This attitude acted to magnify distrust on the part of those international investors who had a clear insight into the weaknesses of the Korean economy. The decisions to convert Kia into a public enterprise and to guarantee the payment of foreign currency liabilities by Korean financial institutions were also made in the mistaken belief that public intervention could heighten international credit-worthiness. In fact, these actions disappointed international investors who wanted market-based solutions to be led by the private sector.

Transitional Problem: Lack of Co-ordination Mechanism

We raised the question of why Korean *chaebol* were so inflexible and slow in adjusting their investment and output in response to the changes in the internal and external environment and kept on expanding their investment. One explanation was that they tended to compete for market share more than for profit and that the rigid and bureaucratic management system, where the decision making was concentrated at the top, made it difficult for the *chaebol* to adjust their investment and production to changes in market conditions as rapidly as they should. Another explanation was that there did not exist a well functioning co-ordination mechanism for an efficient allocation of investment that could prevent over-investment. The transition to an unfettered free market system is still not complete, and at present there is no mechanism, either through the market or government industrial policy, which could screen out bad investment projects.

The government's "visible-hand" industrial policy was widely recognized as no longer capable of generating economic and financial stability since the 1980s. The new government that came to power early in 1993 mounted a campaign of market deregulation and opening as it was determined to rely more on the market for the management of the economy. The World Trade Organization (WTO) agreement did not leave much room for industrial policy, and market liberalization took away what was left of the government's control of the production and investment activities of the large conglomerates and enterprises. The deregulation efforts succeeded in freeing the *chaebol* from the government, but without instituting either an internal or external mechanism to monitor and control their management which could assume the government's former role.

VII. SUMMARY AND CONCLUSION

Looking back on the Korean development experience over the last three decades, it seems clear that the Korean economy has faced endless challenges and that it has somehow properly responded and successfully adapted to them. In the 1960s Korea enjoyed the dynamic gains from expanded trade by following an outward-oriented development strategy. In the 1970s, however, the Korean economy experienced economic deterioration mainly due to excessive government intervention and the over-ambitious heavy and chemical industrialization drive. The 1980s was a period of structural adjustment aimed at the promotion of continued economic growth with price stability. As the development experience of the Korean economy shows, adaptation inevitably involves much uncertainty and risks. The Korean experience seems unique in overcoming these risks and successfully adapting to the changes in the economic environment during the last three decades.

Korea's economic development process during this period has been generally described as following a government-led export promotion strategy. It can be said that the Korean government has played an active role in resource mobilization even though the degree has, of course, fluctuated during the development period, depending on the situation faced by the country. The government has been actively involved in almost every important aspect of economic decision-making and the private sector has followed the signals given by the government. The government-led order has always taken precedence over the spontaneous market order.

In the context of maximum utilization of economic resources, the economic development process usually entails two interrelated aspects of resource utilization. One is how to mobilize economic resources, and the other is how to allocate economic resources. On economic resource allocation, there has been a lively discussion on the optimal degree of government intervention, and the consensus seems to be that the market order is superior to government intervention in guiding resource allocation in general, except in the special cases of the so-called "market failures". However, practically speaking, it is very difficult to resolve the issue as to what extent and how the government intervention should be exercised to optimally promote resource allocation for economic development, which of course has long been a subject for debate.

On the allocation of resources, the Korean government intervened directly in the microeconomic resource allocation through discriminatory policies, such as favouring certain sectors and certain groups of economic agents. The government controlled the financial resource allocation with regulations on interest rates and lending activities of financial institutions. In the earlier stage of development — until the 1970s — the large business groups and the heavy and chemical industries sector were favoured. The government has been substituting for the role of market competition as a discovery procedure in making the important allocation decisions such as what business lines the large business groups can engage in and what kind of businesses the financial institutions can lend money to. This pattern of direct intervention into the private decision area has been ameliorated through the liberalization process in recent years.

On the other hand, little attention has been paid to the possible side effects of emphasizing the active role of government in resource mobilization. It has been the case that the mobilization drive tends to create a detrimental environment for macroeconomic management. In general, once priority is given to domestic resource mobilization, even macroeconomic policies such as monetary, fiscal and exchange rate policies tend to be "mobilized" as instruments to support economic development, thereby eroding the macroeconomic stabilization role. Low interest rates, base money creation and tax-and-expenditure instruments all tend to be utilized to support policy loans for important industries. Exchange rate management also tends to be constrained by the concern for export promotion. How to mobilize available macroeconomic policy instruments to support economic development becomes the dominant concern rather than how to improve macroeconomic stability. This can explain why Korea had the highest inflation rate among Asian NICs over the last three decades and direct controls on important individual prices and even on economic activities within the private realm became widely utilized as the main instruments for maintaining macroeconomic stability.

The experience of Korea points out that for government intervention to have a positive effect on economic development it is necessary that the government follow developmental objectives and that there is a bureaucracy capable of formulating and implementing policies aimed at these objectives. Korea's economic policy environment has undergone a drastic change in recent years, forcing the reform of the existing economic management system. As a result of the world-wide trend of financial market globalization and the inexorable increase in the complexity and market orientation of the Korean economy, there are limits to the role of government in managing the financial system. Ensuring the operation of the fundamental principle of capitalism — the survival of the fittest — must begin in the financial sector. Economic problems are caused by the inefficiency that results from the misallocation of resources. In a capitalist economy the flow of resources is followed by the flow of funds. As such, that misallocation of resources can be prevented only by normalizing the financial system so that funds may flow freely. The fact that failure to resolve the nation's backlog of non-performing bank loans led to eventual IMF bail-out illustrates that the government does not have much informational superiority in the globalized financial market.

The government's "visible-hand" industrial policy was widely recognized as no longer capable of generating economic and financial stability since the 1980s. The Korean government mounted a campaign of market deregulation and opening as it was determined to rely more on the market for the management of the economy. The WTO agreement did not leave much room for industrial policy, and market liberalization took away what was left of the government's control of the production and investment activities of the large conglomerates and enterprises. However, the deregulation efforts succeeded in freeing the *chaebol* from the government, but without instituting either an internal or external mechanism to monitor and control their management which could assume the government's former role.

NOTES

1. Sum of substandard, doubtful and bad loans.
2. The roll-over ratio of the seven largest commercial banks fell to 58.8% in November 1997 from 86.5% in October.
3. Though the daily fluctuation band had been widened gradually with the progress of financial liberalization, it remained at only ±2.25% just before the crisis.
4. This accord was introduced in April 1997 to prevent chain insolvencies. If an ailing firm's application for protection under the accord was approved, banks would defer the dishonouring of its bills.

REFERENCES

Amsden, Alice. *Asia's Next Giant*. New York: Oxford University Press, 1989.
_____. WIDER Stabilization and Adjustment Programmes. Country Study, no. 14, Republic of Korea. World Institute for Development Economics Research, 1987.
Bank of Korea. Financial Crisis in Korea — Why It Happened and How It Can be Overcome. Seoul, July 1998.
Cargill, Thomas F. "The Political Economy of Financial Liberalization in Korea". Economic Papers 1, no. 2 (September 1998).
Chang, Ha-Joon. "A Crisis From Underregulation". *Los Angeles Times*, 31 December 1997.
_____. "Reform for the Long Term in South Korea". *International Herald Tribune*, 13 February 1998.

Collins, Susan M. and Barry P. Bosworth. "Economic Growth in East Asia: Accumulation versus Assimilation". *Brookings Papers on Economic Activity* 2 (1996): 135–203.

Economist, "Economic Growth: The Poor and the Rich", 25 May 1996.

Edward J. Lincoln. "Some Missing Elements". *Brookings Papers on Economic Activity* 2 (1996): 351–55.

Electronic Industries Association of Korea. *Statistics of Electronic Industries*, various issues. Seoul, various years.

_____. *Junjasanup-40-nyunsa 1959-1999* [40-year history of electronics industry]. Seoul, 1999

Fischer, Stanley. "Lessons from East Asia and the Pacific Rim". *Brookings Papers on Economic Activity* 2 (1996): 345–50.

Hwang, Sang-In. "Economic Impact of Foreign Debt in Korea". KIEP Working Paper, no. 97–07. Seoul: Korea Institute for International Economic Policy, 1997.

Ito, Takatoshi. "Japan and the Asian Economies: A 'Miracle' in Transition". *Brookings Papers on Economic Activity* 2 (1996): 205–72.

Jwa, Sung-Hee. "The Role of Government in Economic Management — Korea's Experiences and Lessons". Unpublished manuscript. Korea Economic Research Institute, 1997.

Kim, Kihwan. *The Korean Economy: Past Performance, Current Reforms, and Future Prospect*. Seoul: Korea Development Institute, 1984.

Kim, Kwang Suk and Sung Duk Hong. *Accounting for Rapid Economic Growth in Korea, 1963-1995*. Seoul: Korea Development Institute, 1997.

Kim, Linsu. *Imitation to Innovation: The Dynamics of Korea's Technological Learning*. Boston: Harvard Business School Press, 1997.

Kim, Wan-Soon. "The Korean Economy in Distress: Major Issues and Challenges in the 1990s". In *East Asian Economies: Transformation and Challenges*, edited by T. Kawagoe *et al.* Singapore: Institute of Southeast Asian Studies, 1995.

_____. "Comments on Public Policies in the Taiwan Economy — The Nurturing of a Market Economy by Chi Schive and Hsien-Feng Lee". Presented at the workshop on Public Policies in East Asian Economies, 1997, in Kitakyushu.

Korea Development Bank. *Industry in Korea*, various issues. Seoul, various years.

Krugman, Paul. "The Myth of Asia's Miracle". *Foreign Affairs* 73, no. 6 (1994): 62–78.

Kwon, Yul. "Korea's Economic Prosperity — Implications for Australia". Inaugural Professorial Lecture, Griffith University, 1997.

Lee, Chung H. "The State and the Market in the Economic Development of Korea and Taiwan: Lessons for Economic Development and Transition". Paper presented at an International Symposium Celebrating the 50th Anniversary of the Department of Economics and the 20th Anniversary of the Economic Research Institute and the Journal of Economic Development, 1995, at Chung-Ang University, Seoul.

Lee, Hyung-Koo. *The Korean Economy: Perspectives for the Twenty-first Century*. Albany: State University of New York Press, 1996.

Lee, Keun and Chaisung Lim. "Technological Regimes, Catch-up and Leapfrogging: Findings from the Korean Industries". Paper presented to the symposium on Development Model of East Asia and Economic Crisis, 1998, held at Seoul National University.

Noland, Marcus. "Restructuring Korea's Financial Sector for Greater Competitiveness". Institute for International Economics. APEC Working Paper, no. 96–14, 1996.

North, Douglas C. *Institutions, Institutional Change and Economic Performance*. New York: Cambridge University Press, 1990.

_____. "Institutions". *Journal of Economic Perspectives*, Winter 1991, pp. 97–113.

Olson, Mancur. "Big Bills Left on the Sidewalk: Why Some Nations are Rich, and Others Poor". *Journal of Economic Perspectives*, Spring 1996, pp. 3-24.

Park, Yung-Chul. "Financial Crisis and Macroeconomic Adjustments in Korea, 1997-98". In *Financial Liberalization and Opening in East Asia: Issues and Policy Challenges*, edited by Yung-Chul Park. Seoul: Korea Institute of Finance, 1998.

Park, Yung-Chul and Jong-Wha Lee. "Exports, Accumulation, and Growth in East Asia". In *Financial Liberalization and Opening in East Asia: Issues and Policy Challenges*, edited by Yung Chul Park. Seoul: Korea Institute of Finance, 1998.

Pyo, Hak Kil. "The East Asian Miracle or Myth: A Reconciliation between the Conventional View and the Contrarian Proposition". *Economic Bulletin*, March 1996, pp. 2–23.

Schive, Chi and Hsien-Feng Lee. "Public Policies in the Taiwan Economy — The Nurturing of a Market Economy". Paper presented at the workshop on Public Policies in East Asian Economies, 1997, in Kitakyushu.

Soh, Changrok. *From Investment to Innovation: The Korean Political Economy and Changes in Industrial Competitiveness*. Seoul: Global Research Institute, Korea University, 1997.

Sohn, Chan-Hyun *et al.* "Korea's Trade and Industrial Policies: 1948-1998". KIEP Working Paper, no. 98–05. Korea Institute for International Economic Policy, 1998.

Song, Byung-Nak. *The Rise of the Korean Economy*. 2nd ed. New York: Oxford University Press, 1997.

World Bank. *The East Asian Miracle: Economic Growth and Public Policy*. New York: Oxford University Press, 1993.

9

The Development Experience of South Korea: Government Policies and Development of Industries — The Case of Electronics Industry

Hojin Kang

I. INTRODUCTION

South Korea's (hereafter "Korea") electronics industry surged so rapidly in one generation that Korea became the fourth largest producer in the world in 1996, after the United States, Japan and Germany and the second largest producer of consumer electronic products and dynamic-random-access memory (DRAM) chips after Japan. The electronics industry has been one of the most important industries in the Korean economy. It accounted for 21% of total manufacturing value added in 1996. It is the leading exporter of Korea, with US$41 billion, accounting for one-third of total exports in 1996.

The electronics industry also epitomizes the pattern of industrial development of Korea: active role of government, growth driven largely by local firms rather than by multinational subsidiaries or joint ventures, helped by a favorable external trade environment, based on well-educated, hard-working domestic human resources. The government played a pivotal role in the development of the electronics industry. It created markets for domestic producers during the early years, and then designated electronics a strategic export industry, offering preferential financial and tax incentives. Unlike that of other developing countries, the growth of the Korean electronics industry has been largely driven by Korean *chaebol* and other local firms rather than by multinational subsidiaries or joint ventures. Korean *chaebol* were willing to make heavy investment in production facilities. Reverse engineering and adaptation efforts of local firms were very important as Korea depended more upon capital goods import than foreign direct investment (FDI) for technology import. The electronics industry has also been heavily dependent upon foreign trade. It has been heavily export oriented. Foreign shipments have accounted for more than 50% of the output of the consumer electronics and semiconductor industry. It has also heavily relied upon imported capital equipment and technology.

In the following section we give a brief historical account of the development of the electronics industry in Korea. The development of the electronics industry in Korea can be divided into two phases, which roughly correspond to the two phases of the economic drive. During the first phase the consumer electronics industry was the dominant sector and driving force of the electronics industry and the government's active interventionistic industrial policy was shaping the industrial development. During the second phase the *chaebol*'s aggressive investment in the electronics industry, particularly in semiconductors, drove the growth of the industry. In section III we discuss the development of the consumer electronics sector, with a focus on the role of the government and technological capability development. The government was very active to make it a strategic export industry and formulated a series of promotional programs for the industry.

In section IV we discuss the development of the semiconductor sector. The experience of the semiconductor sector illustrates the aggressive commitment of the Korean *chaebol*. Although the government formulated promotional programs for this industry, the success in the semiconductor industry had been attributable to business initiative rather than state initiative. The role of the government was different in this case. A discussion of the industrial sector development with the government's role follows in section V.

II. HISTORICAL OVERVIEW OF ELECTRONICS INDUSTRY

Korea's first consumer electronics product was produced in 1958. In a small-scale garage operation, foreign components and parts were assembled into the first vacuum tube AM radio in the country through imitative reverse-engineering of a Japanese model. The producer, later called LG Electronics, soon developed expertise in imitation and began producing other home appliances such as electric fans and refrigerators without foreign assistance.

During the early years the electronics industry developed as an import-substitution industry. The government's import-substitution policy and tight control of foreign investment and contraband goods in the black market created attractive business opportunities for local entrepreneurs to enter the protected market in the early 1960s.

Then, the Korean electronics industry really got its start in the mid-1960s with the production of black and white television sets and audio equipment through the international transfer of production technology. In 1965 LG entered into a licensing agreement with Hitachi of Japan to import packaged technology for black and white television-set production. Assembly of other consumer electronics, such as cassette recorders and simple audio systems, was added to the line of business. Three other television set producers started at about the same time with a similar agreement, and new entrants increased the number of producers.

In the mid-1960s Korea's semiconductor industry also started with multinational firms that attempted to relocate the operation of assembling integrated circuits (ICs) to take advantage of cheap labor in the East Asian region. Wholly owned foreign subsidiaries of multinationals imported all the parts and components from the parent companies and assembled them utilizing cheap labor in Korea, then re-exported the output abroad. This simple assembly operation of ICs was a major export activity of Korea's electronics industry in the late 1960s.

The growth of the electronics industry entered a new stage when the government designated electronics a strategic export industry in late 1969. The government promulgated the Electronics Industry Promotion Act in 1969 and released an ambitious Long-term Electronics Industry Promotion Plan, offering comprehensive incentive measures, including preferential financing, tax concessions and foreign loan guarantees. The plan included the government's determination to promote the electronics industry as a leading exporter. In 1969, when the industry was still exporting a mere US$42 million, the government set the goal at US$400 million for 1976, the last year of the plan. It turned out that exports exceeded US$1 billion in 1976, almost 259% of the established target, illustrating the successful transformation of the electronics industry from an import-substitution industry into a major export industry.

In the 1970s many local and foreign firms entered the industry. The government's strong will to promote the electronics industry as a major exporter and growing domestic demand due to the rapid economic growth encouraged new firms to enter the industry. As many local and foreign companies entered the industry, electronics production and exports grew very rapidly in the 1970s. As income levels continued to rise due to the rapid growth, the domestic market for consumer electronic products, such as black and white television sets, refrigerators and washing machines, expanded very rapidly.

Helped by the ambitious export drive of the government, exports increased very rapidly, too. In the 1970s exports of the electronics industry were mainly labor-intensive products and more than half of them were shipped to the United States. Major export items were ICs, radios, black and white television sets, condensers and cathode ray tubes (CRTs) in 1970. In 1979 radio cassettes and colour television sets were added to this list, reflecting the changes in consumption pattern and the advances in the technological capability of Korean producers.

After a brief setback in 1980 due to the second oil crisis and domestic political instability after the assassination of President Park, the electronics industry rebounded with the beginning of colour broadcasting of domestic channels. The government allowed domestic channels to start colour broadcasting in 1980 and it provided the industry with a stable base of domestic demand. In the 1980s, colour television sets and new products became the new engine of growth.

The government also implemented various forms of promotional measures such as the establishment of the electronics promotion fund and long-term development plan of the industry. The exemption of special consumption tax on some electronics products boosted domestic consumption of electronics products and helped the electronics industry to grow rapidly.

Another notable development in the 1980s was that the semiconductor industry became a new strategic sector. Korean firms led by Samsung made the strategic choice to invest in the manufacture of memory chips, which was dominated by Japanese firms. In the mid-1980s Samsung, Hyundai and LG embarked on very large-scale integrated circuits (VLSIC) production based on design process technology acquired from small, financially troubled U.S. semiconductor makers.

Favourable external conditions created by the appreciation of the Japanese yen and a temporary disruption of the worldwide supply of 256K

DRAM in 1988 provided the Korean electronics industry with an excellent opportunity, and the industry had booming years in the mid-1980s.

However, the consumer electronics industry began to lose its competitiveness in the world market in the 1990s. There had been sharp rise in domestic labor cost stemming from developing labor shortages. The appreciation of the Korean won due to a substantial current account surplus in the late 1980s also eroded the price competitiveness of Korean products. Lack of product innovation capability among Korean firms worsened the situation further. Consequently, the industrial electronics sector led the growth of the industry in the 1990s. The consumer electronics sector had experienced relative stagnation due to the high cost of domestic firms and structural changes in international competition such as Japanese overseas investment and the rise of the electronics industry in Southeast Asian countries and China.

One of the most significant developments in the 1990s was the rise of the industrial electronics sector. Until the early 1990s the leading sectors in Korea's electronics industry were consumer electronics and electronic components, which includes semiconductors. The industrial electronics sector had lagged behind other electronics sectors in both output and exports. In the 1990s, however, the industrial electronics sector showed high growth. Consequently, the industrial electronics sector surpassed the consumer electronics sector in both production and exports in 1996. A number of developments provided a favourable environment for the high growth in the industrial electronics sector. Commercial development of new mobile communication services stimulated domestic demand for communication equipment. There took place active investments in computerization by the governmental, financial and educational sectors in accordance with the government's second National Basic Information System project. Together with these, the expansion of new media markets brought about rapid developments of information technology (IT)-related products.

Table 9.1 shows the growth profile of the electronics industry in Korea between 1970 and 1996. In 1970 the number of firms producing electronic products was only 505. Total employment in the electronics industry was 39,538 persons, accounting for 2.1% of the total manufacturing jobs. The industry expanded very rapidly between 1970 and 1990. Total employment grew at an average of 19% per annum during the 1970s and at 8% during the 1980s (Table 9.2). It accounted for 16.5% of total manufacturing employment in 1996.

TABLE 9.1   Korea: Growth of Electronics Industry, 1970–96

	1970	1980	1990	1993	1996
No. of firms	505	1,601	6,921	8,844	9,913
Total output (billion won)	55	2,770	27,072	41,600	73,829
Value added (billion won)	22	975	11,172	17,399	36,342
No. of workers (1,000)	40	221	473	448	479
Total wages (billion won)	7	357	3,013	4,269	6,874
Total fixed asset (billion won)	4	201	9,273	16,410	26,619
Exports (US$ million)	44	1,910	17,816	24,233	41,223
Imports (US$ million)	38	1,640	10,935	14,225	27,850

SOURCE: Report on Mining and Manufacturers, Office of Customs Administration, Korea.

TABLE 9.2   Korea: Growth Rate per Annum of Electronics Industry (in percentages)

	1970-80	1980-90	1990-96
No. of firms	12.2	15.8	6.2
Total output	47.9	25.6	18.2
Value added	46.1	27.6	21.7
No. of workers	18.8	7.9	0.2
Total wages	49.1	23.8	14.7
Total fixed asset	48.6	46.7	19.2
Exports	45.8	25.0	15.0
Imports	45.7	20.9	16.9

SOURCE: Report on Mining and Manufacturers, Office of Customs Administration, Korea.

Value added of the industry grew rapidly between 1970 and 1980 when the consumer electronics sector went through its booming decade. From 1980 to 1990 value added of the electronics industry kept on growing at the same speed. In terms of nominal value, the growth rate seemed to have dropped from 46% during the 1970s to 28% in the 1980s. However, there took place significant changes in the nature of economic growth in Korea between the 1970s and after. In the 1980s the Korean economy became more successful in taming inflation. For example, the rate of inflation measured by the GNP deflator was 7.1%

TABLE 9.3   Korea: Share of Electronics Industry in Total Manufacturing (in percentages)

	1970	1980	1990	1996
No. of firms	2.1	5.2	10.0	10.2
Total output	4.1	7.6	15.3	18.4
Value added	4.0	8.2	15.8	20.9
No. of workers	4.6	11.0	15.7	16.5
Total wages	4.8	10.3	15.4	16.2
Total fixed asset	3.6	6.8	12.2	14.2
Exports	6.8	12.1	28.9	33.9

SOURCE: Report on Mining and Manufacturers, Office of Customs Administration, Korea.

in the 1980s whereas the corresponding figure was 20.6% in the 1970s. Therefore, there was not much slow-down in real terms.

Table 9.3 shows the share of the electronics industry in total manufacturing, measured in various dimensions. In terms of value added, the share of the industry stood at 4.0% in 1970 and doubled to 8.2% in 1980. It doubled again in the next decade to 15.8% in 1990. In the 1990s semiconductors and industrial electronics showed rapid growth and led the growth of the electronics industry. The share of the industry reached 20.9% in 1996.

In terms of employment, the share of the electronics industry showed a steady upward trend. Its share stood at 4.6% in 1970 and steadily climbed to 11.0% in 1980, 15.7% in 1990 and further to 16.5% in 1996. In 1970 and 1980 the share of employment was larger than that of value added. It became comparable in 1990 and far lower in 1996. This suggests that the nature of the electronics industry is changing from a traditional labor-intensive industry to one that is technology-oriented but not necessarily capital intensive, because the share of total fixed asset did not increase as much as employment. It is shown below that labor productivity in the electronics industry is increasing more rapidly *vis-à-vis* the rest of the manufacturing sector. This is because the electronics industry is becoming a more technology- and information-intensive and high value added industry.

The share of exports accounted for by electronics products also showed a steady upward trend. The industry was designated as a

TABLE 9.4   Korea: Productivity of Electronics Industry *vs* All Manufacturing

	1970	1980	1990	1996
Value added/Workers, electronics (A)	0.555	4.413	23.638	75.940
Value added/Workers, all manufacturing (B)	0.639	5.885	23.486	60.122
A/B (%)	87.0	75.0	100.6	126.3

SOURCE: Report on Mining and Manufacturers, Office of Customs Administration, Korea.

strategic export industry from the late 1960s. In fact, the share of the electronics industry is more pronounced in exports than in any other dimensions, indicating that the electronics industry has been more export-oriented than the manufacturing sector as a whole.

Table 9.4 shows that the labor productivity of the electronics industry has improved very rapidly in recent years. Compared to the labor productivity of the manufacturing sector as a whole, the electronics industry lagged behind the average until 1990. labor productivity of the electronics industry was 87% and 75% of the manufacturing sector average in 1970 and 1980, respectively. However, it reached a par level in 1990, and surpassed the average by 26% in 1996, as high value added products such as semiconductors and IT-related products became more important.

The composition of the electronics industry shifted markedly throughout the years. Table 9.5 breaks down the electronics industry into sub-sectors and shows each sector's output and relative share over time. One of the most discernible trends is the dominant position of consumer electronics in the 1970s and 1980s and the rapid decline of its share in the 1990s. It accounted for more than 40% of the industry's output until 1990 and declined to 27.6% in 1996. The most dramatic change of the electronics industry was the rise of the semiconductor sector to the central stage of the industry scene. It surpassed consumer electronics to claim 33.3% of total value added of the electronics industry in 1996. The last change to note is that the products usually classified under the heading of industrial electronics, including computers and telecommunication equipment, finally surpassed consumer electronics in 1996.

TABLE 9.5 Sectoral Composition of Electronics Industry in Korea (in million won)

Subsector	1970		1980		1990		1996	
Computers and peripherals	0	(0.0)	0	(0.0)	88,759	(0.3)	5,182,887	(7.0)
Telecommunication equipment	12,487	(22.6)	256,145	(9.2)	2,497,592	(9.2)	6,511,424	(8.8)
Consumer electronics	23,162	(42.0)	1,278,457	(46.1)	11,537,773	(42.6)	20,412,873	(27.6)
Other industrial electronics	9,820	(17.8)	288,670	(10.4)	3,300,352	(12.2)	9,079,116	(12.3)
Semiconductors	0	(0.0)	552,562	(19.9)	4,021,573	(14.9)	24,551,388	(33.3)
Other electronics components	9,727	(17.6)	394,624	(14.2)	5,623,496	(20.8)	8,090,975	(11.0)
Total	55,196	(100.0)	2,770,458	(100.0)	27,069,545	(100.0)	73,828,663	(100.0)

NOTE: Figures in parentheses indicate percentages.
SOURCE: Report on Mining and Manufacturers, Office of Customs Administration, Korea.

TABLE 9.6 Korea: Output Growth of Key Products (in US$ million)

Key Product	1985	1990	1996	Growth Rate per Annum (%)
Computer	217	1,328	1,406	18.5
Computer peripherals	301	1,831	6,422	32.1
Colour television set	672	2,027	3,680	16.7
Video cassette recorder	317	1,567	1,938	17.9
Microwave oven	258	687	934	12.4
Cathode ray tube	380	1,256	2,677	19.4
Integrated circuit	1,154	4,410	18,225	28.5
Condenser	147	470	931	18.3
Magnetic tape	280	1,116	1,303	15.0
Printed circuit boards	49	389	1,123	32.9

SOURCE: Electronics Industries Association of Korea.

This change is more noticeable at the product level reported in Table 9.6, which shows output growth of key products since 1985. These industrial electronics products were the top ten products in 1996. Although consumer electronic products such as colour television sets, videocassette recorders (VCRs), microwave ovens and magnetic tapes remain significant, their rate of growth lags behind other products. On the other hand, IT-related products such as printed circuit boards (PCBs), personal computers (PCs) and peripherals, ICs and CRTs showed relatively higher growth for the last ten years and led the growth of the electronics industry. For example, although production of PC peripherals were less than half that of colour television set production in 1985, it grew to be almost twice that of colour television sets in 1996.

Korea's electronics industry is highly concentrated. Table 9.7 shows the concentration structure of the industry. Large firms employing more than 500 workers have accounted for almost two-thirds of the industry's output since 1970. Although small and medium-sized firms have mushroomed, four *chaebol* — LG, Samsung, Daewoo and Hyundai — have dominated production and exports. The oligopolistic market structure led to a significant competition among them. LG Electronics is the pioneer of Korea's electronics industry and a pillar of the LG *chaebol*. Samsung joined the industry in 1969, 11 years after LG. Investing

TABLE 9.7 Korea: Concentration Structure of Electronics Industry by Employment Size (output in million won)

No. of Workers	1970		1980		1990		1996	
<50	5,782	(10.5)	137,532	(5.0)	2,662,216	(9.8)	8,424,246	(11.4)
50–99	2,614	(4.7)	125,547	(4.5)	1,625,915	(6.0)	4,075,769	(5.5)
100–199	2,337	(4.2)	180,987	(6.5)	1,813,654	(6.7)	5,253,004	(7.1)
200–499	8,943	(16.2)	434,180	(15.7)	3,043,165	(11.2)	8,225,064	(11.1)
500 and above	35,482	(64.3)	1,892,212	(68.3)	17,917,684	(66.2)	47,850,580	(64.8)
Total	55,158	(100.0)	2,770,458	(100.0)	27,062,634	(100.0)	73,828,663	(100.0)

NOTE: Figure in parentheses indicate percentages.
SOURCE: Report on Mining and Manufacturers, Office of Customs Administration, Korea.

heavily in technology and human-resource development, it became a multibillion-dollar, Korea-based multinational electronics firm. Samsung is considered the most technologically aggressive with the largest pool of engineers. Daewoo entered the industry in 1983 by acquiring the dwindling Electronics Division of Taehan Electric Wire Company. After the takeover, Daewoo Electronics, with an aggressive globalization strategy, grew rapidly. Daewoo is the most enterprising of the *chaebol* in exploring emerging markets. Hyundai Electronics, the youngest and smallest of the four electronics industry *chaebol* does not produce consumer electronics. Hyundai has been the most active in acquiring high-technology companies in advanced countries in an attempt to gain access to cutting-edge technology.

III. DEVELOPMENT OF THE CONSUMER ELECTRONICS INDUSTRY

During the first phase of the development consumer electronics was the leading sector of the electronics industry. An active intervention by the government, protection of the domestic markets in the early 1960s and export promotion since the late 1960s were pivotal for the development of the industry.

Korea's first consumer electronics producer, LG Electronics, was established in 1958 by the owner of a small, rudimentary face cream and plastic houseware company, which sensed an attractive business opportunity in the import-substitution policy. Lacking technological capability, the company hired an experienced German engineer. In a small-scale garage operation foreign components and parts were assembled into the country's first vacuum tube AM radio through imitative reverse-engineering of a Japanese model. LG Electronics soon developed expertise in imitation and began producing other home appliances such as electric fans and refrigerators without foreign assistance.

During the early years the electronics industry developed as an import-substitution industry. The government tried to help create a domestic market. It imposed import restrictions and encouraged a campaign to send radios to farming and fishing villages. The government's import-substitution policy and tight control of foreign investment and contraband goods in the black market created attractive business opportunities for local entrepreneurs to enter the protected market in the early 1960s. Export of radios was also tried with the help of explicit export subsidies.

The Korean electronics industry really got its impetus in the mid-1960s with the production of black and white television sets and audio equipment through the international transfer of production technology. In 1965, after realizing that it was beyond its capability to imitate by reverse-engineering, LG entered into a licensing agreement with Hitachi of Japan to import packaged technology for black and white television set production. The agreement included not only assembly processes but also product specifications, production know-how, parts/components, training and technical experts, transferring a significant volume of explicit and tacit knowledge to LG Electronics, which sent seven experienced engineers and technicians to Hitachi for intensive training. Even though it invested enough for licensing and overseas training, LG decided to have Japanese engineers supervise the installation and start-up of the television set production systems to minimize trial-and-error time. These people played the most vital role in the initial implementation of transferred Japanese technology by transferring their knowledge to LG engineers.

LG Electronics was able to apply the manufacturing competence accumulated over the years to subsequent assembly of other consumer electronics, such as cassette recorders and simple audio systems, without foreign assistance. Three other television set producers that started at about the same time acquired and assimilated production ability the same way from foreign firms such as Sharp of Japan and RCA of the United States. Subsequent entrants raised the number of television set producers to more than ten by 1975 and increased the production level very rapidly to surpass 1 million units in 1974.

Subsequent entrants, on the other hand, lured experienced engineers and technicians from existing firms, resulting in an effective diffusion of tacit knowledge from established firms to new ones. LG Electronics, as the first and largest producer, was a major source of such personnel for new entrants. A similar pattern is evident in other electronic products of the same period.

The growth of the electronics industry got a new momentum when the government designated electronics a strategic export industry in late 1969. The government promulgated the Electronics Industry Promotion Act in 1969 and released an ambitious Long-term Electronics Industry Promotion Plan for 1969–76. It created the Electronics

Industry Promotion fund, offering preferential financing to foster scale economies in production as well as grants to develop and upgrade public support systems for standardization and research and development (R&D). The government also targeted 95 products for promotion, offering preferential financing and other incentives to their manufacturers. Yearly production targets were established. Progressive local content requirements were set to promote the parts and components industry. End products for the local market were completely protected from foreign competitors. Foreign investment was allowed largely in the production of parts and components and for re-export.

The plan exhibited the government's determination to promote the electronics industry as a leading exporter. In 1969, when the industry was still exporting a mere US$42 million, the government set the goal at US$400 million for 1976, the last year of the plan. Preferential financing, tax concessions, foreign loan guarantees and the control of entry by new firms formed the crux of the export drive. The government not only set specific export goals and directives, forcing local firms to be competitive in both price and quality in the international market, it also provided incentives. This scheme induced a crisis, compelling local firms to acquire technological capability quickly while providing support to make the crisis creative rather than destructive. Since marketing was largely in the hands of buyers from foreign original equipment manufacturers (OEMs), the local firms concentrated mainly on the acquisition of product design and production capabilities.

The government also began to undertake investment in the infrastructure relating to the electronics industry: establishment of an industrial park, overhauling of the product quality review system and establishment of research institutes to develop technological capability. The government created an industrial estate for electronics in Kumi to foster inter-firm efficiency. Several governmental research institutes were designated for electronics promotion and actively engaged in reviewing the quality of the products and technological guidance. The government also took the initiative in organizing a yearly electronics show in an attempt to promote the diffusion of technological ideas in the economy and international marketing for Korean firms.

It turned out that exports exceeded US$1 billion in 1976 (Table 9.8), almost 259% of the established target, illustrating the successful transformation of the electronics industry from an import-substitution industry into a major export industry. In short, while the government

TABLE 9.8   Korea: Electronics Industry Exports in the 1970s (in US$ million dollars)

	1970	1973	1976	1979
Electronics total	54.9	369.3	1,036.9	1,845.3
Consumer electronics	8.8	104.5	389.9	914.5
Colour television sets			7.8	71.4
Black and white television sets	2.1	23.4	63.0	231.1
Radios	6.1	16.0	66.5	49.5
Cassette recorders	0.6	30.3	91.6	288.4
Industrial electronics	0.4	18.0	56.2	110.7
Electronic components	45.6	246.8	590.8	820.2
Semiconductors	31.4	173.4	297.8	406.3

SOURCE: Electronics Industries Association of Korea.

played an important role in all strategic industries, its role in the electronics industry was extraordinary in the early years. Under this public policy environment the electronics industry has grown rapidly as a highly export-oriented industry.

The government's strong will to promote the electronics industry as a major exporting industry and the growing domestic demand due to rapid economic growth encouraged new firms to enter the industry. Many local and foreign firms began to enter the industry. Samsung, the biggest of the *chaebol*, joined the industry in 1969 and many Japanese joint ventures began operation in the early 1970s. Between 1968 and 1974 about 30 new firms entered the industry annually, whereas an average of only four new firms entered the industry each year before 1967. For example, the number of producers of black and white television sets increased to more than ten by 1975 and competition among the domestic producers became intense.

As many local and foreign companies entered the industry, electronics production and exports grew very rapidly in the 1970s. As income levels continued to rise due to the rapid growth, the domestic market for consumer electronic products, such as black and white television sets, refrigerators and washing machines, expanded very rapidly. During the 1970s the penetration rate of black and white television sets increased very rapidly, reaching 90% and saturating the domestic market.

Helped by the ambitious export drive of the government, exports increased very rapidly, too. Exports of electronics products jumped from US$55 million in 1970 to US$1,845 million in 1979. In the 1970s exports of the electronics industry were mainly labour-intensive products and more than half of them were shipped to the United States. Major export items were ICs, radios, black and white television sets, condensers and CRTs in 1970 while electronic components such as ICs accounted for more than 80% of total electronics industry exports. During the 1970s, the rapid growth of consumer electronics industry drove the export of the electronics industry. In 1979 almost 50% of the total electronics exports were accounted for by consumer electronics products. Radio cassettes and colour television sets were added to the list of major export items, reflecting the changes in consumption pattern and advance in technological capability of Korean producers.

When black and white television sets, which had been the workhorse of electronics exports in 1970s, eventually encountered a rapid decline in the export market, the colour television set became the next leading electronics appliance to sustain increasing exports. Although colour television sets were first produced in 1974 by a joint venture with National Electric of Japan, they became major export item when *chaebol* such as LG and Samsung entered the field in 1977 after acquiring the technology through licensing.

Colour television is an illustrative example of the Korean government's export drive. The Korean government was not willing to allow domestic channels to start colour broadcasting on social grounds in the 1970s. At the same time it wanted to exploit the potential of the growing export market for colour television sets. Therefore, colour television set producers had to export from the start, while for black and white television sets, the Korean companies had moved up the production learning curve on the strength of the protected local market prior to competing in the export market. Korean companies had difficulty acquiring technology from abroad, since no foreign colour television set maker was willing to license technology to Korean makers to help them invade the U.S. market anew. Therefore, the early production and export of colour television sets were undertaken by joint-venture firms established under the proviso that the whole output would be exported. Korean firms had to accumulate enough knowledge and experience in colour television technology through searching and mastering foreign literature, and reverse-engineering foreign colour television sets. The experience gained from producing black and white receivers and learning from joint research enabled them to strengthen their bargaining power in licensing core patents held by RCA in 1974. The colour television set became a major export in 1977 when domestic *chaebol* such as LG and Samsung began production. Then, Korea became a major exporter of colour television sets in the late 1970s even though Korean channels did not broadcast in colour until 1980.

At the end of the 1970s the electronics industry experienced a setback due to adverse developments in the external economic environment such as the second oil crisis and import restrictions imposed by industrial countries. A sudden rise in crude oil prices in 1979 brought about economic recessions in major Western industrial countries, a major export market of Korea. This naturally reduced the market for Korean electronics products. In addition, many countries tried to impose import restrictions on electronics, further reducing the export market. Domestically, coupled with political instability and the oil crisis, the Korean economy showed negative growth in 1980, which meant a very reduced domestic market for the electronics industry. Due to this unfavourable market condition, the electronics industry recorded a negative growth rate of 13.1% in 1980.

In the 1980s the colour television set and new products became the new engine of growth. To help the industry rebound from this setback, the government took the initiative in allowing domestic television channels to start colour broadcasting and implementing various policy measures to boost domestic demand. The government allowed domestic channels to start colour broadcasting in 1980 and it provided the industry with a stable base of domestic demand. The government also implemented various forms of promotional measures such as the establishment of the electronics promotion fund and long-term development plan of the industry. The exemption of special consumption tax on some electronics products boosted domestic consumption of electronics products and helped the electronics industry to grow rapidly.

Daewoo, another major *chaebol*, entered the industry in 1983 by acquiring the dwindling Electronics Division of Taehan Electric Wire Company and oligopolistic competition among domestic firms became more intense. Korean firms kept on accumulating technological capability through processes similar to the production of television sets. When foreign firms were reluctant to transfer technology to emerging Korean competitors, Korean firms reverse-engineered the technology. It was only after these firms successfully commercialized the products that foreign firms reluctantly licensed the technology to them. The purpose of licensing was not to learn new technology but to pave the way into the export market. The VCR and the microwave oven went through a similar process. Korean firms initially acquired the necessary technological proficiency through reverse-engineering and subsequently became major players in the world market. As Korean electronics firms kept on expanding their lines of production to colour television sets, VCRs, microwave ovens, etc., the consumer electronics industry led the growth of the electronics industry and the Korean economy.

The start of colour broadcasting of domestic television channels and the government's will to implement the plan for advancement of the electronics industry brought about vigorous investment in the electronics industry. Depressed investment in the electronics industry in 1979 and 1980, which was less than 7% of the total manufacturing sector, bounced back in the early 1980s to account for a quarter of total manufacturing investment in 1984. It stabilized in the late 1980s at the 20% level. The consumer electronics industry rapidly expanded the existing production capacity of colour television sets and made new investment in production facilities of VCRs and microwave ovens, which emerged as the next target products to sustain the export increase.

Favourable external conditions created by the appreciation of the Japanese yen provided the Korean electronics industry with excellent opportunities and the industry had booming years in the mid-1980s. Consumer electronics has been the leading export sector of Korea and Korea was for some time the world's second largest exporter, second only to Japan. However, after 1988, the peak year, export growth slowed and China replaced Korea as the world's second largest exporter. Since the 1990s Korean producers have been putting more emphasis on the domestic market, modifying their products to capture Korean-specific tastes and demand.

The erosion of competitiveness of Korean products in the world market brought about such change. The erosion of competitiveness came from the erosion of price competitiveness of Korean products. A rapid rise in domestic labor cost stemming from developing labor shortages and the appreciation of the Korean won due to the substantial current account surplus recorded in the late 1980s eroded the price competitiveness of Korean firms in the world market in the 1990s. The other contributing factor was the lack of product innovation capability of Korean firms, which made Korea somewhat sandwiched between the advanced countries and the next tier newly industrialized economies (NIEs). This is related to the pattern of technological development and innovation in the Korean consumer electronics industry.

In the 1970s the main channel of technology transfer was through direct foreign investment, and Koreans were able to learn from their joint-venture partners. As foreign investors gradually lost their interest in their Korean businesses owing to the export-oriented government policies and continuing denial of access to the domestic market, the Koreans took over the businesses and began independent production from the late 1970s. Thus, the channel of technology transfer changed from informal learning from partners to formal absorption by licensing. During the 1980s Korean producers, mostly *chaebol* firms, imported low-level technology which enabled them to produce marginal parts locally. At this stage the role of the government was critical in encouraging localization of parts production as well as restricting foreign penetration by making restrictive FDI and import policies.

The pattern of technological development and innovation in the Korean consumer electronics industry evolved from the stage of duplicative imitation of standardized products at their mature stage in the product life cycle to creative imitation of new products since the mid-1980s. During the duplicative imitation stage Korean *chaebol* used imported production facilities to carry out mass production of standardized products. Any innovation was mainly process-oriented based on learning by doing, and there was reliance on economies of scale to maintain price competitiveness. The second step in the duplicative imitation process was localization of generic-use parts requiring low-level technology, where there was also some learning by doing in parts production.

After duplicative imitation came the stage of creative imitation of new products. The Korean producers tried to imitate and locally produce, with lower costs, new products, not mature products, developed by advanced economies like Japan. Localization of the marginal parts and, more recently, some core parts also started initially with imitation. Some effort to add "Koreaness" to the Japanese-developed products was also made so that it may be called creative imitation.

However, at this stage of creative imitation Korean producers increasingly felt that product innovation, namely design and creation of new products, and production of core parts required higher technological capability than they possessed. It was becoming more difficult to import high-level technology by licensing, as the forerunners in the advanced countries became more reluctant to do this. At the same time, Korean firms had not made sufficient investment for the development of their own capabilities in product innovation. This can be seen from the composition of the R&D expenditure by the Korean firms. In the average consumer electronics firm, expenditure for basic research accounted for only 8.2% and development for mass production was 65.9% of total R&D expenditure. Lack of product innovation capability has become more acute as the nature of consumer electronics industry in Korea changes over time. As the product life cycles get shorter and the Korean producers move up the economic ladder, consumer electronics has increasingly become science-based rather than supplier-dominated.

In the 1990s as technology licensing became more difficult to acquire, Korean firms had to resort to technology imports and learning to utilize overseas R&D outposts and/or international mergers and acquisitions (M&A) and strategic alliances. At the same time their interests had turned more to the domestic market, and their product innovations had mostly been adaptive ones to capture Korean tastes. For example, LG developed a refrigerator that was especially suited to storing Korean foods. Of course, this meant a smaller market and a market that could be preserved only as long as foreign rivals did not develop and sell Korean-specific products or were forbidden to enter the market itself.

IV. DEVELOPMENT OF SEMICONDUCTOR INDUSTRY

Korea's semiconductor industry has been an illustrative story of a stage-skipping catch-up effort of the Korean economy. Korea leapfrogged from a mere assembler of discrete devices to a major player in DRAM chips in only a decade. It emerged as the second largest memory chip producer after Japan and the third largest semiconductor producer in the world, after Japan and the United States. The industry's total output grew, on average, tenfold every decade, from less than US$40 million in 1970 to US$4.4 billion by 1990 and in five years quintupled to US$23.2 billion in 1995 (Table 9.9). Exports grew from US$32 million to US$21.2 billion during the same period, and its products became the

TABLE 9.9   Growth of Semiconductor Industry in Korea (in US$ million)

	1981	1985	1990	1995	1996
Production	342	1,154	4,410	23,194	18,225
Export	342	1,062	4,079	21,154	16,766

SOURCE: Electronics Industries Association of Korea.

single largest export item from Korea, accounting for 17% of total exports.

While the consumer electronics industry started with assembly operation of local firms with technology licensing, Korea's semiconductor industry started with multinational firms that attempted to relocate the operation of assembling ICs to take advantage of cheap labor in the East Asian region.

In the mid-1960s several multinational firms began assembling discrete devices in Korea to take advantage of cheap local labour. In 1965, Komy Corporation of the United States got the first investment permission. In 1966 wholly owned subsidiaries of Signetics and Fairchild were established. Motorola followed in 1967. Operations consisted merely of simple packaging processes — bonded assembly operations by the wholly owned foreign subsidiaries with all parts and components imported from the parent companies and re-exported to the consignors. These simple assembly operations of ICs were a major export activity of Korea's electronics industry in the late 1960s.

The assembly operations transferred little design and engineering technology to Korea. In the 1970s a few Korean firms began modest-scale production of wafers to meet in-house demands in consumer electronics. The firms absorbed low-level technology and took the form of the FDI firms or private OEMs with the facilities provided by the foreigners.

In 1975 the government, as part of its heavy and chemical industries (HCI) drive, formulated a six-year plan to promote the semiconductor industry. Although many *chaebol* showed great enthusiasm in entering it, the difficulty in obtaining foreign technology and high market risk associated with increasingly short product life cycles chilled the potential entrants' zeal, unlike other HCIs. Investment in the semiconductor industry was quite below the planned level; most of the firms chose to pursue consumer electronics.

At this time the major government involvement was some R&D assistance from a government research institute (GRI) called the KIET [now known as the Electronics and Telecommunications Research Institute (ETRI)] equipped with R&D and VLSIC production processes. Although the government R&D turned out to be not flexible and dynamic enough to adapt to rapidly changing technology in semiconductors, it made a very important contribution to the development of the industry in later decades by providing experienced manpower. It helped produce a large number of R&D engineers experienced in semiconductors who moved to the private sector and played important roles.

The late 1970s to the early 1980s was the period of absorption of high-level technology when all foreign companies sold their shares to Korean firms and Korean *chaebol* like Samsung took over these firms. Through its own initiatives without government help, Samsung first started to produce 64K bit DRAM chips in the early 1980s.

The Korean firms' stake in semiconductors grew substantially in 1983 when the four largest *chaebols* — Samsung, Hyundai, LG, and Daewoo — were ready to start VLSIC production. In the mid-1980s Samsung, Hyundai and LG embarked on VLSIC production based on design process technology acquired from small, financially troubled U.S. semiconductor makers.

The time when Korean firms, including Samsung, were considering production of 16K bit DRAM was the transition period in the world DRAM industry from 16K to 64K. Samsung was able to buy 64K bit DRAM design technology from Microelectronic Technology, a small U.S.-based venture company, and manufacturing technology from the Japan-based Sharp. In the case of Hyundai it bought design technology from Vitelic but tried, without success, to develop its own manufacturing technology. Later, Hyundai had to license manufacturing technology from Texas Instruments.

A couple of years after starting to produce DRAM using licensed manufacturing technology, Korean firms began to develop their own circuit design technology, first developing and producing 256K bit memory chips in the mid-1980s. Samsung chose to develop its own design technology for 256K or higher DRAM as it was not easy or cheap to buy the design. In this process the role of overseas R&D outposts in the Silicon Valley and Koreans who returned home was critical. It was observed that Samsung's 256K DRAM by its Silicon Valley team turned out to be better than the Japanese counter parts.

In 1988, when Korea's semiconductor industry was experiencing heavy losses typical in the semiconductor industry during the initial investment stage, it got unexpected relief from the temporary worldwide shortage of 256K DRAM. Since an enormous amount of facility investment was needed to achieve economies of scale, demand and supply disruptions often developed when the expectations of the producers were not fulfilled in the market. In 1985 the volume of demand for 256K DRAM was below the level expected by the producers and the DRAM price plunged due to the excess supply of the chip. Major suppliers cut back their production of 256K DRAM and hastened to move up to the next generation of chips, making heavy investment in the production facilities for 1M DRAM. However, the 1M DRAM market was not established as planned due to reliability problems and the high prices of new-generation chips in 1988. Sustained market demand for 256K DRAM with reduced supply created temporary worldwide shortages of 256K DRAM and the excess demand had to be filled by new entrants at higher prices. Until 1989, when the price of 1M DRAM eventually stabilized, Korean firms enjoyed high growth and profitability, which provided financial capability to undertake new investment for the next generation chips.

Korean firms have concentrated on the production of memory ICs in general, and DRAM in particular, to meet growing domestic and foreign demand. Due to this strategy, Korea has gone from a near-negligible position just ten years ago, to one of the world's leading suppliers of DRAM with amazing speed. Korea's strategic focus on semiconductor memory products has been extremely successful. Korean semiconductor production enjoyed a high growth rate in the 1990s, enough to accomplish a five-fold increase in just three years from 1992, rising to US$23 billion in 1995. Along with the high increase in production, exports soared to a record US$21.2 billion in 1995, thanks to the rise in world demand for DRAM. Korea is one of the world leaders in the production of DRAM. Led by Samsung Electronics, Korean-produced DRAM accounted for 37.6% of world production in 1996, making Korea the second-largest producer of DRAM behind Japan.

The Korean firms' success in the DRAM industry can be explained in terms of technological characteristics of the industry and relative strength of Korean firms. In the DRAM industry technological innovation within the same generation chip is oriented towards process innovation to reduce unit costs, and thus scale matters in this respect.

Furthermore, transferability of technological knowledge between different generations is not so strong as to pose serious handicaps to late entries. These features imply that conglomerate-style latecomer firms which build production facilities on a large enough scale for the new generation chips can enter and claim some shares in the market without much interference from the existing firms.

The above features of the DRAM industry gave important advantages to the Korean firms as latecomers. A firm's innovation effort is affected not only by its own technological capability but also by expected additional profits from the next-generation chip business. Existing leading firms are less strongly inclined to initiate next-generation chip development since they want to fully exploit profits from the current generation chip. In contrast, additional profits from the next-generation chip business are bigger for the current followers than for the current leaders, relatively speaking.

Owing to their size as conglomerates with strong capability to mobilize financial resources at hand, Korean firms, especially Samsung, have found it easy to enter this market. Korean firms are very experienced in process innovation-driven competition and also strong in scale-intensive R&D and production. The DRAM industry is the kind of industry where the advantages of latecomers are strong owing to the special nature of the technology and Korean firms exploited this advantage. Korean firms, especially Samsung, watched the growth of the DRAM industry, led by the forerunners like Intel, and entered the market only after the market size of the industry was sufficient for the large conglomerate firms to be able to enjoy some of the advantages. Late entry by the conglomerate firms after watching development was possible since they had the financial capability.

One of the most important characteristics of the Korean semiconductor industry is its rapid growth. The Korean semiconductor industry has grown rapidly since the mid-1980s by bold and brash investment in production facilities. It has made a strenuous effort to upgrade the quality of products through R&D and the acquisition of foreign technology. The Korean semiconductor industry has invested heavily in new capital equipment and facilities. According to the Korea Semiconductor Industry Association (KSIA), from 1992 to 1995 Korean companies spent an average of 45% of annual revenue on capital equipment and facilities. Most of the facility investment was had been on the construction of semiconductor fabrication plants since developing the 64K DRAM in 1983. In the 1990s semiconductor manufacturers sustained the investment for the expansion of memory chip facilities such as those for 4M DRAM and 16M DRAM. Facility investment in 1996 amounted to US$9.9 billion and Korea's share of world investment increased to more than 20 per cent.

Facility investment underwent a major adjustment starting in 1996 to bring worldwide semiconductor overproduction in line with demand. Semiconductor manufacturers delayed or cancelled new plants and closed older ones, especially for DRAM. Along with this, the industry has expanded overseas investment for technical co-operation and joint production to cope with trade barriers and with the growing investment risk associated with mass production and the costs of R&D.

Another characteristic of the Korean semiconductor industry is a high export rate and a heavy dependence on imports for its equipment and core parts. Korean semiconductor production is concentrated on memory devices. However, domestic demand is primarily for non-memory devices, such as custom ICs, microprocessors, application specific integrated circuits (ASICs) and compound semiconductors, which are not made in large amounts in Korea.

As a result, Korean semiconductor producers export about 90% of their domestic production, while more than 70% of the domestic demand for semiconductors is met with imports. This implies that the Korean semiconductor industry is structurally dependent on imports and has a weak link between domestic supply and demand.

A sudden drop in DRAM prices in the world market forced the Korean semiconductor industry to decrease its production in 1996. Production decreased by 21.4% to US$18.2 billion, and exports also declined by 20.7% to US$16.8 billion. Korea's semiconductor production accounted for about 9% of world production in 1996, down from 11.2% in 1995. Semiconductors are Korea's single largest export item. Of the total electronics exports, semiconductors accounted for 43.3% in 1996, with their share in total exports rising from 8.9% in 1992 to 17.7% in 1996.

By item, ICs accounted for about 96% of total semiconductor production and most IC products were MOS memory ICs in 1996. Such an excessive dependence on memory device exports made Korea vulnerable to the drop in DRAM prices in 1996 and 1997, which was a main factor in its worsening current account deficit.

Presently, about 50% of total semiconductor exports go to the United States and Japan, while 30% go to Asia and 20% are bound for European Union countries.

The Korean semiconductor industry has been an illustrative example of a stage-skipping, catch-up effort that relied upon access to the external knowledge base in the form of licensing and overseas R&D outposts and took advantage of the mass production and investment capability of conglomerate firms. The special characteristics of DRAM provided the latecomers with some advantages associated with the fact that the innovation path and hence catch-up target was well defined. Continuous development of the new-generation chips involved some explicit knowledge, and the Korean firms overcame this gap with help from the government, overseas R&D posts and Koreans returning from the United States.

V. INDUSTRIAL ELECTRONICS INDUSTRY

The early growth of the Korean electronics industry centred largely around the development of consumer electronics and the semiconductor industry, and the industrial electronics sector had lagged behind these sectors. The output of the industrial sector was US$494 million, less than one-third that of consumer electronics, which was US$1,598 million in 1981. Since the 1980s the growth of the industrial electronics sector has accelerated due to the rapid growth in computers and peripherals. In the 1990s it continued to show high growth while the consumer electronics sector showed relative stagnant growth, and exceeded consumer electronics in both production and exports in 1996. The output of the industrial electronics sector in 1996 was US$14,563 million while that of consumer electronics was US$13,668 million and its exports of US$8,400 million surpassed consumer electronics exports of US$7,836 million (Table 9.10).

While the government's role in semiconductors was rather indirect and focused on providing R&D support, its involvement in personal computers (PCs) and cellular phones was more direct. The PC industry in Korea started with simple assembly in the late 1970s. Small venture companies, like Sambo and Quenix, manufactured an 8 byte PC by reverse-engineering. At that time no foreign companies were interested in investing in the Korean market through joint ventures, but were

TABLE 9.10 Korea: Changes in Export Composition of Electronics Industry (in US$ million)

	1981	1985	1990	1995	1996
Electronics total	2,210	4,590	17,224	43,592	41,223
Industrial electronics	145	905	3,481	7,666	8,400
Consumer electronics	1,124	1,860	5,725	7,861	7,836
Electronic components	941	1,825	8,016	28,065	24,987

SOURCE: Electronics Industries Association of Korea.

more interested in exporting to the Korean market. Thus, Korean producers had to stand on their own feet. However, with the shift to the 16 byte PC after 1984, they felt the need to import higher technology by licensing since they realized that it was very difficult to produce the 16 byte PC by reverse-engineering only. Thus, most Korean PC firms switched to OEM producers targeting exports.

Then, the government also designated the PC as a target for promotion and took active measures to create a growing domestic market for the computer industry in the early 1980s. The government imposed import restrictions on PCs and peripherals, creating a protected market for small local firms to enter and survive long enough to gain by first-stage experience in PC manufacturing.

In addition, the government issued its own procurement order to create an early domestic market, announcing in 1982 that it intended to purchase 5,000 PCs for public schools in 1983 and increasing the number thereafter. The government then created the National Administration Information System (NAIS), investing a substantial amount of funds and creating a demand for main computers and workstations. In addition, the government launched the computerization of the postal system, the tax system, the national defence system and the education-research network system, each of which required as much investment in both hardware and software as the NAIS. In procuring merchandise, the government first set technical specifications and targets for the local content ratio, then awarded contracts to the firms that met the requisites. These announcements attracted many newcomers to the industry and induced aggressive investment for in-house R&D to meet the government requirements.

As with semiconductors, the government played a significant role in providing R&D support. Several GRIs were set up several years prior to the private sector's entry into computers in an attempt to gain first-stage experience in R&D on new technology and to produce experienced researchers.

During the second half of the 1980s Korea emerged as the favourite site for worldwide OEM production of PCs, exploiting economies of scale in the large conglomerates. This change was triggered by the adoption of open PC architecture by IBM, which allowed worldwide licensing of IBM PC BIOS. Numerous manufacturers of IBM-compatible PCs thrived all over the world. Riding this new wave most successfully were the Korean producers who had accumulated some know-how in large-scale assembly in electronics and price-based competition with some learning by doing effect.

However, even during this growth period most Korean firms were OEM producers doing SKD-based assembly, and thus were able to acquire only low-level technology. With technological capability increasing, they switched from simple OEM to private OEM, and at the same time the Korean firms realized the limits of OEM production as a window for technology absorption. It acted rather as a hindrance since the foreign partner firms designated the specific manufacturers' parts to be used in assembling the PCs and therefore locally made parts were hardly ever used. Furthermore, the foreign partners were reluctant to contract further licensing of more advanced technology.

Thus, Korean producers felt the need to conduct their own R&D, and at the same time the role of the government also changed from simple market protection to R&D support and demand creation by government procurement. The public and private R&D collaboration began and the Korea Computer Research Association was set up in 1985. The government lifted the restriction on PC imports in 1987 and subsequently the import restriction on PC-related peripherals was also abolished in July 1988. In the late 1980s and the 1990s Korean producers succeeded in the local production of PC motherboards, memory chips and other peripheral parts, such as hard disk drives.

Since the early 1990s the Korean PC industry has faced a relative stagnation; exports have plummeted, and Korea is no longer a dominant exporter of PCs (Table 9.11). Korean producers have switched to PC peripherals such as monitors, hard drives and CD-ROM drives.

TABLE 9.11   **Trends in Korean Computer Exports** (in US$ million)

	1981	1985	1990	1995	1996
Computers					
Production	18	217	1,341	1,395	1,444
Export	1	159	633	223	159
Computer monitors					
Production	12	177	1,250	3,537	4,328
Export	11	168	1,116	3,116	3,537

SOURCE: Electronics Industries Association of Korea.

CRT terminal is the most important product of the industrial electronics sector. Korea is also the largest maker of CRTs in the world. However, competitively expanding their production capacities, CRT makers oversupplied the world market in 1996. Korean CRT manufacturers are implementing a strategy to make higher value-added products in Korea and lower ones in Asia where they can take advantage of cheaper labor force. Therefore, less value-added cathode picture tube lines have been relocated to other Asian countries or if they remain in Korea, they are changed to cathode display tube lines, especially for bigger tubes such as 15 inches and 17 inches.

Several factors can be identified as causing the sudden downfall of Korea as a PC system provider. First, the importance of the large-scale assembly process declined with the rise of chipsets which integrated the different functions of several chips into one chip. Thus, Korea lost its comparative advantage as an assembly site. Secondly, Korean producers did not respond well to the rapid shortening of life cycles in PCs. For example, the PC industry around the world switched very promptly from the 286 PC to the 386 PC. However, Korean firms, because of the huge investment made by Korean *chaebol* in the 286 PC assembly lines, continued too long with the 286 PC and were left behind. Thirdly, the rising royalty was also a burden for assembly-oriented PC firms in Korea.

During the 1990s one of the most important developments in the electronics industry and Korean society was the rapid proliferation of mobile phone usage among Koreans. Although mobile communication services started with car phones in 1984, they had been perceived as

TABLE 9.12   Korea: Growth of Mobile Communication Subscribers and Exports of Mobile Phones

	1989	1991	1993	1995	1997	1998
No. of subscribers (1,000)	40	166	472	1,641	6,820	13,989
Exports (US$ million)	147	116	201	508	853	1,433

SOURCE: Electronics Industries Association of Korea.

being only for the well-to-do during the 1980s. Total subscribers remained at the level of 80,000 until 1990. However, the number of mobile communication subscribers skyrocketed in the 1990s, surpassing the 1 million mark in 1995 and reaching 14 million in 1998 (Table 9.12). The growth of mobile communication services in the 1990s was attributable to the steady increase in demand for the services due to a steady increase in the income level to the extent that mobile communication services became highly income elastic. But the amazing speed at which the services proliferated was brought about by the government's active intervention in the industry. In the case of the cellular phone system, the government's role was direct and critical. One was the government's competition policy of allowing many service providers and the other was the government's technology policy on the kind of system to be adopted.

In the 1990s the government made mobile communication service a very competitive industry. The government first allowed new firms to provide cellular phone services, which were formerly monopolized. Then, it allowed a new kind of mobile communication service called PCS, which used a different bandwidth from the existing service. In the end five service providers competed in the market and their fierce competition to lure potential customers and to serve at low rates helped the number of subscribers to increase very rapidly.

Another role was the government's initiative in deciding the kind of cellular phone system to be adopted. When the Korean firms and the government authorities considered the development of the cellular phone system, the analogue system was (and still is) dominant in the United States, and the TDMA-based GSM system was the dominant system in Europe. However, the Korean authorities (Ministry of Information and Telecommunication) were monitoring the emerging CDMA technology with its higher efficiency in frequency utilization and higher quality and security in voice transmission. Thus, despite great uncertainty over the development of the world's first CDMA system as well as the strong reservations expressed by the telephone service providers and the system manufacturers, the Ministry and the ETRI decided to go along with CDMA. One of the main reasons for the decision was reported to be the consideration that if Korea just followed the already established TDMA (GSM), the gap between Korea and its forerunners would never be reduced and thus catch-up would take even longer. Thus, Korea chose a shorter but riskier path and succeeded.

Although it was in 1995 that the first test of the CDMA system was conducted, the Korean government first designated the CDMA system development as a national R&D project as early as 1989. It turned out that the Korean authorities were quite well informed in the trend of telecommunications technology and had foresight. In 1991 the contract to introduce the core technology from, and to develop the system together with, the U.S.-based Qualcomm was forged. In 1993 the Ministry declared CDMA to be the national standard in telecommunications. In achieving the leapfrogging by taking a different path, the role of the government was very critical in taking the initiative to form a R&D consortium with private firms and pushing them ahead.

The commercial development of new mobile communication services stimulated domestic demand for communication equipment. There took place active investment in computerization by the governmental, financial and educational sectors in accordance with the government's second National Basic Information System project. Together with these, the expansion of new media markets brought about rapid developments of IT-related products.

Among these, the cellular phone had shown tremendous growth in production and export. Until the early 1990s, the cellular phone market was dominated by multinationals like Motorola, Nokia and Ericsson. They accounted for almost 80% of domestic sales. In the mid-1990s Korean firms increased their marketing effort with localized products which sacrificed the quality of voice signal for better communicability in mountainous region, a typical Korean topography. They succeeded in capturing the domestic market and tried to repeat their success in the export market. As Korea was one of the first countries that successfully commercialized the CDMA system and other countries began to adopt the system, Korean firms were able to take advantage of their reputation as suppliers of an established product. Exports increased very rapidly in the late 1990s. They reached US$1.4 billion in 1998 and the cellular phone became one of Korea's top five export items.

VI. SUMMARY AND CONCLUSION

Korea's electronics industry surged so rapidly in one generation that Korea became the fourth largest producer in the world in 1996, after the United States, Japan and Germany and the second largest producer of consumer electronic products and DRAM after Japan. The electronics industry has been one of the most important industries in the Korean economy. It accounted for 21% of total manufacturing value added in 1996. It is the leading export of Korea, with US$41 billion, accounting for one-third of total exports in 1996.

The electronics industry also epitomizes the pattern of industrial development of Korea: active role of the government, growth driven largely by local firms rather than by multinational subsidiaries or joint ventures, helped by a favourable external trade environment, based on well-educated, hard working domestic human resources. The government played a pivotal role in the development of the electronics industry. It created markets for domestic producers during the early years. The nation's import-substitution policy provided an attractive business opportunity for local entrepreneurs to enter the protected electronics industry. Then, the government designated electronics a strategic export industry, offering preferential financial and tax incentives. The ambitious goals of the government's export drive pushed the industry to transform itself technologically and become competitive in price and quality in the international market. This can be applied to the development of the consumer electronics industry in the 1960s and the PC industry in the 1980s.

The role of the government has changed over time, from acting as a development state to playing an indirect promotional role as Korea entered the technologically dynamic environment. The government played important roles in the process of technological transformation in the electronics industry. It was effective in the demand side of technology by creating a market through procurement. In this case the release of technical specifications stimulated the industry to expedite learning to meet the specifications in time for procurement. One illustrative example was the technical specifications of the cellular phone system in the 1990s. Despite great uncertainty over the development of the world's first CDMA system as well as the strong reservations expressed by the telephone service providers and the system manufacturers, the government decided to go along with CDMA. Whether this kind of decision making was desirable or not, there is no doubt that this was one of the deciding factors for the tremendous growth in the cellular phone market and exports. In addition, the government played an important role in the supply side of technology by strengthening public R&D capability and promoting joint research between industry and R&D institutes and between industry and academia.

Unlike that of other developing countries, the growth of the Korean electronics industry has been largely driven by Korean *chaebol* and other local firms rather than by multinational subsidiaries or joint ventures. Reverse-engineering and adaptation efforts of local firms were very important as Korea depended more upon capital goods imports than FDI for technology imports. When technology was mature and simple, local firms reverse-engineered foreign products. When technology was beyond the capacity of local firms, pioneering firms relied on foreign licensing and technical personnel, as they did with television sets. Local firms did, however, pursue efforts to assimilate the imported technology in the shortest possible time.

The rapid growth of the DRAM industry can be explained by the Korean *chaebol*'s initiative to take advantage of the technological characteristics of the industry. In the DRAM industry technological innovation within the same generation chip is oriented towards process innovation to reduce unit costs, and thus scale matters in this respect. The Korean *chaebol* were in a strong position to generate the necessary financial resources through internal earnings as well as foreign credit and syndicated loans. They used these mechanisms to enter the highly capital-intensive VLSIC production and succeeded in capturing a substantial share of the world market.

The electronics industry has also been greatly dependent upon foreign trade. It has been heavily export oriented. Foreign shipments have accounted for more than 50% of the output of the consumer electronics and semiconductor industries. It has also relied heavily upon imported capital equipment and technology. The Korean government's determination to promote the electronics industry as a major export sector was instrumental in the development of the industry since electronics products have been the most heavily traded products in the world market. At the same time the nature of economic openness made the role of the government as a promoter of an industry rather limited. As shown in the case of consumer electronics and PCs, a shift in the structure of international competition makes industries vulnerable to the emergence of low-cost producers such as the new NIEs and new developments in product innovations among the producers from advanced countries.

10

The Hong Kong Model of Development Revisited

Stephen W.K. Chiu and Tai-Lok Lui

I. INTRODUCTION

Hong Kong, as one of the East Asian NIEs (newly industrialized economies), shares several similarities with the other NIEs (Singapore, South Korea and Taiwan). Not only has it enjoyed a remarkable near double-digit growth for the past three decades, it has also shared with the others the pattern of export-oriented industrialization, under which manufactured goods have accounted for the lion's share of the total merchandise exports. Nevertheless, Hong Kong is also unique among the East Asian NIEs in the state's relatively non-interventionist strategy of development. In contrast to the other NIEs, Hong Kong's colonial state is said to have refrained from adopting an active industrial policy in pushing for the industrialization, and it has largely allowed the market mechanism to allocate resources and private firms to make their own investment decisions.

As such, Hong Kong appears to conform, much more than the other East Asian countries, to the neo-liberal model of economic development as espoused by the World Bank and other liberal economists. For example, in the World Bank's *East Asian Miracle*, it is found that total factor productivity (TFP) growth for Hong Kong is much higher than the other East Asian economies (World Bank 1993, p. 64).[1] The estimate for technical efficiency change is also the highest for Hong Kong compared with other Asian economies (World Bank 1993, p. 69). Similarly, in its discussion of the labor market, the World Bank attributes the flexibility in Hong Kong's labor market to its decentralized enterprise bargaining which is also a result of the absence of state interventions in the labor market (World Bank 1995, p. 83).

An analysis of the Hong Kong experience of industrial revolution, therefore, will help us put the World Bank's neo-liberal model of economic development in proper perspective. As Hong Kong most resembles the ideal type of East Asian development model than the other East Asian countries, examining the Hong Kong model of development allows us to decipher the complexities of developmental experiences in the region. In this chapter we shall review in the following three sections the historical and institutional contexts of Hong Kong's post-war industrial takeoff and the recent restructuring of the economy. What constitutes the Hong Kong model of industrial development and what are the long-term effects of this model will be the focus of this chapter. In the fifth section we shall discuss the relationship between the political regime and development strategy in the post-war era. Finally, the impact of the recent financial crisis and the response of the government are briefly discussed. In another chapter (Chapter 11 in this book) we shall pursue the argument developed in this chapter by examining the development of two major industries in Hong Kong's post-war development: garment-making and electronics.

II. THE REGIONAL AND GEOPOLITICAL ROOTS OF HONG KONG DEVELOPMENT

Before World War II the Guomindang (GMD or the Nationalist Party) government in Nanjing began to recover sovereignty over a number of foreign settlements and treaty ports in China. Hong Kong, however, remained a British colony. Britain was determined to hold on to this Far East colony because Britain conducted a prosperous entrepôt trade with China and Southeast Asia through Hong Kong. As a result of a century of entrepôt development, Hong Kong on the eve of World War II had developed a sophisticated institutional framework of commerce and finance as well as comprehensive infrastructural supports (Haggard 1990). A dominant capitalist class, headed by British-origin merchants and bankers, became entrenched in the economy and enjoyed a cosy alliance with the colonial state (Chiu 1994). In addition, manufacturing industries also began to emerge to serve entrepôt activities as well as the consumer demands in the South China hinterland and the Southeast Asian region.

The Japanese wartime occupation disrupted the Hong Kong economy momentarily, but the rehabilitation process was swift enough to allow normal entrepôt activities to recover less than a year after the war ended. In 1949, after the Chinese communists defeated the GMD and "liberated" the mainland, Hong Kong experienced a sudden influx of refugees. Hong Kong's population jumped from 1,600,000 in 1941 to over 2,360,000 in 1950 as a result. Hambro (1955, p. 162) estimated that in 1954 alone about 667,000 mainland refugees fled to Hong Kong for political and economic reasons. This massive population increase subsequently imposed a back-breaking burden on the colony in the early 1950s.

The Korean War dealt another blow to Hong Kong's entrepôt economy. In June 1951 the war prompted the United Nations to impose an embargo on Chinese trade, which crippled the Hong Kong economy, since China was the colony's largest trading partner. In 1954 Hong Kong's total value of trade was a meagre 60% of its 1948 level (Szczepanik 1958, p. 45). Apart from the embargo, entrepôt trade with China also declined in the 1950s because of the communist regime's rigid control of foreign investment, imports and exports. The immediate effects of the embargo and the decline in entrepôt trade were disastrous. Including the direct loss of earnings from entrepôt trade and of indirect earnings through warehousing, transport, banking and insurance services, Hong Kong's real GDP fell by 5.5% in 1951 (Ho 1979).

Despite the serious economic problems in the early 1950s, the changing nature of the post-war capitalist world economy and the East Asian region changed the fortune of the Hong Kong economy. After World War II the United States emerged as the new hegemonic power in the capitalist world economy. Under American leadership the post-war world economy became much more liberal, multilateral and interdependent, resulting in a global expansion in trade under American free-trade policy. These conditions provided an excellent opportunity for developing countries to strive for upward mobility in the world economy.

In response to the Chinese communist revolution in East Asia, the United States initiated several actions that indirectly fostered the economic development of East Asian NIEs. The United States sent warships to protect the defeated GMD in Taiwan, dispatched soldiers to fight against the communists in Korea, supported counter-revolutionary activities in China, froze mainland Chinese assets in the United States, imposed an economic embargo on mainland Chinese products, prevented mainland China from gaining a seat in the United Nations and waged ideological attacks on Chinese "communist totalitarianism" in the mass media.

In order to build up a strong capitalist Asia as a bulwark against the spread of communism, the United States provided economic aid, industrial contracts and open American markets to its East Asian allies. While other colonial powers controlled East Asia before the war, now the United States, as the new dominant power, built up a dollar bloc in the area.

Hong Kong in particular benefited from America's East Asian order. In fact, Hong Kong owed its continued existence to the Cold War. Without U.S. intervention in the Cold War, there would neither be two Chinas nor two Koreas; Hong Kong would have been returned to China long before 1997. As a result of American hegemony in East Asia, Hong Kong was gradually pulled into the new international division of labor in which the capitalist states in East Asia supplied consumer products to advanced industrial countries in exchange for technology, capital and producers' goods. However, also behind the push for Hong Kong to enter the U.S.-led world economy was the regional dynamics in East Asia, whereby the isolation of communist China from the capitalist world economy closed off possibilities of a more regionalist development trajectory in East Asia. The United Nations' embargo on Chinese trade put an abrupt halt to trade between mainland China and its trading partners — Hong Kong, South Korea, and Taiwan — pushing them away from links with the big Chinese hinterland and towards the U.S-led world economy. Furthermore, the process of decolonization in Southeast Asia brought into existence a number of nationalist regimes which installed import barriers to protect their domestic markets. This closing off of Southeast Asian markets further pushed Hong Kong to search for new markets in the Western industrial states in the late 1950s.

Several "windfall profits" from the Chinese communist revolution also enabled Hong Kong to start its industrial revolution. For example, the "liberation" of Shanghai by the Chinese communists prompted a large number of Shanghainese textile firms to divert their production to Hong Kong (Vogel 1991; Wong 1988). In addition, the massive inflow of refugees from China, many of whom had industrial employment experience, created a pool of potential entrepreneurs willing to work hard and take the risk of setting up manufacturing firms. The result was a mushrooming of small firms with low-level capital investment and technology, firms which tapped into the extensive commercial networks established throughout Hong Kong's entrepôt history, as well as into the abundant supply of cheap and diligent refugee workers. This particular conjuncture of refugee capital, refugee labour, and pre-existing entrepôt trading networks provided the impetus for Hong Kong's export-oriented industrialization in the early 1950s. Ironically, in other words, the best of socialist China's assets in capital and labor suddenly became transplanted in Hong Kong to reap the benefits of the post-war economic upswing of the capitalist world-economy. Coupled with its solid pre-war foundation in trade and manufacturing, Hong Kong thus gained a head start over the other East Asian NIEs in promoting export-oriented industrialization. Additionally, in the 1950s South Korea and Taiwan were still preoccupied with their import-substitution industrialization, while Singapore was caught up with its decolonization turmoil.

This voluntary flight from socialism, however, was only a part of the larger conflict between the United States and the emergent Chinese socialist state. In the midst of the Cold War, U.S. policy makers supported the Nationalist government in Taiwan, sent troops to Korea and imposed an economic blockade on China. Such heightened hostility from the capitalist power bloc explained why China did not reclaim control of Hong Kong right after the communist revolution. Due to its colonial status, Hong Kong was the only port where China had access to foreign currency to buy the necessary foreign equipment. As a result, China was very willing to supply food products, raw materials and even water to Hong Kong in exchange for this needed foreign currency — earning an estimated 30 to 40% from its foreign currency from the Hong Kong trade (Pye 1983, p. 461). Observing this peculiar policy of China, Kraus (1979, p. 256) insightfully remarks that "geographical isolation permits the People's Republic of China to benefit from bourgeois skills [of Hong Kong] without sustaining the cost of internal capitalist institutions". The "unequal exchange" of low-priced food from socialist China and the Hong Kong currency also subsidized the Hong Kong economy, lowered Hong Kong's cost of living and strengthened the competitive power of Hong Kong in the world market (Youngson 1983).

III. THE INSTITUTIONAL CONTEXT: THE LAISSEZ-FAIRE STATE

The role of the colonial state in Hong Kong's industrial development was facilitating rather than guiding and indirect rather than direct (Chiu 1994). Indeed, a low level of state intervention in the economy had been the dominant style of economic management in the early period of industrialization, that is, in the 1950s and 1960s. What the colonial state actually did to promote industrial growth reveals a relatively limited scope of state action, and a very low level of assistance to the development of industrial firms. Most of the promotion efforts were connected with the marketing of products overseas. The first one was the establishment of a system of certification of origin of Hong Kong manufactured exports. The other important aspect of industrial promotion by the Hong Kong government was an extensive publicity campaign about Hong Kong's manufacturing industries. The first such venture was Hong Kong's participation in the 1948 British Industries Fair. Subsequently, Hong Kong had an exhibit at the annual fair for the next seven years. From 1954 onwards, the colonial state arranged displays of local manufactured products in Seattle, Toronto, Frankfurt and New York. Apart from participation in trade fairs, the colonial state published various guides for foreign buyers, furnishing them with commercial information concerning Hong Kong. From 1953 the state also published the *Commerce, Industry and Finance Directory*, an irregular publication containing useful information about Hong Kong's economy for foreign buyers. Then in 1954, the Commerce and Industry Department began to publish a monthly *Trade Bulletin*, circulating among overseas businessmen.

Certification of origin, participation in trade fairs and trade publications more or less exhausted what the colonial state did to selectively promote industrial growth. Still, we do not agree with the portrayal of Hong Kong as a totally *laissez-faire* economy, in which the state had no significant impact on the economy. While the Hong Kong state was a far cry from the development states in East Asia, it did play a major facilitating role with respect to economic growth in general. First, it offered an attractive regulatory framework in which businessmen could operate. Laws and statutes followed the British system, with its unambiguous commitment to and definition of private property. The statutes regulating the economy were also clear and simple, facilitating business calculations. The formation of companies, public or private, limited or unlimited, was easy and straightforward. Second, the colonial state still supplied the basic infrastructure for economic activities. It built and managed roads, railways, harbours, an airport and other transport facilities. It was also the owner of the most precious factor of production in Hong Kong, land. Third, and perhaps most important, it provided low-cost housing to the majority of working-class households, contributing significantly to the socialization of collective consumption and to the prevention of a wage spiral in the course of rapid industrialization. The public health system provided cheap medical services to all citizens and operated the largest hospital system in the territory. Most of the primary and secondary schools in Hong Kong were subsidized by public funding, and almost all the universities were publicly funded. The state-subvented education system was the most important agent of human resources development.

On labor-market policies the colonial state was also remarkably hands-off. In contrast to other East Asian NIEs, where the state maintained a heavy-handed presence in industrial relations, the Hong Kong state preferred to stay away from directing the setting of wages and other terms of employment. It clung on to the "voluntarist" tradition and let employers and workers negotiate between themselves for the terms of buying and selling labor power. It established a "voluntarist" framework of industrial relations in which no legal compulsion was imposed to govern the relations between employers and employees. It imposed few controls on trade union activities but neither did it encourage them. Collective bargaining was allowed but there was no legal provision for union recognition and collective agreements, even if they were concluded, carried no legal status. During the first few decades of industrial development, the state only established a minimal statutory floor of employment conditions regarding safety and health and the employment of women and child workers. Only in the 1970s did it progressively expand the scope of legal protection of workers' rights (Chiu and Levin 1996). As a result, industrial relations in Hong Kong were highly decentralized and informal, with few traces of state intervention.

The point, however, is not whether Hong Kong was *laissez-faire* or not. In contrast to the other East Asian states, the colonial state was especially reluctant to offer *selective* assistance to the development of manufacturing industries. What is more conspicuous from a comparative perspective, however, is not what the colonial state had done, but what it had not done. In fact, whatever it had done for industrial development, the other East Asian states had done more. It offered services which were available universally to all sectors and firms, but had not practised the kind of industrial targeting implicit in East Asian industrial policies. For instance, it had no role, direct or indirect, in industrial financing and declined repeatedly the calls for the establishment of an industrial bank. State ownership of public enterprises was also a rare phenomenon. It maintained a low tax environment for *all* enterprises and meted out no special tax relief for the manufacturing industries.

Chiu has illustrated the operation of Hong Kong's non-interventionist industrial policy with two public policies in the 1950s (Chiu 1994). First, during the mid-1950s the shortage of land for industrial development prompted the state to develop new industrial areas in the outskirts of the urban area. Industrialists demanded that such new land should be sold to them by private tender individually. This would have allowed the state to offer land for industries or firms which were deemed particularly desirable, just as what the Singaporean state did. Nevertheless, the state rejected the proposal and insisted on selling the newly available land by public auction. Second, for the entire 1950s industrialists complained about the inadequate supply of fund to manufacturing by the commercial banks. They wanted the state to follow the practice of many developing countries and establish an industrial bank with the function of lending long-term loans to industries at low interest rates. Again, the state rejected the proposal and manufacturers had to rely on self-financing and the limited lending from commercial banks to finance their operations.

IV. DE-INDUSTRIALIZATION AND ECONOMIC RESTRUCTURING SINCE THE 1980S

Boosted by rapid industrial and export growth (reviewed in Chapter 11), Hong Kong's economy enjoyed near double-digit growth from the 1960s. Stepping into the 1990s, however, the Hong Kong economy appeared to have settled down to a pattern of slow growth. Real economic growth rates in the first few years of the 1990s were obviously lower than the late 1980s (see Table 10.1). Average GDP annual growth

TABLE 10.1 Overview of the Hong Kong Economy, 1998–97

	1988	1989	1990	1991	1992	1993	1994	1995	1996	1997
Nominal GDP (HK$ billion)	455.0	523.9	582.5	668.5	779.3	897.5	1,010.9	1,077.1	1,192.6	1,339.1
Real GDP growth (%)	8.0	2.6	3.4	5.1	6.3	6.1	5.4	3.9	4.7	5.3
Private consumption	8.3	3.4	5.7	8.6	8.5	7.5	6.7	1.6	4.4	6.6
Government consumption	3.7	5.2	5.5	7.7	7.2	2.2	3.9	3.2	4.6	2.4
Gross domestic capital formation	6.5	3.5	8.1	9.3	9.2	3.7	15.7	10.7	11.1	15.9
Total exports of goods	27.3	10.6	9.6	17.3	19.8	13.5	10.4	12	4.8	6.1
Domestic exports	9.0	0.1	-0.5	0.5	0.2	-4.5	-2.3	2	-8.4	2.1
Re-exports	45.7	18.6	16.0	26.5	28.3	19.6	13.8	14.3	7.5	6.8
Imports of goods	26.6	8.9	11.4	19.0	22.2	12.7	14.0	13.8	4.3	7.1
Exports of services	9.9	2.3	3.6	4.7	10.6	8.0	6.5	4.8	6.2	-0.6
Imports of services	15.5	5.7	12.1	11.3	9.7	5.8	8.8	2.1	2.0	4.2
Per capita GDP (HK$1,000)	80.9	92.1	102.1	116.2	134.7	152.1	167.5	174.9	188.9	206.0
Population (million)	5.7	5.7	5.7	5.8	5.8	5.9	6.0	6.2	6.3	6.5

NOTE: Real figures measured in constant 1990 dollars.
SOURCE: Census and Statistics Department (1998c).

rates from 1985 to 1989 and 1990 to 1994 were 6.96% and 5.22% respectively. GDP growth rebounded from the cyclical low of 2.6% in 1989 and rose steadily to 6.3% and 6.1% in 1992 and 1993 respectively. Such a revival was, of course, much less spectacular than the ones which Hong Kong was accustomed to in the previous decades but the economy had apparently become more stable. The real GDP growth rate appeared to exhibit a long-term downward trend, dropping steadily to 4.7% in 1996. With the Asian financial crisis inducing high interest rates and a (property and stock) market slump, GDP growth began to slacken in 1997. While the annual figure still recorded a 5.3% growth, the economy slipped into recession from October 1997. Government statistics show a 5.2% decline in the second quarter of 1998 compared with the previous year (Census and Statistics Department 1998d). According to a forecast by the International Monetary Fund (IMF), real GDP would contract by 5% in 1998 and stabilize at zero growth in 1999 (IMF 1998, p. 25).

On the external trade front, total exports of goods continued to grow in real terms, albeit at a much slower rate. Out of this, re-exports rose by only 7.5% in 1996, significantly below the double-digit growth in the previous years. In addition, domestic exports also declined significantly by 8.4% in 1996, only to increase by 2.1% in 1997. In fact, domestic exports have been stagnant since 1989, only to be compensated by robust growth in re-exports. This appears to signal Hong Kong's transformation from an export-oriented economy to a transhipment centre. Gross domestic fixed capital formation recorded an impressive growth rate of 15.9% in 1997 after a long period of slow growth in the 1980s, while the public sector played an important role in this revival of investment. Government infrastructural projects and private sector property development before the bursting of the bubble economy contributed to the high 15.9% growth in 1997. Growth in private consumption expenditures, on the other hand, began to slacken in 1995 and 1996, but 1997 saw a rebound in private consumption owing to the hand-over celebrations and the bubble economy. Government consumption had been holding steady and continued to be an important component of overall economic growth.

More importantly, the cyclical downturn coincided with the tremendous structural transformation the economy was undergoing. In the 1980s the share of manufacturing industries in the national product declined relative to other sectors. The tertiary sector also overtook manufacturing as the high-growth sector. In terms of contribution to the GDP, financing and business services had very impressive growth rates in the past few years, as had the commerce (wholesale, retail, export and import trades, and hotels and restaurants) sector (Table 10.2).

The structural transformation of the Hong Kong economy is partly a reflection of the restructuring in the manufacturing sector since the mid-1980s. While the employment implications of the industrial restructuring will be discussed in the next section, here we will focus on the underlying mechanism of the process: massive outward relocation of manufacturing production (see also Lui and Chiu 1993; Lui 1994). Due to the cultural and geographical proximity, most of the outward investment naturally went to China. In 1990, when a survey included a question asking the locations of the respondents' overseas plants, 92% said they were in China with Guangdong province accounting for 85%. An abundant supply of low-cost land and labor and the implementation of market reforms have prompted manufacturers in Hong Kong to relocate their production bases across the border. Direct investment in both directions between Hong Kong and China has further tied the two economies together. So besides the inflow of Chinese investment to Hong Kong, Hong Kong investment topped all other countries and grew at a rapid rate. As at the end of 1995 the value of realized Hong Kong direct investment in China was US$20.4 billion. Some 42% of all foreign direct investment came from Hong Kong (China Statistical Yearbook 1996, p. 598). In Guangdong province alone, Hong Kong manufacturers operated 25,000 processing factories and employed three million workers in 1993 (Federation of Hong Kong Industries 1993, p. 3).

The prime variable in Hong Kong's labor market changes undoubtedly is the dazzling pace of industrial restructuring and structural change. The magnitude of change can perhaps be gauged by the sectoral distribution in employment, as shown in Table 10.3. Even in absolute terms, the number of workers employed in manufacturing was dwindling in the 1980s. In line with the relocation of manufacturing production to low-cost countries, the number of workers engaged in manufacturing, as reported by the General Household Survey was almost halved from 918,600 in 1987 to 558,300 in 1994. The commerce sector (wholesale and retail trade and import/export) now becomes the largest employer, increasing its employment from 627,900 to 849,000 during the same period. The financial and business services sector also re-

TABLE 10.2 Hong Kong: GDP by Sector (in percentages)

Year	Agriculture, Fishing and Quarrying	Manufacturing	Electricity and Water	Construction	Wholesale, Retail and Import/ Export Trades, and Hotels Restaurants	Transport, Storage and Communications	Financing, Insurance, Real Estate and Business Services	Community, Social and Personal Services	Ownership of Premises	Charges of Financial Intermediation Services (indirectly measured)	GDP at Factor Cost (HK$ million, production-based estimates)
1986	0.5	22.6	2.8	4.8	22.3	8.2	17.0	16.0	10.2	-4.4	296,008
1987	0.5	22.0	2.6	4.6	24.3	8.6	17.9	14.5	9.8	-4.9	366,795
1988	0.4	20.5	2.3	4.7	25.1	9.1	18.9	13.9	9.9	-4.9	438,255
1989	0.3	19.3	2.2	5.2	25.0	9.0	19.5	14.1	10.3	-4.8	498,935
1990	0.3	17.6	2.3	5.4	25.2	9.5	20.2	14.5	10.6	-5.5	559,446
1991	0.2	15.4	2.1	5.5	25.9	9.6	22.7	14.9	10.9	-7.3	631,514
1992	0.2	13.6	2.1	5.1	26.1	9.7	24.4	15.1	11.1	-7.5	732,120
1993	0.2	11.2	2.1	5.2	27.0	9.5	25.8	15.7	10.8	-7.6	830,169
1994	0.2	9.2	2.3	4.9	26.2	9.7	26.8	15.9	12.2	-7.4	950,172
1995	0.1	8.8	2.3	4.9	27.4	9.8	24.9	17.1	12.7	-8.0	1,016,115
1996	0.1	7.3	2.4	5.8	26.6	9.8	25.2	17.6	13.0	-7.9	1,193,072

SOURCE: Census and Statistics Department (1998c).

TABLE 10.3   Hong Kong: Distribution of Employment by Sector (in percentages)

Year	Manufacturing	Construction	Commerce	Transport and Communications	Finance and Business	Services	Others	Total (1,000)
1981	39.2	8.8	20.8	7.0	5.0	17.3	1.9	2,407.0
1982	37.2	8.5	21.5	7.6	5.3	18.0	1.8	2,404.1
1983	36.3	8.1	21.8	7.7	5.5	18.8	1.8	2,426.7
1984	37.0	7.6	22.1	7.9	5.3	18.5	1.6	2,505.2
1985	36.1	7.5	22.6	8.1	5.8	17.5	2.3	2,543.3
1986	35.0	7.7	23.0	8.3	6.2	17.6	2.3	2,625.4
1987	34.2	8.0	23.4	8.5	6.4	17.3	2.3	2,688.5
1988	32.0	8.5	24.3	9.0	6.8	17.6	1.9	2,740.7
1989	29.7	8.4	24.9	9.6	7.4	18.2	1.8	2,748.6
1990	27.7	8.3	25.9	9.9	7.7	18.9	1.6	2,741.0
1991	26.1	8.2	26.7	10.0	8.3	19.3	1.5	2,793.8
1992	23.9	8.5	27.4	10.7	8.4	19.6	1.4	2,787.2
1993	21.5	8.0	28.5	11.2	9.5	20.0	1.3	2,865.0
1994	18.8	7.9	28.6	11.4	11.5	20.2	1.5	2,968.5
1995	17.5	8.1	28.9	11.4	11.6	21.5	1.1	3,012.7
1996	15	9.4	29.8	10.9	12.1	21.6	1.1	3,063.2
1997	14.1	9.7	30.2	11.0	12.7	21.2	1.0	3,144.7

NOTE: Figures before 1997 are fourth-quarter figures. The figures for 1997 are quarterly averages.
SOURCES: Census and Statistics Department, *Quarterly Report on General Household Survey*, various years.

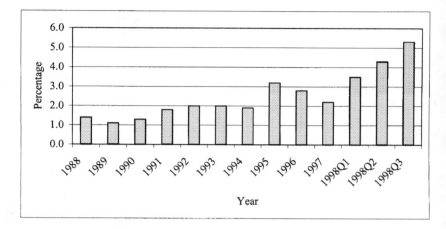

FIGURE 10.1 Hong Kong: Unemployment Rates, 1988–98.
SOURCES: Census and Statistics Department, Report of Employment, Vacancies and Payroll Statistics (1991, 1998).

corded a growth in workers engaged. In the decade before 1994 manufacturing employment slumped by 39.2%, while that for financial and business services and transport and communications increased by 132% and 64% respectively. The growth rates were equally impressive for commerce and community services. The trend continued well into 1997, with the share of manufacturing employment dropping further while that of the commerce sector increased.

After a period of having a tight labor market, unemployment began to rise in the 1990s. Between 1992 and 1994, 181,000 more persons entered the labor market than those who left. Coupled with the relocation of low-skill manufacturing jobs overseas, the level of unemployment climbed steadily (Figure 10.1). The unemployment rate in 1995 was 3.2%, which was the highest figure since the mid-1980s. The unemployment rate began to drop in 1996. However, since the onset of the Asian financial crisis, unemployment began to rise again. In the third quarter of 1998 the unemployment rate stood at 5.3%, an all-time high in recent decades. The IMF estimated that the unemployment rate would average 5% for the four quarters of the year and reach 5.7% in 1999 (IMF 1998, p. 25).

TABLE 10.4   Growth of Real Wages 1990–98 (in percentages)

	1990	1991	1992	1993	1994	1995	1996	1997	1998 (first quarter)
Craftsmen and operatives	2.4	–1.1	0.0	1.7	–2.1	–3.6	1.9	1.4	–2.1
Non-production workers to supervisory level	2.9	–0.8	0.4	2.6	1.5	–1.3	0.9	1.7	0.2
Middle management and professionals	14.3	3.8	3.5	4.6	4.1	3.8	3.3	3.5	—

NOTE: Wages for craftsmen and operatives and other non-production workers are September figures. Figures for managerial employees refer to Real Salary Index (B) in June of the year. SOURCES: Census and Statistics Department, *Report of Employment, Vacancies and Payroll Statistics* (1991, 1998).

As seen in Table 10.4, real wages grew at a slow rate for craftsmen and operatives, and actually declined in 1991, 1994 and 1995. Middle-level employees like clerical and sales workers enjoyed a more healthy growth, but their wages also dropped 1.3% in 1995. The high inflation rate, as discussed, has continued to erode the growth in money wages. Aggregate figures are likely to mask divergent trends across different sectors, as Hong Kong experienced the rapid structural transformation. Operatives in the manufacturing industries, for example, suffered a real decline in wages over the last decade, while clerical, technical and supervisory employees in the same industries had a handsome growth (Census and Statistics Department 1998a). In retailing wages increased quickly, but restaurants and fast-food shops had only sluggish growth. The banking and insurance industries also saw a faster wage increase. The differentiation of the market position between rank-and-file workers and managerial and professional employees is also becoming obvious, as pay rises for the latter categories have exceeded those for all workers in the past few years. The Asian crisis also had a greater adverse impact on lower-level employees, as the wages for operatives and craftsmen dropped by 2.1% in March 1998 from the previous six months, although wages for supervisory employees were also stagnant.

Hence the effects of the economic restructuring on the labor market are highly differentiated. Some growth sectors enjoyed higher than average growth in real wages, while the sluggish or declining sectors had a long-term decline or stagnation. Yet the differences between sectors are still less apparent than those between different ranks and occupations. From 1994 the less-skilled occupations like service workers or operatives began to see their real wages turning from stagnation to a decline. Economic restructuring in Hong Kong, therefore, widened the differentiation and inequality in the labor market.

On the whole this section shows that the *laissez-faire* development strategy managed to capitalize on the favorable international and domestic conditions in the post-war years and generate rapid growth between the 1960s and 1980s. Yet as the colonial state clung on to the same set of policies in the 1980s, a process of de-industrialization and economic restructuring set in and the economy shifted from a manufacturing and export-oriented to a service-centred one. In Chapter 11 we are going to further discuss the impact of the *laissez-faire* strategy on the industrial sector. In the following sections we will be examining some of the political underpinnings of the continuation of the policy. While economic growth can still be regarded as respectable for most of the 1990s until the Asian crisis of 1997, we can still discern the accentuation of inequality and rising employment problems since the 1990s.

V. POLITICAL REGIME AND ECONOMIC DEVELOPMENT

A critical issue in the debate over the East Asian miracle has been the relationship between the form of the political regime and economic development. Free market advocates, for example, have argued that liberal democracy comes hand in hand with a free market and a limited government, which are necessarily conducive to economic growth. More guarantees in individual liberty, in this view, appear to be consonant with the protection of private property and freedom of business. The statistics, on the other hand, contend that state intervention is not necessarily a bad thing, and hence by implication, restriction of individual liberty is sometimes a necessary evil. The unfettered market is merely a myth, so public authority must step up to protect the public interest. At times this line of argument is echoed in the arguments for the "Asian Way" in which a strong but benign government becomes the custodian of the long-term national interest and pushes forward economic growth. Whether this government is democratic or authoritarian is immaterial because a high level of consensus is present in the society. Hence the level of social support for and legitimacy of the strong state is high.

The Hong Kong case does not seem to conform to these two polar views. To begin with, it had long been an authoritarian regime but Hong Kong is unique in terms of its state-society relationship. The other East Asian industrializing states, as described by Cumings (1987), are largely characterized by authoritarianism and repression, allowing these states to constrain social consumption and popular demand as well as maintain political stability. However, in sharp contrast to the bureaucratic-authoritarian regime of other Asian NIEs, the colonial state of Hong Kong was relatively liberal, exhibiting a high degree of political tolerance towards dissent. It is often pointed out Hong Kong is a free society whose people enjoy various civil rights — its citizens are free to criticize the Hong Kong state, free to form political organizations, free to protest, etc. Furthermore, as noted above, trade unions in Hong Kong were given a freedom to operate unsurpassed in the other East Asian NIEs.

Business interests, however, were well represented in the policy-making process. In Ngo's (1997) words, there was a process of "institutionalization of business in politics" through the co-optation of business representatives into the political establishment. Chiu (1994) describes this system as an alliance between the colonial state and the dominant commercial-financial bourgeoisie with the industrialists as a secondary partner in the coalition. The *laissez-faire* strategy or the absence of selective intervention therefore represented the dominance of commercial and financial interests. Ngo (1997), on the other hand, depicts this not in terms of state-business collusion but as the presence of a "substantive consent" among the ruling élite. In this view there is a consensus over a definite set of policy options available to the bureaucrats and a specific range of privileges for the business élite. Hence the acceptance of the *laissez-faire* policy represented a kind of self-restraint on the part of the business élite towards rent-seeking behaviour. No public resources were devoted to the pursuit of private interests in a private manner, fearing that this would have fuelled conflicts among the business élite.

In one way or another, however, these views agree that business interests had been well served under the authoritarian colonial governance. Choi (1997), for example, highlights the authoritarian side of the colonial state as a repressive agent (albeit an semi-autonomous one) *vis-à-vis* the working class. Chiu (1994) also delineates the series of working-class challenges to capitalist and colonial rule as a context for the consolidation of the state-business alliance before World War II. Social welfare provisions, especially the redistributive kind without direct economic benefits, were kept to a minimum and protection of labor rights had been making only incremental improvements (Chiu and Levin 1996). Only after the popular turmoil in 1966 and 1967 did the colonial state move steadily to increase its protection of labor rights. Only on the last day (literally) of colonial rule did the colonial state pass an ordinance giving statutory rights of collective bargaining to trade unions.

Authoritarianism and business interests thus appeared to be in perfect harmony in Hong Kong. On the other hand, however, the authoritarianism and the narrowness of the social bases of the colonial regime also help account for the stubborn upholding of the *laissez-faire* strategy which led to the specific pattern of economic restructuring described in the previous section. As mentioned, *laissez-faire* was clearly a result of the close relations between the business élite and the colonial state. Under the closed colonial regime, it appeared that the only social group that mattered was the business community. The state élite needed only to forge an alliance (or "substantive consent" in Ngo's words) with the business élite in order to ensure the latter's continual investment in Hong Kong. As for the popular classes, the colonial regime provided for little linkages between the state and the masses. The primary objective of the state towards the masses was not to solicit active support through elections but acquiescence. If the working class were content to pursue their individual material gains in a colonial capitalist system, then colonial rule would remain unchallenged by popular pressures. Only when popular pressures became mounted, such as in 1967, would the state move to enlarge its own role in social welfare provisions or setting legal regulations of employment.

Under such kinds of relationship with the various social groupings, *laissez-faire* became the ideal way for the colonial state to cement its alliance with the business community while generating a reasonable level of growth and employment that satisfied the masses. Even when the *laissez-faire* strategy seemed to be running out of steam in the 1980s and became inimical to the upgrading of local industries, the state remained unconcerned. The business community, especially its commercial and financial wing, appeared to be happy in making profits in real estate or other commercial activities. Although the manufacturers did demand state assistance in upgrading, they had at the same time sought to resolve their own problems without the state's help. Past experience told them that it would be unlikely for the state to come to their assistance. Hence their dominant response to changes in the business environment was to look for cheaper locations of production rather than invest in upgrading. The resultant expansion in production volume in the new production sites allowed many manufacturers to enjoy a long spell of prosperity. The growing integration of China through both investment from China and investment from Hong Kong to China then further fuelled the bubble economy *and* the real sector. Therefore, while local manufacturing production suffered from decline and did not experience much technical upgrading, the business community, including manufacturers, was enjoying a period of steady growth before the handover of sovereignty in 1997.

As mentioned, the party that appeared to have suffered from this process consisted of the workers. Without upgrading in the industry, local production continued to shrink. With manufacturing suffering from absolute decline, workers were displaced from manufacturing employment. Some of them had been working in manufacturing for over ten or even 20 years. Without a proactive strategy of restructuring, the colonial state allowed the market mechanism to dominate the process of de-industrialization. When the restructuring process ran its course, workers suddenly realized that their long experience in manufacturing production as well as their renowned production skills had become obsolete. Little was done to ease their transition to other sectors. State policy on retraining began in 1992. And even then, efforts at retraining were too little, too late.[2]

What is more, without a tradition of tripartite co-operation and a long-term vision, the colonial state found its hands tied when it tried to prolong the life of some of the labor-intensive manufacturing industries in Hong Kong. Under the employers' claims of labor shortage, the state attempted to import foreign workers into designated sectors.[3] Nevertheless, the trade unions cried foul and resisted steadfastly. They claimed that there was no shortage and the employers merely wanted to replace local workers with cheaper foreign workers. In the end only a very small-scale scheme of importing foreign workers was implemented, which pleased neither side. Trade unions continued to criticize the program while employers gave up hope of producing in Hong Kong. A major problem in this case is that neither side was willing to accept the importation of foreign workers as a temporary measure for long-term upgrading. Employers merely claimed that they could not hire enough workers, masking their concurrent move of switching production to other countries. Neither the manufacturers nor the state was willing to come out and say that cheaper labor power was necessary to ease the process of restructuring in order to push companies towards long-term upgrading. The trade unions, on the other hand, saw little benefits in accepting the importation scheme. They were accused of short-termism by the employers, but they had to, for there was no institutional mechanism to generate a long-term perspective. The colonial state, being a closed one, allowed no role for the trade unions in policymaking. The trade unions had practically no experience of co-operating with employers and the state for a long-term objective.

Under such circumstances a stalemate was produced while manufacturing continued to shrink from the 1980s. In deference to the free market no long-term development strategy was proposed. The major partner to the colonial state, the business community, also saw no immediate need or feasibility for such a strategy. The manufacturers eventually settled on a short-term, individualistic strategy of relocation. The colonial bureaucrats were insulated from popular demands of workers for guarantees of their long-term employment opportunities. The masses were not organized, so protests were rare. Without the need to answer to the public through elections, the absence of social protests or conflicts was sufficient for the colonial bureaucrats to stick to the tried *laissez-faire* strategy. In fact, the trade unions were the most vocal advocates for a more active industrial policy in the last decade. Unfortunately their lack of institutional linkages to the colonial state rendered their lobbying efforts futile.

Thus the Hong Kong experience demonstrated that authoritarianism could be compatible with free-market economic growth if there was an efficient bureaucracy coupled with sufficient allowance for individual and civil liberty. Nevertheless, it also demonstrated how the authoritarian regime failed to respond to popular demand and change to a more activist approach in assisting the upgrading of local industries. The net result is short-term gain for local capitalists but long-term loss in good employment opportunities for lower-level employees. With the current economic downturn and the bursting of the bubble economy, it also appears that the long-term prosperity of the Hong Kong economy rests on shaky grounds.

VI. CONCLUSION: FUTURE DEVELOPMENT PROSPECTS AND THE CHANGING ROLE OF THE STATE

The financial crisis in East and Southeast Asia finally hit Hong Kong by the end of 1997. In order to defend attacks on the linked exchange rate system between the U.S. dollar and the Hong Kong dollar, the Monetary Authority raised the interest rate to deter speculators from borrowing Hong Kong dollars and re-selling them in the open market. As a result, the stock market suffered. Fearful of the high interest rate and a plan of the government to increase the supply of houses, the property market also collapsed. The bursting of the property bubble thus led to a recession in the economy, which long depended on do-mestic consumption as a source of growth. At the same time a string of bad news was also released by local corporations, mainly about their failed ventures in Southeast Asia. For example, the Peregrine group, which invested heavily in an Indonesian project, was liquidated as the Indonesian economy suffered from a meltdown.

From the perspective of this chapter, the current economic problems that Hong Kong is facing are a result of both structural and cyclical factors. It is certainly a result of the reversal in the business cycle as all the East and Southeast Asian economies are experiencing a down-turn. It is, without doubt, beyond anyone's prediction and the government could do little about it. Unfortunately, however, the recession also co-incided with a long structural trend of the economy in shifting from a relatively more balanced mix of manufacturing and services to an eco-nomic structure that skewed heavily towards finance and services. Elsewhere we have voiced concern over the particular path of restruc-turing in the Hong Kong economy which resulted in little upgrading but massive relocation (Chiu, Ho and Lui 1997). Here we can only add that the current economic crisis reveals in the starkest manner the danger of such a strategy.

The government, along with a chorus of liberal economists, has claimed that the Hong Kong way of restructuring is efficient in that it has been guided predominantly by the free market and individual business decisions unfettered by state interference. They have argued that the loss of manufacturing jobs would be temporary and that services would provide more and better employment opportunities. In this view Hong Kong industries would also emerge as leaner, more advanced and highly competitive. All these predictions now appeared to be in jeopardy. On their part, liberal economists attributed Hong Kong's troubles to a piece of state intervention, the system of linked exchange rates, saying that the need to defend the pegged rate resulted in more intervention by the state in raising interest rates. One solution, they suggested, is to "Americanize" the Hong Kong dollar, by making the U.S. dollar the legal tender in Hong Kong. In monetary terms this will effectively make the Hong Kong economy a part of the United States, hence immune from the financial turbulence in the region.

The merit or feasibility of the scheme does not concern us here. What is important from our vantage point is that neoclassical economics always have a way of explaining away empirical difficulties. When Hong Kong's economy was growing, they had no trouble of attributing the prosperity to the free market that existed in Hong Kong. Yet when Hong Kong's economy witnessed a reversal, they also easily attributed this to too much state intervention. Our position, on the other hand, is that Hong Kong's current trouble is a result of letting the market dictate the course of economic development. Individual entrepreneurs and corporations, therefore, make strategic decisions on the assumption that they could expect little assistance from the state except the most universal kind. Hence their short-term calculations prevail and little effort has been placed on cultivating local technological competence or the skills of local workers. It is this failure to upgrade local production and the overwhelming dependence on finance and services that account for Hong Kong's vulnerability to the financial crisis.

In 1997, a team of researchers from the Massachusetts Institute of Technology (MIT) released a report commissioned by a consortium of public and private organizations in Hong Kong to examine the former colony's industrial future (Berger and Lester 1997). The most interesting part of the book is the analyses of the strengths and weaknesses of Hong Kong industry. We are in broad agreement with their assessment, which makes several criticisms of the Hong Kong government and manufacturing industry. They highlighted, *inter alia*, the insufficient investment by firms in human resources development, the lack of links between higher education and industry, the low investment in new technology development, the limitations of family ownership of business enterprises, the scarcity of specialized technological knowledge in government and the high labor and land costs in Hong Kong. On the other hand, they also rightly pointed out the unique strengths of Hong Kong industry in its flexibility in production, the ability to co-ordinate production processes in decentralized sites, the quality and abundance of managers, the quality of public institutions and the internationalism among companies and in the community.

One of the most outstanding features concerning the recommendations made in the book is how the authors attempted to strike a balance between working within the existing framework and breaking away from it. Given Hong Kong's renowned market-oriented non-interventionist economic policy, especially on manufacturing industry, the book's recommendations have not amounted to a radical break from this tradition. It recommended largely the strengthening of the existing institutions and an improvement of current practices. It did propose an increased level of state activity, but interventionism has no place in its vision of the Hong Kong government. This dose of realism is laudable, but still most of the recommendations read more like moral exhortations than practical programs of action. The major problem in this area is the voluntarism in the book's recommendations and the lack of an analysis of the political basis for the implementation of its recommendations. Given the inertia of firms and the government, why should public and private sector actors adopt its proposals? What is the likelihood, in the authors' own view, of the implementation of their recommendations? To be fair, the status of the book as a commissioned study would not allow the MIT team to conduct a thorough political analysis, but such an analysis is certainly useful and necessary for the understanding of the future shape of industrial policy in Hong Kong.

In this chapter we have attempted to outline an argument that given the present political structure and power alignment in the Special Administrative Region (SAR) government, it is difficult for the government to make an about-turn in terms of industrial policy unless the exogenous environment changes dramatically. The government has set up a Commission on Innovation and Technology to examine the possibility of developing high-technology industries in Hong Kong. The Chief Executive does repeatedly express his verbal support on technology development, but there has been hardly any serious attempt on the part of the state to articulate a clear direction for initiatives. In the end the constituency for state actions in technological and industrial development now does not appear to be active after so many years of production in the mainland; it no longer feels the need to do research and development (R&D) in Hong Kong. China, with its more abundant supply of technical and engineering personnel, appears to be a much more favourable location for such endeavours. The impetus and urgency for a policy change on technology and manufacturing fail to secure enthusiastic support from the business community.

Nevertheless, the onset of the Asian crisis and the downturn of Hong Kong's economy have accentuated the sense of urgency. As mentioned earlier, in 1998 Hong Kong's unemployment rate rose to over 5%, both the stock market and property market crashed, and the economy was set to record a decline. That Hong Kong has become dangerously dependent on the service and finance industries is apparent. In an opinion poll conducted in October 1998 on the citizens' attitudes towards industrial development, it was found that the vast majority of respondents (88.2%) agreed that Hong Kong's long-term development needed manufacturing. They also thought that the government should give financial assistance to manufacturing enterprises (87.9%) and that the government should support technological development and transfer the results to the private sector (71.7%).[4] While the public was still concerned about the question of fairness to other sectors if an active industrial promotion policy was pursued, the level of support for manufacturing was quite remarkable.

Under this circumstance, in September 1998 the Commission on Innovation and Technology released its first report and in October the Chief Executive gave his second policy address. In both cases signs of a change in the approach to industrial development could be detected, given the extraordinary change in the environment caused by the Asian crisis. The Commission's report (1998) puts forth a vision of Hong Kong as a centre of innovation and technology. More specifically, it envisions Hong Kong becoming a leading city in the world for the development and use of information technology, a regional centre for multimedia-based information and entertainment services, a world centre for the development of health food and pharmaceuticals based on Chinese medicine, and a leading supplier in the world of high value-added components and products. Towards this end, it proposes the establishment of an Innovation and Technology Fund with an initial injection of HK$5 billion to meet the requirements in the short to medium term. Furthermore, it proposes the setting up of a publicly funded Applied Science and Technology Research Institute to focus on midstream R&D and commercialize innovative ideas. The Chief Executive's 1998 Policy Address (Tung 1998) basically reiterates the proposals of the Commission. While details of both proposals have not been disclosed, both the fund and the institute mark a major departure from established policies. Although a variety of other funds have been established to support industries of various kinds, this one stands out by its scale. The institute also breaks off from the tradition of funding only more basic research conducted at the universities.

These initiatives are clearly more aggressive than the pre-existing policy paradigm on industrial development. Nevertheless, the government is still cautious in distancing itself from a selective policy when it insists that technology and innovation should not be exclusive to manufacturing. This is a healthy acknowledgement of the reality in Hong Kong where manufacturing is fast diminishing in importance. Yet the government has not offered a future vision for manufacturing proper in Hong Kong. Does it envision that manufacturing *production* of any kind has no future in Hong Kong, or should it exist only in very small niches? In an attempt to muddle through its policy on innovation and technology, the government fails to address some critical issues on the blueprint of Hong Kong's development. Given the fact that its technological innovation pertains to both manufacturing and services, will the new policy amount to another stimulant for the development of service industries? While it is arguable that in the age of information technology, services and manufacturing could no longer be distinguished clearly in all instances, do more conventional manufacturing activities no longer have a place in Hong Kong? Will the high-technology industries provide jobs for the multitude of unemployed?

From this perspective, South Korea or the Southeast Asian economy has an advantage over Hong Kong because their export industries are still dynamic and thriving. Given that the Western markets are less affected by the crisis in the region, it is possible for the South Korean or Southeast Asian countries to export their way out of the crisis, making export industries the dynamo of growth again. Even though their financial sectors have suffered a devastating blow, they still have export industries to count on. Yet what is left of Hong Kong? When the corporate dominoes have fallen one by one, it is difficult to imagine how

Hong Kong could still enjoy continual prosperity except wait for the financial storm to pass away. Given the initial reactions of the government, it appears that their *laissez-faire* predisposition is still very much guiding its policies. When the Chief Executive was questioned on the SAR government's strategy of getting Hong Kong out of its troubles, he merely responded that the fundamentals of Hong Kong's economy were still very sound and the people only needed to take a longer-term view of the problems. As a conclusion, we can only say that we disagree with this view and we think that there are some fundamental problems in Hong Kong's economy. The government's (past) inaction, if not its policy blunder, is one of the factors that have contributed to this malaise. We hope that the government would review its own approach to economic development and give the private sector a sense of direction. Which way is Hong Kong going and where should it be going? What is the government's vision for the future? What are the implications for alternative trajectories of development? We cannot say that the Hong Kong government has done nothing in this regard, but obviously what it has done is not enough in view of the current developments. The initiatives in recent months are promising, but we still have to wait for the details before we could assess their potential benefits.

NOTES

1. This refers to the TFP growth estimates for the sample of high-income economies only.
2. For the impact of the restructuring on women workers, see Chiu and Lee (1997).
3. See Chiu (1996a) for an account of the state's policy on the importation of foreign workers.
4. Stephen Chiu and Sunny Kwong, "Citizens' Attitude towards Industrial Development in Hong Kong: Telephone Survey Report", on behalf of the Faculty of Social Science and Hong Kong Institute of Asia-Pacific Studies, the Chinese University of Hong Kong, October 1998. In the survey 818 Hong Kong adults were randomly selected and interviewed.

REFERENCES

Berger, S. and R. Lester, eds. *Made By Hong Kong*. Hong Kong: Oxford University Press, 1997.

Best, M.H. *The New Competition: Institutions of Industrial Restructuring*. Cambridge: Polity Press, 1990.

Census and Statistics Department, Hong Kong. *Quarterly Report on General Household Survey*. Hong Kong: Government Printer, various years.

_____. *Report of Employment, Vacancies and Payroll Statistics*. Hong Kong: Government Printer, various years.

_____. (various years), *Survey of Industrial Production*. Hong Kong: Government Printer, various years.

_____. "Trading Firms with Manufacturing-Related Functions". *Hong Kong Monthly Digest of Statistics, August 1996*.

_____. "Trading Firms with Manufacturing-Related Functions". *Hong Kong Monthly Digest of Statistics, September 1997*.

Chan, T.S. *Distribution Channel Strategy for Export Marketing: The Case of Hong Kong Firms*. Ann Arbor: UMI Research Press, 1984.

Chiu, S.W.K. "The Politics of Laissez-Faire: Hong Kong's Strategy of Industrialization in Historical Perspective". Hong Kong Institute of Asia-Pacific Studies, Chinese University of Hong Kong, Occasional Paper no. 40, 1994.

_____. "The Changing labor Market and Foreign Workers in Hong Kong". *International Employment Relations Review* 2 (1996a): 55–76.

_____. "Unravelling Hong Kong's exceptionalism: the politics of laissez-faire in the industrial takeoff". *Political Power and Social Theory* 10 (1996b): 229–56.

Chiu, S.W.K and T.L. Lui. "Hong Kong: Unorganized Industrialism". In *Asian NIEs and the Global Economy*, edited by G. Clark and W.B. Kim. Baltimore: Johns Hopkins University Press, 1995.

Chiu, S., K.C. Ho and T.L. Lui. *City-States in the Global Economy*. Boulder: Westview Press, 1997.

Chiu, S.W.K. and C.K. Lee. "After the Hong Kong Miracle: Women Workers under Industrial Restructuring". *Asian Survey* 37 (1997): 752–70.

Chiu, S.W.K. and D. Levin. "Prosperity Without Industrial Democracy? Developments in Industrial Relations in Hong Kong Since 1968". *Industrial Relations Journal* 27, no. 1 (1996): 24–37.

Choi, A.H. "The Political Economy of Industrial Upgrading: A Lost Opportunity". *China Information* 12, nos. 1 and 2 (1997): 157–88.

Clifford, M. "Price of independence: Taiwanese firms weigh cost of screen technology". *Far Eastern Economic Review*, 23 December, 1993, pp.52–3.

Commission on Innovation and Technology. *The Commission's First Report to the Chief Executive*. Hong Kong, 1998. (http://www.info.gov.hk/cit/eng/er/report.htm)

Cumings, B. "The Origins and Development of the Northeast Asian Political Economy: Industrial Sectors, Product Cycles, and Political Consequences". *The Political Economy of the New Asian Industrialization,* edited by F.C. Deyo. Ithaca: Cornell University Press, 1987.

Department of Audit, Hong Kong. "The Government's funding schemes for promoting technology development in industry". *Report of the Director of Audit on the Results of Value for Money Audits*. Hong Kong: Government Printer, 1997.

Dicken, P. *Global Shift: The Internationalization of Economic Activity*. New York: Guilford Press, 1992.

Federation of Hong Kong Industries. *Hong Kong's Offshore Investment*. Hong Kong: Industry and Research Division, Federation of Hong Kong Industries, 1990.

_____. *Hong Kong's Industrial Investment in the Pearl River Delta*. Hong Kong: Industry and Research Division, Federation of Hong Kong Industries, 1993.

Gereffi, G. "The Organization of Buyer-Driven Global Commodity Chains: How U.S. Retailers Shape Overseas Production Networks". In *Commodity Chains and Global Capitalism*, edited by G. Gereffi and M. Korzeniewicz. Westport: Praeger, 1994.

Gereffi, G. and M. Korzeniewicz. "Commodity Chains and Footwear Exports in the Semiperiphery". In *Semiperipheral States in the World Economy*, edited by W.G. Martin. Westport: Greenwood Press, 1990.

_____, eds. *Commodity Chains and Global Capitalism*. Westport: Praeger, 1994.

Germidis, D., ed. *International Subcontracting*. Paris: OECD Development Centre, 1980.

Haggard, S. *Pathways from the Periphery*. Ithaca: Cornell University Press, 1990.

Hambro, E. *The Problem of Chinese Refugees in Hong Kong*. Leyden: A.W. Sijthoff, 1955.

Harvey, D. *The Condition of Postmodernity*. Oxford: Blackwell, 1989.

Ho, H.C.Y. *The Fiscal System of Hong Kong*. London: Croom Helm, 1979.

Hong Kong Trade Development Council. *Survey on Hong Kong's Domestic Exports, Re-exports and Triangular Trade*. Hong Kong: Research Department, Hong Kong Trade Development Council, 1991.

_____. *Profiles of Hong Kong's Major Manufacturing Industries*. Hong Kong: Research Department, Hong Kong Trade Development Council, 1997.

Industry Department, Hong Kong. *Hong Kong's Manufacturing Industries*. Hong Kong: Government Printer, various years.

Kim, L. *Imitation to Innovation: The Dynamics of Korea's Technology Learning*. Boston: Harvard Business School Press, 1997.

Kraus, R.C. "Withdrawing from the World-System: Self-Reliance and Class Structure in China". *The World-System of Capitalism*, edited by W.L. Goldfrank. Beverly Hills: Sage, 1979.

Kwong, K.S. *Technology and Industry*. Hong Kong: City University of Hong Kong Press, 1997.

Kwong, K.S., L. Lau and T.B. Lin. "The Impact of Relocation on the Total Factor Productivity of Hong Kong Manufacturing". Manuscript. 1997.

Levy, B. "Transaction Costs, the Size of Firms, and Industrial Policy". *Journal of Development Economics* 34 (1990): 151–78.

Liu, S.J, and J.F. Lee. "Liquid Crystal Display Industry in Taiwan". *International Journal of Technology Management* 13, no. 3 (1997): 308–325.

Lui, T.L. and S. Chiu. "Industrial Restructuring and labor Market Adjustment under Positive Non-Interventionism". *Environment and Planning* A 25 (1993): 63-79.

Lui, T.L. *Waged Work at Home: The Social Organization of Industrial Outwork in Hong Kong*. Aldershot: Avebury, 1994.

Mody, A and D. Wheeler. *Automation and World Competition*. New York: St. Martin's Press, 1990.

Murray, R. "Fordism and post-Fordism". In *New Times*, edited by S. Hall and M. Jacques. London: Lawrence & Wishart, 1989.

Ngo, T.W. "Changing Government-Business Relations and the Governance of Hong Kong". Paper presented at the international conference on Hong Kong in Transition, 15 December 1997 in London.

Piore, M. and C. Sabel. *The Second Industrial Divide: Possibilities for Prosperity.* New York: Basic Books, 1984.

Pye, L. "The International Position of Hong Kong". *The China Quarterly* 95 (1983): 456–68.

Sit, V. and S.L. Wong. *Small and Medium Industries in an Export-Oriented Economy: The Case of Hong Kong.* Hong Kong: Centre of Asian Studies, University of Hong Kong, 1989.

Sit, V.F.S., S.L. Wong and T.S. Kiang. *Small Scale Industry in a Laissez-faire Economy.* Hong Kong: Centre of Asian Studies, University of Hong Kong, 1979

So, A.Y. and S.W.K. Chiu. *East Asia and World Economy.* Newbury Park: Sage, 1995.

State Statistical Bureau, People's Republic of China. *China Statistical Yearbook 1996.* Beijing: China Statistical Publishing House, 1996.

Szczepanik, E. *The Economic Growth of Hong Kong.* Oxford: Oxford University Press, 1958.

Thornton, E. "Made in Japan: Taiwan vies for a piece of the other big screen market". *Far Eastern Economic Review*, 11 January 1996, pp.52–53.

Tung, C.H. *The 1998 Policy Address.* 1998. (http://www.info.gov.hk/pa98/english/speech.htm).

Vogel, E.F. *The Four Little Dragons.* Cambridge, Mass.: Harvard University Press, 1991.

Ward, M. "Fashioning the Future: Fashion, Clothing, and the Manufacturing of Post-Fordist Culture". *Cultural Studies* 5, no. 1 (1991): 61–76.

Wong, S.L. *Emigrant Entrepreneurs: Shanghai Industrialists in Hong Kong.* Hong Kong: Oxford University Press, 1988.

_____. "Chinese Entrepreneurs and Business Trust". *University of Hong Kong Gazette Supplement* 37, no. 1 (1990): 25–34.

World Bank. *The East Asian Miracle: Economic Growth and Public Policy.* New York: Oxford University Press, 1993.

World Bank. *World Development Report 1995: Workers in an Integrating World.* New York: Oxford University Press, 1995.

Yau, K.C. "The Precarious Symbiosis: Inter-organizational Relations in Hong Kong's Production System". Unpublished Master's thesis, Sociology Department, Chinese University of Hong Kong, 1995.

Youngson, A.J. "Introduction". In *China and Hong Kong*, edited by A.J. Youngson. Hong Kong: Oxford University Press, 1983.

Yu, T.F.L. *Entrepreneurship and Economic Development in Hong Kong.* London: Routledge, 1997.

11

Hong Kong: Garment and Electronics Industry Case Studies

Stephen W.K. Chiu and Tai-Lok Lui

I. INTRODUCTION

Elsewhere we have described industrial development in Hong Kong as a case of unorganized industrialism (Chiu and Lui 1995). Such a depiction serves the purpose of highlighting the effects of the institutional arrangements on the shaping of the course of development of Hong Kong's manufacturing industries. By unorganized industrialism, we suggest that the key features of the institutional environment structuring industrial development in Hong Kong are as follows: (1) a selectively non-interventionist state which stays aloof from actively steering industrial development; (2) an institutional separation of financial and industrial capital, leaving most of the local small manufacturers on their own to deal with problems arising from financial difficulties and raising money for expansion or new initiatives; and (3) underdevelopment in the organizing of business and labor interests, retarding capital and labor in the creation of an effective mechanism for the facilitation of concerted actions. Given that the focus of this chapter lies in the role of the state in industrial development, we shall not dwell upon the notion of unorganized industrialism here (but see Lui and Chiu 1993; Lui 1994; Chiu and Lui 1995; Chiu, Ho and Lui 1997). What we intend to do in this section is to report on the state of industrial development in Hong Kong. This is intended to illustrate the impacts of the institutional setting on industrial development in Hong Kong. In order to sharpen the focus of our discussion, we shall examine the development of garment and electronics manufacturing, the two leading local industries, instead of a general review of the manufacturing sector in Hong Kong.

Before coming to our discussions on the development of garment making and electronics manufacturing, a brief note on the major characteristics of Hong Kong's manufacturing industries is in order. Essentially, Hong Kong's manufacturing establishments are mainly run by small local capital. Their average size in 1995 was 12 employed persons (Industry Department, *Hong Kong's Manufacturing Industries* 1996, p. 8). Among the 31,114 manufacturing establishments in 1995, 88.5% of them employed 19 persons or less. In the same year only 430 manufacturing establishments were identified as either wholly or partly owned by foreign capital (Industry Department, *Hong Kong's Manufacturing Industries* 1996, p. 13). Most of the local manufacturing establishments are original equipment manufacturers (OEM) for exports. They receive their orders through local import-export houses which, in their turn, are connected with overseas buyers through the global commercial networks (Chu 1988; Sit, Wong and Kiang 1979; Sit and Wong 1989; Yau 1995).

II. THE GARMENT-MAKING INDUSTRY

The garment industry developed rapidly in the 1950s (see Table 11.1) and since the early 1960s has overtaken the textile industry as the leading export earner and employer among the manufacturing industries. It reached its peak in the mid-1970s. In 1975 there were 8,047 establishments in the industry (25.9% of the total number of manufacturing establishments), employing 37.9% of the manufacturing workforce (Table 11.1).

The spectacular growth of Hong Kong's manufacturing sector in general, and the garment industry in particular, through export-led industrialization is essentially conditioned by the restructuring of the world economy in the post-war decades (Lui and Chiu 1993; Dicken 1992; So and Chiu 1995). As a result of such restructuring, there has been a relocation of manufacturing production. During this process of relocation some developing economies emerged as the sites for export manufacturing. For the Hong Kong economy, this reorganization of the world economy is the precondition for industrialization. Under the new economic order of the changing world economy, it is possible for Hong Kong's export-oriented industries to be competitive internationally. Also, the emergence of the global subcontracting network has facili-

TABLE 11.1 Hong Kong: Number of Establishments and Persons Engaged in the Garment Industry, 1950–95

Year	No. of Establishments	No. of Persons Engaged	Average No. of Persons Engaged per Establishment	
			Garment Industry	All Manufacturing Industries
1950	41 (2.8)	1,955 (2.4)	47	55
1955	99 (4.1)	4,261 (3.9)	43	45
1960	970 (18.1)	51,918 (23.8)	54	41
1965	1,514 (17.5)	87,454 (25.6)	58	39
1970	3,491 (21.1)	158,025 (28.8)	45	33
1975	8,047 (25.9)	257,595 (37.9)	32	22
1980	9,499 (20.9)	275,818 (30.9)	29	20
1985	10,307 (21.4)	292,789 (34.5)	28	18
1986	10,392 (21.4)	299,932 (34.5)	29	18
1987	10,556 (20.9)	298,377 (34.1)	28	17
1988	10,412 (20.6)	286,659 (33.9)	28	17
1989	9,672 (19.4)	274,732 (34.2)	28	16
1990	9,746 (19.9)	251,746 (34.5)	26	15
1991	8,837 (19.1)	224,925 (34.4)	25	14
1992	6,980 (16.6)	186,607 (32.7)	27	14
1993	6,943 (17.7)	167,273 (32.9)	24	13
1994	5,628 (16.5)	137,287 (31.3)	24	13
1995	4,926 (15.8)	111,917 (29.0)	23	12

NOTES: 1. Figures in parentheses denote the percentage share of all manufacturing industries in the respective year.

2. The figures for 1992 do not include hosiery, knitted underwear and wristwatch bands.

SOURCE: Industry Department, *Hong Kong's Manufacturing Industries* (1996), p. 70.

tated the incorporation of Hong Kong into the world manufacturing system (Chu 1988; Dicken 1992; Germidis 1980).

Given the absence of natural resources and the limited size of the domestic market, it can be argued that Hong Kong had no alternative other than to develop export-oriented industries when entrepôt trade was adversely affected by the United Nations' trade embargo on China. But, obviously, the lack of an alternative to industrialization does not explain the success of Hong Kong's take-off in manufacturing. In this regard Chu's (1988) study of the development of the garment industry in Hong Kong helps throw light on the effects of the changing global economy on its industrialization. The gist of her argument is this. First, although it is true to say that the influx of Shanghainese industrialists brought capital and skills which facilitated the growth of manufacturing in general, and particularly the textile industry, their influence on the industrialization process should not be overstated. There is no evidence to support the view that the textile industrialists have taken an active role in the development of garment production (Chu 1988, p. 121). The influence of these industrialists on other production activities is more limited than is supposed.

Second, though the British merchants and their Commonwealth connections were pertinent to the development of markets for local exports in the early 1950s, their role became less significant as the United States emerged as the major importer of garment products from Hong Kong. Third, foreign direct investment in manufacturing has been rather insignificant for at least the initial stage of the industrialization process. The results of Chu's close scrutiny of the validity of the above explanations suggest that the major factor that brought about Hong Kong's industrial development lies elsewhere. Her suggestion is that "it is the multinational trading groups or the 'commercial form' of international subcontracting system that has been at work" (Chu 1988, p. 74). Put it slightly differently in the growing literature on global commodity chains (Gereffi and Korzeniewicz 1990 and 1994), Hong Kong's incorporation into the global economy through the buyer-driven global commodity chains has provided local manufacturers with the opportunities to develop low-cost, labour-intensive, export-oriented industries. The rapid growth of the garment industry is a case to illustrate how Hong Kong's industries become successful in such a context of the changing global economy.

From the mid-1970s the industry continued to grow in absolute terms until 1986. The subsequent drop in the numbers of establishments and

TABLE 11.2   Hong Kong: Growth of Garment Industry, 1980–95 (in HK$ million, at 1990 constant price)

Year	No. of Firms	No. of Employees	Value Added	Total Wages	Gross Addition to Fixed Asset	Gross Output
1980	8,090	276,299	13,429	10,528	1,197	46,189
1981	9,198	295,754	15,561	11,709	1,695	52,260
1985	9,704	276,342	17,788	14,151	955	54,585
1990	8,938	220,901	18,924	13,765	1,416	63,232
1993	4,703	129,992	13,511	8,989	536	48,202
1995	3,117	80,545	9,369	6,402	357	33,994

NOTE: Real value obtained by using the GDP deflators.
SOURCES: Census and Statistics Department, *Survey of Industrial Production*, various years.

persons employed in garment making reflects the changing conditions of the industry. That production remains labour-intensive exposes the industry to fierce competition from other newly industrialized economies (NIEs). Also largely because of the failure of moving beyond labour-intensive production, local manufacturers have turned to look for the possibility of offshore production. The decline, in absolute terms, in the number of garment-making establishments and employment in the industry best shows the impact of restructuring. In Table 11.2 it is also clear that since the late 1980s the industry's output and value-added have declined in real terms. Yet the industry has not declined relative to other manufacturing industries, as the other industries have been experiencing a decline at the same time (Table 11.3). As for the

TABLE 11.3   Hong Kong: Share of Garment Industry in Total Manufacturing (in percentages)

	1980	1985	1990	1995
Output	22.8	21.5	19.6	14.8
Value added	25.3	24.7	20.5	14.5
Employment	29.5	30.4	29.0	21.9
Export	34.1	34.6	31.9	31.9

SOURCES: Industry Department, *Hong Kong's Manufacturing Industries,* various years.

TABLE 11.4   Hong Kong: Composition of Output of Garment Industry (in percentages)

Subsector	1980	1985	1990	1995
Outer garments	75	76	82	80
Under garments	6	6	8	11
Leather and fur clothing	10	10	6	3
Gloves	4	2	1	2
Headgear	1	1	0	0
Others	6	5	3	5
Total (HK$ million)	24619	38100	63232	44464

SOURCES: Census and Statistics Department, *Survey of Industrial Production*, various years.

composition of the industry, it is found that the share of outer garments has actually increased over the years while that of leather and fur clothing has decreased. Underwear, a high value-added product, also increased its share in the output of the entire industry (Table 11.4). Corresponding to the process of de-industrialization and relocation, the percentage of small firms in the total number of firms increased from 82% in 1980 to 88% in 1995 (Table 11.5). This is because most enterprises have shrunk in size owing to the relocation of production lines overseas.

TABLE 11.5   Hong Kong: Distribution of Garment Enterprises by Number of Employees (in percentages)

No. of Employees	1980	1981	1985	1990	1995
<50	82.03	83.18	84.64	88.43	88.16
50-99	10.87	9.60	9.55	6.00	7.31
100-199	4.91	4.94	3.97	4.15	3.08
200-499	1.73	1.87	1.48	1.21	1.09
500-999	0.28	0.23	0.24	0.15	0.26
1,000 and above	0.19	0.18	0.12	0.06	0.06
Total	8,090	9,198	9705	8,938	3,117

SOURCES: Census and Statistics Department, *Survey of Industrial Production*, various years.

The garment industry has not been particularly successful in increasing its capital intensity and moving up to producing higher value-added products. Indeed, value-added per person engaged is consistently below the average of all manufacturing industries (see Table 11.6). As noted by the government, "productivity of the clothing industry amounted to $134,000 in 1994, lower than that for the manufacturing sector ($200,000). Its productivity increased at an average annual rate of 11.0% during 1984 and 1994, also lower than the rate of 13.7% for all manufacturing industries" (Industry Department, *Hong Kong's Manufacturing Industries* 1996, p. 60). Also, labor costs as a proportion of total production costs of the industry (between 21.9% and 25.3% in the period 1981-89) were higher than the average (between 17.4% and 20.8% in the same period) of the manufacturing sector. The figure dropped to 18.9% in 1993 and then rose slightly to 19.1% in 1994 (see Table 11.7). Yet, it was still slightly higher than the average (19.0% in 1994) for the manufacturing sector. At the same time it is observed that investment in the industry, measured in terms of gross additions to fixed assets, dropped to 8.0% (HK$563 million) of the total investments in all manufacturing industries in 1994, a significant decrease (−39.7%) from that of the previous year (Industry Department, *Hong Kong's Manufacturing Industries* 1996, p. 73). In short, there are few signs to show that garment-making manufacturers have reshaped the production structure of the industry. High labor intensity and low value-added largely sum up the major problems of garment making.

Given the declining cost advantage of garment manufacturing in Hong Kong, some firms are phasing it out. This is especially true for some of the older and larger firms that owned the premises for their plants. With this "land bank", they started branching out into real estate development. However, beneath the surface of this picture of stagnant development, there have been manoeuvres to find niches for the development of the industry and to maintain its competitiveness. First, although Hong Kong's garment making continues to be heavily dependent on the U.S. market (in 1995 it absorbed 48.1% of all the industry's domestic exports), efforts have been made to break into other markets (in 1995 Germany and the United Kingdom absorbed 20.8% of all garment exports and China 8.0%). Furthermore, a handful of firms have turned back from markets in the advanced industrialized countries to the domestic and regional markets. Since Hong Kong and the East Asian and Southeast Asian economies are in the fastest-

TABLE 11.6 Hong Kong: Value Added of the Garment and Electronics Industries, 1981–94 (in HK$1,000)

Value Added per Person Engaged	1981	1984	1985	1986	1987	1988	1989	1990	1991	1992	1993	1994
Clothing	31	47	47	54	67	74	84	91	102	122	127	134
Electronics	29	62	51	72	91	111	126	149	185	241	255	309
All manufacturing	36	55	55	67	80	94	108	121	142	165	181	200

NOTES: 1. The 1985 figure for the garment industry does not include one minor item, ISIC 3274-Hosiery.

2. The 1990 and 1993 figures for the garment industry do not include one minor item, HSIC 3277-Knitted underwear.

SOURCE: Industry Department, *Hong Kong's Manufacturing Industries* (1996), pp. 72 and 88.

TABLE 11.7 Hong Kong: Labor Costs in the Garment and Electronics Industries, 1981–94 (in HK$)

	1981	1985	1986	1987	1988	1989	1990	1991	1992	1993	1994
Garment industry	7,534	11,336	13,357	15,154	15,397	16,736	16,945	16,178	16,064	14,121	12,782
	(22.5)	(25.3)	(23.8)	(21.9)	(22.3)	(21.9)	(22.0)	(20.0)	(20.3)	(18.9)	(19.1)
Electronics industry	2,572	4,001	4,411	5,123	6,018	6,430	6,455	5,829	6,063	6,164	6,138
	(15)	(13.6)	(11.6)	(10.4)	(10.1)	(11.5)	(11.8)	(11.7)	(11.2)	(11.9)	(12.6)

NOTE: Figures in parentheses denote the percentage share of total production costs in the industry.

SOURCE: Industry Department, *Hong Kong's Manufacturing Industries* (1996), pp. 73 and 89.

growing region in the world, their market potential is considerable (Kurt Salmon Associates 1996, p. 11). Second, in response to increasing protectionism and the problem of producing low value-added products, Hong Kong's manufacturers have expanded their production in non-quota products and increased their outputs in higher unit value products, such as woven blouses in silk and wool (Lau and Chan 1991, p. 7).

Generally speaking, garment manufacturers in Hong Kong have been more successful in finding new market niches for exports and responding quickly to market changes by manufacturing new products than in restructuring the character of the industry. Part of the problem of the industry lies in its failure to apply advanced technology in production. A recent survey of 120 garment manufacturers reports that only 30.0% of the surveyed plants have applied automatic equipment in local production. Also, among the same group of respondents, 18.3% used computer-aided systems in their Hong Kong-based production (Lau and Chan 1991, p.11). For most local garment manufacturers, automation is a high-cost option (Industry Department 1990, p. 39). The fact that garment making is dominated by small establishments (the average size of garment-making establishments in 1995 was 12 employed persons) partly explains why most local manufacturers are reluctant to (if not incapable of) adopt the automation strategy. Without suggesting that size *per se* is indicative of organizational capacity, it is safe to say that given the limited capital of most small manufacturers, many would find it difficult to afford to restructure their production by technological upgrading.

The fact that the garment industry has made little effort to upgrade technologically is not surprising. First, the industry generally has made little progress in applying new technology to the assembly process (Mody and Wheeler 1990, p. 38). Most of the technologically sophisticated and automated processes (such as computer-aided design linked to marking and cutting) are found in the pre-assembly and post-assembly stages. In terms of computerization and automation, Hong Kong is no exception. Computer-aided pattern grading and marker making are commonplace. But "only limited automation of sewing operations has so far taken place" (Industry Department, *Hong Kong's Manufacturing Industries* 1992, p. 39). Second, the application of linked automation to garment-making processes makes it difficult to match the needs of volatile markets. In a case reported in the *Report on Industrial Automation Study* commissioned by the Industry Department (1992, p. 19), the garment manufacturer has an integrated computerized system of pattern grading, marker planning and cutting. However, in order to realize the advantage of the automated system, production has to be based on large orders and the cutting of fabrics not requiring any pattern matching. Those producing fashion garments and working for small orders will not find such automation attractive (also see Bailey 1993, pp.38–39).

Third, very often the restructuring of garment production involves shop-floor reorganization rather than technological sophistication. For instance, the so-called modular production system, that is, the formation of self-contained work units of five to 20 persons for the assembly of an entire garment, is a new form of workplace organization, which, according to the Industry Department's suggestions, helps reduce in-process inventories, improve productivity by "between 10% and 40%" and reduce "'throughput time to one or two days" (Industry Department, *Hong Kong's Manufacturing Industries* 1992, p. 39). According to the findings of the survey carried out by Lau and Chan (1991), only ten out of the 120 manufacturers interviewed used the modular system for production. At one point of time, such new production strategies have been promoted as innovations for enhancing productivity and level of production sophistication. However, it should be immediately pointed out that even in the area of workplace reorganization, Hong Kong garment manufacturers are far less than innovative. Berger discusses the failure of establishing new production systems in the report of the Massachusetts Institute of Technology (MIT) project on Hong Kong's manufacturing industries (Berger and Lester 1997, pp.159–60):

> The Clothing Technology Demonstration Centre tried for many years to promote such a system [that is, team-based modular production], even building a pilot factory within its own walls to demonstrate the feasibility and superiority of modular production. Modular production requires teamwork among multi-skilled workers. There were a number of Hong Kong companies that tried it out, but as one by one they moved their plants into China and shifted to the low-cost labor model, they abandoned their experiments, and today no one in Hong Kong is using modular production.

The failure to use advanced technology and develop innovative production strategy partly reflects the present impasse of the garment-making industry in Hong Kong. Indeed, the failure of upgrading is only partially shaped by the financial constraints of small manufacturers. It is also partly an outcome of the inertia of local garment manufacturers. The major business strategy of local garment manufacturers has long been that of product imitation (Yu 1997, chapter 5). As well put by Yu (1997, pp. 93–94) in his study of entrepreneurship in Hong Kong:

> Most textile and garment firms in Hong Kong do not aim at creating new fashions. ... In my survey, 88% of the manufacturers replied that similar garments were sold both in Hong Kong and in overseas markets by other firms while only 8% of them regarded their products as unique in Hong Kong and overseas markets. ... Imitation has been a short cut to their success. The case of Goldlion (Far East) Co. Ltd. supports this. ... Specifically in the tie market, France and Italy possess many first-class designers and supply world markets with ties of new designs and styles. Goldlion simply sent its staff overseas and adopted these new designs by paying licence fees. In the Hong Kong factory, the new designs were rapidly modified into Goldlion's products and then put into mass production.

In other words, Hong Kong garment manufacturers show little interest in innovation. The main concern of garment manufacturers lies in the need to keep production costs low and, at the same time, maintain a high degree of flexibility in production. As mentioned above, automation as a measure to increase efficiency and to reduce production costs is simply beyond small manufacturers' abilities. Furthermore, automation does not necessarily keep production costs low in the short run. In an industry that is dominated by small local capital, alternative strategies are often formulated within a framework of short-term calculations — these small manufacturers have no control over product markets and have to be responsive to rapid market changes. But most critical of all is the opening of China. The availability of a new option that allows them to continue labor-intensive production makes innovation in local production redundant.

With the progress of economic reforms in mainland China, relocation constitutes a viable option for Hong Kong's industries, which facilitates the continuation of their labor-intensive production. The abundant supply of low-wage labor, low production costs and proximity are the attractions of relocating production to the Pearl River Delta. Yet, despite a trend of increasing industrial relocation to mainland China by local manufacturers (Federation of Hong Kong Industries 1990), the garment-making industry remains relatively closely tied to its base in Hong Kong. The study of industrial investment in the Pearl River Delta by the Federation of Hong Kong Industries (1993) reveals that garment manufacturers are among the least likely investors in the region (26.2%, well below the average figure of the survey, 40.7%). The major reason why garment manufacturers have chosen not to relocate their production, at least partially, has to do with the origin rules in force in Hong Kong. For those products exported to restrained markets, "special outward processing arrangement is administrated by the Hong Kong Government Trade Department to ensure that goods manufactured in Hong Kong but partly processed in China only qualify for Hong Kong origin status if they fully meet Hong Kong's origin rules" (Industry Department 1990, p. 40). As a result of such institutional restrictions, unless products produced are targeted at local consumption or unrestrained markets, garment manufacturers have to continue their production in Hong Kong. This explains why garment manufacturers had been vocal in asking for imported labor and in urging the government to review the business environment of local industries in the late 1980s and the early 1990s.

Given the institutional restrictions on relocation, the structural constraints on technological upgrading and protectionist market restrictions, garment manufacturers find themselves increasingly locked into a system of flexible production for volatile export markets. Except for the very few manufacturers who possess the required quotas, obtain adequate orders for mass production and therefore are able to turn to offshore production or adopt automation to enhance their competitiveness in large-scale production, most Hong Kong manufacturers have to make every effort to increase their production flexibility in order to keep pace with rapid changes in styles and tastes in fashion and garment retailing. The survival of garment making in Hong Kong hinges upon its success in fighting its battles on two fronts. On the one hand, it relates to local manufacturers' abilities to maintain their ties with the commercial subcontracting network of global capitalism. That Hong Kong's garment-making industry had its origin in strong commercial ties is an advantage (Chu 1988). It shapes local manufacturers' sensitivity to the needs of importing markets, especially at the level of retailing. As a result of economic restructuring in advanced industrial societies, production has been increasingly conditioned by the needs of the retailing market (Harvey 1989; Murray 1989). And this is especially true for fashions and garments (Ward 1991). In this new world of consumption, the ability to handle such a volatile market is the basic requirement for success. On the other hand, to match the need of responding quickly to changes in the consumption sphere, Hong Kong's garment manufacturers have to obtain a high level of flexibility in production. One way to measure the manufacturers' ability to cope with the above issues is to check their manufacturing lead-time. A study of Hong Kong's garment manufacturing in the mid-1980s (Kurt Salmon Associates 1987, p. 143) shows that from the time a customer order is placed until the goods are ready for shipment, small firms in "cut and sew" need 14 days while large firms need 30 days. And as regards the typical lead times for knitwear production, they are 17.5 days and 35 days for small firms and large firms respectively. On the whole, local manufacturers are competitive with other international competitors in terms of manufacturing lead-time both in "cut and sew" and knitwear (Kurt Salmon Associates 1987, p. 144).

In other words, the continuing development of garment making in Hong Kong depends on the strength of its commercial network in international subcontracting and its flexibility in production. Research on Hong Kong industries has long emphasized the role played by trading firms and sourcing agents in the facilitation of industrial development (see, for example, Chan 1984; Chu 1988; Sit and Wong 1989). What is pertinent to our discussion is that such a well-developed commercial network provides local manufacturers with the means to reach the international fashion and garment markets. More important, however, is whether local manufacturers can organize their production flexibly to meet the demands of such volatile markets. Previously, the comparative advantage of Hong Kong's garment making lay in the structure of the industry. The development of garment making in Hong Kong has long been characterized by the dominance of small firms which are interconnected through the subcontracting network. Also, various forms of informal work (such as internal contracting and outwork) have been widely used and are well integrated into the production system of the industry (Lui 1994). Whereas larger establishments are likely to farm out part of their production to subcontractors, small establishments rely heavily on such subcontracting activities to maintain their production and, in turn, shift part of the burden of risk to outworkers. The point is that in the development process of Hong Kong's garment making, there evolved a network of subcontracting activities and informal work, which constitutes the mechanism for flexible production. The long history of export-oriented, small workshop production gives rise to the unintended effect of building up a network of interdependent producers permeated with notions of personal connections and trust (cf. Wong 1990). The existence of such a network makes various forms of subcontracting and labour-contracting activity transaction cost efficient (cf. Levy 1990). Moreover, under such an industrial structure, flexible labour-intensive production fits in well with the needs of local small garment manufacturers to respond to market changes and to keep production costs to the minimum.

However, with the deepening of economic reform and the liberalization of business environment in China, more and more local manufacturers, including those in garment making, find relocation an attractive option. In the context of massive relocation of production across the border, many garment manufacturers have also moved, at least parts, of their production offshore. Indeed, there are signs suggesting that more and more garment manufacturers, in consideration of rising production costs, would adopt the relocation strategy and move their production lines to South China as well. In the *Survey of Hong Kong's Manufacturing Industries: 1990* carried out by the Industry Department (1990, p. 34), only 22.0% of garment manufacturer respondents answered that they had plant or production facilities outside Hong Kong (the average for all respondents in that year was 27.2%). In 1996 the survey findings suggested that 34.4% of interviewed garment manufacturers had gone offshore (the average figure for that year was 26.8%) (Industry Department, *Hong Kong's Manufacturing Industries* 1996, p. 298). It seems that relocation is gradually becoming the main production strategy as well.

Although the garment industry has a stronger tendency (or, to put it differently, is more restricted by existing regulations concerning product origins) of maintaining its production in Hong Kong, the trend of moving production processes to China, gradually in this case, inevitably means some new arrangements of division of labor in the industry. Given the strength of Hong Kong's garment manufacturers in market intelligence, the "industry has adopted a strategy of investing in mass production factories with a large number of employees overseas, and smaller, fast and flexible factories in Hong Kong" (Kurt Salmon Associates 1996, p. 85). It is "today characterised by many companies who are strongly involved in trading and manufacturing in other Asian countries. Locally, Hong Kong's clothing companies have re-engineered their production to small units answering the customers' demand for fast and flexible product sampling" (Kurt Salmon Associates 1996, p. 107).

Such developments in the garment industry should be understood in the broader context of the restructuring of Hong Kong's manufacturing sector. There is a process of restructuring Hong Kong's manufacturing into more of a commercially oriented business networking centre. Hong Kong is becoming more of a centre for playing the "role as the 'manager' and 'controller' of sourcing in the region" (Kurt Salmon Associates 1996, p. 58) than a production base in the narrow sense of the term. The findings of a survey of manufacturers and traders carried out by the Hong Kong Trade Development Council in 1991 largely confirmed the above observation. When the respondents were asked of their future operations in Hong Kong, 83% mentioned controlling headquarters, 81% documentation, 73% business negotiation and 72% trade financing (Hong Kong Trade Development Council 1991, p. 13). The Hong Kong Trade Development Council (1991, p. 12) underlined that:

> [A]pparently, operations performed by surveyed companies in Hong Kong in the future would concentrate on trade and manufacturing-related services, including marketing, merchandising, business negotiation, transportation, warehousing and distribution, quality control, testing and certification, product design, R&D, sample-making, prototyping, market research and after sale service.

In brief, the strength of the Hong Kong manufacturing economy lies in acting as a node of business networking.

Recent studies of manufacturing-related activities by the Census and Statistics Department (1996 and 1997) further show that a growing number of import/export trading firms are now having subcontract processing arrangement in China (SPAC). Their number increased from 12,580 in 1992 to 24,860 in 1995, an increase of 97.6%. A number of them (7,910 in 1995) were previously established as manufacturing firms. Activities under the SPAC include all contractual agreements with a China counterpart to carry out production processing in China.

It is pointed out that while some manufacturers retain those processes involving higher skills in their local operation,

> [i]n a greater number of other cases, essentially all manu-facturing processes are moved to the mainland of China, leaving only such functions as marketing, orders process-ing, materials sourcing, design, product development, prototype making and quality control with the local firms. That is, the local firms have shifted their operational status from that of manufacturing to that of trading, albeit the fact that they may provide technical support services to the pro-duction in the mainland of China…. Besides, many traditional import/export firms have also become engaged in SPAC to take advantage of cheap and abundant labor and land resources in the mainland of China. They too render different technical support services in varying degrees to the manufacturing activities in the mainland of China. Fur-thermore, quite a large number of new firms are also set up in recent years to serve as a local base for new manufactur-ing firms in the mainland of China, operating in a way different from traditional importers/exporters. (Census and Statistics Department 1997, FA3)

Among the supporting services rendered in connection with SPAC by trading firms with manufacturing-related functions, nearly all pro-vide the service of "sourcing of raw materials". Other major services include "product design" (77%) and "sample and mould making" (76%) (Census and Statistics Department 1997, FA7).

The analysis of manufacturing-related activities carried out by the Census and Statistics Department does not provide us with a detailed breakdown of industries engaged in such activities. However, it does show that in 1995 among those trading firms engaged in manufactur-ing-related activities, 33% of them were importers/exporters of "clothing, footwear and allied products" (Census and Statistics Depart-ment 1997, FA6). Capitalizing on the history of being an entrepôt and the established institutional structure facilitating business networking, local garment manufacturers have come to shape Hong Kong into "a regional centre for sourcing garments, where orders can be placed but with production allocated to neighbouring territories according to cost, level of sophistication and quality required and availability of quota" (Hong Kong Trade Development Council 1997, p. 15; also see Birnbaum 1993). To put it differently, Hong Kong's garment manufacturers are now playing the role of a middleman in the process of global sourcing. They have changed from being the primary production contractors for overseas buyers into being the agents of "triangle manufacturing" (Gereffi 1994, p. 114). In this connection, Hong Kong is "an ideal base and contact point for foreign companies wishing to penetrate the regional market" (Hong Kong Trade Development Council 1997, p. 12). And local garment manufacturers have been quite successful in making use of such strategic advantages in restructuring their own businesses. For example, Yangtzekiang Garment Manufacturing Company Ltd. employed 1,500–2,000 workers in the 1980s. By 1989–90 the employment figure had fallen to just over 1,000 workers. Contraction continued after 1990 and retrenchment was carried out in four stages. In 1994 it employed only 50 production workers in the sample room. Among the 160 employees in its office, 80 were merchandizers and more than ten materials sourcing agents. Essentially the local office of the company was transformed into a garment trading firm distributing various well-known brand name products. The company has long since gone offshore, with investments in Sri Lanka, Myanmar, Malaysia, mainland China and Macau. In addition to servicing customers around the world, it also serves as a buying office for Yangtzekiang Garment Manufacturing International Ltd. The Hong Kong office is now sourcing from countries like China, Indonesia, Mauritius, Poland and Bangladesh.

In the same direction as capitalizing on Hong Kong's strategic advantages in commercial intelligence, market sensitivity and global business networking, another strategy practised by local garment manufacturers is to move beyond manufacturing. That is, they work at three different levels: manufacturing, wholesale and retail (Keenan 1995, p. 46). One notable example of Hong Kong garment manufacturers moving towards high-end fashion retailing is Toppy International. Since its opening in 1986, the Episode line has "grown to more than 100 outlets in 16 countries" (Keenan 1995). And Toppy, spawned from the Fang Brothers knitting and textile group, also markets other brand names with varying styles for different segments of the women's fashion market.

The development of the garment industry best illustrates how individual manufacturers in Hong Kong strive for success in an environment where they largely have to survive on their own. Being left on their own, particularly without assistance in production upgrading, local garment manufacturers focus on those strategies through which they can manage with limited resources, that is, product imitation and flexibility in production and marketing. In the face of rising production costs and fierce competition from other NIEs, they work on the strategic advantages offered by the existing institutional settings of the Hong Kong economy and shift to take up the role of a middleman in the global sourcing of garment. Their experience in networking with global buyers helps them to integrate the functions of manufacturing and trading.

III. THE ELECTRONICS INDUSTRY

Hong Kong's electronics industry began with the assembly of simple transistor radios using imported components. It really took off when some leading American electronics companies came to Hong Kong and set up their plants for the assembly of discrete components. From then the industry moved quickly to the assembly of cassette recorders and into the production of other fashionable electronic products. The electronics industry grew rapidly in the 1960s. There were only four electronics establishments in 1960. By 1970, there were 230 establishments; the industry grew at an average annual rate of 50% in that decade. Electronics production continued to expand in the 1970s and the early 1980s, achieving "at an annual growth of 12.3% to 1,304 [establishments] in 1985" (Industry Department, *Hong Kong's Manufacturing Industries* 1994, p. 60). Thereafter, the industry experienced a lower rate of growth, and the number of persons employed fell from 109,677 in 1988 to 99,455 in 1989 (see Table 11.8). From 1989 onwards, the industry has been contracting in terms of both number of establishments and employment. Again, like what is observed in the garment industry, these statistics reveal the impacts of restructuring and relocation. A similar trend shows in the figures available from the *Survey of Industrial Production* (Table 11.9). In terms of the real gross output and value-added, the industry has been contracting since the late 1980s. Yet, as in the case of garment making, the relative share of electronics in total manufacturing has in fact increased since the 1980s, as the magnitude of decline in other sectors has been higher than in electronics (Table 11.10).

Whereas garment making in the 1980s experienced few changes in its character, electronics has significantly improved its value-added per person and level of capital intensity (see Table 11.6 above). Also, labor costs as a proportion of total production costs of electronics manufacturing fell from 15.0% in 1981 to 10.1% in 1988, only to climb back to the range of 11.2–12.6% in 1989–94 due to wage pressures (see Table 11.7). Despite such improvements in production, it is quite clear that Hong Kong's electronics manufacturing has fallen behind South Korea, Taiwan and Singapore, and at the same time has been increasingly threatened by Thailand and Malaysia as competitors (Dataquest Inc. 1991; Boston Consulting Group International Inc. 1995). For example, in 1989 the average value-added and output per worker of electronics manufacturing in Hong Kong were US$16.1 and US$79.1 respectively, lagging far behind Singapore's level of US$30.6 and US$108.5. The problem with the industry lies its failure to upgrade production as well as to catch up with its competitors. In a recent comparative assessment of the performance of the electronics industry in East Asia, Hong Kong's status was found to be problematic (Boston Consulting Group International Inc. 1995, p. 199):

> The Hong Kong domestic electronics industry is among the smallest in the region, and is the only one which has been contracting in real value over the past five years.... In terms of capabilities, the Hong Kong industry is grouped with the new low-cost manufacturing bases in Thailand, Malaysia and China as a cost-based competitor with relatively few capabilities in product innovation and development. The other four industries in the region have, or are developing, capabilities at a much higher rate and face the future as value based competitors.

Essentially, Hong Kong's electronics manufacturers turn out products like complete electronic watches and clocks, television receivers, communication equipment, industrial apparatus and computing machinery and equipment; electronics parts and components such as integrated microcircuits and semiconductors; and electronic watch/clock movements. In a world of speedy development of electronic and information technology, Hong Kong is not doing particularly well in catching up with the development of sophisticated electronics products.

TABLE 11.8 Hong Kong: Number of Establishments and Persons Engaged in Electronics Industry, 1960–95

Year	No. of Establishments	No. of Persons Engaged	Average No. of Persons Engaged per Establishment	
			Electronics	All Manufacturing Industries
1960	4	183	46	41
	(0.1)	(0.1)		
1965	35	5,013	143	39
	(0.4)	(1.5)		
1970	230	38,454	167	33
	(1.4)	(7.0)		
1975	490	53,833	110	22
	(1.6)	(7.9)		
1980	1,316	93,100	71	20
	(2.9)	(10.4)		
1985	1,304	86,115	66	18
	(2.7)	(10.1)		
1986	1,823	103,796	57	18
	(3.7)	(11.9)		
1987	1,949	106,835	55	17
	(3.9)	(12.2)		
1988	1,939	109,677	57	17
	(3.8)	(13.0)		
1989	2,009	99,455	50	16
	(4.0)	(12.4)		
1990	1,815	85,169	47	15
	(3.7)	(11.7)		
1991	1,633	71,466	44	14
	(3.5)	(10.9)		
1992	1,446	60,653	42	14
	(3.4)	(10.6)		
1993	1,413	53,591	38	13
	(3.6)	(10.5)		
1994	1,176	45,896	39	13
	(3.5)	(10.5)		
1995	1,109	44,078	40	12
	(3.6)	(11.4)		

(*cont'd overleaf*)

TABLE 11.8 *(cont'd)*

NOTES: 1. Figures from 1986 onwards include the item HSIC 3893—Manufacture of electronic watches and clocks, which were classified under the watches and clocks industry before 1986. The number of establishments and persons engaged in the electronics industry excluding electronics watches and clocks are as follows:

Year	No. of Establishments	No. of Persons Engaged
1990	1,303	71,779
	(2.7)	(9.8)
1991	1,129	59,341
	(2.4)	(9.1)
1992	1,009	50,933
	(2.4)	(8.9)
1993	960	43,980
	(2.4)	(8.7)
1994	803	38,422
	(2.4)	(8.8)
1995	782	36,643
	(2.5)	(9.5)

2. Figures in parentheses denote the percentage share of all manufacturing industries in the respective year.

SOURCE: Industry Department, *Hong Kong's Manufacturing Industries* (1996), p. 86.

TABLE 11.9 Hong Kong: Growth of Electronics Industry, 1981–96 (in HK$ million, at 1990 constant price)

Year	No. of Firms	No. of Employee	Value Added	Total Wages	Gross Addition to Fixed Asset	Gross Output
1981	1,933	120,394	6,014	4,419	904	40,105
1985	1,304	86,115	8,152	5,732	1,288	43,642
1990	1,502	85,045	12,644	6,455	2,379	60,272
1993	892	52,536	11,292	5,202	1,938	49,360
1995	807	41,374	11,867	4,605	2,257	46,583

NOTE: Real value obtained by using the GDP deflators.
SOURCE: Census and Statistics Department, *Survey of Industrial Production*, various years.

TABLE 11.10   Hong Kong: Share of Electronics in Total Manufacturing
(in percentages)

	1981	1985	1990	1995
Output	17.1	17.2	18.7	20.3
Value added	9.7	11.3	13.7	18.4
Employment	12.0	10.1	11.2	11.2
Domestic export	19.7*	20.8	25.9	27.7

* 1980.
SOURCES: Census and Statistics Department, *Survey of Industrial Production;* and Industry Department, *Hong Kong's Manufacturing Industries,* various years.

The following characteristics of electronics manufacturing sum up the present status of the industry (Dataquest Inc. 1991; Industry Department, *Hong Kong's Manufacturing Industries*, various years; Hong Kong Trade Development Council 1997). First, most local manufacturers producing end products are involved in the OEM business. Those who manufacture products under their own brand names are more likely to be companies of overseas investments. So, unlike garment making, which is essentially dominated by local manufacturers producing for export, the electronics industry can be roughly divided into two sectors — one occupied by local producers engaging in OEM business and commercial subcontracting activities with overseas buyers, and the other by foreign firms which incorporate their Hong Kong plants in their global production networks.

Second, the size structure of electronics establishments reflects the presence of foreign investment in the industry. In 1995 there were 70 companies with foreign investment engaged in electronics manufacturing, employing 20,863 workers (Industry Department, *Hong Kong's Manufacturing Industries* 1996, p. 15). Compared with the average size of all manufacturing establishments (12 persons) and that of all electronics establishments (40 persons), it is quite clear that manufacturing establishments under foreign investment are generally larger in size.

Third, electronics manufacturers rely heavily upon imported parts and components. Between 1984 and 1986, on average the value of imported parts and components was about 60% of the gross output of the industry. Also, less than half of the total purchased materials are composed of locally available parts. Critical components have to be imported from Japan, Taiwan, South Korea, the United States and Europe.

Fourth, the industry is weak in research and development (R&D) and product design. In a survey report on electronics manufacturers in 1987 (Dataquest Inc. 1991, Appendix IV-20), it is stated that "[m]ost of the respondents were involved in electronic system designs and the design of mechanical parts. In most cases, the designs were worked out according to the product specifications and product cosmetics provided by the parent companies or the customers. Only half of the respondents performed product cosmetic designs for some of their products, and design of tooling and molds were not widely provided by the respondents."

The same phenomenon is still observed in a more recent techno-economic and market research study on Hong Kong's electronics industry (Boston Consulting Group International Inc. 1995, pp. 80–81):

> The majority of establishments in the Computers & Peripherals sector in Hong Kong assemble products from the key component level and do not themselves hold any significant proprietary technologies. The products manufactured in Hong Kong are usually "mature" (i.e. essentially commodities) or in the consolidation stage, with the Hong Kong companies generally belonging to the lower tier group of competitors who compete on a cost basis. Only a few firms have the capacity to develop proprietary elements and to compete on any basis other than commodity/low cost, i.e. to design a computer system from the component (chip) level. But even they lack the resources to venture into other products such as advanced peripherals. A few medium sized companies which may have the necessary resources generally choose to be OEMs, thus confining themselves to mature and consolidating products for which key elements have ceased to be proprietary to the developer.

As a result, for local manufacturers as well as foreign investors, rising product costs are problematic to the continuation of their relatively labour-intensive production. Three points are pertinent here. First, as mentioned above, in terms of R&D, infrastructural support and industrial linkages, Hong Kong is falling behind the development in the other three "Little Dragons". That state support of high-technology development is limited and the government still keeps clear of providing leadership and direction in industrial development leave the burden of technological upgrading primarily on the shoulders of individual manufacturers. The consequence is that, given the limited capability of small local manufacturers, the industry in general capitalizes on its existing competitive edges instead of moving up to the more sophisticated product lines.

In fact, given the larger size of electronics firms relative to other manufacturing firms in Hong Kong, they already have better access to the well-developed local capital market. In recent years a number of electronics manufacturers have raised new capital by going public in the stock exchange. Obviously, however, their size and capitalization are still too small compared with the large foreign conglomerates in South Korea, Japan and the United States which have the capabilities to engage in R&D and technological upgrading.

Second, and relating to the above discussion of the failure to make significant advances in technological upgrading, electronics manufacturing has been more successful in moving quickly into "the production of fashion products invented elsewhere" (Industry Department 1990, p. 51). Hong Kong manufacturers have been shifting from the production of calculators, watches and clocks in 1975, television games in the late 1970s, talking toys in the mid-1980s, to facsimile machines and memory goods in the late 1980s (Table 11.11). By importing purpose-built parts and components and concentrating on assembly, local manufacturers are able to respond swiftly to changes in the product market. Indeed, the production of fashion electronic products shows that Hong Kong manufacturers can continue to find niches in the world market without launching any R&D. They catch up with recent developments in parts and components by acquiring them in the market instead of internalizing such processes of production. Their strength lies in their ability to adapt and respond to changes in the market — most producers can complete product designs in less than 12 months and can produce from the time of order confirmation to shipment in less than six months (Dataquest Inc. 1991, Appendix IV-15). They are more reliant on market intelligence than advancement in core technological development for survival. For example, one should not be misled by the subsectoral changes reported in Table 11.11 showing that such subsectors as computing equipment and parts and components have increased their share in the industry's output. While this certainly suggests a long-term shift away from low-end, low value-added products towards higher value-added products, it does not imply a dramatic increase in the technological capability of the industry. For example,

TABLE 11.11   Hong Kong: Composition of Output in Electronics Industry (in percentages)

Major Subsector	1980	1985	1990	1995
Computing equipment	4.4	9.0	29.8	32.0
Transistor radios	14.5	5.2	1.0	0.7
Television receivers and communication equipment	3.1	14.2	8.9	2.2
Sound reproducing and recording equipment and apparatus	24.4	13.6	3.3	0.5
Parts and components	27.3	23.1	17.5	31.5
Electronic industrial apparatus	0.4	0.4	0.2	0.2
Watches and clocks	19.4	28.1	23.1	19.7
Electronic toys	5.5	0.8	3.4	1.5
Others	0.9	5.5	12.7	11.6
Total (HK$ million)	17,208	30,462	60,272	60,931

SOURCES: Census and Statistics Department, *Survey of Industrial Production*, various years.

Hong Kong mainly produces peripheral computing products such as computer cases and keyboards, not those most lucrative products like memory chips, storage devices and monitors.

Indeed, this is the major strategy by which Hong Kong's electronics manufacturers have been able to survive without significant upgrading in technology. There are two components in this strategy. On the one hand, it is to find niches in OEM production:

Hong Kong electronics companies predominantly serve the OEM market. Under the current model, companies manufacture mature products when prices have eroded to the point where original producers can no longer make an acceptable profit margin. Since Hong Kong companies can quickly ramp up lower cost manufacturing of these products, they can enjoy a higher profit margin. Through continuous improvement of their manufacturing techniques Hong Kong companies can significantly extend the time over which an acceptable profit margin can be achieved. After the product price erodes beyond an acceptable profit margin the companies find new mature products to begin the cycle again. (Berger and Lester 1997, p. 188)

At the same time Hong Kong manufacturers need to develop their sensitivity to market and product changes and to be able to improve products that have already been established. Yu (1997, p. 126) reports on the case of Vtech:

> First, Vtech strove to improve the product design, with new models much more efficient than original ones from overseas. Second, the company could tailor products quickly to meet market needs. ... Third, the improved products were sold more cheaply than their rivals. ... [T]he company established R&D centres in the USA, Canada, UK, China and Hong Kong. Their functions were to review constantly the marketplace for emerging trends and opportunities and to "adapt leading-edge technologies in order to create exciting and inventive consumer products". ... [O]nly a minor portion of the R&D money was spent on new product design, while the bulk went into redesigning and improving products as well as making them easier and cheaper to produce.

It must be noted that, as we have also shown in our discussion of the garment industry, this failure of really making significant progress in upgrading production processes is a general problem of Hong Kong's industry. A study of the total factor productivity (TFP) (using output quantity instead of value added as the output concept) of Hong Kong's manufacturing in 1984–93 (Kwong, Lau and Lin 1997; Kwong 1997) shows that:

> the TFP index for the manufacturing sector turned out to be slowly declining between 1984 and 1993. ... In other words, if the manufacturing sector had been using the same amount of inputs in 1993 as in 1984, only about 87% of the 1984 output could have been produced. ... [I]n the manufacturing sector of Hong Kong, despite the fast accumulation of capital, output growth has been stagnant. (Kwong, Lau and Lin 1997, pp. 21–22)

Generally speaking, Hong Kong's manufacturing fails to make significant progress in restructuring and upgrading the production processes in terms of technological sophistication. The above exercise of TFP measurement largely confirms the observations noted in various studies of local industries we have mentioned earlier. Of course, there are variations among industries in their output performances and the ability of improving technology. The electronics cluster is found by Kwong, Lau and Lin (1997, p. 230) to be among those industries which have been able to improve their technology. However, that said, it should be noted that, while being in the league of improving industries, the electronics cluster does not score that well in terms of TFP growth. Indeed, its score is lowest among other improving industries. This observation is consistent with the picture we have developed in our discussion in this section. On the whole, the electronics industry does have difficulties in making significant technological upgrading and catching up with competitors within the region. Yet, at the same time, being OEM producers, they have to restructure their production in order to ensure that they can obtain orders from abroad. In other words, they are led by their buyers to upgrade their production. Also, as pointed out earlier, many electronics producers have moved towards product redesign and repackaging to meet market demands. Their success in those processes also brings about TFP growth.

Third, given the above characteristics of the industry, electronics manufacturers are quick to capitalize on the abundant supply of low-wage labor in mainland China. Indeed, the leading restructuring strategy of the industry is relocating production to mainland China, particularly the region of the Pearl River Delta (Industry Department, *Hong Kong's Manufacturing Industries* 1991, Appendix IV-28). Among the electronics establishments we had interviewed in 1992 (see Chiu and Lui 1995), 52% of them carried out offshore production. More interesting is that 18% of our respondents did not have any production in Hong Kong and simply had all the manufacturing activities done in their plants in mainland China. The study on industrial investments in the Pearl River Delta conducted by the Federation of Hong Kong Industries also confirms the trend of relocation. Almost 70% (69.4 per cent) of the electronics establishments covered by the study have investment in the region (Federation of Hong Kong Industries 1993, p. 63). And it is suggested that:

> Such a significant extent of investment can be explained by the labour-intensive nature of the industry. In Hong Kong, electronics products are turned out through many component-assembling processes which are mostly done manually. Since full scale automation is still uncommon, a large number

of workers, particularly young workers, are needed. Faced with a severe shortage of labor in Hong Kong, which is complicated by the reluctance of the younger generation to enter the industrial workforce, the electronics industry has a strong incentive to take advantage of the abundant supply of labor across the border.

(Federation of Hong Kong Industries 1993)

The same study reports that the relocated establishments have an average workforce of 905 workers (Federation of Hong Kong Industries 1993, p. 69). However, in terms of investment electronics firms in the Pearl River Delta tend to concentrate in two clusters (Federation of Hong Kong Industries 1993, p. 67). At the one end, there are small and medium-sized firms with a capital size of less than HK$5 million (39.2%). And at the other, there are larger firms with a capital size of more than HK$20 million (20.8%). These findings suggest that the strategy of going offshore is by no means confined to larger firms. Given the geographical proximity between Hong Kong and the Pearl River Delta, many small and medium-sized firms can "make use of the abundant supply of labor there to reduce production cost" (Federation of Hong Kong Industries 1993).

Our 1992 survey findings also show that there is no significant association between the employment size of local establishments and that of offshore plants. In other words, there is no necessary connection that those running larger establishments in Hong Kong will have proportionately larger plants across the border. Although our survey data do not warrant us to go into a sophisticated statistical analysis of the strategic moves behind relocation, the answers solicited from our open-ended questions do allow us to discern, albeit tentatively, three possible strategic considerations in deciding relocation. First, it is the strategy of reducing assembly processes in Hong Kong, reorganizing the local plant into a R&D section and sending the more labour-intensive processes to offshore production. Among our respondents in the electronics industry, there is a significant association ($X^2 = 6.93570$, df = 1, p < .01) between investment overseas and conducting internal R&D. This suggests that it is more likely to find those manufacturers who have started offshore production to carry out R&D in their Hong Kong establishments. More sophisticated processes are retained in their Hong Kong premises and assembly is done in their offshore plants. However, it is important to note that only about one-third (34%) of our respondents are estimated to have adopted this restructuring strategy. The extent to which Hong Kong electronics manufacturers have adopted such a restructuring strategy should not be overestimated. Indeed, in terms of technological sophistication, Hong Kong's electronics industry falls behind its East Asian competitors. As pointed out in the review of industrial automation by the Industry Department (1992, p. 37), "[o]n the whole, the industry only invests in hard automation equipment if forced to by their buyers, instead of continually seeking out opportunities to add extra value for, and hence extract extra value from, their customers". Most of the electronics manufacturers are OEM producers. Their R&D activities are more related to product modifications than core technology development. In this regard, the progress of technological upgrading achieved by the electronics industry has to be interpreted with caution (see Table 11.11; also Lui and Chiu 1994). The second strategy is similar to the above except that the local establishment concentrates on trading instead of R&D. In our survey of electronics establishments, 36% of the sampled establishments do not have their own factory production in Hong Kong. And among these establishments, 50% of them rely solely on their offshore plants for production, one-third carry out the production through relocated plants and subcontracting out to local or offshore factories, and the rest have all their production finished by subcontractors. While some of these establishments have retained the product development process in their local plants, many have more or less changed into trading firms. In some cases, they assume the role of sourcing agent for transnational corporations. Given their business contacts with local subcontractors and manufacturers based in mainland China, they can be commercial agents in facilitating international subcontracting.

Last but not least is the strategy of expanding production capacity by relocation. This is a strategy adopted by many medium-sized firms which see the advantages of the abundant supplies of cheap labor and cheap land across the border and try to make profits by expanding the scale of production rather than moving towards technological sophistication (Industry Department, *Hong Kong's Manufacturing Industries* 1991, Appendix IV-61). For the electronics industry as a whole, this strategy has the danger of further hindering the upgrading of production technology and thus will reduce the competitiveness of the industry in the long run. However, for individual manufacturers this strategy allows them to hold on to labour-intensive production and make lucrative profits by a significant increase in sales volume.

The relocation of electronics production is now in full swing. As expressed by some local producers, relocation is "the only means for the electronics manufacturers to survive. In order to stay cost competitive, they have to move to PRC" (Industry Department, *Hong Kong's Manufacturing Industries* 1991, Appendix IV-28). And in the case of a small telecommunications manufacturer reported in a recent study of the electronics industry (Boston Consulting Group International Inc 1995, p. 53), "[m]ost of our manufacturing steps are done manually and we must move to China to remain competitive. Automation is not an alternative because our products are low-end, low value." In the light of this change of production location, it is then not difficult to understand why there has been a reshaping of subcontracting networks in local production. Indeed, if local manufacturers are still looking for production strategies to reduce costs and enhance flexibility, they turn to setting up their own plants in the Pearl River Delta or finding subcontractors across the border. A Hong Kong-based production strategy is losing its attractiveness.

IV. CONSTRAINTS ON TECHNOLOGICAL ACQUISITION: THE LCD INDUSTRY

Liquid crystal display (LCD) is a major high-technology sector within the electronics industry and has spearheaded the upgrading of the electronics industry in Japan and South Korea. In Hong Kong the LCD sector developed early in the late 1970s but since the mid-1980s it has declined in relative competitiveness against other countries.[1] While LCD components were gradually extended to more high-end applications, Hong Kong manufacturers did not capitalize on the new growth opportunities. Instead, they became marginalized in the sense that they left the mainstream applications, either voluntarily or involuntarily, in favour of niche markets. Hence it is a good case to illustrate the constraints on technological acquisition among Hong Kong manufacturers.

For example, few, if any, Hong Kong firms considered automation to be a feasible alternative. The attitude of C.W. Chua, managing director of Display Technology is illustrative here: "Automation is not practical for a company of our size. The advantage of remaining semi-automated is that we are highly flexible and can change products rapidly.

This is a major selling point because it also means we can offer short lead time."[2] Even multinational corporations (MNCs) investing in Hong Kong adopted the same approach, as Dr H.U. Beyeler, managing director of Videlic (HK) said: "With constant changes in volumes we must have optimum flexibility. To automate too much would inhibit flexibility, so we are trying to find the best balance."[3]

A shift to flexible production did enable local firms to survive and indeed to grow, but the avoidance of automation already illustrated how a low capital base could deter firms from keeping abreast of the mainstream development in LCD industry. Since the mid 1980s huge R&D and capital investments have pushed the technology frontier further ahead, so that Hong Kong firms could stay in the game only as niche players (cf. Liu and Lee 1997, p. 310). Japanese giants have made huge investments in the development of active-matrix technology since the mid-1980s when twisted nematic (TN) still dominated the marketplace. Passive-matrix super twisted nematic (STN) technology first established itself for high-resolution applications by the late 1980s, though active-matrix thin film transistor (TFT) was already up-and-coming at that time. This is a sharp contrast to the majority of Hong Kong firms which were still sticking to the TN technology, with Varitronix being the notable exception.

LCD for lap-top computers became the primary development focus at the turn of the 1990s, and Hong Kong had virtually no role in this technology race. Meanwhile, South Korean conglomerates, latecomers in LCD production, leapfrogged into STN technology. The Taiwan government took the initiative to lend a hand to upgrade the island's LCD industry. In contrast, Hong Kong firms concentrated on TN production for such niche markets as industrial instruments and electronic gadgets, while the government played little or no role in guiding or coordinating the industry. Statistics illustrate well the relative decline of Hong Kong's LCD industry in the 1980s.

As shown in Table 11.12, nominal production value grew at a slow pace from HK$515 million in 1987 to HK$639 million in 1990. To put it in real terms, local production was no better than stagnant from the late 1980s to the early 1990s, with the 1992 figure even lower than the 1987 one. Stagnant growth was the price to pay for staying with TN while the dominant industry standard switched to STN. Nevertheless, into the 1990s it appeared that the fortunes of the Hong Kong LCD industry were changing again.

TABLE 11.12   Major Statistics of Hong Kong's LCD Industry
(in HK$1,000)

Year	Production Value		Domestic Exports		Re-exports	
	Nominal Value	Real Value[1]	Nominal Value	Real Value[2]	Nominal Value	Real Value[3]
1986	n.a.	n.a.	203,282	223,030	98,019	113,215
1987	514,556	741,475	258,932	275,856	104,966	118,594
1988	668,905	885,095	295,044	307,384	195,268	213,393
1989	619,353	666,052	381,489	386,501	201,997	208,108
1990	639,081	639,081	433,011	433,011	197,957	197,957
1991[4]	330,985	303,013	362,721	356,394	222,937	218,277
1992	829,929	692,567	464,000	450,733	272,557	265,124
1993	1,002,146	770,730	629,300	612,683	405,986	396,449
1994	1,672,878	1,203,920	974,400	931,000	593,639	573,070
1995	3,363,607	2,245,653	1,743,100	1,627,893	954,374	897,501
1996	n.a.	n.a.	2,136,200	1,994,824	1,271,771	1,206,429

NOTES: 1. Real production value is measured in constant 1990 dollar using the GDP deflator computed by the Census and Statistics Department.

2. Real domestic export value is measured in constant 1990 dollar using the deflator for domestic export value used in GDP statistics.

3. Real re-export value is measured in constant 1990 dollar using the deflator for re-export value used in GDP statistics.

4. We consulted the Census and Statistics Department about the data discrepancy between production value and domestic exports in 1991. They replied that as production value was collected by a sample survey instead of an industrial census, sampling error may be quite large for a small industry like LCD production.

SOURCE: Unpublished statistics from Hong Kong Census and Statistics Department.

The 1990s saw the rise of TFT LCD, with South Korea, and to a lesser extent Taiwan, catching up in the technology race with Japan. Interestingly, Hong Kong benefited from the room in the low- to mid-range market left behind by its counterparts who were keen to focus on the high-end market. The market was also stimulated by the increasing use of LCDs in more and more applications such as hand-held electronic games, dictionaries and even audio and video products. This enlarging room at the bottom of the market (or at the rear of the race) even attracted a few new entrants into the industry in Hong Kong, including Truly and Yeebo.

While production value grew by 60% from HK$515 million in 1987 to HK$830 million in 1992, a threefold increase was recorded in only two years from 1993 to 1995 (Table 11.12). In 1995 production value topped HK$3,364 million, six times higher than the 1987 figure. The domestic exports show a similar growth rate: it took seven years from 1986 to 1993 to triple the export value, but only three years from 1993 to 1996 for another triple growth. In 1996 domestic exports reached HK$2,136 million, ten times the 1986 figure. Not only was the growth dramatic in nominal values, but putting all figures in real terms also shows a comparable phenomenon.

The rejuvenation of Hong Kong's LCD industry corresponds closely with the rise of mainland China as a production base. China had long absorbed the bulk of Hong Kong's LCD exports and re-exports from the mid-1980s to the early 1990s, but the mainland replaced Japan as the primary origin of LCD re-exports from 1994. The 1990s also saw Hong Kong diversifying its export markets away from China to other countries, primarily Southeast Asian ones. The share of China in both Hong Kong's exports and re-exports shrank significantly in the 1990s, particularly in the case of exports. The changes were a result of two strategies of Hong Kong's LCD industry: first, massive relocation to China; and second, emergence of its middleman role between overseas buyers and LCD firms in China.

Despite the tremendous growth, Hong Kong did not join the technology race in the 1990s when constant improvements were being made in LCD technology in general and TFT in particular. Almost all the Hong Kong firms are now still sticking to passive technology like TN and STN. Japan remained the leader through the 1990s, but top South Korean firms such as Hyundai and Samsung later became alternatives to Japanese suppliers in the TFT LCD marketplace (Kim 1997). Huge investments were again the driving force behind the technological development. For example, in the three years prior to 1992 Japan's LCD suppliers spent at least US$2.5 billion on plants and tools.[4] Samsung spent US$375 million on a plant producing flat panel displays by 1995, and emerged as a market leader along with the Japanese. There were few real efforts pushing for TFT technology in Taiwan until the mid-1990s when the Industrial Technology Research Institute (ITRI) led the development of large-size applications. A few large groups like Nan Ya Plastics and Chunghwa Picture Tubes also began to diversify into the field.

Hong Kong companies certainly could not hope to match the deep pockets of their competitors in the region. Varitronix, the leading Hong Kong LCD producer, had only US$8 million in paid-up capital when listed in 1991. In the same year another company, Truly, was evaluated as being worth US$3.8 million in paid-up capital when listed. The entire stock of fixed assets of Varitronix was evaluated at US$36.6 million in 1996 while Truly's was valued at US$66 million in 1995. Even if we think that comparison to the South Korean *chaebol* would be unfair, Hong Kong's LCD companies are minnows in terms of the capital base even compared with their Taiwanese counterparts. Picvue, a Taiwanese company dedicated to production of LCDs, had a capital base of US$97.5 million in 1995 (Lee and Pecht 1997, p. 136). The other Taiwanese LCD makers which were subsidiaries of larger groups such as Chunghwa and Nan Ya of course had even stronger financial support.

Hence, among the four "Little Dragons" Hong Kong apparently lags behind in terms of the technological upgrading of its manufacturing industries. The LCD industry appears to trek the same path of development. As discussed above, even though it had an early start relative to the other neighboring economies and had decades of dynamic growth, by the 1990s Hong Kong's electronics industry largely remained low-technology and labour-intensive, relying on the low-cost production in China to compete in the international marketplace.

Simply put, the early entrants have survived without chasing after the technological frontier, while the late entrants are primarily engaging in the low-end market. By contrast, in South Korea and Taiwan early entrants were replaced by other newcomers when the LCD industry became a prosperous one in the late 1980s and the early 1990s. In the case of Taiwan those late entrants include Nan Ya Plastics, Chunghwa, Picvue, Unipac and Prime View; and in the case of South Korea, Samsung, Hyundai, LG and Daewoo. In most of these cases the new entrants clustered in the middle to higher end of the market rather than choosing to enter the lower-end market.

As our previous discussion suggests, one of the major factors for the Hong Kong model of development has been the government's passive industrial policy (Chiu 1996; Tuan and Ng 1995). The consequences of this hands-off approach to industrial development have been heavy. Suffice to stress here that all the major public institutional bodies (the Industry Department, Trade Development Council and Productivity Council) have a relative narrow scope of activity, a small budget and a largely passive relationship with manufacturers (Chiu, Ho and Lui 1997). For LCD makers in particular, their views of these institutions are particularly dim. When asked about these institutions, their typical response was that they had no contact with them or did not think they were useful.

Before the 1990s the government also persistently refrained from directly promoting industrial development through any form of selective incentive (Chiu 1996b). For example, despite high land costs which raised production costs considerably for manufacturers, the government remained committed to selling industrial land mainly by open bidding. Only belatedly was industrial land provided to designated high-technology sectors through publicly funded industry-support organizations. First, the Hong Kong Industrial Estates Corporation offers accommodation at development costs to advanced industries in the three industrial estates located in suburban areas. Second, the Hong Kong Industrial Technology Centre Corporation offers business incubation services and accommodation to technology-based companies at the Technology Centre in Kowloon Tong near the city centre (Department of Audit 1997). Also due to the reluctance of the government to subsidize industry and hence limited public funding for the Productivity Council, the latter's services are often provided on a cost-recovery basis and its role in promoting technological diffusion is often quite limited (Chiu, Ho and Lui 1997; Berger and Lester 1997).

Yet a slight change in the government's approach since the early 1990s is detectable. In the case of the LCD industry the government funded HK$14 million for the establishment of the Centre for Display Research in 1996. Located in the new Clearwater Bay campus of the Hong Kong University of Science and Technology (HKUST), the centre is equipped with facilities for TN/STN module prototyping, complete LCD testing, failure analysis, LCD electronics packaging (chip-on-glass) and microelectronics fabrication for active matrix LCD. The centre has defined its mission as being to provide technical support for local LCD manufacturers, perform research in advanced display techniques and train students with hands-on experience in LCD manufacturing for the local industry. It has a major project to develop "image on a chip" technology, together with Varitronix.

The government also set up several funds designated for the promotion of industries. Four of the five are relevant to manufacturing industries, including the New Technology Training Scheme (NTTS) which provides grants to assist training in new technologies; the Ap-

plied Research and Development Scheme (ARDS) which provides loans
or equity participation to assist applied research and development
projects; the Industrial Support Fund (ISF) which provides grants to
finance projects which are beneficial to the technological development
of industry; and the Cooperative Applied Research and Development
(CARDS) program which provides loans or equity participation to assist
applied R&D projects involving mainland China and Hong Kong experts. Nevertheless, there are doubts concerning the efficacy of these
programmes. For example, their operation has been roundly criticized by
an internal audit report within the government (Department of Audit
1997). The report queried whether training courses supported by NTTS
meet the original objective, while it pointed out that the number of projects
assisted under ARDS was much lower than expected. Hence the Director
of Audit "considers that there is a need to conduct an overall strategic
review of the various funding schemes in order to ensure that these
schemes meet the long-term needs of Hong Kong".[5] Furthermore, with
the exception of the ISF, the funds are simply too small to have any
significant impact on the overall development of industries.[6]

   This puts Hong Kong in sharp contrast to the other NIEs in the
promotion of the LCD industry. The South Korean *chaebol* of course
benefited from the selective credit allocation from the government-
controlled commercial banks and from the official guarantee of foreign
loans they raised. Without such financial support, it is inconceivable
that the *chaebol* could grow so large in such a short period of time.
Even in Taiwan the state has "strategic loan schemes" to help designated high-technology industries. More importantly, the publicly funded
ITRI has played a critical role in fostering high-technology industries.
The Singapore government also provides many incentives for the
development of designated high-technology industries, through the
activities of the Economic Development Board and, since the 1990s,
the National Science and Technology Board.

   Without public financial support, Hong Kong LCD makers have to
raise funds from private sources. Nevertheless, the absence of well-established venture capital funds makes it difficult for them to raise capital
to develop new technology (Chiu, Ho and Lui 1997; Berger and Lester
1997). Even local banks are not known to be warm to R&D efforts
among high-technology firms, as noted by an MIT research group led
by Suzanne Berger and Richard Lester that "manufacturing or manufacturing-related activities make up only a small fraction of bank's business....

Most banks could give only one single example of high tech company they have financed (Berger and Lester 1997, p. 305).

Before the 1990s industrial firms also found it difficult to tap the capital market by becoming listed (Chiu, Ho and Lui 1997). Only in the 1990s, when there was a boom in the stock market, did initial public offerings (IPOs) by industrial firms become easier. For example, all three of the listed LCD makers secured listing in the 1990s. To become publicly quoted has made in easier for them to borrow from banks, as Truly admits: "It has been much easier to obtain loans since we became listed." Hence the institutional separation between industry and finance that has been entrenched in Hong Kong since the very early years of its industrial development continues to plague the LCD industry. Current proposals to establish a NASDAQ-type second board may help smaller firms to raise fund.

Since it is clear that investment in advanced LCD technology, such as active-matrix TFT technology, is beyond the resources of any of the Hong Kong firms individually and it is equally clear that public agencies in Hong Kong are not prepared to underwrite the necessary investments, then one might ask why firms do not join forces in collaborative ventures to make the needed investments. In this respect Hong Kong's LCD industry also suffers from a more fundamental problem, namely the lack of an institutional framework to foster collaborative R&D and to co-ordinate among different institutions and actors. There is no R&D collaboration among industrialists in Hong Kong. Nearly all of them do their own product research by themselves. Truly, for example, prefers to develop the technology in-house as compared with collaborative efforts. Executive director James Wong discloses: "We choose instead to try to do our own R&D in-house." Previous efforts by the Productivity Council to create a collaborative consortium to develop new products also failed to produce tangible results (Chiu, Ho and Lui 1997). There are exceptions, such as the collaborative program between Varitronix and the Centre for Display Research at HKUST, but these are rare.

While inter-firm collaboration sounds logical, collaborative R&D actually requires certain preconditions to work — such as a dense and close-knit personal and social network, or strong leadership from the public sector. In Hong Kong it is clear that both these factors are lacking. Among local LCD makers, personal contacts with other manufacturers have been minimal, and they do not customarily befriend other electronics producers in the same line of business. In other words, while vertical ties with suppliers or buyers are important and treasured, horizontal ties have not been a valued asset among LCD makers in particular or Hong Kong manufacturers in general. Yes, they may occasionally get together to have meals and share information, but collaborative ventures are not normally considered among firms in the same product sector. They see each other more as competitors than potential partners.

While this contradicts much of the talk about business network in Chinese communities, the "atomistic" nature of local manufacturing firms must be traced to the absence of an institutional infrastructure that facilitates and underwrites collaborative efforts. In Hong Kong industry associations play a minimal role in fostering collaboration. For example, senior managers of Truly said they did not have much contact with the electronics industry associations, nor did they think of them as of much relevance in actually devising business strategy. Varitronix's Chang is a vice-chairman of an industry association, but he regards it more as a community service than actually helping his own enterprise (Interview transcript).

The state also has not played much of a role as matchmaker or linchpin for a collaborative network on R&D among industrialists. As mentioned, the Productivity Council has attempted without much success to build a consortium for developing new products. Firms jealously guard their commercial secrets and genuine collaboration is difficult. To change this mentality, the public sector needs to play a much bigger role in encouraging and underwriting collaborative efforts. For example, in the "Third Italy" local governments and industry associations play a major role in helping small firms to get finance and developing joint ventures in training and technology development (Best 1990; Piore and Sabel 1984).

A contrast with neighboring Taiwan is probably more appropriate, however. In Taiwan the state works mainly through the ITRI to promote technological diffusion in high-technology electronics industries. Its success in fostering the semiconductor industry in Taiwan is already well known. It has also taken the lead to develop TFT technology and foster an alliance of LCD makers. In 1993, for example, it co-ordinated a consortium —which included United Microelectronics Corp., Taiwan Semiconductor Manufacturing, Unipac Optoelectronics and Picvue — to develop the technology (Clifford 1993); this however had few results. In 1995 the Electronics Research Organization (ERSO) of the

ITRI was successful in jointly developing Taiwan's first-generation 10.4-inch TFT colour LCD. We are not saying that Taiwan's collaborative efforts produce runaway successes; there are reports of early problems in the projects (Thornton 1996, p. 72). Yet such collaboration did stimulate the further upgrading of Taiwanese firms. For instance, PrimeView, one of the two Taiwanese manufacturers who pioneered the production of TFT LCDs, acquired the technology from the ITRI. The other firm producing TFT LCDs, on the other hand, was also a joint venture established in 1990 among several major Taiwanese semiconductor firms (Lee and Pecht 1997, pp. 102–103).

The Centre for Display Research at HKUST is perhaps the only exception in the otherwise absence of institutional ties between LCD firms and public institutions. Yet it also bears the limitations of industry-university collaboration in general in Hong Kong. According to the MIT study of Hong Kong industry, a common complaint among Hong Kong industrialists is that "the universities hold themselves aloof from the industrial sector and do not tailor their teaching and research activities closely enough to its needs" (Berger and Lester 1997, p. 66). While the Centre for Display Research has set its mission as helping the local industry, interaction between the centre and local industry is not as yet well developed. Currently two collaboration research projects are active, one with Varitronix on reflective active-matrix displays and one with Motorola (HK) Ltd. on chip-on-glass technology. By contrast, Truly confessed to having no linkage with the centre; it has instead established co-operation with Tsinghua University in China in preference to collaborating with institutions in Hong Kong.

V. SUMMARY

We presented case studies of the two leading industries in Hong Kong, garment-making and electronics, in order to illustrate their general path of development and relationship to the overall institutional settings. In both cases the industries thrived with flexible production and market sensitivity, using mature technology to mass produce labor-intensive commodities at low cost. Later in the 1980s, when cost became too high locally to sustain this kind of strategy, they resorted to relocation to overseas but did not change their production method fundamentally or acquire more sophisticated technology. The decentralized production helped individual firms to maintain high profitability, but inevitably the industries' local production shrank in size.

The commercial origin of Hong Kong's manufacturing contributed to this strategy by endowing local firms with an extensive global commercial network. Market intelligence and connections enable local firms to search constantly for new market niches without having to change their core technology. The colonial state's passive industrial policy also reinforced this path of development by not offering incentives or support for the technological upgrading of local industries. Focusing on the LCD industry, we have illustrated how the absence of financial support and limited technological assistance from the public sector partly explain the industry's marginalization in global technological development.

NOTES

1. This section is partly based on materials in Chiu and Wong (1998).
2. *Electronic Components*, October 1986, p. 46.
3. *Electronic Components*, June 1984, p. 102.
4. *Far Eastern Economic Review,* 2 July 1992, p. 38.
5. Department of Audit (1997), p. 402.
6. The breakdown of grants/loans disbursed by each scheme up to March 1996/97 is as follows: HK$5 million by NTTS, HK$34 million by ARDS, HK$635 million by ISF and HK$8 million by CARDS.

REFERENCES

Bailey, T. "Organizational Innovation in the Apparel Industry". *Industrial Relation* 32 (1993): 30–48.

Berger, S. and R. Lester, eds. *Made By Hong Kong*. Hong Kong: Oxford University Press, 1997.

Best, M.H. *The New Competition: Institutions of Industrial Restructuring*. Cambridge: Polity Press, 1990.

Birnbaum, D. *Importing Garments Through Hong Kong*. Hong Kong: Third Horizon Press, 1993.

Boston Consulting Group International Inc. *Report on Techno-Economic and Market Research Study on Hong Kong's Electronics Industry 1993-1994, Volume 2: Phase 1 Study — Industry Analysis*. Hong Kong: Government Printer, 1995.

Census and Statistics Department, Hong Kong. *Survey of Industrial Production*. Hong Kong: Government Printer, various years.

_____. "Trading Firms with Manufacturing-Related Functions". *Hong Kong Monthly Digest of Statistics*, August 1996.

_____. "Trading Firms with Manufacturing-Related Functions". *Hong Kong Monthly Digest of Statistics*, September 1997.

Chan, T.S. *Distribution Channel Strategy for Export Marketing: The Case of Hong Kong Firms*. Ann Arbor: UMI Research Press, 1984.

Chiu, S.W.K. "The Changing labor Market and Foreign Workers in Hong Kong". *International Employment Relations Review* 2 (1996*a*): 55–76.

_____. "Unravelling Hong Kong's Exceptionalism: The Politics of Laissez-Faire in the Industrial Takeoff". *Political Power and Social Theory* 10 (1996*b*): 229–56.

Chiu, S.W.K. and T.L. Lui. "Hong Kong: Unorganized Industrialism". In *Asian NIEs and the Global Economy*, edited by G. Clark and W.B. Kim. Baltimore: Johns Hopkins University Press, 1995.

Chiu, S., K.C. Ho and T.L. Lui. *City-States in the Global Economy*. Boulder: Westview Press, 1997.

Chiu, S.W.K. and K.C. Wong. "The Hong Kong LCD Industry: Surviving the Global Technology Race". *Industry and Innovation* 5 (1998): 51–71.

Chu, Y.W. "Dependent Industrialization: the Case of Hong Kong Garment Industry". Unpublished M.Phil. Thesis, Sociology Department, University of Hong Kong, Hong Kong, 1988.

Clifford, M. "Price of Independence: Taiwanese Firms Weigh Cost of Screen Technology". *Far Eastern Economic Review*, 23 December 1993, pp. 52–53.

Dataquest Incorporated. *Techno-economic and Market Research Study on Hong Kong's Electronics Industry 1988-1989*. Hong Kong: Government Printer, 1991.

Department of Audit, Hong Kong. "The Government's Funding Schemes for Promoting Technology Development in Industry". *Report of the Director of Audit on the Results of Value for Money Audits*. Hong Kong: Government Printer, 1997.

Dicken, P. *Global Shift: The Internationalization of Economic Activity*. New York: Guilford Press, 1992.

Federation of Hong Kong Industries. *Hong Kong's Offshore Investment*. Hong Kong: Industry and Research Division, Federation of Hong Kong Industries, 1990.

_____. *Hong Kong's Industrial Investment in the Pearl River Delta*. Hong Kong: Industry and Research Division, Federation of Hong Kong Industries, 1993.

Gereffi, G. "The Organization of Buyer-Driven Global Commodity Chains: How U.S. Retailers Shape Overseas Production Networks". In *Commodity Chains and Global Capitalism*, edited by G. Gereffi and M. Korzeniewicz. Westport: Praeger, 1994.

Gereffi, G. and M. Korzeniewicz. "Commodity Chains and Footwear Exports in the Semiperiphery". In *Semiperipheral States in the World Economy*, edited by W.G. Martin. Westport: Greenwood Press, 1990.

Gereffi, G. and M. Korzeniewicz, eds. *Commodity Chains and Global Capitalism*. Westport: Praeger, 1994.

Germidis, D., ed. *International Subcontracting*. Paris: OECD Development Centre, 1980.

Harvey, D. *The Condition of Postmodernity*. Oxford: Blackwell, 1989.

Hong Kong Trade Development Council. *Survey on Hong Kong's Domestic Exports,*

Re-exports and Triangular Trade. Hong Kong: Research Department, Hong Kong Trade Development Council, 1991.

_____. *Profiles of Hong Kong's Major Manufacturing Industries*. Hong Kong: Research Department, Hong Kong Trade Development Council, 1997.

Industry Department, Hong Kong. *Survey of Hong Kong's Manufacturing Industries: 1990*. Hong Kong: Government Printer, 1990.

_____. *Report on Industrial Automation Study*. Hong Kong: Government Printer, 1992.

_____. *Hong Kong's Manufacturing Industries*. Hong Kong: Government Printer, various years.

Keenan, F. "The Latest Thing: Hong Kong Garment Makers Must Sell as Well as Sew". *Far Eastern Economic Review*, 8 June 1995, pp. 46–47.

Kim, L. *Imitation to Innovation: The Dynamics of Korea's Technology Learning*. Boston: Harvard Business school Press, 1997.

Kurt Salmon Associates. "Final Report on Techno-Economic and Market Research Study on the Textiles and Clothing Industries for Hong Kong Government Industry Department". Mimeographed, 1987.

_____. *Techno-Economic and Market Research Study on Hong Kong's Textiles and Clothing Industries. Vol 2*. Hong Kong: Government Printer, 1996.

Kwong, K.S. *Technology and Industry*. Hong Kong: City University of Hong Kong Press, 1997.

Kwong, K.S., L. Lau and T.B. Lin. "The Impact of Relocation on the Total Factor Productivity of Hong Kong Manufacturing". Manuscript. 1997.

Lau, H.F. and C.F. Chan. "Structural Adaptation: the Response of Hong Kong Garment Manufacturers". Paper presented at the Symposium on Industrial Policy in Hong Kong, 1991, organized by Hong Kong Institute of Asia-Pacific Studies, Chinese University of Hong Kong.

Lee, C.S. and M. Pecht. *The Taiwan Electronics Industry*. Boca Raton: CRC Press, 1997.

Levy, B. "Transaction Costs, the Size of Firms, and Industrial Policy". *Journal of Development Economics* 34 (1990): 151–78.

Liu, S.J. and J.F. Lee. "Liquid crystal display industry in Taiwan". *International Journal of Technology Management* 13, no. 3 (1997): 308–25.

Lui, T.L. *Waged Work at Home: The Social Organization of Industrial Outwork in Hong Kong*. Aldershot: Avebury, 1994.

Lui, T.L. and S. Chiu. "Industrial Restructuring and labor Market Adjustment under Positive Non-Interventionism". *Environment and Planning* A 25 (1993): 63–79.

_____. "A Tale of Two Industries: the Restructuring of Hong Kong's Garment-Making and Electronics Industries". *Environment and Planning* A 26 (1994): 53–70.

Mody, A. and D. Wheeler. *Automation and World Competition*. New York: St Martin's Press, 1990.

Murray, R. "Fordism and Post-Fordism" In *New Times*, edited by S. Hall and M. Jacques. London: Lawrence & Wishart, 1989.

Piore, M. and C. Sabel. *The Second Industrial Divide: Possibilities for Prosperity*. New York: Basic Books, 1984.

Sit, V. and S.L. Wong. *Small and Medium Industries in an Export-Oriented Economy: The Case of Hong Kong*. Hong Kong: Centre of Asian Studies, University of Hong Kong, 1989.

So, A.Y. and S.W.K. Chiu. *East Asia and the World Economy.* Newbury Park: Sage, 1995.

Thornton, E. "Made in Japan: Taiwan Vies for a Piece of the Other Big Screen Market". *Far Eastern Economic Review*, 11 January 1996, pp. 52–53.

Tuan, C. and L.F.Y. Ng. "Evolution of Hong Kong's Electronics Industry under Passive Industrial Policy". *Managerial and Decision Economics* 16 (1995): 509–23.

Ward, M. "Fashioning the Future: Fashion, Clothing and the Manufacturing of the Post-Fordist Culture". *Cultural Studies* 5, no. 1 (1991): 61–76.

Wong, S.L. "Chinese Entrepreneurs and Business Trust". *University of Hong Kong Gazette Supplement* 37, no. 1 (1990): 25–34.

Yau, K.C. The Precarious Symbiosis: Inter-organizational Relations in Hong Kong's Production System". Unpublished Master's thesis, Sociology Department, Chinese University of Hong Kong, 1995.

Yu, T.F.L. *Entrepreneurship and Economic Development in Hong Kong.* London: Routledge, 1997.

12

The Role of the State in Singapore's Industrial Development

Poh-Kam Wong

I. INTRODUCTION

This paper aims to provide an analysis of the role of the state in the industrial development experience of Singapore. While the East Asian Miracle (EAM) study took as its starting point the commonality of factors that account for the apparent success of a diverse range of economies of East Asia, even a cursory analysis of these countries suggest that there are marked differences among them in terms of the role of the state in general and the specific development strategies and policies pursued in particular. Moreover, the EAM focus on economic growth as the main performance criterion differentiating East Asian countries from other developing countries also tends to mask significant differences in other dimensions of economic performance within the group of high-growth East Asian economies, firstly between Japan and the four Asian NIEs, and secondly between the NIEs and China and other ASEAN countries.

We believe that a deeper understanding of the development experience of the diverse economies of East Asia can only be obtained by asking not only where their commonality lies, but also why and how they differ in the ways they achieved rapid economic growth. Instead of one universal set of policy prescriptions and institutional approach, might there be diverse paths to economic success, at least up to the NIE-income stage, that other developing countries can pursue? Instead of one East Asian Miracle, might the experience of the four Asian NIEs suggest four different ones instead? As the economies of the NIEs further advance, will their development paths converge or further diverge? And which model of development will prove to be more resilient in coping with the transition from NIE to advanced nation? This last question is particularly intriguing in the light of the recent financial turmoil in East Asia that has affected the different countries in the region differently.

The development experience of Singapore is interesting in this comparative institutional perspective. Like the other three Asian NIEs, Singapore has achieved remarkable economic growth over the last four decades. Between 1960-2000, Singapore's GDP grew by an average of 8.2% per annum in real term (Table 12.1), with per capita GNP in current prices rising more than 60 times from US$435 in 1960 to US$27,000 in 1999 (PPP-adjusted), highest in Asia and globally was only behind Luxembourg, the US, and Switzerland (World Bank, 2001). Like Hong Kong, the other successful city-state in Asia, Singapore has evolved over the years into a major financial, transport, communications and business hub in the Asia-Pacific region. Unlike Hong Kong, however, Singapore has not experienced significant de-industrialization and "hollowing" out of manufacturing employment in recent years: Significantly, the manufacturing sector of Singapore grew even faster than the economy as a whole over 1960-99 (9.4% vs. 8.3%), and currently accounts for about one-quarter of total GDP. Manufacturing activities in Singapore have also witnessed very rapid technological development, moving from labor-intensive, simple assembly industries to increasingly capital-intensive and technologically complex industries.

While Singapore thus shares a similar pattern of high economic growth with sustained industrial development as Taiwan and Korea, Singapore's strong manufacturing performance differs from these two NIEs in that it has relied heavily on the investment of foreign multinational corporations (MNCs). Foreign- and majority foreign-owned manufacturing firms consistently accounted for more than 70% of the total manufacturing output throughout the 1970s, 1980s and 1990s. This pattern of MNC-led manufacturing development stands in strong contrast to Taiwan and Korea, where indigenous manufacturing firms predominate over foreign firms — numerous SMEs in the case of Taiwan, large chaebols in the case of Korea.

This chapter is organized as follows. In Section I, we present an overview of the key phases of economic development of Singapore, highlighting the main development policies of the government in response to the historical political-economic contexts and external environment under which Singapore had to operate. Section II focuses on the development performance of the manufacturing sector and the specific government policy interventions and institutional mechanisms that have influenced it. A summary interpretation is provided in the Concluding Section (Section III). A more detailed case study of two manufacturing industries — electronics and shipbuilding/repair — will be given in the next chapter (Chapter 13).

II. OVERVIEW OF ECONOMIC DEVELOPMENT STRATEGY

1. The Genesis of Singapore as a Colonial Entrepot

The development of Singapore as a modern city-state owes her histori-cal root to her strategic geographic position in South East Asia. Under the British Empire, Singapore was developed as a major port com-manding the main sea-way between the Indian Ocean and the Pacific world, the commercial hub of a rich primary producing region and the administrative capital and garrison of the British empire in Southeast Asia. As documented by Huff (1994), Singapore grew rapidly as an entrepot trading hub for the hinterland of Peninsular Malaya and the Indonesian Archipalego in the late 19th century and early 20th century, as a result of the opening of the Suez Canal in 1869 and the rapid increase in world demand for primary products like tin and rubber that the Malayan region could produce. By the time of the Second World War in 1939 and certainly by the time of withdrawal of British rule in 1959, Singapore was already a major metropolis with the most devel-oped transport, communications, administrative and business services infrastructure in Southeast Asia.

2. The Early Years of Political Independence (late 1950s to mid-1960s)

When self-government was attained in 1959, Singapore was faced with a very uncertain future. Its role as the commercial hub of the region was severely threatened. The colonial era, especially the Pax Britannia under which Singapore had existed for 140 years, had irretrievably come to an end. The newly independent nations of Southeast Asia were in a mood of assertive nationalism. They sought to bypass the middle-man entrepot trading role of Singapore, the mainstay of its economy, which was viewed with suspicion as a colonial arrangement for their economic exploitation. British Malaya, of which Singapore was the primal city, had attained a separate independence two years earlier. The world had undergone a kaleidoscopic change and new political and economic equations were being written for Southeast Asia. Singapore appeared in danger of being left high and dry by the receding tide of colonial withdrawal.

Domestically, a bitter political struggle took place within the ruling People's Action Party (PAP) over the future political orientation of Singapore, and by extension, its economic role in the changing world. A group under the then Prime Minister, Lee Kuan Yew, which advocated that Singapore's economic future could best be guaranteed by industrialization in the context of a pan-Malayan common market, and hence some form of political merger with the Federation of Malaya, emerged victorious. The Federal government in Kuala Lumpur was then also keen for some form of political union that could give it a degree of control over a small but volatile southern neighbor to which it had his-torically been closely linked. Britain was also looking for an arrangement whereby it could tie up all its remaining colonial territories in Southeast Asia for divestment. The result was the formation of Malaysia in 1963.

President Sukarno of Indonesia, denouncing Malaysia as a neo-colonialist plot, embarked on a policy of Confrontation against it. Indonesia had been part of the commercial hinterland of Singapore and the disruption of Confrontation to Singapore's economic life was se-vere. Trade which accounted directly for a third of Singapore's GDP in 1963 fell by 17.6% in 1964 and Financial and Business Services which accounted for another 12% of GDP fell by 5.9%. In spite of increased British military spending, GDP overall fell by 4.3% in 1964. Meanwhile, unfortunately, the predominantly Chinese population of Singapore fitted rather uneasily into the delicate balance of politics in Peninsula Malaya which was premised on an implicit recognition of continued Malay dominance, and in 1965 Singapore was expelled from Malaysia in an independence it did not desire.

Singapore's foray into Malaysia thus appeared to have ended disas-trously. Its economic situation in 1965 had deteriorated as compared to 1959. Unemployment topped 10% with population and labor force growing annually by 3.3% and 5.0% respectively. Social conditions were as bad and demands on state resources remained as high as before. On the other hand, state coffers were empty. Furthermore, political relationships with Indonesia and Malaysia, Singapore's top trading partners were badly soured.

Singapore's venture into the formation of Malaysia, however, did not result in totally negative fallouts. From the point of view of development strategy, it did confer a few important, if perhaps unintended, benefits. First, on the strength of the economic arguments for merger, the PAP 'moderates' under Lee Kuan Yew were able to take the political offensive against their left wing and pro-Communist opponents who, for political reasons, could not accept merger as their political base was in Singapore and they feared repression by a right-wing central government in Kuala Lumpur. As a result they were gradually discredited, lost support and ultimately politically eclipsed. Second, the traumatic few years in Malaysia, which saw two racial riots and the economic disruption of Indonesian Confrontation before culminating in Singapore's expulsion, created a sense of siege and shared hardship among the population which bound it to the political leadership. This siege mentality was further sharpened by Britain's announcement in 1967 to accelerate military withdrawal from Singapore by 1971. British military expenditure in 1966 accounted for a hefty 16.3% of GDP and directly and indirectly for about 20% of employment, the imminent loss of which created much apprehension. The dire economic outlook caused the population to rally around the PAP government and, via a resounding 84% of votes in the 1968 elections, gave it the necessary mandate to impose a level of control, social discipline and political acquiescence necessary for the success of the low-wage export manufacturing drive subsequently embarked upon. Finally, the Indonesian Confrontation and the economic fallout of its break-up from Malaysia underlined for Singapore the fragile dependence of its economy on the goodwill of its neighbours and forced it to look further afield for economic sustenance.

3. Beginning of DFI-Driven, Export-Led Industrialization (1965 to late 1970s)

Short of surrendering its sovereignty for economic security in some international Cold War alignment (like Cuba, for example), the economic options facing Singapore in 1965 were narrow. With a population of 1.9 million on some 600 square kilometers of land, it had only its strategic location and the resourcefulness of its population to fall back upon. Faced with an unfriendly regional market, Singapore had to look beyond to the open international market. The development strategy thus adopted was to turn Singapore into a global city through export led industrialization on the basis of the freest flow of international capital, goods and services in its domestic economy. From 1969 to 1973, various defensive duties, imposed in the wake of separation from Malaysia, were removed, and Singapore, for all practical purposes, became a free trading economy.

The central thrust of Singapore's development strategy switched to attracting MNCs to set up operations in Singapore for export markets (Lee 2000). Local businesses (which were mainly engaged in trade related services) were felt to lack both the expertise and the long term view necessary to mount an industrialization drive on a scale sufficient to achieve the pressing national objectives of job creation and income generation. Besides, the PAP government, in its drive to political ascendance was not beholden to nor did it need the political support of local business classes. MNCs, with their massive resources and international networks, appear capable of offering jobs, productive capacity, technology, management know-how and export markets, in a single and continuous package, quickly, and seemingly without limit. To attract MNCs and mobilize them for national economic development, however, required certain preconditions, viz., political stability, industrial peace, a stable free market framework, serviceable infrastructure, as well as supporting institutions. A panoply of measures was taken. Harsh legislation such as the Employment Act of 1968 (to standardize terms and conditions of employment and keep a lid on labor cost) and the Industrial Relations Act of 1968 (to strengthen management control over recruitment, transfer, dismissal, work organization and job assignment, and also to give the state greater powers in the maintenance of industrial peace) were enacted. Further, the Economic Expansion Incentives (Relief from Income Tax) Act of 1967 provided fiscal incentives to investors. Institutionally, various supporting agencies were created to take over the specialized functions performed by the Economic Development Board (a government agency set up in 1961 to spearhead Singapore's industrialization drive). These include the Jurong Town Corporation to develop and manage industrial land, the

Development Bank of Singapore to provide long-term industrial finance, the Singapore Institute for Standards and Industrial Research (SISIR) to ensure quality and promote industrial research, and the Technical Education Department of the Ministry of Education to oversee industrial manpower development. Through the coordinated efforts of these institutions, a comprehensive support framework was put in place to promote and direct Singapore's externally oriented industrialization drive.

The industrialization drive was a great success, at least in regard to the main objectives of employment and income creation. In the late 60s and early 1970s, the world economy was booming. There was a tremendous upsurge in international direct investment as MNCs, first from the USA and then Europe and Japan, came under increasing competitive pressure to seek low cost manufacturing bases overseas. In adopting an open trading system and providing a favourable business environment, Singapore was able to attract multinational firms whose scale of operation was largely directed toward the international market. Between 1967 and 1973, foreign-owned gross fixed assets in Singapore's manufacturing sector grew from S$303 million to S$2,659 million. Over this same period, manufacturing value-added increased annually by 19.3% and GDP by 13%. Despite some 40,000 workers released by the British military withdrawal, the spectre of unemployment, which loomed so menacingly in 1965, was effectively dispelled in 1973 when unemployment stood at 4.5%.

The end of the labor-surplus stage in Singapore's industrialization called for a change in development strategy. This was marked in 1972 by the establishment of the tripartite National Wages Council (NWC) comprising organized labour, employers' associations and the government. With full employment, the task of the NWC was to ensure that the inflationary pressure generated by a tight labor market would not jeopardize Singapore's international competitiveness and its industrialization drive. The attainment of full employment also led to a greater concern for efficient labor deployment and improving the quality of the labor force by education and training. Around the same time, the Economic Development Board also began exercising greater selectivity in the promotion of industries, and was drawing up a list of priority industries in 1975.

The pursuit of a more selective and directed industrial strategy was, however, undermined by the oil-crisis of 1973 and the worldwide recession it precipitated in 1974-75. Manufacturing sector growth slowed to 3.9% in 1974 and 4.0% in 1975. Because of the great concern over maintaining international competitiveness and sustaining the growth of the manufacturing sector, through the NWC and a liberal policy on the import of foreign workers, wages were kept low. Largely because of an increase in foreign investment, manufacturing and GDP growth picked up strongly after 1976. The quality of industrial growth, however, left much to be desired. As a result of wage restrain (average real earnings increased by only 2.3% per annum), labor productivity in manufacturing increased by a mere 0.4% per annum from 1973 to 1979 as compared to 3.0% for the whole economy over the same period. labor productivity in manufacturing as a percentage of average economy-wide productivity fell from 95.0% in 1973 to 81.8% in 1979. This was made possible, to some extent, by an increase in female labor force participation (37.3% in 1973 to 44.2% in 1979), as well as by an influx of foreign unskilled workers, mainly from Malaysia but increasingly from further afield.

4. Transition to NIE (late 1970s to late 1980s)

Because of the increasing perception that the manufacturing sector might have been caught in a low-wage trap, as well as concern over the negative social consequences of a further increase in foreign labor inflow, the government launched a new industrial strategy in 1979. This was dubbed the 'Second Industrial Restructuring' and its objective was to promote higher value-added, skill and technology-intensive industries. The cornerstone of this new strategy was a three-year corrective high wage policy from 1979 to 1981. This high wage policy continued up to 1984 because of a tight labor market and heightened expectations. The full arsenal of policy instruments comprising fiscal and other incentives as well as institutional support ranging from credit and financing to manpower and education were also activated in pursuance of these new industrial objectives.

The high wage strategy initiated in 1979 together with the greater availability of trained manpower quickened the pace of automation. As a result, the level of gross fixed assets per worker in 1983 grew to almost double that in 1979 and productivity growth in 1979 to 1984 averaged 5.9% per annum compared to 0.4% per annum in 1973 to

1979. The price of this high wage strategy, however, was a marked deceleration in the rate of manufacturing growth which fell from 8.1% in 1973–79 to 5.1% in 1979–84, despite a higher GDP growth in the later period (8.5% per annum compared to 7.3% per annum). This higher GDP growth was achieved despite a sluggish world economy because of a rapid expansion of the financial and business services sector as Singapore made great strides in its development as an international financial centre, and because of a domestic construction boom partly initiated by the government as a counter-cyclical measure. Also, in the aftermath of the second oil shock, the primary commodity-based regional economy was relatively buoyant and Singapore benefited from the spillover.

Growth of the above nature, however, could not be sustained and as the construction boom flattened out, and the regional economy collapsed in tandem with falling primary commodity (especially oil) prices in 1985, the Singapore economy went into a free fall. From 8.3% in 1984, GDP growth fell to –1.6% in 1985 — the first time since 1964 that Singapore had experienced negative growth.

The first casualty of the 1985 economic downturn was the high wage policy, blamed in particular by the private sector, for reducing Singapore's international competitiveness. The severity of the downturn and its largely unanticipated suddenness, led to a questioning of more than the high wage policy. It precipitated the beginnings of a serious examination into various aspects of the fundamentals of Singapore's post-independence development strategy. In response to the situation, a high level Economic Committee chaired by the then Minister of State for Trade and Industry, and comprising civil servants, trade unionists, as well as a broad cross section of private sector interests was formed in April 1985 to review the progress of the Singapore economy, and to identify new directions for its future growth (The Economic Committee,1986). The Committee recommended various short term cost cutting measures, the implementation of which resulted in a quick rebound of the economy, from a mere 1.9% GDP growth in 1986, to 8.8% in 1987, and 11.0% in 1988.

Despite the manufacturing sector's role as the leading sector of the economy, its growth appeared to have been much more dependent on low wages as compared to that of the service sector. The experiences of the 1970s and early 1980s have shown that Singapore's comparative advantage in labor intensive manufacturing was temporary. Dramatic declines in bulk transport costs imply that geographical proximity to markets has become less important over time, and therefore that labor intensive industries can afford to be increasingly footloose. Furthermore, as a result of the sharp recession of the mid-1980s, continued low primary commodity prices and mounting problems of debt servicing, both Indonesia and Malaysia had embarked upon radical programs of economic liberalization and deregulation to attract MNC capital for export-oriented manufacturing.

Changes in the structure of manufacturing costs, together with increased competition from neighbouring labour-surplus countries inevitably resulted in comparative advantage shifts over time. It was inevitable that labor intensive industries which were production costs oriented would choose to relocate. The above manufacturing location trends in Singapore (reflecting changes in cost structures) paralleled those of cities elsewhere where higher land and labor costs had caused firms to relocate the more labor intensive stages of manufacturing further away from central cities. The comparative advantage of larger cities, with their higher costs of living and wages, increasingly lie, not in the labor intensive manufacturing activities, but in skill-intensive and knowledge-based manufacturing activities as well as in the provision of a diversified range of specialized services.

It can, however, be argued that the development of the manufacturing sector was necessary to create the needed jobs and was an essential stage in the acquisition of modern production skills and technology. Besides the manufacturing sector accounted for more than 50% of Singapore's foreign exchange earnings, and other sectors, such as transport and communication and commerce are heavily dependent on the growth of manufacturing. While activities such as international financial services and tourism may be independent sources of foreign exchange earnings, they are more volatile and less dependable than manufacturing.

5. From NIE to a Developed Economy (late 1980s to late 1990s)

While Singapore's development strategy up to the late 1970s had centered on the manufacturing sector as the key engine of growth, increasingly other sectors of the economy were also promoted to support and complement the manufacturing sector so as to give a more diversified base to the economy. This diversification strategy received greater impetus after the mid-1980s recession, with government emphasis increasingly shifting from promoting Singapore as a manufacturing hub to that of promoting Singapore as a global 'total business centre'. As a reflection of this reorientation in strategy, the government increasingly described its development strategy as one of maximizing Singapore's 'connectivity' as a 'strategic node for global companies in the Asia-Pacific region' (*The Straits Times*, 26 Oct. 1988). As such, services ranging from financial services and manufacturing services like product design, supply chain management and sales supports, to new services like healthcare, leisure and entertainment were targeted for active promotion.

The financial and business services sector, which already experienced steady expansion throughout the 1970s, grew particularly rapidly in the 1980s and 1990s. In 1970, the sector contributed only 16.7 % to GDP. This rose slightly to 18.9% in 1980, but subsequently accelerated to account for 25.5% by 1990. By 1997, its contribution had further risen to 26.2 %, overtaking manufacturing as the single largest sector of the economy. This rapid growth of Singapore's financial services since the late 1970s was driven mainly by the enormous expansion of international trade and investment in East Asia in general and Southeast Asia in particular throughout most of the 1980s and the first half of 1990s. Regional growth was particularly boosted after the Plaza Accord in 1985, which led to a great influx of Japanese DFI into the region. The increasing financial liberalization of the regional economies throughout much of the period was also an important facilitating factor in Singapore becoming a major financial and services hub in the region. However, active government policies had also contributed significantly to strengthening Singapore's regional hub position. For example, Singapore sought as early as 1968 to establish a role for itself in this area with the launching of the Asian Dollar Market. The government also sought to attract foreign investment into Singapore as a offshore banking centre through the provision of a liberal framework for the free flows international funds, low taxation, and good supporting infrastructure such as telecommunications and a transparent legal environment. The government also consciously cultivated a reputation for sound and prudent banking system through the establishment of a tight supervisory control system.

Tourism also emerged as another important sector of the economy. As the hub of Southeast Asia, for centuries the cross-roads of Chinese, Indian, middle-Eastern and Western cultural influences, Singapore is a microcosm of, as well as gateway to a culturally rich, varied and touristically attractive region of the world. With jet travel and rising incomes, tourist arrivals in Singapore rose from some half million in 1970 to more than 7 million in 1995, contributing to more than 10% of GDP.

In 1990, the political premiership of Singapore was passed from Lee Kuan Yew to Goh Chok Tong, who put forth his new vision to Singapore as a developed nation in a document called The Next Lap (Government of Singapore, 1991). The document envisioned Singapore joining the ranks of advanced, developed nations by the year 2000. Soon after the release of The Next Lap, the government announced the formulation of a Strategic Economic Plan (SEP) to guide the future economic development of the country (MTI, 1991). By themselves, the broad strategic thrusts identified in the SEP represent nothing radically new. The challenge, however, was to translate the strategic intentions into concrete policies and programs. Besides a new focus on integrated promotion of strategic industrial clusters (rather than individual industries) and a stronger emphasis on promoting technological innovation and R&D capabilities, other notable policies recommended include the development of Singapore as a "total business hub", expansion of the privatisation program initiated in the 1980s, various policies aiming at containing health care and social insurance costs, and a call to 're-engineer' the civil service to improve flexibility and quality of the public sector as a whole.

The vision of "The Next Lap" was thus of an expanding world economy with Singapore as the technopolis of Southeast Asia, a gateway for the region to connect with the world economy. In the process of its transformation, Singapore had to convince the neighbouring countries that her growth would be beneficial to them rather than at their expense. Towards this end, the Singapore government pioneered in the early 1990s the concept of a "growth triangle" linking the southern state of Peninsular Malaysia (Johor) and the Riau Islands of Indonesia as a new approach to hasten sub-regional cooperation and integration. The strategic intent of the concept was to find new space to support the relocation of labor-intensive manufacturing activities from Singapore to areas that are geographically proximate to facilitate management and logistic control. By leveraging the different factor endowments of Singapore and her neighbours, the growth triangle concept can arguably strengthen the attractiveness of the sub-region as a whole through greater specialization and synergy. A related goal was to encourage outward DFI from Singapore to go to her immediate neighbours, thereby demonstrating Singapore's commitment to promote the economic growth and social welfare of her neighbours. The initial responses of Malaysia and Indonesia to this Singapore inspired concept had been positive, resulting in a significant expansion of Singaporean investments into Johor State and the Riau Islands in the ensuing years. However, further development of the growth triangle may be stalled by the recent financial crisis that has adversely affected both Malaysia and Indonesia.

During the colonial era, Singapore had developed as the commercial and service centre of an outward-looking primary produce-exporting Southeast Asia. For a brief period in the early 1960s, Singapore had entertained hopes of becoming the 'New York' of an industrializing Malaysia. However, after 1965, as the surrounding countries embarked upon direct trading and inward-looking industrialization, Singapore was forced to become an offshore manufacturing base for multinational corporations. With the countries of the region started to pursue outward-looking, export-oriented industrialization since the late 1970s, the opportunity once again presented itself to Singapore to become the service centre of the region, though now linking the region and the global economy through a different vector of activities. It was to exploit this regional services hub opportunity that underpinned much of the diversification strategies towards a "total business hub" as proposed in the SEP.

Another major new strategic thrust to help establish Singapore as an advanced country was the exploitation of the growing importance of information technology (IT) in the global economy. As far back as the early 1980s, the government already foresaw the growing importance of IT. In 1985, a National IT Plan was launched to promote the diffusion and adoption of IT as well as the development of a strong IT industry encompassing computer-related manufacturing, software development and IT services (Wong, 1996b). With rapid computerizastion already achieved by the early 1990s and sensing the emerging opportunities created by advances in computer network technologies, the Singapore government launched a bolder initiative called the IT2000 Plan in early

1992 to turn Singapore into an "intelligent island" at the end of the
century. Despite some false starts, the implementation of the plan to
connect all households and businesses into a nation-wide high-speed
network, and to proliferate the growth of new internet-based applications and industries, has reached an advanced stage by the late 1990s.

Despite these new strategic thrusts to diversify the economy, the SEP
did not envisage a hollowing out of the manufacturing sector. Instead,
the plan specifically emphasized the need to maintain a strong manufacturing base in Singapore, albeit one that will be innovation and
R&D-intensive. Shortly after the SEP, a Manufacturing 2000 Plan was
announced to promote the continued expansion of the manufacturing
sector by at least 7% a year, and to maintain the sector's contribution
to GDP at a minimum of 25% up to the end of the century.
A new 5-year National Technology Plan (NTP) was also announced in
1991, followed by a more ambitious 5-year National Science and
Technology Plan (NSTP) in 1996, to boost investment in R&D and
technological innovation to support this shift towards technology-
intensive manufacturing.

That Singapore had successfully transited from an NIE into an advanced economy by the late 1990s can be seen from the fact that, by
1997, Singapore had earned the distinction of being ranked number 1
in the world in terms of GNP per capita as measured by purchasing
power parity (PPP) (World Bank,1998). At US$29,000 in terms of PPP,
Singapore overtook the US and Switzerland. In 2000, despite the negative impacts of the Asian financial crisis over 1997–98, Singapore's
PPP-adjusted GNP/capita of US$27,000 still ranked the highest in Asia,
and globally was only behind Luxembourg, the US, and Switzerland
(World Bank, 2001). Singapore has also been consistently ranked as
among the most competitive nations in the world for the last few years,
despite the impacts of the Asian financial crisis. For example, WEF
ranked Singapore No.1 in its 1998 and 1999 Global Competitiveness
Report, while IMD ranked Singapore No.2 for five years in a row from
1996 and 2000 (see Annex Table 12I and 12J).

6. Responding to the Regional Financial Crisis

The severity of the regional economic crisis that resulted from the
initial financial crisis in Thailand in mid-1997 caught virtually all

analysts by surprise. Although the Singapore economy had not been affected by the panics of capital flight as experienced by Thailand, Malaysia, Indonesia and Korea, her economic growth had not remained unscathed. After turning in a credible GDP growth rate of 7.8% in 1997, the economy slowed to 6.1% in Q1 of 1998, 1.6% in Q2, and −1.5% in Q3, the first negative growth in 13 years since the last recession in 1985. By the end of third quarter of 1998, unemployment had climbed to 4.5%, with 20,000 retrenchment in the first 9 months of 1998 alone vs. less than 9,000 in the whole of 1997 (*The Straits Times*, 30 Oct. 1998).

As a regional business hub, Singapore's strong trade and investment linkage with the region has been a contributor to Singapore's strong economic growth prior to the Asian financial crisis. However, the same regional dependence has dragged down Singapore's economic growth after the Asian financial turmoil savaged several key economies in the region. In 1997, about half of Singapore's export went to the 6 worst affected regional economies (Indonesia, Malaysia, Thailand, Korea, Hong Kong and Japan). Recession in all these economies in 1998 therefore had significant negative impacts on Singapore's exports. According to the World Bank (2001), the Indonesian economy contracted by 13.1% in 1998, Thailand 10.8%, Korea 6.7%, Malaysia 7.4%, Hong Kong 5.3% and Japan 1.1%. The consequent drastic slowdown in regional imports and intra-regional trades had significant negative impacts on a wide range of Singapore's regional hub services, from financial services to transportation, communications and business services like regional technical support. Singapore's tourism receipts also dropped substantially (−1% in 1997, −17% in the first 9 months of 1998), led by decline of tourists from Japan and the region.

A significant proportion of Singapore's rapid outward direct foreign investment (DFI) and outward portfolio investments since the late 1980s has also gone to the region (Wong, 1996a). Singapore has been among the largest investors in Thailand, Indonesia and Malaysia. As a result of the financial crisis, this regionalization strategy has resulted in various negative fall-outs. Firstly, there has been an increase in non-performing loans arising from the bursting of the regional asset bubbles and severe recession in the real sector of these regional economies. Statistics suggest that the six local Singapore banks had non-performing loans (NPL) amounting to S$5.9 billion, or 17% of their loan portfolios in the five worst hit countries in the region as of end of August 1998, up sharply from a year ago. Nonetheless, due to the conservative banking supervisory environment in Singapore, all the banks remain healthy despite their regional exposure. Overall, the NPL represented only 6.1% of all the loans by Singaporean banks, much less than for the banking sector in other regional economies (e.g. 35–55% for Korea, Thailand, Malaysia and Indonesia). Secondly, many DFI projects in the region by Singaporean companies have also been negatively affected. The worse hit were those targeting the domestic markets, which have collapsed in many of these regional economies.

The rapid depreciation of regional currencies relative to the Singapore dollar (which has lost less value vs. the US dollar than most other regional currencies) had also worsened Singapore's loss of cost competitiveness versus her regional neighbors. Between July 1997 and Oct. 1998, the Singapore dollar depreciated 13.6% vs. the US dollar and 9.9% vs. the Japanese Yen, compared to 17.5%–66.9% and 13.4%–65.7% respectively for seven other regional currencies (ASEAN-4, Korea, Taiwan and India); only the Hong Kong dollar and the Chinese Renminbi had depreciated less (Freris, 1998). Particularly hard hit were the manufacturing operations of various local small and medium enterprises.

Last, but not least, the initial financial panic has led to a massive flight of capital from the region as a whole, as foreign fund managers as well as local investors shifted their funds to perceived safer havens in US and Europe. This had particularly battered Singapore's stock market, as the perception of high risk in the region due to the political uncertainties and social unrest that have been triggered by the financial crisis spilled over to Singapore as well.

In addition to the effect of regional recession, three other special factors further contributed towards the negative sentiments towards Singapore in 1998. First and foremost was the growing political-economic friction with Malaysia over the last two years. Diplomatic relations between the two countries have steadily worsened over a series of events — Malaysia's strong objections to remarks by Singapore's Senior Minister Lee Kuan Yew, the raising of levy on cargo trucks from Johor to Singapore to discourage Malaysian exporters from using the port of Singapore, alleged re-negation by Malaysia over the Point of Agreement for the redevelopment of Malayan Railways in Singapore and the subsequent tit over the relocation of the customs check-point of the Malayan Railways in Singapore, the suspension of Singapore's CLOB operation, the publication of SM Lee's memoir that contains unfavourable accounts of certain past UMNO leaders, and most recently, Malaysia's withdrawal of her airspace for use by Singapore's Armed Forces and the Malaysian pull-out of a recent military exercise under the Five Power Defence Agreement (FPDA). Although not aimed at Singapore, the decision by the Malaysian government to impose capital controls in 1998 also had significant repercussions on Singapore. It did not help matters that the Malaysian government accused the Singapore government of deliberately causing capital flights from Malaysia by offering high interest rates for ringgit deposits in Singapore-based banks (the Singapore government insisted that this was a purely market-driven phenomenon). More recently, the Malaysian government was also unhappy with Singapore over press coverage of the arrest of the former deputy prime minister, Anwar Ibrahim.

The second factor is the concern over growing political uncertainties and social unrest in Indonesia and their possible negative repercussions on Singapore. Not only are Singapore's substantial investment in Indonesia (especially the Riau Islands of Batam and Bintan) at stake, more importantly, many foreign analysts fear the prospect of an increase in illegal migrants entering Singapore, if political and social turmoil were to escalate in Indonesia and the downward spiral of the Indonesian economy fails to be arrested.

Last, but not least, the vulnerability of Singapore's high dependence on several key electronics industry sectors was exposed when these sectors experienced severe cyclical downturns in their global business cycles in 1998, just when the regional financial crisis hit. Particularly hard hitting was the downturn in the global magnetic hard disk drive and semiconductor industry, which together accounted for almost a quarter of Singapore's manufacturing output. Coupled with a softening of the global demand for computers and a drastic reduction in regional demand for electronics goods in general, Singapore's electronics industry — which accounted for more than 60% of Singapore's non-oil domestic manufactured exports — experienced negative growth and accounted for a large part of the significant rise in retrenchments in recent months.

Such drastic slowdown in growth in 1998 notwithstanding, the Singapore economy managed to recover remarkably strongly in 1999 and 2000. From 0.6% growth in Q1 of 1999, economic growth accelerated to 6.7% in Q2 and Q3, and over 8% in Q4, resulting in an overall annual growth of 5.9% for the whole of 1999. Growth continued to surge in 2000, with the annual growth rate of reaching 9.9%. Thus, compared to all other East Asian economies with the exception of Taiwan and China, Singapore not only suffered the least from the Asian financial crisis, but was among the fastest to recover in 1999.

The ability of Singapore to weather the regional crisis better than most other East Asian countries can be attributed not only to the strong fundamentals of its underlying economic structure, but also by a series of significant government-coordinated policy responses to cope with the regional recession, particularly the reduction of business cost to help companies survive and to protect jobs (Wong, 1999a). In Sept. 1997, even before the magnitude of the regional recession was clear, the government already set up a high-level committee to identify means to enhance Singapore's competitiveness in the medium term future. With the worsening regional situation, the committee was also tasked with coming out with immediate short term measures to cope with the emerging recession. In Nov. 1998, the Committee on Singapore Competitiveness (CSC) released its report, calling for a sweeping coordinated program of action by the public and private sector to implement cost reduction of up to S$10 billions. A large part of this was to come from reduction of wage costs through a combination of a 10% cut in CPF contributions (out of 40%) and recommended 5–8% cuts in the variable component of wages. Both these proposals had been negotiated and eventually endorsed by the tripartite National Wage Council (NWC). To provide the lead, the government announced that the public sector would implement the wage cut policy in the public sector with immediate effect. Other sizable cost cutting came from the reduction of a variety of public services charges, ranging from rentals for industrial and commercial properties operated by statutory boards, to lower corporate and personal income taxation and indirect taxes on various items like petrol and properties.

In addition to these short-term cost cutting measures, the political leadership announced a series of medium to long-term policy initiatives to further bolster the position of Singapore as a major regional hub in the global knowledge based economy. Among the new policy initiatives aimed at such long-term strategic positioning include:

Policies to Enhance Singapore as a Financial Services Hub

First and foremost, the government announced major new policy measures in 1998 and 1999 to further deregulate her financial system to stimulate innovation, even as some of her regional neighbours were learning to tighten their supervisory control system. The Singapore government calculated that she could afford to do so as her reputation for prudent financial supervision had been enhanced as a result of the crisis. As part of this policy shift, the government hastened the process of consolidation of local banks to better compete regionally by announcing the merger of the national postal savings bank (POSB) with DBS, one of the big four local banks. The government also announced a plan to merge the local stock exchange (SES) with the commodity and futures exchange (SIMEX), and to de-mutualize the exchanges. At the same time, listing requirements on the local stock exchange were relaxed to make it easier for technology and internet start-ups to IPO. The government also succeeded in jumpstarting the long-term bond market by attracting regional issuers to issue long-term bonds in Singapore, in addition to pushing public statutory boards to issue long-term bonds. More initiatives would likely to emerge over the next twelve months as the recommendations from a high-level committee tasked by the government to look into financial liberalization were being released and adopted.

Policies to Enhance Singapore as a Regional Trading and Business Services Hub

Singapore's standing as a trading and business services hub in Asia was also likely to be enhanced through a major push by the government to promote the development of information infrastructure and other supporting services for enabling electronic commerce (EC for short). Having established the most advanced physical communications networks and technical manpower base in the region to support EC, the government launched new supporting policy measures, including a new Cyberspace Trading Act and Computer Crime Act to provide the necessary legal framework, a new cyber trader incentives scheme for MNCs to use Singapore as their regional EC hub, a new digital signature certification authority and mutual recognition agreement with other countries to support secure EC cross-border transactions, the building up of a host of EC-ready government services/applications, and the promotion of a sizable base of EC-ready merchants through a number of industry consortia (Online Technologies Consortium, EC Consortium). A five-year EC-masterplan was released to promote the roll-out of EC on a big scale. In the mean time, the time-table for liberalization of the telecommunications market of Singapore has also been accelerated to enable greater competition and innovation in internet and EC-related activities. Restrictions on foreign ownership of telecommunications services companies were completely lifted in early 2000.

Policies to Develop Singapore as a Regional Knowledge and Innovation Hub

Besides financial reform, a key element in the region's ability to regain sustained long-term economic growth will be an increase in the intensity of investment in technology and innovation to spur total factor productivity growth. In this regard, the Singapore government is intensifying efforts to strengthen her position as a regional hub for technological innovation activities. On the one hand, the government is offering new investment incentives like Manufacturing Headquarter and subsidies like the Research Incentive Scheme for Companies (RISC) to encourage more MNCs to set up regional R&D labs, world product mandate product development centres, lead manufacturing plants for technology-intensive, high value add products, and applications software design and development in Singapore. On the other hand, the government intensified investment in public research institutions and centres (PRICs) and universities to increase indigenous innovation capability and to accelerate the transfer of technology to industry.

Besides efforts to further deepen the technological intensity of her existing cluster of electronics industry, the Singapore government has also been aggressively promoting another major industry cluster centred around chemical and healthcare products. In 1998, the contribution of the chemical industry cluster to total manufacturing value add in Singapore climbed to almost half of that of electronics, up sharply from less than one-quarter just four years ago. More recently, in 2000, in response to the completion of the Genome Mapping project, the government announced a S$1 billion initiative to promote R&D in life sciences.

Besides R&D-based activities, the Singapore government also actively promoted content publishing and media development. Besides investment incentives, the government also offered the nation-wide high-speed network infrastructure and a liberal regulatory policy as a strong inducement. Indeed, over the last few years, Singapore has already gained significantly at the expense of Hong Kong as a regional centre for media broadcasting, including pre- and post-production houses, satellite uplink/downlink, and editorial offices. Singapore may be arguably ahead of Hong Kong in multimedia publishing and web-based content development, thanks to the superior development of broadband networks and manpower. The government also actively promoted Singapore as a major educational hub in the region with a plan to attract up to 10 leading such institutes in the world to establish branch operation in Singapore or to enter into strategic alliances with local institutions. Recent developments along this line include the establishment of a branch campus by INSEAD and the University of Chicago Business School, the development of a new private university (SMU), major expansion of post-graduate programs in the existing universities, a five-year, multi-million engineering and science education and research co-operation program with MIT, and establishment of major research presence in Singapore by Georgia Tech (logistics) and John Hopkins (medicine).

Last, but not least, from late 1998, the Singapore government started to promote the development of Singapore as a "technopreneurial" hub in Asia in a big way through a new initiative called Technopreneurship 21 (T21). The political leadership had evidently become increasingly convinced of the Silicon Valley model of high tech innovation (including the successful Israeli and Taiwanese variants) as the key to success in the global knowledge-based economy of the 21st century, and hence the need for Singapore to supplement the MNC-leveraging model of technological development with another model based on nurturing technopreneurship (Wong, 2001a). First articulated by the deputy prime minister, Dr. Tony Tan, in late 1998, the T21 strategy established a new public US$1 billion technopreneurship fund to stimulate the development of Singapore as a regional venture capital hub. In addition, sweeping changes to a wide range of existing business regulations that were found to stifle local start-ups were announced. These include changes to the existing bankruptcy laws, revision of existing regulations and taxation rules governing company stock options, and new tax offset provision for loses incurred by business investors in local high tech start-ups. The breadth and comprehensiveness of the policy changes being proposed or under consideration clearly shows that the government may have come to the realization of the importance of promoting local technopreneurship somewhat late, but that it was able to move quite decisively once the decision was taken to shift direction.

III. THE GROWTH AND TRANSFORMATION OF MANUFACTURING

Having reviewed how the broad development strategies of Singapore has evolved over the years, we turn now to examine the growth and transformation of the manufacturing sector in Singapore over the last four decades, and what government roles have contributed towards the sector's development.

1. Overview of Manufacturing Performance

In assessing the state of the economy shortly after independence, Singapore's political leaders had decided that a vibrant manufacturing sector had to be added to the largely commerce-based economy. The United Nation team, invited to look into Singapore's development, was of the view that the country's unemployment problem then could be solved by promoting labour-intensive manufacturing, which could not only provide jobs but also skill training for the population. Since then, although the manufacturing sector has undergone drastic structural transformation, it has remained as the key growth engine of the economy. Some indicators of the performance and transformation of the economy and the manufacturing sector in particular are presented in Table 12.1.

During the period 1960–99, the Singapore economy grew at an average rate of 8.1% per annum in real terms. In comparison, the manufacturing sector grew at a faster rate of 9.4% per annum during the same period. Manufacturing growth was particularly rapid during the first two decades (1960–80), but slowed to less than 2% per annum during 1980-85, due mainly to the recession in 1985, during which manufacturing was the hardest hit. After the recession, it bounced back strongly, registering an average of 12.5% per annum growth in the next five years. Growth rate moderated to 5.8% during 1990–99, due primarily to the onset of the Asian financial crisis which cut manufacturing growth in 1998 to virtually zero, before recovering to 5.8% in 1999 [Table 12.1(b)]. Despite attempts since the early 1980s to diversify the

TABLE 12.1 Performance of Singapore's Economy, 1960–2000
(a) Aggregate Economic Growth Performance, 1960–2000

					% real growth p.a				
	1960–70	1970–80	1980–90	1990–2000	1990–97	1997	1998	1999	2000
GDP	8.7	9.4	7.1	7.5	8.4	8.5	0.1	5.9	9.9
Labour productivity	n.a	4.3	4.8	3.4	3.6	2.3	-2.7	6.3	5.6ᴾ
					(S$ at current prices)				
	1960	1970	1980	1990	1997	1998	1999	2000	
GNP per capita	1,330	2,825	9,941	20,090	39,310	38,418	39,721	42,212ᴾ	

NOTE: ᴾPreliminary figures.

SOURCES: Calculated from MTI (1990); Department of Statistics, *Yearbook of Statistics Singapore*, various years; Ministry of Trade and Industry, *Economic Survey of Singapore*, various years. Mid-year population estimate for 2000 obtained from Singstat website, http://www.singstat.gov.sg/FACT/KEYIND/keyind.html.

TABLE 12.1 *(cont'd)*
(b) Overall GDP vs. Manufacturing GDP growth rates
(in percentage growth per annum)

Sectoral Growth	1960–70	1970–80	1980–85	1985–90	1990–99
Manufacturing	13.7	10.9	1.6	12.5	5.8
Construction	15.8	6.0	15.2	–6.1	11.2
Commerce	8.0	7.4	4.0	9.2	7.3
Finance and Business Services	11.3	11.1	12.5	7.0	5.8
GDP Growth	9.1	9.0	6.2	8.1	7.2

SOURCES: Calculated from MTI (1990); Department of Statistics, *Yearbook of Statistics Singapore*, various years; Ministry of Trade and Industry, *Economic Survey of Singapore*, various years.

TABLE 12.1 *(cont'd)*
(c) Singapore GDP Distribution by Sectors, 1960–2000
(in percentages)

Industry	1960	1970	1980	1990	1995	1999	2000
Agriculture & Mining	3.9	2.7	1.5	0.4	0.2	0.2	0.1
Manufacturing	11.7	20.2	28.1	28.0	26.3	25.0	25.9
Utilities	2.4	2.6	2.1	1.9	1.6	1.9	1.7
Construction	3.5	6.8	6.2	5.4	7.0	7.8	6.0
Commerce	33.0	27.4	20.9	16.3	17.3	17.3	19.1
Transport & Communication	13.6	10.7	13.5	12.5	12.4	11.1	11.1
Financial & Business Services	14.4	16.7	18.9	25.5	25.5	26.2	25.3
Other Services	17.6	12.9	8.7	9.9	9.8	10.8	10.9
Total	100%	100%	100%	100%	100.0	100.0	100.0

NOTES: 1. Figures may not add up to 100 due to rounding.
2. Total GDP excludes owner-occupied dwellings and calculations for taxes and duties on imports and imputed bank service charge.

SOURCES: Calculated from MTI (1990); Department of Statistics, *Yearbook of Statistics Singapore*, various years; Ministry of Trade and Industry, *Economic Survey of Singapore*, various years.

TABLE 12.2   Growth of Labour Productivity and Capital Intensity in Singapore's Manufacturing Sector, 1960–99

Year	Real Value Added Per Worker ($'000 in 1985 prices)	Capital/Labour Ratio ($'000)
1960	17,816	16,973[1]
1970	23,574	23,090
1980	34,738	30,414
1990	55,000	43,784
1995	72,822	55,086
1997	80,900	77,450
1999	104,620	89,600
Growth rates (%):		
1960–70	2.8	4.6[2]
1970–80	4.0	2.8
1980–90	4.7	3.7
1990–99	7.4	8.3

NOTES: 1. 1963 figure.
                  2. Figure for 1963-70.
SOURCES: Calculated from Economic Development Board, *Census for Industrial Production*, various years, using deflators from Ministry of Trade and Industry, *Economic Survey of Singapore*, various years.

economy into a transport, communications and financial and business services hub, manufacturing has remained the single most important sector, consistently accounting for over one-quarter of the national GDP since the late 1980s. It was not until the second half of the 1990s that financial and business services reached parity with manufacturing in terms of direct contribution to GDP.

The expansion of the manufacturing sector has been accompanied by a high rate of technological upgrading, as shown in Table 12.2. Manufacturing labor productivity (value added per worker measured in real terms) grew at 4.6% per annum over 1960–99, increasing steadily over the years from 2.8% per annum over the initial industrial take-off phase (1960–70), to as much as 7.4% per annum over the last ten years (1990–99). The steady increase in labor productivity performance has been achieved partly through intra-industry upgrading, and partly through shifting production from labor-intensive to technologically more advanced and capital-intensive industries. As can be seen from Table 12.2, capital-labor intensity had also been increasing since the 1970s, accelerating in particular over the last 10 years (1960–99) due to the rapid growth of a number of highly capital-intensive industries, especially chemical processing and semiconductor wafer fabrication. As can be seen from Table 12.3, the share of labor-intensive industries such as food and beverage, textile and apparel and wood-based industries declined steadily from 45% of manufacturing value added in the early 1960s to less than 14% by 1980, and just over 4% by 1999. On the other hand, the chemicals/petroleum sector increased its value added share significantly from 7% in 1960 to 27% in 1970, driven primarily by the growth of petroleum refining. Although still expanding in absolute terms, the share of this sector's output had declined steadily to about 17% of total manufacturing output by 1995, before starting to expand again, reaching 23% in 1999 as a result of the increasing investment of heavy chemical processing and pharmaceutical production in recent years.

The star performer within the manufacturing sector, one that has grown the fastest since the early 1970s, has been the electronics industry (Wong, 2001a). In the early 1960s, the electronics industry accounted for less than 6% of manufacturing value added. The share doubled to 11.7% by 1970, and further increased to close to 20% by 1980. By 1990, the sector had accounted for 36% of total manufacturing value added. It share continued to increase in the first half of the 1990s, before reaching a plateau of around 43% in the second half of the 1990s (Table 12.3). In terms of output, the share of electronics in total manufacturing had been even higher, typically exceeding 50% in the second half of the 1990s. As in the chemicals and petroleum industry, the growth of the electronics industry has been most strongly driven by the inflow of foreign direct investment, which also brought along with it successive waves of technological upgrading.

The remarkable growth of Singapore's manufacturing sector can be gauged in terms of how the industry fared relative to the advanced OECD countries and other Asian NIEs. As can be seen from Annex Table 12A, although Singapore's manufacturing labor productivity level was only half of the OECD average in 1980, by 1994 she has almost attained parity. Singapore's average labor productivity in 1994 was also higher than those of the other Asian NIEs, particularly that of Hong Kong.

Another indicator of the global competitiveness of the manufacturing sector in Singapore is the relatively high profitability of the sector over the years. As can be seen in Annex Table 12C, return on equity (ROE) in the manufacturing sector has consistently outperformed not only the average of all firms in the economy as a whole, but also the expected international norms for manufacturing investments. In particular, the electronics manufacturing industry has achieved remarkably high ROEs.

While the above overall performance statistics are indeed impressive, it becomes less so when one recognizes that, unlike in Korea or Taiwan where domestic firms dominate manufacturing, it is the subsidiaries of foreign MNCs that contributed the bulk of the manufacturing output and value add in Singapore. The high degree of dependence of Singapore's manufacturing sector on foreign direct investment is evident in Table 12.4. Except for the recession period of 1985–86, local firms' share in total manufacturing output has been less than 30% since the mid-70s and less than 25% in the 1990s. Foreign majority-owned firms were on average significantly larger, as their average output per firm had consistently exceeded ten times that of local firms since the late 1980s. Among the 20 largest non-petroleum based manufacturing firms in Singapore in 1996 in terms of sales, there was only three Singaporean majority-controlled firms (Datapool, 1998).

In terms of new capital investment among the larger manufacturing establishments, the share of local equity capital has been similarly low, generally less than 30% in most years, occasionally exceeding 40% but sometimes dipped as low as 10% (Table 12.5). Overall, for the manufacturing sector as a whole, the cumulated stock of foreign equity capital accounted for close to 70% of total manufacturing equity capital since the late 1980s, although it dipped lower in the first half of the 1990s (see Table 12.6). In comparison, the foreign share of total equity capital in the entire economy has been consistently much lower at around one-third. The persistently high presence of foreign firms in Singapore's manufacturing activities reflects the attractiveness of Singapore as a manufacturing hub for global MNCs, despite rapid increase in labor cost. As can be seen from Annex Table D, foreign firms consistently earned very high average rate of returns on equity (ROE) or returns on asset (ROA).

The presence of local firms in the manufacturing sector varied significantly across different industries. Table 12.7 shows the share of

TABLE 12.3 (a) Output Composition of Singapore's Manufacturing Sector (in percentages)

Sectors	1960	1970	1980	1990	1995	1996	1997	1998	1999
Food & Beverage	33.0	18.4	6.6	4.0	3.3	3.0	3.0	3.0	2.5
Textile & apparel	3.3	5.2	4.5	3.1	1.3	1.0	0.8	0.9	0.9
Timber & furniture	8.5	5.4	3.1	1.2	0.7	0.2	0.2	0.3	0.2
Printing & paper products	10.3	3.5	2.6	3.6	3.2	3.2	3.0	2.8	2.6
Chemicals/petroleum	17.6	36.6	41.4	25.0	17.6	19.6	21.0	21.0	22.5
Non-metallic mineral products	3.7	2.3	2.0	1.4	1.8	2.0	2.1	1.8	1.3
Basic metals	1.1	1.9	1.7	1.1	0.7	0.5	0.5	0.4	0.4
Metal products/machinery	20.6	23.6	36.6	59.0	70.7	69.4	68.2	68.8	68.8
Electronic products	3.7[1]	7.3[1]	16.9	39.1	51.4	50.8	49.7	49.4	51.4
Other Manufacturing Industries	1.9	3.1	1.6	1.6	0.7	1.1	1.1	0.9	0.8
Total Manufacturing	100	100	100	100	100	100	100	100	100.0

NOTE: 1. Includes electrical products.

SOURCE: Economic Development Board, *Census for Industrial Production*, various years.

TABLE 12.3   (b) Value Added Composition of Singapore's Manufacturing Sector (in percentages)

Sectors	1960	1970	1980	1990	1995	1996	1997	1998	1999
Food & Beverage	31.04	12.44	4.97	4.40	3.64	3.56	3.57	2.9	3.0
Textile & apparel	5.46	5.14	5.36	3.23	1.27	1.00	0.94	0.96	0.9
Timber & furniture	8.03	6.50	3.11	1.21	0.24	0.22	0.24	0.25	0.2
Printing & paper products	18.57	5.81	4.37	5.90	5.95	5.73	5.80	5.45	4.5
Chemicals/petroleum	6.84	26.69	24.64	20.41	16.97	17.64	18.41	20.5	23.0
Non-metallic mineral products	3.84	3.04	2.33	1.53	1.95	2.05	2.02	1.83	1.4
Basic metals	1.34	2.03	1.80	1.15	0.55	0.48	0.45	0.4	0.4
Metal products/machinery	23.62	35.70	51.86	60.93	68.22	68.21	67.37	66.85	65.9
Electronic products[1]	5.55	11.65	19.58	35.71	43.47	44.55	43.44	43.12	44.4
Other Manufacturing Industries	1.25	2.65	1.56	1.23	1.22	1.09	1.19	0.85	0.8
Total Manufacturing	100	100	100	100	100	100	100	100	100.0

NOTE: 1. Includes electrical products.
SOURCE: Economic Development Board, *Census for Industrial Production*, various years.

TABLE 12.4 Composition of Manufacturing Output by Foreign and Local-Controlled Firms, 1976–99

Year	Number of Firms		Output ($mn)			Average Output per firm ($mn)	
	Local	Foreign	Local	Foreign	(% Local)	Local	Foreign
1976	1,955	550	4,121.3	11,196.2	(26.9)	2.11	20.36
1977	2,036	602	4,665.9	12,852.3	(26.6)	2.29	21.35
1978	2,306	640	5,597.7	14,069.0	(28.5)	2.43	21.98
1979	2,376	746	6,639.1	18,657.6	(26.2)	2.79	25.01
1980	2,521	834	8,328.7	23,329.2	(26.3)	3.30	27.97
1981	2,540	899	8,825.0	27,962.1	(24.0)	3.47	31.10
1982	2,674	912	9,581.9	26,885.5	(26.3)	3.58	29.48
1983	2,855	761	10,601.4	26,620.2	(28.5)	3.71	34.98
1984	2,883	765	11,968.6	29,109.3	(29.1)	4.15	38.05
1985	2,767	737	11,422.7	27,081.9	(29.7)	4.13	36.75
1986	2,748	701	11,443.9	25,814.8	(30.7)	4.16	36.83
1987	2,725	788	11,522.1	34,420.4	(25.1)	4.23	43.68
1988	2,806	818	14,105.6	42,364.5	(25.0)	5.03	51.79
1989	2,767	843	15,110.7	48,772.4	(23.7)	5.46	57.86
1990	2,837	866	17,215.6	54,117.6	(24.1)	6.07	62.49
1991	2,921	864	18,435.2	56,139.9	(24.7)	6.31	64.98
1992	3,062	855	19,936.2	57,339.8	(25.8)	6.51	67.06
1993	3,135	858	21,810.3	65,828.7	(24.9)	6.96	76.72
1994	3,150	863	24,697.3	75,924.8	(24.5)	7.84	87.98
1995	3,178	858	26,734.0	86,624.1	(23.6)	8.41	100.96
1996	3218	850	28567.1	91301.8	(23.8)	8.9	107.4
1997	3236	872	30215.9	96315.0	(23.9)	9.3	110.5
1998	3171	833	27598.1	93834.9	(22.7)	8.7	112.6
1999	3109	819	29661.7	103915.7	(22.2)	9.5	126.9

% Growth	Number of Firms		Output $mn	
	Local	Foreign	Local	Foreign
1980-90	1.2	0.4	7.5	8.8
1990-99	1.0	−0.6	6.2	7.5

NOTE: No corresponding data available for 1975 and earlier.
SOURCE: Economic Development Board, *Census for Industrial Production*, various years.

TABLE 12.5   Share of Manufacturing Investment by Local and Foreign Firms, 1972–2000

| Year | Manufacturing Investment Commitment | | |
	Foreign ($mn)	Local ($mn)	(% Local)
1972	156.0	38.0	(19.5)
1973	224.0	72.0	(24.3)
1974	169.0	123.0	(42.1)
1975	247.0	60.0	(19.6)
1976	260.0	43.0	(14.2)
1977	362.0	34.0	(9.4)
1978	765.0	47.0	(5.8)
1979	823.0	120.0	(12.7)
1980	1,189.1	224.4	(15.9)
1981	1,221.4	641.6	(34.4)
1982	1,162.5	542.0	(31.8)
1983	1,269.8	506.0	(28.5)
1984	1,334.7	493.7	(27.0)
1985	888.0	232.4	(20.7)
1986	1,190.6	259.4	(17.9)
1987	1,448.0	295.0	(16.9)
1988	1,657.8	349.6	(17.4)
1989	1,625.4	333.4	(17.0)
1990	2,217.9	269.5	(10.8)
1991	2,461.1	472.9	(16.1)
1992	2,733.0	758.6	(21.7)
1993	3,177.0	748.0	(19.1)
1994	4,327.5	1,437.2	(24.9)
1995	4,852.4	1,956.7	(28.7)
1996	5716.3	2368.9	(41.4)
1997	5963.8	2524.6	(29.7)
1998	5213.5	2615.9	(33.4)
1999	6257.1	1780.3	(22.2)
2000	7235.3	1973.6	(21.4)

SOURCES: Economic Development Board, *The EDB Yearbook*, various years; Department of Statistics, *Singapore Statistics Yearbook*, 1998 and 2000.

TABLE 12.6   Foreign Share of Equity Investment in Singapore, 1984–98
(in percentages)

	1984	1987	1990	1993	1994	1995	1996	1997	1998
Manufacturing	65.0	70.8	69.4	60.2	62.6	66.9	67.9	68.8	69.8
Total Economy	na	39.6	37.2	33.2	32.8	31.5	32.1	33.2	35.1
Electronics Industry	na	na	na	85.3	84.8	87.2	86.4	88.1	86.9

SOURCES: Department of Statistics, *The Extent and Pattern of Foreign Investment Activities in Singapore*, 1995; Department of Statistics, *Foreign Equity Investment in Singapore*, 1997 and 2000.

local equity capital in the cumulative investment by manufacturing sub-sectors in Singapore in 1980 and 1989 (the latest year for which such data were published). While the more labor-intensive industries such as textile, food and beverage, wood, rubber and plastic products generally have high local equity participation, the more technologically advanced and capital intensive industries like industrial chemicals, petroleum refining, electrical/electronics and precision equipment tend to have rather low local equity share. Some exceptions are the basic metal industries and transport equipment, mainly ship-repair and maintenance, which exhibited relatively high local capital participation due to the presence of state-owned enterprises.

The high dependence on foreign direct investment notwithstanding, it is nonetheless still remarkable that Singapore was able to increase the labor productivity of her manufacturing industries to catch up with those of advanced industrial countries like UK, Canada and Italy in such a short period of time. The significant structural shift in Singapore's manufacturing into medium and high tech sectors by the mid-1990s can be seen from Annex Table E, which shows the composition of Singapore's manufacturing value added in terms of OECD definition of technology intensity as well as Pavitt's classification. On both classification, Singapore's manufacturing industry exhibited a higher technological intensity than the average for the G-5 as well as that of the Scandinavian countries. Such rapid growth in labor productivity and technological upgrading over a period of less than four decades requires a concomitant significant upgrading of skills, a massive amount of capital investment, and a high degree of technological absorption

TABLE 12.7 Local Share of Cumulative Investment in Manufacturing, 1980 vs 1989 (in percentage of local capital in cumulative investments)

Sectors	1980	1989
Food, beverage & tobacco	60.9	59.0
Textile	45.2	51.5
Garment & footwear	70.3	82.6
Leather & rubber products	37.9	45.9
Wood products & furniture	63.0	64.5
Paper & paper products	74.1	67.8
Industrial chemicals	37.1	11.7
Other chemical products	25.7	15.1
Petroleum	1.4	1.3
Plastics products	70.1	58.8
Non-metal mineral products	61.3	46.1
Basic metal industries	73.2	70.7
Fabricated metal products	50.4	43.1
Machinery (except electrical)	31.8	29.1
Electrical/electronic machinery	9.0	6.8
Transport equipment	71.1	69.1
Precision equipment & optical	18.1	9.4
Total Manufacturing	32.9	27.2

SOURCE: Low *et al.* (1993).

and learning. These could not have occurred without some significant government policy intervention, which we turn to next.

2. Role of the State in Industrial Development

In contrast to the *lassiez faire* policy of the Hong Kong government, the Singapore government engaged in a wide range of policy interventions in all the key factor markets, ranging from land, labor and capital to infrastructure and related supporting industries. Although some of these policies might have been described as "market-friendly" in the jargon of EAM, it would be misleading to characterize Singapore as largely conforming to the market friendly paradigm; in many instances to be described below, the Singapore government had certainly deliberately "got the prices wrong" in the jargon of Amsden (1989). In this sense, the Singapore government could be characterized as having an interventionist industrial policy. Our account below aims to show that, while there certainly had been obvious policy mistakes, many of the industrial policies introduced by the government had been largely positive in the sense that they either contributed towards ameliorating market failures or otherwise enhancing the working of the various factor markets. Other policies contributed towards establishing an overall favourable business environment and efficient infrastructure that encouraged foreign investment. Some of them may also have served to reduce coordination costs in certain instances (Stiglitz, 1996).

State Intervention Through Investment Promotion

First and foremost, Singapore has been outstandingly successful in attracting foreign direct investment to use Singapore as an offshore production platform through the investment promotional effort of the Economic Development Board (EDB), a government agency set up as early as 1961 to promote and manage the economic development process (Low *et al.*, 1993). While the offering of tax incentives has been a major policy tool to attract DFI, the capability of EDB to market Singapore to foreign investors went significantly beyond such financial subsidies. In essence, it performed the entreprenuerial function of identifying potential investors, developing a package of incentives and grants tailored to fit the interest of the investors (but hopefully not giving too much away unnecessarily), and serving as a "one-stop" agency to handle all requirements of investors, including helping them in finding facilities for their factories, in recruiting and training their workforce, provide whatever infrastructure (e.g., power supply, communication facilities, etc.) that was needed. In short, the EDB were tasked to solve all problems that might arise, not only during the initial phase of investment, but also subsequently as these manufacturing operations expanded.

To enable EDB to play such a comprehensive coordinating role, it was set up as a statutory board to provide it with the independence that it needed. The success of the organization in fulfilling the missions given to it over the years has resulted in the chairman of EDB enjoying the confidence and support at the highest political level, which further contributed to its ability to adapt and change.

Since its early days of attracting labor-intensive industries to set up operation in Singapore, the role of EDB has indeed changed significantly over the years. The economic success of the late 1960s and 1970s led to higher wages, which made Singapore non-competitive in labour-intensive manufacturing operations. The EDB thus shifted its focus to selectively attracting high-technology industries such as electronics, chemical products, and industrial electronic equipment manufacturing. The role of the EDB was expanded to include industrial policy management. Not only must the EDB promote investments, it must attract the right investments that are compatible with the national objectives of becoming a high-technology manufacturing centre. In the 1990s, the EDB's tasks are further expanded to include co-investment in targeted industries to share risk. An example of industrial targeting is the promotion of semiconductor wafer fabrication facilities in Singapore. Besides setting up the infrastructure, the EDB also made direct equity participation in Tech Semiconductor, a joint venture with foreign MNCs, to jumpstart Singapore's entry into the industry. Such co-investment became necessary because of the high capital cost and risk involved; without the Singapore government committing substantial equity capital to share risk, it is unlikely that the venture would have taken off. Besides semiconductors, the EDB has also actively involved in biotechnology business ventures.

It is not possible to conduct an empirical cost-benefit assessment of the tax incentives and expenditures on promotional activities by the EDB, as the necessary data on the exact amount of incentives granted are often not disclosed to the public. Methodologically, the "over-determination" of policy inputs also mean that any such attempt at impact assessment should ideally involve a comparative analysis across countries; a limited attempt at doing so by McKendrick et al. (2000) and Wong(1999b) in the case of the development of a particular industry — the hard disk drive industry — showed that public policy in Singapore indeed had been much more comprehensive and beneficial than was found in Malaysia and Thailand. In general, it is no doubt possible that some of the direct foreign investment into Singapore's manufacturing sector would have taken place any way without the tax incentives and/or promotional efforts of EDB. It is also likely that some of the investment projects may prove to have negative social rate of returns as the effective subsidies they received might have enabled them to bid up resources away from other more economic use. The only publicly available evidence is the fact that many senior managers of companies that have invested in Singapore have praised the role of EDB

(Schein, 1996), many of these investments have been profitable, and that increasingly sophisticated foreign investment have continued to pour into Singapore despite keen competition from elsewhere offering perhaps even higher tax incentives. On balance, therefore, it is hard not to assign to EDB a significant contribution to much of the impressive growth in foreign direct investment into a wide range of increasingly high value-adding sectors in the Singapore economy.

State Intervention in Labor Market

The Singapore government has also intervened extensively in the market of labor and skills. In the early years of independence, because the communists had infiltrated the labor unions, labor unrest and industrial actions were frequent, which seriously undermined Singapore's attractiveness for manufacturing investors. The government thus had no choice but to intervene in the labor market to encourage cooperative behaviour from all parties and to foster an atmosphere conducive to foreign investment. To this end, all trade unions were brought under an umbrella body called the National Trade Union Congress (NTUC), which cooperated closely with the government in securing a stable labor market condition for the benefits of all parties. In recent years, the position of Secretary-General of the NTUC has been held by a government minister (without portfolio) who devotes much of his time to explaining and defending government policies to his union members (Peebles and Wilson, 1996, p.15).

Further, a wage setting mechanism was instituted in 1972, with the formation of the National Wages Council (NWC), a tripartite body comprising representation from the government, employer unions, and the NTUC. The National Wages Council has been playing a mediating role by recommending annual non-mandatory wage increase guidelines. In essence, the NWC sought to play an information coordination role by bringing in line wage increase expectations of all parties with the aim to help ease the upward pressure on wages as a result of a tight labor market.

The NWC was used in the late 1970s and early 1980s by the government to introduce a deliberate high wage increase policy with the hope of inducing firms to invest in industrial productivity upgrading. The policy turned out to be a failure as the government later discovered that many firms were unable to achieve the kind of productivity upgrading to match the pace of wage increase driven by the NWC. The drastic slowdown in manufacturing investment and the consequent sharp recession of 1985 was partly blamed on this high wage policy.

After reviewing the situation in the aftermath of the 1985 recession, the high wage policy was dropped by NWC, and a new wage policy was introduced to increase the flexibility of wages. The policy called for having a significant variable component to the total wage compensation package. This flexi-wage policy was to ensure that wage levels could be more easily lowered during economic downturns, thereby reducing the magnitude of job loss. The government took the lead by implementing the flexi-wage system throughout the civil service system.

Besides attempting to influence the wage adjustment system in the labor market, the government also intervened in terms of the supply of labor and skills. When the Singapore economy reached full employment in the 1970s, the shortage of labor was mitigated somewhat by the influx of foreign workers. However, this inflow was regulated by the government through the use of a dependency ceiling, which placed a limit on the number of foreign workers that each company could employ, and a foreign worker levy, which was a pricing mechanism. While there are no official data on the number of foreign workers, it was estimated that in 1994 there were about 300,000 foreign workers employed in the Singapore economy (*The Straits Times*, 4 March 1995).

The dependency ceiling and foreign worker levy amount had been used to allocate different categories of foreign labor supply to different sectors of the economy and over time. In particular, to cope with the demand for professional skills, the government adopted a very liberal policy of exempting the hiring of high-skill professionals from both the dependency ceiling and foreign worker levy. Indeed, recognizing the severe limitation of the national pool of manpower skills and talents at the start of Singapore's initial industrialization drive, the Singapore government had allowed foreign MNCs to freely bring in foreign managers and technical professionals to fill the crucial technical and management gap. Since then, the government had consistently wooed foreign talents to work (and eventually settle) in Singapore. The Economic Development Board is probably among the first government investment promotion agencies in the world to establish an International Manpower Division to attract foreign talents to Singapore. Such foreign technical manpower supply has been particularly important in the electronics and IT industry; for example, a recent survey of IT manpower in Singapore 1995 found 24% of the IT professionals in Singapore were non-Singaporean (NCB,1996). The proportion of foreigners among R&D scientists and engineers in Singapore is even higher.

In addition to their effect on the quantity of labor supply, government policies on education and skills training also had a direct impact on the quality of labor supply. At the time of political independence, Singapore inherited a labor force structure heavily skewed towards unskilled and lowly-educated. Such under-investment in education was attributed to the British colonial policy of neglect. Despite increasing efforts by the post-colonial government to invest in education, Singapore continued to exhibit below average proportion of workforce with post secondary and tertiary education compared to other Asian NICs up to the mid-1980s (see e.g., Lim *et al.*, 1988, p.167). The policy of persistently high investment in human resource development — expenditure on education was consistently the second largest item of government expenditure (next to defense) and typically exceeded 20% of government operating expenditure in the 1980s and 1990s — only began to be reflected in a significant catching up of the educational profile of Singapore's workforce to the average of other Asian NIEs in the 1990s. The percentage of students enrolled in tertiary institutions has increased most markedly in recent years, rising from 7.7% in 1985 to 15% in 1995. Even then, Singapore still has some way to go before catching up to the norms of the advanced industrial countries.

Besides greatly increasing the supply of tertiary trained manpower, the government also introduced major policies to speed up vocational training of the adult workforce (Soon,1992). In the 1970s, to prepare the cadres of technicians and skilled workers necessary to meet the requirements of industry, the government (through EDB) set up many industrial training centres and institutes, often in collaboration with MNCs and foreign governments. In fact, the EDB pro-actively sought out MNCs to enter into jointly sponsored training programs. For the less skilled workers, their training and skill upgrading have been financed by the Skills Development Fund (SDF), set up by the government from a compulsory tax (currently 1%) on the payroll of less skilled workers. The government also provided direct financial assistance to workers pursuing upgrading in designated technical skills (e.g. CNC machining). As the skills training demand of industry became more advanced over time, government policies to promote such training also became correspondingly more specialized and sophisticated: e.g. automation and robotics training program for operators, new initiatives in advanced technologies (called the InTech program) to subsidize training of engineers in new, advanced technologies, a Local Industry Upgrading Program (LIUP) to facilitate transfer of technology and best management practices from the leading MNCs operating in Singapore, a number of S&T manpower schemes to train R&D engineers and scientists, and various scholarship schemes to attract the best and brightest to manufacturing and R&D activities. Since the early 1990s, the Economic Development Board (EDB) has also established a Manpower and Capability Development Division to focus specifically on identifying potential skills and technical know-how gaps and devising training programs to address these gaps. Recent examples of this is the accelerated training program implemented to increase the supply of engineering skills to support the semiconductor wafer fabrication industry and the wireless communications industry respectively.

State Intervention in Land Market

The Singapore government had also consistently intervened in the land market to ensure that sufficient industrial land were made available to accommodate the anticipated needs of manufacturing industries. Like Hong Kong, the Singapore government has ownership and control over large amount of land, and has enacted legislatures that allows the state to compulsorily acquire private land for development purposes. Consequently, the state could engage in long-term land-use allocation planning. However, unlike Hong Kong where state control over land allocation has resulted in commercial land-use driving out industrial land-use, thus contributing to the large-scale industrial hollowing out observed over the years, the Singapore state has consistently placed a strategic focus on sustaining manufacturing growth in Singapore, by subsidizing the cost of industrial land where necessary. This is in recognition of the substantial externalities or multiplier impacts that manufacturing activities have in sustaining Singapore as a regional business hub. For example, the rentals and land lease terms of industrial factories or lands provided by the state-owned Jurong Town Corporation (JTC) had been used as a policy instrument, reduced in times of industrial difficulties, and revised upward when industrial profitability revives. Another example of proactive government industrial land policy is the development of science park as early as the beginning of the 1980s to stimulate R&D-based

activities in Singapore. A third example of pro-active government industrial land policy is the recent acquisition and assembly of a large parcel of land to support the anticipated development of a major cluster of semiconductor wafer fabrication plants in Singapore. By clustering these plants together, economies of scale in infrastructural facilities such as water supply and treatment can be reaped.

The government has of course intervened in the land market for other purposes besides promoting industrial development. Indeed, the government had long recognized the potential constraints that land scarcity may have on economic growth, and hence had been careful to undertake long-term land-use planning ever since the late 1960s. A long-term land-use plan, the 1971 Ring Concept Plan, was developed with the assistance of the United Nations Development Programme. This was replaced in 1991 by the New Concept Plan, which provided the framework for the physical development of the island to accommodate a population of 4 million by the year 2030. To facilitate the supply and efficient use of land for economic development, the state, where and when necessary, acquired land from the private sector. The Land Acquisition Act of 1966 conferred powers on the state and its agencies to acquire land for any residential, industrial, commercial or public purposes. Between 1973 and 1987, land was acquired at the market value as at November 30, 1973 (the statutory date) or at the date of gazette notification, whichever was lower. The statutory date for the determination of compensation for acquired properties is currently January 1, 1995. The Land Acquisition Act therefore greatly reduces the cost and simplifies the process of providing public housing, setting up industrial estates, infrastructure development and improvement, and urban renewal.

To manage the development and planning of land for different uses, the government established several state agencies including the Jurong Town Corporation, the Urban Redevelopment Authority and the Housing and Development Board. However, effective planning controls and coordination were imposed on the different agencies to ensure that their respective development functions (industrial estates and flatted factories, urban commercial/office redevelopment, and public housing) are synergized to optimize the land-use pattern and traffic flow. The state also leases land to the private sector for commercial, residential and recreational developments. This has become an important revenue source for the government. In 1995, for example, the capital receipts for land sales amounted to $11.7 billion or 10% of GDP.

It was the state's significant control over land resource that enabled the PAP political leadership to embark on the major public housing programs in the initial years that crucially helped the PAP leadership to consolidate and sustain their electoral popularity among the working class in Singapore. Although not directly related to industrial policy, the wide and equitable provision of highly affordable public housing has been an important factor that enabled the PAP to garner the strong support that it did among the working class to go along with the various industrial policies outlined earlier, including the significant control over industrial relations. Over the years, Singapore's public housing program has been recognized as one of the best in the world. With over 80% of Singaporean population now living in their own public housing, this state intervention over land continues to exert significant influence over the life of the majority of Singapore citizens.

State Intervention Through Pro-Active Infrastructure Development

Singapore has been consistently ranked as having the best infrastructure in the world for businesses by the World Competitiveness Report in recent years (IMD, various years). Besides having the best sea-port and airport facilities in the world, Singapore has among the most efficient telecommunications infrastructure, power systems and water utilities. The island has also been well served by public transport services, including the Mass Rapid Transit network, and road infrastructure. Traffic congestion has been contained through motor vehicle quotas on ownership and an Area Licensing Scheme designed to reduce congestion by imposing charges for travel in busy areas and during peak hours. The manual pricing system has since been replaced by an electronic road pricing system, the first of its kind in Asia if not the world. The development of all these extremely high quality infrastructural facilities have not come about by accident, but through a consistent government policy to invest, often pro-actively, in having the most efficient and highest quality infrastructure facilities and operations as a source of competitive advantage in attracting foreign MNCs against other competing locations in the region.

An illustrative example of this pro-active approach to infrastructure development is the Singapore government's early focus on investing in a new generation of nation-wide advanced broadband information network (Wong, 1996b). One and a half year before the Clinton Administration announced the "Information Superhighway" program initiative, the Singapore government was first in the world to advance the concept of a National Information Infrastructure (NII), and produced a strategic plan called *IT2000: Vision of an Intelligent Island* in 1992 to guide the nation's information infrastructure development for the next decade. While many other countries have similarly announced national information infrastructure program initiatives since (e.g. Korea, Japan and Taiwan), Singapore is probably among the most advanced in actually implementing the infrastructure investment program: By the middle of 1997, Singapore was already launching an actual island-wide market trial for broadband multimedia services ("Singapore ONE"). Singapore was also the first country in Asia to launch a new test-bed for a second generation of advanced multi-megabits internet II technology, launched to link Singapore-based R&D companies to a similar experimental networks linking a consortium of leading universities and research labs in the US.

Although the government was somewhat cautious in liberalizing the telecommunications markets in Singapore and privatizing the public telecommunications monopoly (Singapore Telecoms) in the early 1990s, it had moved decisively to accelerate the pace of liberalization in recent years when it became clear that the explosive growth of internet would render the old competition models obsolete. Despite its privatisation, however, Singapore Telecoms as a "Government-Linked Corporation" (GLC) was committed by the government to a program to connect all Singaporean homes and offices with optical fibres by the year 2005 (Wong, 1996b). More recently, the government announced removal of restriction on foreign ownership of telecommunications services companies.

State Intervention in Science and Technology Development

Up until the late 1980s, government policies towards science and technology focused primarily on promoting effective technology absorption rather than technology development (Wong, 1994, 1995b, 2001b). The emphasis was on facilitating industrial technology transfer and diffusion from MNCs, and effective learning and absorption capacity of Singaporean engineers, technicians and workers. Major efforts of the government to facilitate the diffusion of technology adoption include the National Automation Masterplan formulated in the late 1980s and the National IT Plan formulated in 1985. The former led to policies, borrowed heavily from the Japanese experience, to provide subsidized funding for the leasing and acquisition of industrial automation equipment and the carrying out automation feasibility studies. The latter involved large-scale effort to promote the computerization of the public sector itself under a Civil Service Computerization Program (CSCP), as well as assistance and subsidized loans to local SMEs to adopt IT. The National Computer Board (NCB) was also set up to spearhead the promotion of IT usage in all sectors of the economy. NCB undertook in particular the development of a number of industry-wide IT applications that proved to have significant beneficial economic impacts. The most publicised of these was the development of TradeNet, an electronic data interchange (EDI) system that enables exporters/importers to file customs documentation electronically. This resulted in significant savings of processing cost and drastically improved processing time. The development of TradeNet serves as a useful illustration of the role of the state in reducing coordination costs among economic agents. Because of the multiple economic actors are involved, an industry solution does not emerge naturally; indeed, Singapore became the first country in the world to introduce such a system, and other competing nations like Hong Kong and Malaysia took substantially longer to adopt such a system despite the demonstrated benefits.

Because of the strong emphasis on promoting technology adoption and diffusion, Singapore has become among the most advanced in the world in terms of adoption propensity for a wide range of high technology products from CNCs, robotics, IT and telecommunications including the internet (World Competitiveness Report, various years). While few empirical studies are available due to data limitations problems, a number of recent studies [see e.g.Wong (2000)] have shown significant positive impact of IT investment on aggregate labor productivity of the economy, as well as in specific sectors (e.g. warehousing, financial services). There is also little doubt that the high level of penetration of IT and industrial automation would have occurred naturally without the active government support and promotion.

The high focus of public policy to promote greater technology usage and diffusion withstanding, public policy on promoting the creation of new technology through R&D has not been very significant until the early 1990s. Although some public R&D institutions were set up by the mid-1980s, the scale and scope of public R&D were modest in comparison to Taiwan and South Korea. It is only since the late 1980s, with the formulation of the first National Technology Plan and the establishment of a National Science and Technology Board (NSTB) in 1991, that public R&D funding has become significant (Wong, 1995c). Among others, the establishment of the Institute of Microelectronics, the Data Storage Institute and the Centre for Wireless Communications, together with the expansion of GINTIC into the Institute for Manufacturing Technology (GIMT) were meant to facilitate the development of R&D capabilities relevant to the key manufacturing industries. Various R&D and innovation incentive schemes such as R&D assistance scheme and Research Incentive Scheme for Companies were introduced to provide generous support for R&D by private companies, particularly in the key manufacturing industries. Significantly, the assistance was made available for both local firms as well as foreign MNCs operating in Singapore.

Since the late 1980s, the EDB's investment promotion efforts were increasingly directed at attracting leading high-technology MNCs to locate their R&D activities in Singapore. The Science Park, launched in the mid-1980s to encourage R&D and software development activities in Singapore, became fully occupied in 1994. A second phase is now well underway. With the completion of the first National Technology Plan (NTP) in 1995, during which S$2 billion was allocated, and largely committed, to funding R&D programs and facilities, the government introduced a second plan called the National Science and Technology Plan (NSTP) for the period 1996-2000, for which funding allocation was doubled to S$4 billion. In addition to expanding the existing public R&D infrastructure and incentive programs, the plan also envisaged more upstream research being promoted at the two local universities, in addition to expanding public R&D institutions. More recently, from 1999, the government started to promote technopreneurship in a big way through the new T21 initiative (see earlier discussion). As a result of these public S&T support programs, R&D expenditure in Singapore had been rising very rapidly in the 1990s, reaching a GERD/GDP ratio of 1.8% by 1999, which was comparable to the level of Taiwan, and higher than several OECD countries (see Annex Table 12F and 12G). Although foreign MNCs still contributed more than half of the private R&D spending in Singapore, the share of R&D expenditure by local firms had been increasing steadily in recent years (see Annex Table 12H).

Because the policy focus on promoting innovation and R&D is quite recent, and because of the long gestation period for R&D investment to translate into quantifiable commercial impacts, it is probably too early to tell if these policies and programs have had a significant positive impact on the economy. Nevertheless, the increased investment in S&T infrastructure and public R&D institutes have been cited as an important factor by many of the MNCs that had decided to invest in R&D activities in Singapore in recent years.

It could be argued that Singapore should have embarked upon a significant program of public investment in R&D much earlier as was the case of Taiwan and Korea. A possible reason for the lower level of investment in public R&D by the Singapore government in the past is that there has been no effective institutional mechanism for promoting long-term S&T capability development, after the Ministry of Science and Technology was abolished in the 1970s. Throughout the 1970s and 1980s, economic development agencies such as the EDB, being more focused on responding to the needs of foreign investors, did not see much demand by manufacturing MNCs for R&D supporting infrastructures, and hence did not lobby for these to be established, while the focus of the local higher institutions of learning has been on training manpower, not industrially-relevant research. There was also few local enterprises entering high-tech sectors that looked to the public sector for new technologies. The situation has been rapidly changing in recent years, however, especially with the announcement of the T21 initiative. High tech spin-offs from public research institutes and universities are rapidly increasing in numbers over the last 2–3 years and are expected to accelerate in the future.

Capital Market Intervention

That the Singapore government intervened extensively in the capital market have been well documented elsewhere (see e.g. Asher, 1995). We will examine its role in (i) the promotion of savings and investments; (ii) the creation and regulation of financial markets; and (iii) the allocation of investments, particularly in the manufacturing sector.

(i) *Promotion of Savings and Investments*

In 1995, Singapore's Gross National Savings (GNS) stood at 51% of GNP, the highest in the world. In contrast, the corresponding figure in 1960 was negative. The dramatic increase in saving rates in Singapore has been due largely to government policies specifically designed to promote savings. The bulk of Singapore's GNS consists of government savings, surpluses of statutory boards and GLCs, and mandatory saving through the Central Provident Fund (CPF) (Asher, 1995):

1. Conservative budgetary policy: Since the early 1970s, the Singapore government has been able to finance its current as well as capital expenditures out of operating revenues in most years. Its strong fiscal position has enabled it to pursue tax and other policies designed to promote growth.

2. Unusual revenue sources: The Singapore government has a number of unusual revenue sources which include levies on the employment of foreign workers, various motor vehicle taxes and charges, leasing of land and substantial investment income. In 1993, revenue from motor vehicle related fees and charges alone accounted for 29.1% of total tax revenue and 22.9% of total operating revenue.

3. The CPF system: The CPF is a fully funded, pay-as-you-go social security system. CPF savings are meant not just for retirement, but other purposes such as housing mortgage payments, medical expenses and insurance, education, and investments in financial assets. Mandatory CPF contributions for about two-thirds of the work force have been increased from 10% of the net wage (net of employer's contribution) in 1968 to a high of 50% in the mid-1980s. It is currently at 40%, with equal contribution from the employer and employee. CPF balances at the end of 1994 were an astounding S$57.0 billion or 72% of GDP, and has become a major planning and social engineering tool.

In effect, a large part of the nation's savings and investment decisions has been concentrated in the hands of the government. Since 1988, GNS has exceeded the amount of domestic investment so that Singapore becomes a net lender abroad. Despite the excess of domestic savings over investment, foreign direct investment continues to be wooed by the government because of their important contributions to technology progress. In defending the government's policy of generating healthy surpluses and having large reserves, the official position was that they were necessary to attract foreign investors to invest in Singapore (*The Straits Times*, March 1994).

The government performs a large part of the financial intermediation process of channelling savings for investment purposes, not only through government capital expenditures, but also through GLCs and the Government of Singapore Investment Corporation (GIC). This partly explains the dominance of GLCs in the economy. Trade-offs do exist under such an arrangement. The government may not always have access to the best investment information available to allocate capital efficiently. This arrangement also requires a certain type of political economy in which the government must behave benevolently, and manage these funds in the overall public interest (Asher, 1995, p.130). Further, monopoly rents made in the process of financial intermediation do exist, although they are difficult to estimate.

(ii) *Development and Regulation of Banks and Financial Markets*

Singapore has established a well-functioning financial system which is supervised and regulated by the Monetary Authority of Singapore. In 1997, financial and business services accounted for 26.2% of GDP. More than 200 international financial institutions are represented in Singapore and operate in the various offshore markets. However, only 35 banks, known as full-licence banks, are authorized to engage in the full range of banking activities. As such, the domestic banking sector, dominated by four big local commercial banks, has been protected from competition through restrictions on the entry of domestic and foreign competitors.

The government controls three important financial intermediaries in Singapore. Besides the CPF Board, a statutory board managing the CPF program, two other government-linked financial institutions are the Development Bank of Singapore (DBS Bank) and the Post Office Savings Bank (POSBank). DBS Bank was established in 1968 to function as a development bank, i.e., to provide loans to industries whose activities were deemed important to the economic development of Singapore. It has since developed into a full-fledged commercial bank and is the largest of the big four local commercial banks.

POSBank was established as a statutory board in 1972 to promote savings by individuals and to mobilise these savings for the purpose of national development. Savings in the POSBank are fully guaranteed by the government and interest on savings account is tax-exempt. However, it is not allowed to accept deposits from the corporate sector and must hold a minimum of 50% of its assets in government securities, loans to statutory boards and government enterprises, or deposits in the domestic banking system — mainly with DBS Bank (Luckett *et al.*, 1994). Over the years, POSBank has developed into one of the largest financial intermediaries in Singapore. In 1995, it had over 5 million accounts and a deposit base of over $22 billion.

Singapore's capital market has three main components: the Stock Exchange of Singapore, the market for government securities excluding Treasury Bills, and the long term commercial paper market. The Monetary Authority of Singapore has played a major role in the development and regulation of these markets. Although the government's fiscal position requires no borrowing, it issues government securities to provide a benchmark risk-free rate so as to create a market for corporate bonds.

The capitalization of the Stock Exchange of Singapore has increased tremendously in recent years, largely due to the privatisation program of the government. In fact, a main objective of the government's divestment of statutory boards and GLCs is "to add breadth and depth to the Singapore stock market by the floatation of GLCs and through secondary distribution of Government-owned shares" (Report of the Public Sector Divestment Committee, 1987, p.12). The privatisation program have allowed the government to withdraw part of its equity from well established and mature industries, but without losing control over them, and invest in new areas of activities (Asher, 1988, p.70). The influence of GLCs in the economy remains strong, and has in fact increased as they become more diversified.

The use of CPF savings for investment has also benefited the Stock Exchange of Singapore. In 1986, CPF members were allowed to use their CPF savings to invest in approved trustee stocks under the CPF Approved Investment Scheme. The rules were further liberalized in 1993 under the CPF Enhanced Investment Scheme. Another investment scheme is the Share-Ownership Top-up Scheme (SOTUS), under which the government provides grants to CPF members to enable them to purchase shares of state enterprises which are divested. This amounts to providing subsidies for purchase of such stocks.

In 1987, a second tier stock market, known as SESDAQ, was set up to provide an opportunity for small- and medium-sized enterprises to tap into the equity market. By October 1996, there were 49 companies listed on SESDAQ with a total market capitalization of over S$3 billion. SESDAQ has since become an important avenue for local firms to raise capital. As a result, the local share of equity investment in manufacturing has been rising steadily since the late 1980s.

(iii) *Government Control over Allocation of Investments*

Because of the significant financial control by the government on national savings, including the persistently large budget surplus of the public sector, the Singapore government has the resources to actively play the role of "picking winners", or a "high tech venture capital corporation" (Asher, 1988, p.71) in the manufacturing sector through the process of directed credit, fiscal incentives for targeted sectors (Lim *et al.*, 1988, p.258), direct investment through GLCs and joint ventures with MNCs, as well as capital subsidies for the development of promising local enterprises (Low *et al.*, 1993, chapter 6). While all these have been practised to a certain extent, overall the government has actually been quite prudent, and much of the savings have actually been used to build up sizable foreign reserves, invest in long-term physical infrastructures, public housing and other social infrastructures, rather than in major industrial projects. The co-investment in semiconductor wafer fabrication mentioned earlier, the recent acquisition of an ailing American disk drive company (Micropolis) and the investment in the Suzhou industrial park projects are the notable exceptions.

Through its conservative budgetary policy as well as various institutions described above, the government has very effectively mobilized savings for the pursuit of various economic development activities in general and the various state intervention policies mentioned earlier in particular. Such high control of the government over national savings has attracted a fair share of criticism. Firstly, such a centralized process of capital allocation has been criticized for being inefficient. Indeed, some economists such as Young (1992) and Krugman (1994) have argued that essentially all the growth in Singapore can be explained by rapid increases in labor and capital inputs. According to Krugman (1994), Singapore's negligible Total Factor Productivity (TFP) growth rate makes it "an economic twin of growth of Stalin's Soviet Union", a "paper tiger" with "capital piling up" that "is beginning to yield diminishing returns".

In arriving at such conclusion, Krugman(1994) used the findings of Young (1992) which however have been shown to be problematic by Rao and Lee (1995) and Hsieh (1997). Taking a more careful approach in their measurement of capital and labor inputs, Rao and Lee (1995) shows that, consistent with previous studies [e.g. Tsao (1985)], the contribution of TFP to aggregate growth prior to 1984 is quite small. However, between 1987 and 1994, there was a significant increase in TFP contribution to growth — in the order of magnitude of 30%. Moreover, their findings are largely invariant to the adjustment of the labor and capital time-series data and are similar if output is disaggregated into manufacturing and services. Hsieh (1997), using the priced-based estimates of TFP growth, also obtained much higher estimates of TFP growth than Young's estimates. Hsieh shows that a combination of three factors — undervaluation of the imputed rent on owner-occupied housing in the official statistics, exaggerated growth rate of private capital, and imperfect competition — can explain the difference between his estimates and Young's. Bosworth and Collins (1996) similarly found higher TFP growth for Singapore than Young (1992) by covering the more recent period of up to 1994. Singapore Department of Statistics (1997) likewise found commendable TFP growth for Singapore between the mid-1980s and mid-1990s. Using a different estimation methodology, Leung (1996,1997) further found reasonably high TFP growth for Singapore economy as a whole as well as for the manufacturing sector alone. Finally, MTI (2001) provided productivity growth estimates for Singapore over 1985–2000, and found TFP to account for over 40% of the growth in output per worker.

In view of the above, the weight of evidence appears not to support Krugman's (1994) extreme conclusion about Singapore's investment efficiency. Nevertheless, it is a valid concern that the continuing high concentration of savings within the control of the public sector may result in less than optimal investment allocation. While such high control may have been important in the early years when savings were scarce, it is likely to become increasingly dysfunctional now that Singapore has become so much more developed. Although the government has so far pursued relatively conservative and prudent policy with respect to investment of public savings, it can be argued that the returns to such investment have not been commensurate with the risk-return preference of individual Singaporean investors.

In view of this, despite Singapore's standing as an international financial centre, Singapore's centralized system of capital allocation is becoming increasingly incompatible with the development of capital markets. Indeed, the high CPF contribution rate was listed as one of the factors resulting in the dearth of private sector entrepreneurs. Writing in the aftermath of the mid-1980s recession, Lim *et al.* (1988, p.269) argued that, "high CPF rates contributed to a scarcity of personal risk and venture capital; in particular, the growth of small business, often the training ground for entrepreneurs, have been hampered by the lack of ready access to the capital market due to poor credit ratings in the absence of business track records." Similar concerns over the effects of "regulatory overdose" on small- and medium-sized enterprises (SMEs) have also been expressed by Lee and Low (1990), who argue that SMEs' main obstacle to growth may not be the access to loans, but rather the cost of loans, besides other factors such as lack of managerial expertise. Another adverse effect of the conservatism of the management of public funds may have been the stifling of financial innovation and consequent underdevelopment of the financial sector in Singapore.

In fairness, the inefficiencies and overly conservatism of the current financial system in Singapore have been increasingly recognized by the government itself as she seeks to position Singapore to become a major financial hub in the world in the 21st century. As mentioned earlier, this has led to the formation of a high powered committee, chaired by the deputy prime minister, to look into greater financial liberalization. Various new policies have already emerged, including the development of bond market, the promotion of the fund management industry, pressure on local banks to merge and to internationalize, liberalization of listing requirements on the local stock exchange, deregulation of commission on stock trading, and further reform in the governance structure and eventual listing of the stock and commodity/future exchanges.

Regionalization and Overseas Investment

Since the late 1980s, the government has also played a key role in Singapore's investment in the emerging regional economies through the Regionalization 2000 program. As Singapore has been rapidly internationalizing through overseas direct foreign investment (DFI) in recent year, the program seeks to form a network of strategic zones in key markets with emphasis on building linkages between Singapore's regional projects and domestic industry clusters. The stock of outward DFI increased 15 fold between 1980 and 1994. By the end of 1994, over 4,000 domestic companies had invested abroad, with the total cumulative stock of outward DFI constituting as much as 36% of total GNP for that year (Wong, 1996). By the end of 1998, the number of overseas investments had increased to 7,494, with the cumulative stock of outward DFI:GDP ratio increased to 54% (DOS, 2000b). More than half (58 percent) of Singapore's outward DFI in 1997–98 were to Asian countries. To provide incentives and assistance for Singapore-based firms to invest abroad, the government provides tax incentives, overseas market access information services, and even the setting up of Singapore international schools to assist overseas relocation of Singapore families.

Another major prong of the regionalization strategy is to invest in and manage the development of large-scale industrial parks in the region in partnership with the national or regional authorities in the respective countries. Such "flagship" projects include Batam and Bintan in Indonesia, Bangalore in India, Wuxi and Suzhou in China, and Ho Chi Minh City in Vietnam. Although government-to-government facilitation is critical to get these joint ventures off the ground, they are usually undertaken by a consortium of Singapore firms, in joint ventures with local partners. These developments were expected to not only enable Singapore firms to export their expertise in infrastructure planning, engineering development and project management, but through equity stake, also allowed Singapore firms to share in the future industrial growth of the regional economies.

These regional industrial park developments form part of a larger government effort to promote regional cooperation between Singapore and major countries in the Asia-Pacific region. Besides the industrial park projects, closer cooperation through regional cooperation such as the ASEAN Free Trade Area and the proposed APEC Free Trade and Investment Area will also facilitate other forms of investment by Singapore-based companies in these countries.

The strategic intent of the government is that, through these efforts, not only are outward DFI by indigenous Singapore firms promoted, but that they also enable the government to play the role of a "one-stop" partner in Asia to help MNCs to invest in the Asia-Pacific region as a whole, not just in Singapore, by leveraging the regional projects that

Singapore has developed throughout the region. In this regard, the experience and expertise of the EDB are instrumental to the success of such a strategy. It is hoped that, through good government relationships and strong local partners, Singapore can promise foreign investors almost the same infrastructural efficiency and transparency of regulations in these regional projects as if they were investing in Singapore.

It is still too early to tell if these regionalization policies will bear fruits in the long run. In the short run, there has been recent reports of significant problems encountered in the development of the Suzhou projects. The onset of the regional financial crisis has also negatively affected quite a few Singaporean investments in the region. Nevertheless, in the longer run, the regional recession may actually provide an opportunity for relatively well-capitalized Singaporean firms to acquire at low price some of the viable but distressed companies and asserts in the region. In the medium term, however, in response to the significant regional slowdown, and the slow progress of implementation of trade liberalization under AFTA, the Singapore government has sought to promote greater investment and trade diversification from Southeast Asia, by initiating new bilateral Free Trade Agreements (FTAs) with Japan, New Zealand and the US.

State-Owned Enterprises

While the government has by and large refrained from direct participation in manufacturing activities, there have been instances where state-controlled (and usually, though not always, state majority-owned) enterprises or "government-linked companies" (GLCs) become industry leaders in specific manufacturing sectors. In particular, in the shipbuilding and repair industry, the three largest companies are all GLCs, and together they accounted for more than half the total industry output. Other manufacturing industries include those that are historically linked to military requirements (aerospace repair/maintenance, ammunition making) or deemed "strategic", such as shipping and steel making. More recently, a listed GLC (the Singapore Technology Holding Group) has ventured into a diverse range of high-technology industries such as wafer fabrication and design, software and systems engineering, telecommunications and magnetic disk drive manufacturing.

In nearly all cases, the involvement of GLCs have been justified on the ground that these industries are of strategic importance to Singapore, yet there are too few local private investors who are prepared to venture into these industries on their own. State-owned enterprises' involvement is therefore necessary to fully exploit the scale, scope or network economies. The general framework under which GLCs operate in Singapore is as follows. The government, as the majority shareholder, is represented in the board of directors, who in turn appoint senior managers. However, the management enjoys significant autonomy in the day-to-day running of the company. All GLCs are subject to the market discipline, be it competition from other GLCs, MNCs, or international competition in the export markets. In many instances, GLCs are also seen arranging financing through the commercial credit market, although in some cases capital financing is obtained from the government.

In essence, although GLCs are directed to sectors in which there is alleged failure of private capital allocation, they are operated as private enterprises in many aspects (e.g. in executive compensation), and their performance are monitored in largely commercial terms. In particular, GLCs are encouraged to list on the local stock exchange so that their performance could be monitored by independent investors through the equity market. This approach has helped to minimize inefficiency and rent capture by management. Unlike state owned enterprises in many other countries which persist despite recurrent losses, GLCs in Singapore have shown willingness to close down unprofitable businesses. A case in point is the recent decision by the Singapore Technology Group to shut down the operation of a disk drive company, Micropolis that it bought less than two years earlier, suffering a substantial loss in the process. In addition, the government has not hesitated to replace management when their performance was deemed unsatisfactory. Increasingly, foreign expatriate managers are brought in to engineer major strategic change or to turnaround poorly performing GLCs (e.g. DBS Bank, NOL).

Although the intent of the government is to have the GLCs to enter only strategic businesses where local entrepreneurship is lacking, there is no doubt that the presence of many large GLCs in different sectors of the economy had a "crowding out" effect on participation by local firms. The negative effects of this crowding out process on the Singapore economy may have been moderated in two ways. On the one hand, the government had sought to apply competition policy to most domestic markets by having more than one GLCs to compete in the same sector (e.g. in shipbuilding, telecommunications services). Such inter-GLC competition helped to keep market somewhat efficient, even if they crowd out competition from local entrepreneurs. On the other hand, the GLC network may have facilitated the formation of strategic alliances among GLCs, or of GLCs and private enterprises, to achieve greater scale economies to compete in international markets and in regionalization effort.

The extent of dominance of GLCs in the Singapore economy is still a matter of debate. A recent US Embassy report claimed that GLCs accounted for as much as 60% of Singapore's GDP. However, according to a recent study by the Department of Statistics of Singapore, the share of GLCs in Singapore's GDP was substantially lower, being only about 10.6% in 1996, although it did show an increasing trend, rising to 11.3% in 1997 and 12.9% in 1998 [DOS(2001)].

With the recent strategic shift towards promotion of high tech entrepreneurship under the T21 initiative, the government is re-thinking the logic of promoting large GLCs in technologically dynamic industries. The recent establishment of the US$1 billion Technopreneurship Fund may be a step in the direction of allocating more government funding of high tech ventures through the venture capital market, rather than through internal allocation by GLC management. In addition, the government is increasingly recognizing the need for Singaporean GLCs to globalize their operations in order to compete effectively in many industries where the major competitors are all highly globalized MNCs; to facilitate such globalization, the government has to reduce its control over these companies. An interesting test case in point is the recent attempt by Singapore Telecoms to acquire Optus, an Australian telecommunications company, which has met with objection from some quarters in the Australian government over concerns of the close link of Singapore Telecoms to the Singapore government.

3. Quality of State Institutions

In summary, our analysis above highlighted significant industrial policy intervention by the state in Singapore. While it has not been possible to quantify the costs and benefits of such policy intervention in details, the broad picture is one of generally positive contributions, with some notable mistakes (e.g. the high wage policy in the late 1970s-early 1980s) and regulatory excesses (e.g. in public control of national savings).

A major contributing factor to the relative effectiveness of state interventions in Singapore is the quality of the state institutions in

Singapore as measured by dimensions of governance such as the political stability, quality of the bureaucracy, the extent of rule of law, the extent of public-private sector cooperation and the incidence of corruption (Weder, 1999). A recent survey (Weder, 1999) ranked Singapore highest in terms of quality of bureaucracy, rule of law, and second highest in terms of low level of corruption and public-private sector cooperation, when compared against Hong Kong, Korea, Thailand and Malaysia. In terms of political stability, BERI had consistently ranked Singapore highly (Annex Table 12K). Despite the extensive intervention by the state in various economic activities, the Heritage Foundation has consistently ranked Singapore highly (see Annex Table 12L) in terms of economic freedom, suggesting that these interventions had not been perceived as adversely affecting the freedom of private economic agents.

To further illustrate how the various government policies and institutions have specifically contributed to the development of competitive manufacturing industries in Singapore, we provide a more detailed analysis of the development of the electronics industry and the shipbuilding and repair industry in Singapore in the next chapter. These two industries illustrate the very different roles that the state has historically played in promoting industrial development — leveraging MNC investments in the former and substantial direct state involvement through state-owned enterprises in the latter.

IV. SUMMARY ASSESSMENT AND CONCLUSION

We started the paper by asking what lessons can be drawn from the development experience of Singapore regarding the role of the state. We would like to conclude here by highlight what we see as the most relevant lessons from our re-examination of the development experience of Singapore. First and foremost, we believe that Singapore's ability to develop an internationally competitive manufacturing sector clearly demonstrated the important role of the state in leveraging direct foreign investment (DFI) not only for capital, but more importantly in terms of technology transfer and access to the home and international markets of the MNCs involved. As Dr. Goh Keng Swee, the key architect of Singapore's early industrial growth, has keenly observed, the early take-off of export-led industrialization is not just a matter of having cheap land, labor or even capital; what is most needed is the presence of an industrial entrepreneur class. The British colonial legacy of entrepot trading did not breed any significant indigenous industrial capital class in Singapore and Hong Kong. While the movement of experienced industrialists from Shanghai after the communist take-over of mainland China helped jumpstart the early industrialization of Hong Kong, no such help was forthcoming in the case of Singapore. Consequently, the state policy of attracting MNCs effectively substituted for the absence of an indigenous industrial entrepreneurial class in the crucial early years of industrial take-off in Singapore.

It should also be noted that the MNC-leveraging strategy of Singapore went significantly beyond just being export-oriented and open to world market competition as recommended by the World Bank's EAM Study (1993); it involved a conscious strategy to upgrade infrastructure and technical skills to attract ever higher-value adding manufacturing operations, and to facilitate the transfer and assimilation of imported technology. It also involved the establishment of an institution like the Economic Development Board (EDB) to actively court MNCs in targetted industries, and to constantly devise policies and adapt incentives to make Singapore attractive to these MNCs despite increasing competition from the region and, increasingly, from the advanced industrial countries themselves. Indeed, it is without exaggeration to say that the success of Singapore in attracting so many world-class MNCs to continuously invest in Singapore over the years owes in no small part to the entrepreneurial and dynamic institutional capabilities of the state in the form of institutions like the EDB to adapt to the changing requirements of marketing Singapore to overseas investors, and to pro-actively invest in infrastructures and skills to promote continuous technological upgrading.

According to Schein (1996), a key characteristics of EDB's success as an institution has been its "strategic pragmatism". EDB is strategic in that it tries to select investments that meet specific objectives deemed of strategic importance to Singapore; but it is pragmatic in that it is not dogmatic about the specific industry targets, and is willing to adapt when environmental changes warrant. For example, EDB's mission in recent years have been broadened to attract investment in services besides manufacturing. EDB was able to quickly identify a whole range of new services that can be promoted to make Singapore into a total business hub. More recently, EDB's mission has been further broadened to cover attracting foreign talents, the development of core capabilities and the promotion of innovation. EDB also has the flexibility and discretionary power to tailor investment incentives to best fit the needs of investors. It is this adaptive institutional capability that sets it apart from other institutions with similar missions in many other developing countries.

Another factor in the strategic pragmatism of EDB is that it sets its objectives broadly in terms of attracting high value-adding jobs and creating technological learning opportunities, rather than being fixated with particular industries per se. Indeed, the bias of EDB is not so much towards MNCs as such, but towards encouraging investment by companies that can provide the advanced technologies and market access that offer the highest value-adding jobs, regardless of the nationality or ownership of the companies. Rather than promoting "national champions", creating high-value adding jobs and technological learning opportunities have been seen as more effective routes to improving the income and living standards of the Singaporean citizenry.

Some analysts have argued that this MNC-led strategy has led to a stunting of local enterprise development. To the extent that MNCs have provided high-paying jobs and careers to many Singaporeans who might otherwise have ventured to start up their own manufacturing enterprises, there has certainly been some adverse effects on local entrepreneurship. Indeed, the greater presence of foreign competition has undoubtedly bid up prices of a wide range of other less easily tradable factor inputs, ranging from labor to industrial land, and hence rendered many local enterprises that did not possess technological capabilities comparable to MNCs less competitive. But this is the basis of Singapore's development strategy: because of the small domestic market and extreme scarcity of labor and land, local firms must be internationally competitive, or otherwise they would be hoarding resources at below market value. Thus, government assistance schemes for local enterprises were not meant to shield them from global competitive pressures, but targeted at assisting firms which show good potential for growth.

The Singapore experience also suggests the importance of science and technology policies that focus not only on technology creation, but also on technology diffusion and utilization (Wong, 1994, 2001b). The presence of many world-class MNCs have induced the development of technological capabilities among indigenous manufacturing firms through supplier-buyer linkages (Wong, 1991). High quality technical training at the polytechnic level as well as in various government training programs in precision engineering, quality management, etc. in the 1970s and 1980s had helped the workforce in skill and technology upgrading, which was crucial in the transformation of the manufacturing sector. In addition, specific technical upgrading programs sponsored by various government agencies further facilitated the diffusion and adoption of technology. It is only in the late 1980s that the government began to promote investment in R&D in a major way, in anticipating the shift towards more R&D-intensive manufacturing in the 1990s. In comparison to Taiwan and Korea, Singapore therefore started emphasizing indigenous R&D much later. While the early emphasis on technology diffusion is correct, I believe nonetheless that the government had underestimated the importance of technology creation and hence been a little late in investing in building up the R&D infrastructure of the country. The government has also been a bit late in promoting the development of local high tech entrepreneurship, but once the T21 initiative was announced in 1998, the pace of investment by the government in stimulating the growth of Singapore as a venture capital hub in Asia has been extremely aggressive.

The Singapore development experience, with its emphasis on maintaining a strong manufacturing base, also shows the importance of long-term strategic considerations in economic policy making. Despite rising costs and increasing regional competition, the government remains firmly committed to promoting manufacturing as a key component of the economy. Manufacturing is seen not only as an engine of economic growth, but more importantly as a means to further the nation's technological capability. Moreover, the political leadership clearly recognized the potential risk of becoming solely a financial, business services and transportation hub for other countries in the region, with no manufacturing base of one's own: Even if Singapore is able to maintain her competitive edge as a servicing centre, there is no guarantee that the neighbouring nations would not resort to protectionist policies to promote their own tertiary industries. Thus, despite the temptation to "hollow out" manufacturing and to become increasingly dependent on financial and business services, the government is determined to keep attracting ever higher value-adding manufacturing to Singapore through various policy measures described earlier. It is this long-term strategic consideration that has set Singapore on a different industrial development path from Hong Kong, which has seen massive de-industrialization.

The experience of Singapore also poses a challenge to the conventional wisdom that state owned enterprises tend to be inefficient. Many state owned enterprises in Singapore have performed well by international standards, including the world's best air and sea ports, one of the most efficient telecommunications systems in the world, and among the world's best airlines. The high performance of Singapore's brand of state owned enterprises suggests that it is the governance mechanism and competitive policy, not ownership per se, that determines enterprise performance. State owned enterprises engaging in internationally competitive markets were given significant management autonomy and were in turn judged on market performance terms. Even for public enterprises in monopoly situation, international benchmarking has been successfully used by the Singaporean government to discipline them in the past, when Singapore was not at the technical frontier and there were obvious international leaders that can be used as benchmarks. In recent years, however, as Singapore approaches closer to the technical frontier, and as innovation becomes more critical than efficiency in improving consumer welfare, the government has resorted to a greater use of competition policy. For example, in the telecommunications market, liberalization of entry has been accelerated, with different state-owned enterprises encouraged to compete. Thus, an industrial policy to ensure a certain degree of indigenous participation in key domestic markets can still lead to an efficient outcome if vigorous competition is permitted among the domestic players.

The Singapore experience also suggests a possible important role of the state in moulding the "social contract" between the various social classes, particularly between employers, workers and civil servants. From a neoclassical economics perspective, institutions like the tripartite National Wage Council (NWC) appears to be inefficient mechanisms that impose unnecessary rigidities on free labor market processes. However, from an institutional economics perspective, it could be a useful mechanism to induce a spirit of information sharing and trust building. Such a tripartite institution may also be a means to arrive at a "fairer" distribution of gains (or pains). To the extent that "trust", "social cohesion" and "team-work" are important social values that increase the dynamic efficiencies of enterprises in a country in the long-run, they may effectively compensate for the possible loss in static inefficiencies in the labor market in the short run.

Last, but not least, the Singapore development experience suggests the importance of developing strong institutional capability when a state wishes to pursue significant visionary goals. This is consistent with the argument in the latest development report of the World Bank that state intervention policies and programs need to be matched to the institutional capabilities of the state (World Bank, 1997). In particular, for a small economy like Singapore, highly integrated into the global economy, a critical institutional capability is the ability to respond fast and flexibly to external environmental changes. Policies enacted under one set of circumstances need to be quickly reversed when those circumstances no longer hold. So far, the state in Singapore has demonstrated that it was quite capable of changing policies in response to environmental changes. Thus, despite some policy mistakes in the past, the Singapore government appears to have been able to recover quickly by making the necessary corrections. Indeed, it is this strategic pragmatism in the role of the state that has arguably contributed the most to the enormous economic progress of Singapore over the last 30 or so years, and upon which her future continued economic success will rest.

In this regard, the recent regional financial crisis and the severe regional recession that it has caused certainly represents an interesting test of Singapore's institutional capability to respond flexibly to adverse external shocks. It is also a test of the capacity of Singapore's tripartite industrial relations institution to achieve pain-sharing as well as gain-sharing. It may be too early to tell if the many established roles of the state in Singapore will continue to be a source of strength for Singapore to weather the storm, or that Singapore will be forced to dismantle many of these state intervention policies, as the minimalist-state, free market paradigm might suggest. On the basis of evidence so far, we are inclined to the former. Indeed, while Singapore had hastened the move towards market liberalization, and had made greater move towards giving more autonomy to state owned enterprises to better cope with globalization, Singapore had so far been able to emerge from the regional recovery with her competitiveness enhanced because of, rather than in spite of, a continuing strong role of the state.

In summary, our analysis of Singapore's industrial development experience largely confirms an important role of the state, even as the economy transitions towards an advanced market economy with increasing reliance on private market mechanisms over time. While not free of mistakes, the intervention of the state has contributed significantly to the development of the country's manufacturing capabilities, especially in the early development stages. In this regard, it should hold interesting lessons especially for other developing countries, especially small countries that are similarly constrained by a lack of natural resources and a small domestic market. The broad lesson, however, is that it is not whether there is a role of the state in development, but what these roles should be, and how can they be tailored to the particular contexts and development stages of the countries concerned. In view of the differences in the development approach adopted by Singapore when compared to Taiwan, Korea and Hong Kong, it is hoped that the experience of Singapore can provide a useful example, from a comparative institutional analysis perspective, on how different East Asian economies, each starting with different unique initial conditions and facing different political imperatives, may achieve economic success through different approaches to economic development. In the context of the Transitional Developmental State Paradigm proposed in Chapter One, Singapore's transitional experience from "Third World to First" [Lee (2000)] appears to conform more closely to the "transitional developmental state" pathway than the "strong developmental state" pathway of Japan and Korea.

Singapore's experience suggests that the recent financial crisis that engulfed much of East Asia does not negate the role of the state in economic development. Indeed, by inducing very different impacts and eliciting very different responses from the different East Asian countries, the recent regional financial crisis is likely to help to bring into sharper relief the differential contributions of the state in these respective countries, thereby amplifying our understanding of the most critical roles of the state. As observed by Ohno and Ohno (1998), the active role of the state is particularly important in early stages of development or in an economic crisis. The fact that Singapore is now increasing the pace of liberalization of her financial and telecommunications services sectors is more in response to the perceived strategic opportunity to strengthen Singapore's position as a viable hub in the global knowledge-based, internet-driven economy, rather than as a reaction to the Asian financial crisis. Even as the state continues to deregulate and liberalize, its visible hands continue to be seen in building the market institutions and infrastructure to support the shift of the economy towards a knowledge-intensive, innovation-driven one.

REFERENCES

Amsden, A. *Asia's Next Giant: South Korea and Late Industrialization*. New York: Oxford University Press, 1989.

Aoki, M., K. Murdock and M. Okuno-Fujiwara. "Beyond the East Asian Miracle: Introducing the Market Enhancing View". World Bank EDI Working Paper, 1995.

Asher, M.G. "An Economic Perspective". In *Privatisation: Singapore's Experience in Perspective*, edited by I. Thynne and M. Ariff. Singapore: Longman, 1988.

Asher, M.G. "Public Policies and Domestic Saving: The Case of Singapore". Report of the conference on Change and Prosperity: The Aspen Institute Program on the World Economy, August 1995, Aspen, Colorado.

Chan, H.C. *The Politics of Survival*. Kuala Lumpur: Oxford University Press, 1965-1967.

Collins, S. and B. Bosworth. "Economic Growth in East Asia: Accumulation versus Assimilation". *Brookings Papers in Economic Activity* 2 (1996): 135–204.

Department of Statistics (DOS). *Yearbook of Statistics, Singapore*. Singapore: Department of Statistics, various years.

Department of Statistics (DOS). "Multifactor Productivity Growth in Singapore: Concept, Methodology and Trends". Singapore: Department of Statistics, Occasional Paper on Economic Statistics, 1997.

Department of Statistics (DOS). *Foreign Equity Investment in Singapore 1997-1998*. Singapore: Department of Statistics, 2000a.

Department of Statistics (DOS). *Singapore's Investment Abroad 1997-1998*. Singapore: Department of Statistics, 2000b.

Department of Statistics (DOS). "Contribution of Government-Linked Companies to Gross Domestic Product". Singapore: Department of Statistics, Occasional Paper on Economic Statistics, 2001.

Economic Development Board (EDB). *Report on the Census for Industrial Production*. Singapore: Economic Development Board, various years.

Economic Development Board (EDB). *EDB Yearbook*. Singapore: Economic Development Board, various years.

Elsevier. *Yearbook of World Electronics Data*. Oxford: Elsevier Advanced Technology, various years.

Goh, K.S. "A Socialist Economy That Works". In *Socialism that Works*, edited by C.V.D. Nair. Singapore: Federal Publications, 1977.

Goh, K.S. "Public Administration and Economic Development in Less Developed Countries". Harry G. Johnson Memorial Lecture No.4. London: Trade Policy Research Centre, 1983.

Goh, K.S. *Wealth of East Asian Nations*, edited by L. Low. Singapore: Federal Publications, 1995.

Goh, K.S. and L. Low. "Beyond Miracles and Total Factor Productivity: The Singapore Experience". *ASEAN Economic Bulletin* 13(1), 1996.

Government of Singapore. *The Next Lap*. Singapore: Government Printers, 1991.

Hsieh, C.T. "What Explains the Industrial Revolution in East Asia? Evidence from Factor Markets". Unpublished paper. Department of Economics, University of California, Berkeley, 1997.

Huff, W.G. *The Economic Growth of Singapore: Trade and Development in the Twentieth Century*. Cambridge; New York: Cambridge University Press, 1994.

Hughes, H. and P.S. You, eds. *Foreign Investment and Industrialization in Singapore*. Canberra: Australian National University Press, 1969.

Kim, J. and L. Lau. "The Sources of Economic Growth of the East Asian Newly Industrialized Countries". *Journal of Japanese and International Economics* 8, no. 3 (1994): 235–71.

Krause, L.B., A.T. Koh and T.Y. Lee. *The Singapore Economy Reconsidered*. Singapore: Institute of Southeast Asian Studies, 1987.

Krueger, A. "East Asian Experience and Endogenous Growth Theory". In *Growth Theories in Light of the East Asian Experience*, edited by T. Ito and A. Krueger. Chicago: University of Chicago Press, 1995.

Krugman, P. "The Myth of Asia Miracle". *Foreign Affairs* 73, no.6 (1994): 62–78.

Lee, K.Y. *The Singapore Story: Memoirs of Lee Kuan Yew*. Singapore: Singapore Press Holdings: Times Editions, 1998.

Lee, K.Y. *From Third World to First: The Singapore Story 1965–2000 — Memoirs of Lee Kuan Yew*. Singapore: Singapore Press Holdings: Times Editions, 2000.

Lee, T.Y. and L. Low. *Local Entrepreneurship in Singapore: Private and State*. Singapore: Times Academic Press, 1990.

Leung, H.M. "Total Factor Productivity Growth in Singapore's Manufacturing Industries". *Applied Economics Letters* 4, no. 8 (1997): 525–28.

Leung, H.M. *Productivity of Singapore's Manufacturing Sector: An Industry Level Non-Parametric Study*. Department of Business Policy, National University of Singapore, 1997.

Lim, C.Y. and Associates. *Policy Options for Singapore Economy*. Singapore: McGraw Hill, 1988.

Lim, C.Y and J.L. Peter, eds. *Singapore: Resources and Growth*. Singapore: Oxford University Press, 1988.

Low, L., M.H.Toh, T.W.Soon, K.Y. Tan and H. Hughes. *Challenge and Response: Thirty Years of the Economic Development Board*. Singapore: Times Academic Press, 1993.

Low,L. and D.M. Johnston, eds. *Singapore Inc.: Public Policy Options in the Third Millennium*. Singapore: Asia-Pacific Press, 2001.

Luckett, D.G., D.L. Schulze and R.W.Y. Wong. *Banking, Finance and Monetary Policy in Singapore*. Singapore: McGraw Hill, 1994.

McKendrick, D.G., R.F. Doner and S. Haggard. *From Silicon Valley to Singapore: Location and Competitive Advantage in the Hard Disk Drive Industry*. Stanford: Stanford University Press, 2000.

Ministry of Trade and Industry, Singapore (MTI). *Economic Survey of Singapore*. Singapore: Ministry of Trade and Industry, various years.

Ministry of Finance, Singapore. *Final Report of the Committee to Promote Enterprise Overseas*. Singapore: National Printers, 1993.

Ministry of Trade and Industry, Singapore (MTI). *Strategic Economic Plan*. Singapore: Ministry of Trade and Industry.

Mirza, H. *Multinationals and Growth of the Singapore Economy*. New York: St. Martins Press, 1986.

Murray, G. and A. Perera. *Singapore: The Global City-State*. Kent: China Library, 1996.

Natarajan,S. and J.M. Tan. *The Impacts of MNC Investments in Malaysia, Singapore and Thailand*. Singapore: Institute of Southeast Asian Studies, 1992.

National Computer Board, Singapore (NCB). *Singapore IT Manpower Survey 1995*. Singapore: NCB, 1996.

National Science & Technology Board, Singapore (NSTB). *National Science and Technology Plan: Towards 2000 and Beyond*. Singapore: NSTB, 1996.

National Science & Technology Board, Singapore (NSTB). *National Survey of R&D*. Singapore: NSTB, various years.

Organisation for Economic Co-operation and Development. *Information Technology Outlook 1997*. Paris: OECD, 1997.

Ohno, K. and I. Ohno, eds. *Japanese Views on Economic Development: Diverse Paths to the Market*. London; New York: Routledge, 1998.

Peebles, G. and P. Wilson. *The Singapore Economy*. Cheltenham; Brookfield: Edward Elgar, 1996.

Porter, M.E. *The Competitive Advantage of Nations*. New York: The Free Press, 1990.

Rao B.V.V. and C. Lee. "Sources of Growth in the Singapore Economy and its Manufacturing and Services Sectors". *The Singapore Economic Review* 40, no. 1 (1996): 83–115.

Rao, V.V.B. and D. Owyong. "Sources of Growth in the Singapore Economy: Some New Results". Paper presentation at Taipei International Conference on Efficiency and Productivity Growth, 1997.

Sandhu, K. and P. Wheatley, eds. *Management of Success: The Moulding of Modern Singapore*. Singapore: Institute of Southeast Asian Studies, 1989.

Schein, E. *Strategic Pragmatism: The Culture of the Economic Development Board of Singapore*. Cambridge: MIT Press, 1996.

Soon, T.W. *Singapore's New Education Systems: Education Reform for National Development*. Singapore: Institute of Southeast Asian Studies, 1988.

Soon, T.W. and C.S. Tan. "Singapore: Public Policy and Economic Development". In *Lessons from East Asia*, edited by D.M. Leipziger. Ann Arbor: The University of Michigan Press, 1997.

Stiglitz, J.E. "Some Lessons from the East Asian Miracle". *The World Bank Research Observer* 11, no. 2 (1996): 151–77.

The Economic Committee. *The Singapore Economy: New Directions*. Singapore: Ministry of Trade and Industry, 1986.

Toh, M.H. and L.Low. "Differential Total Factor Productivity in the Four Dragons: The Singapore Case". *The Journal of International Trade and Economic Development* 5, no. 2 (1996): 161–81.

Toh, M.H. and K.Y. Tan, eds. *Competitiveness of the Singapore Economy*. Singapore: Singapore University Press, 1998.

Tsao, Y. "Growth Without Productivity: Singapore Manufacturing in the 1970s". *Journal of Development Economics* 18 (1985): 25–38.

United Nations Industrial Development Organization. *Industrial Development Global Report 1997*. Oxford: Oxford University Press for the United Nations Industrial Development Orgnization, 1997.

United Nations Conference on Trade and Development. *World Investment Report 1997: Transnational Corporations, Market Structure and Competition Policy.* New York, United Nations, 1997.

Urban Redevelopment Authority. *Living the Next Lap: Towards a Tropical City of Excellence.* Singapore: Urban Redevelopment Authority, 1991.

Wade, R. *Governing the Market: Economic Theory and the Role of the Government in East Asian Industrialization.* Princeton: Princeton University Press, 1990.

Wong, P.K. *Technological Development Through Subcontracting Linkages.* Tokyo: Asian Productivity Organization, 1991.

Wong, P.K. "Singapore's Technology Strategy". In *The Emerging Technological Trajectory of the Pacific Rim*, edited by D.F. Simon. New York: M.E. Sharpe, 1994.

Wong, P.K. "Technology Transfer and Development Inducement by Foreign MNCs: The Experience of Singapore". In *Industrial Strategy for Global Competitiveness of Korean Industries*, edited by K.Y. Jeong and M.H. Kwack. Seoul: Korea Economic Research Institute, 1995a.

Wong, P.K. *National Innovation System: The Case of Singapore.* Seoul: Science and Technology Policy Institute, 1995b.

Wong, P.K. "From NIE to Developed Economy: Singapore's Industrial Policy to the Year 2000". *Journal of Asian Business* 12, no. 3 (1996a): 65–85.

Wong, P.K. "Implementing the NII Vision: Singapore's Experience and Future Challenges". *Information Infrastructure and Policy* 5, no. 2 (1996b): 95–117.

Wong, P.K. "Technology Acquisition Pattern of High-Tech Firms in Singapore". *Singapore Management Review* 20, no. 1 (1998a): 43–64.

Wong, P.K. "Leveraging the Global Information Revolution for Economic Development: Singapore's Evolving Information Industry Strategy". *Information Systems Research* 9, no. 4 (1998b).

Wong, P.K. "Singapore's Strategic Positioning for a Stronger Regional Hub Role after the Regional Economic Recovery". In *Trends and Issues in East Asia 1999*, edited by C.Y. Ng and C. Griffy-Brown, pp. 147–59. Tokyo: Foundation for Advanced Studies on International Development, 1999a.

Wong, P.K. "Dynamics of HDD Industry Development in Singapore". San Diego: Information Storage Industry Centre, Univ. of California, San Diego Working Paper, 1999b

Wong, P.K. "The Contribution of IT to the Rapid Economic Development of Singapore". In *Information Technology, Productivity, and Economic Growth: International Evidence*, edited by M.Pohjola, pp. 221–41. Oxford Univ. Press, 2000.

Wong, P.K. "Globalization of American, European and Japanese Production Networks and The Growth of Singapore's Electronics Industry". *International Journal of Technology Management* (2001a), forthcoming

Wong, P.K "Leveraging Multinational Corporations, Fostering Technopreneurship: The Changing Role of S&T Policy in Singapore". *International Journal of Technology Management* (2001b), forthcoming.

Wong, P.K., S.Y. Phang *et al. Development of Internationally Competitive Indigenous Manufacturing Firms in Singapore.* Tokyo: Foundation for Advanced Studies of International Development, 1997.

World Bank. *The East Asian Miracle: Economic Growth and Public Policy.* New York: Oxford University Press, 1993.

World Bank. *Bureaucrats in Business.* New York: Oxford University Press, 1995.

World Bank. *The State in a Changing World.* New York: Oxford University Press, 1997.

World Bank. *Knowledge for Development.* New York: Oxford University Press, 1998.

World Bank. *World Development Indicators 2001*, Washington, D.C.: World Bank, 2001.

Young, A. "A Tale of Two Cities: Factor Accumulation and Technical Change in Hong Kong and Singapore". *NBER Macroeconomic Annual 1992.* Cambridge: MIT Press, 1992.

Young, A. "Lessons from the East Asian NICs: A Contrarian View". *European Economic Review* 38, nos. 3-4 (1994): 964–73.

Young, A. "The Tyranny of Numbers: Confronting the Statistical Realities of the East Asian Growth Experience". *Quarterly Journal of Economics* 110, no. 3 (1995): 641–68.

ANNEX TABLE 12A   Labour productivity of Singapore manufacturing vs. OECD and other NIEs

Country	Value Added/Labour of Total Manufacturing (US$)		Structural Indices for Degree of Specialisation	
	1980	1994	1980	1994
OECD:				
Australia	25280	70383	11.1	12.1
Austria	22681	61797	9.7	10.5
Belgium	30556	61596	12.5	13
Luxembourg	28479	53895	38.2	13.6
Canada	32187	58465	10.3	12.4
Denmark	31187	54677	14.8	15.6
Finland	26845	61365	13.3	15.2
France	30101	65118	10.4	11.4
Germany	36739	88680	12.1	15
Greece	16204	33368	11.8	12.4
Iceland	18864	38630	26.5	34.6
Ireland	25118	32017	14.9	23.6
Italy	28784	46871	10	12
Japan	30912	117764	11.8	15
Netherlands	29285	69616	15	14.5
New Zealand	16711	32618	14.6	16.4
Norway	19129	45828	12.2	14.5
Portugal	8087	14917	11.2	9.3
Spain	20475	43162	8.4	11.1
Sweden	36206	58602	15.4	17
Switzerland	40009	66570	11.6	15
Turkey	13617	25991	14.3	13.3
UK	25117	57635	11.1	12.5
US	40078	93199	11.9	12.8
Average of OECD	**26360**	**56365**	**13.88**	**14.70**
Singapore	**13942**	**56329**	**19.9**	**28.2**
Other NIEs:				
Hong Kong	7840	26436	24.2	19.5
South Korea	9545	52760	9.1	11.2
Taiwan	7470	33766	9.5	12.5
Average of other NIEs	**8285**	**37654**	**14.27**	**14.40**
Malaysia	**8060**	**15317**	**15.5**	**18.5**

SOURCE: United Nations Industrial Organization, *Industrial Development Global Report*, 1996 and 1997.

ANNEX TABLE 12B   Manufacturing Growth in Singapore, 1959–99

Year	No. of Firms	Output $mn	No. Workers	Value Added $mn	Fixed Asset $mn	Val.Add/ Labor $	Val.Add/ Output %	Capital/ Labor $
1959	531	398.94	25607	142.78	na	5576	35.8	na
1960	548	465.57	27416	142.14	na	5185	30.5	na
1961	562	518.37	27562	174.36	na	6326	33.6	na
1962	605	660.30	28642	201.68	na	7041	30.5	na
1963	858	843.75	36586	252.57	214.21	6903	29.9	5855
1964	930	927.93	41488	282.46	248.36	6808	30.4	5986
1965	1000	1086.36	47334	348.36	317.31	7360	32.1	6704
1966	1123	1325.78	52807	415.04	420.01	7860	31.3	7954
1967	1200	1687.23	58347	478.63	502.12	8203	28.4	8606
1968	1586	2175.67	74833	611.76	574.77	8175	28.1	7681
1969	1714	3213.90	100758	856.63	810.89	8502	26.7	8048
1970	1747	3891.01	120509	1093.72	1071.30	9076	28.1	8890
1971	1813	4699.25	140552	1366.52	1458.86	9723	29.1	10379
1972	1931	5722.22	170352	1782.28	1810.84	10462	31.1	10630
1973	2079	7938.07	198574	2540.60	2538.20	12794	32.0	12782
1974	2179	13346.91	206067	3528.22	3165.71	17122	26.4	15363
1975	2385	12610.14	191528	3411.13	3579.25	17810	27.1	18688
1976	2505	15317.44	207234	3961.81	3888.99	19118	25.9	18766
1977	2638	17518.25	219112	4475.46	4181.46	20425	25.5	19084
1978	2946	19666.68	243724	5162.92	5226.70	21183	26.3	21445
1979	3122	25133.69	269334	6412.93	5744.60	23810	25.5	21329
1980	3355	31657.90	285250	8521.89	7461.07	29875	26.9	26156
1981	3439	36787.10	281675	9720.55	8837.45	34510	26.4	31375
1982	3586	36467.44	275450	9355.94	10118.74	33966	25.7	36735
1983	3616	37221.52	271106	9822.09	11224.39	36230	26.4	41402
1984	3648	41077.86	274391	11106.27	13144.36	40476	27.0	47904
1985	3504	38495.09	253510	10702.27	12874.56	42216	27.8	50785
1986	3449	37258.70	246682	11899.97	12519.71	48240	31.9	50752
1987	3514	46084.04	276309	14470.82	13162.75	52372	31.4	47638
1988	3624	56470.01	324713	17918.21	14516.93	55182	31.7	44707
1989	3660	63626.32	337575	19675.68	16581.40	58285	30.9	49119
1990	3703	71333.22	351674	21606.82	18030.61	61440	30.3	51271
1991	3785	74575.03	358274	23449.89	18722.34	65452	31.4	52257
1992	3917	77275.89	358394	24908.97	20222.88	69502	32.2	56426
1993	3993	87639.04	355175	28287.17	22338.43	79643	32.3	62894
1994	4013	100622.09	365588	31453.95	24117.99	86037	31.3	65970
1995	4036	113358.00	370281	34882.40	26435.01	94205	30.8	71392
1996	4068	119868.96	368055	36881.35	29099.15	100206	30.8	79062
1997	4108	126530.9	366696	38688.06	37033.2	105504	30.6	100992
1998	4004	121433.1	352289	38782.9	37246.4	110088	31.9	105727
1999	3928	133577.4	338885	45113.8	38603.3	133124	33.8	113913

ANNEX TABLE 12B *(cont'd)*

			% Average Growth p.a.				
1960–70	12.29	23.65	15.96	22.64	25.85[1]	5.8	6.1[1]
1970–80	6.74	23.32	9.00	22.79	21.42	12.7	11.4
1980–90	0.99	8.46	2.12	9.75	9.22	7.5	7.0
1990–99	0.7	7.2	–0.4	8.5	8.8	9.0	9.3
	1.70	8.5	0.60	8.7	10.8	8.0	10.2

NOTE: 1. 1963–70.
SOURCES: Economic Development Board, *Report on the Census for Industrial Production,* various years.

ANNEX TABLE 12C   Return on Equity (ROE) in Singapore's Manufacturing Industry, 1987–98 (in percentages)

Year	Electronics Manufacturing	All Manufacturing	All Economic Sectors
1987	31.5	18.7	8.9
1988	24.7	21.8	11.7
1989	19.7	17.2	14.2
1990	20.8	18.3	12.6
1991	22.4	17.8	11.3
1992	21.3	16.9	10.4
1993	31.0	19.7	14.3
1994	19.7	16.2	12.9
1995	25.1	17	10.4
1996	22.3	14.5	11.4
1997	25.7	14.9	5.4
1998	16.5	11.8	1.4

SOURCES: For 1987 to 1994 ROE is calculated by the Department of Statistics as the ratio of current year's earnings to the average of the stock of equity capital invested in the current & preceding year. For 1995 to 1998 data is obtained from Department of Statistics, *Foreign Equity Investment in Singapore,* various years.

ANNEX TABLE 12D   Pretax ROE and ROA of Singapore's Manufacturing Industry (in percentages)

Year	ROE		ROA	
	Locally-controlled Company	*Foreign-controlled Company*	*Local*	*Foreign*
1990	15.6	26.7	8.4	15.3
1991	13.8	29.7	7.6	16.2
1992	14.2	23.0	7.5	12.2
1993	14.3	29.0	7.8	15.0
1994	9.9	24.8	5.7	13.2
1995	10.9	26.3	6.2	14.5
Ave 1990-95	13.1	26.6	7.2	14.4
1997	2.8	20.4	n.a.	n.a.
1998	–0.9	17.4	n.a.	n.a

SOURCES: Department of Statistics, *Performance of Singapore Companies*, 1997; Department of Statistics, *Foreign equity investment in Singapore*, 2000a.

ANNEX TABLE 12E   Manufacturing Value Add (MVA) by Technology Group and Pavitt Classification, 1995 (in percentages)

Share of MVA by Technology Group	*Singapore*	*G-5[1]*	*Small Industrialized Countries[2]*
High-technology industries	49.2	21.5	14.3
Medium-technology industries	39.7	31.7	26.9
Low-technology industries	11.1	46.8	58.8
Total	100.0	100.0	100.0

Share of MVA by Pavitt classification	*Singapore*	*G-5[3]*	*Small Industrialized Countries[4]*
Resource-intensive industries	10.8	21.8	28.8
Labor-intensive industries	8.7	19.9	10.8
Scale-intensive industries	19.7	31.2	37.2
Specialized-supplier industries	32.0	16.7	16.7
Science-based industries	28.8	10.4	6.5
Total	100.0	100.0	100.0

NOTES: 1. Figures for 1994.
2. Includes Denmark, Finland, Netherlands, Norway & Sweden. Figures for 1994.
3. Excludes Germany. Figures for Japan & UK are for 1994; figures for France are for 1993.
4 Includes Denmark (1994 figures), Netherlands, Norway (1994 figures) & Sweden.

SOURCES: Estimated by author from United Nations Industrial Development Organization, *International Yearbook of Industrial Statistics*, 1996.

ANNEX TABLE 12F International Comparisons of R&D Intensity

Grouping	Country	Year	R&D/GDP (%)	RSE per 10,000 Labor Force
G-5	Japan	1998	3.1	96
	Germany	1998	2.3	60
	U.S.A	1999	2.8	74 (1993)
	U.K	1998	1.8	55
	France	1997	2.2	61 (1996)
	Finland	1999	3.1	94 (1998)
	Switzerland	1996	2.7	55
	Sweden	1997	3.9	86
Industrialized Small Countries	Ireland	1997	1.4	51
	Netherlands	1996	2.1	46
	Denmark	1998	2.1	59 (1997)
	Norway	1997	1.7	76
	Australia	1996	1.7	66
	New Zealand	1996	0.9	35 (1995)
	Korea	1998	2.5	48
Asian NIEs	Taiwan	1998	2.0	66
	Hong Kong	1996	0.3	na
	Singapore	1999	1.8	70

SOURCES: National Science & Technology Board, *National Survey of R&D*, various years; Organization for Economic Co-operation and Development, *STI Outlook*, 1996 & 1998; Organization for Economic Co-operation and Development, *STI Scoreboard* 1999; Pacific Economic Cooperation Council and Asia Pacific Economic Cooperation, *APEC/PECC Pacific S&T Profile* 1995; *Far Eastern Economic Review*, May 14, 1998; National Science Board, *Science & Engineering Indicators*, 1998; and various national sources.

ANNEX TABLE 12G R&D Expenditure by Sectors, Singapore, 1978–1999

Year	Private Sector ($mn)	Higher Education Sector ($mn)	Government Sector ($mn)	Public Research Institutes ($mn)	Total ($mn)
1978	25.5	8.2	4.1	—	37.8
1981/82	44.2	24.3	12.5	—	81.0
1984/85	106.7	69.6	38.0	—	214.3
1987/88	225.6	95.4	53.7	—	374.7
1990	309.5	119.7	99.4	43.1	571.7
1991	442.1	147.1	96.8	70.8	756.8
1992	577.6	156.0	105.0	110.8	949.5
1993	618.9	157.3	106.5	115.5	998.2
1994	736.2	179.5	142.1	117.2	1175.0
1995	881.4	193.4	110.4	181.4	1366.6
1996	1133.4	238.7	166.8	253.2	1792.1
1997	1314.5	277.7	216.1	296.2	2104.6
1998	1536.1	305.8	299.8	350.5	2492.3
1999	1670.9	310.0	304.9	370.6	2656.3
1978	67%	22%	11%	—	100%
1984/85	50%	32%	18%	—	100%
1990	54%	21%	17%	8%	100%
1991	58%	20%	13%	9%	100%
1992	61%	16%	13%	12%	100%
1993	62%	16%	11%	12%	100%
1994	63%	15%	12%	10%	100%
1995	65%	14%	8%	13%	100%
1996	63%	13%	9%	14%	100%
1997	63%	13%	10%	14%	100%
1998	62%	12%	12%	14%	100%
1999	63%	12%	12%	14%	100%

SOURCE: National Science & Technology Board, *National Survey of R&D in Singapore*, various years.

ANNEX TABLE 12H   Foreign Company's Share of Private R&D Spending in Singapore
(in percentages)

Year	Share in Total Private R&D
1993	67.6
1994	74.5
1995	64.3
1996	67.0
1997	61.2
1998	55.8
1999	55.8

SOURCE: National Science & Technology Board, *National Survey of R&D in Singapore*, various years.

ANNEX TABLE 12I   Global Competitiveness Report Overall Ranking, 1998 and 1999

Countries	1999	1998
Singapore	1	1
US	2	3
Hong Kong	3	2
Taiwan	4	6
Canada	5	5
Switzerland	6	8
Luxembourg	7	10
UK	8	4
Netherlands	9	7
Japan	14	12
Norway	15	9
Malaysia	16	17
Korea	22	19
Thailand	30	21
Philippines	33	33
Indonesia	37	31

SOURCE: World Economic Forum, *Global Competitiveness Report*, 1998 and 1999.

ANNEX TABLE 12J   World Competitiveness Yearbook Ranking, 1997 and 1999

Countries	Overall		
	1999	*1998*	*1997*
US	1	1	1
Singapore	2	2	2
Hong Kong	7	3	3
Japan	16	18	9
Taiwan	18	16	23
Malaysia	27	20	17
China	29	24	24
Philippines	32	32	
Thailand	34	39	29
Korea	38	35	
Indonesia	46	40	39

SOURCE: International Institute for Management Development, *World Competitiveness Yearbook*, various years.

ANNEX TABLE 12K   BERI Low-Risk Ranking, 1998

Countries	Ranking	Present Composite Score
Switzerland	1	83
Singapore	2	76
Taiwan	3	76
Japan	4	74
Netherlands	5	74
Germany	6	72
Norway	7	71
Austria	8	69
US	9	69

SOURCE: *BERI Report*, 1998-II.

ANNEX TABLE 12L Economic Freedom Ranking of Singapore (Heritage Foundation), 1997 and 2000

Countries	Ranking		Score	
	2000	1997	2000	1997
Hong Kong	1	1	1.3	1.25
Singapore	2	2	1.45	1.30
New Zealand	3	4	1.7	1.75
Bahrain	4	3	1.8	1.7
US	4	6	1.8	1.90
Luxembourg	4	7	1.8	1.95
Ireland	7	7	1.85	2.0
Switzerland	8	5	1.9	1.90
UK	8	7	1.9	1.95
Taiwan	11	7	2.0	1.95
Japan	19	12	2.15	2.05
S. Korea	33	28	2.4	2.3
Thailand	46	28	2.7	2.4
Malaysia	46	28	2.7	2.4
Philippines	58	48	2.85	2.65
China	100	124	3.4	3.75
Indonesia	110	65	3.5	2.85
India	127	120	3.8	3.70

SOURCE: Heritage Foundation website, *The 2000 Index of Economic Freedom.*

ANNEX TABLE 12M Labour Force Evaluation Measure (LFEM) 1998

Top 5 Workforces Advanced Economies	Present Composite Score
Singapore	82
Switzerland	76
Japan	74
Belgium	72
US	69

SOURCE: *BERI Report*, 1998.

Annex Table 12N World Competitiveness Yearbook Ranking, 1998 and 1999

Countries	Overall		Domestic Economy		International-ization		Government		Finance		Infrastructure		Management		Science & Technology		People	
	1999	1998	1999	1998	1999	1998	1999	1998	1999	1998	1999	1998	1999	1998	1999	1998	1999	1998
US	1	1	1	1	1	1	15	13	1	1	1	1	1	1	1	1	6	8
Singapore	2	2	18	2	2	2	1	1	9	10	13	15	4	2	12	9	4	1
Hong Kong	7	3	36	17	5	3	2	2	7	9	19	19	5	4	22	25	14	13
UK	15	12	26	19	4	5	19	10	12	6	17	17	20	18	14	17	24	25
Japan	16	18	29	15	21	34	23	27	25	23	20	21	26	24	2	2	13	11
Taiwan	18	16	20	8	27	32	11	14	23	19	21	26	9	7	10	7	15	18
Malaysia	27	20	41	3	29	24	3	3	30	28	24	24	25	22	32	24	36	34
China	29	24	6	5	18	20	16	5	36	42	42	40	36	30	25	13	27	24
Philippines	32	32	39	23	20	28	21	19	35	40	45	44	28	27	33	32	45	40
Thailand	34	39	40	16	34	37	17	22	40	44	43	41	41	41	46	43	33	35
Korea	38	35	43	34	40	46	37	34	41	45	30	31	42	34	28	28	31	22
Indonesia	46	40	45	9	39	36	34	24	46	35	44	38	46	44	47	42	46	44

SOURCE: International Institute for Management Development, *World Competitiveness Yearbook*, 1998 and 1999.

13

Singapore: Electronics and Shipbuilding/ Repair Industry Case Studies

Poh-Kam Wong

I. INTRODUCTION

As highlighted in the previous chapter, DFI by multinational corporations (MNCs) has played a very important role in Singapore's rapid industrial development and technological upgrading. The significant presence of MNCs in Singapore's manufacturing growth and technological transformation is not accidental, but the results of conscious government policies and incentives to attract and leverage DFI. This facilitating role of the state is best illustrated by examining in greater details in this chapter the development of the electronics industry in Singapore.

Besides the important contribution of this MNC-leveraging strategy, the Singapore government has also been instrumental in promoting the growth of a number of industrial sectors through the direct involvement of state-owned enterprises. This approach to industrial development is best illustrated by examining the development of the shipbuilding and repair industry in this chapter.

II. DEVELOPMENT OF SINGAPORE'S ELECTRONICS INDUSTRY

1. Overview of the Electronics Industry

The electronics industry in Singapore represents a key driver of manufacturing growth in the economy, whether measured in terms of output produced, value added, goods exported, or technology spillover to the rest of the economy. For example, the industry accounted for almost 10% of the country's GDP, over 44% of the manufacturing value added, over 60% of domestic exports, and attracted over 55% of total private-sector R & D expenditure in 1999. In addition, the electronics industry has also stimulated the development of a whole host of other related supporting industries and services through backward linkages. The electronics industry is also responsible for stimulating the development of Singapore as a major regional logistics, marketing and technical support services hub through forward linkages. In 1996, Singapore was the third largest exporter of electronics goods in the world, after Japan and USA (Elsevier, 1998). The following is a brief account of the industry's historical development [see Wong (2001) for a more detailed treatment].

The development of the electronics industry in Singapore can be divided into three phases, which roughly correspond to the three phases of technology development the economy went through. The first phase covers the period up to about 1980, the second phase is from 1980 to 1989, and the third phase is from 1990 onwards. Some broad indicators for the industry during these three phases are presented in Table 13.1.

During the first phase, the EDB successfully attracted foreign MNCs to engage in the manufacturing of simple electronics in Singapore to take advantage of the low costs of production, particularly low wages. Most electronics goods produced were consumer electronics, which were destined for MNCs' export markets. As is evident in Table 13.1,

TABLE 13.1   Growth Performance of Singapore Electronics Industry, 1960–99 (in percentages)

	Phase 1		Phase 2	Phase 3
Average Growth Rate Per Annum (Compounded)	*1960–70*	*1970–80*	*1980–90*	*1990–99*
Industrial output	28.7	38.0	18.0	10.5
Value added	28.8	32.6	16.5	11.2
Employment	24.6	20.3	5.5	−1.6

NOTE: Growth rates are in current prices.
SOURCE: Economic Development Board, *Report on the Census for Industrial Production*, various years.

TABLE 13.2 Labor Productivity Trends of Singapore's Electronics Industry, 1960–99 (in S$ thousand)

Value Added Per Worker	1960	1970	1980	1990	1999
Electronics	6.3	9.4	23.3	62.8	189.2
All Manufacturing	5.2	9.1	29.9	61.4	133.1

NOTE: Values are in current prices.
SOURCE: Economic Development Board, *Report on the Census for Industrial Production*, various years.

electronics employment grew dramatically at an average of 25% p.a. over the 1960s and 20% p.a. over the 1970s to reach over 70,000 by 1980. Reflecting the labor-intensive nature of much of this growth, however, labor productivity in the electronics industry remained low, growing at only about 4.1% p.a. over the 1960s (Table 13.2); although labor productivity growth increased to 9.5% p.a. over the 1970s (in current prices), it actually lagged behind overall manufacturing labor productivity.

By the end of the 1970s, the electronics industry had become the largest employer in manufacturing, accounting for over one-quarter of total manufacturing employment. Although there had been steady upgrading of production technology throughout the 1970s, the major push for technological development came only in Phase II, as Singapore rapidly evolved from a labor surplus economy in the 1960s/early 1970s towards one with significant labor shortages. The government deliberated encouraged a high wage policy through the National Wage Council in the first half of this second development phase to force many electronics firms to upgrade their production technology. Most labour-intensive manufacturing activities were relocated to low-wage countries in the region. This quickened the pace of technology advancement and brought about an industry-wide adoption of capital-intensive production processes. Employment growth during the second phase thus slowed down considerably to only 6% p.a., while the growth in output and value added slowed down in a much less drastic fashion (Table 13.1). Labor productivity growth in the electronics sector rose to 10.4% p.a. in the 1980s, exceeding the average achieved for manufacturing as a whole. By the end of the 1980s, the sector employed 123,000 people, or 35% of total manufacturing employment (Annex Table 13D).

The slowing down of employment was even more pronounced during the third phase (the 1990s), with total employment actually fell by 1.6% p.a.; in contrast, output and value added continued to achieve double-digit growth (Table 13.1). The growth of the electronics industry in this period is thus driven primarily by more capital-intensive and higher-technology processes and products. Labor productivity in this period rose to 13.1% p.a., higher than the 9% p.a. achieved by the manufacturing sector as a whole (Table 13.2).

The rapid technological upgrading of Singapore's electronics industry is accompanied by significant transformation of the compositional structure of electronics products being manufactured. Table 13.3 depicts the changing composition of electronics production output over the four decades of rapid output and employment growth, while Table 13.4 compares and contrasts the output, value added and employment growth rates of the key electronics sub-sectors. As can be seen, the consumer electronics (audio-video equipment) manufacturing sub-sector, which was generally more labor-intensive and involved less advanced manufacturing process technologies, figured most prominently in the early industrialization phase and indeed accounted for a significant share of the growth in output and employment of the electronics industry from the late 1960s to 1970s. While Philips and General Electric were the early foreign investors in consumer electronics assembly in Singapore, much of the growth in the 1970s were driven by Japanese consumer electronics firms such as Matsushita, Hitachi, Aiwa, and Sanyo. However, this sub-sector began to decline in relative importance over the period of 1980–90, and in absolute terms from 1990 onwards; by 1999, the relative share of this sub-sector had dropped to a mere 3.4%.

In contrast, the computers and peripheral equipment sub-sector had been the key growth drivers in the second and third phase, as Singapore grew to become a major regional production hub for the global PC industry that emerged since the early 1980s. This sub-sector registered average value added growth of nearly 40% per year over 1980–90, before moderating to about 11% p.a. over 1990–99. Although assembly of computers by global players such as Apple Computers and Compaq had played a part, the most significant contributor had been magnetic hard disk drive production, which grew to be the single

TABLE 13.3   Sectoral Composition of Singapore's Electronics Industry, 1970–99 (in percentages)

Sub-sectors	1970	1975	1980	1990	1998	1999
Consumer electronics	100	30.6	38.8	17.7	3.7	3.4
Electronics components	0	69.4	54.4	35.2	27.7	29.6
Computers & peripherals	0	0	5.4	42.3	54.7	42.1
Telecom & others	0	0	1.2	4.8	13.9	24.9
Total	100	100	100	100	100	100

NOTES:

For 1970-90:
1. Consumer electronics include TV sets and other audio and video equipment.
2. Electronics components include semiconductor devices, capacitors and resistors, connectors, PCBs and PCB Assembly.
3. Computers and peripherals include computers and data processing equipment, disk drives, printers and other office equipment.
4. Telecom and others include communication equipment, electronic security system, and other electronics.

For 1998:
1. Consumer electronics include TV sets and other audio and video equipment.
2. Electronics components include semiconductor devices, capacitors and resistors, connectors and PCBs.
3. Computers and peripherals include computers and data processing equipment, disk drives, and printers.
4. Telecom and others include communication equipment, electronic security system, and other electronics.

For 1999:
1. Consumer electronics include TV sets and other audio and video equipment.
2. Electronics Components include wafer fabrication, other semiconductor devices, capacitors and resistors, connectors, PCBs and contract manufacturers.
3. Computers and peripherals include computers and data processing equipment and disk drives.
4. Telecom and others include communication equipment, electronic security system, and other electronics.

SOURCE: Calculated from Economic Development Board, *Report on the Census of Industrial Production*, various years.

largest sub-sector in Singapore's electronics industry and accounted for more than half of the world's total disk drive output throughout the late 1980s–mid-1990s (Wong, 1999; Wong and McKendrick, 2000). Other major computer peripheral products include ink-jet printers, CDROMs, and multimedia soundcards, where Singapore also became

TABLE 13.4   Growth Performance of Singapore's Electronics Industry by Sectors (in percentages)

	Output	Value Added	Employment
Audio-video equipment			
1980-90	11	8	–4
1991-99	–8.9	–5.6	–12.8
Computers and office equipment			
1980-90	45	39	29
1991-99	11.1	7.9	–2.6
Semiconductor devices			
1980-90	5	2	–2
1991-99	19	23	6

NOTE: Growth rates are in current prices.
SOURCE: Economic Development Board, *Report on the Census of Industrial Production*, various years.

the largest producers in the world. Overall, the computer-related sector had achieved significantly higher labor-productivity than the consumer electronics sub-sector. While continuing to be dominated by foreign investments, especially US, this sector had witnessed an increasing presence of local enterprises in recent years (see more details below).

The semiconductor components sub-sector also played a major role in the first phase of development of the industry, when Singapore emerged as a major offshore production location for labor-intensive semiconductor assembly and test operations by the leading global players like National Semiconductor, Texas Instruments, SGS-Thomson and NEC in the 1970s. In 1975, this sub-sector contributed close to 70% of electronics output, from virtually zero in 1970. Although still growing in relative terms, this sub-sector declined in relative importance in the second phase, over-taken by the explosive growth of computer and peripheral assembly. However, this sub-sector began to stage a gradual turn around in 1995 after the government's effort in promoting semiconductor wafer fabrication finally picked up momentum. By 1997, the semiconductor sector had expanded its share to over 17%, from less than 15% in 1990. With the shift from the more labor-intensive semiconductor assembly and testing operations to the more

capital intensive activities of semiconductor wafer fabrication, there
was also a marked increase in labor productivity in this sub-sector, as
shown by the steep increase in value added per worker during the third
phase.

Annex Table 13F shows the emerging structure of Singapore's electronics industry at the end of the 1990s. The four leading industry
sub-groups in terms of share of value-added were disk drives, semiconductor testing and assembly, computer equipment, and
semiconductor wafer fabrication. In terms of labor productivity (value
added per worker), computer ranked highest, followed by communications equipment, semiconductor wafer fabrication, and semiconductor
testing and assembly. As the process of technological upgrading continues into the 2000s, it is these high labor-productivity industry groups
that can be expected to expand further. Already, the number of semiconductor wafer fabrication plants had increased with new investments
by TSMC and UMC from Taiwan, while a new Toshiba LCD fabrication plant had begun construction.

2. The Pivotal Role of MNCs

As can be seen from the above account, until recently, the growth of
all three sub-sectors of the industry has been driven largely by MNCs.
Indeed, Singapore first emerged as an attractive offshore production
locations for American semiconductor MNCs in the late 1960s–early
1970s. These industries were looking for cheap labor locations overseas to perform the highly labor-intensive semiconductor assembly
operations. Although Taiwan, Korea and Hong Kong were the early
favourites, Singapore and Malaysia in Southeast Asia became more
attractive for a variety of reasons — the increasing restriction on
foreign investment in Korea, lack of English-educated workers in
Taiwan, and political uncertainties over Hong Kong (and Northeast
Asia in general) arising from the turmoil of the cultural revolution in
China.

The government's investment promotional policies and the effective
implementation of infrastructural and other support programs to accommodate the needs of industrial investors had been widely credited
with helping to turn Singapore from just another labor-surplus economy
into a highly attractive regional hub for offshore manufacturing produc-

tion (Schein, 1996). Other conducive factors include an English-educated labor-force, a more liberal policy towards the employment of expatriate managerial and technical staff, political stability and government restraints on industrial strife. Compared to other regional economies, Singapore was not only able to attract a larger share of foreign investments, but more importantly, induce foreign MNCs to pursue higher value-added and technologically more advanced activities. Throughout the 1970s and 1980s, Singapore was able to extend her superiority in telecommunications and transportation infrastructures over other competing countries, thereby consolidating her role as the most advanced regional production hub in Southeast Asia for US, Japanese and European electronics manufacturing MNCs. With the trend towards mechanization and miniaturization in electronics, Singapore's emphasis on technical training, industrial automation and infrastructure development makes manufacturing investments in the country more attractive.

Despite some temporary setbacks in the mid-1980s due to an over-ambitious technological upgrading program through a high-wage policy, Singapore quickly recovered its attractiveness for electronics industry through government interventions that have resulted in lower operating and wage costs and reduced rigidities in the labor market. In the second half of the 1980s, the rapid growth of the computer and related industries helped spurred another wave of new investment in Singapore, in particular in the manufacturing and assembly of disk drives, personal computers, computer monitors and printers.

By the late 1980s, although Singapore had become increasingly uncompetitive in the more labor-intensive stages of electronics production, three developments helped make Singapore attractive for continuing investment in electronics manufacturing. First, the increasing shift towards "time-base" competition in electronics products means that global supply chain management capability becomes increasingly critical, thus Singapore's superior logistics infrastructure becomes an important advantage. Increasingly, electronics MNCs use Singapore as their regional logistics hub, integrating the flow of parts, components and finished products from throughout Southeast Asia via Singapore. Secondly, as part of this shift towards globalization of production, there is an increasing trend towards outsourcing of production by many electronics OEMs to specialized, dedicated contract manufacturers (Wong, 2000). Singapore quickly became a major hub for some of the

TABLE 13.5   Growth Trend of Private Sector R&D Expenditure in Singapore, 1981–99

Year	Total Private Sector R&D Expenditure (S$mn)	Private Sector R&D Expenditure in Electronics & IT (S$mn)	%
1981	44.2	27.5	62.2
1984	106.7	53.4	50.0
1987	225.6	147.1	65.2
1990	309.5	177.6	57.4
1991	442.0	273.9	62.0
1992	577.5	324.2	56.1
1993	618.9	338.1	54.6
1994	736.2	385.2	52.3
1995	881.4	475.3	53.9
1996	1133.4	706.9	62.4
1997	1314.5	760.3	57.8
1998	1536.1	882.6	57.5
1999	1670.9	933.0	55.8

NOTE: Figures from 1993 onwards exclude electrical products but include IT and Communications.
SOURCE: National Science & Technology Board, *National R&D Survey,* various years.

leading contract manufacturers in the world, including a number of home-grown firms, due to a combination of superior transport and communications infrastructure and a critical mass of supporting industries providing various manufacturing services. Thirdly, as the government intensified investment in public R&D and the supply of technically-competent R&D manpower since the early 1990s, an increasing number of electronics MNCs have found Singapore an attractive location for product and process R&D activities. Some MNCs like HP, Philips and Motorola have given Singapore "world product mandate" in selected product lines that cover responsibility from design to marketing and technical support. As evident in Table 13.5, private sector R&D in the electronics and IT industry had increased sharply in recent years, rising from less than S$200 million in 1990 to over S$900 million in 1999.

TABLE 13.6   Ownership Structure of Singapore's Electronics Firms, 1993

Ownership Structure	Number of Firms	%
100% Local	50	18.9
> 50% Local	62	23.5
50:50 Joint Venture	4	1.5
> 50% Foreign	16	6.1
100% Foreign	132	50.0
Total	264	10

SOURCE: *Report on the Census for Industrial Production* 1993 (unpublished).

The continuing dominance of MNCs in Singapore's electronics industry can be gauged from various statistical indicators. As can be seen from Table 13.6, although only 56% of the electronics firms in production in 1993 were majority or wholly owned by foreign firms, these firms were substantially larger in size than local firms, and accounted for as much as 85% of the equity capital investment in the electronics, a much higher than the figure of 60% for the manufacturing sector as a whole, or the 33% figure for all private sector industries (see Table 13.7). Despite the rapid growth of indigenous firms in the 1990s, the share of foreign equity in Singapore's electronics sector had remained above 85%. Similarly, Annex Table 13A shows that the top 20 foreign electronics MNCs in Singapore had a combined sales of about S$50 billion in 1998, versus about S$12.3 billion by the top 20 local electronics firms as listed in Annex Table 13B. If we combine both foreign

TABLE 13.7   Foreign Share of Equity Investment in Singapore, 1984–98
(in percentages)

	1984	1987	1990	1993	1994	1995	1996	1997	1998
Manufacturing	65.0	70.8	69.4	60.2	62.6	66.9	67.9	68.8	69.8
Total Economy	na	39.6	37.2	33.2	32.8	31.5	32.1	33.2	35.1
Electronics Industry	na	na	na	85.3	84.8	87.2	86.4	88.1	86.9

SOURCE: Singapore Department of Statistics, *The Extent and Pattern of Foreign Investment Activities in Singapore*, 1995; Singapore Department of Statistics, *Foreign Equity Investment in Singapore*, 1995–96 and 1997–98.

and local electronics firms in a single ranking table by sales, only four local firms make it to the top 20.

A number of studies have documented in greater details the specific role of government policies in attracting foreign electronics firms to establish their production in Singapore, and to subsequently upgrade their product and process technological capabilities over time. For example, Wong (1999) and Wong and McKendrick (2000) showed in details the role of government in attracting successive waves of investment by hard disk drive assemblers in Singapore in the 1980s and 1990s, making Singapore the single largest assembly hub for hard disk drive in the world. Schein (1996) also provided examples of how MNCs responded to the investment incentives and promotional efforts of EDB. Similarly, Wong, Wang and Singh (1999) provided detailed case studies of how several leading global electronics MNCs like HP, ST Microelectronics (formerly SGS-Thomson Microelectronics) and Matsushita progressively transferred technologies to their Singapore operations and deepened their local technological capabilities, and the role that supporting government policies and complementary programs played in facilitating these technological upgrading efforts. Another study by Wong and He (2001) showed that firms that were that received public R&D support had higher innovation performance than firms that did not.

3. The Development of Indigenous Electronics Firms

The role of indigenous firms in the electronics industry has largely been negligible until the 1980s. Unlike Taiwan and Hong Kong, Singapore lacked an initial injection of experienced manufacturing entrepreneurs from Mainland China during the early years of political independence. Neither did Singapore witness the large number of students going to the United States for training in electronics technology as compared to Taiwan, Hong Kong and South Korea. While the influx of foreign manufacturing investments did provide training and exposure to a large number of Singaporean engineers and technicians, much of this was in manufacturing process technology, not in product technology know-how which, by and large, still reside in the corporate headquarters in US, Japan and Europe. It is thus not surprising that the transfer of technological know-how induced through these manufacturing investments translated more significantly into the development of indigenous firms in the electronics contract manufacturing (i.e., "OEM") and supporting industries, rather than in Original Design Manufacturing or Original Brand Manufacturing.

In spite of this, a number of indigenous electronics firms did emerge in recent years, particularly in the computer-related sectors where the barriers to entry are arguably lower than, say, in mass consumer electronics and semiconductors. As can be seen in Annex Table 13B, at least 20 indigenous electronics firms had emerged with annual sales of S$100 millions or more by 1998. Among them are Creative Technology, the world leaders in sound-card technology; GES, which is manufacturing and selling their own brands of personal computers as well as being a contract manufacturers for others; ASA, ASTI and Ellipsiz, which provide semiconductor assembly equipment and services; and a large number of contract manufacturing firms such as Venture Manufacturing, Flextronics, JIT, Omni Industries and Natsteel Electronics.

In addition, a number of indigenous semiconductor manufacturers have also emerged through a different route: they were created in the early 1990s as GLCs, specifically to carve out an indigenous position in the global semiconductor industry-Chartered Semiconductor Manufacturing (CSM) to compete in the "third-party" ASIC wafer-foundry market, Tech-Semiconductor (a joint venture with Texas Instruments, Canon, and Hewlett Packard) in the DRAM market, and Tri-Tech in the IC design market. The formation of Tech-Semi is significant as it was a new attempt by the government to attract high-tech investment by MNCs through the offering of not only tax incentives, but also equity capital to share the risk with foreign investors. CSM has rapidly expanded to become the third largest semiconductor pure foundry company in the world, with major joint investment in new wafer fabrication plants with Hitachi and HP. Tri-Tech was also established by the government-controlled Singapore Technology group to enter the global IC design services business, although the company later chose to exit the market to avoid a law-suit by an incumbent US firm on alleged patent infringement.

The above direct state involvement notwithstanding, Singapore's indigenous electronics firms were otherwise mainly private-sector driven. Nearly all the other companies listed in Annex Table 13B are local private companies formed by local entrepreneurs, many of whom had previously worked as employees in the MNC subsidiary operations in Singapore. Although many of these companies may have benefited from various forms of government assistance schemes and technology transfer from public R&D institutes, all of them, by and large, had to face full competition in the world market, as the government provides no protection whatsoever against foreign competition. In particular, Singapore had been able to spawn a number of globally competitive indigenous contract manufacturers which had grown rapidly to become among the top contract manufacturers in the world (Wong, 2000). These contract manufacturers started initially by exploiting their geographic proximity to serve the electronics OEMs operating in Singapore, but rapidly internationalized their operations to cater to the global manufacturing needs of their customers.

More importantly, in addition to the growth of indigenous firms in the electronic industry proper, there has also been a significant growth of a large number of firms that supply various inputs and services to the industry. Because of extensive subcontracting of electronics firms to the various supporting industries, a more complete picture of the growth of indigenous capabilities in the electronics industry will emerge only after we take into account the growth of the latter.

4. Development of Electronics Supporting Industries

The importance of the large electronics MNCs in stimulating the growth of local enterprises can best be seen by examining the growth of the electronics supporting industry. The following supporting industries can be identified: plastic moulding, metal stamping/tool and die making, precision parts and components, electroplating and finishing, mold making, jigs and fixtures, casting, printed circuit boards, and industrial automation equipment. They are mostly dominated by local small- and medium-sized enterprises (SMEs).

Table 13.8 shows the growth trend of the aggregate electronics supporting industry over the last three decades. The supporting industry achieved an average value-added growth of about 28% in 1970–80 before moderating to about 21% in 1980–90, and further falling to 9.8% over 1990–99. While part of the reason for the slower growth rates since 1980 is due to the lower growth of the electronics majors itself, a more significant factor is the trend towards relocation of the

TABLE 13.8   Growth of Singapore's Electronics Supporting Industry, 1970–99 (in percentages)

Average Growth Rate per Annum (Compounded)	1970–80	1980–90	1990–99
Industrial output	27	19	10.1
Value added	28	21	9.8
Employment	14	12	5.7

NOTE: Electronics supporting industries include 1996 SSIC 25216 (plastic precision parts), 28914 (metal stamping), 28915 (die casting), 28921 (electroplating and plating of metals & formed products), 28997 (metal precision components), 29223 (dies, moulds, tools, jigs and fixtures).
SOURCE: Economic Development Board, *Report on the Census of Industrial Production*, various years.

more labor-intensive electronics supporting activities to neighbouring countries, particularly Malaysia and China.

Pressured by their MNC customers to constantly upgrade quality and reduce cost, the electronics supporting industry achieved significant productivity gains from the late 1970s right through to the late 1990s. A process of "induced technological upgrading", whereby the growth of increasingly sophisticated operations of MNCs stimulated technological development among their subcontractors was found to occur (Wong, 1992). For example, the magnetic hard disk drive industry was found to have stimulated the growth and development of a large number of component suppliers, subcontract manufacturers, and engineering service providers (automation design, clean room design, tools and dies makers, etc.) (see Wong, 1999; Wong and McKendrick, 2000). Further facilitating the technological upgrading process was the various financial aid and technical training programs that were put in place to assist the electronics supporting industry, especially after the recession in 1985-86. Most notable among these assistance programs were the Local Industry Upgrading Program (LIUP), and the various subsidies for technological upgrading's (SITAS), manpower development (In-Tech), R&D (RDAS, RISC) and innovation (IDS). Partly as a result of these government efforts, and more importantly because of the constant waves of MNC investment into technologically more advanced operations that had more stringent demand on subcontractors and suppliers, a highly competitive cluster of electronics supporting industries were induced in Singapore by the late 1980s.

Annex Table 13C lists some of the largest indigenous firms in the various electronics supporting industries in Singapore. About 30 of these firms have grown to medium size, with annual sales of over S$30 million. Many of these have been publicly listed on the local stock exchange in recent years, and all of them have regionalized their operations, particularly to Malaysia, to stay competitive. Besides serving multinationals' manufacturing operations in Singapore, these companies also increasingly supplied to MNCs in Malaysia and around the region, and in some cases, world-wide (Wong, 1999). Like the contract manufacturers, these component suppliers and precision engineering firms also started initially to exploit the close geographic proximity to the many electronics MNC assembly firms in Singapore. As their customers started to relocate their more labor-intensive operations to other lower cost countries like China and Malaysia, these supporting services firms likewise moved their operations to be close to their customer plants.

5. Summary Assessment

The development of Singapore as a major regional hub in the global electronics production networks is a dramatic demonstration of the success of the export-oriented, MNC investment-led industrial development strategy. With a population of only 3 million and starting with virtually no natural resources and industrial technological capability, Singapore has today become the fourth largest producer of electronics and IT goods in the world, after only the US, Japan and Korea, and the world's third largest exporter of computer products. The success of Singapore has derived from her ability to ride the waves of technological change emanating from the advanced industrial countries, absorbing and leveraging the technology transferred from MNCs to continuously advance the technological capabilities of her workforce (Wong, 2001). By plugging into the global electronics production networks of global MNCs from US, Japan and Europe, Singapore has been able to develop not only a strong base of advanced manufacturing by large MNCs, but through them, the development of her own internationally-competitive indigenous firms over time, initially through contract manufacturing and component supplies, but increasingly through new entrepreneurial start-ups and technology strategic alliances between government-linked firms and MNCs.

III. DEVELOPMENT OF SINGAPORE'S SHIPBUILDING AND REPAIR INDUSTRY

1. Overview of the World Marine Industry

The world's modern marine industry began with the launch of steam-engine ships in the 19th century. Since then, the industry has undergone several metamorphoses, as new technologies emerged and world trade demand conditions change. In the first-half of the 20th century, steam engines gradually gave way to diesel ones, while the introduction of assembly-line manufacturing techniques to the building of standard ships drastically changed the management of shipyards. The second-half of the 20th century also witnessed the emergence of specialized ships such as oil tankers, container ships, and specialized chemical carriers. In geographic terms, there also occurred a major shift in ship-building activities, from the traditional maritime countries in Western Europe to Asia (e.g., Japan in the 1950s and 1960s, South Korea in the 1970s and 1980s) and later to developing countries in Asia (e.g., China) and Latin America (e.g., Brazil) [Todd (1991), Cho and Porter (1986)].

A salient feature of the shipbuilding industry is the persistently cyclical nature of the industry (Stopford, 1988, p.300). During the eighty-year period 1901–1981, the average percentage reduction of output from peak to trough averaged 50%. Notably, such fluctuations were not restricted to war times; for example, from 1975 to 1980, a 60% reduction in world shipbuilding output was registered. Furthermore, these cycles could be very long, e.g., the duration from peak to peak lasted as long as 17 years. The volatility of the shipbuilding and ship-repair markets is due in part to the aggressive expansion in capacity by state-sponsored shipyards, and in part to the volatility of shipping freight rates, which is in turn a reflection of the fluctuations in the volume of world trade.

Such volatility is evident in the industry's post world war II history. After the war, merchant ship losses resulted in high demand for new ships and repair of existing ships. This, and the subsequent boom in world trade, led to a quick expansion of world shipbuilding capacity. The closure of Suez cannel in 1956 further fuelled the demand for larger (and faster) ships, particularly oil tankers. Under such a favourable demand condition, Japan, with the active involvement of the Japanese government, overtook Western European countries and became the leading shipbuilder in the world in 1958. Except for a brief period between 1958-61, the world shipbuilding industry continued its expansion well into the 1970s, during which the 1973 oil crisis further fuelling the demand for large oil tankers. However, the subsequent depression following the oil crisis resulted in a sharp fall in world trade, which adversely affected the health of the industry. The situation was further aggravated by the large-scale entry of South Korea in the 1970s, which intensified the price competition. Compared to the peak in 1975, output fell by as much as 60% by 1979. The industry managed to stage a recovery in the early 1980s, although that proved to be short-lived, however. The recession in the mid-1980s, coupled with excess tonnage in the world shipping fleets, caused freight rates to remain weak, which caused major reduction of capacity for many shipyards. From the mid-1980s to the mid-1990s, the industry went through another business cycle, with the recovery in the second half of 1980s reaching a peak in 1991, followed by a significant down-turning trend throughout 1991-95, before a gradual recovery from 1997.

As is evident throughout maritime history, government involvement was, to a great extent, responsible for the over-capacity problems. During periods of slackening demand, many shipyards were able to remain afloat through government interventions. Such interventions, although costly, were often justified by the strategic advantages of maintaining an adequate shipbuilding capacity, not just for military purposes, but also for the industry's linkages with other industries, such as steel and heavy engineering.

2. Growth and Maturation of Singapore's Shipbuilding/ Repair Industry

In 1997, more than 130,000 ships totaling 808 million gross tons called at the port. Of which, 2886 vessels docked in the port for repair. With such high sea traffic, Singapore also has the highest concentration of ship repair yards in the world, with deadweight aggregating some 3 million tons and growing. Despite the economic downturn, Singapore's yards have performed reasonably well. Total gross turnover of the country's ship-repair sector stood at S$1.55 billion, approximately 4.4% of worldwide ship-repair work value estimated at S$35 billion a year. The development of the shipbuilding/repair industry in Singapore began right after the country achieved independence in 1965. Shipbuilding and repair was identified by the United Nation advisory team as an industry with good growth potential. In part, this was due to the industry's synergistic relationship with the country's single most important industry then — the entrepot trade. As unemployment was a pressing problem in the 1960s, the industry was developed with a view to generate employment for the country's largely unskilled workforce.

The development of the marine industry, particularly ship repair, owed very much to Singapore's location as a major seaport and an important trading hub for the region. Because ships which undertake repairs in Singapore do not have to deviate from their normal routes, this significantly reduces the opportunity cost of repairs. Thus, large oil tankers which ply the Middle East-Japan route have found Singapore a convenient stopover for repair and maintenance. This potential advantage, together with the relatively cheap labor costs, was seized by the Singapore government to turn Singapore into the world's top-ranking ship-repair centre in the 1970s.

As in the case of the electronics industry, the development of Singapore's shipbuilding and repair industry can be divided into three distinct phases. The first phase of development covers the period from independence to about 1980, during which the industry experienced a period of steady growth. Phase II covers the period 1980-91, which was a period of slump and recovery. Phase III started around 1991, when the process of structural transformation began, and is still ongoing today. Figure 13.1 depicts the industry output and value added trend, while Figure 13.2 shows the trend of average labor productivity during the three phases. Some broad indicators of the industry during each phase can be found in Table 13.9. In that table, the second phase was further subdivided into two halves, the first-half being the period of slump while the second half corresponding to the period of recovery. In terms of tonnage, Singapore's shipbuilding and repair capacity jumped from 750,000 dwt in 1972 to 2.82 million dwt in 1983, an increase of 2.7 times. The total capacity was further increased to 3.89 million dwt in 1996, accounting for about 23% of Asia's total capacity.

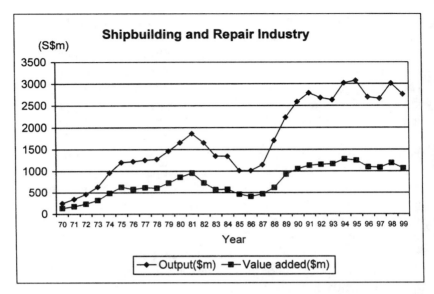

FIGURE 13.1 Growth Trend of Shipbuilding & Repair Industry, 1970–99 (in S$ million).

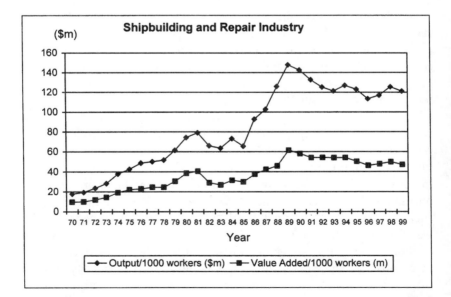

FIGURE 13.2 Labor Productivity of Shipbuilding and Repair Industry, 1970–99 (in S$ million).

TABLE 13.9   Shipbuilding and Repair Industry in Singapore, 1970–99
(in percentages)

Year	Employment Growth	Output Growth	Value-Added Growth
1970-80	4.7%	20.8%	20.2%
1980-86	−11.2%	−7.9%	−11.6%
1986-91	14.0%	22.5%	22.6%
1991-99	1.0%	−0.1%	−0.7%

NOTE: SSIC 38511-14 for 1970–91; 1996 SSIC 33201-33204 for 1995–98.
SOURCE: Economic Development Board, *Report on the Census of Industrial Production*, various years.

During the early years of phase I, from independence up till 1974, shipbuilding was an insignificant part of the marine industry in Singapore, the major component was the labour-intensive ship repair activities, which flourished because of Singapore's location advantage. As a whole, marine industry employment during the period 1970–74 was growing at slightly over 14% per annum, while the yearly ship repair revenue was around three times that of shipbuilding. The picture, however, began to change in the mid-1970s, due primarily to an increasing worldwide demand for new ships, and to the government's active promotion and support of shipbuilding. By 1976, shipbuilding revenue actually overtook that of ship-repair for the first time. However, the growth of shipbuilding was somewhat halted from 1977 to 1980, because of the decline in world trade during the recession years following the 1973 oil crisis. Ship-repair, on the other hand, continued to enjoy healthy growth throughout this period (see Figure 13.3). In contrast to the first half of the 1970s, employment growth during the second-half (1976–80) was actually negative. Workers who left the industry were readily absorbed by other manufacturing industries such as electronics. Operating margin for the industry as a whole was rather healthy throughout the period, with operating surplus fluctuating between 20–30% of sales (Figure 13.4). The industry also enjoyed healthy growth in labor productivity, notably during the second-half of the 1970s. For example, in 1980, the industry's value added per thousand workers was some 65% higher than that of the electronics industry. On the whole, the government was actively involved in promoting and nurturing the

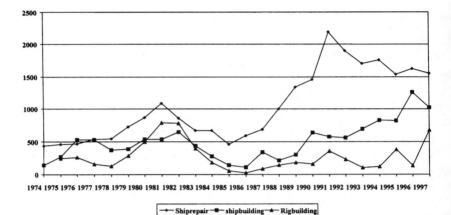

FIGURE 13.3 Singapore Marine Industry Revenue by Sectors, 1974–97, 1970–99 (in S$ million).

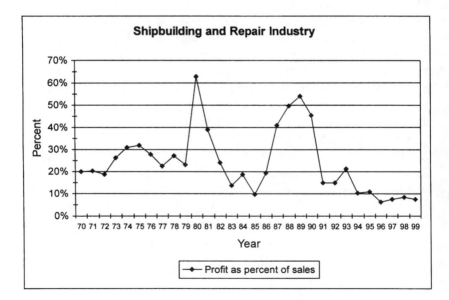

FIGURE 13.4 Profitability of Shipbuilding and Repair Industry, 1970–99.

industry during this phase. In particular, local shipyards were actively encouraged to import and adapt foreign technology to improve productivity.

The second phase covering the 1980s was a difficult period for the marine industry as a whole, and for shipbuilding in particular. As shown in Figure 13.1, throughout the period 1981–86, both industry output and value added were falling steadily and by 1986, they had actually fallen back to the 1974 levels. Shipbuilding was the hardest hit, due to the worldwide shipping slump, which saw new orders gradually drying out. In 1985, the situation was so difficult that an agreement was reached among the major shipyards in Singapore to scale back capacity. Employment was also falling rapidly as a result of the reduction in capacity, and this somewhat cushioned the fall in average product and labor productivity (see Figure 13.2). The wage correction policy introduced by the government did not help matter. Operating margin was squeezed from both the input and output ends, and was fluctuating between 10%–20%, hitting a low of 10% in 1985 (see Figure 13.4).

The industry began to recover around 1987, and a period of rapid growth followed during 1988–91. However, as Figure 13.3 shows, the industrial composition began to change during this period, as ship-repair was growing by leaps and bounds, while shipbuilding stagnated as the world shipbuilding industry continued to be plagued by over-capacity. Figure 13.2 shows that, despite the increase in industry output and value added during this period, both average product and labor productivity started to decline after 1989, indicating that growth was achieved largely through increased in employment. Indeed, employment growth was respectively 20% and 16% for the years 1990 and 1991. A drastic increase in operating margin was registered during the period 1987–90, with margin reaching a high of more than 50% in 1989. The decline, however, was equally swift, by 1991 the margin was back to about 15%.

Since 1991, the industry experienced severe structural problem. Even though output and value added expanded for a brief spell in 1994 and 1995, the industry output had largely stagnated below S$3 billion throughout the second half of the 1990s. Moreover, profit margin had become exceedingly low in the 1990s. In 1994, for example, as labor and other operating costs soared, operating surplus had dropped to a mere 10% of sales; since then, the operating surplus ratio had hovered below 10% (Fig. 13.4). With competition from other low-cost developing countries from the Middle East (for ship-repair) and East Asia (for shipbuilding) intensifying, output prices had been permanently depressed in the second half of the 1990s. Furthermore, it is increasingly difficult to rely on imported technology to boost productivity, as technology progress in a mature industry like shipbuilding and repair had been limited and required increasingly the development of indigenous R&D capability. Although increasing investments were indeed made in R&D, the industry had responded more by concentrating on developing niches in high value-added jobs such as ship conversions and rig-building. The major shipyards also began to relocate their labour-intensive operations to neighbouring countries such as the Philippines and Vietnam to increase cost competitiveness. In addition, a significant process of industry consolidation had taken place through mergers and acquisition to remove excess capacity from the industry.

In more recent years, with the depreciation of the Singapore dollar against the U.S. currency since the Asia's economic meltdown, the country's larger yards have become more competitive in their core Very Large Crude Carrier (VLCC) business for the Middle East. Also, the faster turnaround time of Singapore dockyards (three weeks against four weeks for a VLCC special survey repair) due to better utilisation of resources has been able to offset the higher labor cost (up to 30% higher) than those in the Middle East. The fear of South Korean shipyards taking Singapore's market share became less apparent, following the collapse of Korean Halla Shipyard in 1997. However, with the devaluation of the won after 1997, shipbuilding orders of South Korean yards were once again on the rise.

While the Asia's economic problems arising from the financial crisis have postponed the demand for new ship building and hence boosted the ship-repairers' activities temporarily, the long-term health of the ship-repair sector is very much dependent on the structural growth trend of the shipping industry. Prior to the Asian economic crisis, competition within the ship-repair market was already intense, as the number of yards continued to grow and the existing yards expanded their facilities. Although the current economic climate has retarded the expansion activities of new facilities, there is still growing interest in such expansion plans, one of which was to establish a VLCC repair facility at South Africa's Richard Bay. In general, there has been a trend for VLCC owners to reduce the amount of work done. However, in the medium term, aging world fleet and an increasingly strict international regulatory regime would create more work per vessel, thereby softening the loss of work for yards in the global market. Nevertheless, even under the most optimistic scenario, the growth prospect of the commodity ship building and repair industry will be limited by the existence of significant capacity, due to the reluctance of existing state-subsidized shipyards to remove their excess capacity and the entry of new capacity from developing countries. To stay competitive, Singaporean shipyards have no choice but to follow the examples of some advanced countries to develop specialist niches in the market.

3. Competition in Offshore Industry

Facing declining ship repair activity (currently contributing less than half of the marine industry's turnover), Singapore yards have turned increasingly to the offshore structure sector. In 1997, offshore contracts accounted for about 24% of the country's shipyard activities, which is equivalent to some $828 million of total revenue. The offshore activities that Singapore yards engaged in constituted mainly of drilling rig, upgrading and repair, as well as converting tankers into various types of floating production units. The global competition for offshore rig building centers on yards of Europe, South Korea, Japan and US. Until the current financial crisis is resolved, the likelihood of rig owners granting big orders to South Korean yards will be capped to some extent. While the Japanese yards are facing a backlog of new ships comprising mainly of tankers, European yards still depends largely on subsidies to secure orders. As the Singapore dollar falls against the pound and the US dollar, Singapore's yards will continue to have a competitive edge over European yards.

In addition to the four world's major oil exploration and production areas comprising of US Gulf of Mexico, Norwegian and North Sea sectors, West Africa and Asia Pacific, which Singapore yards receive orders from, the emergence of a fifth new major market in the shape of Brazil will further boost the prospect of the offshore sector. As at December 1997, the world-wide offshore rig utilization rate was at 96.6%. The rising demand for energy from Asia and the lack of rigs built over the last 10 years has led to a surge in rig demand. As rig utilization rates reaching almost near capacity, more laid rigs will be reactivated for services, hence creating opportunities for more repairs and upgrading work. By the year 2000, about 35% of the current rig fleet would be 20 years old. This would imply a rise in demand for new-builds over the next few years as drilling operators prepare themselves to capitalise on the high rig charter rates. For traditional rig building and rig repair specialist Keppel FELS, and Jurong Shipyard, prospect for offshore activities appears promising as they continue to venture into offshore-related repair and upgrading work.

4. The Development of Major Government-Controlled Shipyards in Singapore

Although there are more than 250 companies involved in the shipbuilding/repair sector in Singapore, the industry had become highly concentrated, with the top five firms-Keppel Corporation Ltd, Jurong Shipyard Ltd, Sembawang Shipyard Ltd, Hitachi Zosen and ST Ship Engineering — accounting for more than 75% of the industry output in 1997. With the exception of Hitachi Zosen, the other four major companies were all government-controlled enterprises, or Government-Linked Companies (GLCs). All four started out as wholly government owned enterprises, and although they were subsequently listed in the Stock Exchange of Singapore during the 1970s and mid-1980s, the government remains the substantial shareholder in all four companies till today. Reflecting the consolidation of the maturing industry, Jurong Shipyard was acquired by Sembawang Shipyard and Hitachi Zozen was acquired by Keppel Shipyard in 1998.

Many shipyards worldwide survived on the back of government subsidy, and many government-owned shipyards had done badly and needed to be rescued through privatization (e.g. in Korea, poorly-run state-owned shipyard was turned around by the Daewoo group). In Singapore, the four GLCs had performed well in spearheading the development of Singapore as a leading ship-repair centre in the world in the 1970s and 1980s, while remaining state-controlled all the time. Moreover, they had done so without substantial direct subsidies from the state, although (as will be elaborated later), they had all derived strategic assistance from the government. The floating of these enterprises on the local stock exchange in the 1980s and their creditable financial performance since are testimony of the management capabilities of these enterprises.

A brief account of the historical development of two major ship-building/repair GLCs-Keppel and Sembawang-is given below to provide insights on the role of the state in fostering the development of internationally competitive indigenous enterprises in the shipbuilding/repair industry in Singapore.

Keppel Corporation

The largest shipyard company in Singapore, Keppel was formed in 1968, to take over the Dockyard Department of the Port of Singapore Authority. Initially, a British ship-repair company, the Swan Hunter Group, was hired to manage the new company for four years. The running of Keppel was reverted back to local managers in 1972. Soon after, favourable market condition for oil tankers due to the oil crisis in 1973 provided the company the opportunity to substantially expand its shipbuilding and repair capacity in the 1970s. The expansion was achieved through the building of new facilities and as well as the acquisition of existing shipyards such as Far East Levingston Shipyards and Singmarine Industries.

The shipbuilding slump in the first-half of 1980s prompted Keppel to diversify to non-marine related businesses. As profit margin from shipbuilding and repair dwindled, the company's other business activities began to assume increasing importance, as shown in Table 10. From 1988 to 1997, the contribution of shipbuilding and repair in total group revenue declined from 62% to 16%. Keppel changed its name from Keppel Shipyard to Keppel Corporation in 1986 to reflect its conglomerate status. In the early 1990s, as labor and other business costs soared, Keppel began relocating its labour-intensive operations to other developing countries such as the Philippines, India, and United Arab Emirates. Today, Keppel has evolved into a multinational business conglomerate, with a group turnover of S$3.5 billion in 1998 (Table 13.11), and activities ranging from shipbuilding and repair, property development, banking and insurance, to telecommunication services. It is also one of the most internationalized Singapore GLCs. Such diversifications notwithstanding, Keppel still maintained a significant presence in the shipbuilding and repair industry. For example, it committed a S$100 million investment in a new drydock in 1994, which became operational in 1996 and expanded its capacity by some 35%.

TABLE 13.10   Sales of Keppel Corp by Business Activities
(in S$ million)

Year	Shipbuilding & Repair	Engineering	Non-Marine Related	Total Sales
1983+	615	*	52 (7.8%)	667
1984+	728	*	80 (9.9%)	808
1985	517	*	99 (16.1%)	616
1986	480	*	96 (16.7%)	576
1987	301.6	51.9	342.2 (49.2%)	695.7
1988	496.1	116.5	188.6 (23.5%)	801.2
1989	670.1	141.8	246.9 (23.3%)	1058.8
1990	898.1	227.7	323.2 (22.3%)	1449.0
1991	1107.1	258.9	431.9 (24.0%)	1797.9
1992	931.5	251.6	503.0 (29.8%)	1686.1
1993	808.3	275.4	581.5 (34.9%)	1665.2
1994	1053.4	329.4	902.6 (39.5%)	2285.4
1995	1107.5	338.1	1,108.0 (43.6%)	2553.6
1996	1226.3	390.4	1,545.1 (48.9%)	3161.8
1997	1289.6	437.9	1,720.3 (49.9%)	3447.8
1998	575.6	1221.4	1,730.9 (49.1%)	3527.9

NOTES: +Estimates from chart presentations.
*Included in Shipbuilding and Repair figures.
SOURCE: Keppel Corporation, *Annual Report*, various years.

Keppel's major investments in shipbuilding and repair activities in the early 1970s was no doubt facilitated by the fact that the company had a strong link to the political leadership. The first chairman of Keppel (from 1968–70) was Hon Sui Sen, who was also at the same time the finance minister as well as the chairman of DBS Bank, which was set up by the government to provide development financing. The second chairman, George Bogaars (from 1970–84), was the head of civil service and permanent secretary of the ministry of defence as well as the chairman of National Iron and Steel (Natsteel), another state-controlled enterprise involved in steel making. Although the big push by Keppel into ship-repair and oil-rig building seems obvious business choices in retrospect, they were risky investments at the time, and it was not obvious that financing would have been readily forthcoming had Keppel been a purely private enterprise with no government link. Indeed, one reason why Far East Levingston Shipbuilding (FELS) —

TABLE 13.11   Keppel Corporation Financial Performance

Year	Total Revenue (S$m)	Pretax Profit (S$m)	Return on Sales (%)
1979	368.6	42.4	11.5
1980	535.9	104.3	19.46
1981	723.3	153.5	21.22
1982	645.8	160.5	24.85
1983	666.9	28	4.2
1984	808	5.4	.67
1985	616.1	−49.9	−8.1
1986	576.3	7.3	1.27
1987	670.7	45.8	6.83
1988	776.5	80.8	10.41
1989	1020.2	155.2	15.21
1990	1400.3	225	16.07
1991	1681.8	270.7	16.1
1992	1559.5	278.9	17.88
1993	1528.9	338.6	22.15
1994	2103.4	416.9	19.8
1995	2404.4	444.9	18.5
1996	2886.0	506.0	17.5
1997	3448	414	12.0
1998	3528	−199	−5.6

NOTE: Company was listed only in 1980; data prior to 1979 not available.
SOURCE: Keppel Corporation, *Annual Report*, various years.

a foreign-owned rig-builder established in 1967 in Singapore — became a subsidiary of Keppel was precisely because of severe under-capitalization. The injection of fund by Keppel after the acquisition in 1971 enabled FELS to quickly expand and become a leading rig-builder in the world.

Keppel's initial capital financing was either provided by or backed by the government. However, rather than in the form of subsidy, these financing arrangements were subjected to the discipline of the capital market. Although government-guaranteed bonds were used in the initial years, later financing were from commercial markets and indeed often represented financial innovations in Singapore. Among these are a public offering of shares in 1980 that saw government ownership reduced to 75%[1], an unguaranteed Asian Dollar Bond in 1997, a commercial paper issued in the US in 1984, a bond issue with warrants in

1986, and a share issue in the United States[2] (Sikorski, 1997). In March 1993 Keppel was one of two local firms to list an option as the options market was introduced in the Stock Exchange of Singapore.

Despite dominant state ownership and close political link, the management of Keppel-indeed, of most GLCs in Singapore-was given significant autonomy in running the company. In effect, GLCs like Keppel are given relatively free-rein to operate as a private enterprise, although strategic business directions may be subject to government approval. Government influence was exercised primarilly through the intermediation of state-owned holding companies (Temasek Holdings in Keppel's case) that holds the government's equity interest, and secondarily through the selection of directors and management personnel. The secondment of senior civil servants to Keppel is a case in point: besides the first two chairmen, the third and current chairman from 1984, Sim Kee Boon, was also the head of civil service prior to his appointment, in addition to senior positions in several other GLCs. Interviews offered by Keppel chairmen over the years suggest that, in many occassions, the management of Keppel was responsible for formulating strategic business plans, while the government as shareholders were being pursuaded to go along (Sikorski, 1997). Beyond broad policy guidance and due-diligence monitoring, there had been relatively little interference from the government, unless the performance of the management was found wanting. In the case of Keppel, which has been relatively successful in terms of financial performance, there appears to have been little direct intervention, except possibly in the mid-1980s when a number of senior management resignations were linked by journalists to a widely publicised acquisition of a British shipping and engineering firm which was alleged to be overpriced.

In addition to management autonomy, GLCs like Keppel also enjoy potential benefits from being an "insider" in a network of mutually supporting relationships between GLCs (and through them, the leveraging of their MNC partners) that seek to promote the collective good of 'Singapore Inc.' For example, Bogaars was also on the board of Sembawang Shipyard when he was chairman of Keppel, an unusual if not illegal arrangement by American standard of business practice (Sikorski, 1997). The interlocking directorates among competing GLCs manifests a national system of cooperative competition. For example, during the industry recession in 1985, the three GLC shipyards and two other major foreign-owned shipyards in Singapore jointly agreed to an across-the-board 20% reduction of dock use by adopting a 24-working day month. More recently, several major internationalization projects and diversification ventures by Keppel were carried out through strategic alliance with other GLCs. For examples, Keppel had jointly pursued contracts in China with Sembawang, with POSB in insurance, Natsteel in steel fabrication, and Singapore Press Holding in mobile phone.

Sembawang Shipyard

After the British withdrawal in 1968, Sembawang Shipyard was formed to take over and commercialize the naval base dockyard on the northern coast. Like Keppel, it was initially managed by the Swan Hunter Group of the U.K. For the first two years, naval contracts kept the yard afloat and its 4000 strong workers employed. Gradually the shipyard began to ventured out to undertake merchant ship-repair. The transition from a naval facility to a commercial shiprepair yard was completed when the company was listed on the local stock exchange in 1973. Soon after going public, the company undertook an aggressive expansion of capacity. A 400,000 dwt drydock, the largest in Singapore, was put into operation by the company in 1978.

Up to the early 1980s, Sembawang (like Keppel) concentrated its expansion in other marine-related sectors, e.g. the entry into the ship salvage and towing business in Singapore and HongKong, and the acquisition of the Singapore subsidiary of Bethlehem Steel to further expansion into rig-building and building of specialized tankers. From the second half of 1980s and especially after the collapse of the oil tanker market, Sembawang further diversified into construction, industrial/aviation engineering, and energy and related infrastructure engineering services (Table 13.12). Sembawang has also pursued a strategy of regionalization since the early 1990s by relocating some of its activities to neighboring countries such as Indonesia. Today, Sembawang has evolved into a large conglomerate with sales of S$3.3 billion from four main businesses-shipbuilding/repair and other marine-related businesses, engineering and construction, property and building materials and heavy industries. A fifth business unit, Sembawang Venture, was established to nurture new businesses. The latest foray of this new business group is into the info-media business, which includes internet service provision and multimedia content development, as well as into property development.[3] To further ration-

TABLE 13.12 Sales of Sembawang Corporation by Business Activities (in S$ million)

Year	Marine Services	Engineering	Shipping	Industrial	Others	Eliminations	Total Sales
1987	143.9	19.4	21.5	—	—	—	184.8
1988	241.7	22.9	19.0	—	0.3	—	283.9
1989	313.1	62.9	20.4	—	0.1	—	396.4
1990	354.6	64.0	16.8	—	0.0	—	435.8
1991	403.2	96.8	8.3	—	1.7	—	510.0

	Shipyard	Engineering	Maritime	Industrial	Others	Eliminations	Total Sales
1992	439.2	213.9	—	54.8	—	—	707.9
1993	387.1	181.6	—	97.4	—	—	666.1
1994	403.7	379.1	155.2	167.2	—	—	1105.2
1995	378.3	349.2	136.7	365.6	9.2	—40.9	1198.2

	Marine/Heavy Industries	Engineering /Construction	Transportation /Logistics	Properties/ Building Materials	Others	New Business	Total Sales
1995	543.9	311.7	129.7	197.8	14.9	0.2	1198.2
1996	466.9	591.3	168.0	230.9	45.0	0.3	1502.3
1997	537.4	1100.7	437.6	229.5	583.4	420.7*	3309

	Infrastructure	Marine Engineering	IT	Lifestyle	Others	Corporate	Total Sales
1997	1767.7	537.4	420.7	502.2	63.2	18.0	3309.3
1998	1722.9	935.3	538.3	579.5	115.6	8.4	3900.1

NOTE: * Includes IT

SOURCE: Sembawang Corporation and Sembawang Shipyard, *Annual Report*, various years.

alize its shipbuilding/repair business, Sembawang in 1998 acquired Jurong Shipyard, the third GLC in the industry, and the least diversified so far.[4]

Like Keppel, Sembawang also had senior civil servants appointed to management positions. Past chairmen and deputy chairmen included permanent secretaries of government ministries, and the current chairman, Philip Yeo (since 1993), also holds the chairmanship of the EDB. Unlike Keppel, which received government financing to venture decisively into shipbuilding and repair in the crucial formative years, Sembawang's initial expansion into merchant shiprepair in the 1970s, including major investment in dry and floating docks, was financed primarily through the equity market and a term loan from commercial market. Indeed, much of the group's subsequent diversification and regionalization efforts have been largely self-financed or on commercial terms, with little or no subsidy from the government. Such financial independence notwithstanding, many of Sembawang's diversification ventures, like Keppel's, benefited from networking and leveraging of other GLCs.

It is worth noting that all three GLCs — Sembawang, Keppel and Jurong shipyard — had been encouraged to venture into commercial shipbuilding and repair almost simultaneously. The fourth GLC, ST Shipbuilding and Engineering (STSE) was initially formed to provide shipbuilding and repair services for the Singapore Navy, but it too was later encouraged to diversify into commercial operations. From the government's perspective, this direct involvement of the state served two important purposes. Firstly, it helped to create the necessary agglomeration economies to capitalize on market opportunities to catapult Singapore into a major shipbuilding/repair centre in the world. Secondly, it was able to create competition that helped keep these GLCs on their toes. While some degree of specialization emerged among the four companies (e.g. Sembawang in ship-repair, while Keppel in rigbuilding), these appeared to have been differentiation strategies adopted by the companies themselves in response to global competition and demand opportunities, rather than through orchestration by the state (the exception was STSE's initial focus on serving the Singapore's naval defence needs). Indeed, around the same time that these GLCs were encouraged to venture into shipbuilding and repair, foreign MNCs and other smaller local firms were not prevented from entering into the same sector. Thus, no artificial barriers to entry was created by the government to shield the GLCs from competition.

5. International Competitiveness of Singapore's Shipbuilding and Repair Industry

The international competitiveness of Singapore's shipbuilding and repair industry rest on different factors during the three different phases which the industry had gone through. In the first phase (pre-1980), the industry benefited from the synergistic relation with the country's entrepot trade, and low labor and operating costs. Given favorable world-wide demand conditions in the 1970s, the country made a successful entry into shipbuilding and repair. During the second phase between 1980 and 1991, despite difficult operating environment, the industry's cost advantage was maintained through importing and adapting foreign shipbuilding and repair technology. Together with the upgrading of marine workers' skills through government initiatives, industrial productivity was maintained at a relatively high level, despite drastic fall in output and value added in the mid-1980s.

In the 1990s, however, the country's cost advantages as a ship-repair center were fast eroding. Rather than relying on price competition, local shipyards instead looked for product differentiation and developing niche markets through technology and innovations to remain competitive. Among the business strategies pursued by the local shipyards were:

- Going regional by relocating the more labor intensive operations to neighboring countries to take advantage of their relatively low labor and land costs. In August 1996, Sembawang Shipyard joined hands with Indonesia's Salim Group to form the joint venture, PT Karimun Sembawang, in order to lower its cost as well as to tap on new market opportunities arising from intra-Asian trade. This new facility has a new 65,000 dwt capacity floating dock and a 400 meter long pier. An additional 400 meter repair pier and a larger floating dock is planned for its second phase expansion. Sembawang Shipyard has also started a joint venture ship-repair in Tianjin in November 1996 with China National Offshore Oil Bohai Corporation. In February 1999, Keppel Corporation's new 40,000 dwt drydock in South Manila, Philippines was completed. Provisions have been made in the yard's dock area to accommodate future expansion of the dock's repair capacity of up to 70,000 dwt. Another joint-venture is set to take place, following Pan-United's announcement to invest up to US$30 million in a new joint-venture shipyard in Batam (Indonesia) with PT Repino Mitra Abadi. The shipyard will be able to handle ships of up to 13,000 dwt and will offer other facilities including a 300 meter long pier. Thus, instead of importing and adapting foreign technology, the country has become an exporter of shipbuilding and repair technology in the 1990s.

- Diversifying into other business activities, such as ship-owning, insurance, banking, property development and telecommunications. Keppel, in particular, had pursued this diversification strategy most aggressively, to the point that ship-building and repair now represents only a small proportion of its total revenue.
- Developing niche markets, e.g., converting oil tankers into floating production facilities, repair of luxury cruise. In pursuing this strategy, both Jurong and Sembawang Shipyards found it to be effective in securing and maintaining market share and profit margin in face of competition from shipyards in low-cost developing countries.

Despite diversification and regionalization, the government and the three GLC shipyards remained committed to competing in the global shipbuilding/repair industry through the third prong, i.e. niche specialization. The success of this strategy, however, will depend very much on the effort of the shipyards in raising labor productivity as well as developing new technological capabilities through R&D. Even though it is already a relatively mature industry, ship-repair is still highly dependent on skilled labour, due to the need to customize to the needs of different repair and new building specifications which standardized machinery is not able to handle. Thus, unlike other mature manufacturing activities, shipbuilding and repair does not allow complete automation and mechanization. Productivity improvement in the industry therefore hinges critically on the skill levels of workers. At the same time, niche differentiation requires investment in specialized skills such as ship design, knowledge of advanced materials, new welding and joining technologies etc., the mastery of which requires substantial indigenous R&D efforts. To help promote technological upgrading, a government-sponsored Marine Technology program was launched in 1994 with the aim to encourage greater automation, develop key engineering design and analysis capabilities, and to build a pool of research and engineering expertise within the marine industry. However, the impact of this program had been little, due to the modest scale of the government funding, and the lack of strong commitment by the industry players.

Table 13.13 Sembawang Corporation Financial Performance

Year	Total Revenue (S$m)	Pretax Profit (S$m)	Return on Sales (%)
1982	214.43	63.41	29.6
1983	108.93	2.84	2.6
1984	114.28	−1.09	−1.0
1985	111	−7.29	−6.6
1986	160.67	15.39	9.6
1987	184.8	21.54	11.7
1988	283.89	37.39	13.2
1989	396.41	61.6	15.5
1990	435.77	70.38	16.2
1991	510	91.47	17.9
1992	707.93	106.89	15.1
1993	666.1	81.34	12.2
1994	1105.19	85.13	7.7
1995	1198.15	34.17	2.9
1996	1502.3	28.39	1.9
1997	3309.3	203.0	6.1
1998	3900.1	213.2	5.5

SOURCE: Sembawang Shipyard, *Annual Report*, various years.

A major problem faced in public efforts to upgrade the industry had been the high reliance of the industry on subcontractors for workers. Improving the technology and skills of subcontractors was thus critical to maintaining the industry's international competitiveness. In this aspect, the industry still lagged behind other manufacturing industries such as electronics. For example, in 1994, marine subcontractors account for about 70% of the total marine workforce, but their value added was only $26,000 per worker, which was substantially lower than that of the shipyards, which stood at over $70,000 per worker. To cope with this problem, the Economic Development Board persuaded and coordinated the five major shipyards to form a Marine Group Local Industry Upgrading Program, with the aim of raising sub-con-tractors' productivity through skills training, improved work methods and mechanization. All three GLC shipyards also invested substantially in improving process quality, and were among the first in the industry to qualify for ISO9000 certification. However, progress in the rest of the industry had been slow due to the high reliance of the subcontractors on foreign workers, and the high turnover of such

Table 13.14   Aggregated Financial Performance of 5 Ship Building and Repair Companies in Singapore

Year	Total Sales (S$m)	ROS (%)	ROE (%)	ROA (%)
1979				
1980				
1981				
1982*	1011.83	25.25	26.46	12.37
1983*	894.60	4.22	3.73	1.31
1984*	1043.10	0.94	1.02	0.37
1985**	892.60	−5.60	−4.38	−2.05
1986**	906.20	3.88	3.01	1.48
1987**	1120.20	8.22	6.62	3.22
1988	1489.60	10.68	10.29	4.46
1989	1998.70	13.56	11.79	5.34
1990	2802.60	14.33	13.19	6.10
1991	3242.50	17.04	15.02	7.05
1992	3117.80	18.23	12.68	5.50
1993	2994.50	19.42	10.51	4.16
1994	4097.70	16.07	9.56	4.06
1995	4485.30	13.15	7.60	3.10
1996	5596.20	11.58	7.18	2.91
1997	7853.47	9.50	6.70	2.41

Compound Growth rate (%)

1982–97	14.6			

NOTES: *Aggregated financial data of 3 companies: Jurong, Keppel, Sembawang.
**Aggregated financial data of 4 companies: Jurong, Keppel, Sembawang, ST.
SOURCE: Companies' Annual Reports and Prospectuses.

workers. Moreover, local technical talents were not attracted to the industry due to the perceived "low-tech" image of the industry.

In view of the limited progress achieved in technological upgrading, the shipyards concerned decided that more drastic rationalization were needed for them to survive global competition in the future. As a result, Sembawang announced a merger with Jurong Shipyard, while Keppel announced a merger with Hitachi Zosen in 1998. Following these two mergers, the country is now left with three major shipyards. The merged entity of Keppel and Hitachi Zosen now operates a total of 1.3 million dwt of docking capacity, equivalent to about 44% of the total docking capacity of the four major repair yards in Singapore. Sembawan Shipyard's acquisition of Jurong Shipyard made it the largest shipyard in South-east Asia with a capacity of 1.8 million dwt.

The mergers of the Singapore yards have reduced competition globally. Besides the two big players in Singapore, other major players competing for large tanker repairs in the Gulf-East route are Arab Ship Repair Yard and Dubai Dockyard in the Middle East, Malaysian Shipbuilding & Engineering and to a smaller extent, Hyundai Mipo in South Korea. In the wake of leaner times ahead, further merger could take place, resulting in a single super shipyard in Singapore. More consolidation is also expected among the smaller local shipyards specializing in making barges and tugs. In 1997, barges and tugs made up 78% of the 130 vessels delivered by local yards, totaling 241,096 gross tons with a total value of $608 million. Some of these yards had successfully diversified into higher value-added activities such as anchor handling tug/supply vessels and customised aluminium boats, while a few had managed to carve out niche markets such as the construction of tugs for oil exploration, but many are not expected to be able to survive in the future.

6. Summary Assessment

The development history of the three largest shipyards in Singapore shares a number of common characteristics. All of them began as government firms, set up to convert and expand colonial dockyards into internationally competitive shipbuilding and repair businesses. Over the years, and despite some difficult times, these GLCs contributed significantly towards making Singapore a major shipbuilding/repair and rig-building centre in the world. Since the 1980s, these GLCs have also evolved from shipyard operations into huge business conglomerates, with interests spanning across a wide spectrum of business activities. To stay competitive in the 1990s, they have adopted, to varying degrees, the strategies of regionalization and business diversification, while seeking to achieve niche specialization within the shipbuilding and repair sector itself.

In the initial formative years, government support and initiatives, whether in financial investment, manpower training or development of market niches, were instrumental in the successful emergence of Singapore as a ship-repair hub in Asia. While luck had certainly played a role in terms of providing Singapore with a window of opportunities in the early 1970s due to her favorable geographic location as a major sea-port in Southeast Asia, the pro-active role of the state was critical in enabling Singapore to seize the opportunities before other countries in the region like Malaysia and Philippines did. Furthermore, the strong commitment of government investment in technological learning and manpower training helped sustain the growth and deepening of the ship-repair industry for the next two decades.

State-owned enterprises in many parts of the world tend to be a financial burden to their governments. Often they do not exit industries even when doing badly, and had to either rely on state subsidy or be eventually rescued through privatization. In marked contrast, Singapore's state-owned enterprises in shipbuilding and repair had not only made significant contribution to the development of an important industrial cluster in the 1970s and 1980s, but had been doing so profitably except for periods of severe cyclical downturns. Recognizing the long-run structural decline in competitiveness of Singapore in this industry in the 1990s, these GLCs have sought to diversify from the marine sector since the late 1980s, and later formed mergers among themselves to rationalize cost and operations, as well as to develop new competitiveness in niche markets through specialization. In coping with the structural decline of their industry, these state-owned firms behaved largely as private entities and responded to competitive market pressures, including the performance monitoring of the stock market where their shares are listed. Although the government provided various assistance, these were generally reduced in scope over the years, and there was no attempt at sheltering them from global competitive pressures. If anything, the government might be faulted by not investing sufficiently in public R&D to support technological upgrading of the industry, rather than providing too much help to the industry.

IV. CONCLUSION

We believe that our examination in this chapter of the development of two very different industries in Singapore — electronics and ship-building/repair — illustrated very well our argument in the earlier chapter that the state can play different industrial policy roles depending on the development contexts. In the case of the electronics industry where technological change is rapid and where markets and competition are global, the policy of attracting leading foreign MNCs to locate their manufacturing operations in Singapore and to transfer increasingly advanced technologies through investment incentives, manpower development subsidies and public provision of infrastructural support services, had been highly successful in accelerating the growth and technological upgrading of the industry. In contrast, in the case of the shipbuilding and repair industry where technological change is more gradual and markets and competition were initially more regionalized, the policy of setting up state-owned firms to quickly seize a window of opportunity and to build a critical mass of productive capacity and trained workforce to exploit agglomeration economies was successful in establishing Singapore as a major regional shipbuilding/repair hub in Asia.

The policy of attracting MNCs by itself need not lead to rapid technological upgrading, as can be seen in the experience of other developing countries (e.g. Malaysia, Thailand) which have similar DFI-friendly investment incentives. Similarly, the policy of using state-owned firms to enter into industries has often been disastrous in many developing countries, due to special protection and subsidies provided to such state entities, and their consequent lack of responsiveness to market pressures to improve performance. Our analysis in this chapter shows that Singapore has been relatively successful in both cases because the government coupled these policies with various complementary policies (investment in manpower development, encouraging competition, etc.).

NOTES

Part of this chapter draws extensively from an earlier paper by Wong, P.K., S.Y. Phang, J.S. Yong and M.K. Chng, "Development of Internationally Competitive Indigenous Manufacturing Firms in Singapore. Report Prepared for Foundation for Advanced Studies on International Development, Tokyo, Japan". In *Asia's Development Experiences: How Internationally Competitive National Manufacturing Firms have Developed in Asia*, edited by T. Kazuo, Tokyo: Foundation for Advanced Studies on International Development, 1998.

1. Keppel was among the first GLCs to be listed in the local stock exchange.
2. Keppel was the second firm in the world to take advantage of the new listing rule in the U.S.
3. The property arm was set up primarily to develop existing dockyard land on prime location into commercial and residential properties once the dockyard operation is relocated to Indonesia.

4. The oldest shipyard in Singapore, Jurong Shipyard was formed in 1963 as a joint venture between the EDB and the IHI Group of Japan, with the former assuming majority ownership. The shipyard was built from scratch on a 60-acre site at Pulau Samulun on the Western coast of Singapore. The joint venture was conceived as part of the government's industrialization plan to exploit the linkages of shipbuilding and repair activities to develop the petrochemical and other heavy engineering industries. The tie-up with the Japanese shipyard also facilitated the transfer of shipbuilding technology and management know-how. Jurong Shipyard was listed in the local Stock Exchange in 1987.

REFERENCES

Association of Singapore Marine Industries. *Annual Report*. Singapore: Association of Singapore Marine Industries, various years.

Association of Singapore Marine Industries. *A Shared Purpose: 30 Years of Linking up the Marine Industry*. Singapore: Association of Singapore Marine Industries, 1998.

Cho,D.S. and M. Porter. "Changing Global Leadership: The Case of Shipbuilding". In *Competing in Global Industries*, edited by M.E. Porter, pp. 539–67. Boston: Harvard Business School Press, 1986.

Economic Development Board (EDB), Singapore. *Census for Industrial Production*, various years. Singapore: EDB.

Elsevier. *Yearbook of World Electronics Data*. Oxford: Elsevier Advanced Technology, various years.

Schein, E. *Strategic Pragmatism: The Culture of the Economic Development Board of Singapore*. Cambridge, Mass: MIT Press, 1996.

Sikorski, D. "Public Enterprise in the Marine Industry: Case Study of a Shipyard in Singapore". Paper presented at the conference on the Asian MNC, 26 February 1997 in Singapore.

Stopford, M. *Maritime Economics*. London: Unwin, 1988.

Todd, D. *Industrial Dislocation: The Case of Global Shipbuilding*. London: Routledge, 1991.

Wong, P.K. "Technological development through subcontracting linkages: Evidence from Singapore". *Scandinavian International Business Review* 1, no. 3 (1992): 28–40.

Wong, P.K. "Competing in the Global Electronics Industry: A Comparative Study of the Innovation Networks of Singapore and Taiwan". *Journal of Industry Studies* 2, no. 2 (1995): 35–61.

Wong, P.K. "Dynamics of HDD Industry Development in Singapore". Information Storage Industry Centre, University of California San Diego, Working Paper, 1999.

Wong, P.K. "Globalization of Electronics Production Networks and the Emerging Roles and Strategies of Singapore Contract Manufacturers", Proceedings of the 19th Annual Hosei University International Conference on Japanese Foreign Direct Investment and Structural Change in the East Asian Industrial System, Tokyo, Oct. 30–Nov. 1, 2000.

Wong, P.K. "Globalization of American, European and Japanese Production Networks and The Growth of Singapore's Electronics Industry". *International Journal of Technology Management* (2001).

Wong, P.K., C.Wang and A.Singh. *Technology Transfer by MNCs in Singapore*, Singapore: CMIT, National University of Singapore: research report commissioned by the Asian Development Bank, 1999.

Wong, P.K. and D.McKendrick. "Singapore", chapter 7 in McKendrick, D.G., R.F.Doner and S.Haggard. *From Silicon Valley to Singapore: Location and Competitive Advantage in the Hard Disk Drive Industry*, Stanford University Press, 2000.

Wong, P.K. and Z.L. He. "The moderating effect of firm's internal innovation climate on the impact of public R&D support: Empirical evidence for Singapore", CMIT working paper, National University of Singapore, 2001.

ANNEX TABLE 13A   Leading Foreign Electronics MNCs in Singapore, 1997/8 (Revenue in S$ million)

Company	1997	1998	Nationality
Hewlett-Packard Singapore (Pte) Ltd	8,263.9	9,788.1	USA
Maxtor	1,224.1	3,672.6	USA
Texas Instruments Singapore (Pte) Ltd	3,892.6	3,428.6	USA
Compaq Asia Pte Ltd	3,330.7	3,264.9	USA
Philips Singapore Pte Ltd	3,427.6	2,634.1	The Netherlands
Western Digital (S) Pte Ltd	2,701.4	2,571.1	USA
Motorola Electronics Pte Ltd	2,312.2	1,986.2	USA
Matsushita Kotobuki Electronics Industries (S) Pte Ltd	2,201.0	1,797.4	Japan
Thomson Multimedia Asia Pte Ltd	1,782.9	1,486.5	France
Sony Singapore	784.3	1,402.2	Japan
Lucent Technologies Singapore Pte Ltd	886.5	1,290.7	USA
Canon Singapore Pte Ltd	903.7	1,026.9	Japan
Adaptec Manufacturing (S) Pte Ltd	1,222.9	971.5	USA
NEC Semiconductors Singapore Pte Ltd	1,160.4	912.2	Japan
Aiwa Singapore Ltd	907.3	776.1	Japan
Hitachi Electronic Devices (S) Pte Ltd	788.0	707.2	Japan
Seagate	7,568.1	na	USA
Siemens Components Pte Ltd	1,913.1	na	Germany
ST Microelectronics Pte Ltd	1,835.9	na	France/Italy
Sanyo Electronics (S) Pte Ltd	841.4	na	Japan

SOURCE: DP Information Network Pte Ltd, *Singapore 1000*, various years; except figure for Seagate, which is derived from company annual report.

ANNEX TABLE 13B Leading Local Electronics Manufacturing Firms in Singapore (Revenue in S$ million)

Electronics Manufacturing	1995	1996	1997	1998	Activity
Natsteel Electronics	710.5	901.2	1231.5	2,458.7	Contract mfg
Flextronics International	336.5	1,185.1	1,339.4	2,235.5	PCBA and contract mfg
Creative Technology	1,679.70	1,846.20	1750.9	2,092.6	PC soundcard & multimedia products
Venture Mfg	249.5	649.1	708	730.7	PCBA and contract mfg
Chartered Semiconductor Mfg	407.8	574	557.3	700.7	Semiconductor fabrication
JIT Electronics	144.5	173.1	396.5	580.2	PCBA and electronic components
ACMA [1]	518.1	559.2	570.4	519.8	Electrical/electronic products
Omni Industries	139.6	263.7	307.4	415.4	PCBA and contract mfg
GES Singapore [2]		252.3	263.1	404.5	PCs
ST E&E [3]	127.3	152.1	311.5	337.7	Industrial electronics/systems integration
Goldtron [1]	553.4	574.5	367.8	254.0	Telecom products and contract mfg
Wearns Technologies [2]	202.1	181.5	254.5	231.8	PCBA and contract mfg
Aztech	662.1	452.9	236.7	210.4	PC soundcard & multimedia products
Tech-Semiconductor	865.9	575.7	427.7	204.8	Semiconductor fabrication
Avimo	92.4	117.9	164.3	194.9	Precision optics & laser equipment
Flextech	70.3	89.5	128.6	180.3	Precision engineering/semicon. packaging
Sunright	106.6	142.6	161.1	178.7	Testing of semiconductors
Gul Technologies	95.2	117.6	127	151.6	PCB
Eltech	101.6	112.2	147.1	128	Contract mfg
CET Technologies [2]	na	101	88.8	103.4	Telecoms products & systems

NOTES: 1. Diversified Group, Revenue from electronics manufacturing not available separately
2. Not publicly listed
3. Singapore Technologies Electronics from 1997

SOURCES: Company Annual Reports; Economics Development Board, *Singapore Electronics Manufacturers Directory*, various years; Stock Exchange of Singapore website, http://www.ses.com.sg; DP Information Network Pte Ltd, *Singapore 1000*, various years.

ANNEX TABLE 13C   Leading Local Electronics-Supporting Manufacturing Firms in Singapore (Revenue in S$ million)

Electronics Manufacturing	1995	1996	1997	1998	Activity
Singapore Shinei Sangyo[1]	213.3	248.5	336.8	460.7	Metal stamping, tools & dies
Amtek Engineering	197.1	251.5	258	281.6	Precision parts machining
Fu Yu Mfg	183.6	208.2	203.4	168.5	Plastic moulding
Micro-Machining Industries	68.0	90.1	113.0	164.7	Disk drive basplates and VCM assembly
Uraco	84.2	116.5	148.4	136.4	Diecasting and precision machining
San Teh	70.8	81.7	101.7	129.4	Rubber products
Giken Sakata	232.8	283.4	133.5	129.1	Floppy disks and electronic components
Li Xin	57.8	57.8	100.4	90.1	Precision moulds
Broadway	50.7	60.7	71.9	72.1	Plastic components
Brilliant Manufacturing	na	83	79.5	71.7	Precision engineering
Seksun Precision Engineering	62.8	57.4	63.7	70.3	Metal stamping & dies
Excel Machine Tools	44.2	53.2	69.5	65.7	CNC machinery
Measurex[1]	33.6	42.6	54.4	58.8	Precision engineering
First Engineering	30	73.6	68	54.6	Tape and reel machines
Heraeus Precision[1]	36.5	39.1	58.1	52.2	Precision engineering
Singapore Precision Industries[1]	74.4	78	85.5	50.4	Precision engineering
ASJ	na	20.1	35.3	49.4	Passive components
Armstrong Industrial	36.8	42	51.4	46.3	Rubber foam products
Sunningdale Plastics[1]	na	33.1	40.3	36.9	Plastic moulding
Hi-P [1]	na	21.4	27.7	33.2	Precision engineering

NOTES: 1. Not publicly listed

SOURCES: Company Annual Reports; Economics Development Board, *Singapore Electronics Manufacturers Directory*, various years; Stock Exchange of Singapore website, http://www.ses.com.sg; DP Information Network Pte Ltd, *Singapore 1000*, various years.

ANNEX TABLE 13D Growth of Electronics Industry in Singapore, 1959–99

Year	Number of Firms	Output ($mn)	Number Employed	Value Added ($mn)	Fixed Assets ($mn)
1959	11	19.36	1,071	11.6	na
1960	13	17.09	1,252	7.88	na
1961	15	17.77	1,300	9.24	na
1962	14	14.43	1,138	6.18	na
1963	23	21	1,381	9.48	5.08
1964	27	19.58	1,276	9.79	4.89
1965	30	25.48	1,454	11.14	6.38
1966	26	33.42	1,611	13.41	6.28
1967	30	42.21	1,856	15.92	8.55
1968	41	53.22	2,312	17.46	10.2
1969	55	122.73	6,845	47.25	11.88
1970	35	212.85	11,251	99.08	na
1971	49	318.97	15,874	141.14	na
1972	53	616.84	27,270	286.65	na
1973	64	1,096.76	39,210	424.69	na
1974	91	1,603.58	46,247	523.45	na
1975	95	1,457.89	32,026	475.02	na
1976	105	1,987.84	43,718	637.71	na
1977	115	2,322.73	46,441	705.05	na
1978	135	2,821.93	53,440	893.30	na
1979	168	4,092.68	66,844	1,273.59	na
1980	172	5,344.00	71,727	1,668.85	585.06
1981	185	5,728.45	69,358	1,625.71	699.86
1982	186	5,297.57	60,760	1,484.45	840.19
1983	203	7,018.61	65,954	1,911.48	1,011.81
1984	214	9,703.39	73,271	2,917.49	1,116.52
1985	207	9,179.04	66,646	2,894.26	1,582.68
1986	194	11,492.72	70,863	3,780.98	1,860.44
1987	236	16,780.68	87,676	5,156.22	2,487.01
1988	239	21,864.59	112,769	6,337.43	2,967.86
1989	233	24,692.26	116,080	6,979.84	3,472.42
1990	240	27,878.13	122,797	7,716.64	3,757.31
1991	243	28,957.67	123,358	8,027.63	3,726.60
1992	247	32,044.35	122,562	8,924.92	4,060.20
1993	247	39,827.43	117,614	11,066.25	4,552.84
1994	246	49,005.93	123,587	12,907.23	5,344.05
1995	239	57,872.75	126,891	15,162.58	6,595.79
1996	238	60,192.84	128,455	16,430.46	8,296.31
1997	238	62,905.23	123,863	16,806.02	9,741.97
1998	225	60,848.75	111,624	16,305.59	10,466.31
1999	205	68,718.52	105,826	20,023.74	11,107.24

SOURCE: Economic Development Board, *Report on the Census for Industrial Production*, various years.

ANNEX TABLE 13E   Growth Performance of Singapore's Electronics Industry, 1970–99

Year	Output S$ million	Value Add S$ million	Employment	% Share of Total Manufacturing		
				Output	Value Add	Employment
1960	17.1	7.9	1,252	3.7	5.5	4.6
1970	283	127.4	13,586	7.3	11.7	11.3
1980	5,344	1,668.9	71,727	16.9	19.6	25.1
1990	27,878.1	7,716.6	122,797	39.1	35.7	34.9
1995	57,872.8	11,987.9	126,891	51.1	44.6	34.3
1996	60,912.8	12,672.2	128,455	51.1	44.9	34.3
1997	62,905.2	16,806.0	123,863	49.7	43.4	33.8
1998	60,848.8	16,305.6	111,624	50.1	42.0	31.7
1999	68,718.52	20,023.74	105,826	51.4	44.4	31.2

	Average Growth % p.a.					
	Electronics Industry			Total Manufacturing		
	Output	Value Add	Employment	Output	Value Add	Employment
1960-70	32.4	32.1	26.9	23.6	22.6	16
1970-80	34.2	29.3	18.1	23.3	22.8	9
1980-90	18.0	16.5	5.5	8.5	9.8	2.1
1990-98	10.2	9.8	−1.2	6.9	7.6	.02
1960-98	24.0	22.2	12.5	15.8	15.9	7.0
1990-99	10.5	11.2	−1.6	7.2	8.5	−0.4
1960-99	23.7	19.9	25.1	15.6	12.4	18.4

SOURCE: Economic Development Board, *Report on the Census for Industrial Production*, various years.

ANNEX TABLE 13F Structure of Singapore's Electronics Industry, 1999

Electronics Subsectors	Number of Firms	Number Employed	Output Added S$ m	Value Assets S$ m	Net Fixed Surplus S$ m	Operating Added S$ m	Value Worker Output %	Value Added/Assets/Worker S$ thou'd	Net Fixed Surplus/Output S$ thou'd	Operating %
Wafer fabrication	8	8,538	4,464.1	1,960.8	4,653.6	−207.1	43.9	229.7	545.0	−4.6
Other semiconductor devices	21	15,583	9,884.8	3,102.4	2,325.6	1,073.5	31.4	199.1	149.2	10.9
Capacitors and resistors	9	3,318	591.4	297.5	168.4	79.2	50.3	89.7	50.8	13.4
Printed circuit boards without electronic parts	22	5,029	1,044.7	500.2	590.6	103.2	47.9	99.5	117.4	9.9
Printed circuit boards with electronic parts	37	3,568	1,142.6	277.3	125.4	78.4	24.3	77.7	35.1	6.9
Contract manufacturers	15	7,442	2,817.2	462.8	228.0	156.7	16.4	62.2	30.6	5.6
Communication equipment	14	4,354	3,640.0	1,271.0	198.8	827.3	34.9	291.9	45.7	22.7
Television sets and other audio and visual equipment	13	6,536	2,365.7	583.8	177.9	128.7	24.7	89.3	27.2	5.4
Computers and data processing equipment	11	4,944	10,221.2	2,915.6	268.5	2,386.5	28.5	589.7	54.3	23.3
Disk drives	7	29,324	18,923.8	3,858.6	1,191.3	1,617.1	20.4	131.6	40.6	8.5
Electronic security system	9	828	159.1	48.9	23.7	−16.3	30.7	59.1	28.6	−10.2
Other electronic products and components nec	39	16,362	13,464.0	4,744.9	1,155.5	2,835.9	35.2	290.0	70.6	21.1
Total electronics products and components	*205*	*105,826*	*68,718.5*	*20,023.7*	*11,107.2*	*9,063.2*	*29.1*	*189.2*	*105.0*	*13.2*

Percentage share of total electronics

Electronics Subsectors	Number of Firms	Number Employed	Output Added	Value Assets	Net Fixed Surplus	Operating Added
Wafer fabrication	3.9	8.1	6.5	9.8	41.9	−2.3
Other semiconductor devices	10.2	14.7	14.4	15.5	20.9	11.8
Capacitors and resistors	4.4	3.1	0.9	1.5	1.5	0.9
Printed circuit boards without electronic parts	10.7	4.8	1.5	2.5	5.3	1.1
Printed circuit boards with electronic parts	18.0	3.4	1.7	1.4	1.1	0.9
Contract manufacturers	7.3	7.0	4.1	2.3	2.1	1.7
Communication equipment	6.8	4.1	5.3	6.3	1.8	9.1
Television sets and other audio and visual equipment	6.3	6.2	3.4	2.9	1.6	1.4
Computers and data processing equipment	5.4	4.7	14.9	14.6	2.4	26.3
Disk drives	3.4	27.7	27.5	19.3	10.7	17.8
Electronic security system	4.4	0.8	0.2	0.2	0.2	−0.2
Other electronic products and components nec	19.0	15.5	19.6	23.7	10.4	31.3
Total electronics products and components	*100.0*	*100.0*	*100.0*	*100.0*	*100.0*	*100.0*

SOURCE: Economic Development Board, *Report on the Census for Industrial Production,* 1999.

GUIDE TO LITERATURE ON EAST ASIA ECONOMIC DEVELOPMENT

Compiled by Poh-Kam Wong and Joyce Lee

General Development Literature Relevant to East Asia

Abramovitz, M. (1986), "Catching up, Forging Ahead, and Falling Behind", *Journal of Economic History* 46(2): 385–406.

Abramovitz, M. (1989), *Thinking About Growth*, Cambridge University Press.

Alston, L.J., Eggertson, T., North, D. (eds.) (1996), *Empirical Studies in Institutional Change*, Cambridge, New York: Cambridge University Press.

Barro, R.J. (1994b), "Sources of Economic Growth", *Carnegie-Rochester Conference Series on Public Policy* 40: 1–46.

Barro, R.J. (1995), *Economic Growth*, New York: McGraw-Hill.

Bartelsman, E.J., Caballero, R.J., Lyons, R. (1994), "Consumer and Supplier-driven Externalities", *American Economic Review* 84(4): 1075–1084.

Best, M.H. (1990), *The New Competition: Institutions of Industrial Restructuring*, Cambridge: Policy Press.

Branson, J. (1970), "Technology Transfer through the International Firm", *American Economic Review* (Papers and Proceedings) 60: 435–440.

Christensen, L.R., Cummings, D., Jorgenson, D.W. (1980), "Economic growth, 1947–73: An international comparison", Kendrick, J.W., Vaccara, B.N. (eds.), *New developments in productivity measurement and analysis*, University of Chicago Press, Chicago, Illinois, pp.595–698.

Clark, C. (1940), *The Conditions of Economic Progress*, London: Macmillan.

Diamond, L. (forthcoming), *Developing Democracy: Towards Consolidation*, Baltimore, Maryland: John Hopkins University Press.

Dicken, P. (1992), *Global Shift: The Internationalization of Economic Activity*, New York: The Guilford Press.

Dixit, A. (1996), *The Making of Economic Policy: A Transaction Cost Politics Perspective*, Cambridge: MIT Press.

Enos, J. (1992), *The Creation of Technological Capabilities in Developing Countries*, London: Pinter Publishers.

Ergas, H., Goldman, M., Ralph, E., Felker, G. (1997), "Technology Institutions and Policies: Their Role in Developing Technological Capability in Industry", *World Bank Technical Paper* No. 383, World Bank.

Feenstra, R., Markusen, J., Zeile, W. (1992), "Accounting for growth with new inputs: Theory and evidence", *American Economic Review*, 82(2): 415–421.

Fukuyama, F. (1992), *The End of History and the Last Man*, N.Y.: Free Press.

Gereffi, G., Korzeniewicz, M. (eds.) (1994), *Commodity Chains and Global Capitalism*, Westport: Praeger.

Germidis D. (ed.) (1980), *International Subcontracting*, Paris: OECD Development Centre.

Gerschenkron, A. (1962), *Economic Backwardness in Historical Perspective*, Harvard University Press.

Gibbons, M. (1988), "The Evaluation of Government Policies for Innovation", Roessner, J.D. (ed.), *Government Innovation Policy: Design, Implementation, Evaluation*, London: Macmillan, pp.135–146.

Grossman, G., Helpman, E. (1991), *Innovation and Growth in the Global Economy*, Cambridge: MIT Press.

Harvey, D. (1989), *The Condition of Postmodernity*, Oxford: Blackwell.

Hikino,T., Amsden, A.H. (1994), "Staying behind, stumbling back, sneaking up, soaring ahead: late industrialization in historical perspective", Baumol, W.J., Nelson, R., Wolf, E.N. (eds.), *Convergence of Productivity: Cross National Studies and Historical Evidence*, NY: Oxford University Press.

Hirschman, A.O. (1958), *The Strategy of Economic Development*, New Haven, Conn.: Yale University Press.

Hirschman, A.O. (1986), "A Dissenter's Confession: The Strategy of Economic Development Revisited", Hirschman, A. O. (ed.), *Rival Views of Market Society*, New York: Viking.

Hollingsworth, J.R., Schmitter, P.C., Streeck, W. (eds.)(1994), *Governing Capitalist Economies: Performance and Control of Economic Sectors*, Oxford University Press.

Huntington, S.P. (1996), *The Clash of Civilizations and the Remaking of World Order*, NY: Simon & Schuster.

Jalilian, H., Weiss, J. (1997), "Bureaucrats, business and economic growth", *Journal of International Development* 9(6): 877–885.

Kozmetsky, G., Yue, P.Y. (1997), *Global Economic Competition*, Kluwer Academic Publishers.

Krugman, P. (1991), "History versus Expectations", *Quarterly Journal of Economics* 106: 651–667.

Kuznets, S. (1957), "Quantitative aspects of the economic growth of nations: II. Industrial distribution of national product and labour force", *Economic Development and Cultural Change*, 5: supplement.

Lall, S. (1990), *Building industrial Competitiveness in Developing Countries*, Paris, OECD Development Centre.

Lall, S. (1992), "Technological capabilities and industrialization", *World Development* 20(2): 165–186.

Lall, S. (1993a), "Understanding technology development", *Development and Change* 24(4): 719–753.

Lin, S.(1994), "Government spending and economic growth", *Applied Economics* 26(1): 83–94.

Lucas, R. (1988), "On the Mechanics of Economic Development", *Journal of Monetary Economics*, pp.3–42.

Maddison, A. (1972), "Explaining economic growth", *Banca Nazionale Del Lavoro Quarterly Review* 22(102): 211–251.

Maddison, A. (1982), *Phases of Capitalist Development*, Oxford: Oxford University Press.

Maddison, A. (1991), *Dynamic Forces in Capitalist Development: A Long-Run Comparative View*, Oxford: Oxford University Press.

Mankiw, N.G. (1995), "The Growth of Nations", *Brookings Papers on Economic Activity* 1: 275–326.

Mody, A., Wheeler, D. (1990), *Automation and World Competition*, New York: St. Martin's Press.

Murray, R. (1989), "Fordism and post-Fordism", Hall, S., Jacques, M. (eds.), *New Times*, London: Lawrence and Wishart, pp.38–53.

Nelson, R.R., Winter,S.J. (1982), *An Evolutionary Theory of Economic Change*, Cambridge, Massachusetts: Harvard University Press.

Nelson, R.R (1993), *National Innovation Systems: A Comparative Analysis*, Oxford: Oxford University Press.

Noll, R.G. (1985), "Government Regulatory Behaviour: A Multi-disciplinary Survey and Synthesis", Noll, R.G. (ed.), *Regulatory Policy and the Social Sciences*, Berkeley, Calif.: University of California Press, pp.9–63.

North, D. C. (1990), *Institutions, Institutional Change and Economic Performance*, New York: Cambridge University Press.

North, D.C.(1991), "Institutions", *Journal of Economic Perspectives*, pp.97–113.

North, D. C., Thomas, R. (1973), *The Rise of the Western World: A New Economic History*, Cambridge, UK: Cambridge University Press.

North, D.C. (1994), "Economic performance through time", *American Economic Review* 84(3): 359–368.

Olson, M. (1982), *The Rise and Decline of Nations*, New Haven, Conn.: Yale University Press.

Olson, M. (1996), "Big Bills Left on the Sidewalk: Why Some Nations are Rich, and Others Poor", *Journal of Economic Perspectives*, pp.3–24.

Olson, M., Sarna, N., Swamy, A.V. (1997), "Governance and Growth: A Simple Hypothesis Explaining Cross-Country Differences in Productivity Growth", IRIS Working Paper. Center for Institutional Reform and the Informal Sector, University of Maryland, College Park, Md.

Pack, H. (1992), "Technology Gaps between Industrial and Developing Countries: Are There Dividends for Latecomers?", Summers, L.H., Shah, S. (eds.), *Proceedings of the World Bank Annual Conference on Development Economics*, Washington: World Bank.

Pack, H. (1987), *Productivity, Technology and Industrial Development*, Oxford University Press.

Pack, H., Page, J., Katz, J., Dahlman, C. (1992), "Technology gaps between industrial and developing countries: Are there dividends for latecomers?", *World Bank Research Observer*.

Page, J. M. (1990), "The Pursuit of Industrial Growth: Policy Initiatives and Economic Consequences", Scott, M.FG., Lal, D. (eds.), *Public Policy and Economic Development: Essays in Honor of Ian Little*, Clarendon Press.

Polanyi, K. (1944), *The Great Transformation*, Boston: Beacon Press.

Porter, M (1990), *The Competitive Advantage of Nations*, N.Y.: The Free Press.

Reynolds, L. (1982), *Economic Growth of the Third World*, New Haven: Yale University Press.

Rodrik, D. (1997), "The 'paradoxes' of the successful state", *European Economic Review*, 41(3–5): 411–442.

Rodrik, D. (1998), "King Kong Meets Godzilla: The World Bank and The East Asian Miracle", *Policy Essay No.11, Overseas Development Council*.

Rodrik, D. (1998), "The Global Fix: A plan to save the world economy", *The New Republic*.

Romer, P. (1986), "Increasing returns and long-run growth", *Journal of Political Economy*, pp.1002–10138.

Romer, P. (1990), "Endogenous technical change", *Journal of Political Economy* 98: S72–102.

Romer, P. (1993), "Two strategies for economic development: Using ideas", Proceeding of the World Bank Annual Conference on Development Economics, pp.63–91.

Romer, P. (1994), "New goods and old goods, and the welfare costs of trade restrictions", *Journal of Development Economics*.

Rothwell, R. (1985), "Evaluation of Innovation Policy", Sweeney, G. (ed.), *Innovation Policies: An International Perspective*, New York: St. Martin's Press, pp.167–188.

Rueschemeyer, D., Evans, P. (1985), "The State and Economic Transformation: Towards an Analysis of the Conditions Underlying Effective Intervention", Evans, P., Rueschemeyer, D., Skocpol, T. (eds.), *Bringing the State Back In*, Cambridge University Press.

Rueschemeyer, D., Putterman, L. (1992), "Synergy or rivalry?", Putterman, L., Rueschemeyer, D. (eds.), *State and Market in Development*, Boulder, CO: Lynne Rienner, pp.243–262.

Sachs, J.D., Warner, A. (1995a), "Economic Reform and the Process of Global Integration", *BPEA*, 1: 1–95.

Sachs, J.D., Warner, A.M. (1997), "Fundamental sources of long-run growth", *American Economic Review* 87(2): 184–188.

Sachs, J. (1998), "Global Capitalism: Making it Work", *The Economist.*

Scott, M. F.G. (1989), *A New View of Economic Growth*, Oxford: Clarendon Press.

Shapiro, H., Taylor, L. (1990), "The State and Industrial Strategy", *World Development* 18(6): 861–878.

Stern, N. (1991), "The determinants of growth", *Economic Journal* 101(404): 122–133.

Stiglitz, J.E. (1990), *The Economic Role of the State*, Oxford: Basil Blackwell.

Teece, D. (1986), "Profiting from Technological Innovation: Implications for Integration, Collaboration, Licensing and Public Policy", *Research Policy* 15: 285–305.

UNCTAD (1997), *World Investment Report 1997: Transnational Corporations, Market Structure and Competition Policy*, New York, United Nations.

UNCTAD (1998), *World Investment Report 1998: Trends and Determinants*, New York, United Nations.

UNIDO (1996), *Industrial Development Global Report 1996*, Oxford University Press.

UNIDO (1999), *International Yearbook of Industrial Statistics 1999.*

Vernon, R. (1966), "International investment and international trade in the product cycle", *Quarterly Journal of Economics* 80: 190–207.

Vernon, R. (1989), "Technological development: the historical experience", Washington, D.C., *World Bank, Economic Development Institute, Seminar paper* No.39.

Weiss, L., Hobson, J. (1995), *States and Economic Development: A Comparative Historical Analysis*, Cambridge: Massachusetts' Polity Press.

Williamson, O.E. (1985), *The Economic Institutions of Capitalism*, NY: Free Press.

Williamson, O.E., Master, S. (eds.) (1995), *Transaction Cost Economics Vol. 1: Theory and Concepts*, E. Elgar.

Wolf, C. (1988), *Markets or Governments: Choosing between Imperfect Alternatives*, MIT Press.

World Bank (1987), *Barriers to Adjustment and Growth in the World Economy/ Industrialization and Foreign Trade*, NY: Oxford University Press.

World Bank(1995), *Bureaucrats in Business*, NY: Oxford University Press.

World Bank (1996), *From Plan to Market*, Oxford University Press.

World Bank(1997), *The State in a Changing World*, NY: Oxford University Press.

World Bank(1998), *World Development Report 1998: Knowledge for Development*, Oxford University Press.

World Bank (1998), *Global Economic Prospects and the Developing Countries: Beyond Financial Crisis,* World Bank Publication.

World Bank (1999), *World Development Report 1999/2000: Entering the 21st Century*, Oxford University Press.

World Economic Forum (1997), *World Competitiveness Report*, Geneva.

WTO (1998), *WTO Focus*, No.28, March 1998.

Young L.H. (1998), "A mixed picture for the world outlook", *Electronic Business*, Vol.24, Iss.1.

East Asia Development: General

Adams, F.G., James, W.E. (eds.) (1999), *Public Policies in East Asian Development: Facing New Challenges*, Westport, Conn.: Praeger.

Akamatsu, K. (1962), " A Historical Pattern of Economic Growth in Developing Countries", *The Developing Economies*, Vol.1.

Amsden, A.H. (1991), "Diffusion of Development of Development: The Late-Industrializing Model and Greater East Asia", *American Economic Review*, Papers and Proceedings 81(2): 282–286.

Amsden, A.H. (1992), "A theory of government intervention in late industrialization", Putterman, L., Ruschmeyer, D. (eds.), *The State and the Market in Development*, Boulder: Lynne Rienner Publishers, pp. 53–84.

Amsden, A.H. (1994), "Why isn't the whole world experimenting with the East Asian model to develop? Review of The East Asian Miracle", *World Development* 22(4): 627–634.

Amsden, A.H. (2001), *The Rise of "The Rest": Challenges to the West from Late-Industrializating Economies*, Oxford; New York: Oxford University Press.

Aoki, M., Murdock, K., Okuno-Fujiwara, M. (1995), "Beyond the East Asian Miracle: Introducing the Market Enhancing View", *World Bank EDI Working Paper*.

Aoki, M., Kim, H.K., Fujiwara, M.O. (1997), *The Role of Government in East Asian Economic Development — Comparative Institutional Analysis*, Clarendon Press, Oxford.

Appelbaum, R.P., Henderson, J. (eds.) (1992), *States and Development in the Asian Pacific Rim*, Newbury Park, California: Sage Publications.

Arndt, H. (1993), "Saving, investment and growth: Recent Asian experience", Arndt, H. (ed.), *50 Years of Development Studies*, Canberra: Australian National University, pp.241–250.

Arrighi, G. (1994), "The Rise of East Asia: World-System and Regional Aspects", Paper prepared for the conference "L'economia mondiale in transformazione", Rome, October 6–8.

Asian Development Bank (1997), *Emerging Asia: Changes and Challenges*, Asian Development Bank.

Balassa, B. (1988), "The Lessons of East Asian Development: An Overview", *Economic Development and Cultural Change* 36 (3rd supplement): S273–S290.

Behrman, J.R., Schneider, R. (1994), "An International Perspective on Schooling Investments in the last Quarter Century in Some Fast-Growing East and Southeast Asian Countries", *Asian Development Review* 12(2): 1–50.

Bell, M., Pavitt, K. (1993), "Technological accumulation and industrial growth: Contrasts between developed and developing countries", *Industrial and Corporate Change* 2(2): 157–210.

Bernard, M., Ravenhill, J. (1995), "Beyond Product Cycles and Flying Geese", *World Politics*, 46, January.

Blomqvist, H.C. (1996), "Critical Issues in Asian Development: Theories, Experiences and Policies", *Economic Journal: The Journal of the Royal Economic Society* 106(438): 1482.

Bosworth, B., Collin, S. (1996), "Economic Growth in East Asia: Accumulation vs. Assimilation", *Brookings Papers on Economic Activity* 2: 135–204.

Bosworth, B.P., Collins, S.M., Chen, Y.C. (1996), "Accounting for Differences in Economic Growth", Kohsaka, A., Ohno, K. (eds.), *Structural Adjustment and Economic Reform: East Asia, Latin America, and Central and Eastern Europe*, Tokyo: Institute of Developing Economies.

Bridsall, N., Ross, D., Sabot, R. (1995), "Inequality and Growth Reconsidered: Lessons from East Asia", *The World Bank Economic Review* 9(3): 477–508.

Bruno, M. (1994), "Development Issues in a Changing World: New Lessons, Old Debates, Open Questions", *Keynote address of the World Bank Annual Conference on Development Economic 1994*.

Campos, J.E., Root, H.L. (1996), *The Key to the Asian Miracle*, The Brookings Institution.

Castells, M. (1992), "Four Asian Tigers with a Dragon Head", Appelbaum, R.P., Henderson, J. (eds.), *State and Development in the Asian-Pacific Rim*, Newbury Park: Sage.

Chen, B.L. (1994), "Limited Diffusion of Technology, Learning Incentives and a Low Level of Industrialization", *Journal of Economic Development* 19, 2.

Chen, B.L., Shimomura, K. (1998), "Self-fulfilling expectations and economic growth: A Model of technology adoption and industrialization", *International Economic Review* 39(1).

Chen, E.K.Y. (1979), *Hyper-growth in Asian Economies: A comparative study of Hong Kong, Japan, Korea, Singapore and Taiwan*, London: Macmillan.

Chen, E.K.Y. (1988), "The economics and non-economics of Asia's four little dragons", Supplement to the *Gazette*, Vol.35(1), March 21, University of Hong Kong, Hong Kong.

Chen, E.K.Y. (1997), "Dynamic Asian economies: Retrospect and prospect", Chan, H.C. (ed.), *The New Asia-Pacific Order*, Singapore: Institute of Southeast Asian Studies.

Chen, T.J., Tang, D.P. (1990), "Export performance and productivity growth", *Economic Development and Cultural Change* 38(3): 577–585.

Chiu, S., Ho, K.C., Lui, T.L. (1997), *City-States in the Global Economy*, Boulder: Westview Press.

Chu, Y.H. (1989), "State Structures and Economic Adjustment in the East Asian NIEs", *International Organisation* 43(4): 647–672.

Coe, D.T., McDermott, C.J. (1997), "Does the gap model work in Asia?", *International Monetary Fund Staff Papers*, 44(1): 59–80.

Collins, S. M., Bosworth, B.P. (1996), "Economic Growth in East Asia: Accumulation versus Assimilation", *Brookings Papers on Economic Activity*, 2: 135–203.

Cumings, B. (1987), "The Origins and Development of the Northeast Asian Political Economy: Industrial Sectors, Product Cycles and Political Consequences", Deyo, F.C. (ed.), *The Political Economy of the New Asian Industrialization*, Ithaca: Cornell University Press.

Dahlman, C.J., Ross-Larson, B., Westphal, L.E. (1987), "Managing technological development: Lessons from newly industrialising countries", *World Development* 15(6): 759–775.

Dahlman, C. J. (1994), "Technology Strategy in East Asian Developing Economies", *Journal of Asian Economics* 5 (Winter): 541–572.

Daly, M.T., Logan, M.I. (1998), *Reconstructing Asia*, RMIT University Press.

Denison, E.F., Chung, W.K. (1976a), "Economic Growth and Its Sources", Patrick, H., Rosovsky, H. (ed.), *Asia's New Giant: How the Japanese Economy Works*, Washington: Brookings.

Deyo, F.C. (1989), *Beneath the Miracle: Labour Subordination in the New Asian Industrialism*, Berkeley: University of California Press.

Dollar, D. (1992), "Outward-oriented Developing Economies Do Grow Rapidly", *Economic Development and Cultural Change*, Vol.40, Nos.1–2.

Drysdale, P., Huang, Y. (1995), "Technological catch-up and productivity growth in East Asia", The Australian National University, mimeo.

Easterly, W. (1995), "Explaining Miracles: Growth Regressions Meet the Gang of Four", Ito, T., Krueger, A. (eds.), *Growth Theories in Light of the East Asian Experience*, University of Chicago Press.

Economist (1996), "Economic Growth: The Poor and the Rich", *The Economist*, May 25, 1996.

Economist (1998), "A Survey of East Asian Economies", *The Economist*, March 7, 1998.

Edward, J.L. (1996), "Some Missing Elements", *Brookings Papers on Economic Activity* 2: 351–355.

Ernst, D., O'Connor, D. (1989), *Technology and Global Competition: The Challenge for Newly Industrialising Economies*, Paris: OECD Development Centre.

Ernst, D., Ganiatsos, T., Mytelka, L. (eds.) (1998), *Technological Capabilities and Export Success in Asia*, Routledge.

Fischer, S. (1996), "Lessons from East Asia and the Pacific Rim", *Brookings Papers on Economic Activity*, 2: 345–350.

Fishlow, A., Gwin, C., Haggard, S., Rodrik, D., Wade, R. (1996), "Miracle or Design? Lessons From the East Asian Experience", *Policy Essay No.11, Overseas Development Council*.

Fransman, M., King, K. (ed.), (1984), *Technological Capability in the Third World*, London: Macmillan.

Galenson, W. (ed.) (1985), *Foreign Trade and Investment: Economic Development in the Newly Industrializing Asian Countries*, University of Wisconsin Press.

Gereffi, G. (1990), "Paths of Industrialization: An Overview", Gereffi, G., Wyman, D.L (eds.), *Paths of Industrialization in Latin America and East Asia*, Princeton: Princeton University Press.

Gereffi, G. (1992), "New Realities of Industrial Development in East Asia and Latin America: Global, Regional and National Trends", Appelbaum, R., Henderson, J (eds.), *State and Development in the Asian-Pacific Rim*, Newbury Park: Sage.

Gereffi, G., Korzeniewicz, M. (1990), "Commodity chains and footwear exports in the semiperiphery", Martin, W.G. (ed.), *Semiperipheral States in the World Economy*, Westport: Greenwood Press.

Goh, K.S. (1972), *The Economics of Modernization and other Essays*, Singapore: Asia Pacific Press.

Goh, K.S. (1983), "Public Administration and Economic Development in Less Developed Countries", Harry G. Johnson Memorial Lecture No.4. London: Trade Policy Research Centre.

Goh, K.S. (1995), *Wealth of East Asian Nations*, Low, L. (ed.), Federal Publications.

Goldstein, S.M. (ed.) (1991), *Mini Dragons: Fragile Economic Miracles in the Pacific*, Boulder: Westview Press.

Greenwood, J. (2000), "The real issues in Asia", *Cato Journal* 20(2): 141–157.

Griffith-Jones, S., Kimmis, J. (1999), "East Asia: What Happened to the Development Miracle?", IDS Bulletin Vol. 30, No.1.

Haggard, S. (1990), *Pathways from the Periphery: The Politics of Growth in the Newly Industrializing Countries*, Ithaca: Cornell University Press.

Hanna, N., Boyson, S., Gunaratne, S. (1996), "The East Asian Miracle and Information Technology: Strategic Management of Technological Learning", World Bank Discussion Paper No.326.

Hara, Y. (1996), *How Should Asian Economic Dynamism be Interpreted?* (mimeo.).

Harbet, T. (1998), "Toughing it out", *Electronic Business*, Vol.24, Iss.5.

Harris, N. (1992), "States, Economic Development and the Asian Pacific Rim", Appelbaum, R.P., Henderson J. (eds.), *State and Development in the Asian-Pacific Rim*, Newbury Park: Sage.

Henderson, J. (1989), *The Globalization of High Technology Production*, London: Routledge.

Henke, H., Boxill, I. (eds.) (1999), *The End of the "Asian model"?* New York: Walter de Gruyter.

Hirata, A., Hiroshi, O. (1990), "Transformation of Industrial Structure and the Role of Trade and Investment", Fukuchi, T., Kagami, M. (eds.), *Perspectives on the Pacific Basin Economy*, Tokyo: Institute of Developing Economies.

Hobday, M. (1994), "Export-led Technology Development", *Development and Change*, Vol.25.

Hobday, M. (1995) "East Asian Latecomer firms: Learning the technology of electronics", *World Development* 23(7): 1171–1193.

Hobday, M. (1995), *Innovation in East Asia: The Challenge to Japan*, Edward Elgar.

Hughes, H. (ed.) (1988), *Achieving Industrialization in East Asia*, Cambridge: Cambridge University Press.

Hsieh, C.T. (1997), "What Explains the Industrial Revolution in East Asia? Evidence from Factor Markets", Unpublished paper, Department of Economics, University of California, Berkeley.

Huang, X. (ed.) (2001), *The Political and Economic Transition in East Asia: Strong Market, Weakening State.* Richmond, Surrey: Curzon.

Ichimura, S.I. (ed.) (1988), *Challenge of Asian Developing Countries: Issues and Analyses*, Tokyo: Asian Productivity Organisation.

Ito, T., Krueger, A. (1995), *Growth Theories in Light of the East Asian Experience*, Chicago: University of Chicago Press and National Bureau of Economic Research.

Ito, T. (1996), "Japan and the Asian economies: A 'miracle' in transition", *Brookings Papers on Economic Activity*, No.2: 205–272.

Ito, T., Krueger, A.O. (eds.) (2000), *The Role of Foreign Direct Investment in East Asian Economic Development*, Chicago: University of Chicago Press.

Johnson, C. (1987), "Political Institutions and Economic Performance: The Government-Business Relationship in Japan, South Korea and Taiwan", Deyo, F.C. (ed.), *The Political Economy of the New Asian Industrialization*, Ithaca: Cornell University Press.

Jwa, S.H. (2000), "A new-institutional economics perspective of corporate governance reform in East Asia", *Seoul Journal of Economics* 13(3): 215–223.

Kawai, K. (1995), "International comparison of economic growth", Urata, H. (ed.), *Trade Liberalization and Economic Development*, Institute of Developing Economies, Tokyo (in Japanese).

Kawai, M. (1998), "Evolving Patterns of Asia-Pacific Financial Flows", presented at the PAFTAD conference on Asia Pacific Financial Liberalization and Reform, May, Chiangmai, Thailand.

Khan, H. (forthcoming), *Innovation and Growth in East Asia*, London: Macmillan.

Kim, J.I, Lau, L. (1994), "The Sources of Economic Growth of the East Asian Newly Industrialized Countries", *Journal of Japanese and International Economics* 8(3): 235–271.

Kim, J., Lau, L.(1996), "The sources of Asian Pacific economic growth", *Canadian Journal of Economics* 29(2): S448–S454.

Kim, S.S. (ed.) (2000), *East Asia and Globalization*, Lanham: Rowman & Littlefield.

Kitamura,K.,Tanaka, T. (eds.) (1997), *Examining Asia's Tigers*, Tokyo: Institute of Developing Economies.

Klitgaard, R. (1991), "Adjusting to Reality: Beyond "State versus Market"", *Economic Development*, Institute for Contemporary Studies Press.

Knowles, J.C., Pernia, E.M., Racelis, M. (1999), "Social Consequences of the Financial Crisis in Asia", Manila: ADB Economics Staff Paper No.60.

Krueger, A. (1995), "East Asian Experience and Endogenous Growth Theory", Ito, T., Krueger, A. (eds.), *Growth Theories in Light of the East Asian Experience*, Chicago: University of Chicago Press.

Krugman, P. (1994), "The Myth of Asia Miracle", *Foreign Affairs* 73(6): 62–78.

Krugman, P. (1999), *The Return of Depression Economics*, New York: W.W. Norton.

Kunio, Y. (2000), *Asia per Capita: Why National Incomes Differ in East Asia*, London: Curzon Press.

Kwon, J. (1994), "The East Asia Challenge to Neoclassical Orthodoxy", *World Development* 22(4): 635–644.

Lall, S. (1993b), "Policies for building technological capabilities: Lessons from Asian experience", *Asian Development Review* 11(2): 72–103.

Lall, S. (1994a), "'The East Asian Miracle' study: Does the bell toll for industrial strategy?", *World Development* 22(4): 645–654.

Lall, S. (1995), *Science and Technology in the New Global Environment: Implications for Developing Countries*, United Nations.

Lall, S. (1996), *Learning from the Asian Tigers in Technology and Industrial Policy*, London: Macmillan.

Lall, S. (1997), "Coping with New Technologies in Emerging Asia", Background paper for *Emerging Asia: Changes and Challenges*, Asian Development Bank, Manila.

Lall, S. (1997), "Technological Change and Industrialization in the Asia NIEs: Achievements and Challenges" (mimeo).

Lall, S. (1998), "Exports of manufactures by developing countries: Emerging patterns of trade and location", *Oxford Review of Economic Policy* 14(2).

Lau, M.L., Wan, H.Y. (1991), "The theory of growth and technology transfer: Experience from the East Asian Economies, *Seoul Journal of Economics* 4: 109–122.

Leipziger, D.M. (1997), *Lessons from East Asia*, University of Michigan Press.

Levy, B. (1990), "Transaction Costs, the Size of Firms and Industrial Policy", *Journal of Development Economics* 34: 151–178.

Lim, Y. (1992), "Export-Led Industrialisation: The Key Policy for Successful Development?, Global Issues and Policy Analysis Branch, UNIDO", Paper prepared for Wilton Park Conference, 14–18 Dec., London, UK.

Lindauer, D., Roemer, M. (1994), *Asia and Africa: Legacies and Opportunities in Development*, San Francisco: Institute for Contemporary Studies.

Liu, L., Noland, M., Robinson, S., Wang, Z. (1998), *Asian Competitive Devaluations*, Institute for International Economics.

Lucas, R.E. JR(1993), "Making a miracle", *Econometrica* 61(2): 251–272.

MacIntyre, A. (ed.) (1994), *Business and Government in Industrializing Asia*, Allen & Unwin.

MacLean, B.K. (1999), "The rise and fall of the 'Crony Capitalism' hypothesis: Causes and Consequences", Working Paper, Department of Economics, Laurentian University, Canada.

Manning, C., Pang, E.F.(1990), "Labour market trends and structures in ASEAN and the East Asian NICs", *Asia-Pacific Economic Literature* 4(2): 59–81.

Masuyama, S., Vandenbrink, D. and Chia S.Y. (eds.) (2001), *Industrial Restructuring in East Asia: Towards the 21st Century*, Singapore: Institute of Southeast Asia Studies; Tokyo: Nomura Research Institute.

Mathews, J.A. (1999), *The Challenge in 1999: Rebuilding institutions in Asia for the 21st Century*, Sydney: The Rench Institute for Asia and the Pacific, University of Sydney.

Matsuyama, K. (1991), "Increasing return, industrialization, and indeterminacy of equilibrium", *Quarterly Journal of Economics* 106: 617–650.

Mizaki, M. (1995), "Growth and Structural Change in Asian Countries", *Asian Economic Journal* 9: 113–136.

Mody, A. (1997), *Infrastructure Strategies in East Asia: The Untold Story*, World Bank.

Mody, A. (1999), "Industrial Policy after the East Asian Crisis — From "Outward Orientation" to New Internal Capabilities?", Policy Research Working Paper, World Bank.

Montes, M.F., Quigley, K.F.F., Weatherbee, D.E. (1997), "Growing Pains: ASEAN's Economic and Political Challanges", *http: //www.asiasociety.org/publications/asean_miracle.html*.

National Science Foundation (1995), *Asia's New High Tech Competitors*, NSF 95–309.

Nelson, R., Pack, H. (1995), "The Asian Growth Miracle and Modern Growth Theory", Unpublished paper, Columbia University and University of Pennsylvania.

Odagiri, H. (1986), "Industrial Policy in Theory and Reality", Jong, H.D., Shepherd, W.G. (eds.), *Mainstreams in Industrial Organization*, Dordrecht: Martinus Nijhoff, pp.387–412.

Oshima, H.T. (1987), *Economic Growth in Monsoon Asia*, Tokyo: University of Tokyo Press.

Ozawa, T. (1999), "The role of government in East Asian economic development: comparative institutional analysis", *The Journal of Asian Studies* 58(2): 453–454.

Page, J. (1994), "The East Asian Miracle: Four Lessons for Development Policy", Fischer S., Rotemberg, J.J. (eds.), NBER *Macroeconomics Annual 1994*, Cambridge, Mass.: MIT Press.

Park, H., Westphal, L.E. (1986), "Industrial Strategy and Technological Change: Theory vs. Reality", *Journal of Development Economics* 22(1): 87–128.

Park, J. (1999), *The Role of Intangible Capital in East Asian Economic Growth*, Ann Arbor, Mich.: University Microfilms International.

Park, Y.C., Lee, J.W. (1998), "Exports, Accumulation and Growth in East Asia", Park, Y.C. (ed.), *Financial Liberalization and Opening in East Asia: Issues and Policy Challenges*, Korea Institute of Finance.

Park, S.R., Kwon, J.K. (1995), "Rapid economic growth with increasing returns to scale and little or no productivity growth", *Review of Economics and Statistics* 77(2): 332–351.

Patterson, A. (1998), "Tigers no more", *Electronic Business*, Vol.24, Iss.1.

Pauw, D.S, Fei, J.C.H. (1973), *The Transition in Open Dualistic Economies: Theory and Southeast Asian Experience*, New Haven: Yale University Press.

Peng, D. (2000), "The changing nature of East Asia as an economic region", *Pacific Affairs* 73(2): 171–191.

Perkins, D. (1994), "There Are at Least Three Models of East Asian Development", *World Development* 22(4): 655–661.

Perkins, D., Roemer, M. (1994), "Differing Endowments and Historical Legacies", Lindauer, D., Roemer, M. (eds.), *Asia and Africa: Legacies and Opportunities in Development*, San Francisco: Institute for Contemporary Studies.

Pezzey, J. (1989), "Economic Analysis of Sustainable Growth and Sustainable Development", Working Paper No. 15. Environment Department, World Bank.

Przeworski, A., Limongi, F. (1993), "Political regimes and economic growth", *Journal of Economic Perspectives* 7(3): 51–69.

Purcell, D.L., Anderson, J.R. (1996), "Economic Growth Revisited", *Industrial and Corporate Change* 3(1): 65–110.

Pyo, H.K.(1996), "The East Asian Miracle or Myth: A Reconciliation between the Conventional View and the Contrarian Proposition", *Economic Bulletin*, March 1996, pp.2–23.

Radelet, S., Sachs, J., Lee, J.W. (1996), "Economic Growth in Asia", Background paper for *Emerging Asia: Changes and Challenges*, Manila: Asian Development Bank.

Ranis, G., (1995), "Another Look at the East Asian Miracle", *The World Bank Economic Review* 9(3): 509–534.

Rao, B.V.V. (2001), *East Asian Economies: The Miracle, a Crisis and the Future*, Singapore: McGraw-Hill.

Ravich, S.F. (2000), *Marketization and Democracy: East Asian Experiences.* New York: Cambridge University Press.

Rhee, Y.W. (1989), "Managing Entry into International Markets: Lessons from the East Asian Experience", Industry and Energy Department Working Paper, World Bank.

Richter, F.J. (2000), *The East Asian Development Model: Economic Growth, Institutional Failure and the Aftermath of the Crisis*, New York: St. Martin's Press.

Robison, R. *et al.* (eds.) (2000), *Politics and Markets in the Wake of the Asian Crisis*, New York: Routledge.

Rodrigo, G.C. (2000), "East Asia's growth: Technology or accumulation?" *Contemporary Economic Policy* 18(2): 215–227.

Rodrik, D. (1998), "King Kong Meets Godzilla: The World Bank and The East Asian Miracle", Policy Essay No.11, Overseas Development Council.

Rodrick, D. (1994), "Trade Straetgy, Investment and Exports: Another Look at East Asia", Working Paper 5339, Cambridge, Mass.: National Bureau of Economic Research.

Roemer, M. (1994), "Industrial Strategies: Outward Bound", Lindauer, D., Roemer, M (eds.), *Asia and Africa: Legacies and Opportunities in Development*, San Francisco: Institute for Contemporary Studies.

Root, H. (1996), *Small Countries, Big Lessons: Governance and the Rise of East Asia*, Oxford University Press.

Rowen, H.S. (1998), *Behind East Asian Growth — The Political and Social Foundations of Prosperity*, Routledge.

Rozman, G. (1992), "The Confucian Faces of Capitalism", Borthwick, M. (ed.), *Pacific Century*, Boulder: Westview Press.

Sarel, M. (1997), *Growth in East Asia: What We Can and What We Cannot Infer*, IMF.

Scully, M.T., Viksnins, G.J. (1987), *Financing East Asia's Success: Comparative Financial Development in Eight Asian Countries*, Macmillan.

Sengupta, J.K. (1993), "Growth in NICs in Asia: Some tests of new growth theory", *Journal of Development Studies* 29(2): 342–357.

Sheridan, K. (ed.) (1998), *Emerging Economic Systems in Asia: A Political and Economic Survey*, St. Leonards, N.S.W.: Allen & Unwin.

Shin, J.S. (1996) *The Economics of the Latecomers: Catching-up, technology transfer and institutions in Germany, Japan and South Korea*, Routledge.

Singh, A. (1996), "Savings, Investment and the Corporation in the East Asian Miracle", Unpublished paper, United Nations Conference on Trade and Development.

Smith, H. (1995), "Industry Policy in East Asia", *Asian-Pacific Economic Literature* 9(1): 17–39.

So, A.Y., Chiu, S.W.K. (1995), *East Asia and World Economy*, Newbury Park: Sage.

Sowinski, L. (1999), "Asia: Prospects for Japan, South Korea & Taiwan", *World Trade* 12(6): 28–32.

Stiglitz, J.E. (1996), "Some Lessons From the East Asian Miracle", *The World Bank Research Observer* 11(2): 151–177.

Stiglitz, J.E. , Uy, M. (1996), "Financial Markets, Public Policy and the East Asian Miracle", *The World Bank Research Observer* 11(2): 249–276.

Sung, G.H. (1997), *The Political Economy of Industrial Policy in East Asia*, Edward Elgar Publishing.

Takahashi, K. (ed.) (1998), *Asia's Development Experiences: How Internationally Competitive National Manufacturing Firms Have Developed in Asia*, Tokyo: FASID.

Takatoshi, I., Krueger, A.O. (eds.) (1995), *Growth Theories in Light of the East Asian Experience*, Chicago: The University of Chicago Press.

Terry, E. (1996), "An East Asian Paradigm?", *Atlantic Economic Journal* 24(3): 183–198.

Thomas, V., Wang Y. (1993), "Government Policy and Productivity Growth: Is East Asia an Exception?", World Bank Working Paper.

Thomas, V., Wang, Y. (1996), "Distortions, interventions and productivity growth: Is East Asia different?", *Economic Development & Cultural Change* 44(2): 265–288.

Tipton, F.B. (1998), *The Rise of Asia: Economics, Society and Politics in Contemporary Asia*, Basingstoke: Macmillan Press; Honolulu: University of Hawaii Press.

Toh, M.H., Tiew C.S. (1999), "A neoclassical analysis of the ASEAN and East Asian growth experience", *ASEAN Economic Bulletin* 16(2): 149–165.

Turner, L., McMullen, N. (eds.) (1982), *The Newly Industrialising Countries, Trade and Adjustment*, London: Unwin.

Tzannatos, Z. , Johnes, G. (1996), "Training and Skills Development in the East Asian NIC's: A Comparison and Lessons for Developing Countries", PSP Discussion Paper Series, Washington, D.C., World Bank.

UNCTAD (1996), " Rethinking Development Strategies: Some Lessons From East Asian Experience", Trade and Development Report 1996.

Vogel, E.F. (1991), *The Four Little Dragons*, Harvard University Press.

Wade, R. (1989), "What Can Economies Learn from East Asian Success?", *Annals of the American Academy of Political Science* 505: 68–79.

Wade, R. (1990), *Governing the Market: Economic Theory and the Role of Government in East Asian Industralization*, Princeton, NJ: Princeton University Press.

Wade, R. (1996), "Japan, the World Bank, and the Art of Paradigm Maintenance: The East Asian Miracle in Political Perspective", *New Left Review* 217: 3–36.

Wade, R. (1996), "Selective Industrial Policies in East Asia: Is The East Asian Miracle Right?", Policy Essay No.11, Overseas Development Council.

Walton, M. (1997), "The Maturation of the East Asian Miracle", *Finance & Development*, World Bank.

Weder, B. (1999), *Model, Myth, or Miracle? Reassessing the role of governments in the East Asian experience*, Tokyo: United Nations University Press.

Western, D.L. (2000), *East Asia: Growth, Crisis and Recovery*, Singapore: World Scientific.

White, G. (1988), *Developmental Studies in East Asia*, St. Martin's Press, New York.

World Bank (1993a), *The East Asian Miracle: Economic Growth and Public Policy*, NY: Oxford University Press.

World Bank (1993b), *Sustaining Rapid Development in East Asia and the Pacific*, University Press.

World Bank (1994), *East Asia's Trade and Investment: Regional and Global Gains from Liberalization*, World Bank Publication.

World Bank (2000). *East Asia: Recovery and Beyond*, Washington, DC: World Bank.

Wu, R.I., Chee, Y.P. (eds.) (1998), *Business, markets and government in the Asia Pacific*, NY: Routledge.

Yamazawa I., Taniguchi, K., Hirata, A. (1983), "Trade and Industrial Adjustment in Pacific Asian Countries", *Developing Economies*, Vol.21, No.4.

Yoshihara, K. (1988), *The Rise of Esratz Capitalism in Southeast Asia*, New York: Oxford University Press.

Young, A. (1992), "A Tale of Two Cities: Factor Accumulation and Technical Change in Hong Kong and Singapore", *NBER Macroeconomic Annual 1992*, Cambridge, Mass.: MIT Press.

Young, A. (1994), "Lessons from the East Asian NICs: A Contrarian View", *European Economic Review* 38: 964–973.

Young, A. (1995), "The tyranny of numbers: Confronting the statistical realities of the East Asian growth experience", *Quarterly Journal of Economics* 110: 641–680.

Zhang, K.H. (2001), "Does foreign direct investment promote economic growth? Evidence from East Asia and Latin America", *Contemporary Economic Policy* 19(2): 175–185.

East Asia Development: Asian Financial Crisis

Akyuz, Y. (1998), "The East Asian Financial Crisis: Back to the Future?", *http: //www.unctad.org/en/pressref/prasia98.html.*

Asian Development Bank (1998), *Asia: Responding to Crisis*, ADB Institute.

Asian Development Bank (1999), *Asian Development Outlook 1999: The Financial Crisis in Asia*, ADB Institute.

Bello, W., Rosenfeld, S. (1990), *Dragons In Distress: Asia's Miracle Economies In Crisis*, San Francisco: A Food First Book.

Bergere, M.C. (1999), The East Asian crisis in historical perspective", EAI Working Paper No. 20, Singapore: East Asian Institute.

Betcherman, G., Islam, R. (eds.) (2000), *East Asian Labor Markets and the Economic Crisis: Impacts, Responses, and Lessons*, Washington, DC: World Bank.

Bhagwati, J. (1998), "The Capital Myth", *Foreign Affairs,* Vol. 77, No.3, May/June.

Camdessus, M. (1999), "Sustaining Asia's Recovery from Crisis", Remarks at the 34th South East Asian Central Banks Governors' Conference, Seoul, Korea.

Claessens, S., Djankov, S., Xu, L.C. (2000), Corporate performance in the East Asian financial crisis, *The World Bank Research Observer* 15(1): 23–46.

Corden, W.M. (1998), "The Asian Crisis: Is There a Way Out? Are the IMF Prescriptions Right", *The Asian Crisis: Is There a Way Out*, Singapore: Institute of Southeast Asian Studies.

Corsetti, G., Pesenti, P., Roubini, N. (1998), "Paper tigers? A model of the Asian. Crisis", Working Paper, Nouriel Roubini Homepage.

Crafts, N. (1999), "East Asian growth before and after the crisis", *International Monetary Fund Staff Papers* 46(2): 139–166.

Crone, D. (1999), "Crisis, half reform and consequences for East Asia", paper presented at FASID Forum on Socio-Economic changes and political trends in East Asia, Oct.20–21, 1999.

Daly, M.T., Logan, M.I. (1998), *Reconstructing Asia*, RMIT University Press.

Economist (1998a), "Why did Asia crash?", *The Economist*, January 10–16, 1998.

Economist (1998b), "A Survey of East Asian Economies", *The Economist*, March 7, 1998.

Feldstein, M. (1998), "Refocusing the IMF", *Foreign Affairs*, Vol. 77, No.2, March/April 1998.

Fischer, S. (1998), "The Asian Crisis and Implications for Other Economies", Speech delivered at the Brazilian and World Economic Outlook Seminar, June 19, 1998.

Fischer, S. (1999), "The Asian Crisis: The Return of Growth", June 17, 1999.

Furman, J., Stiglitz, J.E. (1998), "Economic Crises: Evidence and Insights from East Asia", *Brookings Papers on Economic Activity* 2: 1–135.

Garnaut, R., McLeod, R. (1998), *East Asia in Crisis: From Being a Miracle to Needing One*, Routledge.

Goldstein, M. (1998), "The Asian Financial Crisis: Causes, Cures and Systemic Implications", *Policy Analyses in International Economics 55*, Institute for International Economics.

Griffith-Jones, S., Cailloux, J., Pfaffenzeller S. (1998), "The East Asian Financial Crisis: A Reflection on its Causes, Consequences and Policy Implications", IDS Discussion Paper 367.

Griffith-Jones, S., Kimmis, J. (1999), "East Asia: What Happened to the Development Miracle?", *IDS Bulletin* Vol. 30, No.1.

Guillermo, P.E., Lederman, D. (1998), *Financial Vulnerability, Spillover Effects and Contagion: Lessons from the Asian Crisis for Latin America*, World Bank.

Harrison, S., Prestowithz, C., Jr. (eds.) (1998), *Asia after the "Miracle"*, Washington D.C.: Economic Strategic Institute.

Hellman, T., Murdock, K., Stiglitz, J. (1997), "Financial Restraint: Towards a New Paradigm", Aoki, M., Fujiwara, M.O., Kim, H. (eds.), *The Role of Government in East Asian Economic Development: Comparative Institutional Analysis*, New York: Oxford University Press.

Henderson, C. (1998), *Asia Falling? Making sense of the Asian currency crisis and its aftermath*, Singapore: McGraw Hill.

IMF, "The IMF's Response to the Asian Crisis – Factsheet", September 1, 1998.

IMF (1999), "Outlook: International Financial Contagion", May 1999.

Johnson, C. (1999), "Let's revisit Asia's 'Crony Capitalism'", *Los Angeles Times*, June 25, 1999.

Katz, S.S. (1999), "The Asian crisis, the IMF and the critics", *Eastern Economic Journal* 25(4): 421–439.

Kawai, M. (1998), "Evolving Patterns of Asia-Pacific Financial Flows", presented at the PAFTAD conference on Asia Pacific Financial Liberalization and Reform, May, Chiangmai, Thailand.

Khan, M., Reinhart, C. (1995), "Capital flows in APEC region", IMF Occasional Paper No.122.

Khan, H. (1999), "Corporate governance of family businesses in Asia", ADB Institute Working Paper No.3, August 1999.

Khan, H. (forthcoming), *Innovation and Growth in East Asia*, London: Macmillan.

Knowles, J.C., Pernia, E.M., Racelis, M. (1999), "Social Consequences of the Financial Crisis in Asia", Manila: ADB Economics Staff Paper No.60.

Krugman, P. (1998), "Will Asia Bounce Back?", *http: //web.mit.edu/krugman/www/suisse.html*.

Kumar, R., Debroy, B. (1999), "The Asian Crisis: An alternate view", Asian Development Bank, Economic and Development Resource Centre: Economic Staff Paper No.59.

Lim, C.Y. (1998), "The Solution to The Asian Currency Crisis", Key-note address by Lim Chong Yah at International Conference "The New Role of Government in a Market Economy", February 1998, Singapore.

Liu, L., Noland, M., Robinson, S., Wang, Z. (1998), *Asian Competitive Devaluations*, Institute for International Economics.

MacLean, B.K. (1999), "The rise and fall of the 'Crony Capitalism' hypothesis: Causes and Consequences", Working Paper, Department of Economics, Laurentian University, Canada.

McKibbin, W.J. (1998), *The Crisis in Asia: An Empirical Assessment, Research School of Pacific and Asian Studies*, The Australian National University and The Brookings Institution.

Mishkin, F.S. (1999), "Lessons from Asian Crisis", NBER Working Paper No. 7102.

Mody, A. (1999), "Industrial Policy after the East Asian Crisis — From "Outward Orientation" to New Internal Capabilities?", Policy Research Working Paper, World Bank.

Normile, D. (1998), "Down and out in Asia", *Electronic Business*, Vol.24, Iss.9.

Park, U.K. (2000), *Balancing Between Panic and Mania: The East Asian Economic Crises and Challenges to International Financing*, Seoul: Samsung Economic Research Institute.

Park, Y.C., Lee, J.W. (1998), "Exports, Accumulation and Growth in East Asia", Park, Y.C. (ed.), *Financial Liberalization and Opening in East Asia: Issues and Policy Challenges*, Korea Institute of Finance.

Radelet, S., Sachs, J. (1998), "The Onset of the East Asian Financial Crisis", Working Paper, Harvard Institute for International Development.

Radelet, S., Sachs, J. (1999), "What Have We Learned, So Far, From the Asian Financial Crisis?", Working Paper, Harvard Institute for International Development.

Rajan, R.G., Zingales, L. (1998), "Which Capitalism? Lessons From the East Asian Crisis", Working Paper, University of Chicago.

Reisen, H. (1998), "After the Great Asian slump: Towards a Coherent Approach to Global Capital Flows", Policy Brief No. 16, OECD Development Centre.

Rodrik, D. (1998), "The Global Fix: A plan to save the world economy", *The New Republic*.

Sachs, J. (1998), "Global Capitalism: Making it Work", *The Economist*.

Sachs, J. (1998), "The IMF and the Asian Flu", *The American Prospect*, March-April, pp.16–21.

Sachs, J., Radelet, S. (1998), "Toward a New Strategy for Asian Recovery", *Singapore Straits-Times*.

Stiglitz, J. (1998), "Boats, planes and capital flows", *Financial Times*.

Stiglitz, J. (1998), "The Asian Crisis and the Future of the International Architecture", *World Economic Affairs*, September 1998.

Sugisaki, S. (1998), "Economic Crisis in Asia", Presentation at the 1998 Harvard Asia Business Conference, January 30, 1998.

Taylor, L. (1998), "Lax public sector, destabilising private sector: Origins of capital market crises", *http: //www.newschool.edu/cepa/papers/archive/cepa0306.pdf.*

Thurow, L. (1998), "Asia: The Collapse and the Cure", *http: //www.nybooks.com/nyrev/WWWfeatdisplay.cgi?1998020522F.*

Tornell, A. (1999), "Common Fundamentals in the Tequila and Asian Crisis", NBER Working Paper No. 7139, May 1999.

Wade, R. (1998), "The Asian Debt and Development Crisis of 1997 — Causes and Consequences", *World Development*.

Wade, R., Vaneroso, F. (1998), "The Asian Financial Crisis: The unrecognised risk of the IMF's Asian Package", *http: //www.russellsage.org.*

Wade, R., Vaneroso, F. (1998), "The Asian Crisis: The high debt model vs the Wall Street-Treasury-IMF Complex", Russell Sage Foundation.

World Bank (1998), *East Asia: The Road to Recovery,* World Bank Publication.

World Bank (1998), *Global Economic Prospects and the Developing Countries: Beyond Financial Crisis,* World Bank Publication.

East Asia Development: Total Factor Productivity Debate

Bosworth, B.P., Collins, S., Chen, Y.C. (1995), "Accounting for Differences in Economic Growth", Brookings Discussions Papers in International Economics No. 115 (October), The Brookings Institution, Washington.

Bosworth, B., Collin S. (1996), "Economic Growth in East Asia: Accumulation vs. Assimilation", *Brookings Papers on Economic Activity* 2: 135–204.

Chen, E.K.Y. (1977), "Factor inputs, total factor productivity and economic growth: The Asian case", *Developing Economies* 15(2): 121–143.

Chen, E.K.Y. (1997), "The total factor productivity debate: Determinants of economic growth in East Asia", *Asian-Pacific Economic Literature* 11(1): 18–38.

Chen, K. (1991), "The Form of Singapore's Aggregate Production Function and Its Policy Implications", *The Singapore Economic Review* XXXVI (1 April): 81–91.

Christensen, L.R., Cummings, D. (1975), *Real product, real factor input, and total factor productivity in the Republic of Korea*, 1960–73, Discussion Paper No.7057, Social Systems Research Institute, University of Wisconsin, Madison, Wisconsin.

Creamer, R. (1972), "Measuring capital input for total factor productivity analysis", *Review of Income and Wealth* 18(1): 55–78.

Currie, D., Pearlman,J., Levine, P., Chui, M. (1996), *Phases of Imitation and Innovation in a North-South Endogenous Growth Model*, ESRC Global Economic Institutions Initiative.

Department of Statistics (1997), *Multifactor Productivity Growth in Singapore: Concept, Methodology and Trends*, Occasional Paper Series, Department of Statistics, Singapore.

Felipe, J. (1997), *Total Factor Productivity Growth in East Asia: A Critical Survey*, EDRC Report Series No. 65, Economics and Development Resource Center, Asian Development Bank.

Goh, K.S., Low, L. (1996), "Beyond "Miracles" and Total Factor Productivity — The Singapore Experience", *ASEAN Economic Bulletin*, Vol.13, No.1.

Hsieh, C.T. (1997), *What Explains the Industrial Revolution in East Asia? Evidence from Factor Markets*, Department of Economics, University of California, Berkeley.

Kim, J.I., Lau, L. (1994), "The Sources of Economic Growth of the East Asian Newly Industrialised Countries", *Journal of the Japanese and International Economies* 8: 235–271.

Kim, J.I., Lau, L. (1994), "The Sources of Economic Growth of the Newly Industrialised Countries on the Pacific Rim", L.R. Klein, Yu, C.T. (eds.), *Economic Development of ROC and the Pacific Rim in the 1990s and Beyond*, World Scientific Publishing.

Krugman, P. (1994), "The Myth of Asia Miracle", *Foreign Affairs* 73(6): 62–78.

Krugman, P. (1996), "Pacific Myths", *http: //www.colorado.edu/cewww/ econ2020/course/topic8/krugman.html.*

Krugman, P., "What ever happ.ened to the Asian Miracle?", *http: //web.mit.edu/ krugman/www/perspire.html.*

Kwon, J.K. (1986), "Capital utilization, economies of scale and technical change in the growth of total factor productivity", *Journal of Development Economics*, No.24, pp.75–89.

Kwong, K.S., Lau, L.J., Lin, T.B. (1997), "The Impact of Relocation on the Total Factor Productivity of Hong Kong Manufacturing", Manuscript.

Lall, A., Tan, R.G.K., Chew, S.B. (1996), "Total factor productivity growth experience of Singapore: an interpretative survey", Lim,. C. Y. (ed.), *Economic Policy Management in Singapore*, Singapore: Addison Wesley, pp.1–22.

Lau, L.J. (1994), "Technical Progress, Capital Formation and Growth of Productivity", Bredahl, M.E., Abbott, P.C., Reed, M.R. (eds.), *Competitiveness in International Food Markets*, Westview Press.

Lau, L.J. (1996), "The Sources of Long-term Economic Growth: Observations from the Experience of Developed and Developing Countries", Landau, R., Taylor, T., Wright, G. (eds.), *The Mosaic of Economic Growth*, Stanford University Press.

Lau, L.J. (1997), *The Sources of and Prospects for East Asian Economic Growth*, Stanford University: Department of Economics.

Lee, T.Y. (1985), "Growth without Productivity: Singapore Manufacturing in the 1970s", *Journal of Development Economics* 18: 25–38.

Lee, T.Y. (1986), "Sources of Growth Accounting for the Singapore Economy", Lim, C.Y., Lloyd, P.J. (eds.), *Singapore, Resources and Growth*, Oxford: Oxford University Press.

Leung, H.M. (1996), "Total Factor Productivity Growth in Singapore's Manufacturing Industries", *Applied Economics Letters* 4: 525–528.

Leung, H.M. (1997), *Productivity of Singapore's Manufacturing Sector: An Industry Level Non-Parametric Study*, National University of Singapore: Department of Business Policy.

Lindauer, D.L., Roemer, M. (1994), "Legacies and Opportunities", Lindauer, D.L., Roemer, M. (eds.), *Asia and Africa, Legacies and Opportunities in Development*, International Center for Economic Growth and Harvard Institute for International Development.

Marti, C. (1996), *Is There an East Asian Miracle?*, Union Bank of Switzerland Economic Research Working Paper (October), Zurich.

Nadiri, M.I. (1970), "Some approaches to the theory and measurement of total factor productivity: a survey", *Journal of Economic Literature* 8(4): 1137–1177.

Nadiri, M.I. (1972), "International studies of factor inputs and total factor productivity: A brief survey", *Review of Income and Wealth* 18(2): 129–154.

Nehru, V. (1994), "New estimates of total factor productivity growth for developing and industrial countries", Policy Research Working Paper No.1313, World Bank, Washington, DC.

Nelson, V. (1981), "Research on productivity growth and productivity differences: Dead ends and new departures", *Journal of Economic Literature* 19(3): 1029–1064.

Okamoto, Y. (1994), "Impact of Trade and FDI Liberalization Policies on the Malaysian Economy", *The Developing Economies* XXXII (4 December): 460–478.

Osada, H. (1994), "Trade Liberalization and FDI Incentives in Indonesia: The Impact on Industrial Productivity", *The Developing Economies* XXXII (4 December): 479–491.

Rao, B., Lee, C. (1995), *Sources of Growth in the Singapore Economy and its Manufacturing and Service Sectors*, Paper presentation at the 20th Federation of ASEAN Economic Associations Conference, Singapore.

Rao, V.V. B., Owyong, D. (1997), *Sources of Growth in the Singapore Economy: Some New Results*, Paper for presentation at the Taipei International Conference on Efficiency and Productivity Growth, June 20–21, 1997.

Rodrik, D. (1997), *TFPG Controversies, Institutions and Economic Performance in East Asia*, NBER Working Paper No. 5914.

Roubini, N. (1998), *What Causes Long run Growth? The Debate on the Asian Miracle*, Stern School of Business, New York University.

Sarel, M. (1997), "Growth and Productivity in ASEAN Countries", IMF Working Paper No. 97/97.

Thomas, V., Wang, Y. (1997), "Government Policies and Productivity Growth: Is East Asia an Exception?", Leipziger, D.M. (ed.), *Lessons from East Asia*, Ann Arbor: The University of Michigan Press.

Toh, M. H., Low, L. (1996), "Differential total factor productivity in the Four Dragons: The Singapore case", *The Journal of International Trade & Economic Development* 5(2): 161–181.

Urata, S., Yokota, K. (1994), "Trade Liberalization and Productivity Growth in Thailand", *The Developing Economies* XXXII (December): 444–459.

Wong, F.C., Gan, W.B. (1994), "Total Factor Productivity Growth in the Singapore Manufacturing Industries During the 1980s", *Journal of Asian Economies* 5(2) (Summer): 177–196.

World Bank, "Economic Growth in East Asia", *http: //www.worldbank.org/ html/edi/edimp/eastasia/prod.html*.

Young, A. (1992), "A Tale of Two Cities: Factor Accumulation and Technical Change in Hong Kong and Singapore", *National Bureau of Economic Research, Macroeconomics Annual*, Cambridge.

Young, A. (1994a), *Accumulation, Exports and Growth in the High Performing Asian Economies*, A Comment, Carnegie-Rochester Conference Series on Public Policy No.40.

Young, A. (1994b), "Lessons from the NICs: A Contrarian View", *European Economic Review* 38: 964–973.

Young, A. (1995), "The Tyranny of Numbers: Confronting the Statistical Realities of the East Asian Growth Experience", *Quarterly Journal of Economics* (August): 641–680.

Young, A. (1998), "Alternative Estimates of Productivity Growth in the NIC's: A Comment on the Findings of Chang-Tai Hsieh", Working Paper 6657, National Bureau of Economic Research.

Hong Kong

Bailey, T. (1993), "Organizational Innovation in the App.arel Industry", *Industrial Relation* 32: 30–48.

Berger, S., Lester, R. (eds.) (1997), *Made By Hong Kong*, Hong Kong: Oxford University Press.

Birnbaum, D. (1993), *Importing Garments Through Hong Kong*, Hong Kong: Third Horizon Press.

Boston Consulting Group International Inc. (1995), *Report on Techno-Economic and Market Research Study on Hong Kong's Electronics Industry 1993– 1994, Volume 2: Phase 1 Study — Industry Analysis*, Hong Kong: Government Printer.

Census and Statistics Department (1993), *Report on 1993 Survey of Industrial Production*.

Census and Statistics Department (1995), *Hong Kong Annual Digest of Statistics*, 1995.

Census and Statistics Department (1995), *Hong Kong Social and Economic Trends*, 1995.

Census and Statistics Department (1996, 1997), "Trading firms with manufacturing-related functions", *Hong Kong Monthly Digest of Statistics*: August 1996 and September 1997.

Chan, T.S. (1984), *Distribution Channel Strategy for Export Marketing: The Case of Hong Kong Firms*, Ann Arbor: UMI Research Press.

Chen, E.K.Y. (1975), "Endogenous technical progress: A survey", *Hong Kong Economic Papers* No.9, Hong Kong Economic Association, pp.18–45.

Chen, X. (1993), "China's Growing Integration with the Asia-Pacific Economy", Dirlik, A. (ed.), *What Is In A Rim?*, Boulder: Westview Press.

Chiu, S. (1994), "The Politics of Laissez-Faire: Hong Kong's Strategy of Industrialization in Historical Perspective", The Chinese University of Hong Kong: Occasional Paper No.40, Hong Kong Institute of Asia-Pacific Studies.

Chiu, S., Lui, T.L. (1995), "Hong Kong: Unorganised Industrialism", Clark, G., Kim, W.B. (eds.), *Asian NIEs and the Global Economy*, Baltimore: John Hopkins University Press.

Chiu, S., Levin D. (1996), "Prosperity Without Industrial Democracy? Developments in Industrial Relations in Hong Kong since 1968", *Industrial Relations Journal* 27(1): 24–37.

Chiu, S.W.K. (1996), "The Changing Labour Market and Foreign Workers in Hong Kong", *International Employment Relations Review* 2: 55–76.

Chiu, S.W.K. (1996), "Unravelling Hong Kong's Exceptionalism: The politics of laissez-faire in the industrial takeoff," *Political Power and Social Theory* 10: 229–256.

Chiu, S.W.K., Lee, C.K. (1997), "After the Hong Kong Miracle: Women Workers under Industrial Restructuring", *Asian Survey* 37: 752–770.

Chiu, S.W.K., Wong, K.C. (1998), "The Hong Kong LCD Industry: Surviving the Global Technology Race," *Industry and Innovation* 5: 51–71.

Choi, A.H. (1997), "The Political Economy of Industrial Upgrading: A Lost Opp.ortunity", *China Information* XII (1/2): 157–188.

Chow, S.C., Papanek, G.F. (1981), "Laissez-faire, growth and equity — Hong Kong", *Economic Journal* 91: 466–485.

Chiu, S., Ho, K.C., Lui, T.L. (1997), *City-States in the Global Economy*, Boulder: Westview Press.

Commission on Innovation and Technology (1998), *The Commission's First Report to the Chief Executive (http: //www.info.gov.hk/cit/eng/er/report.html)*.

Chu, Y.W. (1988), "Dependent Industrialisation: The Case of Hong Kong Garment Industry", unpublished M. Phil Thesis, Sociology Department, University of Hong Kong, Hong.

Dataquest Incorporated (1991), *Techno-economic and Market Research Study on Hong Kong's Electronics Industry 1988–1989*, Hong Kong: Government Printer.

Department of Audit (1997), "The Government's funding schemes for promoting technology development in industry," *Report of the Director of Audit on the Results of Value for Money Audits* October, Hong Kong: Government Printer.

Enright, M., Scott, E., Dodwell, D. (1997), *The Hong Kong Advantage*, Oxford University Press.

Federation of Hong Kong Industries, Industry & Research Division (1990), *Hong Kong's Offshore Investment*, Hong Kong: Federation of Hong Kong Industries.

Federation of Hong Kong Industries, Industry & Research Division (1992), *Hong Kong's Industrial Investment in the Pearl River Delta*, Hong Kong: Federation of Hong Kong Industries.

Hambro, E. (1955), *The Problem of Chinese Refugees in Hong Kong*, Leyden: A.W. Sijthoff.

Ho, H.C.Y. (1979), *The Fiscal System of Hong Kong*, London: Croom Helm.

Ho, Y.P. (1992), *Trade, Industrial Restructuring and Development in Hong Kong*, Honolulu: University of Hawaii Press.

Hong Kong Trade Development Council (1997), *Profiles of Hong Kong's Major Services Industries*, 1997.

Hong Kong Trade Development Council Research Department (1991), *Survey on Hong Kong's Domestic Exports, Re-exports and Triangular Trade*, Hong Kong Trade Development Council.

Hong Kong Trade Development Council Research Department (1997), *Profiles of Hong Kong's Major Manufacturing Industries*, Hong Kong Trade Development Council.

Howe, C. (1983), "Growth, Public Policy and Hong Kong's Economic Relationship with China", *The China Quarterly* 95: 512–533.

Industry Department (1990), *Hong Kong's Manufacturing Industries*, Hong Kong: Government Printer.

Industry Department (1992b), *Report on Industrial Automation Study*, Hong Kong: Government Printer.

Keenan, F. (1995), "The latest Thing: Hong Kong Garment Makers Must Sell as Well as sew," *Far Eastern Economic Review* June 8: 46–47.

Kraus, R.C. (1979), "Withdrawing from the World-System: Self-Reliance and Class Structure in China", Goldfrank, W.L. (ed.), *The World-system of Capitalism*, Beverly Hills: Sage.

Krause, L.B. (1988), "Hong Kong and Singapore: Twins or kissing cousins?", *Economic Development and Cultural Change*, Vol. 36, No.3, April Supplement.

Kurt Salmon Associates (1987), *Final Report on Techno-economic and Marketing Research Study on the Textiles and Clothing Industry for Hong Kong Government Industry Department*, Mimeo.

Kurt Salmon Associates (1992), *Techno-economic and Market Research Study of Hong Kong's Textiles and Clothing Industries: 1991–1992*, Hong Kong: Government Printer.

Kurt Salmon Associates (1996), *1995 Techno-economic and Market Research Study on Hong Kong's Textiles and Clothing Industries* Vol.II, Hong Kong: Government Printer.

Kwong, K.S. (1997), *Technology and Industry*, City University of Hong Kong Press.

Kwong, K.S, Lau, L., Lin, T.B. (1997), "The Impact of Relocation on the Total Factor Productivity of Hong Kong Manufacturing", Manuscript.

Lau, H.F., Chan, C.F. (1991), "Structural adaptation: The response of Hong Kong garment manufacturers", Paper presented at the Symposium on Industrial Policy in Hong Kong, Hong Kong Institute of Asia-Pacific Studies, The Chinese University of Hong Kong.

Lau, S.K. (1982), *Society and Politics in Hong Kong*, Hong Kong: The Chinese University of Hong Kong.

Lee, M.K. (1995), "Community and Identity in Transition in Hong Kong", Kwok, R., So, A.Y. (eds.), *The Hong Kong-Guangdong Link*, Almonk: M.E. Sharpe.

Leung, C.C. (1997), "Hong Kong: A Unique Case of Development", Leipziger, D. (ed.), *Lessons from East Asia*, University of Michigan Press.

Levin, D., Chiu, S. (1993), "Dependent Capitalism, Colonial State and Marginal Unions: The Case of Hong Kong", Frenkel, S. (ed.), *Organized Labour in the Asian-Pacific Region*, Ithaca: ILR.

Lui, T.L. (1994), *Waged Work at Home: The Social Organisation of Industrial Outwork in Hong Kong*, Aldershot: Avebury.

Lui, T.L., Chiu, S. (1993), "Industrial restructuring and labour market adjustment under positive non-interventionism", *Environment and Planning* A 25: 63–79.

Lui, T.L., Chiu, S. (1994), "A tale of two industries: The restructuring of Hong Kong's garment making and electronics industries", *Environment and Planning* A 26: 53–70.

Maruya, T. (1992), "Economic Relations between Hong Kong and Guangdong Province", Maruya, T. (ed.), *Guangdong*, Hong Kong: Centre of Asian Studies, the University of Hong Kong.

Milby, K.C., Mushkat, M. (1989), *Hong Kong: The Challenge of Transformation*, Hong Kong: Centre of Asian Studies, University of Hong Kong.

MIT Hong Kong Study Research Team (1997), *Made By Hong Kong*, Oxford University Press.

Naughton, B. (1997), *The China Circle: Economics and Electronics in the PRC, Taiwan, and Hong Kong*, Brookings Institute Press.

Ng, L. F.Y. et al. (1997), *Three Chinese Economies: China, Hong Kong and Taiwan: Challenges and Opportunities*, Chinese University Press.

Ngo, T.W. (1997), "Changing Government-Business Relations and the Governance of Hong Kong", Paper presented at the International conference on "Hong Kong in Transition", London.

Pye, L. (1983),"The International Position of Hong Kong", *The China Quarterly* 95: 456–468.

Scott, I. (1989), *Political Change and the Crisis of Legitimacy in Hong Kong*, Honolulu: University of Hawaii Press.

Scott, I. (1989), "Administration in a small capitalist state: The Hong Kong experience", *Public Administration and Development* 9: 185–199.

Sit, V.F.S. (1989), "Industrial Out-Processing — Hong Kong's New Relationship with the Pearl River Delta", *Asian Profile* 17: 1–13.

Sit, V., Wong, S.L. (1989), *Small and Medium Industries in an Export-Oriented Economy: The Case of Hong Kong*, Hong Kong: Centre of Asian Studies.

Sit, V., Wong, S.L., Kiang, T.S. (1979), *Small Scale Industry in a Laissez-faire Economy*, Centre of Asian Studies, University of Hong Kong.

Sung, Y.W. (1992), *The China-Hong Kong Connection*, Cambridge University Press.

Szczepanik, E. (1958), *The Economic Growth of Hong Kong*, Oxford University Press.

Tuan, C., Ng, L.F.Y. (1995), "Evolution of Hong Kong's Electronics Industry under Passive Industrial Policy," *Managerial and Decision Economics* 16: 509–523.

Tung, C.H. (1998), *The 1998 Policy Address*.

Wong, S.L. (1988), *Emigrant Entrepreneurs: Shanghai Industrialists in Hong Kong*, Hong Kong: Oxford University Press.

Wong, S.L. (1990), "Chinese entrepreneurs and business trust", *University of Hong Kong Gazette Supplement* XXXVII 1: 25–34.

Yau, K.C. (1994), "The precarious symbiosis: Inter-organizational relations in Hong Kong's production system", unpublished M. Phil. Thesis, Sociology Department, The Chinese University of Hong Kong.

Yau, K.C. (1994), "Business and Politics in Hong Kong during the Transition", Leung, B.K.P., Wong, T.Y.C. (eds.), *25 Years of Social and Economic Development in Hong Kong*, Centre of Asian Studies, University of Hong Kong.

Young, A. (1992), "A Tale of Two Cities: Factor Accumulation and Technical Change in Hong Kong and Singapore", *NBER Macroeconomic Annual 1992*, Cambridge, Mass.: MIT Press.

Youngson, A.J. (1982), *Hong Kong: Economic Growth and Policy*, Oxford University Press.

Youngson, A.J. (1983), "Introduction", Youngson, A.J. (ed.), *China and Hong Kong*, Oxford University Press.

Yu, F.L.T. (1997), *Entrepreneurship and Economic Development in Hong Kong*, London: Routledge.

Japan

Akamatsu, K. (1935), "Trade of Woolen Products in Japan (in Japanese)", *Studies of Commerce and Economy*, No.13: 129–212.

Ando, A., Auerbach, A. (1988), "The Corporate Cost of Capital in Japan and the United States: A Comparison", Shoven, J.B. (ed.), *Government Policy towards Industry in the United States and Japan*, Cambridge: Cambridge University Press, pp.21–49.

Angel, D.P., Savage, L. (1997), "Globalization of R&D in the Electronics Industry: The recent experience of Japan", Lee, R., Wills, J. (eds.), *Geographies of economics*, New York: Arnold.

Beason, R., Weinstein, D.E. (1996), "Growth, Economies of Scale, and Targeting in Japan (1955–1990)," *Review of Economics and Statistics* 78(2): 286–295.

Belderbos, R. (1997), *Japanese electronics multinationals and strategic trade policies*, New York: Clarendon Press.

Boskin, M.J., Roberts, J.M. (1988), "A Closer Look at Saving Rates in the United States and Japan", Shoven, J.B. (ed.), *Government Policy towards Industry in the United States and Japan*, Cambridge: Cambridge University Press, pp.121–143.

Brown, C.G., Watanabe, C., Fujisue, K. (forthcoming), "Technology spillovers and informatization in Japan: An analysis of information technology diffusion in large versus small and medium-sized enterprises", *International Journal of Technology Management* (forthcoming).

Brunello, G. (1989), "Bonuses, Wages and Performance in Japan: Evidence from Micro Data", Discussion Paper No.359, Centre for Labour Economics, London School of Economics.

Callon, S. (1995), *Divided Sun: MITI and the Breakdown of Japanese High-Tech Industrial Policy, 1975–1993*, Stanford University Press.

Cho, D.S., Kim, D.J., Rhee, D.K. (1998), "Latecomer Strategies: Evidence from the Semiconductor Industry in Japan and Korea", *Organization Science*, Vol.9, No.4, July-August 1998.

Dempa Publications (1996), *Japan electronics almanac*.

Denison, E.F., Chung, W.K. (1976), *How Japan's Economy Grew So Fast: The Sources of Postwar Expansion*, Washington: Brookings.

Doane, D.L. (1984), "Two Essays on Technological Innovation: Innovation and Economic Stagnation, and Interfirm Cooperation for Innovation in Japan", Ph.D. dissertation, Yale University, Department of Economics.

Dore, R. (1986), *Flexible Rigidities: Industrial Policy and Structural Adjustment in the Japanese Economy 1970–80*, London: Athlone Press.

Eads, G.C., Yamamura, K. (1987), "The Future of Industrial Policy", Yamamura, K., Yasuba, Y. (eds.), *The Political Economy of Japan, Vol.1: The Domestic Transformation*, Stanford, California: Stanford University Press, pp.423–468.

Economist (1997), A Survey of Japanese Finance, *The Economist*, June 28th.

Electronics Association of Japan (1986), *Electronics in Japan*.

Electronic Industries Association of Japan (1995), *Profile of the Electronic Industries Association of Japan*.

Electronic Industries Association of Japan (1995), *Perspective on the Japanese electronics industry*.

Electronic Industries Association of Japan (1995), *Facts and figures on the Japanese electronics industry*.

Fallows, J.M. (1989a), "Containing Japan", *Atlantic Monthly*, May 1989, pp.40–54.

Fransman, M. (1991), *The Market and Beyond: Cooperation and Competition in Information Technology Department in the Japanese Systems*, New York: Cambridge University Press.

Fransman, M. (1999), "Where are the Japanese? Japanese information and communications firms in an internetworked world", *Telecommunications Policy*, Vol.23, Iss.3/4.

Friedman, D. (1988), *The Misunderstood Miracle: Industrial Development and Political Change in Japan*, Ithaca, N.Y.: Cornell University Press.

Fruin, M. (1989), "History, Strategy and the Development Factory in Japan: Production for Competitive Advantage", Unpublished, INSEAD.

Fujishiro, N. (1988), "Computer Sangyo ni Okeru Kyodo-Kenkyu no Yakuwari" (The Role of Joint R&D in the Computer Industry), Unpublished master's thesis, University of Tsukuba.

Goto, A., Wakasugi, R. (1988), "Technology Policy", Komiya, R., *et al.* (eds.), *Industrial Policy of Japan*, Academic Press.

Goto, A., Odagiri, H. (1997), *Innovation in Japan*, Oxford University Press.

Gregory, G. (1986), *Japanese Electronics Technology: Enterprise and Innovation*, Tokyo: Sophia University.

Hane, G. J. (1992), "Research and Development Consortia in Innovation in Japan: Case Studies in Superconductivity and Engineering Ceramics", Ph.D. dissertation, Harvard University.

Hoddar, J.E. (1988), "Corporate Capital Structure in the United States and Japan: Financial Intermediation and Implications of Financial Deregulation", Shoven, J.B. (ed.), *Government Policy towards Industry in the United States and Japan*, Cambridge: Cambridge University Press, pp.241–263.

Imai, K. (1986), "Japan's Industrial Policy for High Technology Industry", Patrick, H. (ed.), *Japan's High Technology Industries: Lessons and Limitations of Industrial Policy*, Seattle: University of Washington Press, pp.137–170.

Inoue, R., Kohama, H., Urata, S. (eds.) (1993), *Industrial Policy in East Asia*, Tokyo: JETRO.

Itaya, S. *et al.* (1990), "A case study of Japan's textiles and electronics industries", prepared for OECD project "New technologies, industry, and trade with special reference to Asian NIEs", Research Institute for International Relations at Nagoya Shoka University.

Ito, T. (1992), *The Japanese Economy*, MIT Press.

Ito, T. (1996), "Japan and the Asian Economies: A 'Miracle' in Transition", *Brookings Papers on Economic Activity* 2: 205–272.

Johnson, C. (1982), *MITI and the Japanese Miracle*, Stanford, California: Stanford University Press.

Johnson, C. (1987), "Political Institutions and Economic Performance: The Government-Business Relationship in Japan, South Korea and Taiwan", Deyo, F.C. (ed.), *The Political Economy of the New Asian Industrialization*, Ithaca: Cornell University Press.

Kaizuka, K. (1973), *Keizai Seisaku no Kadai (Tasks of Economic Policy)*, Tokyo: University of Tokyo Press.

Kikuchi, M. (1983), *Japanese Electronics: A Worm's-Eye View of its Evolution*, Tokyo: Simul Press Inc.

Komiya, R., Okuno, M., Suzumura, K. (eds.) (1988), *Industrial Policy of Japan*, San Diego: Academic Press.

Komiya, R. (1990), *The Japanese Economy: Trade, Industry and Government*, University of Tokyo Press.

Lynn, L.H. (1982), *How Japan Innovates*, Boulder, Colo.: Westview Press.

McGrath, M.E. (1997), "What happened to Japan", *Electronic Business*, Vol. 23, Issue 11.

McIntyre, J.R. (ed.) (1997), *Japan's technical standards: Implications for global trade and competitiveness*, Westport, Conn: Quorum Books.

Motai, H. (1998), "Japan's market outlook for 1999 and beyond", *Semiconductor International*, Vol.21, Iss.13.

Murakami, Y. (1987), "Technology in Transition: Two Perspectives on Industrial Policy", Patrick, H. (ed.), *Japan's High Technology Industries: Lessons and Limitations of Industrial Policy*, Seattle: University of Washington Press, pp.211–242.

Nagaoka, S. (1989), "Overview of Japanese Industrial Technology Development", Departmental Working Paper No.10583, Industry Development Division, Industry and Energy Department, World Bank.

Nageswaran, K., Kumiko, M. (1999), "An integrated network app.roach to systems of innovation — The case of robotics in Japan", *Research Policy*, Vol.28, Iss.6.

Nobuo, K. (1990), *Modern Political History of Japan* (Chinese translation by Zhou, C.C., Lu, W.H., *et al.*), Vols.2, 3, Taipei: Guei-Guan.

Odagiri, H. (1989), "Government Policies towards Industrial R&D: Theory, Empirical Findings, and Japan's Experience", Neumann, M. (ed.), *Public Finance and Performance of Enterprises*, Detroit: Wayne State University Press, pp.211–226.

Odagiri, H., Iwata, H. (1986), "The Impact of R&D on Productivity Increase in Japanese Manufacturing Companies', *Research Policy* 15: 1 (Feb.): 13–19.

Odagiri, H. (1992), *Growth Through Competition, Competition Through Growth*, Oxford University Press.

Odagiri, H., Goto, A. (1993), "The Japanese System of Innovation: Past, Present and Future", Nelson, R.R. (ed.) *National Innovation Systems: A Comparative Analysis*, Oxford University Press.

Odagiri, H., Goto, A. (1996), *Technology and Industrial Development in Japan*, Oxford University Press.

Ohkawa, K., Rosovsky, H. (1973), *Japanese Economic Growth: Trend Acceleration in the Twentieth Century*, Stanford, California: Stanford University Press.

Ohkawa, K., Shinohara, M. (eds.) (1979), *Patterns of Japanese Economic Development: A Quantitative Appraisal*, New Haven: Yale University Press.

Ohkawa, K., Kohama, H. (1989), *Lectures on Developing Economies: Japan's Experience and its Relevance*, Tokyo: University of Tokyo Press.

Ohno, K. (1996), *Creating the Market Economy: The Japanese View on Economic Development and Systemic Transition*, World Bank WD97 Project.

Ohno, K., Ohno, I. (eds.) (1998), *Japanese Views on Economic Development: Diverse paths to the market*, Routledge.

Okimoto, D.I., Rohlen, T.P. (eds.) (1988), *Inside the Japanese System: Readings on Contemporary Society and Political Economy*, Stanford University Press.

Okimoto, D. (1989), *Between MITI and the Market: Japanese Industrial Policy for High Technology*, Stanford University Press.

Ozaki, R.S. (1985), "How Japanese Industrial Policy Works", Johnson, C. (ed.), *The New Industrial Policy Debate*, San Francisco: ICS Press, pp.47–70.

Peck, M.J., Levin, R.C., Goto, A. (1988), "Picking Losers: Public Policy towards Declining Industries in Japan", Shoven, J.B. (ed.), *Government Policy towards Industry in the United States and Japan*, Cambridge: Cambridge University Press, pp.195–239.

Porter, M.E., Takeuchi, H. and Sakakibara, M. (2000), *Can Japan Compete?* Basingstoke, Hampshire: Macmillan.

Prestowitz, C. (1988), "Japanese vs. Western Economics: Why Each Side Is a Mystery to the Other", *Technology Review* 91(4): 27–36.

Robert, C. (1996), *Korea's economic miracle: The crucial role of Japan*, New York: St. Martin's Press.

Saxonhouse, G.R., Okimoto, D.I. (1987), "The Political Economy of Japan: Technology and the Future of the Economy", Yamamura, K., Yasuba, Y. (eds.), *The Political Economy of Japan, vol.1, The domestic Transformation*, Stanford University Press.

Scientific American, "We were burning: Japanese entrepreneurs and the forging of the electronic age", *Scientific American*, Vol.280, Iss.4.

Shin, J.S. (1996), *The Economics of Latecomers: Catching-up, technology transfer and institutions in Germany, Japan and South Korea*, Routledge.

Shinohara, M. (1982), *Industrial Growth, Trade and Dynamic Patterns in the Japanese Economy*, Tokyo: University of Tokyo Press.

Shoven, J.B. (ed.) (1988), *Government Policy towards Industry in the United States and Japan*, Cambridge: Cambridge University Press, pp.21–49.

Sigurdson, J. (1986), "Industry and State Partnership in Japan: The Very Large Scale Integrated Circuits Project", Research Policy Institute, University of Lund, Sweden, Discussion Paper no.168.

Stenberg, L. (1993), "Technological Strengths Needs and Feeds a New Research Infrastructure in Japan", Aspray W. (ed.). *Technological competitiveness: Contemporary and historical perspectives on the electrical, electronics and computer industries*, New York: Institute of Electrical and Electronics Engineers.

Suzuki, K. (1985), "Knowledge Capital and the Private Rate of Return to R&D in Japanese Manufacturing Industries", *International Journal of Industrial Organisation* 3(3): 293–305.

Taira, K. (1970), *Economic Development and the Labour Market in Japan*, New York: Columbia University Press.

Takamiya, S. Thurley, K. (eds.) (1985), *Japan's Emerging Multinationals*, Tokyo: University of Tokyo Press.

Takenaka, H. (1997), "Changing Asia-Pacific and the Japanese economy", Keio University, mimeo (in Japanese).

Taketoshi, R. (1984), "Waga Kuni Seizogyo no Gapp.ei ni Kansuru Kenkyu" (A study on Mergers in Japanese Manufacturing Industries), Unpublished Master's thesis, University of Tsukuba.

Takeuchi, K., Shimada, H., et al. (1997), *Made in Japan: revitalizing Japanese manufacturing for economic growth*, Cambridge, Mass: MIT Press.

Trevor, M. (1983), *Japan's Reluctant Multinationals*, London: Frances Printer.

Trevor, M., Schendel, J., Wilpert, B. (1986), *The Japanese Management Development System*, London: Frances Printer.

Trezise, P.H. (1983), "Industrial Policy is Not the Major Reason for Japan's Success", *Brookings Review*, pp.13–18.

Van Wolferen, K. (1989), *The Enigma of Japanese Power: People and Politics in a Stateless Nation*, New York: Vintage Books.

Wade, R. (1996), "Japan, the World Bank, and the Art of Paradigm Maintenance: The East Asian Miracle in Political Perspective", *New Left Review* 217: 3–36.

Wakasugi, R. (1986), Gijutsu Kakushin to Kenkyu Kaihatsu no Keizai Bunseki (*Economic Analysis of Technological Innovation and R&D*), Tokyo: Toyo Keizai Shinpo Sha.

Wakasugi, R. (1988), "A Consideration of Innovative Organization: Joint R&D of Japanese Firms", Staff Paper Series 88–05, Faculty of Economics, Shinshu University.

Wakasugi, T., Nishina, K., Kon-ya, F., Tsuchiya, M. (1984), *Measuring the Profitability of the Nonfinancial Sector in Japan*, Holland.

White, M., Trevor, M. (1983), *Under Japanese Management*, London: Heinemann.

Woronoff, J. (1992), *Japanese trageting: Success, failures, lessons*, New York: St. Martin's Press.

Yamawaki, H. (1991), "The Effects of Business Conditions on Net Entry: Evidence from Japan", Geroski, P.A., Schwalbach, J. (eds.), *Entry and Market Contestability: An International Comparison*, Oxford: Basil Blackwell.

Yamamura, K. (1982), "Joint Research and Antitrust: Two Perspectives on Industrial Policy", Patrick, H. (ed.), *Japan's High Technology Industries: Lessons and Limitations of Industrial Policy*, Seattle: University of Washington Press, pp.171–210.

Yoshihara, H., Sakuma, A., Itami, H. and Kagono, T. (1981), Nihon Kigyo no Takakuka Senryaku (*Diversification Strategies of Japanese Firms*), Tokyo: Nihon Keizai Shimbun Sha.

Yoshihara, K. (1994), *Japanese Economic Development*, Kuala Lumpur: Oxford University Press.

Young, L.H. (1997), "Japan's economy hits the skids", *Electronic Business*, Vol.23, Iss.12.

Young, L.H. (1998), "Japan's economy holds back electronics", *Electronic Business*, Vol.24, Iss.2.

Yuko, A. (1998), *From fortress Japan to global networks: Locational specificity of globalization for the Japanese electronics industry in the 1990s*, University Microfilms International.

Korea

Ahn, C.S. (1994), "The state, society and democratization in South Korea: The impact of deepening industrialization", Nagel, S.S. (ed.), *Asian Development and Public Policy*, London: St. Martin's Press, pp.32–43.

Amsden, A.H. (1989), *Asia's Next Giant: South Korea and Late Industrialization*, New York: Oxford University Press.

Amsden, A.H. (1987), *WIDER stabilization and adjustment programmes country study 14*, Republic of Korea, World Institute for Development Economics Research.

Archambault, E.J. (1991), "Small is beautiful, Large is Powerful: Manufacturing Semiconductors in South Korea", unpublished M.Sc Thesis, SPRU, University of Sussex.

Bank of Korea (1998), "Financial Crisis in Korea — Why it happened and how it can be overcome", July 1998.

Bloom, M. (1991), "Globalisation and Korean Electronics Industry", Paper presented to EASMA conference, INSEAD, Fontainbleu, 17–19 Oct.

Bloom, M. (1992), *Technological Change in the Korean Electronics Industry*, Paris: OECD.

Branscomb, L.M., Choi, Y.H. (1996), *Korea at the turning point*, Praeger Publishers.

Cargill, T.F. (1998), "The Political Economy of Financial Liberalization in Korea", *Economic Papers*, Vol.1, No.2, Sept. 1998.

Castley, R.J. (1998), "The Korean Electronics Industry: The Japanese Role in its Growth", *Asia Pacific Business Review* 4(2/3): 29–47.

Chang, H.J. (1997), "A Crisis from Underregulation", *Los Angeles Times*, Dec. 31, 1997.

Chang, H.J. (1998), "Reform for the Long Term in South Korea", *International Herald Tribune*, Feb. 13, 1998.

Cho, D.S., Kim, D.J., Rhee, D.K. (1998), "Latecomer Strategies: Evidence from the Semiconductor Industry in Japan and Korea", *Organization Science*, Vol.9, No.4, July-August 1998.

Chris, R., Bae, J.S. (1998), "Special Issue: Korean Businesses: Internal and External Industrialization", *Asia Pacific Business Review*, Issues 4.2& 3.

Collins, S.M. (1987), "Comment on Dornbusch and Park, Korean growth policy", *Brookings Papers on Economic Activity* No.2, pp.389–454.

Dahlman, C.J., Sercovich, F.C. (1984), "Local Development and Exports of Technology: The Comparative Advantages of Argentina, Brazil, India, the Republic of Korea and Mexico", World Bank Staff Working Paper *No. 667*, World Bank.

Electronic Industries Association of Korea (1990), *Statistics of Electronic & Electrical Industries* 1990.

Enos, J., Park, W.H. (1987), *The Adaptation and Diffusion of Imported Technologies in the Case of Korea*, London: Croom Helm.

Haggard, S. (1988), "The politics of industrialization in the Republic of Korea and Taiwan".

Hughes, H. (ed.), *Achieving Industrialization in East Asia*, Cambridge: Cambridge University Press.

Hobday, M. (1998), "Latecomer Catch-up Strategies in Electronics: Samsung of Korea and Acer of Taiwan", *Asia Pacific Business Review* 4(2/3): 47–83.

Hwang, S.I. (1997), "Economic Impact of Foreign Debt in Korea", KIEP Working Paper 97–07, Korea Institute for International Economic Policy.

Jacobsson, S. (1993), "The length of the learning period: Evidence from the Korean engineering industry", *World Development* 21(3): 407–420.

Johnson, C. (1987), "Political Institutions and Economic Performance: The Government-Business Relationship in Japan, South Korea and Taiwan", Deyo, F.C. (ed.), *The Political Economy of the New Asian Industrialization*, Ithaca: Cornell University Press.

Jones, L.P., Sakong, I. (1980), *Government, Business and Entrepreneurship in Economic Development: The Korean Case*, Cambridge, MA: Harvard University Press.

Jun, Y.W., Kim, S.G. (1990), "The Korean Electronics Industry: Current Status, Perspectives and Policy Options", Report Prepared for OECD Development Centre Project, *Technological Change and the Electronics Sector — Perspectives and Policy Options for Newly Industrialising Economies*, Paris: OECD.

Jwa, S.H. (1997), "The Role of Government in Economic Management — Korea's Experiences and Lessons", unpublished manuscript, Korea Economic Research Institute.

Kang, D.C. (1995), "South Korean and Taiwanese Development and the New Institutional Economics", *International Organisation* 49(3): 555–587.

Kenny, M. (1995), *Learning and coping with competitive pressure: The Korean electronics industry at the dawning of the 21st century*, Institute of Government Affairs, University of California, Davis.

Kim, H.R. (2000), "Korea's economic governance in transition: Governance crisis and the future of Korean capitalism", *Korea Observer* 31(4): 553–577.

Kim, J.H. (1991), "Korea: Market Adjustment in Declining Industries, Government Assistance in Troubled Industries", Patrick, H. (ed.), *The Political Economy of the New Asian Industrialism*, Ithaca: Cornell University Press.

Kim, J.H. (2000), "Economy of austerity in Korea in the early 1980s: To repeat or not", *Korea Observer* 31(1): 41–72.

Kim, K. (1984), *The Korean Economy: Past Performance, Current Reforms, and Future Prospect*, Seoul: Korea Development Institute, 1984.

Kim, K., Park, J.K. (1985), *Sources of Economic Growth in Korea*, Korea Development Institute.

Kim, K., Leipziger, D. (1997), "Korea: A Case of Government Led Development", Leipziger, D. (ed.), *Lessons from East Asia*, University of Michigan Press.

Kim, K.S., Roemer, M. (1979), *Growth and Structural Transformation, Studies in the Modernisation of the Republic of Korea: 1945–1975*, Cambridge, Massachusetts: Harvard University Press.

Kim, K.S., Sung, D.H. (1997), *Accounting for Rapid Economic Growth in Korea, 1963–1995*, Seoul: Korea Development Institute.

Kim, L.L. (1980), "Stages of Development of Industrial Technology", Park, G.K. (ed.), *Macroeconomics and Industrial Development in Korea*, Seoul: KDI.

Kim, L., Dahlman, C.J. (1992), "Technology Policy for Industrialisation: An Integrative Framework and Korea's Experience", *Research Policy* 21: 437–452.

Kim, L. (1993), "National System of Industrial Innovation: Dynamics of Capability Building in Korea", Nelson, R. R. (ed.), *National Innovation Systems: A Comparative Analysis*, Oxford University Press.

Kim, L. (1997), *Imitation to Innovation: The Dynamics of Korea's Technological Learning*, Boston: Harvard Business School Press.

Kim, K.S., Roemer, M. (1979), *Growth and Structural Transformation: Studies in the Modernization of the Republic of Korea, 1945–1975*, Harvard University Press.

Kim, S.R. (1996), "The Korean System of innovation and the semiconductor industry: A governance perspective", SPRU/SEI-Working Paper.

Kim, W.S. (1995), "The Korean economy in distress: Major issues and challenges in the 1990s", Kawagoe T. (ed.), *East Asian Economies: Transformation and Challenges*, Singapore: Institute of Southeast Asian Studies.

Kim, Y.H., Campbell, N. (195), "Strategic control in Korean MNCs", *Management International Review* 35(1): 95–108.

Korea Development Bank (1995), *Recent Trends of Korean Electronics Industry*, http: //www.kol.co.kr/~kdbmst/focus/elec_ind.html.

Lau, L. (ed.) (1990), *Models of Development: A Comparative Study of Economic Growth in South Korea and Taiwan*, San Francisco: ICS Press.

Lee, C.H. (1995), "The State and the Market in the Economic Development of Korea and Taiwan: Lessons for Economic Development and Transition", A paper presented at an International Symposium Celebrating the 50th Anniversary of the Department of Economics and the 20th Anniversary of the Economic Research Institute and the *Journal of Economic Development* at Chung-Ang University, Seoul, Korea, unpublished manuscript.

Lee, H.K. (1996), *The Korean Economy: Perspectives for the twenty-first century*, Albany: State University of New York Press.

Lee, K.S. (1972), *The Bruno production function, factor market disequilibrium, and factor contributions to growth in the Korea industrial sectors*, KDT WP7208, Seoul: Korea Development Institute.

Leipziger, D. (1987), *Korea: Managing the Industrial Transition*, World Bank.

Levy, B., Kuo, W.J. (1991), "The Strategic Orientations of Firms and the Performance of Korea and Taiwan in Frontier Industries: Lessons from Comparative Case Studies of Keyboard and Personal Computer Assembly", *World Development* 19(4): 363–374.

Mason, E.S. *et al.* (1980), *The Economic and Social Modernization of the Republic of Korea*, Cambridge, MA: Harvard University Press.

Mathews, J.A.(1995), *High-Technology Industrialisation in East Asia: The Case of the Semiconductor Industry in Taiwan and Korea*, Chung-Hua Institution for Economic Research, Tzong-shian Yu.

Ministry of Science and Technology, Korea (1995), *Report on the Survey of Research and Development in Science and Technology*, 1995.

Ministry of Science and Technology, Korea (1995), *Science and Technology in Korea 1995*.

Mody, A. (1989), "Institutions and Dynamic Comparative Advantage: Electronics Industry in South Korea and Taiwan", Industry and Energy Department Working Paper, Industry Series Paper No.9, World Bank.

Moreira, M.M. (1994), *Industrialization, Trade and Market Failures: The Role of Government Intervention in Brazil and the Republic of Korea*, London: Macmillan.

Mytelka, L., Ernst, D. (1998), "Catching up, Keeping up and Getting ahead: The Korean Model under pressure", Ernst, D., Ganiatsos, T., Mytelka, L. (eds.), *Technology Capabilities and Export Success in Asia*, London: Routledge.

Noland, M. (1996), "Restructuring Korea's Financial Sector for Greater Competitiveness, Institute for International Economics", APEC Working Paper 96–14.

Otsuka, S. (1987), "Korean Parts and Components Suppliers", Sakong, I. (ed.), *Macroeconomic policy and Industrial Development Issues*, Seoul: KDI.

Park, Y.C (1998), "Financial Crisis and Macroeconomic Adjustments in Korea, 1997–98", Park, Y.C., *Financial Liberalization and Opening in East Asia: Issues and Policy Challenges*, Seoul: Korea Institute of Finance.

Pecht, M., Bernstein, J.B., Searls, D., Peckarer, M. (1997), *The Korean Electronics Industry*, New York: CRC Press.

Pecht, M.G., Bernstein, J., Searls, D., Peckerar, M. (1998), "Korea's Focus on Market Dominance", *Semiconductor International*, pp.119–122.

Pilat, D. (1995), "Comparative productivity of Korean manufacturing", *Journal of Development Economics* 46(1): 123–144.

Rhee, Y.W., Ross-Larson, B., Pursell, G. (1984), *Korea's Competitive Edge: Managing the Entry into World Markets*, Baltimore: John Hopkins Press.

Robert, C. (1996), *Korea's economic miracle: The crucial role of Japan*, New York: St. Martin's Press.

Rodrick, D. (1995), "Getting intervention right: How S. Korea and Taiwan grew rich", *Economics Policy*, pp.55–107.

Rowley, C., Bae, J.S. (1998), "Special Issue: Korean Businesses: Internal and External Industrialization", *Asia Pacific Business Review*, Issues 4.2 & 3.

San, G. (1993), "A Comparison of Economic Development Between Taiwan and Korea and Taiwan Enterprises' Strategies in the 1990s", Brundenius, C., Goransson, B. (eds.), *New Technologies and Global Restructuring: The Third World at the Crossroads*, London: Taylor Graham Publishing.

Schive, C. (1990), "The Next Stage of Industrialization in Taiwan and Korea", Wyman, D.L., Gereffi, G. (eds.), *Manufacturing Miracle*, Princeton University Press.

Schive, C. (1990b), "The Next Stage of Industrialization in Taiwan and Korea", Wyman, E.L., Gereffi, G. (eds.), *Development Strategies in Latin America and East Asia*, Princeton: Princeton University Press, pp.267–291.

Scitovsky, T. (1986), "Economic Development in Taiwan and South Korea", Lau, L., Klein, L. (eds.) *Models of Development: A Comparative Study of Economic Growth in South Korea and Taiwan*, San Francisco: ICS Press.

Shin, R.W., Ho, A. (1997) "Industrial transformation: Interactive decision-making process in creating a global industry (Korea's electronics industry)", *Public Administration Quarterly* 21(2): 143–195.

Shin, R.W., Ho, A. (1997), "The role of science and technology in creating Korea's electronics industry", *Asian Affairs: An American Review*.

Shin, J.S. (1996) *The Economics of the Latecomers: Catching-up, technology transfer and institutions in Germany, Japan and South Korea,* Routledge.

Soh, C. (1997), *From Investment to Innovation?: The Korean Political Economy and Changes in Industrial Competitiveness*, Global Research Institute, Korea University.

Sohn, C.H., *et al.* (1998), "Korea's Trade and Industrial Policies: 1948–1998", KIEP Working Paper, 98–05, Korea Institute for International Economic Policy.

Sakong, I. (1993), *Korea in the World Economy*, Institute for International Economics.

Song, B.N. (1997), *The Rise of the Korean Economy*, 2nd edition, New York: Oxford University Press.

Stern, J.J., Kim, J.H., Perkins, D., Yoo, J.H. (1995), "Industrialization and the State: The Korean Heavy and Chemical Industry Drive", *Harvard Studies in the International Development*, Harvard Institute for International Development.

Tong, X.S., Zhao, H.X., Wong, P.K. (1996), "Technological development Strategies and International Patenting: Cases of South Korea and Taiwan", Department of Business Policy, National University of Singapore.

Tran, V.T. (1988), "Foreign capital and technology in the process of catching up by the developing countries: The experience of the synthetic fibre industry in the Republic of Korea", *Developing Economics* 26(4): 396–402.

Westphal, L.E. (1978), "The Republic of Korea's Exeperince with Export Led Development", *World Development* 6: 347–382.

Westphal, L.E., Kim, L., Dahlman, C.J. (1985), "Reflections on the Republic of Korea's Acquisition of Technological Capability", Rosenberg, N., Frischtak, C. (eds.), *International Transfer of Technology: Concepts, Measures and Comparisons*, New York, NY: Praeger.

Westphal, L.E., Rhee, Y.W., Pursell, G. (1988), "Korean Industrial Competence: Where It Came From", World Bank Staff Working paper 469.

Westphal, L.E. (1990), "Industrial Policy in an Export-Propelled Economy: Lessons from South Korea's Experience", *Journal of Economic Perspectives* 4(4): 41–59.

Whang, I.J.(1992), "Economic management for structural adjustment in the 1980s", Corbo, V., Suh, S.M. (eds.), *Structural Adjustment in a Newly Industrialized Country: The Korean Experience*, Baltimore, MD: Johns Hopkins University Press.

Woo, J.E. (1991), *Race to the Swift: State and Finance in Korean Industrialization*, NY: Columbia University.

Singapore

Asher, M.G. (1988), "An Economic Perspective", Thynne, I., Ariff, M. (eds.), *Privatisation: Singapore's Experience in Perspective*, Singapore: Longman.

Asher, M.G. (1995), "Public Policies and Domestic Saving: The Case of Singapore", *Report of the conference, Change and Prosperity: The Aspen Institute Program on the World Economy*, August 19–23, 1995, Aspen, Colorado.

Castells, M. (1988), *The developmental city state in an open economy: The Singapore experience*, Berkeley: University of California, Berkeley Roundtable on the International Economy.

Chan, H.C. (1971), *The Politics of Survival, 1965–1967*, Kuala Lumpur: Oxford University Press.

Chia, S.Y. (1971), "Growth and pattern of industrialisation", Seng, Y.P., Yah, L.C. (eds.), *The Singapore Economy*, Singapore: Eastern Universities Press.

Chia, S.Y. (1986), "Direct foreign investment and the industrialisation process in Singapore".

Yah, L.C., Lloyd, P.J. (eds.), *Singapore: Resources and Growth*, Singapore: Oxford University Press, pp.79–117.

Chiu, S., Ho, K.C., Lui, T.L. (1997), *City-States in the Global Economy*, Boulder: Westview Press.

Chng, M.K., Low, L., Tyabji, A., Tay, B.N. (1986), *Technology an Skills in Singapore*, Singapore: Institute of Southeast Studies.

Clammer, J. (1985), *Singapore, Ideology, Society, Culture*, Singapore: Chopman Enterprises.

Department of Statistics (1998), *Singapore Statistical Yearbook*.

Department of Statistics (1997), "Multifactor Productivity Growth in Singapore: Concept, Methodology and Trends", Occasional paper on economic statistics.

Deyo, F. (1991), "Singapore: Developmental paternalism", Goldstein, S.M. (ed.), *Mini Dragons: Fragile Economic Miracles in the Pacific*, Boulder: Westview Press.

Economic Development Board (EDB), Singapore (1996). *Electronics Industry in Singapore*, Singapore.

Economic Development Board (EDB), Singapore (1996). *Report on the Census for Industrial Production*, Singapore.

Economic Development Board (EDB), Singapore (1996). *EDB Yearbook*, Singapore.

Ermisch, J.F., Huff, W.G. (1999), "Hypergrowth in an East Asian NIC: Public Policy and Capital Accumulation in Singapore", *World Development* 27(1): 21–38.

Giordano, R., Kato, S. (1993), "Singapore: The most successful 'Asian dragon'", Goldman Sachs (ed.), *The International Economics Analyst* 8(2): S.01–S.12.

Goh, K.S. (1977), "A Socialist Economy That Works", Nair, C.V.D. (ed.), *Socialism that Works*, Singapore: Federal Publications.

Goh, K.S. (1995), *The Practice of Economic Growth,* Singapore: Federal Publications.

Goh, K.S. (1995), *Wealth of East Asian Nation*, Singapore: Federal Publications.

Goh, K.S., Low, L. (1996), "Beyond Miracles and Total Factor Productivity: The Singapore Experience", *ASEAN Economic Bulletin* 13(1).

Griffith, W.H. (1987), "Can CARICOM countries replicate the Singapore experience?", *Journal of Development Studies* 24(1): 60–82.

Han, F., Fernandez, W., Tan, S. (1998), *Lee Kuan Yew: The Man and his Ideas*, Singapore: Times Ed.

Hobday, M.G. (1994), "Technological learning in Singapore: a test case of leapfrogging", *Journal of Development Studies* 30(4): 831–858.

Huff, W.G. (1994), *The Economic Growth of Singapore: Trade and Development in the twentieth century*, Cambridge University Press.

Huff, W.G. (1995), "The developmental state, government, and Singapore's economic development since 1960", *World Development* 23(8): 1421–1438.

Hughes, H, You, P.S. (eds.) (1969), *Foreign Investment and Industrialization in Singapore*, Canberra: Australian National University Press.

IMF (1999), "Singapore: Selected Issues", IMF Staff Country Report No.99/35, April 1999.

International Monetary Fund (1995), *Singapore: A Case Study in Rapid Development*, IMF, Washington, D.C.

Islam, I., Kirkpatrick, C. (1986), "Export-led development, labour market controls and distribution of income: The case of Singapore", *Cambridge Journal of Economics*, Vol. 10.

Koh, A.T. (1987), "Saving, Investment and entrepreneurship", Krause, L.B., *et al.* (eds.), *The Singapore Economy Reconsidered*, Singapore: Institute of Southeast Asian Studies, pp.78–106.

Krause, L.B., Koh, A.T., Lee, T.Y. (1987), *The Singapore Economy Reconsidered.* Singapore: Institute of Southeast Asian Studies.

Krause, L.B. (1988), "Hong Kong and Singapore: Twins or kissing cousins?", *Economic Development and Cultural Change*, Vol. 36, No.3, April Supplement.

Lee, H.L. (1986), "Singapore's economic policy: Vision for the 1990s", Speech at the Commonwealth Institute, London.

Lee, K.Y. (1998), *The Singapore Story: Memoirs of Lee Kuan Yew*, Singapore: Singapore Press Holdings: Times Editions.

Lee, K.Y. (2000), *From Third World to First: The Singapore Story, 1965–2000: Memoirs of Lee Kuan Yew*, Singapore: Singapore Press Holdings: Times Editions.

Lee, T.Y. (1982), "Growth and productivity in the Singapore economy: A supply side analysis", PhD dissertation, Harvard University, Cambridge, USA.

Lee, T.Y. (1985), "Growth without Productivity: Singapore Manufacturing in the 1970s", *Journal of Development Economics* 18: 25–38.

Lee, T.Y. (1986), "Sources of growth accounting for the Singapore economy", Lim, C.Y., Lloyd, P. (eds.), *Singapore Resources and Growth*, New York: Oxford University Press, pp.17–44.

Lee, T.Y., Low, L. (1990), *Local Entrepreneurship in Singapore: Private and State*, Singapore: Times Academic Press.

Lee, T.Y. (1994), *Overseas Investment: Experience of Singapore Manufacturing Companies*, Singapore: McGraw-Hill.

Lee, T.Y., Arun, M. (eds.) (1998), *Singapore: Re-engineering Success*, Singapore: Institute of Policy Studies, Oxford University Press.

Lim, C.Y. and Associates (1988), *Policy Options for Singapore Economy*, Singapore: McGraw Hill.

Lim, C.Y, Peter, J.L. (eds.) (1988), *Singapore: Resources and Growth*, Singapore: Oxford University Press.

Lim, L. (1983), "Singapore's Success: The Myth of the Free Market Economy", *Asian Survey* 23(6).

Lim, L., Pang, E.F. (1984), "Labour strategies and the high-tech challenge: The Case of Singapore", *Euro-Asia Business Review* 3(2): 27–31.

Lim, L., Pang, E.F. (1986), *Trade, Employment and Industrialisation in Singapore*, International Labour Organisation, Geneva.

Lim, L. (1987), "Capital, Labour and the state in the internationalisation of high-tech industry: The case of Singapore", Douglass, M., Friedmann, J. (eds.), *Transnational Capital and Urbanisation on the Pacific Rim*, Centre for Pacific Rim Studies, UCLA, pp.1–62.

Lim, L., Pang, E.F., Findlay, R. (1993), "Singapore", Findlay, R., Wellisz, S., (eds.), *Five Small Open Economies*, Oxford: Oxford University Press for World Bank, pp.93–139.

Low, L. (1984), "Public enterprises in Singapore", You, P.S., Lim, C.Y. (eds.), *Singapore: Twenty-five Years of Development* , Singapore: Nan Yang Xing Zhou Lianhe Zaobao, pp.253–287.

Low, L. (1991), *The Economies of Education and Manpower: Issues and Policies in Singapore*, Singapore: McGraw-Hill.

Low, L. (1998), *The Political Economy of a City-State: Government-made,* Singapore: Oxford University Press.

Low, L. & Johnston, D.M. (eds.) (2001), *Singapore Inc.: Public Polity Options in the Third Millennium*, Singapore: Asia Pacific Press.

Low, L., Toh, M.H., Soon, T.W., Tan, K.Y., Hughes, H. (1993), *Challenges and Response: Thirty Years of Economic Development Board*, Singapore: Times Academic Press.

Ministry of Finance, Singapore (1993), *Final Report of the Committee to Promote Enterprise Overseas*, Singapore National Printers.

Ministry of Trade and Industry (MTI), Singapore (1991), *Strategic Economic Plan (SEP)*, Singapore Government Printers.

Ministry of Trade and Industry (MTI), Singapore (1998), *Economic Survey of Singapore*.

Ministry of Trade and Industry (1998), *Committee on Singapore's Competitiveness*, Singapore: MTI.

Mirza, H (1986), *Multinationals and Growth of the Singapore Economy*, New York: St. Martins Press.

Murray, G., Perera, A. (1996), *Singapore: The Global City-State*, Kent: China Library.

Natarajan, S., Tan, J.M. (1992), *The Impacts of MNC Investments in Malaysia, Singapore and Thailand*, Singapore: Institute of Southeast Asian Studies.

National Computer Board (1992), *A Vision of an Intelligent Island: IT2000 Report*, Singapore: NCB.

National Computer Board (1996), *Singapore IT Manpower Survey 1995*, Singapore: NCB.

National Science and Technology Board (1991), *National Technology Plan*, Singapore: NSTB.

National Science and Technology Board (1996), *Securing our Future: National Science and Technology Plan*, Singapore: NSTB.

National Science & Technology Board, Singapore (1994), *National Survey of R&D*, Singapore: NSTB.

Pang, E.F. (1987), "Foreign investment in the state of Singapore", Cable, V., Persaud, B. (eds.), *Developing with Foreign Investment*, London: Croom Helm.

Pang, E.F., Tan A. (1981), "Export-led industrialisation: the experience of Singapore", Amjad, R. (ed.), *The Development of Labour-intensive Industry in ASEAN Countries*, ILO, Geneva.

Peebles, G., Wilson, P. (1996), *The Singapore Economy*, UK: Edward Elgar.

Rao, V.V.B., Lee, C. (1996), "Sources of Growth in the Singapore Economy and its Manufacturing and Services Sectors", *The Singapore Economic Review* 40(1): 83–115.

Rao, V.V. B., Owyong, D. (1997), "Sources of Growth in the Singapore Economy: Some New Results", Paper presentation at Taipei International Conference on Efficiency and Productivity Growth.

Rodan, G. (1989), *The Political Economy of Singapore's Industrialization: National State and Interest Capital*, London: McMillan.

Rodan, G. (ed.) (1993), *Singapore Changes Guard: Social, Political and Economic Directions in the 1990s*, New York: St. Martin's Press.

Sandhu, K., Wheatley, P. (eds.) (1989), *Management of Success: The Moulding of Modern Singapore*, Singapore: Institute of Southeast Asian Studies.

Schein, E. (1996), *Strategic Pragmatism: The Culture of the Economic Development Board of Singapore*, MIT Press.

Soon, T.W. (1988), *Singapore's New Education Systems: Education Reform for National Development*, Singapore: Institute of Southeast Asian Studies.

Soon, T.W., Tan, C.S. (1993), "Singapore: Public Policy and Economic Development", Leipziger, D.M. (ed.), *Lessons from East Asia*, The University of Michigan Press.

Tan, A.H.H., Ow, C.H. (1981), "Singapore", Balassa, B. (ed.), *Development Strategies in Semi-industrial Countries*, Baltimore: John Hopkins University Press.

The Economic Committee (1986), *The Singapore Economy: New Directions*, Singapore: Ministry of Trade and Industry.

Toh, M.H., Low, L. (1996), "Differential total factor productivity in the Four Dragons: The Singapore case", *The Journal of International Trade and Economic Development* 5(2): 161–181.

Toh, M.H., Tan, K. Y. (eds.) (1998), *Competitiveness of the Singapore Economy*, Singapore: World Scientific/Singapore University Press.

Urban Redevelopment Authority (1991), *Living the Next Lap: Towards a Tropical City of Excellence*, Singapore.

Vennewald, W. (1994), "Technocrats in the state enterprise system of Singapore", Asia Research Centre, Murdoch University, Working Paper No.32, November.

Wong, K.P (1986), "Saving, Capital inflow and capital formation", Lim, C.Y., Lloyd, P.J. (eds.), *Singapore: Resources and Growth*, Singapore: Oxford University Press.

Wong, P.K. (1991), *Technological Development Through Subcontracting Linkages*, Tokyo: Asian Productivity Organization.

Wong, P.K. (1992), "Technological Development Through Subcontracting Linkages: Evidence from Singapore", *Scandinavian International Business Review*, 1(3): 28–40.

Wong, P.K. (1994), "Singapore's Technology Strategy", D.F. Simon (ed.), *The Emerging Technological Trajectory of the Pacific Rim*. New York: M.E. Sharpe.

Wong, P.K. (1995a), "Competing in the Global Electronics Industry: A Comparative Study of the Innovation Networks of Singapore and Taiwan", *Journal of Industry Studies* 2(2): 35–61.

Wong, P.K. (1995b), "Technology Transfer and Development Inducement by Foreign MNCs: The Experience of Singapore", Jeong, K.Y., Kwack, M.H. (eds.), *Industrial Strategy for Global Competitiveness of Korean Industries*, Seoul: Korea Economic Research Institute.

Wong, P.K. (1995c), *National Innovation System: The Case of Singapore*, Seoul: Science and Technology Policy Institute (STEPI).

Wong, P.K. (1996a), "From NIE to Developed Economy: Singapore's Industrial Policy to the Year 2000", *Journal of Asian Business* 12(3): 65–85.

Wong, P.K. (1996b), "Implementing the NII Vision: Singapore's experience and future challenges", *Information Infrastructure and Policy* 5(2): 95–117.

Wong, P.K. (1997), "Creation of a Regional Hub for Flexible Production: The Case of Hard Disk Drive Industry in Singapore", *Industry and Innovation*, Vol.4, No.2.

Wong, P.K. (1998a), "Technology acquisition pattern of high-tech firms in Singapore", *Singapore Management Review* 20(1): 43–64.

Wong, P.K. (1998b), "Leveraging the Global Information Revolution for Economic Development: Singapore's Evolving Information Industry Strategy", *Information Systems Research*.

Wong, P.K. (1999), "The dynamics of HDD industry development in Singapore", Information Storage Industry Centre, University of California, San Diego, Research Report 99–03, July.

Wong, P.K. (2000), "Riding the waves: Technological change, competing US-Japan production networks and the growth of Singapore's electronics industry", in M. Borrus, S. Haggard and D. Ernst (eds.), *International Production Networks in Asia: Rivalry or Riches?*, London: Routledge, pp.176–197.

Wong, P.K. (2000), "The contribution of IT to the rapid economic development of Singapore", in M. Pohjola (ed.), *Information Technology, Productivity, and Economic Growth: International Evidence*, Oxford University Press, pp.221–241.

Wong, P.K. (2001), "From Using to Creating Technology: The Evolution of Singapore's National Innovation System and the Changing Role of Public Policy", forthcoming in *Technological Development in East Asia*, Oxford University Press.

Wong,P.K. (2001), "Globalization of American, European and Japanese Production Networks and The Growth of Singapore's Electronics Industry", *International Journal of Technology Management*, forthcoming.

Wong,P.K. (2001), "Leveraging Multinational Corporations, Fostering Technopreneurship: The Changing Role of S&T Policy in Singapore", *International Journal of Technology Management*, forthcoming.

Wong,P.K., McKendrick, D., *et al.* (2000), "Singapore", in D.G. McKendrick, R.F. Doner and S.Haggard, *From Silicon Valley to Singapore: Location and Competitive Advantage in the Hard Disk Drive Industry*, Stanford: Stanford University Press, pp.155–183.

Wong,P.K. and Singh, A.A. (2000), "The Role of Foreign MNCs in the Technological Development of Singaporean Industries", in J.Legewie and H. Meyer-Ohle (eds.), *Corporate Strategies for Southeast Asia After the Crisis*, Houndmills, Basingstoke, Hampshire: Macmillan Press, pp.40–54.

World Maker Design (1997), *Towards Tomorrow: The Singapore Technologies Story*, Singapore: Singapore Technologies.

Young, A. (1992), "A Tale of Two Cities: Factor Accumulation and Technical Change in Hong Kong and Singapore", *NBER Macroeconomic Annual 1992*, MIT Press.

Taiwan

Amsden, A.H. (1984), "Taiwan", *World Development* 12(5/6): 491–503.

Amsden, A. (1985), "The State and Taiwan's Economic Development", Evans, P. Rueschemeyer D., Skocpol, T. (eds.), *Bringing the State Back in*, Cambridge University Press.

Arensman, R. (1998), "Advantage Taiwan", *Electronic Business*, Vol: 24, Iss. 3, March 1998.

Chan, S. Clark, C. (1992), *Flexibility, Foresight and Fortune in Taiwan's Development: Navigating between Scyll and Charybdis*, Routledge.

Chan, V.L., Chen, B.L., Chueng, K.N. (1995), "External Economies in Taiwan's Manufacturing Industries", *Contemporary Economic Policy*, No.13: 118–130.

Chao, J.C. (1985), *The Use of the US Aid to Taiwan* (in Chinese), Taipei, Taiwan: Llien-Ching Press.

Chaponniere, J.R., Fouquin, M. (1989), "Technological Change and the Electronics Sector — Perspectives and Policy Options for Taiwan", Report Prepared for OECD Development Centre Project, *Technological Change and the Electronics Sector — Perspectives and Policy Options for Newly-Industrialising Economies*, Paris: OECD.

Chen, B.L. (1996), "Picking the Winners and Industralization in Taiwan", *Journal of International Trade and Economic Development*, No.5: 137–159.

Chen, B.L., Hsu, M. (1997), 'Technology Adoption and Industrialization: Different experiences of man-made fibre in Taiwan and Korea", mimeo., Institute of Economics, Academia Sinica.

Chen, P.C., Chu, Y.P. (1994), "The Present State and Prospect of the Taiwan Economy: Structural Adjustment and Its Implication for Changes in the Pattern of International Division of Labour", Presented at the 1994 conference of the East Asian Economic Association, Taipei.

Chen, T.J. (1992), "Technical Change and Technical Adaptation of Multinational Firms: The Case of Taiwan's Electronics Industry", *Economic Development and Cultural Change*.

Chen, T.J., Tang, D.P. (1990), "Export performance and productivity growth: The case of Taiwan", *Economic Development & Cultural Change* 38(3): 577–585.

Chen, T.J., Wang, W.T. (1994), "Wai T&C Ch'ang Shang Te Pen Tu Hua: Mei Jih Den Tzu Ch'ang Te Pi chiao Yen Chiu" (*Localization of Foreign Firms: A Comparative Study of American Cover*).

Chen, Y.Y. (1992), "The Technology Derivation Mode for Enhancing the Transfer of Industrial Technology Research and Development in Taiwan", Khalil, T., Bayraktar, B. (eds.), *Management of Technology II*, Institute of Industrial Engineers.

Chen, Y.Y., Liang, S.K., Yuan, B., Chen, M.R. (1992), "Crucial Management Principles of High-Tech Companies in Taiwan", Khalil, T., Bayraktar, B. (eds.), *Management of Technology II*, Institute of Industrial Engineers.

Chiang, J.T. (1990), "Management of National Technology Programs in a Newly Industrialized Country — Taiwan", *Technovation*, 10(8): 531–554.

Chien, J.C. (1988), "Den Tze Ling Tso Chien Yeh Fa Chan Ch'e Lieh Yen Chiu Pao Kao (Development Strategy of Electronic Components Industry)", Project report, Taipei: Taiwan Institute for Economic Research.

Chu, C.H. (1975), "Tai-wan chih Den Tze Kung Yeh" (The Electronics Industry in Taiwan), *Taiwan Bank Quarterly* 26(1): 112–130.

Chu, Y.P. (1994), "Taiwan's External Imbalance and Structural Adjustment: A General Equilibrium Analysis", *Asian Economic Journal*, No.8: 85–114.

Chow, P.C.Y. and Gill, B. (eds.) (2000), *Weathering the Storm: Taiwan, its Neighbors, and the Asian Financial Crisis*, Washington D.C.: Brookings Institution Press.

Clark, C. (1989), *Taiwan's Development: Implications for Contending Political Economy Paradigms (Contributions in Economics and Economic History, No. 100)*, New York: Greenwood Press.

Clifford, M. (1993), "Price of Independence: Taiwanese firms weigh cost of screen technology," *Far East Economic Review*, December 23, pp.52–53.

Council for Economic Planning and Development (CEPD) (1988), Ad Hoc Committee for the Improvement of Economic and Social Legislation, *Review and Recommendations on Taxation of the Statute for the Encouragement of Investment*, Taipei, Taiwan: CEPD.

Council for Economic Planning and Development (1997), *Taiwan: 2006: Plan for National Development into the Next Century*, Executive Yuan, Republic of China.

Council for Economic Planning and Development (CEPD) (1998), "Current Economic Situation (in Chinese)", report submitted to the Executive Yuan, Taiwan Council for Economic Planning and Development (CEPD), *Final Report on the Impact of the APROC Plan on Taiwan's Economic Development*, Chung Hwa Institution for Economic Research (in Chinese), July 1998.

Dahlman, C. J., Sananikone, O. (1997), "Taiwan, China: Policies and Institutions for Rapid Growth", Leipziger, D.M. (ed.), *Lesson from East Asia*, Ann Arbor: University of Michigan Press.

Davidson, J. (1903), *The Island of Formosa: Past and Present*, NY: MacMillian.

Directorate-General of Budget (1991), *The Report on 1991 Industrial and Commercial Census Taiwan-Fukien Area*, The Republic of China.

Dolven, B. (1998), "Taiwan's Trump", *Far Eastern Economic Review*, August 6, 1998.

Economist (1998), "The Flexible Tiger", *Economist* Vol. 346, Iss. 8049.

Fei, J. C.H, Ranis, G., Kuo, S.W.Y. (1979), *Growth with Equity: The Taiwan Case*, London: Oxford University Press.

Fei, J., Kuo, S.W.Y., Ranis, G. (1981), *The Taiwan Success Story: Rapid Growth with Improved Ditsribution in the Republic of China, 1952–79*, Westview.

Galenson, W. (ed.) (1979), *Economic Growth and Structural Change in Taiwan*, Ithaca: Cornell University Press.

Gee, S., Kuo, W.J. (1998), "Export Success and Technology Capability: Textiles and Electronics in Taiwan Province of China", Ernst, D., Ganiatsos, T., Mytelka, L. (eds.), *Technological Capabilities and Export Success in Asia*, Routledge.

Gold, T.B. (1986), *State and Society in the Taiwan Miracle*, NY: M.E. Sharpe.

Haggard, S. (1988), "The politics of industrialization in the Republic of Korea and Taiwan".

Hughes, H. (ed.), *Achieving Industrialization in East Asia*, Cambridge: Cambridge University Press.

Hattor, T., Sato, Y. (1996), *Kankoku Taiwan no Hatten Mekanizumu* (*The Development Mechanism in Korea and Taiwan*), Tokyo: Institute of Developing Economies.

Ho, S.P.S. (1978), *Economic Development of Taiwan, 1860–1970*, New Haven: Yale University Press.

Hou, C.M., Gee, S. (1993), "National Systems Supporting Technical Advance in Industry: The Case of Taiwan", Nelson, R.R. (eds.), *National Innovation Systems: A Comparative Analysis*, Oxford University Press.

Hsia, A., Fung, F. (1993), "Management of Innovation: A view from Taiwan's High-Tech Industry", *APO Productivity Journal,* Spring 1993.

Hsiao, F.H. (1994), *Industrial Policies and Industrial Development in Taiwan* (in Chinese), Taipei: Far East.

Hsiao, F.H. (1995), "Tsung Shih Chang Ching Ju Chang Ai Tan Tao Tai Wan Kao Ko Chi Chan Yeh Fa Chan Tse Lueh — Chi Ti Tien Lu Chan Yeh Chih Ko An Yeh Chiu" (A Study on Industrial Development Policy from the Viewpoint of Entry Barriers — The Case of the IC Industry), *Industry of Free China.*

Hsieh, C.H., Wang, K., Sun, P. (1997), "The development of capability for tackling R&D issues in small companies: A case of a CNC-controller manufacturer in Taiwan", *International Journal of Technology Management*, Vol. 13, Iss. 5,6.

Hsu, S.K. (1996), "On the Contribution of Taiwan's Industrial Policy: 1960–90 (in Chinese)", Academia Sinica: Institute of Economics, Discussion Paper No.8502.

Hu, M.W., Schive, C. (1998), "The Changing Competitiveness of Taiwan's Manufacturing SMEs", *Journal Small and Medium-sized Business*, 1998.

Hwang, Y.D. (1991), *The Rise of a New World Economic Power: Postwar Taiwan*, Greenwood.

Industrial Development and Investment Center (1968), "The Electronics Industry in Taiwan", *Industry of Free China* 29(3): 32–44.

Investment Commission (1980), Wo-Kuo Den Tze Den Chih Chih Tsao Yeh Chih Su Ho Tso Chen Kuo Tiao Ch'a Pao Kao (*Survey Report on Technology Cooperation Programs in the Electronics Industry*), Taipei: Investment Commission, Ministry of Economic Affairs.

Industrial Technology Research Institute (1987), "Chi Ti tien lu Chuan An Chi Hua Tui Chan Yeh Ying Hsiang Chih Chui Tsung Yu Fen His" (*An Assessment of Government R&D Projects on the Development of the IC Industry*), *Project Report*, Taipei: ITRI.

Jacoby, N.H. (1966), *U.S. Aid to Taiwan*, NY: Praeger.

Jan, F.G., Schive, C. (1997), "WTO and Taiwan's Financial Liberalization and Internationalization (in Chinese)", presentation at a conference in memory of Kuo-Shu Liang.

Johnson, C. (1987), "Political Institutions and Economic Performance: The Government-Business Relationship in Japan, South Korea and Taiwan", Deyo, F.C. (ed.), *The Political Economy of the New Asian Industrialization*, Ithaca: Cornell University Press.

Kang, D.C. (1995), "South Korean and Taiwanese Development and the New Institutional Economics", *International Organisation* 49, 3: 555–587.

Kim, W.S. (1997), "Comments on Public Policies in the Taiwan Economy — The Nurturing of a Market Economy by Chi Schive and Hsien-Feng Lee", Presented at the Workshop on Public Policies in East Asian Economies, Kitakyushu.

Klein, L.R. *et al.* (1994), *Economic Development of ROC and the Pacific Rim in the 1990s and Beyond: Taiwan R.O.C. May 25–28, 1992: 10th Anniversary of the Asia and the Pacific Co*, World Scientific.

Klintworth, G. (1995), *New Taiwan, New China: Taiwan's Changing Role in the Asia-Pacific Region*, New York: St. Martin's Press.

Ko, C.M. (1993), *The Creation, Operation and Productive Organisation of Taiwan's Urban Small-scale Manufacturing* (in Chinese), Taipei: Institute of Ethnology, Academia Sinica.

Kraemer, K.L., Dedrick, J. (1995), *Entrepreneurship, Flexibility and Policy Coordination: Taiwan's Information Technology Industry*, Centre for Research on Information Technology and Organisations, University of California.

Kuo, S.W.Y. , Ranis, G., Fei, J.C.H. (1981), *The Taiwan Success Story: Rapid Growth with Improved Distribution in the R.O.C. 1952–1979*, Boulder: Westview Press.

Kuo, S.W.Y. (1983), *The Taiwan Economy in Transition*, Boulder: Westview Press.

Kuo, S.W.Y. (1997), *Economic Policies: The Taiwan Experience 1945–1995*, Taipei: Hwa-Tai.

Kuo, C.T., Tsai, T.J. (1998), "Differential Impact of the Exchange Crisis on Taiwan, Japan, and South Korea: A Politico-Institutional Explanation", Presented at the Conference on The East Asian Economic Crisis: One Year After, organized by the ASEAN Institute of Strategic and International Studies and the Institute of International Relations, Taiwan, Taipei.

Kuznets, S. (1979), "Growth and structural shifts", Galenson, W. (ed.), *Economic Growth and Structural Change in Taiwan*, Cornell University Press, Ithaca, NY.

Lai, V.S. (1972), "Tai-wan Den Tze Kung Yeh Chih Yen Chiu (Taiwan's Electronics Industry)", Masters Thesis, National Taiwan University.

Lau, L. (ed.) (1990), *Models of Development: A Comparative Study of Economic Growth in South Korea and Taiwan*, San Francisco: ICS Press.

Lee, C.H. (1995), "The State and the Market in the Economic Development of Korea and Taiwan: Lessons for Economic Development and Transition", A paper presented at an International Symposium Celebrating the 50th Anniversary of the Department of Economics and the 20th Anniversary of the Economic Research Institute and the *Journal of Economic Development* at Chung-Ang University, Seoul, Korea, unpublished manuscript.

Lee, C.S., Pecht, M. (1997), *The Taiwan Electronics Industry*, Boca Raton, Florida: CRC Press.

Levy, B., Kuo, W.J. (1991), "The Strategic Orientations of Firms and the Performance of Korea and Taiwan in Frontier Industries: Lessons from Comparative Case Studies of Keyboard and Personal Computer Assembly", *World Development* 19(4): 363–374.

Li, K.T., Yu, T.S. (eds.) (1982), *Experiences and Lessons of Economic Development in Taiwan*, Institute of Economics.

Li, K.T. (1988), *Economic Transformation of Taiwan, ROC*, London: Shepheard-Walwyn.

Li, K.T. (1995), *The Evolution of Policy Behind Taiwan's Development Success*, Singapore: World Scientific.

Liang, C.Y. (1989), *The sources of growth and productivity change in Taiwan's industries, 1961–1981*, Discussion Paper No. 8903, Institute of Economics, Academia Sinica, Taipei.

Liang, K.S., Hou,C.I. (1988), "Development Policy Formation and Future Policy Priorities in the Republic of China", *Economic Development and Cultural Change*, Vol.36, No.3, Supplement.

Lin, C.Y. (1973), *Industrialization in Taiwan*, NY: Praeger.

Lin, H.M. (1987), "Ai Fa Chung Kuo Chia Hsin Hsing Chan Yeh Fa chan Kuo Cheng Chih Yeh chiu — Wo Kuo IC Kung Yeh Shih Li Tan Tao" (Newly Emerged Industries in Developing Countries — The Case of Taiwan's IC Industry), Master Thesis, Graduate Institute of Business, National Taiwan University.

Lin, O.C.C. (1994), "Development and Transfer of Industrial Technology in Taiwan, R.O.C.", Lin, O.C.C., Shih, C.T. , Yang, J.C. (eds.), *Development and Transfer of Industrial Technology*, Elsevier Science B.V., ITRI.

Little, A.D. (1974), "The Electronics Industry in Taiwan", *Industry of Free China* 42(1): 21–34.

Liu, C.Y. (1993), "Government's role in developing a high-tech industry: the case of Taiwan's semiconductor industry", *Technovation* 13(5): 299–309.

Liu, S.J, Lee J.F. (1997), "Liquid crystal display industry in Taiwan", *International Journal of Technology Management* 13(3): 308–325.

Liu, T.Y. (1985), "Jih Shang: Lai Hua Tou Tzu Tui Wo Kuo Ching Chi Chi Yin Shiang (Economic Impacts of Japanese Investment in Taiwan)", *Taipei: Project Report to Research and Development Council*, Executive Yuan.

Lu, C.Y. (1995), "Wo Kuo Tzu Wei Mi Pan Tao Ti Chi Chi Shu Fa Chan Chi Chan Wang" (The Development of Submicron Semiconductor Technology in Taiwan and Future Perspectives), Unpublished manuscript.

Lundberg, Erik (1979), "Fiscal and Monetary Policies", Galenson, W. (ed.), *Economic Growth and Structural Change in Taiwan*, Ithaca, NY: Cornell University Press, pp.308–383.

Mathews, J. (1995), *High-Technology Industrialization in East Asia: The Case of the Semiconductor Industry in Taiwan and Korea*, Taipei: Chung-Hua Institution for Economic Research.

McDermott, M.C. (1991), *Taiwan's Industry in World Markets*, The Economist Intelligence Unit

Mody, A. (1989), "Institutions and Dynamic Comparative Advantage: Electronics Industry in South Korea and Taiwan", Industry and Energy Department Working Paper, Industry Series Paper No.9.

Moore, J. (1997), "Taiwan's New Grail: Innovation", *Business Week*, Iss. 3541, August 25, 1997.

National Science Council (1995), *Indicator of Science and Technology,* Republic of China.

National Science Council (1998), "A Status Report on the Study of National Innovation Systems in Taiwan: A Catching-up Economies Framework and Perspective", National Science Council Research Team on National Innovation Systems.

National Science Council (1998), "Knowledge Flow and Industry Innovation", APEC/OECD Innovation Project.

Naughton, B. (1997), *The China Circle: Economics and Electronics in the PRC, Taiwan, and Hong Kong*, Brookings Institute Press.

Ng, L. F.Y. *et al.* (1997), *Three Chinese Economies: China, Hong Kong and Taiwan: Challenges and Opportunities*, Chinese University Press.

O'Connor, D., Wang, C. (1992), "European and Taiwanese Electronics Industries and Cooperation Opportunities", Paper presented at Sino-European Conference on Economic Development.

Pang, C.K. (1992), *The State and Economic Transformation: The Taiwan Case (Developing Economies of the Third World)*, New York: Garland Publication.

Park, A., Johnston, B. (1995), "Rural Development and Dynamic Externalities in Taiwan's Structural Transformation", *Economic Development and Cultural Change* 44(1): 181–208.

Ranis, G. (1979), "Industrial Development", Galenson, W. (ed.), *Economic Growth and Structural Change in Taiwan*, Ithaca: Cornell University Press.

Ranis, G. (1992), *Taiwan: From Developing to Mature Economy*, Westview Press.

Rodrick, D. (1995), "Getting intervention right: How S. Korea and Taiwan grew rich", *Economics Policy*, pp.55–107.

San, G. (1989), "A Comparison of the R&D Efforts of National Firms and Foreign Direct Investment Firms in the ROC — A Study of the Electronics Industry" (in Chinese), *Academia Economic Papers*, Taipei: Institute of Economics, Academia Sinica.

San, G. (1990), "The Status and an Evaluation of the Electronics Industry in Taiwan", Technical Papers No.29, OECD Development Centre.

San, G. (1993), "A Comparison of Economic Development Between Taiwan and Korea and Taiwan Enterprises' Strategies in the 1990s", Brundenius, C., Goransson, B. (eds.), *New Technologies and Global Restructuring: The Third World at the Crossroads*, London: Taylor Graham Publishing.

San, G. (1995), " Policy priorities for industrial development in Taiwan", *Journal of Industry Studies* 2(1): 27–55.

Schive, C., Barlow, M. (1989), "Policy Reform in Taiwan's Economic Development: 1950–1965", Conference on Democracy in China, Pacific Culture Foundation and Carnegie Council on Ethics and International Affairs, New York.

Schive, C. (1995), *Taiwan's Economic Role in East Asia*, Washington D.C.: Center for Strategic and International Studies.

Schive, C., Lee, H.F. (1997), "Public Policies in the Taiwan Economy — The Nurturing of a Market Economy", Presented at the Workshop on Public Policies in East Asian Economies, Kitakyushu.

Schive, C. (1990), "The Next Stage of Industrialization in Taiwan and Korea", Wyman, D.L., Gereffi, G. (eds.), *Manufacturing Miracle*, Princeton University Press.

Schive, C., Yeh. R.S. (1980), "Direct Foreign Investment and Taiwan's TV Industry", *Economic Essays* 9(2): 261–291.

Schive, C. (1990a), *The Foreign Factor: The Multinational Corporation's Contribution to the Economic Modernization of the Republic of China*, Stanford: Hoover Press.

Schive, C. (1990b), "The Next Stage of Industrialization in Taiwan and Korea", Wyman, E.L., Gereffi, G. (eds.), *Development Strategies in Latin America and East Asia*, Princeton: Princeton University Press, pp.267–291.

Schive, C. (1994), "How did Taiwan Solve its Dutch Disease Problem?", Research in *Asian Economic Studies, Vol.5 of Asia-Pacific Economies: 1990s and Beyond*, London: JAI Press, pp.183–202.

Schive, C. (1995), "Industrial Policies in a Maturing Taiwan Economy", *Journal of Industry Studies* 2(1): 5–25.

Schive, C. (1998), "Taiwan's Move Toward 2000: Economic Liberalization and Regional Operations", *Review of Pacific Basin Financial Markets and Policies* 1(1): 99–116.

Schive, C. (1998), "Taiwan's Economic Role After the Financial Crisis", Presentation at Conference in Memory of Professor Kuo-Shu Liang.

Schive, C. (1998), "How was Taiwan's Economy Opened Up? The Foreign Factor in Appraisal", *The Political Economy of Taiwan's Development into the 21st Century: Essays in Memory of John C.H. Fei*, Vol.2, Edward Elgar Publishing Limited.

Scitovsky, T. (1986), "Economic Development in Taiwan and South Korea", Lau, L., Klein, L. (eds.) *Models of Development: A Comparative Study of Economic Growth in South Korea and Taiwan*, San Francisco: ICS Press.

Scott, M. (1979), "Foreign Trade", *Economic Growth and Structural Change in Taiwan*, Galenson, W. (ed.), Ithaca, NY: Cornell University Press, pp.263–307.

Shieh, G. S. (1992), *Boss Island: The Subcontracting Network and Micro-Entrepreneurship in Taiwan's Development*, NY: Peter-Lang.

Simon, D.F., Kau, M.Y.M. (eds.) (1992), *Taiwan: Beyond the Economic Miracle (Taiwan in the Modern World)*, New York: M.E. Sharpe.

Simon, D.F., Kau (1992), "Taiwan's Emerging Technological Trajectory: Creating New Forms of Competitive Advantage", Simon, D.F., Kau, M.Y.M. (eds.) *Taiwan: Beyond the Economic Miracles*, NY: M.E. Sharpe.

Thorton, E. (1996), "Made in Japan: Taiwan vies for a piece of the other big screen marker", *Far Eastern Economic Review*, January 11, pp.52–53.

Tong, X.S., Zhao, H.X., Wong, P.K. (1996), "Technological development Strategies and International Patenting: Cases of South Korea and Taiwan", Department of Business Policy, National University of Singapore.

Tsai, M.C. (1996), *The Politics of Transition to Neoliberal Economy: The Case of Taiwan*, Department of Sociology, National Chung Hsing University.

Tsiang, S.C. (1985), "Reasons for the Successful Economic Takeoff of Taiwan", *Industry of Free China*, September.

Wang, F.Y. (1990), "Reconsidering the East Asian model of development: The link between exports and productivity enhancement, evidence from Taiwan, 1950–87", PhD dissertation, University of California, Los Angeles.

Wang, J.C. (1993), "Cooperative Research in a Newly Industrialised Country: Taiwan", *Research Policy* 23: 697–711, Elsevier Science B.V.

Weiss, L. (1994), "Government-Business Relations in East Asia: The Changing Basis of State Capacity", Taipei: Chung-hua Institution for Economic Research, Occasional Paper Series No. 9407.

Wong, P.K. (1995), "Competing in the Global Electronics Industry: A Comparative Study of the Innovation Networks of Singapore and Taiwan", *Journal of Industry Studies*, Vol.2, No.2, Dec. 1995.

Wu, Y.P. (1994), Ko Hsueh Yuan Chu Chi Ti tien Lu Chan Yeh Hsien Kuang Fen His Chi Wei Lai Fa chan Mu Piao Yu Tse Lueh (*Analysis of the Current Status of the IC Industry in the Hsinchu Science-Based Industrial Park and Future Perspectives*), Hsinchu Science-Based Industrial Park Administration.

Yanaihara, T. (1929), *Taiwan under Imperialism* (Chinese translation by Chou, H.-W., published by Pamir, Taipei), Tokyo: Iwanami Shoten.

Yang, S.C. (1991),"Strategy and Experience of Industrial Development in Taiwan, ROC — Supporting Infrastructure: Case Study of Taiwan", Seminar on developing physical and supporting infrastructure for industrial restructuring.

Yin, K.Y. (1963), *My View of Taiwan's Economy* (in Chinese), Taipei: Council for Economic Planning and Development, p.89.

Yu, T.S. (1996), "The Myth of the effect of Industrial Policy: The case of Taiwan", Chung-Hua *Institution for Economic Research Newsletter*, Vol.3, No.5.

Yu, T.S. (1994), "Does Taiwan's Industrialization have its own paradigm", *Journal of Asian Economics*, Vol.5, No.4.